THE DEVELOPMENT OF HUMAN RIGHTS LAW BY THE JUDGES OF THE INTERNATIONAL COURT OF JUSTICE

The jurisprudence of the International Court of Justice generally demonstrates that no rule of international law can be interpreted and applied without regard to its innate values and the basic principles of human rights. Through its case-law the ICJ has made immense contributions to the development of human rights law, and in so doing continues to provide solutions to mounting international problems, such as terrorism and unilateral use of force. Part I of the book argues that the legislative spirit of contemporary international law lies in the doctrine of human rights and that the spirit of human rights doctrine lies in the principle of human dignity. Furthermore it argues that the processes of international legislation and international adjudication are inseparable, and that there is no norm of international law which does not intertwine the fundamental principle of human dignity with human rights doctrine. Hence human rights law is more a school of law than merely a normative branch of international law, and the ICJ's willingness to engage in the development of human rights law depends upon which judicial ideology its judges subscribe to. In order to evaluate how this human rights spirit is manifested, or occasionally not manifested, through the vast jurisprudence of the ICJ, Parts II and III critically examine the Court's principal contentious and advisory cases in which it has treated human rights questions. The legal reasoning of the Court and the opinions appended to its decisions by its individual judges are analysed in light of the principle of human dignity and the doctrine of human rights.

Studies in International Law: Volume 10

The Peace Palace in the Hague

The Development of Human Rights Law by the Judges of the International Court of Justice

Shiv R S Bedi

·HART·
PUBLISHING
OXFORD – PORTLAND OREGON
2007

Published in North America (US and Canada) by
Hart Publishing
c/o International Specialized Book Services
920 NE 58th Avenue, Suite 300
Portland, OR 97213-3786
USA
Tel: +1 503 287 3093 or toll-free: (1) 800 944 6190
Fax: +1 503 280 8832
E-mail: orders@isbs.com
Website: www.isbs.com

Hart Publishing, 16C Worcester Place, Oxford, OX1 2JW
Telephone: +44 (0)1865 517530 Fax: +44 (0) 1865 510710
E-mail: mail@hartpub.co.uk
Website: http://www.hartpub.co.uk

British Library Cataloguing in Publication Data
Data Available
ISBN-13: 978-1-84113-576-2 (hardback)
ISBN-10: 1-84113-576-3 (hardback)

Typeset by Hope Services Ltd, Abingdon
Printed and bound in Great Britain by
Biddles Ltd, King's Lynn, Norfolk

To my revered teachers, Charan Singh and Gurinder Singh
and
to my inspiration, Prem

CONTENTS

Part III The Development of Human Rights Law by the International Court of Justice: Advisory Cases

1

INTRODUCTION

> There are no limits to the heights that a human being can attain, nor to the depths that he can sink. It is *for you to choose* between the heights of bliss and happiness or the depths of pain and agony. (emphasis added).
>
> (Maharaj Charan Singh[1])

THIS JURO-MYSTIC POSTULATE with its two contrasting scenarios is emphatic about mankind's strong determination to set priorities. If we do not go forward we go backwards, for life does not stand still. If we do not rise we fall; it is always for us to choose and set our priorities.

Looking at the post 9/11[2] world in the perspective of the preceding postulate we can see international human rights as the pinnacle of the collective legislative spirit of *'We, the people of the United Nations'* and the frequent flagrant violations of human rights as the depths to which the conscience of man will sometimes sink.

The international scene of today is well described by Judge Weeramantry, a former Vice-President of the International Court of Justice: 'We live in the midst of terrorism, genocide, racism, torture, narcotics, militarism, arms races, hijacking, environmental devastation, and human rights violations of every kind.'[3] The terrorist attack on the World Trade Organization's building on 11 September 2001 represents the worst aspect of the sunken and perverted spirit of man. Yet instead of prudently admitting their failure to strengthen the protective mechanism of collective security based on force, which is the monopoly of the international community, States are still choosing primitive and disastrous mechanisms for self-defence as well as overt or covert military alliances, the corollary of rights springing from the old concept of absolute sovereignty[4], of the pre-Charter era. *9/11* needs to be seen as a wake-up call. The assassination of Archduke Franz Ferdinand in 1914 which ignited the First World War, the *blitzkrieg* by Germany which ignited WWII in Europe, and the Japanese attack on *Pearl Harbour* in 1942 were similar moments in history when war was taken to the rest of the world. The post

[1] MC Singh, *Quest for Light, Radha Soami Satsang Beas,* 4th edn, (Panjab, India, 1988) 54.

[2] The terrorist attack on the World Trade Organisations' building on 11 September 2001 has popularly become to be known as 9/11.

[3] CG Weeramantry, *The Lord's Prayer: Bridge to a Better World* (Liguori, MO, Triumph, 1998) 3.

[4] Jessup opines: 'Those who still preach the traditional license of absolute sovereignty as an excuse for disregarding the interest of the world community, sound a discordant note . . .', see PC Jessup, 'A Half Century of Efforts to Substitute Law for War' (1960) 99 *Recueil des Cours* 1, 20.

9/11 events are in danger of repeating the old scourge. All this is the reverse of the heights at which the post-WWII signatories of the UN Charter and the International Bill of Human Rights aimed on behalf of all mankind. Amidst the turmoil there are signs that the whole of humanity is once again willing to engage in warfare as it did during the two world wars. Yet if it is for man *to choose* between the heights and depths then *what is the choice* between these two contrasting scenarios? History provides ample evidence. *The path of the law based on respect for human rights and human dignity is the choice* is well described in the words of Prof Jessup, a former Judge of the International Court of Justice:

> We lawyers do not have the arrogance to assert that the path of the law is the only way to peace. We do confidently assert that no human society has ever discovered an ordered substitute for violence save through the use of law and legal institutions whether the law in question be secular or religious. It is the same in international community. Those who look realistically at what often seems to be an international anarchy and who suggest the solutions of economics, of political or of science, come first or last to rely upon some agreement, some treaty, even though they may ignore the fact that a contractual obligation is essentially one of the simplest and one of the most pervasive manifestations of the acceptance of the very spirit of law. Whatever form of organisation they propose, it must be in structure and in operation a legal phenomenon, because law can be defined as a description of the way people organise and act.[5] (emphasis added).

To those who think that the role played by international law in international relations has never proved so successful, the words of Judge Manfred Lachs, a former President of the ICJ, may provide a satisfactory answer: 'Though imperfect and inadequate in many respects, international law is honoured more in the observance than the breach.'[6] The inherent juridical sense of man, respecting his fellow human beings at the personal level of a single individual—for law in its antiquity was personal—or at the level of nation States, or internationally at the level of the UN always shows a determination to follow the path of righteousness, which we call humanity; virtue in the Republic of Plato and human rights in the United Nations Charter. That the spirit of man is always, unless clouded and perverted, capable of distinguishing between right and wrong—is capable of legislating the path from within his own reason and spirit; and, is capable of implementing his own legislation and if needs be passing a judgment on his own actions—is his dignity. Every individual is a living parliament (billions of cells in his brain engaged in constant deliberation and decision-making), a living executive (constantly implementing his own decisions) and a living court of justice (reviewing and judging his own actions consciously and conscientiously according to his *dharma*, the chosen path of action) unto himself. It is also the dignity of man to respect the spirit and the path of his fellow human beings and to live a life of peaceful

[5] Ibid, p 4.

[6] M Lachs, 'Thoughts on the Recent Jurisprudence of the International Court of Justice' (1990) 4(1) *Emory International Law Review* 78. Judge Lachs also mentions: 'If you look at the world at large, law is vital and essential part of the daily affairs of nations. Without it, our daily life would be impossible. Without it, all routine events we so frequently take for granted would be impossible.' (*Ibid*, pp 77–78).

co-existence. When in contact, or even in conflict, people similarly legislate for themselves, implement their laws and adjudicate upon the matters in contention. The organised life of human beings has long since moved from the level of numerous nation States to the international community level of the UN. The path *'we the peoples of the United Nations'* enacted for ourselves is provided in the UN Charter. Historically, every democratic rule of law proves that the secret of success of a legal system lies in respect for the rights of its subjects and the protection of those rights, if necessary by force. It is not hard to see that the root cause of the relative imperfection and inadequacy of international law, and the consequent flagrant violations of human rights worldwide (including by means of terrorism) lies in the failure of *'we the peoples of the United Nations'*—rulers and ruled alike—to establish the conditions for the institutionalisation of the use of force monopoly held by international society. The primitive practices found in the outdated international rights of States, such as the right of self-defence and collective security based on alliances, which disregards the possibility of establishing a workable system of force monopoly within international society, is detrimental to the very concept of collective security based on force monopoly in the international community in the age of international human rights. The very core of the legislative spirit of the UN Charter reflects this and needs to be recalled here briefly.

Every constitution is imbued with a spirit and philosophy that animates the path chosen by its people and enacted as legislation by its legislators. One does not become a legislator simply by getting elected to that office by the people. The legislator must pursue the spirit and philosophy of the people's constitution to a point that the law is enforced by a strong executive and guarded by an impartial judiciary. One does not become a judge simply by getting elected to that office. Handsome is he who handsome does and similarly, justice is he who justice does. The spirit and the school of law, reflected in the judicial ideology of the judge go a long way to create the proper conditions for decision-making in the field of human rights. The judge must mould his judicial conscience in accordance with the spirit and philosophy of the path prescribed in the constitution and adopted by the people of his society. Every element of his reasoning must conform to them. Detailed adjudication speaks louder and clearer than the frequently terse language of constitutions. Judgements are even more potent. Adjudication by a Court must bear the hallmark of the legislative spirit and the legislature must strengthen the executive to facilitate compliance with judicial pronouncements. The juridical conscience of a community often lies in the preamble to its constitution and the United Nations Charter is, for all practical purposes, such a constitution for the international community. It is to the Preamble to the Charter that we must therefore look. The Charter opens with the words *'We, the peoples of the United Nations'*, and not with *We, the sovereign States of the United Nations.* That choice of the universality of the *collective human conscience* of *'We'* showed the UN's determination to follow the path of human rights prescribed by the UN Charter. Even a brief analysis of the Charter reveals what the *'peoples'* were *'determined'* to achieve for themselves and for coming generations: the *four key 'ends'*. First: 'to save succeeding generations from the scourge of war, which twice in our lifetime has brought untold sorrow to mankind. Second: 'to reaffirm faith in the fundamental *human rights, in the dignity and worth of the human person,* in the equal rights of men and women and of nations large and small.' (emphasis added). Third: 'to establish conditions under which justice and respect for the obligations arising from treaties and other sources of international law can be maintained.' And the fourth: 'to promote social progress and better standards of life in larger freedom.' All the four ends perceived in a circle reflect the spirit of the doctrine of human rights and human dignity at the centre of that circle. The first two ends speak of achieving peace based on human rights and human dignity. The third end speaks of establishing an international rule of law, a condition for the achievement of peace based on human rights. The fourth signifies the promotion of social welfare and civil liberty, well enshrined now in the UN Charter and its associated instruments popularly called the International Bill of Human Rights.

And further, to achieve 'these ends', the preamble speaks of adopting *four means.* First: 'to practice tolerance and live together in peace with one another as good neighbours.' Second: '*to unite our strength* to maintain international peace and security.' (emphasis added). Third: 'to ensure, by the acceptance of principles and institutions of methods, that *armed forces shall not be used, save in the common interest.*' And the fourth: 'to employ *international machinery* for the *promotion of the economic and social advancement of all peoples.*' The most striking of these means to achieve peace based on human rights is the element of '*to unite our strength*' clearly standing for the promotion of the system of force monopoly of international society. The concept of '*Armed forces shall not be used, save in the common interest*' read together with the concept of '*to unite our strength*' created a cardinal characterization of means aiming to limit the recourse to use of force in the forms of self-defence and alliances and to promote the collective use of force monopolized in the hands of the peoples of international society. The human rights spirit in the four means of achievement is exactly commensurate to the same spirit in the four ends. It is the humanity of man, in the form of human rights and human dignity, which stands at the core of this octagon of eight fundamental concepts, the first four representing the ends of the Charter and the other four standing for the means to be adopted. The position of human rights and human dignity in the UN Charter and the contemporary sources of international law are so central that any application and interpretation of any principle of law in disregard of the principles of human rights would need careful scrutiny.

The success, or failure, of the path of human rights, is something for which many can claim credit or be equally held responsible, respectively—States, individuals, the United Nations, etc—yet some are more praiseworthy and responsible than the others. Who actually is responsible for the present failed state of affairs in which the international legal system is not as effective as national legal systems? Is it the General Assembly of the UN? Is it the UN Security Council? Is it the International Court of Justice? Or, is it nation State leaders, mass-media or peoples themselves? Perhaps the best answer is to pose a counter-question: who does not have a hand in it? The place of the judiciary in any society is always conspicuous. Therefore, the Charter provided for an international judiciary. To judge in full accordance with the legislative spirit of human rights and human dignity a judge must be sufficiently broadminded, human and humane in the core of his mental judicial faculty. The Statute of the International Court of Justice is an integral part of the Charter of the United Nations. In adjudicating upon any case, be it a judgment in a contentious case or an advisory opinion in an advisory case, the Court being an integral part and principal judicial organ of the United Nations, is bound to interpret and apply international law keeping constantly in mind the *ends and means*, described also as *purposes and principles*, enshrined in the UN Charter. Doing full justice to the common good of mankind, and the co-existence of '*we the peoples of the United Nations*', the drafters of the Court's Statute carefully devised the following formula of method and qualifications to be followed when electing the judges of the principal judicial organ of the United Nations: 'at every election, the electors shall bear in mind not only that the persons to be elected should individually possess the qualifications required, but also that in the body as a whole the representation of the main forms of civilization and the principal legal systems of the world should be assured.'[7]

And further, in order to strongly imprint in *the conscience* of every single judge the following provision was provided: 'Every Member of the Court shall, before taking up his duties, make a solemn declaration in open court that he will exercise his powers impartially and conscientiously.'[8]

Looking at the above provisions of the Court's Statute and the qualities of judgeship recounted therein one perceives that there are two cardinal concepts in the ICJ Statute, governing its adjudication process—1) *the concept of the main forms of civilization and the principal legal systems of the world* (Article 9 of the Statute), and 2) *the concept of deciding impartially and conscientiously* (Article 20 of the Statute)—which have great relevance to the eight fundamental concepts of the UN Charter.

Seen in the light of the above eight fundamental concepts in the UN Charter and the two cardinal concepts in the ICJ Statute, every principle developed by the International Court of Justice during the course of its adjudication is expected to be a super refined and clarified voice of the *human rights oriented international legislative spirit* of international community. To disregard that would be tantamount to betraying the trust of '*we the peoples of the United Nations*'. To pay due regard to this is to epitomize the *spirit of human rights and human dignity*.

Spirit is something constant (fixed) in man whereas the expression and meaning of his *conscience* is dynamic, depending always how *conscious* the man is about his own living essence of *spirit*, The Greeks used the word *logos*; in teutonic language it was *lag*, which later came to be known as *law*. And, in *that* spirit and conscience lies the defining stuff of the principle of human dignity. Hence; *we may*

[7] Article 9 of the Statute of the International Court of Justice.

[8] Article 20 of the Statute of the International Court of Justice.

also define the principle of human dignity as respect for the spirit and conscience of the man, for the man and by the man individually; and, respect for the spirit and conscience: of the people, for the people and by the people collectively. These are *'the elementary considerations of humanity'*, to use the language of the International Court of Justice. And these, applied to practical human conduct, either in the form of a right or a duty, run *erga singulum* as well as *erga omnes*, to use again the terms of the Court's jurisprudence. Depending upon the field of action and the actors involved—for instance legislation and legislators or the adjudication and the judges—it is the substance (human dignity) of the principle which matters most, the form being subservient.

Profoundly striking is the truth: *'Legislative and judicial processes are inseparable'*.[9] The traditional view that judges only find and apply the law, and do not make it, is not only rapidly losing ground in national judicial circles but hardly has a place in international adjudication, particularly the International Court of Justice, whose founding fathers expected from its judges the ability to develop international law to the extent of delivering to posterity an *'empire of justice'*. That is not to reflect that the international judges have taken over the role of legislature on the international plane of 'global governance', and neither is it to maintain the view that the judiciary in general has become more powerful than the legislature. It is simply to recognize an existing fact—the result of constant historical, legal and political development, generally and in all national jurisdictions, but certainly and particularly in the international community—that legislative and judicial processes are getting so interwoven and interdependent that their complementarity is something to be taken notice of and to be appreciated in a positive spirit. It is a *'creative act'* on the part of the judiciary and not a *'conspiracy'* against the legislature.[10]

'Jurists are the Judges and guides of the Judges.'[11] A prominent jurist turned judge of the ICJ, Judge Hersch Lauterpacht (UK), writing on the International Court of Justice as an agency for developing the law, posed a question: *'What . . . is the explanation of the wide recognition of the achievement of the Court?'*[12] His own spontaneous answer to the question he posed for himself was: *'The explanation is that, debarred from directly acting as an important instrument of peace, the Court has made a tangible contribution to the development and clarification of the rules and principles of international law.'*[13] That the Court has played a significant role by contributing to the orderly development of international law is a well-known fact. It is also well known that several pronouncements of the Court have had a considerable impact on the development of the law of the sea, the law of the treaties,

[9] JL Brierly, H Lauterpacht and H Waldock, (eds), *The Judicial Settlement of International Disputes: The Basis of Obligation in International Law* (London, 1958) 98.

[10] *Ibid.*

[11] Justice VR Krishna Iyer, Human Rights (A Judge's Miscellany, 1995) p 52.

[12] Sir H Lauterpacht, *The Development of International Law by the International Court of Justice* (London, Stevens & Sons, 1958) 5.

[13] *Ibid.*

international economic law, the law of decolonization, the law of the international organizations, environmental law and so on.[14] However, what is less known is the fact that the International Court of Justice, though not a special human rights court as such, has also made, and sometimes also failed to make, an important contribution to the development of human rights law. Though there are some articles[15] published on this particular subject, and some publications on the case law of the International Court which cover the subject briefly, mainly mentioning the principle of self-determination and the concept of obligations *erga omnes*, yet there is not a single monograph[16] to be found in the English literature which comprehensively covers the development of human rights law by the International Court of Justice.

Regularly engaged in the research in the Court's jurisprudence, and frequently noticing the lack and need of an account of such a nature, I had often felt it worthy of research. It is no exaggeration to state that whenever I carried out an analytical study of the reasoning of any decision of the Court, particularly involving human rights issues, the reasoning preceding its decisions, as well as the independent opinions appended by individual judges to those decisions, repeatedly impressed upon me that any theoretical principle of human rights law enshrined in any human rights instrument is more like a tiny legal seed which goes through a

[14] See particularly: 1) Judge Sir H Lauterpacht, *The Development of International Law by the International Court of Justice* (London, Stevens & Sons, 1958); 2) Judge N Singh, *The Role and Record of the International Court of Justice* (Dordrecht, Nijhoff, 1989); 3) Judge Mohamed Shahabuddeen's *Precedent in the World Court* (1996); 4) JN Singh's *International Justice: Jurisprudence of the World Courts* (1991); 5) JHW Verzijl's *The Jurisprudence of the World Court*, vol II (1967); 6) E McWhinney, *The World Court and the Contemporary International Law-Making Process* (Alphen aan den Rijn, Netherlands, Sijthoff & Noordhoff, 1979); 7) Judge Jimenez de Arechiga's 'The Work and the Jurisprudence of the International Court of Justice 1947–1986' (1987) 58 *British Year Book of International Law* 1–38; 8) Judge Manferd Lach's two articles: a) 'Some Reflections on the Contributions of the International Court of Justice to the Development of International Law' (1983) 10 *Syracuse Journal of International Law and Commerce*, Nr 1, p 239, and b) 'Thoughts on the Recent Jurisprudence of the International Court of Justice' (1990) 4 *Emory Journal of International Dispute Resolution* 193–236; and 9) E Hambro and AW Rovine's, *The Case Law of the International Court of Justice*, 8 vols, 1952–76.

[15] Strictly speaking, comprehensively dealing with the subject are, to my knowledge, are the following five articles: 1) by Judge R Higgins, 'The International Court of Justice and Human Rights' in K Wellens, (ed), *International Law: Theory and Practice: Essays in Honour of Eric Suy* (The Hague, Martinus Nijhoff, 1998) 694; 2) by Judge SM Schwebel, 'Human Rights in the World Court' in RS Pathak and RP Dhokalia, (eds), *International Law in Transition, Essays in Memory of Judge Nagendra Singh* (New Delhi, Lancer Books, 1992) 267–90. (The latter also published in (1991) 24 *Vanderbilt Journal of Transnational Law* 945–70); 3) by Judge SM Schwebel, 'The Treatment of Human Rights and Aliens in the International Court of Justice' in V Lowe and M Fitzmaurice, (eds), *Fifty Years of the International Court of Justice: Essays in Honour of Sir Robert Jennings* (Cambridge, CUP, 1996) 327–51; 4) M Bedjaoui, 'À propos de la place des droits de la personne humaine dans la jurisprudence de la Cour internationale de Justice' in P Mahoney, *et al*, (eds), *Protecting Human Rights: The European Perspective* (Köln, Carl Heymanns Verlag KG) 87–93; 5) K Wellens, 'La Cour internationale de justice et la protection des droit de l'homme' in *Les incidences des jurisprudences internationale sur les droits Néderlandais et Français notamment sur les Droits de l'Homme* (Paris, Presses Universitaires de France) 41–81.

[16] However, there appeared in 2002 for the first time a monograph in French, ie, R Goy, *La Cour Internationale de Justice et les Droits de l'homme* (Brussels, Nemesis Bruylant, 2002).

circular process of adjudication—application-interpretation and interpretation–application; no–yes; yes–no; until the impartial and conscientious reasoning faculty of judges convincingly hear the inner voice which says: a) there is for me now clear, convincing, sufficient and conclusive evidence, and b) beyond any reasonable doubt this is my inner conviction—it appears in the form of a gigantic tree whose every leaf, branch, flower or fruit sparkle with the human rights spirit which was encased in the tiny seed. The blossom of a rose, its delicate perfume, the soft moisture of open petals, are experiences and manifestations of its essence hidden in the seed. The principle of equality for instance produced the legal reasoning of 503 pages in the joint cases concerning *South West Africa.*[17] The simple principle of State responsibility was expressed in 128 pages in the case concerning *Corfu Channel*,[18] developing the principle of *elementary considerations of humanity*, manifesting the very substance and application of human rights, finding its place in 1949 Geneva Conventions and in the international law for the protection of environmental needs. At the heart of the 357 page judgment in the *Barcelona Traction*[19] case, dealing with diplomatic protection to shareholders, the Court developed the most revolutionary concept, that *'human rights run erga omnes.'* Just to mention one more case in which the Court adjudicated upon the question of the legality and illegality of nuclear weapons,[20] the advisory opinion of the Court amounted to 368 pages. These pages, including individual opinions of several judges, contain a boundless treasury on international humanitarian law and human rights law. As a matter of fact the Court's record on international human rights adjudication, like most of its jurisprudence, shows a refined and developed form of the spirit of international human rights legislation, something *'we the peoples of the United Nations'* must know. However, when, on occasion the Court has spoken with a voice which is conservative, formal and proceduralist, the light of the law has been missing and the concept of human dignity was thereby dimmed. Fortunately, individual opinions of the judges have meant that the Court has never been completely formal and proceduralist; for instance, thanks to the dissenting opinions (290 pages)[21] of exactly half the Court's members in the *South West Africa* cases, its human rights interpretation and the extensive elaboration of the principle of equality prevailed in the long run despite its casting vote and conservative decision in the *dispositif.* 185 judges on the bench of the Court (including 91 judges *ad hoc*) delivering 89 judgments in 107 contentious cases, giving 25 advisory opinions in 24 advisory cases, making 429 orders altogether, and appending hundreds of individual opinions to all these decisions[22]—producing forests of gigantic jurisprudential trees

[17] Judgment of 18 July 1966 in the joint cases of South West Africa, ICJ Reports 1966, pp 4–505.

[18] Judgment of 9 April 1949 on Merits of the case concerning *Corfu Channel (United Kingdom v Albania)*, ICJ Reports 1949, pp 4–131.

[19] Judgment of 5 February 1970 in the case concerning *Barcelona Traction, Light and Power Company, Ltd*, New Application: 1962 *Belgium v Spain*, ICJ Reports 1970, p 3.

[20] Advisory Opinion of 8 July 1996 in the case concerning Legality of the Threat or Use of Nuclear Weapons, ICJ Reports 1996, pp 226–593.

[21] Judgment of 18 July 1966 in the joint cases of South West Africa, ICJ Reports 1966, pp 216–505.

[22] Statistics are as they stand on 8 April 2005; for details see the bibliography at the end of this book.

from the legislative seeds on the aforementioned branches of international law, including human rights law, makes the Court worthy of profound and critical study aimed at uncovering what lies in its jurisprudence which will aid the development of human rights law. Hence this book.

This book aims at: a) surveying the Court's jurisprudence and analysing its case law in order to highlight the contribution of the judges of the International Court of Justice to the development of human rights law; *and* b) to point out at the same time its failures, as pointed out by the judges in their independent opinions appended to the Court's rulings. For this purpose, the book is divided into three parts.

Part 1 concentrates on two enquiries: 1) *the legislative role of the judge:* do judges legislate?; what do we mean by the development of law by judges?; the relationship between development of law and judicial ideologies; and 2) *the relation between human rights and international law* in the context of the equation: the principle of human dignity versus the traditional doctrine of State sovereignty.

Part II examines and analyses the *principal contentious cases* in which the International Court has treated *human rights issues and allied questions.*

Part III examines and analyses the *principal advisory opinions* delivered by the Court in which *human rights issues and allied questions* have been dealt with.

Finally, the concluding chapter offers a *summary and general conclusion.*

Part I

Perspective: Legislative Role of the Judge and Human Rights Law

2

Legislative Role of the Judge: A Vital Role in the Life of the Law

> Judgment is a process of mind that some claim to know and others continue to discover. Each judgment is either a step forward or a step backward in the development of law. As a result, since each judgment is the product of the minds of several individuals—how each understands and interprets the law—judges cannot avoid being vital force in the life of the law. (Judge Manfred Lachs[1])

> The Jurisprudence of the Court develops and strengthens the law concerning human rights: Moreover, apart from the legal attribute of binding obligations which can now be said to be associated with human rights, the International Court of Justice has not hesitated to refer to the general concept of human rights in its judgments whenever an opportunity has suitably offered itself in a case brought before the Court. Again, if the Court has ever omitted to refer to the concept of human rights or failed fully to deal with it in a case, the Members of the Court have, at no point, failed to elaborate that aspect in their independent or separate supporting opinions, or even give vent to their thinking in dissenting opinions which fact is quite remarkable.[2] (Judge Nagendra Singh)

The above words of Judge Lachs (Poland), a former President of the International Court of Justice were uttered during an address delivered at the Syracuse University College of Law on 30 September 1982. I have chosen these words at the outset and italicized them for their plain truth: '*judges cannot avoid being a vital force in the life of the law.*' Whether in enacting the law or applying it, judges will apply reason to unearth any underlying source(s) of law as part of the process of finding the rules to be applied. Any process of legislation takes fully into consideration all existing relevant judicial precedents on the enactment in question. And any process of adjudication takes into consideration all the existing relevant legislation concerning the issue(s) to be decided. This is what made a world renowned jurist remark, when considering the problem of sources of law: 'Where does the judge obtain the rules by which to decide cases? In this sense, among the sources of law will commonly be listed: statute, judicial precedents, custom, the opinion of experts, morality and equity.'[3]

[1] M Lachs, 'Some Reflections on the Contribution of the International Court of Justice to the Development of International Law' (1983) 10(2) *Syracuse Journal of International Law and Commerce* Nr 1, 239.

[2] N Singh, *Enforcement of Human Rights in Peace and War and the Future of Humanity* (Dordrecht, Nijhoff, 1986) 29.

[3] LL Fuller, *Anatomy of the Law* (1968) 69.

The second quote from another former President of the International Court of Justice, Judge Nagendra Singh (India), has been particularly selected for mention at the outset to highlight the fact that *although the ICJ is not a human rights court as such, yet its contribution to the development of human rights law, hitherto not very well known, is by no means negligible.*

But do judges really legislate? The controversy centred on this issue is perhaps as old as jurisprudence itself. However, whatever position is taken on this controversy, the following brief discussion is intended to reveal that Judge Lachs statement that 'judges cannot avoid being a vital force in the life of the law' is irrefutable. That being said, it remains to be seen to what extent the judges of the International Court of Justice, not being a special human rights court such as the European Court of Human Rights, end up being a vital force in the life of human rights law.

'*The judge is nothing but the law speaking*'[4] is an old proverb. And an equally old maxim about judges is that '*Laws should be made by legislators, not by judges*'.[5] The legislative role of the judge is, and has always been, a question of great controversy. Speaking about discovery and creation in the judicial process, Bodenheimer also thinks that 'the role which the judge plays in the processes of adjudication is the subject of disagreement and debate'.[6] Actually, according to Bodenheimer, there are two theories about this controversial matter which he describes as the old theory and the new theory. 'Many famous figures in the history of English law, such as Coke, Hale, Bacon and Blackstone, were convinced that the office of the judge was to declare and interpret the law, but not to make it',[7] says Bodenheimer. He continues and observes:

> The newer theory, initiated by Bentham and carried to a radical conclusion by John Chipman Gray, asserted that judges produce law just as much as legislators do; in the view of Gray, they even make it more decisively and authoritatively than legislators, since statutes are construed by the courts and such construction determines the true meaning of the enactment more significantly than its original text.[8]

Gray himself was very fond of quoting enthusiastically Bishop Hoadly's words: 'whoever hath an absolute authority to interpret any written or spoken laws it is he who is the Law giver to all intents and purposes and not the person who first wrote or spoke them.'[9] It certainly reflects a bit of exaggeration. To this Judge Shahabuddeen adds himself: 'Some exaggeration does not diminish a certain *core truth*'[10] (emphasis added). Such a brief, but truth-laden, comment from a former

[4] B Whichcote, *Moral and Religious Aphorisms*, 1753 in D Shrager and E Frost, (eds), *The Quotable Lawyer* (1992) 141.

[5] *Ibid*, p 144.

[6] E Bodenheimer, *Jurisprudence: The Philosophy and Method of the Law*, 2nd edn, (1997) p 439.

[7] *Ibid.*

[8] *Ibid.*

[9] J Chipman Gray, *The Nature and Sources of Law* (1931) 125, 172, cited in M Shahabuddeen, *Precedent in the World Court* (1996), p 89.

[10] Shahabuddeen, *ibid.*

judge of the International Court of Justice (at present a judge at the International Criminal Tribunal for the Former Yugoslavia) might clear up doubt in the minds of many about the question, do judges legislate? And if they do, what is their legislative role? What is the 'core truth'? Keeping in mind these fascinating questions, I wish to concentrate in this book on the legislative role of the judge at the ICJ, reflecting the development of human rights law by the judges of the International Court of Justice.

I. The Core Truth: All Roads Lead to Rome

There are different terms used to describe the one reality that judges do play a legislative role, for instance: judicial legislation, judicial law-making, judge made law, development of law by judges, the creative role of judges, judicial creativity, judicial activism, etc, etc. With some degree of difference between the use, meaning and role played by these terms, and also the type of judiciary, national or international, with which these terms are associated, together within the context of their respective statutes or constitutions, the average minimum common meaning describes one concrete concept: the legislative role of the judge in the given context in general and the given framework of powers drawn, for instance the powers of judicial review and the guardian of the constitution, in particular from the relevant constituting document. Judge Hersch Lauterpacht has offered a meaning for the term 'judicial legislation' which perhaps could be applied to all the terms mentioned above. According to him:

> Judicial legislation, conceived as a process of changing the existing law, is not a legal term of art. It is a convenient term in legal philosophy and political science. A system of law expressly sanctioning judicial legislation would be a contradiction in terms. At the same time, the fact remains that judicial law-making is a permanent feature of administration of justice in every society . . .[11]

Part III of his book bears the title 'Judicial Legislation', and the five ways, in which he saw the International Court of Justice expressing its judicial legislation function are described in the five chapters of Part III under the following headings: chapter 9: Judicial Legislation through Application of General Principles, chapter 10: Judicial Legislation through Application by Reference to Parallel Development in International Law, chapter 11: Judicial Legislation on Account of Generally Accepted Law, chapter 12: Judicial Legislation and the Jurisdiction of the Court, and chapter 13: Judicial Legislation and Adjudication *Ex Aequo et Bono*.

Similarly, an Indian jurist, Prof Saraf, writing in the Indian adjudicational context, has the following to say:

[11] Sir H Lauterpacht, *The Development of International Law by the International Court of Justice* (London, Stevens & Sons, 1958) 155.

> Judicial creativity at present is being defended on three grounds. First, it has been suggested that in a federal set up with a written constitution which purports to create a delicate balance of several conflicting interests, the courts are not merely interpreters of the law but also instrumentality to ensure that there is no erosion of the terms of compact both in letter and spirit. Second, social change considerations necessitate our looking at the law not as a set of immutable rules of conduct but self-evolving enterprise directed towards realization of societal goals. Although it is the duty of the legislature to adapt the law to the needs of a changing society, a court of law has also its own obligation in this regard. Last, but not the least important consideration is that rules developed by the courts regarding the role of judges in the judicial process are applicable essentially to private law litigations; public law litigation being of a different nature the courts would be justified in acting upon policy arguments for arriving at sound decisions.[12]

United States doctrine and case law is studded with glittering examples of judicial activism. With the appointment of Earl Warren as Chief Justice in 1953, along with other judges like Black, Douglas and Brennan, a new creativity emerged in the US. *Brown*[13] in 1954, for instance, was a judicial revolution which swept away obstacles of race and colour in the field of education. As a result the principle of desegregation was established as an individual right to be enforced by the State. Justice Oliver Holmes is popularly known to have moulded law just as Marshall is known to have moulded constitutional law. The following famous expression of Holmes has become a cardinal point in the philosophy of judicial legislation: 'I recognize without hesitation that judges do and must legislate, but they can do so only interstitially; they are confined from molar to molecule.'[14]

Though spoken in a national context, but equally valid for international judges, the following words of a former Chief Justice of Indian Supreme Court, Justice Bhagwati, addressing the Commonwealth Law Conference at London, hit the nail right on its head:

> Law-making is an inherent and inevitable part of the judicial process. Even where a Judge is concerned with interpretation of a statute, there is ample scope for him to develop and mould the law. It is he, who infuses life and blood into the dry skeleton provided by the Legislature and creates a living organism appropriate and adequate to meet the needs of the society and by thus making and moulding the law, he takes part in the work of creation. A Judge is not a mimic. Greatness on the bench lies in creativity. The process of judging is a phase of a never ending movement and something more is expected of a Judge than mere imitative reproduction, lifeless repetition of a mechanical routine. It is for this reason that when a law comes before a Judge, he has to invest it with meaning and content and in this process of interpretation he makes law.[15]

[12] DN Saraf in KL Bhatia, (ed), *Judicial Activism and Social Change* (1990) 76.

[13] *Brown v Board of Education* 394 US 294 (1954).

[14] *Southern Pacific Co v Jensen* 244 US 205(1917) at 221. See also in the F Rigaux, *La Loi des Juges* (Paris, Editions Odile Jacob, 1997) 247; and also in E Bodenheimer, *Jurisprudence: The Philosophy and the Method of the Law* (1974) 442. Neil MacCormick has given a good commentary on the Holmes' expression of 'interstitially' in his book *Legal Reasoning and Legal Theory* (Oxford, Clarendon Press, 1978) pp 122 and 187–88.

[15] Cited by Justice RP Sethi in KL Bhatia, (ed), *Judicial Activism and Social Change* (1990) 40.

None of this means that judges legislate by enacting the law. They do so only by developing the law. During the process of application and interpretation of law they develop, or create, law. Judge Shahabuddeen describes the reality aptly, saying: 'It is of course an exaggeration to suggest that the Court is a legislator; it is also an exaggeration to assert that it cannot create any law at all.'[16] Hence, for lack of the right term which conveys the right meaning of the fact that judges legislate from within the existing legislation, several terms are being used, often creating panic in the legislators' circles that judges are perhaps swaying over them. While engaged in judicial process when judges develop and create law from within the existing law, and/or when judges legislate from within the existing enacted legislation, this phenomenon can well be described as judgislation It is time that we coined this new term: judgislation.

II. The Core Truth in Retrospect: An International Perspective

Before we move to survey the role played by the judges of the International Court of Justice, it would simply be proper to see in retrospect how at the beginning of the 20th century, during and after the First World War period, people looked at the need and role of international judiciary.

'Government is required not simply because men are in conflict but also because they are in contact.'[17] The words are equally true for the judicial organ of any organization, be it a State or an International Organization like that of the United Nations. Judge Sir Robert Jennings (UK), a former President of the International Court of Justice, has described the importance of the development of law by a permanent international court in these words:

> The historical endeavour, extending from the First Hague Conference of 1899 until eventual success in 1920, to establish a permanent international court as distinct from *ad hoc* tribunals, was inspired by the belief that only a court established on a permanent basis could, besides deciding disputes, make an adequate contribution to the progressive development of international law as a working system of law.[18]

Having seen the horrors of war President Wilson outlined the idea of the League of Nations. With this idea he authorized his friend Colonel House to prepare a plan which he did in the form of a draft 'Covenant of the League of Nations'. The same was carefully edited by the President. The preamble ran as follows: '*International civilisation proved a failure because there has not been a fabric of law* to which nations have yielded with the same obedience and deference as individuals submit to

[16] *Ibid*, p 86.
[17] C Ins Jr, *Swords into Plowshares*, 1971, p 216.
[18] See the Foreword by Judge Jennings for Judge Shahabuddeen's book *Precedent in the World Court*, p xiii.

intra-national laws . . . .'[19] The Permanent Court of International Justice was established in 1921 in accordance with the provisions of Article 14 of the Covenant of the League of Nations reading: 'The Council shall formulate and submit the members of the League for adoption plans for the establishment of a Permanent Court of International Justice.' The Council accordingly on 13 February 1920 formed a Committee of Jurists, with Baron Descamps (Belgian), as its President, entrusted with the task of preparing a draft Statute of the Court. Right during the summer of 1920, on 16 June to be precise, when history was about to deliver the first world judiciary to its mankind, Mr Leon Bourgeois, an experienced French and international legislator, administrator and lawyer, delegated by the Council of the League of nations to open the meeting of the Committee of Jurists in The Hague, addressed the drafters with the following closing words:

> You are about, Gentlemen, to give life to the *judicial power of humanity.* Philosophers and historians have told us of the laws of the growth and decadence of Empires. We look to you, Gentlemen, for laws which will assure the perpetuity of the only empire which can show no decadence, *the empire of justice,* which is the expression of *eternal truth.*[20]

The voice of national and international legislature, executive and judiciary, combined in Bourgeois, it is symbolic of what it was expecting from the judges of the Permanent Court of International Justice. It was clearly admitting the failure of traditional political power of 'empires' and asking to release and deliver the 'judicial power of humanity' in order to construct a 'fabric of law' for the 'international civilisation' as conceived by President Wilson. In a nutshell, a very active and creative role was expected to be played by the judges of the PCIJ. It was well observed by Judge Hersch Lauterpacht in his words: 'the necessity of providing for a tribunal developing international law by its own decisions had been the starting-point for the attempts to establish a truly permanent international court as distinguished from the Permanent Court of Arbitration'.[21]

And the similar role was visualized at San Francisco of the judges of the International Court of Justice, who have inherited, with minor modifications, the same Statute of its predecessor, the PCIJ. The words of the Report of the Rapporteur of Committee I of Commission IV on Judicial Organizations reflect: '1945 Statute will garner what has come down from the past. To make possible the use of precedents under the old Statute the same numbering of the articles has been followed in the new Statute.'[22]

A tribute was paid to the development of international law by the judges of the PCIJ in his publication *The Development of International Law by the Permanent*

[19] MP Tandon, *International Relations*, 4th edn, (Allahabad, India, Allahabad Law Agency) 33.

[20] Permanent Court of International Justice, Advisory Committee Jurists: Proces-Verbaux of the Proceedings of the Committee, 16 June–24 July 1920, p 11.

[21] H Lauterpacht, 'The So-called Anglo-American and Continental Schools of Thought in International Law' (1931) 12 *British Year Book of International Law* 59.

[22] Documents of the United Nations Conference on International Organization, London, 1945, XIII, p 384.

Court of International Justice, published in 1934. And a revised edition, including the development of international law by the International Court of Justice, was published in 1958 under the title *The Development of International Law by the International Court.*

III. Legislative Role of the ECJ and the ECHR

The communication between the legislature and the judiciary in any democratic system is not only indispensable but unceasing and constantly developing. The links of communication are mainly democratic values and human rights principles. In no way these both are inseparable.

> . . . law is not something which is (completely) made at one point in time, and afterwards simply 'applied' by officials, by citizens and by judges to concrete cases. *Law is constantly made, adapted and developed in legal practice*, and most prominently by judges. If a court adapts, and even changes, the content of a legislative rule, it is not, in so doing, usurping its role, but in most cases rather fully assuming its tasks and duties. Legislators cannot foresee everything, nor can they constantly adapt every statute to changed circumstances. It is precisely the task and the duty of the judges to fill in the gaps which every legislator must inevitably leave.[23]

Nowhere these words of Prof Van Hoecke can be more aptly evident than in the legislative role of the two European Courts, the European Court of Justice and the European Court of Human Rights.

After centuries of bloodshed and trampling over the human dignity of the individual on the European soil, particularly the six years of World War II, the path of action chosen by the peoples and leaders of Europe was laid in the *Treaty Establishing the European Community*.[24] The spirit of the path of action reflected in the words: *'DETERMINED to lay the foundation for an ever closer union among the peoples of Europe'*.[25]

However, nowhere did the EEC treaty provide for the principles that: either the EC law should stand *supreme* to the national law of its member States, or, that it should be *directly effective* on the peoples and governments of its members. Neither the treaty made any straightforward commitment to the protection of human rights. No union, howsoever much 'closer' it may be in theory, can achieve the desired objective of the legislator if there is, in practice, no established judicial legitimation of the principle of popular sovereignty of its peoples and institutions. The greater union is obviously supreme to the national sovereignties of its peoples and institutions.

Newly created, but also weak legal systems in theory, like any social system such as international law, in their infancy are so fragile to establish themselves

[23] M van Hoecke, *Law as Communication* (Oxford, Hart Publishing, 2002) 176.

[24] Title as amended by Article G(1) of the Treaty on European Union (TEU) signed at Maastricht, Netherlands in December 1991. The previous title of the treaty, signed in 1957, was European Economic Community Treaty. The same is also popularly known as Treaty of Rome.

[25] Preamble to the EEC-cum-TEU treaty.

effectively over the already existing independent legal systems that the failure of a constructive communication between the higher (in the making) and the lower courts (already well established) may result in doomed legislative spirit of the visionary legislators. In furthering this delicate task and turning it into success the creative role of the judges implementing the higher law is indispensable. One of the greatest contribution of the judges of the European Court of Justice is that by applying the teleological approach of interpretation to the EC Treaty, they have brought to life a fully fledged and active European legal system to which national courts and other individual State institutions have accepted in reality, though sometimes willy-nilly.

The European Community Treaty is a framework treaty to which the substance is being constantly provided by the European Court of Justice. While there are several landmark judgments[26] delivered by the Court but the boldness of decisions in two cases, highlighting the European vision of the Court, stand conspicuous: *Van Gend en Loos*[27] and *Costa v ENEL.*[28] Even out of these two the pride of place goes to the first one. 'No decision in Community law is more important than the following: *Van Gend en Loos v Nederlandse Administratie der Belastingen (Case 26/62).*' This is how Stephen Weatherill opens his chapter on 'The Nature of Community Law: Direct Effect'.[29]

Van Gend en Loos was the first case in which the Court had to deal with the direct effect of the Treaty provisions on a national legal system. A private company, named Van Gend en Loos, had imported unreaformaldehyde from Germany into the Netherlands. The company was made to pay customs duty. It was according to the company a violation of the principle of the free movement of goods between Member States, more particularly Article 12 of the Treaty of Rome. Hence, the company, seeking to rely on European Community law against Netherlands' customs authorities, claimed reimbursement of the amount before a Dutch court. This created a conflict between Article 12 of the Treaty and a prior Netherlands' legislation on the matter. The Dutch Court made a reference to the European Court of Justice under Article 177 in order to find whether the company could rely on that Article 12. The European Court held in an Article 177 reference that Article 12, prohibiting Treaty members from introducing new customs duties between themselves, was directly effective on the member States and could, therefore, be relied on before the Dutch courts of law. The real significance of the ECJ's decision in this case lies in the words:

> 'The Community constitutes a new legal order in international law, for whose benefits the States have limited their Sovereign rights.'[30]

[26] For instance Case 262/88 *Barber v Guardian Royal Exchange Assurance Group.*

[27] Case 26/62.

[28] Case 6/64.

[29] S Weatherill, *Cases and Materials on EC Law*, 2nd edn, (London, Blackstone Press, 1995) 60.

[30] Case 26/62 *Van Gend en Loos v Nederlandse Administratie der Bleastingen* [1963] ECR 1; S Weatherill, *Cases and Materials on EC Law*, 2nd edn, (London, Blackstone Press, 1995) 61.

The Court, by the legal force of this *kort en krachtig* (a Dutch expression which may be translated as *brief and strong*) statement, at once declared the supremacy of European Community law over national law.

In the seminal case of *Costa v ENEL* the ECJ further developed its reasoning of *'limitation of sovereign rights'*. Mr Costa held shares in an Italian electric company. The company was nationalized by an Italian legislation enacted after the Italian Government passed its Ratification Act incorporating European Community law into Italian law. Mr Costa refused to pay his electricity bill. His claim was that the Italian legislation contravened numerous provisions of the EEC Treaty. The matter of priority of law was in question. The Italian Court referred the question to the European Court of Justice. The Court held that the *Community law has priority* over a unilateral subsequent national legislation. The significance of the decision of the ECJ lies in the following statement of the Court: 'The transfer, by member states, from their national orders in favour of the Community order of the rights and obligations arising from the Treaty, carries with it a clear limitation of their sovereign right upon which a subsequent unilateral law, incompatible with the aims of the Community, cannot prevail.'[31]

This landmark decision clearly further solidified and developed the 'higher law' of the Treaty, boldly declared earlier in the *Van Gend en Loos* case. The successful role played by European judges in the above two cases was well recognized by Federico Mancini:

> In view of the risk of government by national and European civil servants, it became the number one priority to define in precise terms a *higher law* on the basis of which their action could be mentioned, even if to do so might raise the spectre of government by judges; or, rather, make that spectre more threatening insofar as the discovery of fundamental rights came shortly after the vindication of principles such as direct effect of Community provisions and the primacy of Community law, which likewise were not written into the Treaties but were enshrined in a number of famous judgments (*Van Gend en Loos*, [1963]; *Costa v Enel*, [1964]).[32]

In so establishing the supremacy of the European legal order and giving direct effect to European Community law the judges of the European Court of Justice have brought a revolutionary constitutional change in the constitutional system of every Member State of the Community. Just one example from a State which has in political discreteness always been more *in* the Union than *of* the Union and *for* the Union: this is how Prof Harris observes the situation in the United Kingdom:

> Before the enactment of the European Community Act 1972 it was a settled feature of the UK customary constitution that Parliament could not bind successor parliaments, at least as to matters of legal content. That Statute provided that legislation emanating from

[31] Case 6/64 *Costa v ENEL* [1964] ECR 585; S Weatherill, *Cases and Materials on EC Law*, 2nd edn, (London, Blackstone Press, 1995) 52.

[32] G Fedrico Mancini, 'Safeguarding Human Rights: The Role of the Court of Justice of the European Communities' in Federico Carpi and Chiara Giovannucci Orlandi (eds) *Judicial Protection of Human Rights at the National and International Level*, International Congress on Procedural Law for the Ninth Centenary of the University of Bologna, vol I (Milano, Dott A Giuffre, 1991) p 504.

> the institutions of what is now the European Union should prevail over UK legislation. If it is now accepted, in any description of UK law, that our parliament could not, constitutionally, repeal the 1972 Act in such a way as to reverse the ranking of European and UK sources, then, at some time between 1972 and the present day, there occurred a change in presupposed constitutional foundations—a change in the basic norm, a technical (Kelsenian) 'revolution'.[33]

The treaties establishing the European Community (now known as the European Union), with few exceptions, did not contain any human rights guarantees. While State constitutions and the European Convention on Human Rights provided for the protection of human rights, but the treaties creating the Community established no parallel protective system against their violation by Community institutions. Since these institutions were of supranational nature and not bound by the domestic constitutional law of any of its Member States, 'the risk existed', observed Prof Buergental, now judge at the ICJ, that they might deprive individuals and companies subject to the jurisdiction of the Community of human rights guaranteed them under their own domestic law and under the European Convention without there being a remedy against such action'.[34]

The ECJ, well aware of the spirit of the 'closer union' which would have no meaning without its associated spirit of human rights, made a 'hesitant start' in that direction in the *Stauder v Ulm* case, the case which arose out of a Community scheme to provide cheap butter for recipients of welfare benefits. The Article 177 reference to the European Court by a German Court in the given case arose out of a concern that a provision of Community legislation infringed fundamental human rights. The Court held: 'the provision at issue contains nothing capable of prejudicing the fundamental human rights enshrined in the general principles of Community law and protected by the Court'.[35] This very brief statement contains dual judicial legislation. First: that *human rights are enshrined in the general principles* of Community law. And the second: that *they are protected by the Court.* This is a great 'legitimation' of creating an obligation concerning the Community's judicial commitment to the protection of human rights law by the Court's very 'deliberative communication'.

The Court added further solid substance to the already developed law when it stated in the *Internationale Handelsgesellschaft*:

> In fact, respect for fundamental rights forms an integral part of the general principles of law protected by the Court of Justice. The protection of such rights, whilst inspired by the constitutional traditions common to the Member States, must be ensured within the framework of the structure and objectives of the Community.[36]

[33] JW Harris, *Legal Philosophies*, 2nd edn, (London, Butterworths, 1997) 76.

[34] T Buergenthal, *International Human Rights Law* (St Paul, MN, West Publishing, 1995) 148.

[35] Case 29/69 *Stauder v Ulm* [1969] ECR 419; S Weatherill, *Cases and Materials on EC Law*, 2nd edn, (London, Blackstone Press, 1995) 37.

[36] *InternationaleHandelsgesellschaft* (Case 11/70) [1970] ECR 1125. J Tillotson, *European Community Law: Text, Cases and Material*, 2nd edn, (London, Cavendish, 1996) 85.

A much more serious commitment to the protection of human rights was made by the ECJ in the *Nold* case. The Court in this case first reiterated the principle that fundamental rights form an integral part of the general principles of law and then further stated:

> In safeguarding these rights, the Court is bound to draw inspiration from constitutional traditions common to the member States, and it cannot therefore uphold measures which are incompatible with fundamental rights recognized and protected by the constitutions of those states. Similarly, international treaties for the protection of human rights on which the member states have collaborated or of which they are signatories, can supply guidelines which should be followed within the framework of Community law.[37]

The Court in this statement makes amply clear: (i) the Court may annul any EC measure conflicting with fundamental human rights enshrined in constitutions of all member states, and (ii) international human rights treaties involving the member states are equally a source of law for the ECJ.

In a nutshell, the development of law by the ECJ shows that the gap created by the absence of reference to human rights guarantees is being well filled by the European Court of Justice. The dual commitment to the pluralization of democracy on the one hand and to the protection of human rights on the other, both enshrined in the grand principle of human dignity, are considered to be the civilized trends of the contemporary ideal State. The ECJ case law has steadfastly adhered to this view in interpreting the spirit of the EC Treaty. And, in doing so has also been in constant legal communication with the ECHR by relying on that Court's case law. This interaction between the two Courts has greatly facilitated the ratification of the European Convention on Human Rights by all member states of the European Union.

In the Preamble of the European Convention on Human Rights, the Contracting States first made an emphatic reference to their '*common heritage of political traditions, ideals, freedoms and the rule of law*' and then reaffirmed '*their profound belief in those Fundamental Freedoms which are the foundations of justice and peace in the world and are best maintained on the one hand by an effective political democracy and on the other by a common understanding and observance of the Human Rights upon which they depend.*'

The health of the communication between the legislature and the judiciary of a democratic system can be well measured by the degree with which the judiciary's interpretation and application of human rights principles are influenced by democratic values and in turn how much the development of human rights law by the courts' decisions have further developed the democratic values. In interpreting that Convention the ECHR has considerably demonstrated that the democratic values and the notion of human rights are the two sides of the same coin, called human dignity.

[37] Case 4/73 *Nold v Commission* [1974] ECR 491; S Weatherill, *Cases and Materials on EC Law*, 2nd edn, (London, Blackstone Press, 1995) 39.

One of the most important cases justifying judicial legislation centred around general principles of law was the *Golder v UK* case. The development of law in this case is mainly significant in two ways.

First: the European Court of Human Rights inferred from Article 6, paragraph 1, of the European Convention on Human Rights, a fundamental right of access to the courts. Mr Golder, a UK citizen in a UK prison petitioned the UK Home Secretary for leave to consult with a view to suing a prison officer. Golder was seeking to exculpate himself of the charge made against him by the prison officer and which had entailed for him unpleasant consequences. The Home Secretary declined to accord the leave request. The Court held that: 'In declining to accord the leave which had been requested, the Home Secretary failed to respect, in the person of Golder, the right to go before a court as guaranteed by Article 6(1).'[38]

Second: the Court held that the general principles of law constitute an independent source of law part of any legal system despite their unwritten nature. General principles of law recognized by civilized nations have been recognized as a source of international law by the provisions of two most authoritative international instruments, Statute of the Permanent Court of International Justice, Article 38, paragraph 1c, and the Statute of the principle judicial organ of the United Nations, International Court of Justice, Article 38, paragraph 1c. However, there was no mention of this as a source of law in the European Convention. The only reference made to general principles by that Convention was to be found in Article 7(2), the provision dealing with the particular issue of retrospective criminal law. Was this a deliberate doing by the European legislature and why? According to Prof Merrills: 'The omission of a provision corresponding to Article 38 was quite deliberate, not because those responsible for producing the Convention wished to withhold access to general principles from those entrusted with its interpretation, but, on the contrary, because they saw the use of general principles as inevitable'. This inevitability and the missing link of the judicial significance of general principles as a source of international law to be applied by the European judicial institutions was well clarified by the European Court of Human Rights in the *Golder* Case. In answering this weighty question with a weighty answer the Court drew considerably legal support from the two considerably important international instruments, Vienna Convention on Treaties and the Statute of the International Court of Justice:

> Article 31(3)(c) of the Vienna Convention indicates that account is to be taken, together with the context, of 'any relevant rules of international law applicable in the relation between parties'. Among those rules are general principles of law and especially 'general principles of law recognized by civilized nations' (Article 38(1)(c) of the Statute of the International Court of Justice). Incidentally, the Legal Committee of the Assembly of the Council of Europe foresaw in August 1950 that 'the Commission and the Court must necessarily apply such principles' in the execution of their duties and thus considered it

[38] Judgment of 21 February 1975 in the case concerning *Golder v UK*, paras 39–40, Publ Court Series A, vol 18, pp 19–20.

to be 'unnecessary' to insert a specific clause to this effect in the Convention (Documents of the Consultative Assembly, working papers of the 1950 session, vol III, no 93, p 982, para 5).[39]

By this *'deliberative communication'*[40] approach the Court killed more birds with one stone. First, it improved and solidified the international legal communication, by applying a juridical cement of common legal principles, among international legal institutions. Secondly, the Court's ruling indicates that general principles of law are as much a source of law as treaty and custom without their being written part of a statute or instrument to be interpreted; in so doing the Court also indicates that this third source is an essential link of communication between the legislators and judges to resolve the problem of *non-liquet* within the continuing framework for the unremitting protection of individual rights and liberties and on the basis of the purpose, object, and thus intention of the law givers.[41] And finally, by adding the further legislative weight to the already existing legislation of the Convention, the Court not only put a seal of judicial legislation on a newly created rule of 'the Commission and the Court must necessarily apply such principles' in the execution of their duties, but at the same time proved that the communication between the legislature and the judiciary is constant and constructive as it is the legislative spirit of the given legislation that the judges expound,[42] clarify, promote and develop. Drawing the clear distinction between recognizing that recourse to general principles is necessary in principle, and deciding that use of a general principle is appropriate in a particular case, and appraising the judicial legislative role of the Court, Prof Merrills sharply commented: 'The latter requires a demonstration that the principle in question will promote and not subvert the development of human rights law and, equally important, that in the particular circumstances use of a general principle is *a justifiable, not an excessive, act of judicial legislation.*'[43]

[39] Judgment of 7 May 1974 in the *Golder Case*, Publ Court, Series A, vol 18, para 35, p 17.

[40] M van Hoecke, *Law as Communication* (Oxford, Hart Publishing, 2002) 176. Prof Van Hoecke's theory of law as something which is not (completely) made at any point in time, and afterwards simply 'applied' by officials, by citizens and by judges to concrete cases. *Law is constantly made, adapted and developed in legal practice*, and most prominently by judges. If a Court adapts, and even changes, the content of a legislative rule, it is not in so doing, usurping its role, but in most cases rather fully assuming its tasks and duties. Legislators cannot foresee everything, nor can they constantly adapt every statute to changed circumstances. It is precisely the task and the duty of the judges to fill in the gaps which every legislator must inevitably leave.

[41] As Judge J Dickson put it:

A constitution . . . is drafted with an eye to the future. Its function is to provide a continuing framework for the legitimate exercise of governmental power and, when joined by a Bill or a Charter of Rights, for the unremitting protection of individual rights and liberties. Once enacted, its provisions cannot easily be repealed or amended. It must, therefore, be capable of growth and development over time to meet new social, political and historical realities often unimagined by its framers.

See in *Hunter v Southam*, [1984] 2 SCR 145, 155; (1984) 11 DLR (4th) 641, 649.

[42] As long back as 1819, the Chief Justice Marshall of the United States made his frequently cited dictum: 'we must never forget that it is a constitution we are expounding', 'a constitution intended to endure for ages to come'. See in *McCulloch v State of Maryland* 17 US (4 Wheaton) 306 at 405–7, 415 (1819).

[43] JG Merrills, *The Development of International Law by the European Court of Human Rights* (Manchester, MUP, 1993) 177.

(Italics added). To use the language of *Law as Communication* theory: 'From this perspective, an active role of the courts is not to be seen as "democratic deficit", but rather as a democratic *benefit*'.[44]

In the case concerning *Belilos v Switzerland* the European Court of Human Rights was called upon to apply Article 64 of the European Convention on Human Rights to an 'interpretative declaration' (reservation)[45] which the Government of Switzerland made in adhering to the Convention. The Court in the given situation was required to decide the preliminary question whether the declaration aiming at limiting the Swiss obligations under Article 6, paragraph 1, of the Convention satisfied the requirements set by paragraphs 1 and 2 of Article 64. The Court concluded that the Swiss 'declaration' was indeed a 'reservation' and that, as such, it was 'invalid' because it failed to meet the requirements of paragraphs 1 and 2 of Article 64.[46] In addressing the question of the effect of the invalid reservation on the continued membership of Switzerland to the Convention, the Court declared that: 'it is beyond doubt that Switzerland is, and regards itself as, bound by the Convention irrespective of the validity of the declaration'.[47]

This is an important case because it sets *an innovative new rule broadening the scope of the European Convention*: the validity of a reservation depends upon the criteria for making reservations as set out in Article 64 of the European Convention. Bourguignon finds in this ruling a new light on reservations to multilateral treaties.[48]

Marcks v Belgium case revolved around an illegitimate child. According to Article 8(1) of the Convention 'Everyone has the right to respect for his private and family life, his home and his correspondence.' But the Convention is silent when it comes to see the provision's relation to illegitimate children. This is another example that no legislation can ever be complete in foreseeing its application to several future situations. Those gaps, in the light of the object of the law, are always to be filled by the judges of the time.

The Court in this case held:

> . . . when the State determines in its domestic legal system the regime applicable to certain family ties such as those between an unmarried mother and her child, it must act

[44] M van Hoecke, *Law as Communication* (Oxford, Hart Publishing, 2002) 204

[45] Although Article 64 of the Convention permits its Member States to attach reservations when adhering to the Convention, it subjects this right to the following two conditions: First: 'Any State may, when signing this Convention or when depositing its instrument of ratification, make a reservation in respect of any particular provision of the Convention to the extent that any law then in force in its territory is not in conformity with the provision. Reservation of a general character shall not be permitted under this article.' (Para 1 of Article 64). And Second: 'Any reservation made under this Article shall contain a brief statement of the law concerned.' (Para 2 of Article 64).

[46] Judge Syed SS Pirzada described such reservation as 'objectionable reservation' and suggested such reservations to be treated 'as severable'. See Judge *ad hoc* Pirzada's Dissenting Opinion appended to the International Court of Justice's Judgment of 21 June 2000 in the case concerning *Aerial Incident of 10 August 1999* (*Pakistan v India*) in ICJ Reports 2000, para 5, p 85.

[47] *Belilos v Switzerland*, Judgment of 29 April 1988, 132 Publ European Court of Human Rights (1988), p 28.

[48] T Bourguignon, 'New Light on Reservations to Multilateral Treaties' (1989) 29 *Viginia Journal of International Law* 347.

> in a manner calculated to allow those concerned to lead a normal family life implies in particular, in the Court's view, the existence in domestic law of legal safeguards that render possible as from the moment of birth the child's integration in his family. In this connection, the State has a choice of various means, but a law that fails to satisfy this requirement violates paragraph 1 of Article 8.[49]

The Court having found that the Belgian law failed to make adequate provision for this integration, it followed that the Convention had been violated.

Within the area of constitutional control 'courts have sometimes explicitly obtained the power to formulate general rules, comparable to legislative powers.'[50] The process of such judicial legislation involves the court's power to decide that a new interpretation of the instrument which the court has posited in its decision will be valid for the future only and could not be invoked for the period which was preceding the decision (unless of course, a trial in which a claim was based on it, started before that date).[51] Such a rule was formulated by the European Court of Human Rights in the present case.

Although the Court held that the Belgian law violated Article 8 of the Convention, nevertheless, it did not fail to acknowledge that:

> difference of treatment between 'legitimate' and 'illegitimate' children, for example, in the matter of patrimonial rights, were for many years regarded as permissible and normal in a large number of Contracting States.... Evolution towards equality has been slow and reliance on the Convention to accelerate this evolution was apparently contemplated at a rather late stage.[52]

Human dignity reflecting through the principle of equality has here been placed in retrospect and prospect. An illegitimate child is not 'illegitimate' by his/her own doing. He/she is simply a 'child' and a human being with inherent dignity as far as law is concerned. But law in the past, such as that of Belgium, did not recognize the individual human dignity in the same light as it does now, for the principle of equality of the time was not as much developed as at present.

Therefore, the Court further held that in the given circumstances the government of Belgium was not under an obligation to reopen legal acts or situations prior to the decision of the Court. Was it necessary that the Court should establish such a rule? Not as far as the current case and the applicant were concerned. Yet, in the interest of the society and to stop the potential flood of future cases of past illegitimacies, the Court found it wise and necessary to take to judicial legislation. This may well be described as a silent communication of discretion and mutual understanding of the legislative spirit between the legislature and the judiciary.

In the *Handyside* case the Court finally laid the very hallmarks of a true and dignified democracy in interaction. And those very hallmarks reflect the concept

[49] Series A, No 31, para 31.
[50] M van Hoecke, *Law as Communication* (Oxford, Hart Publishing, 2002) 175.
[51] *Ibid.*
[52] Series A, No 31, para 58.

of human dignity in its entirety at every level and in every form of human interaction and communication.

> The Court's supervisory functions oblige it to pay the utmost attention to the principles characterising a 'democratic society'. Freedom of expression constitutes one of the essential foundations of such a society, one of the basic conditions for its progress and for the development of every man. Subject to paragraph 2 of Article 10, it is applicable not only to 'information' or 'ideas' that are favourably received or regarded as in offensive or as a matter of indifference, but also to those that offend, shock or disturb the State or any sector of the population. *Such are the demands of that pluralism, tolerance and broadmindedness without which there is no 'democratic society'.* This means, amongst other things, that every 'formality', 'condition', 'restriction' or 'penalty' imposed in this sphere must be proportionate to the legitimate aim pursued.[53] (italics are mine).

The Court in this case developed a paramount principle: that without pluralism, tolerance, and broadmindedness, democracy is not worth its name and spirit.

In dealing with the expression 'prescribed by law' in Article 10(2), the Court held in the Sunday Times case that the 'prescribed by law' has no meaning if it does not fulfil at least two requirements:

> Firstly, the law must be adequately accessible: the citizen must be able to have an indication that is adequate in the circumstances of the legal rules applicable to a given case. Secondly, a norm cannot be regarded as a 'law' unless it is formulated with sufficient precision to enable the citizen to regulate his conduct: he must be able—if need be with appropriate advice—to foresee, to a degree that is reasonable in the circumstances, the consequences which a given action may entail.[54]

Human dignity and dignity of human interaction were further promoted in the *Young, James and Webster* case. The Court, within the context of 'closed shop agreement', explained:

> . . . pluralism, tolerance and broadmindedness are hall-marks of a 'democratic society'. Although individual interests must on occasion be subordinated to those of a group, democracy does not simply mean that the views of a majority must always prevail: a balance must be achieved which ensures that the fair and proper treatment of minorities and avoid any abuse of a dominant position. Accordingly, the mere fact that the applicants' standpoint was adopted by the very few of their colleagues is again not conclusive of the issue now before the Court.[55]

Speaking about the legislative role of the European Court of Justice (within the European Union) and the European Court of Human Rights (within the ambit of the European Council) Prof Van Hoecke wrote:

> In the absence of any strong legislator at both European levels, courts have filled in the gap and established, through the interpretation of the respective European treaties, new

[53] Series A, No 24, para 49.
[54] Series A, No 26, para 31.
[55] Series A, No 44, para 63.

general rules with a much broader scope, and sometimes a different content, compared that which the parties to those treaties originally had in mind.[56]

In brief, paraphrasing the Chief Justice Marshall, the judges of the two European Courts have expounded the European legislative spirit intended to endure for ages. No intended 'closer union among the peoples', their unification or harmonization, has ever been reached so smoothly in legal and political history. But, one may—considering the judicial injection given by the European courts to the theoretical political will (at times shaky) of European leaders and peoples—declare confidently that the most critical stage towards their 'union' has long passed. No matter how rough and turbulent the political tides of today and tomorrow may be the hardest part of the individual national sovereignties have melted down into the European human pot for good. It is now more human and European than German, French or British and therein lies the dignity and popular will of its individual(s) which owes a great deal to the judges of the European Courts. In other words, the transfer of power from the member States to the European Community has reached the point of irreversibility.

IV. Legislative Role of the International Court of Justice

Speaking about the judicial law-making role of the International Court of Justice, Judge Jennings, a former President of the ICJ, has the following message to give:

> And here the message I want to convey is that the International Court of Justice, the Principal Judicial Organ of the United Nations, has a dual role to play. It is readily and generally thought of as being well suited to the settlement of disputes. But in so doing, it has also a vital role in the development and elaboration of general law. A glance at, for example, the near now 90 volumes of the *International Law Reports* demonstrates very clearly the extent to which judicial decisions are now an important source of international law. Moreover, a glance at virtually any report of a decision by the International Court of Justice itself, will show the extent to which the decision is indebted to the 'jurisprudence' of previous decisions.[57]

In the above article, Judge Jennings, while emphasizing that new international law for the protection of the environment needs urgently to be developed and also mentioning about the important role the International Court can play in this development, brings to light the fact, citing an example of the very first contentious case concerning *Corfu Channel* brought before the ICJ, of how this development of environmental law can draw upon the case law. For instance, he says:

[56] M van Hoecke, *Law as Communication* (Oxford, Hart Publishing, 2002) 175.

[57] Sir Robert Jennings, *The Role of the International Court of Justice in the Development of International Environmental Law* (1992) 241.

> it is an important elementary principle that a State may not knowingly permit its territory to be used to inflict serious injury on other States—a proposition which, incidentally, owes its prominence if not its origin to a Judgment of the ICJ in the *Corfu Channel* case—but such general rules originated at a time before global problems such as climatic change were perceived at all.[58]

The Court had not yet finished with the *Corfu Channel* case, that the history making case in judicial law-making, the advisory case concerning *Reparation for Injuries Suffered in the Service of the United Nations* was brought to the Court by the Secretary-General of the United Nations. By his letter dated 4 December 1948, filing on 7 December 1948, he transmitted the General Assembly Resolution of 3 December 1948. In that Resolution the General Assembly requested an Advisory Opinion of the Court on two questions:

> I. In the event of an agent of the United Nations in the performance of his duties suffering injury in circumstances involving responsibility of a State, has the United Nations, as an Organization, the capacity to bring an international claim against the responsible *de jure* or *de facto* government with a view to obtaining the reparation due in respect of the damage caused (a) to the United Nations, (b) to the victim or to persons entitled through him?
>
> II. In the event of an affirmative reply on point 1(b), how is action by the United Nations to be reconciled with such rights as may be possessed by the State of which the victim is national?[59]

In reaching its conclusion on the answer to first question that the United Nations was a subject of international law and could make an international claim, the Court stated:

> The subjects of law in any legal system are not necessarily identical in their nature or in the extent of their rights, and their nature depends upon the needs of the community. Throughout its history, the development of international law has been influenced by the requirements of international life, and the progressive increase in the collective activities of States has already given rise to instances of action upon the international plane by certain entities which are not States. This development culminated in the establishment in June 1945 of an international organization whose purposes and principles are specified in the Charter of the United Nations. But to achieve these ends the attribution of international personality is indispensable.[60]

In answer to the second question asked by the General Assembly the Court advised:

> When the United Nations as an Organization is bringing a claim for reparation damage caused to its agent, it can only do so by basing its claim upon a breach of obligations due to itself; respect for this rule will usually prevent a conflict between the action of the

[58] Sir Robert Jennings, *The Role of the International Court of Justice in the Development of International Environmental Law* (1992) 241.

[59] ICJ Reports, 1949, p 175.

[60] *Ibid*, p 178.

> United Nations and such rights as the agent's national State may possess, and thus bring about a reconciliation must depend upon considerations applicable to each particular case, and upon agreements to be made between the Organization and individual States, either generally or in each case.[61]

'Thus', says Judge Lachs, 'for the first time in history, an institution other than a State was recognized as a subject of international law.' Judge Lachs also described this legislative act of the ICJ as a 'landmark in the development of international law'.[62] Appreciating the judicial law-making by the International Court of Justice, Friedmann writes: 'Outstanding, in this writer's opinion, is the Advisory Opinion in which the International Court, by a strong majority, bestowed full international legal personality upon the United Nations as a condition of its capacity to demand reparation for injury suffered by one of its servants (Count Bernadotte).'[63] Further, recognizing the solid development of international law on legal personality made by the Court while deciding the above Advisory Opinion case Friedmann says:

> In going beyond the wording of article 104 of the UN Charter, which cautiously refrained from declaring such international legal personality, the Court firmly established the advance from a system of international law in which states are the sole subjects, to one in which international organizations, without being super states, live and function as personalities in their own right.[64]

There is another area of international law, Human Rights law, in which the Court has substantially contributed by its judicial law-making process. As a matter of fact, Judge Higgins sees the contribution of the World Court to the development of human rights law going as far back as 1920s. She thinks that it is fair to say that in the early 1920s, and indeed right through the 30s, the idea of human rights was synonymous with the idea of minority rights. The great post-war instruments, commencing with the Universal Declaration of Human Rights, were yet to come. But it had been realized that the redrawing of territorial frontiers at the end of World War I would necessitate some protection for those who found themselves in a new country. The great inter-war Minority Treaties sought to alleviate the human condition, within a framework that represented the realities of the day. The Minorities Treaties system became both important in its own right and an important beginning in developing our ideas on human rights. It was the permanent Court of International Justice that was called upon to provide the necessary judicial underpinning to the minority Treaties system. An immense case law came into being by the discharge of this duty. The jurisprudence of the Permanent Court showed a profound insight into what was necessary for the protection of national minorities and its findings contained ideas that have had a lasting

[61] ICJ Reports, 1949, p 188.

[62] M Lachs, *ibid*, pp 252–53.

[63] W Friedmann, *Law in a Changing Society*, 2nd edn, (New Delhi, Universal Book Traders, 1996) 86.

[64] *Ibid*.

importance in human rights law. Of particular importance, in this field, are the following few cases: 1) *German Settlers in Poland*,[65] 2) *Rights of Minorities in Polish Upper Silesia* (Minority Schools).[66] The Third case concerning Minority Schools is a famous case for the equality between a majority and a minority. Albanian government decided to shut all minority schools and not just Greek schools in order to prove that there was no minority discrimination in Albania. The PCIJ was not impressed by that. The Court in this case linked that proposition to the entitlement of equality in fact and as well as equality in law. According to the Court, special needs and equality in fact 'are indeed closely interlocked, for there would be no true equality between a majority and a minority if the latter were deprived of its own institutions, and were consequently compelled to renounce that which constitutes the very essence of its being a minority.'[67]

Just to mention one more important aspect of human rights, the concept of self-determination, Judge Higgins writes:

> The Court has clearly played a major and critical role in the development of the concept of self-determination. We take that legal concept for granted today, but it must be remembered that when the Court addressed this matter in the *South West Africa*, *Namibia* and *Western Sahara* cases, there were still those who insisted that self-determination was nothing more than a political aspiration.[68]

There are other areas—Law of the Sea, Law of Treaties, Economic Law, law concerning frontier disputes, etc—that the ICJ has played an impressive role in the development of international law. To describe all these here is not within the scope of this chapter.

V. The Development of Law and Judicial Ideologies

Professor Merrills is of the view that the extent to which the decisions of an international tribunal develop the law depends in large measure on which of the two general judicial ideologies—1) the ideology of judicial restraint and 2) the ideology of judicial activism—the members of the Court subscribe to.[69]

And further Prof Merrills finds that when an international court develops the law, the direction, the subject matter, in which it does so is again influenced by two of the specific ideologies—1) tough conservatism and 2) benevolent liberalism.[70] The advocate of judicial restraint believes that the judge's job is to apply law and

[65] Advisory Opinion, 1923, PCIJ Series B, No 6.

[66] PCIJ Series A, No 15.

[67] Minority Schools in Albania, Advisory Opinion, 1935, PCIJ Series A/B, No 64, p 17.

[68] R Higgins, 'The International Court of Justice and Human Rights' in K Wellens, (ed), *International Law: Theory and Practice: Essays in Honour of Eric Suy* (The Hague, Martinus Nijhoff, 1998) 694.

[69] JG Merrills, *The Development of International Law by the European Court of Human Rights* (Manchester, MUP, 1993) 229.

[70] *Ibid.*

not to make it. He sets considerable store by precedent. Although he agrees that an element of legal development occurs as a natural part of the judicial process, his particular concern for the 'rule-book', authoritative legal materials, makes him uncomfortable with doctrinal innovation. In a nutshell he minds his own business of applying the law and reacts with 'great hostility' to anything which can be regarded as 'politicisation' of judicial process, or any attempt to suggest that moral, social or economic factors should play a part in decision-making.[71]

The judicial activist is diametrically opposed to the above position of the advocate of judicial restraint. To the activist, what the Court decides is more important than how it decides. He emphasises using of the rules and developing them to achieve results. Activist, as opposed to believer of judicial restraint, interprets constraints on the judicial role very liberally. The activist is keen to consider what the law ought to be. For him courts are part of the political process and the adjudication always a political act. He sees law as much more than a matter of rules. The activist judge does not ignore the law which has been laid down, but he equally considers as part of his job that he must be ready to develop and, if necessary, change it. In short the activist judge is a supporter of doctrinal innovation.[72]

The advocate of tough conservatism is obviously not only a conservatist but a tough conservative. He is concerned with the preservation of existing institutions and attaches considerable importance to history, tradition and established social values. He is slow to recognize the need for change. In short the tough conservative is happy with the *status quo* and has no great faith in either the merits or the practicality of schemes for improvement No doubt that most advocates of judicial restraint must be tough conservatives when it comes to develop the human rights law.[73] *Tough conservative would go for maximum rights of States.* When an international judge, advocating judicial restraint, hence also tough conservatism, and engaged in adjudicating on subjects involving human rights issues, his ideological bent in the balance of State sovereignty versus human dignity is most likely to tilt to the side of the doctrine of sovereignty in its traditional sense as against the principle of human dignity, for instance in the second phase of the *South West Africa* cases decided by the International Court of Justice.[74]

The benovelent liberalist represents two qualities, he is liberal and he is benevolent. His liberal ideology takes its starting point the value of the individual. The liberal sees the authority of State as inherently oppressive which he finds as irksome restraint on the individual's realization of his potential. He does not deny the necessity of the State's authority but he does not share the tough conservatist's exaggerated fear of anarchy. The liberal is not anarchist but a firm believer of individual's freedom and development. The benevolent aspect of the benevolent liberal is bound up with the role of the State in achieving the liberal's goals. The value which benevolent liberal places on the individual puts fairness and equality

[71] *Ibid*, pp 230–31.
[72] *Ibid*, pp 231–33.
[73] *Ibid*, p 239–40.
[74] *South West Africa* (Second Phase), Judgment of 18 July 1966, ICJ Reports 1966, p 6.

high on its agenda and the State is expected to take steps to bring this about by, for example, outlawing discrimination. *Benevolent liberal goes for maximum rights of individuals.* By virtue of the benevolent stand, however, the conception of rights is broadened. Benevolent liberalism could therefore be summed up, according to Merrills, by saying that those who support this ideology are not at all happy with the way things are, and believe that the change is essential if the individual's worth is to be recognized. They also regard the task of social improvement as never ending and see State action as having a central role in virtually all aspects of the individual's welfare.[75] When an international judge, advocating judicial activism, hence also benevolent liberalism, and engaged in adjudicating on subjects involving human rights issues, his ideological bent in the balance of State sovereignty versus human dignity is most likely to tilt to the side of the principle of human dignity as against the doctrine of State sovereignty in its traditional sense, for instance in the case concerning *Military and Paramilitary Activities in and against Nicaragua* decided by the International Court of Justice.[76]

VI. Appraisal

In our foregoing reflections, a cursory glimpse of some cases decided by the International Court of Justice, and its predecessor the PCIJ, we have seen that the judges of the International Court of Justice have been considerably contributing to the development of international law.

Describing about the ICJ's contribution to the development of the international law which it applies, Court's Handbook mentions:

> By interpreting the international law in force and applying it to specific cases, the Court's decisions clarify that law, and thereby frequently pave the way for progressive development of international law by States, since the Court's decisions are in themselves legal acts and are known both to States and to the international agencies entrusted with the continuing task of codification and progressive development of international law, particularly under the auspices of the United Nations. Those who carry out this task owe an immense debt to the jurisprudence of the Court.[77]

Describing further the judicial legislative role or the contribution of its judicial law-making actively participating in the legislation of the General Assembly through the drafts prepared by the International Law Commission, the Handbook recognizes: Indeed, the role of the ICJ has institutional shape, to some degree, in the statute of the International Law Commission of the United Nations, according to which the Commission prepares its draft articles and submits them to the General Assembly of the United Nations with a commentary which includes a full

[75] Merrills, *ibid*, pp 240–42.

[76] Military and Paramilitary Activities in and against Nicaragua (*Nicaragua v USA*), Judgment on Merits, ICJ Reports 1986, p 14.

[77] *The International Court of Justice 1946–96* (*Court's Handbook*), pp 93–94.

summary of the precedents and other relevant material, including the 'judicial decisions'. As will be seen from the drafts of the International Law Commission, the decisions of the International Court of Justice take pride of place in the Commission's presentation of the relevant judicial decisions.[78]

According to Prof Dhyani, Judges in a conservative country like England boast that they do not make law. They only interpret it. However, he says, this is not borne by facts. And he quotes the following words of one of the most eminent English judges, Lord Denning, to bring the truth to light:

> This is an illusion which they (judges) have fostered. But it is notion which is now being discarded every where. Every new decision—on every new situation—is a development of law. Law does not stand still. It moves continually. Once this is recognised then the task of the judge is put on a higher plane. He must consciously seek to mould the law so as to serve the needs of the time. He must be an architect—thinking of structure as a whole—building for society a system of law which is strong, durable and just. It is on his work that civilized society depends.[79]

These remarks of Lord Denning concerning the legislative role of the judge cannot be simply for judges of national courts. They equally apply to any judge, irrespective of his or her sphere of concern. In closing, to see how true is the core truth may perhaps best be deduced from the following words of a world famous non judicial leader, Theodore Roosevelt, a former President of the United States of America:

> The chief lawmakers . . . may be, and often are, the judges, because they are the final seat of authority. Every time they interpret contract, property, vested rights, due process of law, liberty, they necessarily enact into law parts of a system of social philosophy; and as such interpretation is fundamental, they give direction to all law-making.[80]

Hence, judges do legislate in the sense that they clarify and develop the law further. And they are in that sense, as Judge Lachs put it, 'a vital force in the life of the law.' How far this vital force of the ICJ judges has contributed to the development of human rights law, or has held back from time to time from developing the law, taking into consideration their judicial ideological advocacies, would be surveyed in Part II and Part III of this book.

[78] *Ibid.*

[79] SN Dhyani, *Fundamentals of Jurisprudence: The Indian Approach* (1997) 335.

[80] Cited in M Cappelletti, *The Judicial Process in Comparative Perspective* (Oxford, Clarendon Press, 1989) 3.

3

Relationship between Human Rights and International Law: Principle of Human Dignity Versus Principle of State Sovereignty

. . . all human rights derive from the dignity and worth inherent in the human person.[1]

'. . . the fundamental principle of State sovereignty,' is a basic tenet, 'on which the whole international law rests,' observed the International Court of Justice.[2]

The development of human rights on the international level is one of the most startling innovations in modern international law, because it has a potential to unleash explosive forces challenging the basic tenet of the system, the principle of state sovereignty.[3]

THE UNIFIED AND uniform judicial idea in the trinity of the above mentioned three citations would constantly find expression throughout the following analysis concerning the relation between human rights and international law. If state sovereignty is the fundamental principle on which whole international law rests, then what is the relation between human rights, which are derived from human dignity and form a new branch of international law, with whole international law. If human dignity is the fundamental principle on which whole human rights law rests then what is the relation between sovereignty and human dignity. This enquiry can be set in several different perspectives. This section aims at first setting the enquiry in general perspective, studying both principles in retrospect and prospect, and then, after a brief appraisal, carrying on the study further in part II and part III in the particular perspective of the case law developed by the International Court of Justice.

[1] The Vienna Declaration and Programme of Action, adopted on 25 June 1993, by the UN-sponsored World Conference on Human Rights. The representatives of 172 States adopted by consensus the Vienna Declaration. Quoted in MJ Perry, *The Idea of Human Rights: Four Inquiries* (Oxford, OUP, 1998) 12.

[2] Military and Paramilitary Activities in and against Nicaragua case (Merits), Judgment of 27 June 1986, ICJ Reports 1986, p 133.

[3] P Malanczuk, *Akehurst's Modern Introduction to International Law*, 7th edn, (London, Routledge, 1997) 211.

The development of human rights law by the International Court of Justice largely depends not only on how its Judges look at the legislative role of the Judge, particularly while advocating certain judicial ideologies, but also how do they advocate the relation between human rights and international law, particularly when the adjudicational matters involve the situations of the principle of state sovereignty versus the principle of human dignity. Having dealt with the legislative role of the Judge in the previous section, in the following pages we will deal with the later aspect.

There is no denying the fact that just as the idea of state sovereignty is bound up with the traditional conception of international law, similarly the idea of human dignity is bound up with the idea of human rights, an integral part of the contemporary international law.

When we ask ourselves the question 'What is the relation between human rights and international law?', we are in fact asking several questions. The first thought would go to the related questions in international law itself: i) the relation between international law and municipal law: monist and dualist doctrines, ii) the basis of international law: natural law school with its offshoot of doctrine of fundamental rights, positive law school and its offshoot of consent theory, etc. Yet, parallel to all this we are also addressing a twofold question: 'What are human rights', and, 'What is international law?' And when we are asking what are they both, we are asking: 'What is their nature and scope?' In answering these questions we counter-question ourselves, a) 'Are they bodies of rules?' b) 'What are the sources of human rights and international law?' Then 'What are their functions?' When we ponder over their sources we look for their individual basis. It also tilts towards the subject-object dichotomy in international law. As a matter of fact we question and counter-question ourselves as if there are questions within the questions. But no matter from which perspective we look at these questions, there does ring a common note, somehow, someway, and in some or other measure, the note of the doctrine of sovereignty. No matter how many radii a circle has they all converge at one point, its centre. Having known the centre we have known the circle. Hence, we ask ourselves an understanding of the concept of human rights and the concept of international law. But human rights law is a branch of international law and not vice-versa. In other words international law is a bigger circle within which there are other smaller circles, such as human rights law, space law, environmental law, etc. At the core of all of them there must be one centre. Perceiving international law in its global circularity, we are now asking a grand old question: 'What is the basis of international law'? There are theories and theories expounded to answer this question. The one which still prevails most is the consent theory centring around the traditional concept of state sovereignty. But if we ask ourselves: 'What is the basis of human rights law?' There are also several theories centring around several concepts, such as human dignity, equality, justice based on fairness, freedom, liberty, etc. The theory which seems reflecting more or less in all other theories is the theory based on the principle of human dignity. If the principle of sovereignty is at the base of international law, then the principle of human dignity must have something common with the principle of sovereignty. In fact the question of our questions leads us to asking what is the relation between the principle of State sovereignty and the principle of human dignity. But there are several definitions about the meaning of the term sovereignty. And, the definitions of the principle of human dignity are still in the making. Law is a dynamic process. Humanity itself is subject to evolution. There are processes within processes. The quest goes on in search of the process of processes. The power of sovereignty resting in the person of an absolute ruler, is now reflecting as human dignity in the *persona* of every individual human being, which used to be considered as an object of the traditional international law, but has now emerged as the subject of contemporary international law. Seen through the lenses of the '*law as communication*'[4] approach the legal-political voice of the individual which was silenced by the absolute ruler of the traditional international legal culture has now become equal part of the general legal-political voice of the global community of the present international legal culture. This new development in legal thinking has given birth to a new school of law, a new doctrine, which may be called a school of human rights law. The school is mainly based on the principle of human dignity. It is so affecting the traditional thinking about international law, centring on the State sovereignty, mainly pioneered by the school of positive law, that one is bound to ponder: what is the relation between human rights and international law?. Reflecting in turn: what is the relation between the principle of human dignity and the principle of State sovereignty? In order to deal with the question we would first reflect briefly on the traditional, but *yet* alive to a degree, basis of international law, the principle of sovereignty.

I. Basis of International Law: The Principle of Sovereignty

The doctrinal debate to identify the basis of obligation in international law, setting naturalist school against positivist school, leads to some reflections on the relation between the basis of human rights law and the basis of international law. Today if we ask the question; 'What is the basis of international law?,' the minds of many

[4] M van Hoecke, *Law as Communication* (Oxford, Hart Publishing, 2002). In his approach Prof Van Hoecke forcefully demonstrates that: 'Law cannot anymore be correctly understood within a paradigm of one-dimensional rationality' (p 10). According to him, in the 'new theories of democracy' . . . the individual is seen less as an atomic entity, which could be isolated from any concrete community, but rather as part of a whole, which does not only offer an added value to the sum of the isolated individuals, but is the necessary condition and framework for any form of individual good life. If this approach is correct, it means that *human interaction and communication* have to be at the centre of any theory of law, rather than individuals or legal systems as such. (pp 10–11).

The dignity of the *Law as Communication* approach lies in the fact that it not only enhances the human dignity by elevating the status of individual to an equal '*part of a whole*' but highlights that the dignity of democracy as a whole lies in seeing intersubjective *human interaction and communication* at the centre of entire legal culture.

of us would instantly jump to the 'consent theory', an outcome of positive law school, and answer the question in the fraction of a second in the words 'the principle of sovereignty.' However, the history and development of international law speaks for the fact that not only the principles of international are derived from the 'law of nature' but except for a short interlude, from the birth of positivist school with Bentham and Austin ideas to the writing of the UN Charter and the Universal Declaration of Human Rights, the law of nature has always been the foundation of international law. With the dominance of positivist thinking, which is still prevailing but rapidly declining, the ancient meaning of the word sovereignty as supreme source of law has been covered by analytical mist. With the dawn of absolute monarchs the sovereignty rested in the monarch. With the dawn of the institution of State the concept of State sovereignty was born. The principle of State sovereignty is defined by Judge Alvarez (Chile) in the *Corfu Channel* case in the following words: 'By sovereignty, we understand the whole body of rights and attributes which a State possesses in its territory, to the exclusion of all other States, and also in its relations with other States. Sovereignty confers rights upon States and imposes obligations on them.'[5] Here too it is the State which dominates the stage of international law.

Major voices still declare that the whole international law rests on the principle of State sovereignty. Defending Nicaragua's right of freedom in her doctrinal choices of political, social economic and cultural aspects of State system, the International Court of Justice observed: '. . . adherence by a State to any particular doctrine does not constitute a violation of customary international law; *to hold otherwise would make nonsense of the fundamental principle of State sovereignty, on which the whole international law rests.*' (italics added)[6] An Indian jurist, Prof Agarwal, sees the relation between law and sovereignty in the following words: 'Law is the vehicle of sovereignty'.[7] If it is true in relation to municipal law, in which sovereignty is a vital attribute of statehood, it is more true in relation to international law, for, as Prof Buergenthal (USA), now a judge at the International Court of Justice, points out: 'When international lawyers speak of states, they mean sovereign or nation-states'.[8]

[5] *Corfu Channel* case (Merits), Judgment of 9 April 1949, Individual Opinion of Judge Alvarez, ICJ Reports 1949, p 43.

[6] Military and Paramilitary Activities in and against Nicaragua (*Nicaragua v USA*), Judgment on Merits, ICJ Reports 1986, p 133. At the face of it the words may sound as if the Court hs defended the traditional doctrine of State sovereignty as against human rights based on human dignity. But that is not the case here. It is actually other way round. The Court stood against the US military intervention in Nicaragua and declared: 'The Court cannot contemplate the creation of a new rule opening up a right of intervention by one State against another on the ground that the latter has opted for some particular ideology or political system.' (*Ibid*). The Court further laid down a matter of principle: 'In any event, while the United States might form its own appraisal of the situation as to respect for human rights in Nicaragua, the use of force could not be the appropriate method to monitor or insure such respect.' (*Ibid*, 134).

[7] RC Agarwal, *Political Theory* (2000) 202.

[8] T Buergenthal, *Public International Law in a Nutshell*, 2nd edn, (St Paul, MN, West Publishing, 1990) 2.

Such forceful statements of the International Court and its judges clearly reflect that how the influence of the positivist school of law, based on the principle of State sovereignty, still dominates the international legal system. However, the positivist school is hardly a century or so old. And, it is indeed to the 'law of nature,' the basis of natural law school, that international law owes its existence. Sir Henry Maine aptly observed: 'the greatest function of the 'law of nature' was discharged in giving birth to modern international law.'[9] The age of what we call international law is hardly more than 500 years. Much of its development however has taken place within the last 250 years. And still more so when we speak about the contemporary international law the greater part of it has developed only during the last 100 years. But when it comes to speak about international human rights law as being part of international law, the date of birth falls in 1946, when the UN Charter came into force. The contemporary legal and political cultures are witnessing the transition from absolute sovereignty of State(s) to popular sovereignty of State(s). Absolute sovereignty stood for 'single will' of the ruler over the people in the State. But the developing pluralization of society seems creating a notion of popular sovereignty. Its link with human dignity and human rights is not that of a 'single will' either at the national or international level, but that of all round interaction and communication in an extensive legal and political process, ceaselessly going on. Prof Van Hoecke observes: 'Popular Sovereignty is not interpreted as a necessarily 'single will' of 'the people' but as an *intersubjective communication power*, exercised . . . 'by means of elections and voting and specific legislative, executive, and judicial organs"[10] (italics added). Hence, this accommodating link of absolute sovereignty to the resulting conception of popular sovereignty is so generating the *intersubjective communication power* at every level of human society that the traditional dichotomies of object and subject are fast disappearing giving way to a simple equal pluralistic participation in all legal and political processes. Legal and political thought has long been, slowly though at times, developing into that direction. One simply needs to glance that in retrospect and prospect.

The nation-State system, established by the Treaty of Westphalia (1648), together with its two corollaries, the doctrine of sovereignty expounded by Jean Bodin in the 16th century and the pristine concept of human dignity has now already entered the 21st century. The present situation seen within the perspective of existing international relations and international law reflect that the institution of State and the doctrine of sovereignty are not the same as they were in the past. The international community of mankind has already entered the age of human rights based on the principle of human dignity.

The concepts of State and sovereignty are integral parts of the nation-state system. They together provide a 'central formula' to rationalize and analyze the municipal legal system of a State and the international legal system of the community of sovereign States.

[9] HO Maine, *International Law* (1915) quoted in SK Verma, *An Introduction to Public International Law* (New Delhi, Prentice Hall of India, 1998) 11.

[10] M van Hoecke, *Law as Communication* (Oxford, Hart Publishing, 2002) 123.

The legal and political historians commonly designate the year of 1648, the year when the Treaty of Westphalia was signed, at the time when the modern nation-state system came into being. However, the institution of State has existed all through the time as far as human memory can take us. In the modern sense, however, the term is a derivation of the Greek word '*polis*' which means a city. Hence, modern system of democracy and the concept of State is the continuation and modification of Greek city-States. The State has been viewed differently by different thinkers in different ages. For Plato the State was a great man in virtue.[11] Aristotle saw it as an association meant for promoting good life.[12] Cicero perceived it as the highest product of virtue and excellence.[13] For Machiavelli the State was the noblest product of human nature.[14] Hegel viewed the State as the highest and noblest realisation of idea of 'Right'.[15] Karl Marx saw this institution in a

[11] *The Republic* (386 BC) is the greatest of the writings of Plato. Plato knew well how his native place Athens had to suffer immense humiliation in the wars of Peloponnesian. He witnessed before his eyes the dstruction caused by Macedonian militarism. He had also experienced the defeat of Athens in wars against Spartas and the resulting tyrannical rule of reactionaries. On top of all this he also saw the execution of his own master, Socrates. No doubt all this made an impact on him and resulted in his quest for ideal State in human virtue and true human knowledge. In *The Republic* he dealt with 'ideal state', 'virtue', 'knowledge', 'education', 'justice', etc. For him the dignity of man and State lied in pursuing the path of virtue which he had learnt from his teacher Socrates. *The Republic* also dealt with subjects such as 'individualism' and the relation between State and the individual. Plato has been described as utopian and his ideal State and philosopher king as utopia. However, the problem is not whether the philosophy is practical or utopian the problem is that we are not willing enough to follow in practice what does not please our senses. 'Virtue' is nothing other than being what law calls 'fair'or 'right' or 'just'. By virtue actually what Plato meant in his time and treatise was that all human interaction and communication at all levels and under all forms must be 'fair', 'right', 'just' and in a nutshell dignified. Hence, virtue was the Platonic term for human dignity and human rights.

[12] *Politics*, consisting of 8 Books, is the only available work associated with the name of Aristotle. Book VII deals with the constitution of an ideal state. Though he believed that it was the duty of the State to promote good life yet he was of the firm view that in a State all could not become citizens and thus he denied this basic right to the bulk of population including women and working classes.

[13] Marcus Tullius Cicero (106–43 BC) saw this virtue and excellence in the eternal equality of man according to eternal law and justice. He was far ahead of his time for a State which would grant human rights and protect human dignity of its citizens. His ideas about the State, law and justice are mentioned in his two treatises, the *Republic* and *Laws*. The following paragraph from his *Laws* is striking in this regard:

> Out of all the material of the philosophers' discussion, surely there comes nothing more valuable than the full realization that we are born for justice, and that right is based, not upon man's opinion, but upon nature. This fact will immediately be plain if you once get a clear conception of man's fellowship and union with his fellow-men. For no single thing is so like another, so exactly its counterpart, as all of us are to one another. Nay, if bad habits and false beliefs did not twist the weaker minds and turn them in whatever direction they are inclined, no one would be so like his own self as all men would be like all others.

Laws, 1, 10, 28–29, CW Keyes (tr); SH George and TL Thorson, *A History of Political Theory*, 4th edn, (1977) 162.

[14] Human nature for Machiavelli was very selfish. His masterpiece accordingly was *The Prince* (1513). Though one cannot fish any pluralism from it, neither human dignity nor human rights, yet in the utmostly depressing political situation of Italy and Europe as a whole at that time no plan of action could have worked better than the one described in *The Prince*. However, as the popular sovereignty of the 21st century stands for the power of the masses, the State and sovereignty conceptions of *The Prince* has nothing to contribute to it.

[15] Hegel's idea of 'Right' implied respect for human dignity and human rights. In his *Philosophy of Right* he mentioned: 'A man counts as a man in virtue of his manhood alone, not because he is Jew, Catholic, Protestant, German, Italian, etc.' (GWF Hegel, *Philosophy of Right*, Section 209, note).

totally different light: as an organisation of one class dominating another.[16] These different views reflect that there are different ways one looks at the State system, either as power system or as welfare system, or both. And yet in the juridical world the State is also viewed as a legal construction or juridical personality. Kelsen, for instance, finds law and State as identical.[17] Whether looked through a political lens or a legal prism, of all the essential attributes of State, sovereignty has always remained at the very basis of its political and legal organization. In other words we can also say that the element of power is and has always been at the core of the concept of sovereignty.

Theoretically speaking, the government of a sovereign State is usually divided into three major organs of legislature, executive and judiciary. History provides the evidence that the power centred in one individual or group of individuals tends to be abused. Montesquieu diagnosed this ill in the State's attribute of sovereignty with power centred in one and prescribed the remedy of his doctrine of 'separation of powers'. The birth of this doctrine of separation of powers can be seen as a dividing line between the absolute sovereignty and popular sovereignty and also in a certain way a dividing line between the power system of State and the welfare system of State. The institution of State, from its tribal stage to the nation State of the modern international community, has undergone a tremendous change. At the very heart of it were the concepts of sovereignty and separation of power in any given time. The change in the function and power of State has always been directly proportional to the changing role of the concepts of sovereignty and separation of power.

The records of antiquity demonstrate the functions of the supreme power in the city-state or tribal-state. The term sovereignty is derived from a Latin word '*superanus*' which means supreme. Hence, it implies the supremacy of the State, internally as well as externally. In the words of Bernard Gilson:

> The subject of State sovereignty is general and controversial. The very basis of political and legal organization in the world is at stake. *Sovereignty is a power which some ruler or*

[16] Time, environment and prevailing conditions play a great role in shaping the thoughts of any thinker. Karl Marx was no exception. Poverty and hardships had haunted him throughout his life. No doubt that salient features of his philosophy became 'materialistic interpretation of history', history of class struggle; 'theory of surplus value' and 'dictatorship of proletariats'. In brief for him an ideal state would be one which would emerge on the debris of the state in which the capitalist will no longer exploit the poor. Of all his works *Das Kapital* (1st edn 1867; 2nd edn 1885; and 3rd edn 1894) became an 'epoch making' publication which may also be described as Marxism in a nutshell. The success or failure of Marxism apart, one cannot deny that it was the absolute sovereignty–cum-poltical despotism of State and the capitalist exploitation of the poor by rich that made human dignity in Marx's time something to laugh at. It was this very dignity in him that made him stand for the dignity of the working and dominated class. This way he chose to communicate with his fellow human beings worldwide to convey: that human dignity is not something which is served in a plate by State rulers and capitalists; people have always to struggle for it. In this light his philosophical communication and the resulting worldwide human interaction made a considerable contribution to the pluralistic conception of State and its sovereihnty.

[17] H Kelsen, Knight, (tr), *Pure Theory of Law* (Berkley, CA, University of California Press, 1967) 68.

> *rulers wield over other men.* It is also a legal criterion of public authority which makes it statelike. The State is sovereign. As such, it has supporters and opponents.[18]

The father of the modern theory of sovereignty was the 16th century French political thinker, Jean Bodin (1530–96). His *Les Six Livres De La République*, published in Paris in 1576, contained the first systematic presentation of his theory. He defined sovereignty as: 'the supreme power over citizens and subjects, unrestrained by law.' It is thus clear that sovereignty from the very outset was identified with royal absolute power. Thomas Hobbes' *Leviathan*, published in 1651, developed the conception of legal sovereign. He defined sovereign as *Leviathan*, ie absolute, final, omnipotent and omnicompetent, his commands being law and citizens owing a duty to obey his laws. England, during the time of Hobbes, was in the jaws of a civil war. He has seen lot of bloodshed. Therefore, he saw man as bloodthirsty and having animal instincts. The circumstances reflected in his conception of sovereignty resting in his great and strong sovereign *Leviathan* before whom all were to bow. Later, the theory of sovereignty was put in a very elaborate and systematic form by Austin. For him the law was 'the command of the sovereign'. Austin defined sovereign as: 'If a determinate human superior, not in the habit of obedience of a like superior, receives habitual obedience from the bulk of a given society, that determinate superior is sovereign in that society, and the society (including the superior) is a society political and independent.'[19]

The above theories of Bodin, Hobbes and Austin can rightly be described as theories of *absolute sovereignty*. They all actually reflect three main characteristics: a) sovereignty is essentially in a State, b) sovereignty is indivisible, and c) sovereignty is unlimited and illimitable.

Later, John Locke (1632–1704) developed the theory of sovereignty of the people and clearly distinguished between political sovereignty and legal sovereignty. Jean Jacques Rousseau (1712–78) developed the conception of *popular sovereignty*. The absolute *Leviathan* was absolutely tamed when the *Declaration of the Rights of Man and of Citizens*, adopted in 1789 by the French National Assembly, declaring that 'the principle of all sovereignty resides in the nation'. It depended on the political balance of power within each nation State whether King or Parliament, or King and Parliament jointly, were considered to be the bearers of the national will.[20] Jefferson became the American apostle of the conception of popular sovereignty. He approved of it in the *American Declaration of Independence*. He created the basic American political philosophy that the will of the people is the only true source of governmental power. The fathers of the *American Constitution of 1787* aimed at no less than an alternative to the omnipotence of the unified State on the one hand and to the impotence of mere confederations on the other. The system of checks and balances between federal organs and the legislative, executive and judicial branches

[18] B Gilson, *The Conceptual System of Sovereign Equality* (Peeter, Leuven, 1984) 1.

[19] J Austin, HLA Hart, (ed), *The Province of Jurisprudence Determined, 1832* (London, Weidenfeld & Nicolson, 1954) Lecture VI, p 195.

[20] G Schwarzenberger, *Power Politics: A Study of International Society* (London, Stevens & Sons, 1951) 86.

of the federal government and between the federation and its member States was carefully planned to form a safeguard against undue concentration of power.[21]

Henceforward, the concept of *popular sovereignty* has been gaining ground.

It became an established trend in the 19th and 20th century that sovereignty rests in the people itself. Sovereignty being the supreme power in the State, the people rule themselves through their representatives. Dicey believed that there are two kinds of sovereigns—the political and legal. Legislature (the Parliament) is the legal sovereign because it has the supreme power of law-making. Behind the legal sovereign there is the political sovereign (the electorate).[22] The theory of Jethro Brown has become very popular in modern times. Brown's approach is sociological and he takes into account the changed concept of the State while propounding his theory. He thinks that the State, as a corporation, is sovereign. It acts through various organs and agents for the achievement of its corporate purpose. The sovereign is not a person or a group of persons distinct and separate from community. The community as such is sovereign and it expresses its general will through the organs of the government.[23] Kelsen in his 'Pure Theory of Law'[24] makes some observations on the sovereignty. He believes that there can be no concept of sovereignty as distinct and separate from and above the law. The State is simply a legal order. The only meaning that can be given to the State sovereignty is that the legal order is a unity distinct from and independent of the other legal orders. Duguit rejects the idea of State sovereignty. He thinks that the State is no way different from other human organisations. The 'social solidarity' is the end of all human institutions including the State.[25] Thus, according to Duguit, State sovereignty is a meaningless term and the State has no supreme and superior powers. The most forceful writer of the pluralist sovereignty is Prof Laski. As early as 1916, he stated: 'the sovereignty of the State will pass, as the divine right of kings has had its day.'[26] And in 1925 he suggested that 'it would be of lasting benefit to political science if the whole concept of sovereignty were surrendered.'[27] The absolute sovereignty of 16th century has become a popular sovereignty of 20th century under municipal law. But there is another side of the law, the international law, developing since the time of Grotius. Co-existence of States has given birth to a conception of *coexisting sovereignties*, internationally. In the words of Bernard Gilson:

> Sovereignty under municipal law belongs to the State and no other person. Under international law, a plurality of States coexist. If there were one world-State, the entire legal

[21] *Ibid*, p 87.

[22] AV Dicey, *Introduction to the Study of the Law of the Constitution*, 10th edn, (London, Macmillan, 1959) 72.

[23] Tripathi, *ibid*, p 102–3.

[24] H Kelsen, Knight, (tr), *Pure Theory of Law* (Berkley, CA, University of California Press, 1967) translation of Kelsen's orginal work *Reine Rechtslehre* (1934).

[25] L Duguit, 'The Law and the State' (1917) 31 *Harvard Law Review* 1.

[26] HJ Laski, *The Problem of Sovereignty* (1916) 209.

[27] HJ Laski, *A Grammar of Politics* pp 44–45.

system of the world would be municipal, domestic, internal. There are in fact a number of States and each of them is sovereign. To that extent *sovereignty fares like personality and freedom.*[28]

The matter, from the point of view of international community, has been well Stated by Judge Huber in the *Island of Palmas Arbitration Case* (1928) between the Netherlands and the United States of America:

> Sovereignty in the relations between States signifies independence. Independence in regard to a portion of the globe is the right to exercise therein, to the exclusion of any other State, the functions of a State. The development of the national organization of States during the last few centuries and, as a corollary, in the development of international law, have established this principle of the exclusive competence of the State in regard to its own territory in such a way as to make it the point of departure in settling most questions that concern international relations.[29]

In his *Recent Theories of Sovereignty*, Cohen mentioned that 'international law finds room for the concepts of joint sovereignty, and the sovereignty of international corporations.'[30] Reflecting the realities of international life, the text of Article 14 of the Draft Declaration on Rights and Duties of States, prepared by the International Law Commission of the United Nations reads as follows: 'Every State has the duty to conduct its relations with other States in accordance with international law and with the principle that the sovereignty of each State is subject to the *supremacy of international law*' (italics added). But this supremacy of international law also subscribes to the notion of human rights which are in turn derived from the concept of human dignity. The same international law, with its partnership with the doctrine of human rights, has made individual human being as subject of international law. This is a hundred and eighty degree turn as compared to the traditional international law, based on the doctrine of sovereignty, which treated individuals only as its object.

The working of the principle of sovereignty at regional level is also in transition. Regionalism has been an important feature of the post-World War II period. The regional organization is a sort of formal association of sovereign States of a particular region with permanent institutions. It is not essential that all States of a particular region must join the existing regional organization(s). For example, the European Union, earlier known as European Economic Community, the most active and well organized regional organization, still does not comprise all European States. But the present membership of 25,[31] with the history of the Union going as far back as 1951[32] has certainly made considerable progress in

[28] B Gilson, *The Conceptual System of Sovereign Equality* (Peeter, Leuven, 1984) 53.

[29] 22 *American Journal of International Law* 875.

[30] HE Cohen, *Recent Theories of Sovereignty* (1937) 85.

[31] As from 1 May 2004; see B Turner, (ed), *The Statesman's Yearbook 2004* (London, Palgrave Macmillan) 53.

[32] On 18 April 1951, subsequent to a proposal by the French foreign minister Robert Schuman (Schuman Declaration), Belgium, France, the then Federal Republic of Germany, Italy, Luxembourg and the Netherlands signed the Treaty of Paris establishing the *European Coal and Steel Community*

pooling their sovereign powers in a manner that would give a new meaning to the traditional working of the principle of sovereignty.

MacCormick, writing in 1993 under the title *'Beyond the Sovereign State'*, asks:

> ... whether there actually are any sovereign States now. My answer is to be a negative one so far as concerns Western Europe . . .. Taking the view of the sovereign State which I suggested, or any reasonable variant on its terms, it seems obvious that no State in Western Europe any longer is a sovereign State. None is in a position such that all the power exercised internally in it, whether politically or legally, derives from purely internal sources. Equally, of course, it is not true that all the power which is exercised either politically or normatively is exercised by, or through, or on the grant of, one or more organs of the European Community. Nor has the community as such the plenitude of power politically or normatively that could permit it remotely to resemble in itself as sovereign State or sovereign federation of States . . .. Where at some time past there were, or may have been, sovereign States, there has now been a pooling or a fusion within the communitarian normative order of some of the States' powers of legislation, adjudication and implementation of law in relation to a wide but restricted range of subjects.[33]

Speaking about the transfer of sovereignty and parliamentary sovereignty of the United Kingdom, Tillotson believes:

> The stage has now been reached where the current legal and political reality is that there has been a transfer of powers to the community. It has already been suggested that the traditional rule that Parliament may not bind its successors is not necessarily irreconcilable with the concept of a transfer of powers to another authority. It may further be suggested that whilst the political reality remains membership of the community, such powers are unlikely in practice to be recovered, and at least to that extent the transfer can be regarded as irreversible.[34]

The intermingling of national and coexisting sovereignties is obvious from another fact of the existing hierarchy of law within the European Union. Institutions of the European Union—European Commission, European Council of Ministers and European Court of Justice—have the power to impose rules and decisions on their Member States, but the whole Union is based on the treaties agreed upon by these States and from which in principle, they could withdraw at any time. Furthermore, these Member States participate directly in the creation of the European rules, with members of their respective governments constituting the European Council of Ministers, which is the main formal legislator in the EU. Thus European law determines State law, and State law determines European law. Can all this be simply dismissed under the title of 'European Private Law'? No.

(ECSC). The present day European Union is founded on the existing European communities set up by the Treaties of Paris (1951) and Rome (1957), supplemented by revisions, the Single European Act in 1986, The Maastricht Treaty on European Union in 1992, the Treaty of Amsterdam in 1997 and the dtaft Treaty of Nice in 2000. See *The Statesman's Yearbook 2004, ibid*, p 52.

[33] Cited in J Tillotson, *European Community Law*, 2nd edn (London, Cavendish, 1999), p 50.

[34] Tillotson, *ibid*, p 57. The idea of irreversibility has been contemplated in an English Judgment: *Blackburn v AG* [1971] All ER 1380. The idea has been rejected as against popular sovereignty by the German Constitutional Court in its Maastricht-Treaty judgment.

What to say of regional law, even the municipal law of a State, in the developing trends of international law, particularly its branch of human rights law, cannot escape the problem of defining its relation with international law. If the source of all human rights everywhere is international law, as Judge Higgins maintains,[35] one wonders what is the legal status of the regional human rights conventions and human rights courts as far as the principle of sovereignty is concerned. All the rivers flow into the sea. Monistic doctrine, given impetus by the doctrine of human rights based on the principle of human dignity, seems to be changing the traditional principle of sovereignty, the basis of international law, into the principle of *superanus* of international law. Reviewing the emerging European law in the perspective of doctrinal debate on the relation between international law and internal law, setting dualist doctrine against monist views, Judge Rigaux also draws his conclusion in the words: 'There too is a question of domains in which universal law—or one with pretensions to such—tends to be installed, but it cannot be qualified as "European".'[36] Hence, international law, the melting pot of several aspects of State sovereignty and internal jurisdictions

It is obvious that at the regional level too the theory and practice of the traditional conception of sovereignty is changing very fast.

The principle of State sovereignty, the basic tenet of the positivist school, as mentioned in this brief account reflects that though it is very much an established basis of the contemporary international law at this moment, yet it has not only seen many changes but its positivist reality as the basis of international law is also not very old. The concept of sovereignty resting in 'higher law' or the 'law of nature' was given a different meaning with the birth of positivist school. Even within this school now the concept of *absolute sovereignty* has been replaced by the concept of *popular sovereignty.* At the international level the concepts of *co-existing sovereignties* and the *sovereign equality* are already beginning to be affected by the new developments in the field of international law, such as human rights. Prof Dixon opines: 'Even though the protection of human rights in concrete cases is not as vigorous as we might like, it is important to appreciate that this is only one way in which international law can defeat the excesses of sovereign states.[37] State sovereignty has constantly been getting conditioned by the evolving new international law. If, as Prof Brownlie states—: 'Sovereignty, or sovereignty and independence, are often the terms used to describe both the legal personality of a state and the incidents of that personality'[38]—then what would be the effect on sovereignty, or in other words how much would it be conditioned by, of the principle of human

[35] R Higgins, *Problems and Process: International Law and How We Use It* (Oxford, OUP, 1994) 96. Prof Higgins (now Judge at the ICJ) speaking about human rights mentions: '... although they may most effectively be implemented by the domestic legal system, that system is not the source of the right. International human-rights law is the source of the obligation, albeit that the obligation is reflected in the content of the domestic law.'

[36] F Rigaux, 'Monism and Dualism within the European Jurisdictions' in M van Hoecke and F Ost, (eds), *The Harmonization of European Private Law* (Oxford, Hart Publishing, 2000) 166.

[37] M Dixon, *Textbook on International Law,* 3rd edn, (London, Blackstone, 1996) 310.

[38] I Brownlie, *Principles of Public International Law,* 3rd edn (Oxford, OUP) 289.

dignity which, by already conditioning the State sovereignty in the first instance, has given birth to a new 'legal personality', the individual human being, in the international law? And, in the 'new international law',[39] these 'Individuals are participants, along with states, international organizations' according to Judge Higgins.'[40] Judge Alvarez (Chile), in his individual opinion appended to the *Corfu Channel* case judgment on merits, also observed the changing conception of the notion of sovereignty:

> This notion has evolved, and we must now adopt a conception of it which will be in harmony with the new conditions of social life. We can no longer regard sovereignty as an absolute and individual right of every State, as used to be done under the old law founded on the individualist regime, according to which States were only bound by the rules which they had accepted.[41]

Prof Verma observes: 'The 20th century saw the revival of the law of nature in a modified and profound manner. The tremendous growth of international law in the field of human rights, which started after the Second World War, is influenced by this.'[42]

How do we perceive the basis of human rights law and its relation with the established basis of international law is the subject to be dealt with in the following pages.

II. Basis of Human Rights Law: The Principle of Human Dignity

> One of the most persistent problems in human rights discourse involves the basis on which rights can be claimed.[43]

From the cave to the computer, and from the Vedic Law[44] to the United Nations Law, the story of law, man and human rights has been a constant one. The concept of human rights is certainly a dynamic one, subject to change and expansion, as is also evident from the constitutional history of Western States.[45] However, it is important to understand the fundamental principle on which the whole human

[39] Judge Alvarez is famous for coining the term 'new international law'.

[40] R Higgins, *Problems and Process: International Law and How We Use It* (Oxford, OUP, 1994) 50.

[41] *Corfu Channel* case (Merits), Judgment of 9 April 1949, Individual Opinion of Judge Alvarez, ICJ Reports 1949, p 43.

[42] SK Verma, *An Introduction to Public International Law* (New Delhi, Prentice Hall of India, 1998) 11.

[43] GM Johnson, 'A Magna Carta for Mankind: Writing the Universal Declaration of Human Rights' in MG Johnson and J Synmonides, (eds), *The Universal Declaration of Human Rights: A History of its Creation and Implementation: 1948—1998* (Paris, UNESCO, 1998) 42.

[44] The law enshrined in the Vedas, the body of ancient Indian sacred writings dating from the second millenium BC.

[45] P Malanczuk, *Akehurst's Modern Introduction to International Law*, 7th edn, (London, Routledge, 1997) 209.

rights law rests. While there is widespread acceptance of the doctrine of human rights, there is considerable confusion as to the basis of human rights law. The question what do we mean by the term 'right' is itself controversial and the subject of intense jurisprudential debate.[46] 'Most famous' and helpful 'is the work of Welsey Newcomb Hohfeld (1879–1918)' in this regard.[47] Further in this chapter we will study the theory of Hohfeld.

In order to assess first the relationship between human rights and international law and second, the contribution the International Court of Justice has made to the development of human rights law, it is imperative to know what it is we take to be the basis of human rights and to have a brief understanding of the prominent theories and thoughts about human rights, propounded by various legal thinkers and judges.

Natural law theory of higher law and human dignity is the oldest as well as the most modern as it has been, sometimes at high ebb and sometimes at low ebb, constantly dominating the entire basis of law. Being value loaded, with its humanising and liberating ideals, even the analytical school cannot claim to have totally escaped its influence. Human rights doctrine of these days is a perfect instance of its constant survival, glorious revival, and tremendous potential. In jurisprudence, generally speaking, the term 'Natural Law' means those rules and principles which are considered to have emanated from some supreme source, other than any political or worldly authority. Though there are several divergent natural law theories, but they all proceed from one common ground that the source of law is not any worldly authority. Some say that it is God, others say it is 'nature; some say it is 'reason' and still others say that it is morality. Hence, different names for the sources of human laws, such as 'Divine Law', 'Moral Law', 'Universal Law', 'Higher Law', 'Natural Law', etc.[48] The term Natural Law has become commonly accepted among jurists to describe this theory.

According to Socrates, man possesses 'insight' and this insight reveals to him the goodness and badness of things. This insight makes man know absolute, eternal and moral laws. Therefore natural lawyers believe in the individual autonomy. In brief, the Natural Law theory begins with the assumption that there are natural laws, both theological and metaphysical, which confer certain particular rights upon individual human beings, granting therewith individual autonomy to every human being. Therefore, human rights find their authority in some higher law of nature.

Natural theory gradually led to natural rights theory. John Locke was undoubtedly the chief exponent of this theory. He saw the birth of human rights in the 17th century humanism. According to Locke the existence of human beings in a state of nature represented a state where men and women were freely enjoying their

[46] MN Shaw, *International Law*, 4th edn, (Cambridge, Grotius, 1997) 196.

[47] M van Hoecke, *Law as Communication* (Oxford, Hart Publishing, 2002) 100; for Hohfeld's work see WN Hohfeld, *Fundamental Legal Conceptions as Applied in Judicial Reasoning* (Westport, Greenwood Press, 1978, reprint, first edn in (1913) 23 *Yale Law Journal* 16).

[48] BNM Tripathi, *Jurisprudence: Legal Theory* (1997) 78.

freedom and equality. There was no subjection to will or authority of any other. In order to end certain hazards and inconveniences they formed a community and set up a body politic. However, in so doing, they retained their natural rights of life, liberty and property. Government was under absolute duty to protect these natural rights of human beings. If government failed to do so, they would lose their legitimate right to govern. As human dignity rings the note of a key concept in the body of human rights law, natural law theory of individual autonomy has surely found its proper place in the concept of human rights.

Natural Law theory of human rights, like that of entire jurisprudence in general, is only accepted as far as the 'primary rules' stage of Prof Hart's ideas are concerned. The abiding difficulty with the natural law approach is that its assumptions, intellectual procedures, and modalities of justification can be employed equally by the proponents of human dignity and the proponents of human indignity in support of diametrically opposed empirical specifications of rights, and neither set of proponents has at its disposal any means of confirming the one claim or of disconfirming the other.[49]

While there is widespread acceptance of the positivistic school of thought in every branch of law, not even the staunchest positivist would deny the elements of natural law principles in the human rights law. Prof Shaw remarks: 'The concept of human rights is closely allied with ethics and morality.'[50] Speaking further about the Natural Law approach, Prof Shaw evaluates: 'Although this approach fell out of favour in the 19th century due to the problems of its non-empirical and diffuse methodology, it has proved of immense value this century in the establishment of human rights within the international community as universal principles.'[51]

The natural law character of human rights in the Universal Declaration and its tributary covenants and conventions is not far to seek. Morsink opines:

> The initial presumption is that the Universal Declaration reflects some sort of natural rights view of human rights. Of the thirty articles of the Declaration, the first twenty-one are devoted to the classical 18th century civil and political rights. The social and economic rights seem, to a casual reader at least, to be tacked on at the end, like 19th century tree. And that same casual reader cannot help but notice certain key 18th century fighting words. The preamble speaks of 'inherent dignity' and of 'equal and inalienable rights'.[52]

The deliberations of the United Nations Human Rights Commissions reflect the arguments championing the proposal that the Preamble to the Universal Declaration must refer in someway to God or nature as the source of all the rights proclaimed in the Declaration. The Netherlands' delegation championed this view. During the course of the UN General Assembly debate, Dr JH van Roijen, the Dutch delegate very much regretted that:

[49] M McDougal, H Lasswell and L Chen, *Human Rights and World Public Order: The Basic Policies of an International Law of Human Dignity* (1980) 73–75.

[50] MN Shaw, *International Law*, 4th edn, (Cambridge, Grotius, 1997) 197.

[51] Shaw, *ibid*, pp 197–98.

[52] J Morsink, 'The Philosophy of the Universal Declaration' (1984) 6 *Human Rights Quarterly* 309.

> man's divine origin and immortal destiny had not been mentioned in the declaration, for the fount of all those rights was the Supremebeing, who laid a great responsibility on those who claimed them. To Ignore that relation was almost the same as severing a plant from its roots, or building a house and forgetting the foundation.[53]

This opinion of the Netherlands' delegate, reflecting at the same time a kind of gratitude to the father of international law, Hugo Grotius, also coincidentally a Dutch jurist, was not altogether without substantial support. It was joining of hands of the positivist delegates and the non-Western delegates, who always interpreted natural law as something Western, that had created a strong opposition to the proposal of Dr van Roijen. The essence of the proposal, however, was not defeated, only its expression. The words '*man's divine origin*' found its essence in the expression of '*inherent dignity*'. This reflects a natural law aspect of human rights law.

The *travaux preparatoires* of the Declaration does reveal that the drafters were of the opinion that Article 1 of the Declaration should become 'a basic statement of principle', the *Grundnorm* in Kelsenian language, from which all other human rights norms should draw their validity. Article 1 reads: 'All human beings are born free and equal in dignity and rights. They are endowed with reason and conscience and should act towards one another in a spirit of brotherhood'. This is a typical 18th century natural law language reflecting *fraternite* character of that time.

The understanding of the natural law theory of human rights, even for a positivist, is an imperative for the proper understanding of human rights law and its development. The best activist judge in the human rights cases must of necessity be a judge overtly or covertly subscribing to the natural law theory in general and its human dignity oriented human rights side in particular. And one former Judge of the International Court, Judge Tanaka of Japan, has become a brilliant jurist of this kind. His dissenting opinion in the 1966 Second Phase Judgment in *South-West Africa* cases has already become a classic in the development of human rights law.[54]

Natural law theory and its contribution to the development of human rights will not be complete without the mention of Kant's theory of inherent dignity of the human personality.

Kant's theory of inherent dignity of the human personality is an outstanding example of the natural law school's contribution to human rights. Immanuel Kant (1724–1804), a German philosopher of Scottish descent, was far ahead of his time in his thinking about human rights, as compared to the present day doctrine of human rights based on human dignity. The emphatic opinion of Edgar Bodenheimer in this matter rightly hitting the nail when he states: 'Kant had a strong belief in the inherent *dignity of the human personality*, and he thought that

[53] General Assembly, Summary Records, p 874. And also in Third Committee, Summary Records, pp 755–56.

[54] ICJ Reports, 1966, pp 248–324.

no man had the right to use another person merely as a means to attain his own subjective purposes; each human individual was always to be treated as an end in itself.'[55]

Individual, according to Kant, was an end in itself and not a means to an end.[56] This high conception of human dignity in Kant's thinking made him also place the individual above the authority of the state. What was the underlying thinking of conceiving human being as an end and placing him above the authority of the State one may wonder? The authority of the state, as described in general political and legal theory, manifests in its trinity of institutions of legislature, executive and judiciary. Similarly, Kant saw that i) an individual is capable of leading a true life, ii) individual possesses a rational will, and iii) he can decide things for himself. In other words, individuals are states within the state. Putting individuals within the framework of state and law, Kant reflects: i) that people are ultimate authority and sovereign in the state, and ii) that all laws flow from the people.

As opposed to Bentham's famous concept of the 'greatest happiness of the greatest numbers', Kant saw the aim of the state not in the greatest happiness of the greatest number of people but in the perfection of man and his development. And, as human being for him was an end in itself, a dignified sovereign, he firmly believed that for the development of personality as a dignified human man must be given certain rights by the state. These rights ought to be rational and must be respected by the state authority. The most basic of these rights, according to Kant, were that of freedom, liberty, and equality. Besides liberty and equality before the law, for Kant the right to freedom was 'the one sole and original right that belongs to every human being by virtue of his humanity.'[57] Kant defined rights as the limitation of the freedom of any individual to the extent of its agreement with the freedom of all other individuals in so far as this is possible by a universal law. According to Professor Dhayani:

> The freedom of will in Kant is nothing more than the human right of self determination as expounded by Rousseau who aroused Kant from his 'dogmatic slumbers'. It is from his theory of free willing individual from which has emerged the concept of free individuals, a collective of free beings with their inherent rights, freedoms and personality which makes man to seek and shape his destiny. It is in this manner that Kant's theory of natural law has greatly influenced the contemporary philosophy of human rights.[58]

Hence, Kant's concept of the inherent *dignity of human personality reflect three important attributes*: i) the original right of freedom belonging to each man in virtue of his humanity, ii) equality before the law, and iii) liberty before the law. Liberty, according to him, associated with the rights of freedom and equality, consists in the power to do anything which inflicts nothing on one's neighbours.

[55] E Bodenheimer, *Jurisprudence: The Philosophy and Method of the Law* (1974) 62.
[56] I Kant, JK Abbot, (tr), *Fundamental Principles of the Metaphysic of Morals* (New York,1949) 46.
[57] I Kant, J Ladd, (tr), *The Metaphysical Elements of Justice* (1965) 43–44.
[58] SN Dhayani, *Fundamentals of Jurisprudence: The Indian Approach* (1997) 79.

The essence of the aforementioned, read together with the wording of the opening paragraph of the preamble of the 1948 Universal Declaration of Human Rights, and the similar wordings in the preambles of the two resulting 1966 Covenants, ICCPR and ICESCR, would evidently reflect that Kant's doctrine of the inherent dignity of human personality and the contemporary human rights doctrine based on 'the inherent dignity of the human person' are not only essentially the same but they also formulate and consolidate the dignity of human person as the fundamental postulate of the human rights as a school of law.

The foregoing in fact reflects the monistic and universal picture of law. Describing the monistic doctrine of relationship between international law and municipal law, Prof O'Connell noted at the outset: 'The monist position is an emanation of Kantian philosophy which favours a unitary conception of law.'[59] There might still be a strong divergence of opinion among some legal thinkers on the question as to whether International Law and Municipal Law can be said to form a unity being manifestations of a single conception of law or whether International Law constitutes a legal system essentially different from the system(s) of Municipal Law. There hardly is any doubt when it comes to the rules and principles emanating from the system of Human Rights Law. International Law is not concerned about the human rights provisions in the individual state constitutions. National laws as far as international law is concerned are simple facts. The Permanent Court of International Justice held: 'With regard to international law and the Court, which is its organ, the national laws are simple facts, manifestations of the will and activity of the States, on the same level as judicial rulings or administrative measures'.[60]

Sir Hersch Lauterpacht's theory of human dignity and sovereignty of man is a modern version of a natural law advocate. He sees man no less than a sovereign state in his *persona.* Sir Hersch, a Polish born British International Law professor, a theorist turned judge, a judge at the international Court of Justice between 1955 and 1959, was one of the earliest writers on human rights particularly well known for his seminal work *An International Bill of the Rights of Man* (1945), becoming the basis of much that is in the 1948 United Nations Declarations of Human Rights, revealed his theory of human dignity in his 1950 publication *International Law and Human Rights*. He saw that the struggle between the powerless individual and the powerful State is an old but constant one. Man has for ages been fighting for his dignity and consideration of utility. Sir Hersch therefore makes it the key concept of his theory of human dignity and states:

> ... For human dignity and considerations of utility alike rebel against the idea of the State as the sole guardian on the interests of man. The purpose of the State is to safeguard the interests of the individual human being and to render possible the fulfilment, through freedom, of his wider duty to man and society. Some of these interests can be effectively

[59] DP O'Connell, *International Law*, 2nd edn, (London, Stevens & Sons, 1970) vol 1, p 39.

[60] Decision No 7, 25 May 1926, Case relative to certain German interests in Polish Upper Silesia, Case of the Factory of Chorzow, Permanent Court of International Justice, Series A No 7, p 19.

> safeguarded by the State in the international sphere. But it is inadmissible that the State should claim, in the conditions of the modern world, that it is the best instrument for protecting all these interests and that it is entitled to exclude from this legal sphere individuals and known governmental bodies which may be created for that purpose.[61]

Sir Hersch Lauterpacht sees individual interests as individual rights in the historical text and realistically observing the historical and political currents and the constant slow and steady progress of human rights notion and describes the current evolving situation of human rights between individual and the State prescribes a realist in the following words:

> The claim of the State to unqualified exclusiveness in the field of international relations was tolerable at a time when the actuality and the interdependence of the interests of the individual cutting across national frontiers were less obvious than they are today. It is this latter fact which explains why the constant expansion of the periphery of individual rights an enduring feature of legal development cannot stop short of the limits of the State.[62]

Lauterpacht sees that humanity gradually, with the shrinking of the globe and the increasing contacts between people has awakened to the fact that their dignity lies not to the brutal subjection to the power of the State. What he finds much more important is the fact that the recognition of the individual, by sheer dint of the acknowledgement of his 'fundamental rights and freedom', as the ultimate subject of international law, is a challenge to the traditional doctrine that State alone is the subject of international law and not the individual. It challenges the absolute moral superiority of the collective agency of the State. Consequently, the emerging scene of the fight for dignity and human rights has considerably changed the relationship between the individual and the State whereas it has become an established fact that it is the duty of the State to treat man with respect and acknowledge the sovereignty of man. In his own words:

> For fundamental human rights are rights superior to the law of the sovereign State. The hope expressed by Emerson, that 'man shall treat with man as a sovereign state with a sovereign state' may be brought nearer to fruition by sovereign States recognizing the duty to treat man with the respect which traditional law exacted from them in relation to other States.[63]

To that vital extent Judge Lauterpacht sees that the recognition of inalienable rights and the recognition of the individual as a subject of international law are synonymous. In this he saw, being a 'Neo-Grotian', the 'recognition of a higher fundamental law', through the medium of international law, on the part of the State as well as on the part of the international community. Much to our surprise has been achieved as foreseen by Lauterpacht in 1950. His theory of human dignity and sovereignty of man conceives the further development of human rights in

[61] H Lauterpacht, *International Law and Human Rights* (London, Stevens, 1950) 68.
[62] *Ibid.*
[63] H Lauterpacht, *International Law and Human Rights* (London, Stevens, 1950) 70.

the direction in which the individual becoming more and more a subject of international law, with more and more dignity, and the law between sovereign States developing more and more as the 'universal law of mankind'.

Judge Tanaka (Japan), the most staunch advocate of natural law school, made clear his approach to human right in his dissenting opinion appended to the 1966 Judgment concerning the *South West Africa* cases. He sees the source of human rights first and foremost in the law of nature:

> . . . human rights which require protection are the same; they are not the product of a particular judicial system in the hierarchy of the legal order, but the same human rights must be recognized, respected and protected everywhere man goes. The uniformity of national laws on the protection of human rights is not derived, as in the cases of the law of contracts and commercial and maritime transactions, from considerations of expediency by the legislative organs or from the creative power of the custom of a community, but it already exists in spite of its more-or-less vague form. This is of nature, *ius naturale* in roman law.[64]

According to Tanaka the principle of equality is at the summit of hierarchy of the system of law as a whole, irrespective of its national or international characteristics and, in his opinion, the real source of the principle of equality is none other than the law of nature. In his own words: '. . . the principle of equality being in the nature of natural law and therefore of a supra-constitutional character, is placed at the summit of hierarchy of the system of law, and that all positive laws including the constitution shall be in the conformity with this principle.'[65] Tanaka maintains the judicial-ideological superiority of human rights within the entire framework of international law which is based on the principle of State sovereignty. Having clearly demonstrated first that the principle of equality is an integral part of the United Nations Charter, and second, that the promotion of human rights being as one of the main purposes of the United Nations, Judge Tanaka, with his teleological interpretation of law, advocated that no treaty, irrespective of its particular human rights character or any other character, can be interpreted in disregard to the principle of equality. Tanaka gives human rights judicial character to all international actions of UN Member States. He states:

> . . . those who pledge themselves to take action in co-operation with the United Nations in respect of the promotion of universal respect for, and observance of, human rights and freedoms, cannot violate, without contradiction, these rights and freedoms. How can one, on the one hand, preach respect for human rights to others and, on the other hand, disclaim for oneself the obligation to respect them. From the provisions of the Charter referring to human rights and fundamental freedoms it can be inferred that the legal obligation to respect human rights is imposed on member States.[66]

[64] K Tanaka, *South West Africa cases (Second Phase)*, Dissenting Opinion of Judge Tanaka, ICJ Reports 1966, p 296.

[65] *Ibid*, p 306.

[66] K Tanaka, *South West Africa cases*, ICJ Reports 1966, p 290.

Does it mean that a State which has not signed the UN Charter, or withdraws from this treaty at its will, can escape from the entire human rights law enshrined in the Charter and other UN covenants, conventions, and declarations. Judge Tanaka has this to answer:

> The existence of human rights does not depend on the will of a State; neither internally on its law or any other legislative measure, nor internationally on treaty or custom, in which the express or tacit will of a State constitutes the essential element . . . A State or States are not capable of creating human rights by law or by convention; they can only confirm their existence and give them protection. The role of the State is no more than declaratory. Human rights have always existed with the human being. They existed independently of, and before, the State.[67]

Of all the sources of international law (international conventions, international custom, and the general principles of law) referred to in Article 38, paragraph 1, of the ICJ Statute, Judge Tanaka gives the primary position to the 'general principles.' Comparing the positivistic position with the natural law position, Judge Tanaka is of the opinion:

> From a positivistic voluntaristic viewpoint, first the convention, and next the custom, is considered important, and general principles occupy merely a supplementary position. On the contrary, if we take the supra-national objective viewpoint, the general principles would come first and the two others would follow them. If we accept the fact that convention and custom are generally the manifestation and concretization of already existing general principles, we are inclined to attribute to this third source of international law the primary position vis-à-vis the other two.[68]

After viewing the entire body of human rights law based on the general principles of law, emanating from natural law, manifested in the international treaties and customs, it will be noted in the jurisprudence of the International Court that the development of human rights law is proceeding more on the perception of this primacy of general principles of law, particularly the principle of human dignity.

Positivist theory of State authority, no matter how tightly it might have been sitting in its water-tight compartment of sovereignty, built mainly by Bodin, Bentham and Austin, the waters of natural law have been constantly leaking into it in some quantity. Even the very father of the theory of sovereignty, Bodin, who defined sovereignty as 'supreme power over citizens and subjects, unrestrained by law', did not put the sovereign above the natural law. Sabine and Thorson state: 'Bodin had no doubt that the sovereign was answerable to God and subject to natural law.'[69] The doctrine of State sovereignty is at the very basis of the positivist school. If there is one expression to describe the entirety of the positivist theory, the expression is 'state authority'. It was the 'command of the sovereign' in Austinian language. The positivist theory of human rights assumes that the most

[67] K Tanaka, *South West Africa cases (Second Phase),* Dissenting Opinion of Judge Tanaka, ICJ Reports 1966, p 297.

[68] *Ibid,* p 300.

[69] GH Sabine and TL Thorson, *A History of Political Theory* (1973) pp 377–78.

important measure of human rights is to be found in the authoritative enactment of a system of law sustained by organized community coercion. This theory finds the authority in the perspective of established officials, and any appeal to a 'higher law' for the protection of individual rights is regarded as utopian or a meta-legal aspiration.

None can deny the greatest contribution of the positive theory in recognizing the importance of bringing organized community coercion, the state's established processes of authoritative decision, to bear upon the protection of human rights. However, the contribution of the positivist school to human rights would remain obscure if the fact is not kept in mind that though the school is very much associated with the name of John Austin, but as a matter of fact it was Jeremy Bentham's ideas which gave birth to the positivist school. Austin did little more than bring together systematically the ideas that were scattered through Bentham's voluminous and not always very readable works. Bentham's plan was to reform the courts by Parliamentary control. He pointed out that legal formalism and artificial rules about admissibility of evidence were largely predicated upon a belief that the substantive law is bad and that government is dangerous, and he argued that, if this belief is indeed true, the reasonable remedy is to improve the law, not weaken the courts. Bentham believed in equality based on justice. His ideal was 'every man his own lawyer.' To this end he urged the substitution for formal pleading of informal proceedings before an arbiter who would aim at conciliation, the universal admissibility of any kind of relevant evidence, and a large measure of judicial discretion, rather than rigid rules, to exclude irrelevance.[70] Even though Bentham's name is very much associated with analytical thinking, yet Sabine and Thorson also notice that the jurist was not altogether without its natural law thinking. They observe: 'When he said that "One man is worth just the same as another man", or that in calculating the greatest happiness each person is "to count for one and no one more than one," he was obviously borrowing the principle of equality from natural law.'[71]

Actually, in the positivistic approach the task of specifying the detailed content of the human rights protected in a community goes forward very much as in the natural law approach—by logical, syntactic derivation. The difference is that, while the natural lawyer takes off from theological or metaphysical absolutes, the positivist takes off from assumptions about the empirical reference of traditional legal concepts.[72]

Hohfeld's theory of jural relations[73] is by no means out of place for human rights. Whether it is human rights or any other rights, one cannot forget first to think of Prof Hohfeld whose theory of jural relations in 1913 brought a revolution

[70] GH Sabine and TL Thorson, *A History of Political Theory* (1973) pp 619–20.

[71] *Ibid*, p 621.

[72] M McDougal, H Lasswell and L Chen, *Human Rights and World Public Order: The Basic Policies of an International Law of Human Dignity* (1980) 73–75.

[73] WN Hohfeld, *Fundamental Legal Conceptions as Applied in Judicial Reasoning* (Westport, Greenwood Press, 1978, reprint, first edn in (1913) 23 *Yale Law Journal* 16).

in the field of analytical jurisprudence. In his *Fundamental Legal Conceptions as Applied in Judicial Reasoning*, Hohfeld expounds the lowest common denominators of the law in terms of legal relations. These consist of two squares of correlation and opposition. Within these squares, every horizontal represents a correlation and every diagonal an opposition. Hohfeld set out his table of jural relations as follows:

Jural Correlatives:			
Right	Privilege	Power	Immunity
Duty	No-right	Liability	Disability
Jural Opposites:			
Right	Privilege	Power	Immunity
No-right	Duty	Disability	Liability

Hohfeld's aim was to analyze what he called '*the lowest common denominators of the law*', including concepts such as legal relations, right, duty, power, privilege, liability, and immunity, as well as to expound the logical relations between these notions. With this he hoped that his conceptions might produce a uniform terminology applicable to the most divergent branches of law. Though not much is talked about the application of the Hohfeld's analysis to the notion and norms of human rights law, yet its utility and probable applicability cannot be denied altogether without a thorough research in the matter. Taken into consideration a general definition of the notion of human rights it does offer the glimmer of a hope that it is possible. One general definition is: 'Human rights are those liberties, immunities, and benefits which, by accepted contemporary values, all human beings should be able to claim "as of right" of the society in which they live.'[74]

As, according to Hohfeld, the term right is used in different sense in different situations, and the strictest of these sometimes is that the *right-holder* being *entitled* to something with a correlative *duty* in another. This relationship is not difficult to discover between the human right(s) of a person, or a group of persons, and the State, or any governing entity. Sometimes the term *right* is used to indicate an immunity from having a legal status altered. Sometimes it also indicates a *privilege* to do something. And also sometimes *right* refers to a *power* to create a legal relationship. According to Shestack: Sometimes scholars classify civil and political rights as types of immunities since they protect against encroachments of government. They are restraints on government in the nature of a command: 'Thou shall not'. Generally, such negative restraints can be secured by fairly simple legislation. Economic, social, and cultural rights, on the other hand, are 'rights' in which affirmative action by the government is necessary. Therefore, they are viewed as claims upon the governments which may or may not be realized depending on such matters as availability of resources and other conditions.

[74] *Encyclopedia of International Law*, vol 2, p 886.

Article 29, paragraph 1, of the 1948 UN Universal Declaration of Human Rights stipulates: 'Everyone has *duties* to the community in which alone the free and full development of his personality is possible'. Hence, according to Morsink, human rights in 'Article 29 . . . admits that rights are balanced by and are correlative with duties. Thus, human rights even when conceived of as natural rights, are not unlimited'.[75]

Since there cannot be a right without a remedy, Hohfeld's theory of jural relations has certainly something to offer to the law of human rights in its various forms and norms.

Judge Higgins' theory of integrity and dignity of human being at once elevates individual human being to the status of an equal partner, along with the State, in international law. In defining the very concept of human rights, Judge Higgins at once perceives the link between human 'rights' and human 'dignity'. According to her: 'Human rights are rights held simply by virtue of being a human person.[76] In other words the ultimate source of human rights is the human person. But question arises what is this *human person* for her? What is that substantive link between human rights and human person, or underlying idea of international law, which has so profoundly shaken the international judicial conscience that human rights are at once at the centre of all jurisprudential thought? Wherein lies the essence of her human person, one might wonder? Without a pause she provides the answer in the words: 'They are part and parcel of the integrity and dignity of the human being.'[77] But this is a fine sounding moral and natural law language which would, without a legal force flowing from the legal source of obligation, remain an empty shell. To give a legal protection to the human rights wrapped in the integrity and dignity of the human being Judge Higgins finds that 'international human-rights-law is the source of obligation.' Although, according to her, human rights may most effectively be implemented by the domestic legal system, yet that system is not the source of these rights. For instance, the prohibition placed upon a government from the use of torture is not dependent upon its own legal system: the obligation is one of international law. Hence, the source of all human rights is international law.

Judge Higgins believes in the universality of the human spirit and the universality of human rights and human dignity. The suggestion of relativism that there are diverse cultural, political and economic systems, she opines, is 'a very state-centred view' which is 'rarely advanced by the oppressed'. The oppressed everywhere is too anxious to benefit from perceived universal standards.

Judge Higgins strongly rejects the traditional view that international law, hence also human rights law, is body of rules. She observes: 'International law is not rules. It is a normative system . . . harnessed to the achievement of common values—values that speak to all of us.'[78] What is the position of the principle of State

[75] J Morsink, 'The Philosophy of the Universal Declaration' (1984) 6 *Human Rights Quarterly* 310.
[76] R Higgins, *Problems and Process: International Law and How We Use It* (Oxford, OUP, 1994) 96.
[77] *Ibid*, p 96.
[78] *Ibid*, p 1–2.

sovereignty in her normative system of international law? She sees law as a decision-making process. According to her: 'International law is no different from domestic law . . . domestic law operates in a vertical legal order, and international law in a horizontal legal order. Consent and *sovereignty* are constraining factors against which the prescribing, invoking, and applying of international norms must operate.'[79]

Ultimately, the relation between the principle of human dignity with that of the principle of State sovereignty in the system of international law reflects in equality: '. . . the main participants in this system, naturally, are sovereign states, though there is no reason of principle to exclude individuals from its reach.'[80] Bidding goodbye to the traditional subject-object dichotomy Judge Higgins sees individual human beings as equal partners with sovereign states: '. . . there are no "subjects" and "objects", but only participants. Individuals are participants, along with states, international organizations (such as the United Nations, or the International Monetary Fund (IMF) or the ILO), multinational corporations, and indeed private non-governmental groups.'[81]

Kelsen's theory of hierarchical norms, applied to human rights, may not have a great deal to offer in the substantive sense of the law, but how the norms of human rights law, in particularly its fundamental principle of human dignity would fare in the hierarchy of norms of international law still remains to be seen. Kelsen is an eminent positivist theorist of present times, famous for his Pure Theory of law. Hans Kelsen developed a theory of law based on hierarchy of legal norms.[82] Kelsen maintains that legal systems are founded on one basic norm, the *Grundnorm*, from which further norms are created and validated. 'Kelsen is theoretician *par excellence* of legal system.'[83] As a matter of fact his theory as a framework or even as a legal system can be applied to any system or field of law, as long as the given *Grundnorm* can stand the test of *minimum effectiveness*.

Human rights, if to be theorized as an international independent system of law, can well trace its *Grundnorm* in the UN Charter. And, as the idea of a Grundnorm which may be said to be the foundation stone of the Kelsen's Pure Theory and the definition of law as the *hierarchy of norms*, a normative theory with emphasis on the human rights norms may also find its *Grundnorm* in the norm of human dignity, or respect for life. However, since Kelsen sees law as a 'normative science' and the Grundnorm as the starting point in a legal system, in his conception of law as a system of normative relations there is no such thing as individual right in law. For Kelsen, duties are the *'essence of law'*. Law is always a system of *'oughts'*. The concept of right is not basically essential for a legal system. In Kelsen's own words: 'The right . . . is but the reflection of the obligation of another individual (or other

[79] *Ibid*, p 1.
[80] *Ibid*, p 95.
[81] *Ibid*, p 50.
[82] For Hans Kelsen's hierarchical theory of norms see his publication H Kelsen, A Wedberg, (tr), *General Theory of Law and State* (1945).
[83] F Ost and M van de Kerchove, *Legal System between Order and Disorder* (Oxford, OUP, 1994) 12.

individuals).'[84] Hence, for him legal right is merely the duty as viewed by the person entitled to require its fulfilments. According to Kelsen, the idea of individual right may disappear from criminal law, contract, etc. Prof Tripathi draws the right conclusion from such conception of law in the following words: 'The implication of this proposition are that there can be no inalienable rights of the individual as some legal theories have established.'[85] Therefore, beyond certain limits of theorization of Human Rights as a legal system, Pure Theory of Kelsen does not seem to offer substantively to the development of Human Rights law as such. On the other hand, his revolutionary monist approach towards relation between international law and municipal law offers considerable prospects for the primacy of international law, hence also international human rights law, over municipal law. Kelsen's single conception of law puts man above the subject-object dichotomy in international law. In his words: 'In the ultimate analysis, individuals alone are the subjects of international law'. Kelsen maintains that the constitution of a State is 'valid' only if the legal order established on the basis of this constitution is, by and large, 'effective'. According to him this general 'principle of effectiveness' is a positive norm of international law which, applied to an individual national legal order provides the basic norm of this national legal order. 'Thus', Kelsen concludes, 'the basic norms of the different national legal orders are themselves based on a general norm of the international legal order'.[86] Thus Malanczuk opines: 'Kelsen's theory led to the conclusion that all rules of international law were supreme over municipal law, that a municipal inconsistent with international law was automatically null and void and that rules of international law were directly applicable in the domestic spheres of States'.[87]

Seen the rules and principles of international human rights law from this perspective, no State can violate human rights of any individual in its jurisdiction, be it a non-UN member or a communist or a military dictatorship. Hence, according to Kelsen's theory, state sovereignty cannot be pleaded against the violation of human rights. This itself is a contribution of great weight.

Hart's positivist-naturalist theory of primary and secondary rules applied to human rights principles, seen as 'universally recognized principles of conduct', the rights would find their basis in *'elementary truths concerning human beings.'* Hart is a 'leading jurist of positivistic school'.[88] But he is equally described as 'an influential moral philosopher'.[89]

[84] H Kelson, RT Tucker, (ed), *Principles of International Law*, 2nd edn, (New York, NY, Holt, Rinehart and Winston, 1967) 7.

[85] BM Tripathi, *Jurisprudence: Legal Theory* (1997) 52.

[86] H Kelson, RT Tucker, (ed), *Principles of International Law*, 2nd edn, (New York, NY, Holt, Rinehart and Winston, 1967) 562.

[87] P Malanczuk, *Akehurst's Modern Introduction to International Law*, 7th edn, (London, Routledge, 1997) 62.

[88] Judge CG Weeramantry, ICJ Reports, 1996, p 298.

[89] By J Shestack, cited in M Dixon and R McCorquodale, *Cases and Materials on International Law*, 2nd edn (London, Blackstone Press), p 193.

Hart propounded his theory of primary and secondary rules in his classic work *The Concept of Law* (1961). To Hart law is a system of rules—primary and secondary. The union of primary and secondary rules explains the nature of law. The primary rules are seen as duty imposing rules, for instance in a primitive society. The secondary rules are power conferring rules, the rules that govern recognition of primary rules and create the power to modify, adjudge, create or even destroy primary rules. This supplementation of primary rules with secondary rules says Hart is the step from pre-legal to legal world. The natural law principles embodied in the 1948 United Nations Universal Declaration of Human Rights and the resulting numerous international covenants and conventions, may thus be seen as primary human rights rules, in the pre-legal world, conferred power by the secondary rules recognizing them as positive human rights law. The secondary rules provide all the three remedies—the rules of recognition, the rules of change and the rules of adjudication for removing the uncertainty, static character and inefficiency inherent in the primary rules and convert the regime of primary rules into an indisputable legal system.

What has earned Hart the title of a positivist and naturalist at the same time is well described by Prof Dhayani:

> In short HLA. Hart at best can be described both a positivist and naturalist as by correlating law and morality he conceived what Austin and Kelsen failed to conceive in legal theory. Hart did not accept the narrow concept of law as enunciated by Kelsen nor supported by Austinian method of judging the validity of law in terms of command, sanction and sovereign.[90]

This particularly facilitates not only the study of human rights principles in a theoretical context, retrospective and prospective, but at the same time offers judges and jurists to develop and elaborate human rights law further. One current example of this is very encouraging. In the *Legality of the Threat or Use of Nuclear Weapons case* (1996), the UN General Assembly asked the advisory opinion of the International Court of Justice, asking whether the threat or use of nuclear weapon is legal or illegal. The Court having replied that according to existing international law it is neither legal nor illegal, Judge Weeramantry (Sri Lanka), dissenting with the Court mentioned in his dissenting opinion that the use of nuclear weapons is a violation of human rights principle of right to life. He at great length quoted Hart from his *The Concept of Law.*

Seeing through the 'rationality' of Hart, Judge Weeramantry remarked:

> all the postulates of law presupposes that they contribute to and function within the premise of the continued existence of the community served by that law. Without the assumption of that continued existence, no rule of law and no legal system can have any claim to validity, however attractive the juristic reasoning on which it is based. That taint of invalidity affects not merely the particular rule. The legal system, which accommodates that rule itself collapses upon its foundations, for legal systems are postulated upon

90 SN Dhayani, *Fundamental of Jurisprudence: The Indian Approach* (Allahabad, India, Central Law Agency, 1997) 21.

> the continued existence of society. Being part of society, they must themselves collapse with the greatest entity of which they are a part. This assumption, lying at the very heart of the concept of law, often recedes from view in the midst of the nuclear discussion.... Hart, a leading jurist of the positivistic school, has, in a celebrated exposition of the minimum content of natural law, formulated this principle pithily in the following sentence: 'We are committed to it as something presupposed by the terms of the discussion; for our concern is with social arrangements for continued existence, not with those of a suicide club.[91]

Further in support of his own argument, Judge Weeramantry cited the reasoning of Hart as: 'His reasoning is that', he continued, 'there are certain rules of conduct which any social organization must contain if it is to be viable. Such rules do in fact constitute a common element in the law and conventional morality of all societies which have progressed to the point where these are distinguished as different forms of social control.'[92]

Judge Weeramantry emphasized that:

> International law is surely such a social form of control devised and accepted by the constituent members of that international society—the nation States. Hart goes on to note that: such universally recognized principles of conduct which have a basis in elementary truths concerning human beings, their natural environment, and aims, may be considered the minimum content of Natural Law, in contrast with the more grandiose and more challengeable constructions which have often been proffered under that name.'[93]

The gist of the whole argument and the applicability of the theory of Hart Judge Weeramantry put in the following words: 'Here is a recognized minimum accepted by positivistic jurisprudence which questions some of the more literal assumptions of other schools. We are down to the common denominator to which all legal systems must conform.'[94]

All this is deeply convincing of the fact that Hart's theory has still much more to offer to 'all legal systems', and human rights system is certainly included. It is still too early to say what has been the impact of Hart's '*minimum content of Natural Law*' on the judges partaking in deciding the human rights cases and the development of human rights law, yet the brilliance and persuasiveness of Hart's theory has not left Judge Weeramantry untouched is obvious.

The very name of Rawl's theory of justice based on fairness itself rings a note of human rights doctrine. 'No theory of human rights can be advanced today without considering Rawls' thesis',[95] said Shestack. This is a great tribute to John Rawls and his book *A Theory of Justice* (1971).

[91] Legality of the Threat or Use of Nuclear Weapons, Dissenting Opinion of Judge Weeramantry, ICJ Reports, 1996, pp 520–21. (For Hart's quotation see HLA Hart, *The Concept of Law* (Oxford, Clarendon Press, 1961) 188.

[92] Weeramantry *ibid*, p 521.

[93] *Ibid.*

[94] *Ibid.*

[95] Shestack cited in M Dixon and R Mccorquodale, *Cases and Materials on International Law*, 2nd edn, (London, Blackstone Press) p 194.

Justice, according to Rawls is the first virtue of social institutions. And he maintains that human rights are certainly an end of justice. Therefore, his theory of justice based on fairness suggests that the role of justice is crucial to understanding human rights.

Rawls' conception of justice rests on his two following cardinal principles:

> *First Principle.* Each person is to have an equal right to the most extensive total system of equal basic liberties compatible with a similar system of liberty for all.
>
> *Second Principle.* Social and economic inequalities are to be arranged so that they are both: (a) to the greatest benefit of the least advantaged, consistent with the just saving principle, and (b) attached to offices and positions open to all under conditions of fair equality of opportunity.[96]

The general conception behind these principles rests on the *principle of fairness*. In deriving these principles Rawls has created in his book a hypothetical situation in which a group of people are to choose a set of principles of justice to govern their own conduct. The principles are to be agreed upon under certain conditions bearing specifically on knowledge and motivation. The knowledge conditions are to guarantee fairness. The choosers are assumed to know general scientific principles but are shielded by a *'veil of ignorance'* from their own knowledge, for instance their own conception of the good, own talents, own society, own position, etc. This is how Rawls formulates his *normative principles of justice based on fairness, and shielded by 'veil of ignorance'*. These two principles, however, are not of equal weight. The first has priority over the second.

According to Delaney this theory of Rawls 'revitalized the long dormant field of political philosophy, and more generally, gave new direction and respectability to normative moral theory'.[97]

Judge Weeramantry of the International Court of Justice found the theory of John Rawls as of 'cardinal value'.[98] As mentioned earlier under Hart's theory that Judge Weeramantry found the use of nuclear weapons irreconcilable with the human rights principle of right to life. After citing Hart in favour of his argument, he turned to the theory of Rawls in this way, 'Another philosophical approach to the matter is along the lines of the 'veil of ignorance' posited by John Rawls in his celebrated study of justice as fairness'. He continues:

> If one is to devise a legal system under which one is prepared to live, this exposition posits as a *test of fairness* of that system that its members would be prepared to accept it if the *decision had to be taken behind a veil of ignorance* as to the future place of each constituent member within that legal system.[99] (italics are mine).

Disagreeing with the Court's indecisiveness in delivering the advisory opinion to the UN General Assembly in the case '*Legality of the Threat or Use of Nuclear*

[96] J Rawls, *A Theory of Justice* (Oxford, OUP, 1971) 302.
[97] CF Delaney's entry on Rawls in R Turner (ed) *Thinkers of the Twentieth Century*', 2nd edn, p 640.
[98] ICJ Reports, 1996, p 523.
[99] *Ibid*, pp 522–23.

Weapons' Judge Weeramantry mentioned in his dissenting opinion that: 'My considered opinion is that the use or threat of use of nuclear weapons is illegal in any circumstances whatsoever'.[100] In reaching his considered opinion he was thoroughly convinced of Rawls theory of justice based on fairness and its 'veil of ignorance'. The following long quotation from his dissenting opinion reflects that:

> A nation considering its allegiance to such a system of international law, and not knowing whether it would fall within the group of nuclear nations or not, could scarcely be expected to subscribe to it if it contained a rule by which legality would be accorded to the use of a weapon by others which could annihilate it. Even less would it consent if it is denied even the right to possess such a weapon and, least of all if it could be annihilated or irreparably damaged in the quarrels of others to which it is not in any way a party.
>
> One would indeed be in a desirable position in the event that it was one's lot to become a member of the nuclear group but, if there was a chance of being cast into the non-nuclear group, would one accept such a legal system behind a *veil of ignorance as to one's position*? Would it make any difference if the members of the nuclear group gave an assurance, which no one could police, that they would use the weapon only in extreme emergencies? The answer to such questions cannot be in doubt. By this test of fairness and legitimacy, such a legal system would surely fail.

Such philosophical insight of Rawls, Judge Weeramantry finds, is of cardinal importance in deciding upon the question of threat or use of nuclear weapons which by all means are *irreconcilable with human rights principles*, particularly the right to life. There is no doubt if the above mentioned application of 'fairness' and 'veil of ignorance' is applied to human rights violations situations, particularly in situations like *NATO v Yugoslavia*[101] where force is used, the decisions would have been different. Hence, when jurists and judges like that of Judge Weeramantry grasp the cardinal value of Rawls' theory and insight the protection of human rights and the development of human rights law would usher a new era of progress. The theory indeed has to offer a great deal to the development of the doctrine of human rights and the principle of human dignity.

Dworkin's theory of equal concern and respect is another version with emphasis on the principle of human dignity with its various civil, political, economic and cultural aspects. Dworkin's book *Taking Rights Seriously* (1977) has earned him a special place as a human rights theorist. According to him 'a general theory of law must be normative as well as conceptual'.[102] In expounding his 'general theory of rights' he refutes the conventional notion that all conventional rights are derivative from general right to liberty and establishes that in fact they are all derivative from the right to equality. Dworkin attacks the positivist conception that law consists solely of rules. Individual rights for him are principles which are required by justice or fairness or some other dimension of morality.[103] Dworkin proceeds from the 'postulates of political morality' and proposes that:

[100] ICJ Reports, 1996, p 433.
[101] See ch 11.
[102] R Dworkin, *Taking Rights Seriously* (Cambridge, MA, Harvard University Press, 1977) vii.
[103] *Ibid*, p 502.

> Government must treat those whom it governs with concern, that is, as human beings who are capable of suffering and frustration, and with respect, that is, as human beings who are capable of forming and acting on intelligent conceptions of how their lives should be lived. Government must not only treat people with concern and respect, but with equal concern and respect.[104]

According to Dworkin: 'Individual rights are political trumps held by individuals. Individuals have rights when, for some reason, a collective goal is not a sufficient justification for denying them what they wish, as individuals, to have or to do, or not a sufficient justification for imposing some loss or injury upon them.'[105]

He sees that rights and goals go hand in hand: 'Arguments of principles are arguments intended to establish an individual right; arguments of policy are arguments intended to establish a collective goal. Principles are propositions that describe rights; policies are propositions that describe goals.'[106]

Dworkin finds the 'right to equal concern and respect' is the right most essential of all the rights. In his own words: 'our institutions about justice presuppose not only that people have rights that one right among these is fundamental and even axiomatic. This most fundamental of rights is a distinct conception of the right to equality, which I call the right to equal concern and respect.'[107] He also propounds that all conventional rights, including right to liberty, are derivative from the right to equality itself.[108] In this sense Dworkin's thought is not different from the principle contained in the opening paragraph of 1948 Universal Declaration of Human Rights. The same declaration also declares that 'the foundation of freedom, justice and peace' is in the 'inherent dignity and of equal and inalienable rights of all members of the human family'. Therefore, Dworkin's theory of 'right to equal concern and respect' may also be classified as a theory based on human dignity. There also is tinge of 'natural rights' in his theory. Prof Dias is of the opinion: 'Although he dislikes the description of his "rights" as "natural", his thesis is not dissimilar to "natural rights" as traditionally conceived'.[109]

In a nutshell, the *Grundnorm* of Dworkin's 'general theory of rights', as he calls it, is the right to equality, which he prefers to call as 'right to equal concern and respect', another expression for the principle of human dignity.

The three authors—McDougal, Lasswell and Chen—have propounded a value oriented theory of human dignity in their co-authored work *Human Rights and World Public Order: The Basic Policies of an International Law of Human Dignity* (1980). Their value oriented approach is based on the key concept of the protection of human dignity. The authors believe that demands for human rights are identical with demands for wide sharing in all human value processes in human community. Drawing from the provisions of four important human rights

104 *Ibid*, p 272–73.
105 *Ibid*, p ix.
106 *Ibid*, p 90.
107 *Ibid*, p xii; see also pp 181–82.
108 Chs 10, 11 and 12 of his book *Taking Rights Seriously* are most descriptive of this.
109 RWM Dias, *Jurisprudence*, 5th edn (London, Butterworths) 501.

documents—1) United Nations Charter, 2) Universal Declaration of Human Rights, 3) International Covenant on Civil and Political Rights, and 4) International Covenant on Economic, Social and Cultural Rights—the authors specify eight interdependent basic values widely cherished: 1) Respect, 2) Power, 3) Enlightenment, 4) Well-being, 5) Health, 6) Skill, 7) Affection, and 8) Rectitude. Human dignity is the key concept in relation to all these values and to the ultimate goal of a world community in which a democratic distribution of values is promoted.[110]

Judge Bedjaoui approaches human rights with his divinity[111] and compassion oriented theory of human dignity. He finds the concept of human dignity at the core of human rights ideology. If seen human dignity in the form of a circle, one sees the divinity as an invariant at the centre of this concept and springing henceforth the human compassion to be seen working on its surface. The circumference appears as a 'circular route' marked with historical milestones of 'progression' and 'regressions'.

Judge Bedjaoui does not however simply rests with the hollow mention of this concept but goes a great length further to explain what the concept of human dignity means and how it works. In order to illustrate this he cites the following words of a great Indian and world renowned leader well known for preaching and practising non-violence, Mahatma Gandhi: 'We are all cast in the same mould; to despise a single human being is to despise the divine which is in us.'[112] The essence of these words is not different from the words of St Paul: 'Know ye not that ye are the temple of God, and that the Spirit of God dwelleth in you?'[113] And divinity is

[110] M McDougal, H Lasswell, and L Chen, Human Rights and World Public Order: The Basic Policies of an International Law of Human Dignity, pp 82–93.

[111] Historically, with the dawn of analytical school of thinking, legal thinkers have often insisted that legal science and divinity are mutually exclusive, but that is not the case. Men of law only need to learn from the eminent scientist of the 20th century, Albert Einstein, when he said: 'It is enough for me to contemplate the mystery of conscious life perpetuating itself through all eternity; to reflect upon the marvellous structure of the universe, which we can dimply perceive, and to try humbly to comprehend even an infinitesimal part of the intelligence manifested in nature.' In response to this, Robert Millikan, dean of American Scientists, declared to the American Physical Society: 'That is as good a definition of God as I need.' (Both quoted in *A Spiritual Primer* (Radha Soami Satsang Beas Publication, 1997) p 8.) If so great a scientific genius and expertise regarding the physics of universe concluded that God must exist, the day is not far that once again the mutual inclusiveness of law and divinity must be recognized, and the beginning of that already is in sight with the dawn of human rights and human dignity thinking springing from the very heart of natural law. However, it may be noted that the reference to judeo-christian tradition which was advanced by German delegation in the Charter of Fundamental Rights of the EU (Nice, December 2000) was struck off as a result of a strong French Opposition.

[112] M Bedjaoui, *Preventive Diplomacy: Development, Education and Human Rights* p 54.

[113] *The Bible*, 2 Cor 6:16. On these words from the Bible an Indian mystic commented: 'But do we understand them and take note? It would seem we do not. Actually, our temples, mosques and synagogues stand as statements of how we try to limit God to the physical. How can we limit the unlimited? . . . God created human beings, and only later did they become Christians, Budhists, Jews, Sikhs, Muslims and so forth' (see *A Spiritual Primer*, Radha Soami Satsang Beas Publication, 1997, p 65). Right to religion and development is directly relevant to what we understand by the principle of human dignity with its unvarying factor. Human dignity lies in this that the preacher must in the first instance teach its audience that the religion was made for man and not the man for religion. Hence, every religioun is a means to one common religious end, ie, God-realization. When religion failed to do this and tried to constraint God by walls of brick and mortar or stone, it did tremendous harm to the school of

something unvarying and universal. It is in the essence of this unvarying divinity that Judge Bedjaoui finds his meaning of human dignity.[114] In his own words: 'Through the diversity of cultures and values, unity and *that which does not vary* must be sought.'[115] This unvarying factor is *human dignity*. Hence, for Judge Bedjaoui, the concept of human dignity is meaningless if its theoretical essence is not translated into action by seeing and realizing its working through the diversity

natural law. As a result the positivistic school was born. With the quest for the meaning of human dignity, it is the meaning of life which is on the agenda. Hence, 'circular rout' of Judge Bedjaoui, from natural law to natural law, is on the legal agenda in the human rights school of law. The human dignity perspective underlying these arguments arises from the experience of unity at the heart of life.

[114] Prof Michael J Perry, an American jurist, also concludes: 'The conviction that every human being is sacred is in my view, inescapably religious (and the idea of human rights, therefore, ineliminably religious', see his book: MJ Perry, *The Idea of Human Rights: Four Inquiries* (Oxford, OUP, 1998) 5. The book is rare 'at a time when legal scholarship is becoming increasingly dull'. Perry seeks idea of human rights and human dignity in Christian teachings. Though Perry has written his book mainly based on teachings of the Bible, I firmly believe, that the essence of truth regarding the human dignity, man's soul being part and parcel of God, is the same in every religion. If God is One, there cannot be millions of Essences. Religion as it exists today is nothing more than Machiavellian version of spirituality. But in order to find real meaning of the terms 'God' and His essence in man 'soul' as Human Dignity, one needs to go to a living Christ, the Socrates of spirituality. Then only the true meaning of Christ's words 'human body is the living temple of God' would match with spiritual-political Socrates' wodrs 'Know thyself.' Just as every politcs has its Machiavelli and Socrates, similarly every theology has its devil (Machiavelli) and saint (Socrates) too. Though politically and legally the world is still passing through the Machiavellian era, so is it with religion and theology. The modern religions, with their rituals and dogmas, are nothing less than perverted spirituality in the form of Machiavellianism of spirituality, hence, have nothing to do with the teachings of their founders, be it Christ, Mohammed or Budha. Their founders taught only one thing: God is one; He is in all of us; if we want to be united (*religare*, Latin word for religion which means to unite) with Him, we have to be initiated by a living God-realized soul (call him/her Christ, Mohammed or Budha). It is not the name but the power of being capable of uniting souls with the Supreme Soul, the God, which matters. It has nothing to do with the race, religion, colour, culture, sex or any other considerations of the living Uniter (Saint), as long as he/she is in a living human body. Such a living being has the power to put us in touch with the '*Logos*' of the Greek, the '*Word*' of the Christians (in New Testament), the '*Tora*' of the Jews (in Old Testament), the '*Kun*' of the Muslims (in Quran), and the '*Shabad*' or '*Naam*'of the Hindus (Vedas). This way he/she connects our life current (soul) with the *Logos* Current, initiates us into the inner realities of man which in biblical language are described as '*if thine eye be single thy whole body shall be full of right.*' Real meaning of the principle of human dignity we will be able to appreciate only when we will be able to have direct perception of our Inner/Higher Being, called by names such as *Word*, *Kun* and *Shabad* or *Naam*, but commonly known as God in English, Allah in Arabic and Persian, Parmatma in Sanskrit. One Indian saint has aptly mentioned: 'Man is half angel and half devil. If he overcomes lust and other beastly qualities, he rises higher than the angels; if lust overcomes him, he falls below the level of the beasts; In this human life you can, if you will, become God or fall to the level of the devil' (see JS Singh, *Science of the Soul*, 7th edn, (Radha Soami Satsang Beas, India) p 224). And when man, initiated by a living perfect Saint (the living Christ or Mohammed), begins to rise to the level of God his state of knowledge is described by another Saint: 'The greater the rise within on the Current, the greater the comprehension of the underlying unity even in the diversity outside, and the greater the understanding of human nature, and consequently the greater the toleration and sympathy.' (See S Singh, *The Dawn of Light*, (1985) p 211. The essence of truth, and the source of human dignity in God in all religions is best described by Dr Julian Johnson in his book: JP Johnson, *The Path of the Masters*, 15th edn, (Radha Soami Satsang Beas Beas, India, 1993). I am strongly convinced that Judge Bedjaoui's theory of human dignity (resting on his thoughts relating expressions such as 'circular route,' 'progression and regression,' 'sacred,' and 'that which does not vary must be sought' (contains a revolutionary potential for the legal thought along the path which was paved with the birth of the principle of human dignity, the principle destined to revolutionize the legal system as a whole.

[115] M Bedjaoui, *Preventive Diplomacy*, *Ibid.* p 54.

of numerous human cultures and values forming integral part of international community and international law. In order to explain this conflict between theory and practice, he mentions boomingly:

> Today, for better or for worse, human rights are a matter for ideological confrontation. May be no one is completely innocent. Many, however, think they are honouring human rights simply by denouncing violations committed by others. In human rights we honour something sacred, but we also blaspheme against it, by our soaring sublimity and our weakness, our generosity and our subterfuges, our greatness and our petty calculation, our demanding consciences and our turning of a blind eye, our solemn declarations and our commonplaces, our lofty discourses and our hollow rhetoric.[116]

As a pioneer in the international law of development, Judge Bedjaoui thinks that 'there is an indissoluble link between underdevelopment and the violation of human rights.' Greater part of the international community in which all are supposed to be entitled to have human rights and be protected from their violation is poverty stricken and underdeveloped in various ways is evident from the fact that four out of five human creatures on this planet suffer from the 'grinding daily poverty.'[117] Reflecting this reality of human indignity versus human dignity within the context of underdevelopment versus human rights, Judge Bedjaoui sees the remedy in human compassion[118] in order to promote human dignity in his following statement:

> When an underdeveloped state is lacking in every kind of necessary resource, it is by definition incapable of protecting the first human rights, the right to life, with all it implies in the way of rights to social protection, work, health, education, etc . . .. There is thus no point in giving the invalid a transfusion of blood or a glucose if one is unable to treat his various organs affected by the disease. It is equally pointless to instill human rights by transfusion into a debilitated social fabric if one cannot remedy the primary, deep-rooted causes of the diseases affecting that social fabric. The primary cause is economic underdevelopment. Let us sow the seeds of development and we shall reap human rights.[119]

[116] M Bedjaoui, 'Report on the Difficult Advance of Human Rights towards Universality' in *Council of Europe: Colloquy on The Universality of Human Rights in a Pluralistic World*, H/Coll (89) 3, Strasbourg, 17–19 April 1989, p 17.

[117] M Bedjaoui, European Council, H/Coll (89) 3, p 1.

[118] Albert Einstein advocated this 'compassion' and 'brotherhood' of mankind in human rights in his words:

> A human being is part of the whole, called 'Universe', a part limited in time and space. He experiences himself, his thoughts, and feelings, as something separate from the rest, a kind of optical delusion of his consciousness. This delusion is a kind of prison for us, restricting us to our personal desires and to affection for a few persons nearest to us. Our task must be to free ourselves from this prison by widening our circle of compassion to embrace all living creatures and the whole nature in its beauty.

Quoted in D Brian, *Einstein, A Life* (New York, NY, Wiley, 1996) 388.

[119] M Bedjaoui, *Preventive Diplomacy*, p 51. Judge Lachs once quoted a Professor saying that a lawyer who knows only law is like a worm in a rotten wood. Similarly, the comprehensive understanding of the principle of human dignity will not just come from judges and jurists alone but from people and professionals in all walks of life.

This is a principle when well understood and applied in practice would enrich the practical meaning of human dignity by protecting the right to development and right to quality of life. No code of conduct can give one all the answers, but if one understands the principles that underpin it, the answers start springing as if from an eternal fountain of law.

Human as an individual is though seen at the centre of human rights, yet human rights as a process is a collective and universal undertaking with its vast moral and spiritual dimensions. Judge Bedjaoui states:

> . . . Cultures and religions all recognize that the human being has an irreducible moral dimension. Values such as respect for life, duties towards future generations, protection of the environment, the duty to help and protect the weak at all levels, from family to global, via the national level, may and must constitute the *ethical core* for which a broad consensus exists.[120]

The fountain-head of all this he sees lying in the concept of human dignity.

Hence, according to Judge Bedjaoui the concept of human dignity, the core of human rights ideology, is not complete without its counterpart in action. In other words for Judge Bedjaoui the human dignity, as far as the school of human rights law is concerned, is static on the one side and dynamic on the other, and therefore, it is divinity in action, manifestation of human compassion, by human beings through human beings and for human beings. In this process of two characteristics if action or dynamic part of dignity is commensurate to its divine part, this according to him is the 'progression' of the process of human rights. And, if the dynamic side as against the static recedes, this according to him is the 'regression' of the process of human rights.[121]

The quest and struggle for human rights is by no means something new; it is as old as the history of mankind. Human rights are, according to Judge Bedjaoui, universal in character, be it *ratione temporis, ratione paersonae* or *ratione materiae.*

This historical process, according to him, in all its aspects, reflects a circular path. About the historical march of the universal character of human rights, he has the following to say: 'this long journey towards universality has followed a circular route in theoretical terms, starting from the dignity of the human individual and proceeding from there to an affirmation of rights which he or she represents to return once again to that same human dignity.'[122] This reflects his opinion that the real source of human rights is ultimately to be traced in the divinity of man, natural law, and in this he sees, therefore, with all its time-to-time 'progression' and 'retrogression,' a revival of natural law school within the context of human rights law school. With 'progression' and 'regression' as a matter of course milestones along the historical 'circular route' of the process of human rights with its fundamental concept of 'human dignity' at the core, invariable in essence and variable in action, the human dignity theory of Judge Bedjaoui may rightly be

[120] M Bedjaoui, European Council, H/Coll (89) 3, p 54.

[121] M Bedjaoui, Report on the Difficult Advance of Human Rights towards Universality, 1989, p 1.

[122] M Bedjaoui, Council of Europe, H/Coll (89) 3, p 1.

described as a divinity and compassion oriented theory of human dignity about human rights.

This theory of Judge Bedjaoui, as part of human rights law, seems developing a broader consensus of the international community, filling and healing the gaps between 'north and south', making it possible to establish human rights acceptable to whole range of cultures and ideologies.

III. Appraisal: Principle of Human Dignity in Retrospect and Prospect

There seems to be one common note in all the theories discussed above virtually all legal thinkers have considered the nature of human rights.[123] An analysis of these theories reveals that they are not actually contradicting with each other but complementing. Their methods of studying human rights are different but at the basis is one single reality, the dignity and worth of human being. A synthesis of all provides that there is one common and fundamental *principle of respect for human persona*, the inherent dignity of human being as provided in the opening paragraph of the Universal Declaration of Human Rights.

When Natural Law theory speaks of man's 'insight' and 'individual autonomy', it is simply in other words asking that man must be treated with respect.

Positivist theory is not at all devoid of moral and natural principles. It is actually the difference between 'primary rules' and 'secondary rules' of Hart. As a matter of fact, the bulk of norms of human rights law are just the transformation of natural law principles of philosophy (primary rules) into the rules of law, by the combination of primary and secondary rules, in various covenants and conventions, hence positive law. The words in the UN Charter's preamble—'to reaffirm faith in fundamental human rights, in the dignity and worth of the human person, in the equal rights of men and women and of nations large and small'—are perfectly natural law language as well as positive law language. What is common again is the human dignity and *respect for human person.* It also gives an impression that natural law principles are gradually being incorporated in treaty form or customary law. Dixon has rightly observed: *'Although the binding force of human rights obligations must rest ultimately in treaty or custom, the inspiration for these obligations lies in "morality", "justice", "ethics" or a simple regard for the dignity of Mankind'.*[124]

Whether we approach this from Kant's man as an end, or the Hohfeld's jural relations, or from Lauterpacht's human dignity in the sovereignty of man; whether we see it through the Kelsen's hierarchy of norms or through the primary and secondary rules of Hart; whether we study it through the Rawls' theory of justice based on fairness or through the Dworkin's right to equal concern and respect;

[123] M Dixon and R McCorquodale, *Cases and Materials on International Law*, 2nd edn (London, Blackstone), p 192.

[124] M Dixon, *Textbook on International Law*, 3rd edn, (London, Blackstone, 1996) 307.

whether we take the Nozick's theory of entitlement or the value-oriented theory of dignity propounded by McDougal-Lasswell-Chen; all we find is that the respect for human persona is at the basis of all the theories. Judge Tanaka sees human dignity in the principle of equality, and the principle of equality as the fountain head of human rights and at the summit of hierarchy of the system of law as a whole. Prof Higgins (now Judge at the ICJ) sees human dignity in the equal partnership of the individual, along sovereign state and international organization, in the decision-making process of the normative system of law. Judge Bedjaoui finds human dignity in the factor of unvarying divinity in man.

A former President of the International Court of Justice, Judge Nagendra *Singh* (India), seems to have rightly hit the nail in describing the reality in the following words: '*The fundamental norm governing the concept of human rights is that of the respect for human personality and its absolute worth*, regardless of colour, race, sex, religion or other considerations'.[125] (emphasis added). It may equally serve as a definition of the principle of human dignity. In this sense, the fundamental principle of human dignity prescribes that the human *persona*, the *superanus* in human being, seen in the image of State sovereignty, be respected in all respect regardless of race, sex, religion or other considerations.

Seen in the Theoretical Framework of Judge Bedjaoui's 'Circular Route' of Human Dignity, which May be Described as Journey Starting from Divine (Natural Law) and Leading Back to Divine (Natural Law), it Would Facilitate Further Understanding of the Principle of Human Dignity and the Development of Human Rights Law, in a Brief Glance Can Establish That the Principle of Human Dignity is as Old as Humanity, Irrespective of the Prevailing Juristic Schools of Natural Law or Positive Law.

'*HUMAN BODY IS THE LIVING TEMPLE OF GOD*'. This is the most fitting tribute ever paid to human dignity. A die-hard positivist might instantly and perhaps arrogantly sweep away this old fashioned theological-cum-natural law statement of Jesus Christ. And, if the sleeping Jeremy Bentham awakens in him our devoted positivist might also reject the statement as 'nonsense on stilts'[126] However, today even the analytical jurist Bentham (1748–1832) who himself coined the term 'international law' and yet found moral human dignity oriented rights of man 'nonsense on stilts' would find himself speechless if he read the modern textbooks of international law and found all of them containing a chapter on human rights law with repeated mentions of words such as '*all human rights derive from the dignity and worth inherent in human person*'.[127] This is how the nature, character and substance of international law has changed, and still evolving, with the changing pace of time and the development of legal doctrine.

[125] N Singh, *Enforcement of Human Rights in Peace and War and the Future of Humanity* (Dordrecht, Nijhoff, 1986) 1.

[126] See R Dworkin, *Taking Rights Seriously* (Cambridge, MA, Harvard University Press, 1977) 184.

[127] The Vienna Declaration and Programme of Action adopted on 25 June 1993 by the World Conference on Human Rights, sponsored by the United Nations, reaffirmed this language of UN Charter and that of the three key documents forming the International Bill of Human Rights.

An earlier writer contributing to international law and the international legal system was a Spanish citizen Francisco Vitoria (1480–1546), a professor of theology. It is remarkable that even at the time when international law permitted Spain and other nations to engage in creating colonies, Vitoria nevertheless argued that Spain was obliged to treat the conquered Indians of the Americas humanely, and he even granted these Indians a limited right to conduct 'just wars' against their cruel conquerors. This may well be seen in the light that even when international law was in its primitive most stage, the idea of human rights based on human dignity, though as feeble as the international law of the day, did still echo in the theory and foundation of international law.[128]

Another Spanish writer, also a professor of theology, Francisco Suarez (1548–1617), though much interested in dealing with the then prevailing trend of independence of States showed his particular concern with the nature of just wars and the rules for their conduct.[129]

In the 17th century, the concept of human rights, known at that time as individuals' natural rights, centred around its central concept of human dignity, began surfacing almost at the same time when in the womb of jurisprudence the conception of international law was taking place. It may well be said that they both were intertwined and were in the early process of their birth as far as present academic understandings are concerned. The fact that the concept of natural rights of *individuals* was gaining significance in legal circles in which the doctrine of social contract was an order of the day it was bound to have impact on the social element of the law as well as the contract. That the law based social reform approaches like that of Bentham sprang in that atmosphere is reflective of the fact that on the one hand the thinking of human rights and human dignity gave birth to socio-legal thinking and on the other hand this socio-legal thinking paved way for the development of the doctrine of human rights based on the concept of human dignity, albeit in the capacity of a group, the society. It was nevertheless the struggle for human dignity, a collective human dignity, between the rulers and the ruled, hence less government and more individual rights with dignity. Kelly rightly describes the situation as follows:

> The most significant 17th century contribution to jurisprudence, alongside the placing of the law of nations on a scientific footing, and the definitive expression of the social contract as one binding the ruler as well as the ruled in a conditional structure of trust, was the concept—to some extent correlative to the doctrine of limited government—of individuals' natural rights.[130]

'Man is born free but is found everywhere in chains': with this, his historic statement of the 18th century, philosopher Jean-Jacque Rousseau found the dignity of man in his inherent right to freedom and the irony of man in his ill-treatment at the hands of the ruling class. At the close of 18th century and the beginning of 19th

[128] W Levi, *Contemporary International Law* (1979) 11.
[129] *Ibid.*
[130] JM Kelly, *A Short History of Western Legal Theory* (Oxford, Clarendon Press, 1992) 227.

century two great legal thinkers left their mark: Immanuel Kant and Jeremy Bentham. Though they both stood for human dignity they propounded opposing theories. Kant found the source of human dignity in natural law. Bentham found it in his theory of hedonistic individualism and analytical positivism.

International law in the centuries prior to the twentieth mainly and primarily concentrated on the rights and duties of states. However, the most striking feature of international law in the 20th century, particularly the second half of the century, has been that the development of rules and principles concerning rights and duties of individual human beings occupied such a significant place in the international jurisprudence that an altogether new branch of law, international human rights law, was added to the main body of international law. This new branch of international law—though equally deriving its legal contents from the generally accepted sources of international law under Article 38(1) of the Statute of the International Court of Justice: customs, conventions and general principles of law—has an added dimension to it as a whole. That 'added dimension', according to Martin Dixon, is the dignity of Mankind. Dixon is of the opinion that: 'Although the binding force of human rights obligations must rest ultimately in treaty or custom, the inspiration for these obligations lies in the "morality", "justice", "ethics" or a simple regard for the dignity of Mankind.'[131] This statement actually implies a lot. No matter how positivistic or formalistic a judge is, if the inspiration of the concept of human dignity as substantive law is indeed in the fields of morality, justice and ethics, any interpretation of a customary or treaty law related to human rights cannot escape in the process of judicial interpretation and application of that law delving into the trinity of the moral-justice-ethics depths of human dignity. And since all branches of international law have a growing human rights aspect, international law cannot escape being coloured by the concept of human dignity. In other words in the long term development of human rights law international law appears more human-dignity oriented than state-sovereignty oriented.

The preamble of the United Nations Charter, a document containing 111 Articles and 19 chapters, opens with the words: 'We the Peoples of the United Nations determined . . . to reaffirm faith in fundamental human rights, in the dignity and worth of the human person, in the equal rights of men and women.' In order to materialize the place of human dignity in the post-war development of international law, and within that framework of the international human rights law, the drafters of the Charter foresaw the development of an International Bill of Rights. This Bill now consists of three monumental documents: 1) the Universal Declaration of Human Rights (1948), 2) the International Covenant on Civil and Political Rights (1966), and 3) the International Covenant on Economic, Social and Cultural Rights (1966). A special care was taken in drafting these three documents so that the central concept of human dignity envisioned by the Charter would find its proper central place and reflection. The Preamble of the UDHR emphatically speaks about human dignity in two ways: 1) 'Whereas recognition of

[131] M Dixon, *Textbook on International Law*, 3rd edn, (London, Blackstone, 1996) 307.

the inherent dignity and of the equal and inalienable rights of members of the human family is the foundation of freedom, justice and peace in the world', and 2) 'Whereas the people of the United Nations have in the Charter reaffirmed their faith in fundamental human rights, in the dignity and worth of the human person and in the equal rights of men and women and have determined to promote social progress and better standards of life in larger freedom'. Both the children of the UDHR, the ICCPR and the ICESCR, commonly proclaim in the same language to uphold the spirit of human dignity enshrined in the UN Charter and that of the UDHR in their respective Preambles: 'in accordance with the principles proclaimed in the Charter of the United Nations, recognition of the inherent dignity and of the equal and inalienable rights of all members of the human family is the foundation of freedom, justice and peace in the world', and then recognise that '*these rights derive from the inherent dignity of the human person*'.

The principle of human dignity in the International Covenant on Civil and Political Rights (1966) is seen by Prof Dixon as: 'All in all, the effect of the Covenant is to provide a framework for the protection of those civil and political rights most commonly regarded as being essential for the dignity and liberty of Man.'[132] Article 1 of the Charter of Fundamental Rights of the European Union of 7 December 2000 reads: 'Human dignity is inviolable. It must be respected and protected'

'When human lives are endangered, when human dignity is in jeopardy, national borders and sensitivities become irrelevant,' spoke Ellie Wiesel at the occasion of Nobel Peace Prize on 10 December 1986.[133] The events in the US on 9/11 and the tragedy of Asian Tsunami are good examples. Human dignity is at the core of any legal system, be it national or international. The fact may have been more or less recognised at different times, but never has it been utterly denied. '*God made man in his own image,*' proclaim Indian Vedas, ancient Indian books.[134] Such is the dignity that religion and natural law both bestow upon man. As we saw, even the catholic jurists of 16th century Spain asserted the natural rights of so-called 'heathen people' not to be maltreated and plundered.

Before the advent of Human Rights Law as a branch of International Law, the individual *qua* human being was not recognized as a subject of international law. In other words in the traditional international law obligations were not owed directly to individuals. What has changed the entire character of international law most strikingly is that to an extent, and in some respects, *the object has become the subject.* Though human beings are still not subjects at the same level as States which directly contribute to the formation of international law, yet the trials of individuals at the Nuremburg and Tokyo military tribunals resulted in judgments which gave birth to modern international criminal law. A careful analysis of these judgments at once indicates that the individuals are subjects of international law

[132] M Dixon, *Textbook on International Law*, 3rd edn, (London, Blackstone, 1996) p 313.

[133] B Stern, 'A Propos de la Competence Universelle' in E Yakpo and T Boumedra, (eds), *Liber Amicorum: Judge Mohammed Bedjaoui* (The Hague, Kluwer International Law, 1999).

[134] This Indian Vedas' dictum is correlated by a massive doctrine of the Greek Fathers of the Catholic Church, and also by Philo of Alexandria.

and not objects. The most often cited words from the Nuremberg Tribunal's judgment are: 'Crimes against international law are committed by men, not by abstract entities, and only by punishing individuals who commit such crimes can the provisions of international law be enforced'.[135] The 1948 Genocide Convention has imposed certain duties directly upon the individual human beings. The 1949 Geneva Convention on Prisoners of War has conferred certain rights upon prisoners of war. Human rights flowing from the adoption of the Universal Declaration of Human Rights in 1948 and its resulting two Human Rights Covenants adopted by the UN General Assembly in 1966 have given individuals a status as subjects in international law. Jurists are equally expressive of the new trend that the individual is no more an object of international law. Old editions of *Oppenheim's International Law* always mentioned the individual as the object of international law. Professor Merrills, at present President of the Yugoslavia Tribunal, during his Summer 2002 general course on international law at the Hague International Law Academy, pointed out however that from the 9th edition onwards the word 'objects' has disappeared altogether. Professor Higgins, now Judge at the ICJ, as noted earlier in this chapter, seeing international law as a process, and not just a body of rules, bids farewell to the traditional subject-object dichotomy and perceives human beings as partners in that process along with States.[136] It is true that the system in international law is not yet as far developed that individuals can bring cases before international courts as States can, yet developments are fast heading in that direction; for instance in the newly created International Criminal Court. At the regional level, Europe is even more advanced; even before the coming into existence of the ICC 800 million European citizens from some 44 States could take their grievances directly to the European Court of Human Rights, many of them complaining against their own governments. In the famous case of *Lawless v The Government of Ireland* both the European Commission on Human Rights and the European Court of Human Rights enquired into the violation of human rights alleged by an individual against his own government. Briefly speaking, the individual is no more an object but a 'participant' subject of the international legal system. McCorquodale has summarized the reality in the following words:

> Individuals may not yet be participating in the international legal system to the same extent as States. But the trend is clear: the role of the individual in this system is continuing to expand, often despite the wishes of States. If, Kofi Annan asserts, the ultimate foundation of the international legal system is 'We, the Peoples', then the role of each State is not to ensure and perpetuate its own power but to enable every individual to live a life of dignity and security and so to ensure human flourishing. The interests of individuals must count for more than the interests of States.[137]

Hence, it is in this meaning—though at present more in theory than practice; but

[135] Cited from: SK Kapoor, *International Law*, 7th edn, (Allahabad, India, Central Law Agency) 118.

[136] R Higgins, *Problems and Process: International Law and How We Use It* (Oxford, OUP, 1994) 50.

[137] R McCorquodale, 'The Individual and the International Legal System' in MD Evans, (ed), *International Law* (Oxford, OUP, 2003) 300, 322.

in practice too developing rather fast—that the individual has become a subject of international law. This 180 degree turnaround in judicial development may appear to have occurred all of a sudden with the signing of the Charter of the United Nations and its ancillary human rights instruments. However, careful analysis reveals that the germ of this change was present in the legal philosophy underlying international law. It simply took time for the seed to germinate and ripen. The transformation of individual from object to subject represents the struggle between the power-wielding ruler (the sovereign State) and the powerless who are ruled (individuals). It is as if humanity was at war with itself. What had shaken the international judicial conscience of humans in power was the inhuman treatment of certain humans (ruled) at the hands of certain other humans (rulers). But this inhuman treatment of human beings did not begin and end during WWII. It was perhaps the climax, the moment when humans repented and realized that humans everywhere are dignified beings. In the bond between ruler and ruled human dignity became the common link and the basis of treatment. As a result, the Charter of the United Nations, at once an internationally binding document, signed on 26 June 1945, pledged an international determination in its preamble 'to reaffirm faith . . . in the dignity and worth of the human person'.

What does the Charter mean by dignity? If we just analyze even the first paragraph of the preamble of the Charter, it refers to dignity as a sub-concept within the words 'faith in fundamental human rights'. This suggests that human rights are nothing without human dignity. In other words, human dignity is at the core of the concept of human rights. Then, after the words 'dignity and worth of the human person' follow the words 'in the equal rights of men and women and of nations large and small'. It signifies the fact that 'dignity of human person' has no meaning without its attribute of 'equal rights'. Of 'men and women' and of 'nations large and small'. What does it signify? It signifies the dignified equal treatment of all human beings at all levels, irrespective of their colour, race, religion, or any such considerations. Further, the preamble finds importance in the fact that faith in human rights and human dignity accompanied by equal rights is an empty affirmation without establishing the necessary conditions for 'justice and respect.' Justice and respect for what? Justice and respect 'for the obligations arising from treaties and other sources of international law'. What is the aim and purpose of establishing these conditions of justice and respect? The preamble gives us the answer: 'to promote social progress and better standards of life in larger freedom'. It all shows that 1) human dignity is at the core of human rights law, 2) human rights law is at the core of international law, and 3) human dignity being at the core of both consists of equality, justice and respect, social progress, better standards of life, larger freedom, etc.

Jurisprudence and legal theory in any given age are the reflection of the prevailing legal thought and culture of the given time. Jurisprudence is said to be the first of the social sciences to be born.[138] The word simply means the knowledge of law

[138] KG Wurzel, 'Methods of Juridical Thinking' in *Science of Legal Method* (Boston, 1917) 289.

and derives its meaning from two latin words, 'juris' (meaning law) and 'prudencia' (meaning knowledge). But, etymologically speaking, the term jurisprudence is not sufficient in itself, for 'prudentia' is not yet systematised. Any branch of knowledge in order to attain the title of a science needs to be systematised, for science is a systematic and formulated knowledge of a given field of life. Jurisprudence is a science as far as the systematic and formulated knowledge of a given school of law is concerned, for instance the analytical school of law. But, the analytical school of law is not the only approach to studying law. The natural law school existed before the former was born, and equally there are other schools of law—the historical school, the philosophical school, the sociological school, the realist school, etc—which approach the study of law in very different ways. All are trying to solve the mystery of the knowledge of law, and yet none of them seems to be providing the fundamental principle which may serve as the basis of all law and provide a core to all knowledge of law. This led Stone to remark: 'jurisprudence seems like a chaos of approaches to a chaos of topics chaotically delimited.'

The term law itself is a term which has been variously defined. One of the definitions suggests that the term is derived from its Teutonic root *lag*. The word *lag* means something which lies fixed or uniform; Judge Bedjaoui's 'unvarying factor in human dignity,' mentioned above, is no different, finding in human rights law this same characteristic of *lag*. Seen in this sense any rule of law must be based in essence on its related underlying fixed and uniform principle. To find those principles various approaches to the study of law have been adopted. Jurists have, reflecting the civilization and conditions of their respective age, propounded numerous approaches to the study of law. The systematic formulation of legal thought about the study of law is often termed a 'school of law.' Every school of law reflects the prevailing thought and conditions of its time. But, in no less measure every school also reflects the viewpoints of the legal thinker(s) associated with it. It all depends the way the given legal thinker understands and interprets the problems of the given time. Therefore, there can be more than one school of law developing and even prevailing at one given time. Two schools of law, analytical and historical, developed almost simultaneously. At present too, parallel to the firmly established analytical school, though often seen as declining, the sociological school has been developing. And, though the realist school of law, mainly associated with the US and Scandinavia, is seen by some as an independent school, it is also seen as a branch of the sociological school. There are still others who like to portray the realist school as an extension of the analytical school with the added role of the courts. However, it is mainly for the sake of clarity and convenience of classification that the viewpoints of legal thinkers are divided into different schools, with different titles. There are jurists who will not fit in strict division or school. Hart, with his 'minimum content of Natural Law,' Fuller with his concept of 'inner morality' of law, and Rawls with his 'justice based on fairness', are thinkers who cannot be classified as belonging to one school of law. Some of the schools are simply a synthesis of two or more approaches.

The post second world war history of legal thought, with its special emphasis on the thinking of human rights, based on the principle of human dignity, does seem to have given birth to a school of law which is not limited to the field of human rights alone but which also enters the thinking of all other jurisdictions and branches of law, national as well as international.

Some think of human rights law as an idea;[139] others think of it as a concept, or a doctrine, or a notion, or sometimes a combination of these. For a positivist thinker human rights law was born only with the 1948 United Nations Universal Declaration of Human Rights. For a philosophical or a historical thinker human rights are as old as human history. A natural law thinker may see no substantial difference between the 'right to life' provisions of positive law and the natural law directive, originating from Bible, of 'thy shall not kill'. The right to life is certainly a concept of human rights law, but it is not the only concept found in human rights law. Human rights law might be seen by a positivist as having its source in the relevant declarations, covenants and conventions, but this does not mean that a jurist from another school of thought may not see the working of this concept as a principle of law in another way. One may see the general and positive international law principle of *pacta sunt servanda* in a more moral, natural, and humanly dignified way—as the idea that one must keep one's promises (human beings must keep their promises to other fellow human beings because this is vital for conscientious reciprocity, which is seen as part of the 'inherent dignity' of man. The concept of the inherent dignity of man, like all the principles of human rights law, is not new. It is simply recognized now in a way which is stronger and clearer than before. It could be argued that a significant part of the bundle of concepts and principles which make up human rights law was already in existence as a part of numerous national and international law documents. Even in the strictest analytical sense of the positivistic school of law, the concepts such as right to life and liberty, right to equality, right to property, freedom of speech, freedom of conscience, etc, etc, were recognized long before 1948 in the legal systems of many civilized nations. What is new about these provisions of human rights law in a new language, and new form? It is in the concept of the inherent dignity of man which reflects in every human rights document. After the greatest human bloodshed in the Second World War, humans have simply started, particularly the rulers, to treat, and think of, their fellow human beings more humanely, more compassionately and more fraternally. With the birth of human rights law, a new thinking has dawned upon humanity in its relevant legal circles, legislative circles as well as judicial circles, judges and jurists' circles, as well as lawyers' circles. This new approach of legal thinking may befittingly perhaps be described as renaissance of legal thinking. This new humanistic thinking about law is by no means limited to the provisions and principles of human rights law alone. Actually, the circles of human rights rules and principles are touching upon and cutting across the circles of rules and principles of every other branch and field of law. Be it national or

[139] MJ Perry, *The Idea of Human Rights: Four Inquiries* (Oxford, OUP, 1998). The book is an excellent study of the idea of human rights as ineliminably religious.

international law; be it civil or criminal law; be it administrative or admiralty law; be it law of torts or trusts; there is no jurisdiction of law, whether it is personal, territorial or material, which is not touched upon by the thinking and principles underlying human rights law. In the very first judgment on merits in the *Corfu Channel* case delivered after the 1948 Universal Declaration of Human Rights, the Court found that the obligations incumbent upon the Albanian authorities consisted in notifying, for the benefit of shipping in general, the existence of a minefield in Albanian territorial waters and in warning the approaching British warships of the imminent danger to which the minefield exposed them; and, in this connection, the Court maintained that:

> such obligations are based, not on the Hague Convention, No VIII, which is applicable in time of war, but on certain general and well-recognized principles, namely: elementary considerations of humanity, even more exacting in peace than in war; the principal of the freedom of maritime communication; and every State's obligation not to allow knowingly its territory to be used for acts contrary to the rights of other States.[140]

It shows that even the remote principles of maritime law cannot remain untouched by the principles of human rights law, in the given case the principle of elementary considerations of humanity developed by the Court itself. In a recent instance, speaking about the application of the environmental protection as a principle of international law in the *Gabcikovo-Nagymaros Project* case, Judge Weeramantry emphasized the fact that the protection of the environment is a vital part of the contemporary human rights doctrine. He considered it as a *sine qua non* for several human rights such as the right to health and even the right to life itself. It is dawning upon the judicial conscience of mankind that damage to the environment anywhere can impair and undermine all the human rights spoken of in the Universal Declaration of Human rights and other human rights instruments.[141] Even this one example provides that how great the bearing of human rights law has on the law of environment. Not only this, in the advisory opinion concerning *Legality of the Threat or Use of Nuclear Weapons* the Court and its individual judges have gone to great lengths demonstrating first the bearing of nuclear weapons on the environment and then of both on all human rights and vice versa.[142] In brief, human rights law thinking has bearing upon every other jurisdiction and field of law. It is emerging as an approach, a new approach, of looking at law, its meaning, nature, scope and purpose, which may rightly be called as human-rights-approach.

A close study of the approaches adopted by various thinkers of human rights and the principles of human rights law embodied in numerous human rights instruments would reveal that not only there is a distinct approach to law of its own in all human rights thinking and instruments but that approach is at the same

[140] *Corfu Channel* case (*United Kingdom v Albania*), Judgment of Merits, ICJ Reports 1949, p 22.

[141] *Gabcikovo-Nagymaros Project* case, Judgment of 25 September 1997, Individual opinion of Judge Weeramantry, ICJ Reports 1997, pp 91–92.

[142] ICJ Reports 1996, p 226.

time a synthesis of several other approaches, called schools of law. Hence, human rights law is not simply a normative system of law, seen in its philosophical and ideological perspectives it is equally a school of law, which may be called Human Rights Law School. It is a school of law because it has a distinct approach to study law, the approach of the principle of human dignity at the basis, under the focus of inherent dignity of human being, the fundamental source of all human rights law, nay all law. It cannot be denied that all international law has its underlying human rights dimension; and, all human rights law has its underlying dimension of human dignity. If, then, the principle of State sovereignty is at the basis of international law, it is the principle of human dignity, the basis of human rights law, which would show the greatest impact on the norms and principles established under the doctrine of State sovereignty.

The law of Human Rights, as compared to the history and development of international law, and that too as from the positivistic theoretical point of way, is a very young branch of the international jurisprudence. The idea was conceived in the 1942 United Nations Declaration. Its seed was enthusiastically sown in the Charter of the United Nations. Its first sprouts were seen in the 1948 Universal Declaration of Human Rights and the 1948 Genocide Convention. Its flowering can now be seen in numerous covenants, conventions, declarations, etc. Of all these instruments the two covenants signed in 1966 and entered into force in 1976—the International Covenant on Civil and Political Rights and the International Covenant on Economic, Social and Cultural Rights—stand conspicuous.

Though a new field of law, human rights were at once international. They were conceived international. They were sown international. They sprouted international. They are growing international. Whatever existence they have known before the signing of the UN Charter and its 1948 Universal Declaration, it was either natural in characteristic, belonging to natural law school of thought, or national in positive law form, to be found in various State constitutions. With their strong and solid appearance on the international stage and their proper recognition in the positive international law, they have not only circumvented and brought within their universal fold all their pigmy forms in national constitutions and other documents but have shown a tendency first to make inroads to, and weaving into, all other branches of national and international law and then to give their own colour to all law, international as well as national, by characterising with their essence, namely the inherent dignity of human beings.

The essence and core of the concept of human rights directly reflect in the above mentioned words in the preamble of the UN Charter. And no less in the opening paragraph of the Preamble of 1948 Universal Declaration of Human Rights, which reads: 'Whereas recognition of the inherent dignity and of the equal and inalienable rights of all members of the human family is the foundation of freedom, justice and peace in the world'.

Judge Nagendra Singh's words 'respect for human personality and its absolute worth' match the words 'inherent dignity and of the equal and alienable rights'. Basing his conception on such an essence of human being, Judge Singh continues and sees the need that: 'These rights are essential for the adequate development of the human personality and for human happiness and progress'.[143] Therefore, we may settle with Judge Singh when he comes to define human rights as: '*Human rights may therefore be said to be those fundamental rights to which every man or woman inhabiting any part of the world should be deemed entitled merely by virtue of having been born a human being.*'[144]

If at the basis of traditional international law was its doctrine of State sovereignty, the emerging new unifying force of legal principles of contemporary international law is the concept of human dignity. If law is the command of sovereign in the language of analytical school, then law is the obligation of the sovereign in the human rights school. In a nutshell the derivation of human rights law from the concept of human dignity provides the basis for the scholastic thought of human rights school which is fast at work in influencing the other schools of legal thought in international law, and therewith also the development of all other branches of international law. The concept of *sovereignty*, no matter what we understand intellectually by this term, the human rights school of law has permanently stamped the jurisprudence, international as well as national, with the idea that sovereignty permeates all human beings. No one human is more, or less, sovereign than any other, this is what we may mean by the term human dignity. Just as human rights law is borne of international law, similarly human dignity is borne of State sovereignty. But the principle of State sovereignty has no place in the human rights law, one branch of international law. Does then the principle of human dignity, at the very basis of judicial ideology of human rights law, have any place in the rest of international law? It is a doctrinal question of relation between the basis of human rights and the basis of international law. The relation of human rights to international law depends not upon what law is treated but how law is treated. State sovereignty is not complete without the individual human sovereignty, as described by Judge Hersch Lauterpacht. Former is the modification of the latter. The latter is the continuation of the former. Under the new ideological trends set by the human rights school the entire body of international law must conform to the human rights law which stands for the human dignity in all its civil, political, economic, and cultural aspects, nationally, regionally as well as internationally. The principle of human dignity seems to be possessing and unleashing such a tremendous legal force that no rules of international law, even under the authority of State sovereignty, will be considered having any validity if they purport to contradict with the principles of human rights. It may sound a premature statement, but the beginning of the development of international law in that direction has already been made. An outstanding example, among many others, in this regard is the development of a founding principle of '*elementary considerations of humanity*' by the International Court of Justice in its very first contentious case

[143] N Singh, *Enforcement of Human Rights in Peace and War and the Future of Humanity* (Dordrecht, Nijhoff, 1986).

[144] *Ibid.*

concerning *Corfu Channel*.[145] It is as if a new school of law resting on the principle of human dignity, a synthesis of State sovereignty and individual human sovereignty, and a synthesis of positive law school and natural law school, is born.

Hence, in brief, an indissoluble ideological link between human rights and international law may be described as follows: Human rights as an ideology of law, with the concept of human dignity at its core, is the legislative spirit of the body of international law. And, the international law, with human rights ideology at its core, is the manifestation of that legislative spirit.

If, during the process of application and interpretation of law, the principle of State sovereignty remains commensurate to its own created ideology of principle of human dignity, hence its own self-refined legislative spirit in the form of human rights ideology, the working of the system and its process may be seen as 'progression' of human rights and human dignity (Judge Bedjaoui's expression) or a 'step forward' towards the development of human rights law (Judge Lach's expression), and if human dignity as against State sovereignty recedes, it may well be seen as 'regression' (again Judge Bedjaoui's expression) of the process of human rights and human dignity, or a 'step backward' (again the expression of Judge Lachs) in the development of human rights law.

The principle of human dignity at the basis of human rights law—and the entire body of principles of human rights law being an integral part of the contemporary international law—is merely a theoretical principle, without any practical meaning, unless it expresses itself in and through judicial processes at the hands of judges. And, how the judges of the International Court of Justice have given expression to this principle and to the ideology of human rights while applying and interpreting the main body of international law, still profoundly based on the doctrine of State sovereignty, would be seen in Part II and Part III of this book.

[145] *Corfu Channel* case, ICJ Reports 1949, p 22.

Part II

The Development of Human Rights Law by the International Court of Justice: Contentious Cases

No account of the international aspect of human rights would be complete without a mention of the views of the International Court of Justice which have been progressive, developmental and helpful to the cause of human rights.[1]

[1] N Singh, *Enforcement of Human Rights in Peace and War and the Future of Humanity* (Dordrecht, Nijhoff, 1986) 27.

Introduction to the Contentious Procedure of the Court

> Vous allez, Messieurs, donner la vie au pouvoir judiciaire de l'huminité. Les philosophes et les historiens nous ont dit les lois de la grandeur et de la decadence des Empires; nous attendons de vous, Messieurs, les lois qui assurent la perpétuité du seul empire qui ne peut connaitre de décadence; l'empire de la Justice, expression de l'éternelle Vérité.[2] (the English translation of this is cited in chapter 2).

This is what Léon Bourgeois—delegated by the Council of the League of Nations to open the meetings of the Committee of Jurists on 16 June 1920, charged with the duty of preparing the Statute of the Permanent Court of International Justice, the predecessor of the International Court of Justice—communicated verbally to the drafters of the PCIJ Statute. The same Statute almost ditto, with minor modifications, was adopted again in 1946 for the ICJ. The words are reflective of the hopes and expectations of the international community and its peoples from the judges, and *ad hoc* judges, engaged in the discharging of their judicial functions. Nothing less than an *'empire of justice'* is expected; and that too which is *perpetual* and which is based on the *'l'éternelle Vérité'* with capital letters V. Actually, the English translation of this as 'eternal truth' should be more accurate and reflective of the original sense if the word truth was also translated with capital T as Truth. For the meaning of 'truth' means which never changes, which is pure in its pristine glory of justice; hence, Léon Bourgeois' using the word *'Verité'* with capital emphatically expects from judges to deliver to mankind an empire of justice, by clarifying and developing the based on the Truth, the Justice, the essence of humanity, hence the essence of human rights and human dignity of man against man.

The question arises: is it possible to live up to such high expectations of the international community when its leaders have not even equipped the Court with jurisdiction not depending upon the traditional principle of consent of the parties? Yet, where there is will, there is way. There are certain aspects of the Court's procedure that make it possible. Those are mainly two aspects: first, the *obiter dicta* part of the Court's decisions, and the second, the system of appending individual opinion of judges to those decisions. As described by Judge Lachs that 'Judgment is a process of mind',[3] in order to appreciate these two aspects it is important to have a cursory glance on the intermediate stages of the Court's contentious procedure leading to these aspects.

[2] Procès-Verbaux of the Proceedings of the Committee: 16 June–24 July 1920, p 11 (a publication of the Permanent Court of International Justice).

[3] M Lachs, 'Some Reflections on the Contribution of the International Court of Justice to the Development of International Law' (1983) 10(2) *Syracuse Journal of International Law and Commerce* Nr 1, 239.

The Court's Statute provides that the Court has a double duty to discharge: a) to settle in accordance with international law the legal disputes submitted by States,[4] and b) to give advisory opinions on legal questions referred to it by duly authorized international organs and agencies.

The Court is composed of 15 Judges representing the main forms of civilization and the principal legal systems of the world.[5]

The most fundamental principle governing the settlement of contentious cases is that the jurisdiction of the Court depends in the last resort on the consent of the States parties to the dispute.[6] When there is no judge on the Bench of the Court, or a Chamber of the Court dealing with a case, possessing the nationality of a State party to a case, that State may appoint a person to sit as a judge *ad hoc* for the purpose of the case.[7]

Only States may be parties in cases before the Court.[8] The jurisdiction of the Court comprises all cases which the parties refer to it.[9] The proceedings may be instituted by means of a unilateral Application[10] or by notification of a Special Agreement[11] by both the Parties.

The procedure followed by the Court in contentious cases is governed mainly by three instruments of the Court, a) the Statute, an integral part of the UN Charter, b) the Rules of Court adopted on 14 April 1978,[12] and the Resolution Concerning the Internal Judicial Practice of the Court adopted on 12 April 1976.[13]

The proceedings are divided into two phases, ie, written proceedings and oral proceedings. The written proceedings comprise the filing of pleading within time-limit fixed in orders made by the Court or, if the Court is not sitting, the President. The pleadings are in principle confined to a Memorial and a Counter-Memorial, though the Court may, if necessary, authorize or direct that there be a Reply and a Rejoinder.[14]

However, the questions incidental to the main proceedings are not uncommon. Or, rather they are very common feature of contentious cases. On the average in two-third contentious cases brought before the Court, the incidental proceed-

[4] Article 38, para 1, of the Court's Statute.

[5] Article 3 and Article 9 of the Court's Statute.

[6] Court's jurisdiction in this respect is defined in Article 93 of the UN Charter and in Articles 34–37 of its own Statute.

[7] Article 31 of the Court's Statute; Articles 7–8; Article 17, para 2; Articles 35–37; Article 91, para 2; and Article 102, para 3 of the Rules of Court.

[8] Article 34, para 1, the Statute of the ICJ.

[9] Article 36, para 1, the Statute of the ICJ.

[10] Article 40, para 1, the Statute of the ICJ; Article 38 of the Rules of Court.

[11] Article 40, para 1, the Statute of the ICJ; Article 39 of the Rules of Court.

[12] The Rules of Court approved on 14 April 1978 came into force on 1 July 1978. These Rules replaced the Rules adopted by the Court on 6 May 1946 and amended on 10 May 1972.

[13] Prior to 1968, the internal judicial practice of the Court was governed by the Resolution of the Permanent Court of International Justice of 20 February 1931 (as amended on 17 March 1936), by virtue of a decision of the International Court of Justice of 1946 to adopt provisionally the practice of the Permanent Court.

[14] Article 43 of the Court's Statute; Articles 44–46 and 48 of the Rules of Court.

ings—dealing mainly with preliminary objections, provisional measures, interventions, counter-claims, etc—were filed.

Not unlike in municipal courts the contentious procedure of the Court provides the Parties with the right to raise preliminary objections or preliminary questions in order to prevent the Court from delivering judgment on the merits of the case.[15] However, Article 36, paragraph 6, of the Court's Statutes provides that in the event of a dispute as to whether the Court has jurisdiction, the matter shall be settled by the decision of the Court. The procedures prescribed in Article 79[16] of the Rules speak: a) the preliminary objections must be filed as soon as possible, and not later than three months after the delivery of the Memorial; b) the filing of these objections will suspend the proceedings on the merits and may be answered by the observations and submissions of the opposing party, to be filed within the time-limit fixed by an order; c) oral proceedings on the objections ensue, the party which raised them is called upon to speak first; d) the Court gives its decision in the form of a judgment; e) if the Court rejects the objections, the proceedings on the merits are resumed from the point of interruption; they are likewise resumed if the Court declares that the objections do not possess an exclusively preliminary character.

Of all the incidental proceedings, though traditionally the most common case has always been that of the preliminary objections raised by the respondent States, the cases filed during the 1990s, and recently, reveal that there is a growing trend that the applicant States bringing the cases are increasing in number to bring frequently, and often together with their applications, the requests for provisional measures (also known as interim measures). The Court has the power to indicate,[17] if it considers that circumstances so require, any provisional measures which ought to be taken *to preserve the respective rights* of either party.[18] It may also decline to indicate the measures requested.[19] A written request for indication of provisional measures may be made by a party at any time during the course of the proceedings in the case in connection with which the request is made. A request for such measures is treated as a matter of urgency.[20] The decision of the Court is announced in an Order of the Court.

The contentious procedure of the Court provides that a third State may request the permission to intervene if it considers that it has an *interest of a legal nature* which may be affected by the decision in the case. It is, however, for the Court to decide upon such a request.[21] The same procedure also provides that if the dispute

[15] Article 79, 1978 Rules of the Court.

[16] As amended on 5 December 2000 and coming into force on 1 February 2001, see Report of the International Court of Justice 1 August 2000–31 July 2001 (General Assembly Official Records 56th Session Supplement No 4 (A/56/4).

[17] As for instance was done in the Application of the Convention on the Prevention and Punishment of the Crime of Genocide case (*Bosnia and Herzegovina v Serbia and Montenegro*), discussed in ch 10 of this book.

[18] Article 41, The Statute of the ICJ.

[19] As for instance in *Legality of Use of Force* cases, discussed in ch 11 of this paper.

[20] Articles 73–78, 1978 Rules of the Court.

[21] See Article 62 of the Statute and Articles 81, 83–85 of the Rules.

relates to the construction of a convention to which States other than those concerned in the case are parties, these States are notified forthwith and have the right to intervene in the proceedings.[22]

Counter-Claims may be filed if they are directly *connected with the subject-matter* of the claim of the other party and come within the jurisdiction of the Court. They are to be made by a party in its Counter-Memorial, as part of the submission in that pleading. In case of any doubt, it is for the Court to decide whether the counter-claim is admissible and shall form part of the proceedings.[23]

Articles 44 and 48 of the Statute are the pillar provisions concerning the conduct of Court's proceedings and making arrangements connected with taking of evidence. In implementation thereof, Articles 31 and 66 contemplate the arrangements of inspection *in loco* or visit *in situ*.

The first time ever request for an inspection *in loco* came from the Respondent (South Africa) in the joint cases of *South West Africa*. The request was made during the oral proceedings and was made subject to certain conditions that 'the Court should visit the Republic of South Africa, and the further proposal then made that the Court should also visit the Applicant States and as well one or two sub-Saharan African countries of the Court's own choosing.' All these proposals were opposed by the Applicants. Having heard the contentions of the Parties, the Court made an Order on 29 November 1965 in which it decided not to accede to the request of the Respondent.[24]

The second such a request was made to an *ad hoc* chamber of the Court in the case concerning *Land, Island and Maritime Frontier Dispute* when, at the hearings of 27 May 1991 and 14 June 1991, El Salvador requested the Chamber to consider exercising its functions pursuant to Article 66 of the Rules of Court with regard to the obtaining of evidence *in situ* in the disputed areas of the land frontier. After deliberation, the Chamber decided that it did not consider it necessary to do so.[25]

The third request for visit *in situ* came in a recent case concerning the *Gabcikovo-Nagymaros Project*. It differed from the previous two cases in the sense that the Agents of both the Parties jointly requested the Court in a letter of 3 February 1997 which contained detailed proposals for the conduct of the visit *in situ*. The Court made an Order on 5 February 1997 in which it accepted these proposals and decided to exercise its functions with regard to obtaining of evidence by visiting a place or locality to which the case related.[26] The Court made this visit from 1 to 4 April 1997; it visited a number of locations along the Danube river and took note of the technical explanations given by the representatives who had been

[22] Statute, Article 63; Rules, Articles 43, 82–84 and 86.

[23] Article 80 of the Rules of Court. As amended on 5 December 2000 and coming into force on 1 February 2001, see Report of the International Court of Justice 1 August 2000–31 July 2001 (General Assembly Official Records 56th Session Supplement No 4 (A/56/4).

[24] *South West Africa* cases, Order of 29 November 1965, ICJ Reports 1965, pp 9–10.

[25] Land, Island and Maritime Frontier Dispute, Judgment of 11 September 1992, ICJ Reports 1992, pp 361–62.

[26] *Gabcikovo-Nagymaros Project*, Order of 5 February 1997, ICJ Reports 1997, pp 4–5.

designated for the purpose by the Parties.[27] This was the first historic visit, setting precedence with regard to obtaining of evidence in accordance with Article 66 of the 1978 Rules of the Court under the umbrella of Article 48 of the Court's Statute.[28]

Upon the closure of the written proceedings, the case is usually ready for oral proceedings. The time-table for the hearings is fixed by the Court, or, if it is not sitting, by the President.[29] Sittings of these hearings are public. At these sittings the judges, and the judges *ad hoc* if any, hear the arguments of counsel and such evidence of witnesses or experts as the parties may call. The Court itself may also arrange for a witness to be heard, entrust any individual, body or organization with the task of giving an expert opinion or decide on and inspection *in loco*.[30]

After the oral proceedings the Court deliberates *in camera* and prepares its judgment to be delivered in public. Judgments in contentious cases are of binding force between the parties.[31]

Reasoning Part of the Judgment

The *handbook*[32] of the Court describes that there are three main parts[33] of the Court's judgment.

[27] *Gabcikovo-Nagymaros Project*, Judgment of 25 September 1997, pp 14 and 191.

[28] For an authoritative and detailed account of this visit see P Tomka and SS Wordsworth, 'The First Site Visit of the International Court of Justice in Fulfillment of Its Judicial Functions' (1998) 92 *AJIL* 133. Dr Tomka was Slovakia's Agent in the case and Mr Wordsworth was Slovakia's Counsel and Advocate. For a brief commentary focused on an analysis of the purpose of this historic visit see F Meadows, 'The First Site Visit by the International Court of Justice' (1998) 11 *Leiden Journal of International Law* 603–8. Ms Meadows was present at the site as a member of the Registry of the ICJ.

[29] Article 54 of the Rules of Court.

[30] Articles 43–46 of the Court's Statute; Articles 48–51 of the Rules of Court.

[31] Article 59 of the Court's Statute.

[32] *The International Court of Justice: 1946–96*, 4th edn, (The Hague, ICJ, 1996) 68–69 (this publication is also known as *Handbook*; its 5th edn is soon to appear).

[33] There are no hard and fast rules or terminology to describe this dividing of a judgment into various parts. Taking into consideration the main statutory regulations concerning a judgment George Schwarzenbergen finds:

> In the Statutes of the two International Courts, five points relating to Judgments are expressly settled: (1) *Reasons*. Judgments are to state the reasons on which they are based. (2) *Names of Judges*. The names of the Judges 'who have taken part in the decision' are to be stated. (3) *Individual Opinions*. If in whole or in part, judgments do not represent the unanimous opinion of judges, any judge may append an Individual Opinion. (4) *Signature*. Judgments are to be signed by the President and the Registrar. (5) *Reading in Open Court*. With due notice to the Agents, *judgments are to be read in open court*.

G Schwarzenbergen, *International Law: As Applied by International Courts and Tribunals* (London, Stevens & Sons, 1986) 674–75.

Another good description of these parts is given by Prof Rosenne in the following words:

A judgment of the International Court . . . contains the following separate components, the total comprising a unity. It commences with a title and a head-note, this latter, as in an English law report, indicating the main issues discussed in the judgment. That is followed by the formal history of the proceedings (the *qualités*), including the submissions of the parties. Frequently overlooked, this is an essential element, since it places what follows in context. After this introductory statement come the

First: an introduction: this part gives the names of judges, judges *ad hoc*, and the representatives of the parties; and further, it summarizes the proceedings without any comment, and gives submissions of the parties.

The second: the grounds for the Court's decision, where those matters of fact and law that have led the Court to its decision are set forth in detail and the arguments of the parties are given careful and balanced consideration. As a decision of the Court must give the reasons on which it is based, in this part the Court thoroughly reasons and gives grounds for its decision. This part includes dual activity of the Court: a) the Court sets forth in details those matters of fact and law that have led the Court to its decision, and b) gives careful and balanced consideration to the arguments of the parties as made in their written and oral proceedings. This is the lengthiest part of the decision which for convenience sake may be called as reasoning part of the Judgment.

The third part is very brief, a paragraph or two or so. It is called *dispositif* or operative part of the decision. In this part, based on the reasons described in its reasoning part, the Court gives its actual decision on the submissions made by the parties.

The individual declarations and opinions follow the operative part of the judgment.

Individual Opinions

Judges who find themselves unable to concur in the decision, or part of the decision, or vote in favour of the decision but their concurrence is not based on the reasoning of the Court, or part of the reasoning of the Court, may append to the decision a separate statement of their individual opinions under one of the three titles: 1) Declaration: a brief indication of concurrence or dissent, 2) Separate Opinion: a statement of a judge who votes in favour or partly in favour of the operative provision(s) but disagrees with whole or part of the reasoning or likes to add more or different reasons and reasoning, and 3) Dissenting Opinion: a statement of a judge who votes either against the *dispositif* or the major part thereof; it includes judge's reasons for disagreement and often also describes the way he/she would have wished the Court to reason and decide on the issues involved. These statements can be individual as well as joint. Judges decide themselves what title they should give to their statements. These individual opinions, irrespective of their titles, contribute immensely to the clarification and development of international law.

narrative of the facts and the legal reasoning. The judgment ends with its operative clause (*dispositif*) preceded by some such wording as 'For these reasons, the Court decides etc', and the signatures. That is the decision itself linked to but distinguished from the reasons. The individual declarations and opinions follow, concurring opinions first in order of the seniority of the judges.

See S Rosenne, *The Law and Practice of the International Court of Justice 1920–1996*, 3rd edn, (The Hague, Martinus Nijhoff, 1997) vol III: Procedure, p 1585.

About the purpose of dissenting opinions a former Chief Justice of the Supreme Court of the United States, who was also a member of the Permanent Court of International Justice, had this to say: 'A dissent in a Court of last resort is an appeal to the brooding spirit of the law, to the intelligence of a future day, when a later decision may possibly correct the error into which the dissenting judge believes the court to have been betrayed'.[34] Similarly about the purpose of separate opinions as compared with dissenting opinions an eminent international legal scholar, and also a former member of the International Court of Justice, Sir Hersch Lauterpacht, had this to say: 'Similar considerations apply to concurring or separate Opinions, which amplify the Judgment or Opinion of the Court, which dissent from some of its reasoning, or which choose a different path for arriving at the same conclusion.'[35] He continues: 'From this point of view it may be difficult to name a case in which an individual Opinion has not been of some interest and which, at least indirectly, has not assisted towards a better understanding of the decision of the Court.'[36]

These views represent liberal and broadminded thinking, an ingredient most required for the development of law. Law cannot be shut in narrow watertight compartments of one particular reasoning of one particular group of people, be it a majority or minority. The justice based on eternal truth, *l'éternelle Vérité*, has its own infinite strength of legal and moral authority to withstand the challenge of any counter reasoning, or reasonings. If the reasoning of any majority decision does not have the capacity to stand firm in the face of its rival reasonings then doubtlessly it is an appeal to the brooding spirit of the law, to the intelligence of a future day, when a later decision may possibly correct the error into which the individual judge(s) believe(s) the court to have been betrayed,[37] since every decision of a court is a process of mind which is either a step forward or a step backward in the development of law,[38] and since basic principles of law are uniform and human nature in its essence is constant.[39]

However, it might well be observed here that though for some commentators the meaning of a dissenting opinion are clear but they find that the separate opinions tend to weaken the authority of the judgment and they question the

[34] CE Hughes, *The Supreme Court of the United States* (1928) 68.

[35] Sir H Lauterpacht, *The Development of International Law by the International Court of Justice* (London, Stevens & Sons, 1958) 69.

[36] *Ibid.*

[37] For instance it can safely be said that the majority decision made possible by a casting vote of the Court's President in the 1966 Judgment in the *South West Africa* cases (see ICJ Reports 1966, p 57) dealing with *apartheid* and discrimination against black people was a betrayal of the Court. And, the appeal of the judges in their individual opinions appended to those cases was an appeal to the brooding spirit of the law, to the intelligence of a future day, the day when on 21 June 1971 the Court corrected the error in its Advisory Opinion in the case concerning *Legal Consequences for States of the Continued Presence of Southn Africa in Namibia (South West Africa) Notwithstanding Security Council Resolution 276* (see ICJ Reports 1971, p 16).

[38] M Lachs, 'Some Reflections on the Contribution of the International Court of Justice to the Development of International Law' (1983) 10(2) *Syracuse Journal of International Law and Commerce* Nr 1, 239.

[39] DP O'Connell, *International Law*, 2nd edn, (London, Stevens & Sons, 1970) vol 1, p 1.

usefulness of them. Judge Bedjaoui for instance, when he was President of the ICJ, expressed concern about their excessive length. Speaking at the ICJ/UNITAR Colloquium to Celebrate 50th Anniversary of the Court spoke: 'One of the most worrying questions now is the proliferation of declarations and other separate or dissenting opinions undeniably weaken the decision given.'[40] Judge Guillaume, also a former President of the ICJ, speaking on the general length of the Court's judgments mentioned: 'A legal argument is more easily accepted within a court, and more convincing outside, when it is short and limited to what is necessary to justify the solution'.[41] Long or short, concerning the collective effect of these individual opinions, Judge Jennings, another former President of the Court, has the following to say:

> The separate or dissenting opinions are not ... independent; they are to be read with the Court's judgment; which is therefore truly the Court's judgment and not merely a majority judgment. That this collegiate responsibility involving every Member of the Court is clearly an important enhancement of the judgment's authority is obvious. It also has implications for separate opinions and even for those separate opinions that may be described as dissents.[42]

Encouraged by the ban on dissenting and separate opinions in the European Court of Justice, Bridge is of the opinion that the International Court of Justice should do the same.[43]

In order to appreciate these seemingly conflicting views it is important to glance briefly at the development of the institution of individual opinions.

1899 Convention for the Pacific Settlement of International Disputes granted judges the right to record their dissent, but not to explain their reasons. This right was withdrawn in by the 1907 Convention.[44]

Conservative thinkers are always reluctant and resistant to change, particularly when it comes to bestow equal and more rights to others. Liberals on the other hand always stand for more freedom and equality. When it came to discuss the question of granting right to national and *ad hoc* judges to sit on the Bench of the Court, there was a tough and strong opposition from conservative members, very much under the influence of 1899 and 1907 thinking, of the 1920 Committee of

[40] M Bedjaoui, 'Presentation by HE Judge Mohammed Bedjaoui' in C Peck and RS Lee, (eds), *Increasing the Effectiveness of the International Court of Justice: Proceedings of the ICJ/UNITAR Colloquium to Celebrate the 50th Anniversary of the Court* (The Hague, Martinus Nijhoff, 1997) 26.

[41] G Gullaume, 'The Future of International Judicial Institutions' (1995) *International Comparative Law Quarterly* 854, cited in C Peck and RS Lee, (eds), *Increasing the Effectiveness of the International Court of Justice: Proceedings of the ICJ/UNITAR Colloquium to Celebrate the 50th Anniversary of the Court* (The Hague, Martinus Nijhoff, 1997) 26.

[42] Sir Robert Jennings, 'The Collegiate Responsibility and Authority of the International Court of Justice' in Y Dinstein and M Tabory, (eds), *International Law at a Time of Perplexity: Essays in Honour of Shabtai Rosenne* (Dordrecht, Matinus Nijhoff) 346.

[43] JW Bridge, 'The Court of Justice of the European Communities and the Prospects for International Adjudication' in MW Janis, *International Courts for the Twenty-First Century* (1992) 97–98.

[44] Procès-Verbaux of the Proceedings of the Committee: 16 June–24 July 1920, p 742 (a publication of the Permanent Court of International Justice).

Jurists which was given the responsibility of drafting the Statute for the Permanent Court of International Justice. The strongest opposition came from the Dutch jurist Loder who believed that by so doing the Court would retain a characteristic of '*essentially belonging to arbitration*'.[45] This not only was undermining the provision of representation of different forms of civilization and legal systems but equally disturbing the working of the principle of equal treatment of judges. When the problem of dissent and the question of granting national and *ad hoc* judges the right to publish their reasoned dissents was discussed the strongest opposition came from the French representative de Lapradelle who stated: 'this was an extremely delicate point, because a national judge would always record his disapproval of a sentence unfavourable to his country.'[46] This again was doubting the conscience of national and *ad hoc* judges and treating them unequally. There are numerous examples that judges have decided against their own native country. The attention to this liberal and conscientious view was drawn by Lord Phillimore of Great Britain. He mentioned this as an example that Sir Robert Webster, arbitrator of Great Britain, who in the *Alaska Boundary Arbitration* case pronounced against his own country.[47] Actually, it is not the question of titular, national or *ad hoc* judge, when it comes to element of conscience involved in the solemn declaration, same for all judges, required to be made, to doubt about the integrity and impartiality of any judge on the basis of their origin and mode of appointment is to treat him not equally. Judge Bastid, an *ad hoc* judge, appointed by Tunisia in the case *Application for Revision and Interpretation of the Judgment of 24 February in the Case concerning the Continental Shelf (Tunisis/Libya)*, did vote against the position of Tunisia,[48] setting an example of conscientiousness, integrity and impartiality among judges *ad hoc*.

Article 56[49] of the Draft Statute for the Permanent Court of International Justice as proposed by the 1920 Committee of Jurists was rather narrow and conservative in its meaning and scope. The provision contained two sentences.

[45] *Ibid*, p 531.

[46] Minutes of the 1920 Committee of Jurists, p 531.

[47] *bid*, p 533.

[48] See Judgment of 10 December 1985 in the case Application for Revision and Interpretation of the Judgment of 24 February in the Case concerning the Continental Shelf (Tunisis/Libya), ICJ Reports 1985, pp 192, 229–31 and 247. Among the titular judges voting against the position of their own country the classic examples are: 1) the then President of the Court, Sir Arnold McNair in the Anglo-Iranian Oil Co case (Jurisdiction), ICJ Reports 1952, pp 115–16; 2) Judge Winiarski in the South West Africa cases (Second Phase), ICJ Reports 1966, pp 51 and 58, Judge Schwebel in a) the case concerning Delimitation of the Maritime Boundary in the Gulf of Maine Area, ICJ Reports 1984, pp 345 and 353; b) the case concerning Applicability of the Application to Arbitrate under Section 21 of the United Nations Headquarters Agreement of 26 June 1947, ICJ Reports 1988, pp 35 and 42; and c) the case concerning the *Military and Paramilitary Activities in and Against Nicaragua (Nicaragua v USA)*, ICJ Reports 1984, pp 442 and 558 and ICJ Reports 1986, pp 146–49 and 259. For a good brief account of all these examples see 'Commentary by Professor Krzystof Skubiszewski' in C Peck and RS Lee, (eds), *Increasing the Effectiveness of the International Court of Justice: Proceedings of the ICJ/UNITAR Colloquium to Celebrate the 50th Anniversary of the Court* (The Hague, Martinus Nijhoff, 1997) 379.

[49] Minutes of the 1920 Committee of Jurists, p 743.

First: 'If the judgment given does not represent, wholly or in part, the unanimous opinion of the judges, the dissenting judges shall be entitled to have the fact of their dissent or reservation mentioned in it'.

And the second: 'But the reasons in it for their dissent or reservations shall not be expressed in the judgment'.

Hence, it is obvious that the Committee was not only against the idea that reasons for dissent might be stated but at the time of drafting the Statute of the Permanent Court of International Justice in 1920 except for the system of dissenting opinion there was no mention of separate opinions or declarations to be appended to the Court's decisions.

Knowing well the value of *'recording the reasons'* in favour or against a judgment, expected to contribute to delivering an 'empire of justice' based on *'l'éternelle Vérité'* in relation to the development of international law, it was again the most benevolent liberal and truly international legal thinker, Léon Bourgeois, the representative of France and rapporteur of the draft of the PCIJ Statute at the Council of League of Nations, who was favourably inclined towards the Swedish proposal, respecting the dignity of other legal thoughts and systems, and opposed the draft scheme of the Hague, mainly Euro-continental-centric. About the Swedish proposal he maintained:

> The observation presented had, however, a much wider bearing: the question of giving to the various legal systems represented by the various States the possibility of collaboration with the Court in *the development of international law.* It must first of all be noted that the Court will contain representatives of the different judicial systems into which the world is divided and the judgment of the Court will therefore be the result of the co-operation of entirely different thoughts and systems. (italics are mine)[50]

'Need we go further?', he paused a while and answered himself: 'The draft scheme of the Hague gives dissenting judges the right to state their opposition or their reservation without recording their reasons. If these judges were permitted to state their opinions together with their reasons, the play of the *different judicial lines of thought* would appear clearly.'[51] This was universal judicial liberalism respecting judicial dignity of all judicial ideologies springing from various legal systems of the world, particularly maintaining the principle that even a lone voice, or some lone voices, of dissent may not be silenced by the majority lest the quest for *'l'éternelle Vérité'* be bereft of any hidden truth the dissent judge(s) may be holding in his judicial treasure of thoughts. The Council approved a provision that 'if the judgment does not express wholly or partially the unanimous opinion of the judges,

[50] Documents concerning the action taken by the Council of the League of Nations under Article 14 of the Covenant and the adoption by the Assembly of the Statute of the Permanent Court (Geneva: League of Nations Publications, 1921) 30.

[51] Documents concerning the action taken by the Council of the League of Nations under Article 14 of the Covenant and the adoption by the Assembly of the Statute of the Permanent Court (Geneva: League of Nations Publications, 1921, p 30.

those dissenting have the right to add to it a statement of their individual opinion'.[52]

The path was still beset with conservatism. In the sub-committee of the Third Committee of the First Assembly, the Dutch representative, seemingly a tough conservative with civil law tradition, Mr Loder, found this liberal idea *'foreign to Continental procedure'* and in his opinion it posed *'danger to the authority of the Court'*, mainly because of national judges.[53] The damage conservative thinking does to the cause of international law and international justice is that it puts on blinkers as against other legal systems and cultures. Universality and pluralization are the main ingredients of international legal thought, interaction and communication. Be it procedural or substantive. Hence, from the melting pot of various legal cultures there must spring-forth an essence of judicial truth which is the same in every system and thought. If continental system is the product of Christian thinking and culture, and there emerged out of that obviously a civilization of law and order worthy of credit, there must be, and obviously are, other legal systems, equally, or perhaps sometimes more or less in degree, the product of other religious thinking and cultures, with their own civilizations of law and order worthy of taking notice of, if we are genuinely engaged in an internal enterprise in quest of an international 'empire of justice' based on genuine international law worthy of its name.

Another little hurdle came from the Italian Council for Diplomatic Litigation which proposed the suppression of the provision. The sub-committee, however, decided to retain the article.[54]

This is how the following language of Article 57 of the PCIJ Statute came into being: 'If the judgment does not represent in whole or in part the unanimous opinion of the judges, *dissenting judges are entitled* to deliver a separate opinion'.[55] (italics are added).

To this Judge Hudson commented: 'The Statute does not seem to envisage concurring opinions, though Article 57 refers to dissents from whole or a part of the judgment.'[56] However, the provision was interpreted very liberally and its working in practice reflected in Articles 62 and 71. The Court confirmed the established practice in its Third Annual Report:

> The practice has been to allow dissenting judges to confine themselves, if they so desire, to a record of the fact of their dissent or partial dissent, appended to the judgment or advisory opinion, the Court having decided that this course is in accordance with the terms of the Statute. This practice is now confirmed in the Rules.

[52] Documents, p 44; Minutes of the Council, 10th session, p 161.

[53] Documents, p 136; Records of First Assembly, Committees, I, p 371.

[54] Documents, pp 138, 213; Records of First Assembly, Committees, I, pp 374–75 and 536.

[55] Series D, No 1, Acts and Documents Concerning the Organization of the Court, Statute and Rules of Court, 4th edn, April 1940, p 26.

[56] MO Hudson, *The Permanent Court of International Justice: 1920–42*, 1943 edn, p 589.

And, the Court continued in its further paragraph: 'Judges concurring in the judgment but not with the whole of the reasoning have been permitted to append *observation* to the judgment'.[57] (italics added). The observation was considered another title for an individual opinion, which in future practice became further established as titles of separate opinion[58] and declaration.

In the earlier years of the practice of the PCIJ, dissenting opinions of judges were sometimes attached to the minutes of the private meeting at which the final vote was taken, no public record of the dissent being made. In 1926 the Court gave attention to the practical disadvantage of such 'unpublished separate opinions'. In revising its Rule 31 the Court stated:

> It was argued that such statements constituted in fact dissenting opinions and the Court would be in a very difficult position, if, in a subsequent case, it wished to take into account one of these opinions appended simply to the minutes which constituted a private record. Under the last paragraph of Article 31, judges are now precluded from adopting this course, once the final vote has been taken (Series D, No 2, Add, pages 201–212 and 214–222)[59]

When the question of amending Article 57 was considered by the 1929 Committee of Jurists, the feeble conservative voice of Mr Fromageot spoke against the system of appending dissenting opinions.[60] However, the PCIJ practice meanwhile had developed in a very liberal way. Hence, Mr Fromageot could not stand the strong liberal voices of Sir Cecil Hurst, Mr Root, Mr Politis and Mr Huber. When Sir Cecil Hurst proposed an amendment to Article 57 which would recognize, in addition to dissenting opinions, separate opinions by judges who found themselves in the majority of the Court but did not agree with the statement of reasons given by the majority's conclusions; he argued in favour of this amendment that the judgments of the Court were unnecessarily long, and that the existing system of the Court weakened the judgments by making it necessary for them 'to embody several views'. To this President Anzilotti stated that *this was already the procedure followed by the Court in practice.* Hence, the 1929 Committee of Jurists decided not to amend Article 57 of the PCIJ Statute. However, several members of the Committee did not fail to comment that the judgments of the Court were indeed too long.[61]

[57] Series E, No 3, pp 216–17.

[58] See for instance the 'Separate Opinion by Mr Hudson' (Judgment of 15 June 1939 in the case concerning *The 'Société Commerciale de Belgique'*, Series A/B No 78, p 183) which begins in the following words: 'While the result which I would reach in this case does not differ greatly from that reached by the Court, the reasoning which I should adopt for reaching it differs on some important points from that which the Court has adopted'. The reasoning of a judge behind his vote and decision is the voice of his/her judicial conscience which no procedural rule or norm should try to curb or condition. It should be more so when the decision of a Court, comprising various legal cultures and systems, is based on the majority votes. If this is right in case of a dissenting judge; it should be right in case of any judge. Hence, to draw distinction between a procedural right of a dissenting judge and any other judge is not justified.

[59] Series E, No 3, p 217.

[60] Documents, p 136; Records of First Assembly, Committees, I, p 371.

[61] Minutes of the 1929 Committee of Jurists, pp 50–66. A good summary of this is to be found in MO Hudson, *The Permanent Court of International Justice: 1920–42*, 1943 edn, 206.

With reference to the then existing PCIJ Rules, Article 62, paragraph 2, and sub-paragraph 10 of paragraph 1 (Article 71) it was agreed by the Court on 1 December 1927 that dissenting opinions' 'object was to show the reasons for which a judge could not agree with the majority and they were not intended to be a reasoned criticism of the judgment or opinion'.[62] Further, in this regard, with reference to Article 57 of the PCIJ Statute, Articles 31, last paragraph, 62 last paragraph, and 71, second paragraph, of the PCIJ Rules, the Court adopted a resolution on 17 February 1928, which stated, *inter alia*: 'dissenting opinions are designed solely to set forth the reasons for which judges do not feel able to accept the opinion of the Court, and this opinion will, as a general rule, be determined as regards all essential points when the draft judgment or opinion has been adopted in the first reading'.[63]

Separate concurring opinions were frequently given, however, sometimes under the title 'observations'. The practice was well confirmed by the Court's resolution of 17 March 1936. Just like a river, the judicial river finds its way with various streams on its own. Five titles of what the PCIJ judges appended to the Court's decisions had developed during the course of practice: 'Declaration', 'Observation', 'Separate Opinion', and 'Statement Dissent'. However, two remained most prevalent: separate opinion and dissenting opinion. It is clear from the total number of their appendages during the PCIJ lifetime: 1 declaration, 2 observations, 25 separate opinions, 42 dissenting opinions, and 5 statements dissent.[64]

It is, therefore, interesting to know that before a formal provision in the ICJ Statute giving right to concurring judges to append individual opinions to judgments came into existence the right was already there in force *by practice*.

It equally shows that *in theory* under the PCIJ Statute the right to append an individual opinion was reserved only for dissenting judges and not for any other judge, including judge *ad hoc*, who would, for instance, have voted in favour of the majority decision in the operative part of the judgment but not for the method of the reasoning in the reasoning part of the judgment by which the majority arrived at its decision, and, hence, would like to record the reasoning by which he/she arrived at the same decision. If only the dissenting judge would have the right of appending a separate opinion and not any other judge then it is obvious that the given language of the provision was not in consistent with the procedural principle of equality.

The *Inter-Allied Committee* which was set up in 1944 to look into the future of the International Court. The Report of the Informal Inter-Allied Committee on the future of the Permanent Court of International Justice shows that during the discussion an unsuccessful and feeble conservative attempt aiming at abolishing the dissenting opinion system was made by some members. However, the majority in the Committee was so enthusiastic about the system that they not only

[62] Series E No 4, p 291.

[63] Series E, No 4, p 291.

[64] A Eyffinger, *The International Court of Justice: 1946–96* (The Hague, Kluwer Law International, 1996) 386.

thought of preserving the system as it had developed during the PCIJ time but thought of recommending to make that more liberal and equal. According to the Committee's Report: 'we would not only *preserve* the system of dissenting judgments, but *go further* than the relevant provision of the existing Statute, which only confers a right on the dissenting judges to deliver a separate opinion. In our view *it should be obligatory* on any Judge who dissents from the majority to state his reasons for so doing'. With some opposition throughout the process of drafting the ICJ Statute, the new version of Article 57 came out to be with the following improved language.

'If the judgment does not represent in whole or in part the unanimous opinion of the judges, *any judge shall be entitled* to deliver a separate opinion'. (italics added).

Hence, the element of inequality was rectified by replacing the words *dissenting judges are entitled* by the words *any judge shall be entitled.*

The Rules adopted by the ICJ on 6 May 1946 reflected this spirit in their Articles 74 (paragraph 2) and 84 (paragraph 2) stipulating: 'Any judge May, if he so desires attach his individual opinion to the judgment/advisory opinion, whether he dissents from the majority or not, or a bare statement of dissent'.

In May 1948 the Court decided that the opinion of a judge who disagreed with a judgment or advisory opinion should be called 'dissenting' opinion; and that a separate opinion given by a judge who supported the view of the majority should be called an 'individual' opinion.[65]

In the revised Rules of 1978 the Court developed further the spirit of the procedural principles of equality and freedom of expression by moderating its language further in the relevant transformed Articles 95 (paragraph 2) and 107 (paragraph 3), respectively as follows:

> Any judge may, if he so desires, attach his individual opinion to the judgment/advisory opinion, whether he dissents from the majority or not; a judge who wishes to record his concurrence or dissent without stating his reasons may do so in the form of a declaration. The same shall also apply to orders made by the Court.

This revision not only drew clear distinction, but with equal rights, between dissenting opinions and concurring opinions (usually called separate opinions) but added a new title of 'declaration', equally providing for all judges to record their dissent or concurrence without stating their reasons.

The developing practice in the face of theory in retrospect and prospect is well summarized by Prof Rosenne in the following words:

> But for a number of complicated reasons it has not been possible to adhere to those definitions and they seem to have been abandoned. Even more striking is the growth of the practice of attaching 'declarations' to judgments and advisory opinions, sometimes combining these with other separate or dissenting opinions. Anxiety has been widespread that the unchecked prevalence of these practices would in the long run impair the

[65] ICJ Yearbook 1947–48, p 68.

standing of the Court and detract in a serious way from the authority of its judicial pronouncements.[66]

However, the practice and theory both reflect: 1) the institution of individual opinions—in the face of the Court representing different legal systems and nationalities, advocating the procedural principle of equality, and responsible to develop the law—is not only desirable but necessary, and 2) the dividing line between dissenting opinions and separate opinions is very thin. This led Judge Jennings to maintain that: 'The capacity of Judges to append separate opinions is desirable' as 'Judges will often wish to explain their votes'. He continues:

> It is obvious that in this kind of situation, the rubrics 'separate' and 'dissenting' can give only an indication of the Judges' attitude, which may be approximate to the point of inaccuracy. Moreover, in the sense of the Court's Statute, a dissenting opinion is merely one sort of separate opinion. Even the term 'separate' is somewhat unhappy one because it suggests something separate from the judgment, whereas in fact ... it is not separate from the judgment but belongs to it. The word used in the French version, 'opinion individuelle' is preferable.[67]

The last paragraph of Article 31 of the revised Rules of the PCIJ, as amended on 31 July 1926, actually already confirmed the reality of practicality in the following words: 'After the final vote taken on a judgment or advisory opinion, any judge who desires to set forth his individual opinion must do so in accordance with Article 57 of the Statute'.[68]

It is true that the excessive length of individual opinions is a matter of concern, yet the institution itself, particularly in view of the different reasoning approaches it supplies not only to appreciate the decision of the Court 'in its full judicial perspective' but to the progressive task of the development of international law, has more advantages than disadvantages. It is interesting to observe that even President Bedjaoui who spoke against the excessive length of these opinions did not fail to mention the positive side of this practice in the following words: 'This practice, of Anglo-Saxon origin, which seeks to ensure a degree of transparency in the work of a judicial organ, is without any doubt a healthy one in itself.' His only reservation, he continued, is 'but not, however, if the texts concerned assume excessive proportions'.[69]

To those who question the utility of the lengthy opinions and to those who maintain that these lengthy opinions weaken the authority of the judgment, the

[66] S Rosenne, *The Law and Practice of the International Court of Justice 1920–1996*, 3rd edn, (The Hague, Martinus Nijhoff, 1997) vol III, p 1580.

[67] Sir Robert Jennings, 'The Collegiate Responsibility and Authority of the International Court of Justice' in Y Dinstein and M Tabory, (eds), *International Law at a Time of Perplexity: Essays in Honour of Shabtai Rosenne* (Dordrecht, Matinus Nijhoff) 347–48.

[68] PCIJ Publication Series D, No 1, Statute of the Court—Rules of the Court (as amended on 31 July 1926), (Leiden, Sijthoff, 1926) 46.

[69] M Bedjaoui, 'Presentation by HE Judge Mohammed Bedjaoui' in C Peck and RS Lee, (eds), *Increasing the Effectiveness of the International Court of Justice: Proceedings of the ICJ/UNITAR Colloquium to Celebrate the 50th Anniversary of the Court* (The Hague, Martinus Nijhoff, 1997) 26.

eminent Finnish Professor of theory and history of international law, Martti Koskennieemi, poses a question: 'The utility of the often numerous and lengthy separate and dissenting opinions in judgments of the Court has been questioned. Would the authority of the Court and the likelihood or expediency of compliance with judgments be heightened if the Court were to abandon this practice?' Then he himself answers the question:

> The ban on dissenting and separate opinions in the European Court is seen by some as one of the principal reasons for the success, independence and authority of this court. However, the disadvantages should not be overlooked: Judgments of the European Court of Justice not infrequently lack in elegance and coherence and it is difficult to estimate the likelihood of changes in the case law as long as the judgments do not reveal whether, why and to what extent the Court is divided. Furthermore, the experience with respect to non-compliance with judgments of the European Court of Justice, as compared to the record of the International Court of Justice or the European Court of Human Rights, clearly does not speak itself in favor of a ban against separate and dissenting opinions.[70]

To the valuable relation between the decision of the Court and the system of appending thereto individual opinions, the system inherited from the PCIJ, the ICJ itself has had occasion to stress:

> *an indissoluble relationship exists between such decisions and any separate opinions,* whether concurring or dissenting, appended to them by individual judges. The statutory institution of the separate opinion has been found essential as affording an opportunity for judges to explain their votes. In cases as complex as those generally dealt with by the Court, with operative paragraphs sometimes divided into several interlinked issues upon each of which a vote is taken, the bare affirmative or negative vote of a judge may prompt erroneous conjecture which his statutory right of appending an opinion can enable him to forestall or dispel . . .. *Not only do the appended opinions elaborate or challenge the decision, but the reasoning of the decision itself, reviewed as it finally is with knowledge of the opinions, cannot be fully appreciated in isolation from them.*[71] (italics are mine).

This is how the 'process of judgment' in the contentious cases culminating in the Court's decisions and individual opinions appended by individual judges together contribute to the development of international law and facilitate the delivery of the 'empire of justice'. In reality, in the process of first setting the matters of fact and law and then parallel to that giving careful and balanced considerations to the arguments of parties and at the same time the process of application and interpretation of law is at full swing, the reasoning part of a decision and the individual opinions appended thereto may be perceived as an ocean of 'judicial power of humanity', churned out by the judges through their process of judgment. The result is an immense clarification and development of the law involved.

[70] M Koskenniemi, 'Commentary by Professor Martti Koskenniemi' in C Peck and RS Lee, (eds), *Increasing the Effectiveness of the International Court of Justice: Proceedings of the ICJ/UNITAR Colloquium to Celebrate the 50th Anniversary of the Court* (The Hague, Martinus Nijhoff, 1997) 347–48.

[71] General Assembly document A/41/591/Add.1 of 5 December 1986, Annex II; cited in the blue-book of the Court 'International Court of Justice: 1946–96', ICJ The Hague, 4th edn, p 72.

No doubt that too lengthy opinions may weaken the authority of the judgment and a straightforward decision given by a vast majority, if not a unanimous decision, would add more weight to it. It is equally true on the other hand that unanimous decisions without its appended individual opinions may not be as transparent about the reasoning of the Court, hence, the appended opinions are the only windows to have the better understanding of the decision. Be this as it may, the history of the institution of individual opinions, irrespective of their concurrence or dissent, is the evidence that the part these opinions have played hitherto in contributing to the development of the international law is by no means negligible. Every following chapter would bear witness to this fact.

4

Corfu Channel Case (*United Kingdom v Albania*)[1] (1947–49)

I. The Principle of Elementary Considerations of Humanity

THIS VERY FIRST ICJ contentious case is generally accepted as having developed a founding principle of '*elementary considerations of humanity*' whose bearing on human rights law is unfolding day by day.

The loss of human life was a significant part of the dispute relating the case concerning *Corfu Channel*. The dispute originated in 1946 out of explosion of mines in the Albanian territorial waters of the North Corfu Channel which badly damaged two British warships and caused loss of lives of some members of the crew. At the outset it might be interesting to mention that the jurisdiction of the Court in the case filed by the government of the United Kingdom on 22 May 1947 was challenged by Albanian government. The case had previously been brought before the Security Council of the United Nations and, in consequence of a recommendation by the Security Council, had been referred to the International Court. The United Kingdom's invoking this recommendation as a basis for the Court's jurisdiction was seen as invalid by Albania. The Court, however, dealing with the question of jurisdiction and admissibility, found. *inter alia*, that a communication dated 2 July 1947, addressed to it by the government of Albania, constituted a voluntary acceptance of its jurisdiction. This was not acceptable to Albania. Giving an activist interpretation to the formula of consent established by its predecessor, the Permanent Court of International Justice, the Court declared: 'While the consent

[1] The composition in the merits phase of the Corfu Channel case was: *Acting President* Guerrero; *President* Basdevant; *Judges* Alvarez, Fabela, Hackworth, Winiarski, Zoricic, De Visscher, Sir Arnold McNair, Klaestad, Badawi Pasha, Krylov, Read, Hsu Mo, Azevedo; *Judge ad hoc*Ečer (see *ICJ Reports*, 1949 p 4).

Judge Alvarez, while concurring in the Judgment of the Court, availed himself of the right conferred on him by Article 57 of the Statute and appended to the Judgment a statement of his individual opinion to the Judgment; Judges Winiarski, Badawi Pasha, Krylov and Azevedo, and Judge *ad hoc* Ečer, declaring that they are unable to concur in the Judgment of the Court, availed themselves of the right conferred on them by Article 57 of the Statute of the Court and appended to the Judgment statements of their dissenting opinions (see *ICJ Reports*, 1949, p 38).

of the parties confers jurisdiction on the Court, neither the Statute nor the Rules require that this consent should be expressed in any particular form'.[2]

This style of establishing jurisdiction for itself is in a way a farewell to the judicial restraint ideology, that too in its very first judgment in a contentious case. This way of very liberal and activist approach, consistently and constantly applied to the disputes involving human rights violations, could prove a great contribution to the development and protection of human rights jurisprudence. This however was not the case, as will be seen later, in the ten cases filed by Yugoslavia against 10 NATO States. The Court in those cases became very conservative and followed the ideology of strict judicial restraint.

The dispute in the *Corfu Channel* case arose out of the explosions of mines by which two British cruisers, namely *Orion* and *Superb*, suffered damages while passing through the Corfu Channel in 1946, in a part of the Albanian waters which had been previously swept in 1944 and 1945. The ships were severely damaged and some members of the crew were killed. The United Kingdom accused Albania of having laid, or allowed a third party to lay, the mines after mine-clearing operations had been carried out by the Allied naval authorities. The case was brought before the International Court of Justice by the United Kingdom on 22 May 1947. As the record would have it, this was the first contentious case to be filed with the ICJ.

One of the two questions to be decided by the International Court was: 'Is Albania responsible under international law for the explosions which occurred on 22 October 1946 in Albanian waters and for the damage and loss of human life which resulted from them and is there any duty to pay compensation.'[3]

As Albania neither notified the existence of the minefield nor warned the British warships of the danger they were approaching, the Court held that Albania had obligations under international law to notify international shipping of the existence of a mine field in Albanian territorial waters. In its Judgement on merits,[4] delivered on 9 April 1949, the Court stated:

> Such obligations are based . . . on certain general and well-recognized principles, namely: *elementary considerations of humanity*, even more exacting in peace than in war; the principle of the freedom of maritime communication; and every State's obligation not to allow knowingly its territory to be used for acts contrary to the rights of other States.[5]
>
> Convincing a very large part of the audience is the hallmark of an effective judgment. In order to convince, the judge must properly identify the audience and familiarise himself with it. He must use arguments which are appropriate to that audience. Where the audience is comprised of diverse elements he must carefully consider all its segments.[6]

[2] *Corfu Channel* case, Judgment of 12 December 1947, ICJ Reports, 1947–48, p 27.
[3] *Corfu Channel* case, ICJ Reports, 1949, p 6.
[4] *Ibid*, p 4.
[5] *Ibid*, p 22.
[6] LV Prott, *The Latent Power of Culture and the International Judge* (1979) 184, cited in JG Merrills, *The Development of International Law by the European Court of Human Rights* (Manchester, MUP, 1993) 30.

The persuasiveness is an essential feature of a good judicial style. In justifying its conclusions judges can appeal to the '*common set of cultural values*'. Judges often use this technique. Prof Merrils noted that 'In the Corfu Channel case the International Court invoked "*elementary considerations of humanity*, even more exacting in peace than in war" to establish Albania's international responsibility.'[7] Obviously the ICJ here appealed to the *common human values*, such as the values of human dignity and respect for human right to life, at the global level the persuasiveness of which stands on firm footing beyond the aura of any doubt.

Commenting on the obvious link between the Albanian obligations and the principle of the 'elementary considerations of humanity', Judge Schwebel (USA) writes: 'The Court . . . has had cause to return to the 'elementary consideration of humanity, even more exacting in peace than in war. The relation of such considerations to the substance and application of human rights requires no elaboration.'[8]

'Each judgment is either a step forward or a step backward in the development of law.'[9] Seen in this perspective provided by Judge Lachs (Poland), the principle of elementary considerations of humanity, highlighted by the Court in its *Corfu Channel* case judgment on merits, has considerably broadened the scope of the human rights law and its link with other fields of international law in particular and municipal and other branches of law in general. One cannot deny the fact that that 'the elementary considerations of humanity' are at the core of every principle and concept of human rights.

II. Judge Alvarez: Manifest Misuse of a Right Not Protected by Law

While being in full agreement with the Judgment delivered by the Court, Judge Alvarez, most famous judicial activist and benevolent liberal judge the Court has known, felt that it was desirable to give prominence to certain considerations of a legal character in support of the Judgment on merits. He touched upon the concept of *misuse of a right* to add more to the principle of elementary considerations of humanity.

The Court's discussion in connection with the passage of the British warships through the Albanian territorial waters on 12–13 October 1946, the subjects of intervention, demonstration of force with a view to intimidation, violation of

[7] Merrills, *ibid*, p 31.

[8] SM Schwebel, 'The Treatment of Human Rights and Alients in the International Court of Justice' in V Lowe and M Fitzmaurice, (eds), *Fifty Years of the International Court of Justice: Essays in Honour of Sir Robert Jennings* (Cambridge, CUP, 1996) 330.

[9] M Lachs, 'Some Reflections on the Contribution of the International Court of Justice to the Development of International Law' (1983) 10 *Syracuse Journal of International Law and Commerce* Nr 1, 241.

sovereignty, etc, were found as somewhat confusing notions by Judge Alvarez. To clarify this matter and provide clarity to the law in question, he mentioned:

> The intervention of a State in the internal or external affairs of another—ie, action taken by a State with a view to compelling another State to do, or to refrain from doing, certain things—has long been condemned. It is expressly forbidden by the Charter of the United Nations. The same applies to other acts of force, and even to a threat of force.[10]

Any act or application of force, be it a threat or use thereof, if not permitted by law, is illegal and is considered as an assault on the victim's dignity. Referring to the contention of the United Kingdom, Judge Alvarez elaborated: 'The Agent for the United Kingdom contented that the mine-sweeping operation known as 'Retail', undertaken by the British ships in the Corfu Strait, was a justifiable act of self-help. That is not correct; the operation was in fact a violation of Albanian sovereignty.'[11] This he found as the *misuse of a right* and stated that 'the misuse of a right had no place in law.'[12] Citing texts of Article 226 of the German Civil Code and Article 2 of the preliminary chapter of the Swiss Civil Code, Judge Alvarez establishes in his individual opinion that 'the manifest misuse of a right is not protected by the law.'[13] Hence, he urged the Court: 'The Court must reaffirm, as often as the occasion arises, that intervention and all other kinds of forcible action are not permissible, in any form or on any pretext, in relation between States; but the Court may excuse such acts in exceptional circumstances.'[14] The Court did indeed reaffirm this, as would be seen, for instance, in the *Nicaragua v USA* case, Judgment of 27 June 1986.[15] Alleged human rights violations in Yugoslavia and NATO's use of force in the operation dubbed 'Strike Against Yugoslavia' may also be scrutinized in the light of this criterion.

[10] *Corfu Channel, ICJ Reports*, 1949, p 47.
[11] *Ibid.*
[12] *Ibid.*
[13] *Ibid.*
[14] *Ibid.*
[15] *ICJ Reports*, 1986, p 133.

5

South West Africa cases[1] (1960–66): Violation of Human Rights Law Led to Formation of Human Rights Law

I. Prelude

'ONE OF THE special characteristics of international law is that violations of law can lead to the formation of new law.[2] Of course, this characteristic is more troublesome for those who regard law as rules, and less troublesome

[1] Two cases were individually filed in 1960 by Ethiopia and Liberia against South Africa. Both Applicants being in the same interest the cases were joined by the Court. Two judgments were delivred. One in 1962 and the other in 1966. The composition of the Court in 1962 judgment was: *President* Winiarski (Poland); *Vice-President* Alfaro (Panama); *Judges* Basdevant (France), Badawi (Egypt), Moreno Quintana Argentina), Wellington Koo (China), Spiropoulos (Greece), Sir Percy Spender Australia), Sir Gerald Fitzmaurice (United Kingdom), Koretsky (then USSR), Bustamante y Rivero (Peru), Jessup (USA), Morelli (Italy); *Judges ad hoc* Sir Louis Mbanaffo (Nigeria), van Wyk (South Africa). (See ICJ Reports 1962, p 319). Judges Bustamante y Rivero and Jessup and Judge *ad hoc* Sir Louis Mbanefo appended to the Judgdment of the Court statements of their Separate Opinions; President Winiarski and Judge Basdevant appended to the Judgment of the Court statements of their Dissenting Opinions; Judges Sir Percy Spender and Sir Gerald Fitzmaurice appended to the Judgment a statement of their Joint Dissenting Opinion; Judge Morelli and Judge *ad hoc* van Wyk appended to the Judgment statements of their Dissenting Opinions. (See ICJ Reports 1962, p 348).

The composition in 1966 judgment was: *President* Sir Percy Spender; *Vice-President* Wellington Koo (China); *Judges* Winiarski ((Poland), Spiropoulos (Greece), Sir Gerald Fitzmaurice (United Kigdom), Koretsky (then USSR), Tanaka (Japan), Jessup (USA), Morelli (Italy), Padilla Nervo (Mexico), Forster (Senegal), Gros (France), *Judges ad hoc* Sir Louis Mbanefo (Nigeria), van Wyk (South Africa). (see ICJ Reports 1966, p 6).

President Sir Percy Spender appended to the Judgment his Declaration (see ICJ Reports 1966, p 51); Judge Morelli and Judge *ad hoc* van Wyk appended to the Judgment their Separate Opinions (see ICJ Reports 1966, p 57); Vice-President Wellington Koo, Judges Koretsky, Tanaka, Jessup, Padilla Nervo, Forster and Judge *ad hoc* Sir Louis Mbanefo appended to the Judgment their Dissenting Opinions (see ICJ Reports 1966, p 58).

[2] Prof Friedmann states: 'The Nuremberg Judgments are a conspicuous example of the making of new international law in the form of judicial fiat.' See WG Friedmann, 'The Jurisprudencial Implications of the South West Africa Cases' (1967) 6 *Columbia Journal of Transnational Law* 1, 6.

for those who regard law as process'.[3] Prof Higgins, at present Judge at the International Court of Justice (British), the first and the only woman judge as of date on the ICJ bench, made this distinction between 'law as rule' and 'law as process' as a fundamental approach in her fifteen lectures forming the General Course in International Law delivered by her at the Hague Academy of International Law, appearing under the apt title of her book *Problems and Process: International Law and How We Use It.* If these words of Judge Higgins are apt description of international law, their aptness gets multiplied when applied to human rights law, and still more so when it comes to law as applied, interpreted and developed in the South West Africa cases.

The *South West Africa* cases, with the policy of *apartheid* at the centre, with the *principle of equality* at the background, and with the *norm of non-discrimination* at the face of it, all fitting in the newly born circle of human rights law as an integral part of the grand circle of international law, provided a context within which there was a tension between the judges representing various conflicting sets of perceptions and conceptions, of ideas and ideologies, and of interpretation techniques. It was not only a tension between the judges representing the approach of *law as rule* and the approach of *law as process*, but also between their two conceptions of international law as *formalist-positivist* and *teleological-sociological.*[4] It was also a tension between *positivists* and *sociologists*, often appearing to represent the two general judicial ideologies of judicial restraint and judicial activism respectively, ending up in their opinions advocating either tough conservatism or benevolent liberalism. It all depends how one sees at the Second Phase Judgment of 1966 which was more concerned with human rights law than perhaps any ICJ judgment so far, and more particularly so when it comes to the norm of non-discrimination, an attribute of the concept of justice. '*Treating equal cases alike is a basic principle of justice*', according to Prof Van Hoecke. 'This equality principle', he continues, 'or non-discrimination principle is written in most constitutions and in several international treaties on human rights. Departing from this equality principle, in order to decide otherwise in a particular case, seems to endanger the principle of justice, conceived as "general justice".'[5]

'La loi ne sera pas differente a Rome et a Athenes, maintenant et plus tard, mais chez tous les peoples et en tout temps la meme loi sera d'application,' opines Judge Rigaux citing Ciceron in *Swift v Tyson*[6] case. Could it be then that the human rights law is different in South West Africa, different in the rest of South Africa, and different in the international community as a whole?! Is the conflict of law

[3] R Higgins, *Problems and Process: International Law and How We Use It* (Oxford, OUP, 1994) 19. For Judge Higgins' analysis of the South West Africa cases, discussing jurisprudential implications and interpretation of international documents of humanitarian character, see R Higgins 'The International Court and South West Africa: The Implications of the Judgment' (1966) 42 *International Affairs* 573.

[4] J Trachtman, 'The South-West Africa Cases and the Development of International Law' (1976) 5(3) *LSE Journal of International Studies* 292.

[5] M van Hoecke, *Law as Communication* (Oxford, Hart Publishing, 2002) 154.

[6] F Rigaux, *La Loi des Juges* (Paris, Editions Odile Jacob, 1997) 151.

relating human rights an acceptable feature of international human rights law?! Can we afford to have a private international human rights law?! A big **NO** as an answer to all these questions is an established fact of international human rights law today. But during the six years (1960–66) of judicial marathon proceedings before the International Court of Justice the law was churned out of the judicial milk in the pot of South West Africa cases. Out of that development of law and its impact on the international legislative processes there emerged an equation:

Equality + non-discrimination = core of human rights law

What is the import of the preceding equation and why? It is all still unfolding in the jurisprudence of human rights. None in the juridical circles would like to disagree with Prof Van Hoecke that to depart from the principal of equality in a particular case would endanger the principle of justice. None, equally, would dare refute Judge Rigaux's opinion. People all over, without any distinction of race, colour, religion, nationality, etc, are entitled to be treated equally and without discrimination. Yet one party in the 1960s, the government of South Africa, occupying a conspicuous place in the history of human rights for its famous policy of *apartheid*, disagreed with this. For that government the place of apartheid had nothing to do with discrimination. It was a political and neutral policy meant to be a means in order to achieve a social end. Why did the common juridical sense not prevail in the legal and political circles of South Africa? Why the International Court of Justice changed its course in 1966 as compared to its reasoning in 1962 judgment? If the Court was really saying that Ethiopia and Liberia could be adjudged in 1962 to have *legal standing* to bring a case but not to be entitled to get an answer in 1966 because of lack of legal interest in the subject-matter then, according to Prof Higgins (later an ICJ Judge), one is entitled to ask the Court: 'What claim could Ethiopia and Liberia present after they had been deemed entitled to proceed in 1962, in order to get an answer from the Court?'[7] Why was the first judgment of 1962 delivered with a narrow majority of 8 against 7 and why was the same judgment over-ruled with a casting vote of the Court's President, the voting being 7 against 7? These are some of the questions which have entered several legal minds and multitudes of laymen. Laymen certainly point the finger in the first instance towards the leaders in political circles. The Legal mind however ponders the prevailing status and situation of the law in question. The law at a given time might be in a state of a moral principle of a moralist jurist, yet until and unless the law is developed, crystallized, and institutionalised to that extent that none in its judicial conscience would dare easily challenge either its efficacy or validity, the law cannot stand as a dominant theme of a given branch of law.

The real state and understanding of the principle of equality and the norm of non-discrimination in the early 1960s was so that beside the non-binding

[7] R Higgins 'The International Court and South West Africa: The Implications of the Judgment' (1966) 42 *International Affairs* 573, 580–81; also cited in WG Friedmann, 'The Jurisprudencial Implications of the South West Africa Cases' (1967) 6 *Columbia Journal of Transnational Law* 1, 13.

Universal Declaration of Human Rights of 1948, and the related UN Charter provisions, there hardly were any positive law documents like the two UN Covenants of 1966 in existence. The 1966 International Covenant on Civil and Political Rights and the 1966 International Covenant on Economic, Social and Cultural Rights were signed five months after the delivery of 1966 ICJ judgment and they were ratified even 10 years later in 1976. Does it mean that there was no international human rights law in existence to remedy the wrong of racial discrimination by South African government? No, that certainly was not the case. The law to be applied by the International Court of Justice is clearly stated in Article 38 of its Statute. The real problem and answer(s) to the aforementioned questions lie in the fact that there was dearth of sound analysis of the principle of equality and the norm of discrimination in the international law literature. This is what the Court and its judges in their individual opinions tried to provide in their two judgments in the South West Africa cases. And this is how the Court and its judges developed the international human rights law in these cases.

The constantly running legal issue at the core of the contentious cases concerning the South West Africa cases (1960–66), in theory as well as in practice, in procedure as well as in substance, is the basic principle of equality and its human rights norm of non-discrimination. The cases present a tough judicial polemics between the judges as representatives of two law schools, positive law school on the one side and natural law school joined by blended positive-cum-natural law school judges on the other. And in the development of human rights law, it is equally at the same time a fight between two judicial ideological camps of judges representing two general judicial ideologies—1) the ideology of judicial restraint and 2) the ideology of judicial activism, and in turn in their specific forms 1) the ideology of tough conservatism and 2) the ideology of benevolent liberalism, respectively.

II. Norm of Non-Discrimination and 1962 Judgement: Court Has Jurisdiction to Adjudicate Upon the Merits

The series of cases on South West Africa, ranging between early 1950s and early 1970s, showed, with the single exception of the 1966 judgment on the cases brought by Ethiopia and Liberia, 'a commitment by the Court to decency, to human rights, and to the use of international law in attaining these objectives'.[8] Of these cases only two cases were contentious, filed separately by Ethiopia and Liberia, respectively. At the core of these contentious cases was the principle of non-discrimination which would promote the principle of justice, if applied, and, would 'endanger the principle of justice', if departed from, as Prof Van Hoecke put

[8] R Higgins, 'The International Court of Justice and Africa' in E Yakpo and T Boumedra, (eds), *Liber Amicorum: Judge Mohammed Bedjaoui* (The Hague, Kluwer International Law, 1999) 343, 359.

it. Whether the justice in these two human rights cases was promoted or endangered would be seen in the following pages.

On 4 November 1960, both the States asked the Court to declare, among other things, that South Africa had modified the terms of the mandate over South West Africa and that it had a duty to stop with immediate effect the practice of *apartheid* in South West Africa. The Court found both Ethiopia and Liberia to be in the same interest and joined the cases by making an Order on 20 May 1961.[9] The Applicants based their jurisdiction on Article 7 of the Mandate of 17 December 1920 for German South West Africa and Article 37 of the Court's Statute. The Applicants asked the Court in their Applications, to adjudge, *inter alia*, that:

> The Union, in administering the territory, has practised *apartheid*, ie, has distinguished as to race, color, national or tribal origin, in establishing the rights and duties of the inhabitants of the Territory; that such practice is in violation of Article 2 of the Mandate and Article 22 of the Covenant; and that the Union had the duty forthwith to cease the practice of *apartheid* in the Territory.

In order to escape the charges of violating the norm of non-discrimination in the form of her policy of apartheid the Union of South Africa made four preliminary objections to the jurisdiction of the Court. The first two objections maintained that the mandate agreement lapsed[10] on the dissolution of the League of Nations and, hence, the Applicants, being no longer members of the League, have no right to bring the case before the Court. In its third preliminary objection the Respondent contended that the dispute brought before the Court was not a dispute as envisaged in Article 7 of the Mandate. And, lastly and finally, the fourth objection by South Africa stated that if at all a dispute existed within the meaning of Article 7, it was not one which could not be settled by negotiation with the Applicants. All of these objections were rejected by the Court by its Judgment delivered on 21 December 1962.[11] The Court found that though the League of Nations and the Permanent Court of International Justice had both ceased to exist, the obligation of the Respondent to submit to compulsory jurisdiction had been effectively transferred to the International Court of Justice before the dissolution of the League of Nations. The Court held that the League had ceased to exist from April 1946 and the Charter of the United Nations had come into force in October 1945. The Court further mentioned that all the three parties to these joint cases, have filed their ratifications to the Charter in November 1945, and therewith became Members of the United Nations. With this, they had been subjected to the obligations under the Charter and equally entitled to the rights flowing from that document. The Court proceedings further screened all the three parties in the framework of Article 92 and 93 of the UN Charter and Article 37 of the ICJ Statute. Article 92 of the Charter states that the ICJ forms an integral part of the UN Charter. Article 93 of the Charter states that all UN Members are *ipso facto* parties

[9] South West Africa, ICJ Reports, 1961, p 13.
[10] South West Africa, ICJ Reports, 1962, p 323.
[11] *Ibid*, p 319.

to the Statute of the International Court of Justice. And, Article 37 of the Statute, which provides that whenever a treaty or convention in force provides for reference of a matter to a tribunal to have been instituted by the League of Nations, or to the Permanent Court of International Justice, the matter shall, as between the parties to the present Statute, be referred to the International Court of Justice. By the effect of all these three provisions, the Court found, that the Respondent had bound itself, by ratifying the Charter at a time when the League of Nations and the Permanent Court were still in existence and when therefore Article 7 of the Mandate was also in full force, to accept the compulsory jurisdiction of the present Court in lieu of that of the Permanent Court. By this very broad and liberal interpretation, the Court has promoted the cause of human rights law in the sense that no State party to a human rights litigation, in this pertaining norm of non-discrimination, before it can escape using strict formalism of law, or strict proceduralism, as a strategy of defence, can escape from its adjudication. The Court found by eight votes to seven that 'it has jurisdiction to adjudicate upon the merits of the dispute,'[12] ie, centring on the alleged South African policy of apartheid in the mandated area of South West Africa, known as Namibia, and the alleged violation of the human rights norm of non-discrimination.

The eight judges who voted in favour were: 1) Judge Alfaro (Panama), the Vice-President, 2) Judge Badawi (Egypt), 3) Judge Moreno Quintana (Argentina), 4) Wellington Koo (China), 5) Judge Koretsky (then USSR), 6) Judge Bustamante y Rivero (Peru), 7) Judge Jessup (USA), 8) Judge *ad hoc* Mbanefo (Nigeria).

The seven judges who voted against were: 1) Judge Winiarski (Poland), the President, 2) Judge Basdevant (France), 3) Judge Spiropoulos (Greece), 4) Judge Spender (Australia), 5) Judge Fitzmaurice (United Kingdom), 6) Judge Morelli (Italy), 7) Judge *ad hoc* Van Wyk (South Africa). All these seven judges seemed to be strict judicial conservatives and adhered to strict formalism and proceduralism of law. Six of them appended their dissents to the judgment (Spender and Fitzmaurice jointly), and the seventh, the Judge Spiropoulos, wrote a declaration. The following question-answer type argument in the declaration of this judge, though written individually, is indeed well reflective of the position taken by all of them for voting against the judgment of the Court: Not agreeing with the reasoning of the Court that it had jurisdiction in the given cases, Judge Spiropoulos posed a rather lengthy question, consisting of a series of questions, in questioning the Court's argument:

> Can it readily be found that the Mandate is a 'treaty or convention' within the meaning of Article 37 of the Statute of the International Court of Justice; that the Mandate, as a 'treaty', survived the collapse of the League of Nations (of which the formal act of 'dissolution' of the League of Nations was the result); that Article 7 of the Mandate—assuming the Mandate to be in force—can be relied on by States none of which is a 'Member of the League of Nations', that organization no longer being in existence?

[12] South West Africa, ICJ Reports, 1962, p 347.

The question as can be seen is reflecting strict thinking of legal formalism. He answered himself his own question in the following words: 'It appears to me that any attempt to give an affirmative answer to these questions, and they are not the only ones which arise, must necessarily be based on arguments which, from the standpoint of law do not seem to me to have sufficient weight.'[13] The judgment was hailed internationally as an act of promoting the cause of human rights law, particularly since it cleared the way to adjudication on the violations of these rights under the South African policy of apartheid. It was also greatly appreciated by the General Assembly of the United Nations. However, it would be seen that the dissenting judges in this judgment took their toll and reversed the judgment, as will be seen further, in the second phase of the case, and therewith stopped the Court to adjudicate on the merits of the case.

III. Judges Jessup and Bustamente: Voting in Favour of 1962 Judgment with Human Rights Additions

Though the judgment of 1962 just cleared the path to go to the merits of the case, yet two judges, Jessup and Bustamante, entirely in agreement with the judgment and voting with the majority, availed an opportunity to develop the human rights law by writing their separate opinions under Article 57 of the Statute.

While fully agreeing with the Court's decision that it had jurisdiction to deal with the merits of these cases, **Judge Jessup** (USA), a perfect blend of a positive law jurist and a natural law jurist, was still, however, of the opinion that the Court did not embrace in its reasoning part of the Judgment all the questions of fact and law which he found essential in reaching the decision of the Court in its operative clause. Hence, he wanted to add more to it and appended a separate opinion to the judgment and during the course of which he embraced the question of States having interest in the violation of human rights. Judge Jessup wrote: 'International law has long recognised that states may have legal interests in matters which do not affect their financial, economic or other "material", or any, "physical" or tangible'[14] interests. Judge Jessup was here indicating the legal interests of Ethiopia and Liberia in the situation in South West Africa created by the discriminatory policies of the government of South Africa. Looking at this recognition as a recognized principal of international law he found it necessary to illustrate the principle in the following words:

> One type of illustration of this principle of international law is to be found in the right of a state to concern itself, on general humanitarian grounds, with atrocities affecting human rights in another country. In some instances states have asserted such legal interests on the basis of some treaty, as for example, some of the representations made to the

[13] *Ibid*,, pp 347–48.
[14] *Ibid*, p 425.

> Belgian Government on the strength of the Berlin Act of 1885, concerning the atrocities in the Belgian Congo in 1906–1907. In other cases, the assertion of the legal interest has been based upon general principles of international law, as in remonstrances against Jewish pogroms in Russia around the turn of the century and the massacre of Armenians in Turkey.[15]

Citing many more examples and going deep into the matter of legal interests of States Judge Jessup came to a firm conclusion, that if not under conventional law, it is certainly and clearly possible for States to assert under the general principles of law a legal interest and concern themselves with violations of human rights in another State.

Judge Bustamante (Peru), known for his sociological interpretation of law, also in the same vein but from a different angle, a social angle indeed, touched upon the question of human rights in his separate opinion. Observing that the basis of four preliminary objections raised by the Republic of South Africa against the jurisdiction of the Court and the admissibility of the Applications of Ethiopia and Liberia were connected with the interpretation of the Mandate agreement for South West Africa, it seemed necessary to Judge Bustamante to examine the nature and characteristics of the legal system of Mandate. Three major characteristics of the Mandate system of the League of Nations were embodied in Article 22 of the Covenant of the League which reflected as following: 1) the system must recognize certain **fundamental rights** as belonging to the inhabitants of the underdeveloped territories, 2) the system must reflect as established 'on behalf of the League of Nations', 3) the system provides for an attribution to States Members of the League of the '**sacred trust of civilization**', namely, the promotion of the well-being and development of the peoples concerned and the **safeguard of their rights.** Putting the mandate system in its broadest socio-legal context the judge saw the system as 'the expression of the influence of a collective state of mind in the post-war world'. According to him at that time the general anti-colonial conscience, which had been at work for some time, became particularly active and the **preservation and protection of human rights** appeared more and more incompatible with the survival of the conquest and maintenance of colonial regimes: 'For these same reasons' Judge Bustamante continued:

> there can be no question, in any view, of qualifying as mere 'humanitarian' or 'moral' recommendations, the provisions of the Covenant of the League of Nations and of the Charter of the United Nations in which the 'sacred trust' of the States Members is described and established in respect of populations of the Mandated or Trusteeship Territories. This approach unjustifiably reduces the scope for the operation and application of the law, and confines within an ambit of mere equitable choice what in fact are clearly characterised **rights frequent with social implications**.

Continuing on this he went on elaborating that the concept of sacred trust is closely associated with human rights. Seeing that the concept of sacred trust and

[15] *Ibid*, p 425.

the notion of human rights are much more than simple moral orders Judge Bustamante wrote:

> The 'sacred trust' relates not only to duties of a moral order but also to legal obligations correlative with the rights recognised as belonging to the inhabitants of those territories by Article 22 of the Covenant and Article 76 of the Charter. By these provisions international law claimed for such peoples the quality of human legal person. This is the same process of legal advance under which the abolition of slavery was first proclaimed and which then led to the promulgation of the Declaration of Human Rights.

He continued further and asserted that: 'By an interesting coincidence all the rights set forth in Articles 22 and 76 for the benefit of the under-developed populations are embodied—as well as many others—in this Declaration.'[16] This is by all means stamping the modern notion of human rights with the old good stamp of the 'sacred trust of civilization', and that is what they in reality are.

IV. Second Phase Judgment: Compositional Politics a Setback to Human Rights

In order to have a clear picture of this betrayal of the Court it is important, firstly, to have a glimpse of the changing and re-changing configurations in the composition of the Court. The compositional equation of this extraordinarily weighty judicial tug-of-war arguing and reasoning out on the question of apartheid and human rights took the following form in 1962 on the roundtable in the deliberation room of the International Court of Justice. The composition of the Court at the time of voting in the judgment of 21 December 1962 was 15 judges, 13 regular Members of the Court and two judges *ad hoc*: 1) Judge Winiarski (Poland), President, 2) Judge Alfaro (Panama), Vice-President, 3) Judge Basdevant (France), 4) Judge Badawi (Egypt), 5) Judge Moreno Quintana (Argentina), 6) Judge Wellington Koo (China), 7) Judge Spiropoulos (Greece), 8) Judge Spender (Australia), 9) Judge Fitzmauricae (United Kingdom), 10) Judge Koretsky (USSR), 11) Judge Bustamante y Rivero (Peru), 12) Judge Jessup (United States), 13) Judge Morelli (Italy), 14) *Judge ad hoc* Mbanefo (Nigeria), 15) *Judge ad hoc* van Wyk (South Africa). The voting equation of these 15 judges was eight votes to seven. The interesting thing to be noticed here is the names of those seven judges who, though obviously forming a big minority, voted against the jurisdiction of the Court to decide the dispute centring around the issue of apartheid. These seven judges were: Judge Spiropoulos (appending a declaration to the judgment), Judge Winiarski (appending a dissenting opinion to the judgment), Judge Basdevant (appending a dissenting opinion to the judgment), Judges Spender and Fitzmaurice (appending a joint dissenting opinion to the judgment), Judge

[16] *Ibid*, pp 355–56.

Morelli (appending a dissenting opinion to the judgment), and *judge ad hoc* van Wyk (appending a dissenting opinion to the judgment).

Before we go further to see how the judicial hardcore positivism of 1962 in the composition of the Court reversed the judgment of 1962 and had their way and sway in the Second Phase judgment of 1966 we should now cast a glance on the composition of the Court in the judgment of 1966. The judges participating then were fourteen, including two *judges ad hoc.* These fourteen judges were: 1) Judge Spender (Australia), President, 2) Judge Wellington Koo (China), Vice-President, 3) Judge Winiarski (Poland), 4) Judge Spiropoulos (Greece), 5) Judge Fitzmaurice (United Kingdom), 6) Judge Koretsky (USSR), 7) Judge Tanaka (Japan), 8) Judge Jessup (United States), 9) Judge Morelli (Italy), 10) Judge Padilla Nervo (Mexico), 11) Judge Forster (Senegal), 12) Judge Gros (France), 13) *Judge ad hoc* Mbanefo (Nigeria), *Judge ad hoc* van Wyk (South Africa).

The decision in the Second Phase judgment of 1966 was taken by the casting vote of the President, the voting being equally divided as 7 to 7. If we give a comparative look at two different compositions of the Court in 1962 and 1966 respectively, what would at once come to the fore is: firstly, the President of the Court in 1966 was judge Spender of Australia, a narrow minded positivist who strongly opposed the judgment of 1962 and heavily vented his anger on the judges who wrote dissenting opinions to append to 1966 judgment. Secondly, 6 out of 14 judges, including President Spender, participating in this judgment were those who were in the opposition in 1962. They were here to settle the old score. Thirdly, Judge Gros of France who replaced Judge Basdevant of France at the Court's Bench stepped into his shoes literally and followed the same judicial course, hence the club of 6 became a club of 7. When at the time of voting the voting equation became 7 against 7, the President of the Court, Judge Spender, found a weapon in Article 55, paragraph 2, of the Court's Statute the text of which reads: 'In the event of an equality of votes, the President or the judge who acts in his place shall have a casting vote.' In order to reverse the judgment of 1962, in which he not only voted against the majority of the Court but also wrote a 99 pages long joint dissenting opinion together with Judge Fritzmaurice of the United Kingdom. This joint dissent was more than three times longer than the Court's judgement which itself was only 28 pages. If one wants to learn an art of taking the development of international law backward to the 19th century Austinian positivism and Holland's international law as the 'vanishing point of jurisprudence, one would find a masterpiece of work in the joint dissenting opinion of two devoted positivist, judges Spender and Fritzmaurice.

One may rightly wonder that in the full composition of the Court other than 2 judges *ad hoc* there are supposed to be 15 judges and not just 12. What happened to the other three and why? Why and how these three votes which were not cast would convert the compositional weight, which indeed was a procedural weight, would turn into a decisive voting weight for the judges who with the strategy of judicial self restraint would defeat the benevolent liberals who were fighting the cause of human rights by attempting to strike at the apartheid, the second worst of the inhuman wrong in history done to African people, the first being slavery? If we discover who those three judges were and if we imagine that they participated in the 1966 judgment and voted against the issue of apartheid the fate of apartheid and the development of human rights law in the given judgment would have been totally opposite to the decision given by the club of 7 lead by judge Spender, and the question of using his power of casting vote under Article 55, paragraph 2, of the Statute of the Court would not have arisen. These three judges could make all the difference and they were: 1) Judge Ammoun of Lebanon, 2) Judge Bustamante y Rivero of Peru, and 3) Judge Zafrulla Khan of Pakistan. Judge Ammoun was elected to succeed Judge Badawi of Egypt who voted with the majority of judges in 1962 but unfortunately died in 1965. Judge Ammoun was a bit too late to join the Court and to participate in the 1966 judgment. He would have, one would imagine, voted the same way as his Egyptian predecessor did, not because both were Arabs but also because both were anti-apartheid judges hailing from the so-called Third World which had strongly stood against the apartheid policy of South Africa. Judge Bustamante was ill all through the oral proceedings of the Second Phase of this case. He had earlier voted with the majority of judges in the 1962 judgment. Hence, he would surely be voting against the Spender club. The third judge, Sir Zafrulla Khan, who joined the Court's Bench second time in 1964 and could have participated in the Second Phase of the case but was persuaded by President Spender to recuse himself for the given case on the basis that he had participated in earlier discussions of the general legal questions at issue in the United Nations General Assembly debates to which he had been a delegate. Given this reason, according to Prof Edward McWhinney:

> Sir Percy Spender, as Court President, took the strict English Common Law attitude to judicial disqualification for 'interest'; though it should be noted that the modern Constitutional Courts, European and non-European, less persuaded of an absolute dichotomy between 'law' and 'policy', take a far more flexible, and pragmatic, and, in the end, facultative approach to such questions.[17]

Taking into consideration the absence of all these three judges, Prof McWhinney concludes:

> Death, disease, and disablement thus reduced a Court that would, with the two ad hoc, 'national' judges, have numbered seventeen, to fourteen, opening the way to the seven-seven voting tie which, with the second, tie-breaking vote of President Spender, became an 8–to–7 majority in effect distinguishing the earlier, 1962, ruling and holding that complainant states, Ethiopia and Liberia, did not have a sufficient legal interest to receive a judgment in the matter.[18]

President Spender has been strongly criticized for his role in inducing Judge Zafrullah Khan for announcing himself for his incompatibility in the 1966 case.

[17] E McWhinney, *The International Court of Justice and the Western Tradition of International Law* (Dordrecht, Martinus Nijhoff, 1987) 68.

[18] *Ibid*, pp 68–69.

Even if the death and disease votes left aside, only the presence of Judge Zafrullah Khan's and his voting against apartheid would have changed the entire voting equation to 8 votes to 7, sufficient to block the President's casting vote and sufficient to defeat apartheid of South Africa. This is how the compositional politics of the Court, lead by President Spender, prolonged the life of strict legal formalism and did damage the development of human rights law by the International Court. Prof McWhinney calls it a decision of 'proceduralism in favour of the extension of Apartheid—a ruling that became a political disaster for the Court.'[19] And, hence, a disaster for the development of human rights law. Prof Falk notices the 1966 judicial myopia in the given situation in the following words:

> It is worth noting that of the ten judges participating in both decisions, all those who voted with the majority in 1962 were in dissent in 1966 and vice versa. It requires a peculiar kind of legalistic myopia to ignore the impression of reversal created by a combination of changes in the voting membership of the Court and these voting statistics

He continues and sees 1966 judgment as 'covert reversal' of 1962 judgment.[20]

Are there any lessons to be learned? If I am asked, after the thorough analysis of the Second Phase of the South West Africa cases, what were the main reasons of the anti-human rights judgment of the Court in 1966? Without hesitation my prompt reply will be: there are two, one procedural and the other ideological. Procedurally, the quorum of the Court was not in balance with Article 9 of the Court's Statute. Ideologically, the judges who reversed the judgment of 1962 and managed not to go into the merits of the case centred around the question of racial discrimination were staunch legal formalists exercising narrow judicial self restraint.

V. Disproportionate Quorum: A Setback to Human Rights

The Court being a collegiate body, in its judicial decision making the substantive law is not the only force behind its decision, sometimes strict proceduralism could become a cause for the destruction of a good substantive decision. Judges would be more careful and conscientious in simply accepting their incompatibility in a case the policy issue wherein is the cause they are actively devoted to. In Judge Zafrullah Khan's case his having been engaged in an anti-apartheid debate in the United Nations General Assembly, which in all conscience of a man is worthy cause for human rights and humanity, may in the conscience of a human rights activist judge, liberal or extreme, not be a reason for not participating in the proceedings of a given case. Since Court's composition in reality is based on geographical division of seats, States parties to a case from one particular region or block, say Africa

[19] E McWhinney, *The International Court of Justice and the Western Tradition of International Law* (Dordrecht, Martinus Nijhoff, 1987) p 69.

[20] RA Falk, 'The South West Africa Cases: An Appraisal' (1967) 21(1) *International Organization* 11.

or even the so-called Third World, when the issue at stake is common and affecting them collectively, at least up to some extent, may request the Court to delay the proceedings in a case as long as the death disease or disability of a judge or some judges are not compensating. With three absent judges from the Third World, the Applicants, with the added backing of several Third World States, could have set a precedence for future by sending a joint petition to the Court to remedy the situation in which the absence of three predictably strong anti-apartheid votes could adversely affect the decision of the Court. Though it is true that Article 25, paragraph 3, of the Court's Statute provides for a quorum of nine judges and Article 20, paragraphs 1 and 3 of the Court's Rules further clarifies its application, yet when it comes to a number of 3 votes in a composition of 15, that too when the three absent judges are predictably in favour of the cause Applicants are seeking justice for, the situation is by no means less serious. It would not be a disrespectful objection to the quorum of the Court when the imbalance in view of Article 9 of the Court's Statute is so great that the three (Ammoun from Lebanon, Bustamante from Peru and Zafrulla Khan from Pakistan) out of a total of five (plus Forster of Senegal and Padilla Nervo of Mexico) regular Members of the Court were unable to vote in as crucial a case of human rights as of racial discrimination, the victim of which historically is mainly the colonial countries of three civilizations—Africa, Asia and Latin America—the civilization more in need of protection of human rights than any other. The text of Article 9 reads: 'At every election, the electors shall bear in mind not only that the persons to be elected should individually possess the qualifications required, *but also that in the body as a whole the representation of the main forms of civilization* and the principal legal systems of the world should be assured.' (emphasis added). The wording of Article 9 itself reflects to a considerable extent the principle of equality in the Court's regular composition. It is not hard to notice that all the judges who voted in favour of the judgment were all European or of European origin (President Spender from Australia, Spiropoulos from Greece, Fitzmaurice from the United Kingdom, Gros from France, Morelli from Italy, Winiarski from Poland, and judge *ad hoc* van Wyk of South Africa with white European white government). Had the proper weight of three absent civilizations added to this voting of pattern 7 against 7, the fate of human rights violations in South Africa would have been totally other way round, hence the victory of human rights provisions in the UN Charter. It is also interesting to note that of the seven judges who voted against the judgment of 1966 only two were from white countries, Judge Jessup from the United States and Judge Koretsky from the then USSR. Perhaps the question of Court's quorum and its relation with Article 9 of the Statute should be given a serious reconsideration in a future revision of the Rules of Court revising reforming its procedures, as Article 30 of the Statute provides that: 'the Court shall frame rules for carrying out its functions. In particular, it shall lay down rules of procedures. The International Court of Justice is still a young Court, a World Court in the making, along with its continuation the required modifications in its procedural provisions are to be made to satisfy the demands of justice. In the academic circles there already is being discussed the question whether a judge *ad hoc* is not at disadvantage by not being always present at the Court in the physical company of his other colleagues who themselves are in constant touch with each other and frequently visits each other's chambers to discuss any issue in a case as and when required. It goes a long way in playing a certain role in the process of judicial decision making, if not judicial law making. In a nutshell, the compositional side of the Court as a factor, be it procedural absence of a vote or the physical absence of a judge, in deciding cases, should not be taken lightly. If striking down of the inhuman evil of apartheid has been delayed and the suffering of South African blacks at the hands of its government of whites has lasted longer the Court's narrow proceduralism of seven judges—following the narrow judicial restraint ideology, strictly understanding the law as rule and having no understanding for the law as process, in a nutshell their tough judicial conservatism—is also somewhere partly responsible for it, no matter to what extent.

However, as Judge Higgins put it sometimes 'violation of law can lead to the formation of a new law'. The seven dissenting judges, providing the opposing compositional weight directly proportional to their seven tough conservative judges, have all together erased the stigma on the development of human rights law by their exhausting individual opinions, appended to the judgment, not only proving that how, why and where their seven colleague were wrong but also that how the Court as a whole should have dealt with the jurisdictional questions and the substantive issues of apartheid, discrimination and the equal treatment of the inhabitants of the South West Africa.

VI. Second Phase Judgment: Legal Formalism Circumvents Human Rights

However, the next phase of the case which was supposed to be concluded with a judgment on the merits of the case became a judgment on the 'Second Phase' which did not go into the merits of the case at all. This twist and turn of the substance and procedure was made possible by the Court's recalling that the Applicants, acting in the capacity of States which were members of the former League of Nations, put forward various allegations of contraventions of the League of Nations Mandate for South West Africa by the Republic of South Africa. The contentions of the Parties covered, *inter alia*, several issues concerning the Mandate for South West Africa.

But, instead of beginning to deal with these issues, the Court considered that there were two questions of an antecedent character, appertaining to the merits of the case, which might render an enquiry into other aspects of the case unnecessary. One was whether the Mandate still subsisted at all and the other was the question of the Applicants' standing in this phase of the proceedings, ie, do they have any legal right or interest regarding the subject matter of their claims.[21]

[21] South West Africa, ICJ Reports 1966, pp 18–19.

Having commenced with the usual summary of arguments and pleadings, the Court proceeded to a short assessment of its 1962 judgment. Soon thereafter, the Court 'skirted the subject' and stated as following:

> . . . there was one matter that appertained to the merits of the case but which had an antecedent character, namely, the question of the Applicants' standing in the present phase of the proceedings—not, that is to say, of their standing before the Court itself, which was the subject of the Court's decision in 1962, but the question, as a matter of the merits of the case, of their legal right or interest regarding the subject matter of their claim . . ..[22]

A close analysis of this statement, which may rightly be described as an *antecedent strategy* of the dissenters of 1962, brings to the fore three essential characteristics of their strategy based on strict legal formalism. First, that the Applicants' *legal standing* before the Court was not in question as, according to this 1966 judgment, that was already upheld by the Judgment of 1962, Secondly, The matter in question in 1966 was the Applicant's *legal right or interest* regarding their claim. And, thirdly, the merits of the case, the subject matter of the Applicants' claim, ie, the racial discrimination of the respondent in the territory of the South West Africa, was ringed by the strategy of division between '*locus standi*' and 'legal interest'. To this divide and prevail judicial trick of legal formalism, Flemming has remarkably described as following:

> The division of the applicants' legal position into *locus standi* (1962) and 'legal interest' (1966) appears to be a medieval and unjustified metaphysical splitting of the conceptual 'atom'; it bears the stamp of Judge Fitzmaurice whose separate opinion in the Northern Cameroons Case contains the conceptual seeds of the present majority opinion.[23]

It may may be recalled that Judge Fitzmaurice was in dissent to the Court's Judgment of 1962. He is also considered by Prof McWhinney and Prof Schwarzenberger as the main architect, together with Judge Spender, the President in the Second Phase Judgment, as the real architect of the 1966 judgment. And, no one can be more tough conservative and legal formalist than Judge Fitzmaurice.[24]

Having thus created a division between the concepts of *locus standi* and *legal interest* the Court, avoiding to adjudicate on the merits, examined the Mandate system. In doing so the Court further divided the provisions of Mandate into two categories, 'conduct provisions' and 'special interest provisions'. With this

[22] ICJ Reports, 1966, p 18.

[23] B Flemming, 'South West Africa Cases: *Ethiopia v South Africa*; *Liberia v South Africa: Second Phase*' (1967) 5 *Canadian Yearbook of International Law* 241.

[24] After his dissenting opinion of 1962, a masterpiece of legal formalism, his separate opinion just a year later in 1963 in the *Northern Cameroons* case, charaterized his tough conservatism and proceduralism in the following words: 'In my opinion, however, a claim which would and *could* only have the outcome described in the Judgment of the Court (assuming even, that there was a finding on the merits in favour of the claim), must itself be regarded as inadmissible.' (See ICJ Reports, 1963, p 101). This certainly is a seed for the 1966 majority judgment in which Judge Fitzmaurice placed a most crucial part.

examination, the Court found that 'the dispute between the parties relates exclusively to the former of these two categories of provisions, and not to the latter.'[25]

The Court then examined the question of jurisdiction under Article 7, paragraph 2, of the Mandate. The main question was whether a dispute regarding 'conduct provision' gave any legal right to the League Members, either individually or collectively, to bring an action. Having reasoned, the Court found:

> Accordingly, viewing the matter in the light of the relevant texts and instruments, and having regard to the structure of the League, within the framework of which the mandates system functioned, the Court considers that even in the time of the League, even as members of the League when that organization still existed, the Applicants did not, in their individual capacity as States, possess any separate self-contained right which they could assert.

The Court continued and concluded, 'This right was vested exclusively in the League.'[26] Having reached the finding that the Applicants did not have any legal right to bring an action the Court circumvented the Applicants with the following statement: 'and if in the time of the League—if as members of the League—the Applicants did not possess the rights contended for—evidently they do not possess them now.'[27] In the human rights terms it amounts to saying that the human rights violation of South Africa in the territory of South West Africa can by no means be challenged by Ethiopia or Liberia.

The Court astonished all and sundry by its 18 July 1966 Judgment on the Second Phase of the case. By the casting vote of the President—the votes having been equally divided (7–7)—the Court found that Ethiopia and Liberia could not be considered to have established any legal right or interest appertaining to them in the subject-matter of their claims, and accordingly decided to reject their claims.[28] Long live apartheid was the contribution of this judgment of seven judges. Actually, the legal formalism defeated the substantive human rights. The casting vote of an advocate of judicial self-restraint, President Spender, gave a major setback to the progressive development of human rights. How much the personal subscription of a judge to a particular judicial ideology can have a bearing on the decision of a court, particularly when the judge is the President of the Court, can well be seen from the following description of Judge Spender given by Prof McWhinney:

> As for the President, Sir Percy Spender, his intellectual position in the cases accords with the general legal thinking of a leader of the Equity bar, which Sir Percy at one time was; and also with the special legal philosophy of judicial self-restraint and of the practical political limits to the role of a Supreme Court judge, developed by the late Mr Justice Felix Frankfurter of the United States Supreme Court who is known to have strongly influenced Sir Percy Spender in his general legal ideas when he was Australian

[25] ICJ Reports, 1966, p 21.
[26] *Ibid*, pp 28–29.
[27] *Ibid*, p 31.
[28] South West Africa, ICJ Reports, 1966, p 51.

Ambassador to the United States in the years immediately prior to his election to the World Court in 1957.[29]

Hence, the judicial self-restraint, a family of judicial conservatism, travelling all the way from the United States, via Australia, reached the ICJ in the Netherlands, and marks its casting vote stamp on the 1966 Judgment which Falk labels as 'the Triumph of Judicial Conservatism.'[30] Accordingly, the Court never reached the merits which as Judge Schwebel put it 'had given rise to exceptionally extended and detailed argument over human-rights issues posed by the practice of an overt an acute form of racial discrimination'.[31]

The judgment met the most angry criticism everywhere, including in the UN General Assembly. This was a sad day for the development of human rights law by the International Court of Justice. Judge Higgins writes: 'The 1966 Judgment is, by common consent, to be regarded as an aberration'.[32] Seen in its entirety of two judgments together with majority versus minority changing the voting equations twice it is a case of, centring on human rights issue of racial discrimination, judicial adjudication versus judicial politics of the Court's composition on the one hand, and, the judicial ideology of legal formalism cum judicial self restraint versus judicial ideology of teleological approach cum benevolent activism on the other. It is a story in which the Court first takes a step forward, in 1962, which promotes the human rights law and then takes a step backward, in 1966, which demotes the human rights law. In this troubled judicial march of going forward and going backward, thanks to the benevolent activist judges, first in majority and then in minority, the contribution to the development of human rights law is far outweighing the unpleasant show of judicial tug-of-war.

However, to this situation of endangered justice there is another side which abundantly compensated for the loss caused by 'taking a step backward' by the Court, that is through the dissenting opinions of seven judges. Judge Singh has rightly pointed out that: if the Court has ever omitted to refer to the concept of human rights or failed fully to deal with it in a case, the Members of Court have, at no point, failed to elaborate that aspect in their independent or separate supporting opinions, or even give vent to their thinking in dissenting opinions which fact is quite remarkable'.[33] The equal and considerable value of the dissenting opinions in contributing to the development of law is well described by Judge Jessup in his dissent in this case. He cites Judge Charles Evans Hughes, a former

[29] E McWhinney, 'The Changing United Nations Constitutionalism: New Arenas and New Techniques for International Law Making' (1967) 5 *Canadian Yearbook of International Law* 68, 75.

[30] RA Falk, 'The South West Africa Cases: An Appraisal' (1967) 21(1) *International Organization* 11, 13.

[31] SM Schwebel, 'The Treatment of Human Rights and Aliens in the International Court of Justice' in V Lowe and M Fitzmaurice, (eds), *Fifty Years of the International Court of Justice: Essays in Honour of Sir Robert Jennings* (Cambridge, CUP, 1996) 327, 334.

[32] R Higgins, 'The International Court of Justice and Africa' in E Yakpo and T Boumedra, (eds), *Liber Amicorum: Judge Mohammed Bedjaoui* (The Hague, Kluwer International Law, 1999) 343, 359.

[33] N Singh, *Enforcement of Human Rights in Peace and War and the Future of Humanity* (Dordrecht, Nijhoff, 1986) 28–29.

judge of the Permanent Court of International Justice, and mentions that: 'A dissent in a court of last resort is an appeal to the brooding spirit of law, to the intelligence of a future day, when a later decision may possibly correct the error into which the dissenting judge believes the court to have been betrayed.'[34]

VII. Judge Tanaka and the Development of Human Rights Law

> The dissenting opinion of Judge Tanaka in the South West Africa cases represents probably the best exposition of the concept of equality in existing literature.[35]
>
> (Prof Abdulrahim P. Vijapur)

Judge Kotaro Tanaka (Japan) has already gone down in the history of the Court's jurisprudence for writing an opinion which has become an extraordinary document on the doctrine of human rights in general and on the norm of non-discrimination in particular. Craven finds that the most coherent discussion of the notion of discrimination is to be found in Judge Tanaka's dissenting opinion in the South West Africa cases Judgment on the Second Phase.[36]

Judge Tanaka came to the International Court of Justice in 1961 and served a full term of nine years. He participated in eight contentious cases but no advisory opinions. In all these cases he appended two joint declarations, two separate opinions, and two dissenting opinions. His dissent appended to the 1966 judgment in the South West Africa case may perhaps be described his best of all his individual opinions and without doubt his greatest contribution to the development of human rights law. He was a passionate **champion of natural law school** and **stood staunchly for the 'sociological or teleological' method** of interpretation, in contrast with strict juristic formalism.[37] This was, according to him an 'attitude of interpretation', known as a method of 'libre recherche' or 'Freirecht', mainly in civil-law countries, which has been since long emancipating judges from the rigid interpretation of written laws and emphasizing the creative role in their judicial activities.[38] In pronouncing against South Africa for its government's violations committed against Mandate provisions particularly its policy of apartheid, Judge Tanaka strongly recognized that the 'social and individual necessity constitutes

[34] South West Africa, ICJ Reports, 1966, p 325–26.

[35] AP Vijapur, *The United Nations at Fifty: Studies in Human Rights* (New Delhi, South Asian Publishers, 1996) 58.

[36] MCR Craven, *The International Covenant on Economic, Social, and Cultural Rights: A Perspective on its Development* (Oxford, Clarendon Press, 1995) 155. For the relevant text for Judge Tanaka's dissent see South West Africa Cases *(Ethiopia v South Africa* and *Liberia v South Africa*), Judgment on Second Phase, Dissenting Opinion of Judge Tanaka, ICJ Reports, 1966, pp 284–316.

[37] ICJ Reports, 1966, p 276.

[38] *Ibid*, p 278.

one of the guiding factors for the development of law by the way of interpretation as well as legislation.'[39]

Answering to the Court's opinion that the Applicants' claims are, on the ground of the lack of any legal right or interests in the dispute, to be rejected, Judge Tanaka wrote:

> There is no reason why an immaterial, intangible interest, particularly one inspired by the lofty humanitarian idea of a 'sacred interest of civilization' cannot be called 'interest' . . .. The historical development of law demonstrates the continual process of the cultural enrichment of the legal order by taking into consideration values or interests which had previously been excluded from the sphere of law . . .. Each Member of a human society—whether domestic or international—is interested in the realization of social justice and humanitarian ideas. The State which belongs as a member to an international organization incorporating such ideas must necessarily be interested. So far as the interest in this case affects the rights and obligations of a State, it may be called a legal interest.[40]

Judge Tanaka herewith criticizes the Court's narrow conception and interpretation of the notion of legal interest. His healthy and realistic activism reflects in the broad interpretation of the concept of legal interest taking into consideration the post world war developments of human rights and such humanitarian developments ideas which, according to him, are the concern of all States and individuals.

The Applicants in this case contended the existence of a norm or standards which prohibit the practice of apartheid. The Respondent, however, denied the existence of such a norm or standard to prohibit the practice of apartheid. Judge Tanaka saw the problem as: 'The question here is whether a legal norm on equality before the law exists in the international sphere and whether it has a binding power upon the Respondent's conduct in carrying out its obligations as Mandatory'. Before setting the context to examine the principle Judge Tanaka found it imperative to clarify the meaning of the words 'international norm or standards'. Regarding non-discrimination, his clarification about the matter forms clear and precise definition of the matter in the following words: 'What is meant by "international norm or standards" can be understood as being related to the principle of equality before the law.'[41] Judge Tanaka, by establishing this link of a so-called 'policy' of apartheid with a 'principle' of law, gave a developmental direction to the law of human rights, which reflects in the thinking of Dworkin.

It seems that Judge Tanaka revisited in Dworkin's 'Taking Rights Seriously'. One might recall that Dworkin's celebrated book '*Taking Rights seriously*' which had appeared six years after the delivery of the 1966 judgment of the International Court of Justice clearly reflects, though Dworkin does not make any reference either to Judge Tanaka or to the *South West Africa* cases, Tanaka's reasoning in his greater part of the book but particularly in his distinction between 'rules,

[39] *Ibid*, p 277.
[40] South West Africa, ICJ Reports, 1966, pp 252–53.
[41] *Ibid*, p 287.

principles, and policies' and his 'theory of hard cases'. His following two remarks, in particular, are worthy of taking note:

> I call a 'policy' that kind of standard that sets a goal to be reached, generally an improvement in some economic, political, or social feature of the community (though some goals are negative, in that they stipulate that some present feature is to be protected from adverse change). I call a 'principle' a standard that is to be observed, not because it will advance or secure an economic, political, or social situation deemed desirable, but because it is a requirement of justice or fairness or some other dimension of morality.[42]
>
> Arguments of policy justify a political decision by showing that the decision advances or protects some collective goal of the community as a whole. The arguments in favour of a subsidy for aircraft manufacturers, that the subsidy will protect national defence, is an argument of policy. Arguments of principle justify a political decision by showing that the decision respects or secures some individual or group right. The argument in favour of anti-discrimination statutes, that a minority has a right to equal respect and concern, is an argument of principle . . . . In the subsidy case we might say that the rights conferred are generated by policy and qualified by principle; in the anti-discrimination case they are generated by principles and qualified by policy.[43]

When putting together the sense conveyed by Judge Tanaka in his words 'policy', 'principle' and 'standards' throughout his dissenting opinion and then comparing that sense conveyed in the same words used by Dworkin it would reveal a matching of two juridical minds.

An international judge at the bench of the International Court of Justice, or at any other international tribunal, particularly when the tribunal established under the auspices of the United Nations, must not forget that his judicial conscience and juridical consciousness belong first and foremost to a time and world which have come into existence with the birth of the United Nations whose jurisdiction extends to 'We, the peoples of the United Nations.' A judge fails in delivering the right judgment only when he fails in his reasoning which makes him take law and facts from particular to general and from general to more general until he can see them in their vastly universal form. Those whose thinking is caught up in narrow procedural circles, and are not broadly philosophical and profoundly historical in their bend of mind and attitude, are prone to make decisions which might do injustice to a given party and situation and prove wrong at a later date when law and facts are weighed in a better and greater rationalization of intellectual depth. In any interpretation of human rights law, an international judge should first set the greatest possible global framework of available legal documents, constantly reminding the purposes they are meant to achieve and serve, the UN charter and its human rights provisions for instance, and then try to establish link of the issues and instruments, contended or contested, and weighting and reasoning out the law and facts available, jogging his conscience and consciousness hard enough, trying to find the integral link between the hierarchy of norms and instruments on

[42] R Dworkin, *Taking Rights Seriously* (Cambridge, MA, Harvard University Press, 1977) 22.
[43] *Ibid*, pp 82–83.

the one hand and constantly searching for the befitting principle underlying the acts and conduct associated with law and facts, and within that widest possible context taking its reasoning from particular to general and from general to more general and from more general to universal. Judge Tanaka continues and mentions that the question is whether the principle of equality before the law can find its place among the sources of international law which are referred to in Article 38, paragraph 1[44] of the Court's Statute. This 'question is intimately related to the essence and nature of fundamental human rights'.[45] Judge Tanaka here reminded the Court that the promotion and encouragement of respect for human rights, under Article 1, paragraph 3 of the Charter of United Nations, constitute one of the *purposes* of the United Nations and therein the principle of equality before the law occupies the most important part. This principle, according to the Applicants' view, as Judge Tanaka also agrees, is antithetical to the policy of apartheid.

Judge Tanaka then proceeded to examine one by one the sources of international law enumerated by the above-mentioned provision of the Court's Statute. Before we proceed further in order to know how Judge Tanaka examines all the sources of international law, it would be in order to know three things about his judicial philosophy. First, according to him: 'We . . . must recognize that social and individual necessity constitutes one of the guiding factors for the development of law by the way of interpretation as well as legislation'.[46] Second, about the legislative role of judges he thinks:

> Of course, judges declare law, but they do not function automatically. We cannot deny the possibility of some degree of creative element in their judicial activities. What is not permitted to judges, is to establish law independently of an existing legal system, institution or norm. What is permitted to them is to declare what can be logically inferred from the raison d'être of a legal system, legal institution or norm. In the latter case the lacuna in the intent of legislation or parties can be filled . . .. These kinds of activities of judges are not very far from those of legislators.[47]

And third, his natural law philosophy about human rights:

> Human rights have always existed with the human being. They existed independently of, and before, the State . . .. If a law exists independently of the will of the State and,

[44] ICJ Reports 1966, p 287. Article 38, para 1, of the Court's Statute reads:

The Court, whose function is to decide in accordance with international law such disputes as are submitted to it, shall apply:

(a) international conventions, whether general or particular, establishing rules expressly recognized by the contesting States;
(b) international custom, as evidence of a general practice accepted as law;
(c) the general principles of law recognized by civilized nations;
(d) subject to the provisions of Article 59, judicial decisions and the teachings of the most highly qualified publicists of the various nations, as subsidiary means for the determination of rules of law.

[45] South West Africa, ICJ Reports, 1966, p 287.

[46] ICJ Reports, 1966, p 277.

[47] *Ibid*, p 278.

accordingly, cannot be abolished or modified even by its constitution, because it is deeply rooted in the conscience of mankind and of any reasonable man, it may be called 'natural law' in contrast to 'positive law'.[48]

Norm of Non-Discrimination is an Integral Part of All Conventional Law as it Flows from the UN Charter

Article 38, paragraph 1(a), of the Statute of the International Court of Justice authorizes the Court to apply international conventions, whether general or particular, establishing rules expressly recognized by the contesting States. During the course of development of international law, particularly in the 20th century, treaties have become a very important source of law. The importance of treaties lies in the fact they embody rules and norms which are binding on the States parties to them. Now Ethiopia and Liberia contending that the norm of non-discrimination exists and South Africa denying its existence, Judge Tanaka, touching first upon international conventions, including the UN Charter, noticed the then prevailing situation of July 1966 when the two human rights Covenants, the Covenant on Civil and Political Rights and the Covenant on Economic, Social and Cultural Rights were still to be adopted by the UN General Assembly only in December 1966 and what to say of their coming into force which was still ten years far from 1976 when the required number of ratifications were filed. Only the 1948 Universal Declaration of Human Rights was in existence but without being binding on its signatory States. He correctly described the situation as: 'Without doubt, under the present circumstances, the international protection of human rights and fundamental freedoms is very imperfect. The work of codification in this field of law has advanced little from the viewpoint of defining each human right and freedom' . . . yet, he opined that, 'the legislative imperfections in the definition of human rights and freedoms and the lack of mechanism for implementation, do not constitute a reason for denying their existence and the need for their legal protection'.[49] Seeing the law making character of international conventions, Tanaka at once proposed to analyse the UN Charter. He pointed out that the Charter provisions repeatedly emphasize the principle of equality before the law. One of the purposes of the Charter, according to its Article 1, paragraph 3, lies in 'promoting and encouraging respect for human rights and the fundamental freedoms for all without distinction as to race, sex language, or religion'. Article 13 of the Charter provides that the General Assembly shall initiate studies and make recommendations for the purpose of . . . promoting international co-operation in the economic, social, cultural, educational, and health fields and assisting in the realization of human rights and fundamental freedoms for all without distinction as to race, sex, language, or religion'. Articles 55(c) and 56 of the Charter provide for the promotion of 'Universal respect for, and observance of, human rights and

[48] ICJ Reports, 1966, p 273.
[49] South West Africa, ICJ Reports, 1966, pp 289–90.

fundamental freedoms for all without distinction as to race, sex, language, or religion'. Article 62 of the Charter empowers the Economic and Social Council of the United Nations that 'It may make recommendations for the purposes of promoting respect for, and observance of, human rights and fundamental freedoms for all.' Not only this, Article 76, (c) of the Charter prescribes for the International Trusteeship System, replacing the Mandate System of the League of Nations, that as one of his its 'basic objectives', in accordance with the purposes of the United Nations laid down in Article 1 of the Charter, is: 'to encourage respect for human rights and for fundamental freedoms for all without distinction as to race, sex, language, or religion, and to encourage recognition of the interdependence of the peoples of the world.

Now the question is that as the United Nations Charter contains a legal norm or standard of non-discrimination, are the Applicants, being parties to the Charter and referring to this norm, entitled to have recourse to the International Court of Justice under the jurisdictional clause of Article 7, paragraph 2, of the Mandate?[50] The respondent's position was that the mandate agreement did not stipulate equality before the law clause, and that this clause did not formally constitute a part of the mandate instrument. Tanaka rejected this view and opined that the equality principle, as an integral part of the United Nations Charter or as an independent source of general international law, can be directly applied to the Mandate either as constituting a kind of law of the Mandate *in sensu lato* or, at least in respect of standards, as a principle of interpretation of the mandate agreement. Hence, seeing the development of international law as per time, and therewith the provisions of the Mandate agreement as an integral part of that law, according to Judge Tanaka 'the dispute concerning the legality of apartheid comes within the field of the interpretation and application of the provisions of the Mandate stipulated in Article 7, paragraph 2, of the Mandate.'

After having established that the principle of equality is an integral part of the United Nations Charter, Judge Tanaka's teleological interpretation of laws concludes the following: 1) Respondent is a member State of the United Nations, hence bound by the Charter, 2) the Respondent is not only a UN member State but also a Mandatory, 3), hence, the Respondent is bound by the Charter not only as a member State but also as a Mandatory State, 4) the Charter being of a special type of international law or a law of the organized international community, must be applied to all matters which come within the purposes and competence of the United Nations, hence Mandate included. This way, Judge Tanaka asks the Court to come to the logic of the *unity of personality*. This principle of unity of personality, according to him, must govern both the conduct of the Respondent as a UN

[50] The text of Article 7, para 2, of Mandate for South West Africa (17 xii 1920) reads:

> The Mandatory agrees that, if any dispute whatever should arise between the MandatoryMember of the League of Nations relating to the interpretation or the application of the provisions of the Mandate, such dispute, if it cannot be settled by negotiation, shall be submitted to the Permanent Court of International Justice provided for by Article 14 of the Covenant of the League of Nations. (Source: ICJ Reports, 1962, p 488).

member State as well as its conduct as Mandatory, 'particularly in the matter of the protection and guarantee of human rights and freedoms.'[51] By this principal of unity of personality, and therewith establishing an hierarchical link between the UN Charter and other treaties, Judge Tanaka has created a legal criterion in the form of a guiding and binding principle of human rights which all States parties to the Charter are bound to follow. He puts it in these words:

> Well, those who pledge themselves to take action in co-operation with the United Nations in respect of the promotion of universal respect for, and observance of, human rights and fundamental freedoms, cannot violate, without contradiction, these rights and freedoms. How can one, on the one hand, preach respect for human rights to others and, on the other hand, disclaim for oneself the obligation to respect them. From the provisions of the Charter referring to human rights and fundamental freedoms it can be inferred that the legal obligation to respect human rights and fundamental freedoms is imposed on member States.

And, South African State is a UN Member State.

Seen in this light, the principle of equality being an integral part of the UN Charter, and the promotion of human rights being as one of the main purposes of the United Nations, no treaty, irrespective of its particular human rights character or any other character, can be interpreted in disregard to the principle of equality. In other words, all treaties and conventions, bilateral as well as multilateral, have the right to equality as an ever present element of human rights law as an integral part of their very letter and spirit, making the norm of non-discrimination as integral part of all conventional law as mentioned in Article 38, paragraph 1(a) of the Statute of the International Court of Justice. This brings human rights law at the heart of entire jurisprudence, national or international, *ratione personae*, *ratione materiae* as well as *ratione temporis*. A clear and profound thinking would reveal that there is no branch or type of law without its human rights connection, someway or another. For instance, an example as remote as the destruction of Iranian oil platforms by the United States missiles has an element associated with it and within itself the violation of the human right to development, and up to some extent even of the right to life as well.

Norm of Non-Discrimination is a Rule of International Customary Law

Generally speaking, the traditional international law prescribes that a custom is the frequent repetition of the same act by States. It grows up by conduct of States. Customs, therefore, are rules which evolve after a long historical process and are validly recognized by the international community through the habitual obedience of States and have, therefore, binding force in international law. The preliminary stage of customs is usages. Usages repeatedly followed by States become

[51] South West Africa, ICJ Reports, 1966, p 290.

customs. One single act is not sufficient to create a binding customary rule. It is the recurrence of an act which carries with it a conviction that the act has not been challenged by other States and has, therefore, been accepted as a customary rule of international law. For instance, there is a customary rule that the consent of the other State is to be sought before the appointment of an ambassador of one State to the other. The Applicants in this case enumerated the United Nations resolutions and declarations which condemn racial discrimination, segregation, separation and apartheid. They contended that the given resolutions and declarations were adopted by majority of States forming international community, giving them a binding force of international customary law. The Respondent however opposed the view.

Coming to the formation of a custom, and concerning the Applicant's contention attributing to the norm of non-discrimination or the non-separation the character of customary international law Judge Tanaka agreed that according to traditional international law, a general practice is the result of the repetition of individual acts of States constituting consensus in regard to a certain content of a rule of law. This process, however, according to him 'is going to change in adapting itself to changes in the way of international life. The custom formation, as he saw it, is no more limited to the frequent repetition in historical march of the same act by States. In the modern era of science and technology when the concepts of time and space have shrunk so much and the institutional development has also greatly taken place, he wanted to bring into light the role of the medium of international organizations in the formation of a custom. According to him: 'In the contemporary age of highly developed techniques of communication and information, the formation of a custom through the medium of international organizations is greatly facilitated and accelerated, the establishment of such a custom would require no more than one generation or even far less than that.' He further states that 'What is required for customary international law is the repetition of the same practice; accordingly, in this case resolutions, declarations, etc, on the same matter in the same, or diverse, organizations must take place repeatedly.' Within the context of this newly developing process at the international stage, he also saw the then 11 UN trust territories agreements, with the UN Member States behind them as a legal weight of practice, each of them containing a provision concerning the norm of official non-discrimination or non-separation on the basis of membership in a group or race, may be considered as contributions to the development of the universal acceptance of the norm of non-discrimination, in addition to the meaning which each provision possesses in each trusteeship agreement, by virtue of Article 38, paragraph 1(a), of the Statute. From all this process and development in the international community of States he conferred: 'we consider that the norm of non-discrimination or non-separation on the basis of race has become a rule of customary international law'.[52] By presenting this new and contemporary process of customs formation, Judge Tanaka has not only

[52] *Ibid*, pp 291–93.

developed a new technique to custom-legislate the greater part of human rights principles but at the same time enriched the international legislative process. Of international law. He has brought forward a fact highlighting that the method of the generation of customary international law, and therewith also customary human rights law, is in the stage of transformation. Its character of 'individualistic process' is fast changing into a 'collectivist process'. This may also be called a teleological process of customs generation as compared to the traditional perhaps positivistic process of customs formation. With the evolution of law and jurisprudence in general one cannot go on putting the new wines in old bottles. In early days, the practice, repetition, and *opinio juris sive necessitatis* were the ingredients of customary law. These ingredients could only be combined together in a very long and slow process extending over centuries. With the development of the United Nations, its principal organs and specialized agencies and other international institutions, in contemporary age, according to Judge Tanaka: 'A State, instead of pronouncing its view to a few States directly concerned, has the opportunity, through the medium of the organization, to declare its position to all members of the organization and to know immediately their reaction on the same matter.'[53] The processes of law making, hence customary law making included, must be seen in the new light of international life. States are not the only legal and political organizations. The medium of international organizations and their relevant role in the customs generation is the reality which Judge Tanaka has brought in the lime light within the context of the development of human rights law on non-discrimination, therewith enriching equally Article 38, paragraph 1(b), of the Court's Statute.

Norm of Non-Discrimination Recognized as General Principle of Law

Article 38, paragraph 1(c), entitles the ICJ to apply the general principles of law recognized by civilized nations. in deciding the international disputes. By general principles of law one generally construes principles of equity, justice and good conscience. General principles are not only of theoretical importance but they are to be resorted to in filling the gaps in law. The Applicants referred to this source of law not only as an independent source for the justification of the norm of non-discrimination but also as a supplement and reinforcement of their other arguments to demonstrate their theory. Judge Tanaka undertook to examine whether the legal norm of non-discrimination or non-separation, denying the practice of apartheid, can be recognized as a principle enunciated in Article 38, paragraph 1(c), of the Statute.

The expression 'General Principles' of law is not defined by the Court's Statue. Law textbooks have given its multiple interpretations, some very strict and others

[53] South West Africa, ICJ Reports, 1966, p 291.

very liberal. The strict adherents restrict the meaning of general principles of law only to private law principles or they see them as principles merely belonging procedural law. Among the liberals, Prof Bin Cheng, a well known international jurist, in his work on general principles of law, sees the jurisprudential gist of these principles as 'juridical truth'.[54] Another liberal, perhaps also most universal, Prof O'Connell, sees the general principles of law in their uniformity: 'Law is a spontaneous generation from the needs and aspiration of man in community. Though its specific details differ from time to time and from place to place, its basic principles are uniform because human nature in its essence is constant.'[55] The *travaux preparatoire* of Article 38, paragraph 1(c), of the Court's Statute enacted in 1920 also reveal that the President of the drafting Committee of Jurists, a Belgian jurist Baron Descamps, described general principles of law as '*la conscience juridique des peuples civilisés*'.[56] Judge Tanaka saw this concept as originating from natural law. It may also be remembered that there was a strong opposition to this natural law concept put forward by Baron Descamps. The opponents were strict positivists led by another member of the Committee of Jurists, an American jurist Mr Elihu Root. The final draft of Article 38, paragraph 1(c), was ultimately adopted as a compromise between two law school, natural law school led by the Belgian jurist and the positivist school led by the American jurist. In the present South West Africa cases, Judge Tanaka also defying the staunch narrow majority of positivists and judicial conservatives, brought the general principles of law as a source of international law and international human rights law to its rightfully interpreted place, the natural law school, while establishing the supremacy of natural law system of human rights. Prof Van Hoecke is also of the similar opinion that: 'human rights are increasingly playing . . . critical role. They are really functioning as a natural law system, even if they have become part of the positive law'.[57]

In view of the various interpretations of the 'general principles of law' Judge Tanaka expressed the view that the 'law' must be understood to embrace all branches of law, including municipal law, public law, constitutional and administrative law, private law, commercial law, substantive and procedural law, etc. Neither would he limit the provision of Article 38, paragraph 1(c), to certain basic principles of law such as the limitation of State sovereignty, third party judgment, limitation of the right to self-defence, *pacta sunt servanda*, respect for acquired rights, liability for unlawful harm to one's neighbour, the principle of good faith, etc. Even in defining the meaning of 'general principles of law', Judge Tanaka adopted a broadest possible approach. According to him the word 'general' may be understood to possess the same meaning as in the case of the '*general* theory of law', 'theory generale de *droit*', 'die *Allgemeine Rechtslehre*', namely common to all

[54] B Cheng, *General Principles of Law as Applied by International Courts and Tribunals* (Cambridge, Grotius, 1987) 24.

[55] DP O'Connell, *International Law*, 2nd edn, (London, Stevens & Sons, 1970) vol 1, p 1.

[56] Permanent Court of International Justice, Advisory Committee Jurists: Proces-Verbaux of the Proceedings of the Committee, 16 June–24 July 1920, 319.

[57] M van Hoecke, *Law as Communication* (Oxford, Hart Publishing, 2002) 168.

branches of law. He maintained that though the principles themselves are very extensive and can be interpreted to include not only the general theory of law, but the general theories of all branches of municipal law, as far as they are recognized by civilized nations, yet it can be established by comparative law studies that virtually all municipal legal systems of civilized nations recognize the presence of laws against racial discrimination and segregation. Judge Tanaka, placing the norm of non-discrimination in the broadest theoretical and juridical context, sees one major qualification needed to qualify the principle of equality and norm of non-discrimination as among the 'general principles' to be counted as sources of international law under Article 38, paragraph 1(c) of the Court's Statute, ie, 'whether the alleged norm of non-discrimination and non-separation as a kind of protection of human rights can be considered as recognized by civilized nations and included in the general principles of law.'[58] Step by step, first the greater generality of law as a whole and the the greater generality of the general theory of law as a whole and then the greater generality of the general principles of law, Judge Tanaka comes to maintain the position that:

> The principle of equality before the law, however, is stipulated in the list of human rights recognized by the municipal system of virtually every State no matter whether the form of government be republican or monarchical and in spite of any differences in the degree of precision of the relevant provisions. This principle has become an integral part of the constitutions of most of the civilized countries in the world.[59]

The manifestation of this recognition, however, is not just limited to the acts of legislation alone. It may well be manifested by the attitude of delegations of UN member States by their participation in resolutions, declarations, etc, against racial discrimination adopted by international organizations. It was so manifested in the past by the member States of the League of Nations and it has been since long so happening in the United Nations forum.

Equality at the Summit of Hierarchy of the System of Law

The principle of equality for Judge Tanaka is not only a universally recognized principle of law but it is at the apex of the legal system as a whole, hence, seen in the Kelsen's image of pure theory of law, the principle is the 'Grundnorm' of the legal system. In his own words: '. . . the *principle of equality* being in the nature of natural law and therefore of a supra-constitutional character, is placed *at the summit* of hierarchy of the system of law, and that all positive laws including the constitution shall be in the conformity with this principle.'[60]

Seen in this light, Judge Tanaka considers the right to equality as the fountain head of all human rights law. In his dissenting opinion during the course of con-

[58] South West Africa, ICJ Reports, 1966, p 299.
[59] *Ibid*, p 300.
[60] *Ibid*, p 306.

sidering the content of the principle of equality which he tried to apply to the question of apartheid, he had developed several different aspects of this principle. In examining this apex character given to this principle he tries to see the principle *vis-a-vis* other two fundamental principles of modern democracy, freedom and justice, respectively. The principle of equality is philosophically related to the concepts of freedom and justice, therefore, he considers, that the concepts of freedom and justice are the two corollaries of the principle of equality. Injustice and the conditions of servitude actually are the consequences of unequal treatment in law, hence discrimination on various accounts. In other words freedom and justice can exist only under the premise of the principle of equality.

Explaining its 'supra-constitutional character', Judge Tanaka expressed no doubts that the principle of equality is binding upon all administrative and judicial organs but he himself raised a question whether legislatures have immunity from this binding nature of the principle. Posing a question to himself, he clarified the doubt in its apt and instant answer in this way:

> Then what about the legislative power? Under the constitutions which express this principle in form such as 'all citizens are equal before the law', there may be doubt whether or not the legislators also are bound by the principle of equality . . .. They are bound not only in exercising the ordinary legislative power but also the power to establish the constitution.[61]

Judge Tanaka here revived and injected into the principle of equality the 17th century judicial spirit of the English Chief Justice, Sir Edward Coke, who, quoting Bracton, affirmed that even a King is under God and Law.[62]

Judge Tanaka's individual opinion of 1966 seems reincarnated in Dworkin's classic work *Taking Rights Seriously* (1977) in which he opines about the principle of equality in these words: 'our institutions about justice presupposes not only that people have rights that one right among these is fundamental and even axiomatic. *This most fundamental of rights is a distinct conception of the right to equality*, which I call the right to equal concern and respect.'[63] And this 'right to equal concern and respect' for the people of South West Africa is all what Judge Tanaka has treated to the utmost legal and philosophical depths in his individual opinion. Only difference being that Tanaka using the word *'treatment'* and Dworkin using the word *'concern'*.

In view of the two contrary standpoints of the Applicants and the Respondent—Applicants who condemned the policy of apartheid as illegal and the Respondent who maintained that apartheid was a neutral policy as a means to achieve a particular end—Judge Tanaka felt that although the existence of the principle of equal

[61] ICJ Reports, 1966, p 306.

[62] It was Sir Edward Coke's celebrated admonition to King James I and his pretension of absolute Royal Prerogative powers that Sir Edward quoted Bracton in the Case of Prohibitions; see E McWhinney, *The International Court of Justice and the Western Tradition of International Law* (Dordrecht, Martinus Nijhoff, 1987) pp 2, 17 and 123.

[63] R Dworkin, *Taking Rights Seriously* (Cambridge, MA, Harvard University Press, 1977) 181–82.

treatment is universally recognized but as for the content of this principle is concerned it was not very clear. In clarifying the content of this principle he saw its working twofold: a) the principle is what is equal is to be treated equally and what is different is to be treated differently, namely proportionately to the factual difference. In elaborating this further he found that: a) the most fundamental point in the equality principle is that all human beings as persons have an equal value in themselves; they are the aim itself and not means for others, b) equality before law cannot be absolute it has to be relative, ie, the principle does permit the different treatment of persons from the consideration of the differences of factual circumstances such as sex, age, language, religion, economic condition, education, etc, c) however, the necessity of different treatment can be justified only by the criterion of justice, ie, reasonableness.

In the particular case of apartheid, Judge Tanaka also found it necessary to define what is reasonable and what is not reasonable. Discrimination based upon race, colour and national or tribal origin, according to him was not considered reasonable and just. All these, he mentioned, do not constitute in themselves factors which can influence the rights and duties of people in the case of sex, age, language, religion, etc. If differentiation be required, he stated, it would be derived from the difference of language, religion custom, etc, not from the racial difference itself. Based on this analysis of the content of the principle of equality he reached his conclusion about the South African policy of apartheid in the following words: 'In the policy of apartheid the necessary logical and material link between difference itself and different treatment, which can justify such treatment in the case of sex, minorities, etc, does not exist . . .. Consequently, the practice of apartheid is fundamentally unreasonable and unjust'.[64]

It would not be an exaggeration to state that when reasoning about the principle of equality Tanaka seems to be clearly reflecting a forerunner of the two cardinal principles of John Rawls' '*A Theory of Justice*' (1971), appearing five years after Tanaka's individual opinion. Hence, I would treat below the development of the content of the principle of equality by Judge Tanaka, mainly in his own words, and putting Rawls' two cardinal principles within the ambit of these words.

In examining the principle of equality Judge Tanaka at the outset considers that 'it is philosophically related to the concepts of freedom and justice'. And, 'freedom can exist only under the premise of the equality principle'. He further mentions that 'all human beings are equal before the law and have equal opportunities without regard to religion, race, language, sex, social groups, etc.' The 'principle of equality constitutes one of the fundamental human rights and freedoms which are universal to all mankind.' Rawls first principle states: 'Each person is to have an equal right to the most extensive total system of equal basic liberties compatible with a similar system of liberty for all'. Equal opportunities of Tanaka and equal right of Rawls are forming one general principal of general equality before law for all persons in all walks of life, political, economic, social, etc. And both derive their

[64] ICJ Reports, 1966, p 314.

raison d'être from the concept of justice, which Tanaka mentioned as based on 'reasonableness' and Rawls mentions as based on 'fairness'.

On the other hand, Judge Tanaka says that: 'human beings, being endowed with individuality, living in different surroundings and circumstances are not alike, and they need in some aspects politically, legally and socially, different treatment'. Hence, he maintains:

> Different treatment must not be arbitrarily; it requires reasonableness, or must be inconformity with justice, as in the treatment of minorities, different treatment of the sexes regarding public conveniences, etc. In these cases, the differentiation is aimed at the protection of those concerned, and it is not detrimental and therefore not against their will.

On this aspect of reasonableness, Judge Tanaka brings forward two considerations:

> 1) one is the consideration whether or not the individual necessity exists to establish an exception to the general principle of equality before the law and equal opportunity. In this sense the necessity may be conceived as of the same nature as in the case of minorities' treaties of which the objectives are protective and beneficial

and 2) 'The other is the consideration whether the different treatment does or does not harm the sense of dignity of individual person'. And now if we come to the second cardinal principal of John Rawls, it reads: 'Social and economic inequalities are to be arranged so that they are both: (a) to the greatest benefit of the least advantaged, consisting with the just saving principle, and (b) attached to offices and positions open to all under conditions of fair equality of opportunity.'

Judge Tanaka's concept of 'different treatment' reflects in Rawls' concept of 'inequalities' and they both are of the same mind in their conceptions of 'minorities' and 'least advantaged' in their basis of thinking 'not against their will' and 'just saving principle' respectively. The entire thinking of both is based on justice, for Tanaka it is based on 'reasonableness' and for Rawls it is based on 'fairness'.[65] One speaks of the protective and beneficial objectives for the minorities and the other for the benefit of the least advantaged. They both are obviously thinking the same thing in different terms and at different times, 1966 and 1971 respectively.

Judge Tanaka's General Observations on Human Rights

During the course of his dissenting opinion mainly analysing and developing the concept of equality and the norm of non-discrimination Judge Tanaka made several considerably pertinent observations on the general nature and character of human rights which are of immense value in understanding the human rights system in general and seeking clarification of international human rights law in particular. Of the numerous observations Judge Tanaka made the following few deserve full and special mention. I would add a comment or two on each of them.

[65] For Tanaka's citations see ICJ Reports, 1966, pp 304–13; and for Rawls' principles see J Rawls, *A Theory of Justice* (Oxford, OUP, 1971) 302.

OBSERVATION:

Well, those who pledge themselves to take action in co-operation with the United Nations in respect of the promotion of universal respect for, and observance of, human rights and fundamental freedom, cannot violate, without contradiction, these rights and freedoms. How can one on the one hand, preach respect for human rights to others and, on the other hand, disclaim for oneself the obligation to respect them? From the provisions of the Charter referring to human rights and fundamental freedoms it can be inferred that the legal obligation to respect human rights and fundamental freedoms is imposed on member States.[66]

COMMENTS:

With these words Judge Tanaka has developed the human rights law jurisdiction, *ratione personae* and *ratione materiae* to that extent that not a single UN member can claim immunity from its jurisdiction. The system of international law is generally based on the concept of consent. But, irrespective of the non-binding nature of the 1948 Universal Declaration of Human Rights and irrespective of whether or not a State member to the United Nations has either signed or ratified a certain human rights treaty of convention, acceptance of international human rights law which finds its origin in the Charter is an acceptance *ipso facto*. Double standards, preaching human rights to others and violating the same oneself, is a contradiction. By signing the UN Charter, one has pledged to respect human rights and fundamental freedoms in all forms everywhere.

OBSERVATION:

. . . the legislative imperfections in the definition of human rights and freedoms and the lack of mechanism for implementation do not constitute a reason for denying their existence and the need for their protection.[67]

COMMENTS:

The Respondent in this case contended that a legal norm or standards of non-discrimination did not constitute a part of the Mandate system. Judge Tanaka found the legislative imperfection in a given system of human rights can now be pleaded as a defence. Human rights are universal and they exist despite any perfect legislation on them in existence. Such a defence argument was made before in the Tokyo and Nüremberg war crimes tribunals and they were not accepted. Human rights and fundamental freedoms have their origin in the considerations of humanity.

OBSERVATION:

. . . human rights which require protection are the same; they are not the product of a particular juridical system in the hierarchy of the legal order, but the same human rights

[66] ICJ Reports, 1966, p 289.
[67] *Ibid*, p 290.

must be recognized, respected and protected everywhere man goes. The uniformity of national laws on the protection of human rights is not derived, as in the cases of the law of contracts and commercial and maritime transactions, from considerations of expediency by the legislative organs or from the creative power of the custom of a community, but it already exists in spite of its more-or-less vague form. This is of nature *jus naturale* in roman law.[68]

COMMENTS:

Judge Tanaka sees here the source of human rights in natural law, hence considering human rights law as a natural law system. He compares human rights with *jus gentium* which is developing into a World Law or a Common Law of Mankind as Prof Jenks mentioned in his book Common Law of Mankind. Human rights law is that branch of law, national as well as international, which has its existence in the humanitarian side of humanity, and which has bearing on all other branches of law which may be described as human rights aspect of a given law of a given branch of law. Hence, there is an underlying humanitarian aspect associated with all kinds and branches of law. That aspect does not draw its existence from a legislature. On the contrary all legislatures and legislations draw their existence from this aspect of law. Human rights law, as a philosophy and a school of law, is not only rapidly becoming an important branch of law in all national and international legal systems but is shaping those systems and branches of law into a human rights law system anchored in humanitarian considerations, or natural law thinking, as a common element in all human relationships.

OBSERVATION:

The existence of human rights does not depend on the will of a State; neither internally on its law or any other legislative measure, nor internationally on treaty or custom, in which the express or tacit will of a State constitutes the essential element . . .. A State or States are not capable of creating human rights by law or by convention; they can only confirm their existence and give them protection. The role of the State is no more than declaratory. Human rights have always existed with the human being. They existed independently of, and before, the State.[69]

COMMENTS:

Here again Judge Tanaka puts human rights as principles of law and human rights as a school of law above the State and above any legislative machinery of a State or States. They are there to be part of the jurisprudence and shape the norms and forms of a given legal system and to be shaped by any legal system or its law maker. The system or the State(s) concerned are to declare them and confirm their existence as binding principles of law.

[68] *Ibid*, p 296.
[69] *Ibid*, p 297.

OBSERVATION:

> If a law exists independently of the will of the State and, accordingly, cannot be abolished or modified even by its constitution, because it is deeply rooted in the conscience of mankind and of any reasonable man, it may be called 'natural law' in contrast to 'positive law'. . .. Provisions of the constitutions of some countries characterize fundamental human rights and freedoms as 'inalienable', 'sacred', 'eternal', 'inviolate', etc. Therefore, the guarantee of fundamental human rights and freedoms possesses a super-constitutional significance.[70]

COMMENTS:

Judge Tanaka considers here human rights to belong to a category of law *jus cogens* as contrasted to *jus dispositivum.* Those who think that several of the human rights provisions in the human rights statutes, for instance two UN covenants of 1966, are already present in several State constitutions, hence are a part of positive law and derive their legal force from the State legislatures, this contrast between *jus cogens* and *jus dispositivum* would provide the clarification that even if there were no positive law enactments of human rights they would exist and be in force nevertheless. Their not having been enacted by State legislation would not mean their non-existence. They are, according to Judge Tanaka, above any constitution and their origin lies in the 'conscience of mankind'. This is revisit of Natural Law school in the individual opinion of a prominent former judge of the International Court of Justice.

Though every judge before entering his judicial office makes a solemn declaration that he or she would perform his or her duties and exercise his or her powers 'conscientiously', yet in no legal document I have seen the definition of the word 'conscience'. Human rights as a school of law, having its source in the conscience of humanity as a whole, is seemingly a school of legal thinking which would ultimately and gradually make positive law thinking to fade into the mists of legal history and deliver to coming generations a system and school of law which is universal in scope and conscientious in spirit, with the meaning of the word 'conscience' defined and developed.

VIII. Judge Jessup: Principle of Equal Rights is Universal and Apartheid is a Justiciable Issue

Judge Jessup (USA), described by Prof McWhinney as a perfect blend of positive law and natural law schools, and a judge well known for having a great respect for the Court, respectfully dissented not only from the legal reasoning and factual interpretations in the Court's judgement with a casting vote but also from its entire disposition. According to him the judgment having avoided a decision on

[70] ICJ Reports, 1966, p 298.

the fundamental issue of human rights—whether the policy or practice of apartheid in the mandated territory of South Africa is compatible with the discharge of 'sacred trust'—was a judgment 'completely unfounded in law'.[71]

Writing an exhaustive dissenting opinion, Judge Jessup greatly emphasized the universality of the principle of equality and equal rights. He mentioned:

> The virtual universally accepted description of other legal characteristics of this actual modern world is written in the Charter of the United Nations. It is a world in which 'friendly relations among nations' are to be 'based on respect for the principle of equal rights and self-determination of peoples', and in which there is to be international co-operation both in solving international problems 'of an economic, social, cultural, or humanitarian character', and 'in promoting and encouraging respect for human rights and fundamental freedoms for all without distinction as to race, sex, language or religion'. (*Cf* Articles 1, 55, 56, 73, and 76.) . . .. Since, as I have explained, I believe the judicial task of the Court in interpreting Article 2 of the Mandate, is to be performed by applying objective standards—as, in other contexts, courts both international have done—. . . the standard to be applied by the Court must be of the contemporary international community.[72]

Here Judge Jessup is obviously speaking against the judicial restraint and tough conservative ideologies adopted by the Court in not adjudicating upon the judicial issue of apartheid. Seeing the matter in the contemporary light of the prevailing and progressing ideologies and standards of human rights, Judge Jessup concludes that 'the task of passing upon the Applicants' third submission which asserts that the practice of *apartheid* is in violation of the Mandatory's obligations as stated in Article 2 of the Mandate and Article 22 of the Covenant of the League of Nations, is a justiciable issue, not just a political situation.'[73] It is further adding the legal weight to the concept of *apartheid*, considered by the government of South Africa as a domestic policy.

Prof McWhinney has best described the historical value of Judge Jessup's dissenting opinion in the jurisprudence of human rights:

> History may well record that the American member of the Court, Judge Philip Jessup, more correctly sensed the 'winds of change' in Africa and the general movement of world history when, in his dissenting opinion, he refused to evade the substantive issue of the legality or otherwise of governmentally-practised racial differentiation or discrimination at international law. In categorizing the World Court majority position as 'completely unfounded in law,' Judge Jessup insisted that international law should not be treated as an outdated collection of dead rules, from some bygone era of world history; but that 'the standard to be applied by the Court must take account of the views and attitudes of the contemporary international community.[74]

[71] *Ibid*, p 325.

[72] South West Africa, ICJ Reports, 1966, pp 440–41.

[73] *Ibid*, p 442.

[74] E McWhinney, 'The Changing United Nations Constitutionalism: New Arenas and New Techniques for International Law Making' (1967) 5 *Canadian Yearbook of International Law* 68, 78–79.

Here Judge Jessup demonstrates not only a healthy blend of positive and natural law, but equally a workable union of *law as rules* and *law as process*, the union typically characterising the jurisprudence of human rights worldwide.

IX. Judge Padilla Nervo: The Principle of Non-Discrimination and Obligation to Promote Respect for Human Rights are Internationally Recognized in Most Solemn Form

Judge Padilla Nervo (Mexico) voted against the decision of the Court because he was convinced that it was established beyond any doubt that the Applicants had a substantive right and a legal interest in the subject-matter of their claim, the practice of apartheid. For him this case involving the issue of apartheid and the principle of equal rights was not an ordinary case but a *sui generis* case with far reaching implications of juridical, social and political nature.

Judge Padilla Nervo was not satisfied that the Court had dealt with just one single question, namely, whether the Applicants have a legal interest in the subject-matter of the claim. And, neither was he satisfied with the Court's finding that the Applicants cannot be considered to have established any legal right or interest appertaining to them in the subject-matter of the claim: and that, accordingly, the Court must decline to reject the claim of the Applicants. He did not share the view that the Court, in the interpretation and application of the provisions of the Mandate, is limited or restricted in its jurisdiction to the narrow term of Article 7, paragraph 2, and has not jurisdiction to consider the existence and applicability of a 'norm' and/or 'standard' of international conduct of non discrimination. Criticizing this narrow interpretation of the Court, Judge Padilla Nervo said:

> The Court cannot be indifferent to the fact that the Mandate operates under the conditions and circumstances of 1966, when the moral and legal conscience of the world, and the acts, decisions and attitudes of the organized international community, have created principles, and evolved rules of law which in 1920 were not so developed, or did not have such strong claims to recognition.

Further continuing, and giving a rightful recognition to a reputed international jurist, he cited Prof Jenks' words that 'the principle of non-discrimination has been recognized internationally in most solemn form'.[75]

Judge Padilla Nervo maintained that the Court must interpret and apply law taking into consideration the prevailing conditions and circumstances created by several international legal instruments since 1920. Since the far away time when the Mandate was drafted, he stressed that the international community has enacted important instruments, such as, the Charter of the United Nations, the

[75] ICJ Reports, 1966, p 467.

Constitution of the International Labour Organization, the Universal Declaration of Human Rights, the Declaration of Elimination of All Forms of Racial Discrimination, and numerous resolutions of the General Assembly and Security Council. All these, according to him, had bearing on the *South West Africa* cases for the interpretation and application of the provisions of the Mandate. The Court, he opined, must keep all these in mind, for, according to him 'All these instruments confirm the obligation to promote respect for human rights'.[76]

Stressing on the legislative role of the Court, Judge Padilla Nervo mentioned: 'There are cases where—in the absence of customary law—it is permissible to apply rules and standards arising from certain principles of law above controversy. The principles enacted in the Charter of the United Nations are—beyond dispute—of this nature.'[77] He was also of the opinion that the resolutions of the General Assembly were of the consequence of the universal recognition of the principles consecrated in the Charter and of the international need to give those principles their intended and legitimate application in the practice of States. We may recall here that Article 38, paragraph 1(c), of the Court's Statute stipulates that the Court shall apply, among others, 'the general principles of law recognized by civilized nations'. This broad and teleological interpretation of Judge Padilla Nervo about the General Assembly resolutions, which are generally considered as not legally binding but just as recommendations, brings to the legal light a fact which carries weight when we come to the understanding that those resolutions are not legal documents in isolation bur are 'the consequence' of the 'principles consecrated in the Charter'. Hence, they are rooted in the Charter which is a universally recognized and binding legal document. According to Judge Padilla Nervo it is not only the States which are bound to observe the provisions of the Charter regarding its 'Purposes and Principles', but also the Court. The Court, being the principal judicial organ of the United Nations, and its Statute being an integral part of the Charter, is not only bound to observe the Charter provisions and principles but also must promote by its activities the aims and purposes of the United Nations, which includes promotion of human rights.

Several issues relating human rights, apartheid for instance in the given cases, are considered political. And this often is used as a strategy to escape the adjudication by a Court of law, as was done in the given cases by the government of South Africa. Judge Padilla Nervo elaborated on the relationship between 'political factors' and 'legal norms'. Referring to the resolutions passed by the General Assembly, he mentioned: 'The Court should also recognize those decisions as embodying reasonable and just interpretations of the Charter, from which has evolved international legal norms and/or standards, prohibiting racial discrimination and disregard for human rights and fundamental freedoms'. He continued: 'Many of the activities of the General Assembly and the Security Council . . . are in the nature of political events concerned with the maintenance of international

[76] *Ibid*, p 468.
[77] *Ibid*, p 468.

peace, which is also the concern of the Court, whose task is the pacific settlement of international disputes'. This way, he concludes that: 'From those activities and under the impact of political factors, new legal norms or standards emerge.' Examining this close interrelationship between the political and legal factors Judge Padilla Nervo makes a considerable contribution not only to the development of international human rights law but to the development of every branch of international law.

Fleming has perhaps best appreciated Judge Padilla Nervo's opinion and the issue of apartheid in the following words: 'Judge Padilla Nervo struck at the majority opinion with conciseness and vigour. He pointed to the time, effort and expense that the Court and the parties had expended in studying '. . . the most explosive issue of the post-war world . . . "apartheid".'[78]

X. Judge Wellington Koo: A Nation is a Developed Nation only if all its Citizens are Treated on the Basis of Equality before the Law

Judge Wellington Koo (China), unable to concur with the 1966 Judgment of the Court, and maintaining the Applicants do have the substantive right in the observance by the Respondent of all its obligations towards the inhabitants of South West Africa, saw the question of apartheid within the context of one of the two cardinal principles of the mandates system, namely 1) the principle of the sacred trust of civilization, and 2) the principle of international accountability.

The first principle, he drew from the wording of Article 22, paragraph 1, of the League Covenant, which provided: 'the principle that the well-being and development of such peoples form a sacred trust of civilization'. Manifestly, according to Judge Wellington Koo, it was consideration of this basis principle of the sacred trust of civilization which accounts for the fact that the very first obligation of the Respondent, the Mandatory, is stated in the second paragraph of Article 2 of the mandate agreement as follows: 'The Mandatory shall promote to the utmost the material and moral well-being and the social progress of the inhabitants of the territory subject to the present mandate.' The policy of apartheid, seen in the light of this primary obligation under the above principle, consecrates an 'unjustifiable principle of discrimination'. And that applied to the life, work, travel and residence of the non-white population in the territory of South West Africa. It was enforced in matters relating, for instance, the ownership of land in the so-called Police Zone, mining and the mining industry, employment in the Railways and Harbours Administration vocational training, education, etc. This policy of apartheid or separate development he found not compatible with the basic prin-

[78] B Flemming, 'South West Africa Cases: *Ethiopia v South Africa*; *Liberia v South Africa: Second Phase*' (1967) 5 *Canadian Yearbook of International Law* 241.

ciple of the 'sacred trust of civilization'. From the ill effects and general detriment produced by the South African policy of apartheid Judge Wellington Koo developed a principle which can be applied to any nation or society to earn one of the necessary qualifications to be entitled to the rank of a developed nation. In his words:

> It is a self-evident truth that a whole consists of its parts and the parts make up the whole. Any nation, community or society is made of its individual members. It can be a contented, progressive and developed nation or community or society only when the mass of its individual members enjoy well-being and achieve progress and advancement on the basis of equality before the law. The individuals' dissatisfaction and detriment arising from their discriminatory treatment by law inevitably produce adverse effects, however marginal, on the collectivity.[79]

The second cardinal principle of the mandate system, according to him was the principle of international accountability for the performance of the sacred trust. He saw it broadly sanctioned by paragraphs 7, 8 and 9 of Article 22 of the League Covenant and more concretely by the provisions of Article 6 and 7 of the mandate agreement. He at great length in his dissenting opinion demonstrated the failure of the government of South Africa to comply with these provisions and hence its failure towards international accountability for the performance of sacred trust.

The above principles, though developed and applied in the context of these two joint *South West Africa* cases to the mandates system, no doubt equally constitute a fundamental feature of the present international human rights system. Human rights are indeed sacred trust of civilization and all States are internationally accountable for the performance of this sacred trust.

XI. Judge Koretsky: Racial Discrimination an Issue of Vital Importance

'I can in no way concur in the present Judgment', this is how Judge Koretsky (former USSR) opened his dissenting opinion appended to the Judgment of 1966.

Reminding the Court of its following words in the reasoning part of the 1962 Judgment—'Protection of the material interests of the Members of their nations is of course included within its compass, but the well-being and development of the inhabitants of the mandated territory are not less important'[80]—Judge Koretsky sought to preserve the 1962 position of the Court. For him there were three things important in this regard. First, according to him, the Judgment has not only a binding force between the parties (Article 59 of the ICJ Statute), it is final (Article 60 of the Statute). Second, he found, being final, it is one may say final for the Court itself unless revised by the Court under the conditions and in

[79] ICJ Reports, 1966, p 234.

[80] Cited from ICJ Reports, 1966, p 344.

accordance with the procedure prescribed in the Statute and the Rules of the Court.[81] Thirdly, he clarified the binding force of the reasoning part of a judgment of the Court. To those who think that in a judgment only its operative part but not the reasons for it has a binding force, he mentioned, that the operative part of a judgment seldom contains points of law. Considering that the 'reason', 'motives' and 'grounds' for a given judgment are its 'reasons part', he stated: 'The two parts of a judgment the operative part and the reasons do not "stand apart" one from another. Each of them is a constituent part of the judgment in its entirety'.[82]

Within this context, he saw that the Court itself, without any question being raised by the Respondent State in its final submissions, 'has now raised the question of "legal interest" and therewith reverted from the stage of merits, meant to deal with the vital issue of discrimination, to the stage of jurisdiction. Strongly rejecting the course the Court had taken, and therewith harming the cause of human rights and racial discrimination, Judge Koretsky stated as following:

> And thus the 'door' to the Court which was opened in 1962 to decide the dispute . . . the decision of which would have been of vital importance for the peoples of South West Africa and to peoples of other countries where an official policy of racial discrimination still exists, was locked by the Court with the same key which had opened it in 1962.

Judge Koretsky found the policy of apartheid inconsistent with the League Covenant and with the 'purpose and principles' of the Mandate. Hence, he concluded that the Applicants' right to apply to the Court to seeing to it trough judicial process that the sacred trust of civilization created by the Mandate is not violated was a right of judicial initiative. In his own words: 'This right is a right of judicial initiative, which one might compare *mutatis mutandis* with legislative initiative.' Therewith, Judge Koretsky put the vital matter of racial jurisdiction in any State a concern of all States.

XII. Judge Mbanefo's Dynamic Interpretation: Mandate and Apartheid

Judge Mbanefo (Nigeria), also among the dissenting judges, wrote in much the same spirit, if not the form. The dynamic, teleological and benevolently liberal approach of Mbanefo reflects from his dissatisfaction with the way the Court interpreted the mandates system and declined to adjudicate upon the issue of *apartheid*.

Not accepting the Court's narrow positivistic off the point interpretation of the system of mandates he first put the matter in a much teleological perspective:

> I feel rather unhappy about the Court's analysis of the mandates system. It pays little attention to the *ideals* of the Mandate and devotes a disproportionate amount of space

[81] Cited from ICJ Reports, 1966, p 240.

[82] *Ibid*, p 241.

> to details. The approach, if I may be permitted to draw an analogy, is like that of an artist who, perhaps unconsciously, has distorted the appearance of a building by over-emphasizing details of sections of it. The emphasis, it seems to me, should be on the appearance and framework and not on the components, some of which might not be necessary to support or characterize the building.[83]

Secondly, placing the ideals of the mandates system at the centre Judge Mbanefo reminded the Court that the responsibility of the Mandatory was 'to promote to the utmost the material and moral well being and the social progress of the inhabitants of the territory'.[84] It is in this way that Judge Mbanefo wanted the Court to judge any action of the Respondent.

And finally, following this up, with this line of interpretation, emphasizing on the *ideals* and *teleological-natural context*, Judge Mbaneffo found that the 'policy of *apartheid inherently incompatible with the mandate* obligations of the respondent and the Respondent by practising apartheid has violated its obligations'[85] under the Mandate.

This way, refusing to draw distinction between law and politics, emphasizing on the teleological and natural elements involved in the policy of apartheid and the system of mandates, Judge Mbanefo contributed a dynamic approach of interpretation conductive to the promotion and prevention of human rights.

XIII. Judge Forster's Bold Teleological-Sociological-Natural Interpretation of Law Condemns Apartheid

Judge Forster also like all other dissenting judges highly emphasized in his dissenting opinion the '*purpose*' of the mandates system.

Citing from the Mandate's provisions, the system as he saw had 'no other purpose' than 'to promote to the utmost the material and moral well-being and the social progress of the inhabitants of the territory'.[86] And this system as 'sacred trust of civilization', was created neither for the benefit of the Mandator nor the Mandatory, but for the people of South West Africa. With his purpose based teleological-sociological approach he proceeded to refute the Court's argument that it should not consider 'moral' questions when interpreting a legal instrument. Linking natural law conception with his starting teleological-sociological approach, he made a bold assertion condemning apartheid in the strongest possible terms:

[83] *Ibid*, p 490.
[84] *Ibid*, p 489.
[85] *Ibid*, p 490.
[86] *Ibid*, p 479.

> It is not playing politics or taking into account only ethical or humanitarian ideals to ascertain whether the Mandatory's policies are a breach of the provisions of the Mandate, which is the subject-matter of the dispute; for a Court seised of a breach of obligations under the Mandate is competent to appraise all the methods used in the application of the Mandate, including the political methods. The Court would be within its powers in declaring whether or not the policy of apartheid on which the laws and regulations applied in the Mandated Territory of South West Africa are based is conductive to the purpose laid down in the second paragraph of Article 2 of the Mandate. In fact by now the Court is the only body which can do so, since the Mandatory has obstinately declined to accept any international supervision.[87]

The legal architect with an amazing blend of teleological-sociological-natural approach to interpretation of a legal instrument brought into its rightful play the moral and social purpose of the Mandate and condemned the policy of apartheid with an astonishing legal force. Judge Forster's forceful assertion, while also refusing to draw distinctions between law and politics, made a lasting contribution to the jurisprudence of human rights by his opinion that when human rights issues as grave as of apartheid are under adjudication the Court is competent to appraise all methods, including the political ones. It creates an awareness in juridical circles that if there are any branches of law in the grand jurisdiction of international law where lines between law and politics are very thin, the law of human rights stands conspicuous.

XIV. Postlude: Violation of Human Rights Law Led to Formation of Human Rights Law

The two joint cases of *South West Africa*, both centred on the question of *apartheid* at large and the norm of *non-discrimination*, had marathon-size volumes of pleadings. The cases occupied the full Court for a span of five years and eight months. The result was two lengthy judgments of 1962 and 1966, the former with votes 8 to 7 and pages 346 and the latter with a tie-breaking casting vote of the Court's President and pages 500. Beating all previous records of the length of judgment, only to undo in 1966 what the Court did in 1962. The final ruling not only 'represented a *watershed* decision for the Court'[88] but also became known as 'politically most controversial'[89] judgment delivered by the Court ever.

[87] Cited from ICJ Reports, 1966, p 481.

[88] E McWhinney, *The International Court of Justice and the Western Tradition of International Law* (Dordrecht, Martinus Nijhoff, 1987) 68.

[89] E McWhinney, *The World Court and the Contemporary International Law-Making Process* (Alphen aan den Rijn, Netherlands, Sijthoff & Noordhoff, 1979) 17. Prof McWhinney writes: 'The International Court of Justice's judgment in 1966 in South West Africa, Second Phase, is no doubt the politically most controversial opinion rendered by the present Court or by its predecessor, the old Permanent Court of International Justice.' (P 17).

Judge Higgins, as noted earlier, regards the judgment as '*an aberration*'.[90] Though it is unfortunately true that the Court never reached the merits in this case as Judge Schwebel put it 'had given rise to exceptionally extended and detailed argument over human-rights issues posed by the practice of an overt and acute form of racial discrimination',[91] yet it was nevertheless fortunately proven up to the utmost mark what Judge Nagendra Singh had mentioned that:

> if the Court has ever omitted to refer to the concept of human rights or failed fully to deal with it in a case, the Members of Court have, at no point, failed to elaborate that aspect in their independent or separate supporting opinions, or even give vent to their thinking in dissenting opinions which fact is remarkable.[92]

In the 'aberration' judgment of 1966 seven judges—Judges Wellington Koo (Vice-President), Koretsky, Tanaka, Jessup, Padilla Nervo, Forster, and Mbanefo (judge *ad hoc*)—forming half the composition of the Court, not only boldly criticized the judgment in their dissenting opinions but all together, while considerably elaborating various aspects of human rights law, looked optimistically 'to the intelligence of a future day, when a later decision may possibly correct the error into which the dissenting judge believes the court to have been betrayed'.[93] And, the 'future day' did arrive soon when on 21 June 1971 the Court delivered its Advisory Opinion in *Namibia* case in which the Court departed from its narrow 'proceduralism' and 'tough conservatism' and took to judicial ideology of 'benevolent-liberalis', making the 1971 Opinion to go down in history as 'the most celebrated advisory opinion which deals with the concept of human rights in more ways than one'.[94]

Of the total number of 500 pages of the 1966 Judgment, 291 pages were written by these seven dissenting judges. The judgment itself was only 45 pages. The rest of the 164 pages were containing a Declaration by President Spender, and two separate opinions by Judge Morelli and Judge *ad hoc* van Wyk. All these three voting in favour of the judgment. Of the 291 pages of the dissenting judges, Judge Tanaka alone occupied 74 pages with its most extended individual opinion written so far contributing to the development of human rights law, forming part of the ICJ Reports.

Dealing with the principle of equality Judge Tanaka took the principle from a total scratch point and proposed to examine whether a legal norm on equality before the law exists in the international sphere. With his *naturalistic and teleological* approach he chose to examine and develop the principle within the framework

[90] R Higgins, 'The International Court of Justice and Africa' in E Yakpo and T Boumedra, (eds), *Liber Amicorum: Judge Mohammed Bedjaoui* (The Hague, Kluwer International Law, 1999) 343, 359.

[91] SM Schwebel, 'The Treatment of Human Rights and Aliens in the International Court of Justice' in V Lowe and M Fitzmaurice, (eds), *Fifty Years of the International Court of Justice: Essays in Honour of Sir Robert Jennings* (Cambridge, CUP, 1996) 327, 334.

[92] N Singh, *Enforcement of Human Rights in Peace and War and the Future of Humanity* (Dordrecht, Nijhoff, 1986) 28–29.

[93] ICJ Reports, 1966, Judge Jessup's Dissenting Opinion, pp 325–26.

[94] See N Singh, *Enforcement of Human Rights in Peace and War and the Future of Humanity* (Dordrecht, Nijhoff, 1986) 31.

of Article 38, paragraph 1, of the Statute of the International Court of Justice. In so doing he not only convincingly established that the principle of equality before the law has its proper place in all the three major sources of international law—international conventions, custom and the general principles—but also at the same time developed a new 'collectivistic process' of the generation of customary international law as compared to the traditional custom-making 'individualistic process'.[95] Citing him in great length, an eminent international lawyer, Prof Condorelli, described this new process highlighted by Judge Tanaka as 'a characteristic feature of our time'[96] According to Judge Tanaka the principle of equality before the law is that part of international law which is binding on all States even without any conventional obligation.

Of all the sources of international law Judge Tanaka gives 'primary position to the general principles of law'. And of all the general principles of law he puts the principle of equality at the summit of hierarchy of the system of law. He made a thorough analysis of the content of the principle of equality before the law. He agreed that the principle of equality does not mean absolute equality. In this regard, his most striking finding is that: 'Equality being a principle and different treatment an exception, those who refer to the different treatment must prove its raison d'être and its reasonableness'.[97]

Judge Tanaka demonstrated in great depth that the norm of non-discrimination has become a rule of customary international law.[98] Prof Craven finds it 'the most coherent discussion of the notion of discrimination'.[99]

Judge Tanaka elevates human rights to a 'super-constitutional significance'. Of all his observations on human rights in general, the following three make three arms forming a strong and sturdy legal triangle at the centre of which human rights law finds a most secure place in all human rights jurisprudence: First arm: Human rights are not the product of a particular juridical system in the hierarchy of the legal order, but the same human rights must be recognized and respected everywhere man goes. Second arm: States are not capable of creating human rights by law or by convention; they can only confirm their existence and give them protection. Third arm: Human Rights have always existed with human beings; they existed independently of, and before, the State.[100]

In a nutshell, perhaps Prof Vijapur seems to appreciate the development of the principle of equality by Judge Tanaka in a most apt way when he says: 'The dissenting opinion of Judge Tanaka in the *South West Africa* cases represents probably the best exposition of the concept of equality in the existing literature'. We may equally paraphrase the words of Prof Vijapur in appreciating the develop-

[95] ICJ Reports, 1966, pp 291–92;

[96] L Condorelli, 'Custom' in M Bedjaoui, (ed), *International Law: Achievements and Prospects* (Paris, UNESCO, 1991) 190.

[97] ICJ Reports, 1966, p 309.

[98] *Ibid*, pp 284–316.

[99] MCR Craven, *The International Covenant on Economic, Social, and Cultural Rights: A Perspective on its Development* (Oxford, Clarendon Press, 1995) 155.

[100] ICJ Reports, 1966, pp 295–98.

ment of human rights law in general, and the principle of equality in particular, and draw the conclusion that the dissenting opinion of Judge Tanaka in the South West Africa cases represents probably not only the best exposition of the concept of equality, in particular, in the existing literature, but equally the best exposition of the concept of human rights in general.

It is true that half (7) the Court's judges in 1966 had failed to examine such vital substantive questions as whether, in contemporary international law, the principles of equality of treatment of different races and non-discrimination had become general international norms by virtue of custom or the principles of the Charter of the United Nations; and, assuming a positive answer to this question, whether South Africa had, by introducing into the administration of South Africa not only the policy of apartheid, but also differential treatment between the various African tribes and racial groups, violated any international legal obligations. But it is equally true that equally half (7) the dissenting judges have taken upon themselves to compensate for the Court's failure by examining these human rights questions and thereby developing the international human rights law. Appreciating the value of these opinions treating the preceding 'substantive questions' of human rights, Friedmann considered them[101] as the 'expressions of opinion of high persuasive authority, and perhaps harbingers of further developments in international law.'

The marathon race of formalist-positivist interpretation v teleological-sociological interpretation of law in the South West Africa cases, and a tug of war between advocates of law as rules and law as process made Prof Pollock to conclude in his 1968 Prize Award Essay that: 'The law is, in short a phenomenon of the human (it is high time to acknowledge our debt to Hegel) Spirit'[102] Doubtless, it is more so when we speak about human rights law. Pollock continued to see this human Spirit in the image of human rights situation in 1966:

[101] WG Friedmann, 'The Jurisprudencial Implications of the South West Africa Cases' (1967) 6 *Columbia Journal of Transnational Law* 1.

[102] But what is human Spirit? And why Pollock writes it with a capital S? Different writers have differently described it in different words. But all are in quest of knowing the meaning of it. I firmly believe it is something static in all the dynamics of law. Judge Bedjaoui calls it 'the unvarying factor in human dignity'. See M Bedjaoui, *Preventive Diplomacy: Development, Education and Human Rights*, p 54). Judge Higgins says: 'I believe, profoundly in the universality of the human spirit' (see R Higgins, *Problems and Process: International Law and How We Use It* (Oxford, OUP, 1994) 97). Well-known 'Renaissance man of modern age', Prof Dewey also referred to this 'spirit'. Once US President William McKinley was addressing a mass of faculty and student at the University of Chicago. Prof John Dewey, then head of the department of philosophy, sat by Dr Julian Johnson. President McKinley made some remark about the educated young men of the country carrying the scientific spirit into all channels of social activity. Prof Dewey turned to Dr Johnson and said: 'that will never be done, until spirit shall vitalize the processes of science. Spirit is the soul of the universe.' See JP Johnson, *The Path of the Masters*, 15th edn, (Radha Soami Satsang Beas Beas, India, 1993) 35. Dr Johnson has described it in the profoundest philosophical-spiritual depths the meaning of the word 'Spirit' in his book. I may add that until the process of jurisprudence (the science of law) in general and the human rights law in particular is vitalized by the 'Spirit' we have neither known the real meaning of the word law nor the meaning of human and rights. The dissenting opinions in the South West Africa Second Phase Judgment, notably that of Tanaka and Jessup, are very much developing the law in that spirit and direction.

> What we can say about the legal Spirit at present is that there is an unresolved tension between the two basic sets of jurisprudential notions with which we are concerned. In terms of the central goals of our jurisprudential alternatives the human Spirit has not made up its collective mind about the relative importance of the sovereignty of the nation-state and the recognition of human rights and about which creates how much obligations.[103]

Just as the villain in a story and the opposition in a democratic parliamentary debate are by no means less important, or are rather equally important, in reaching the right end and the right decision, similarly the role of tough *judicial conservatism* as against *benevolent-liberalism* in these cases is by no means insignificant. They have given a tremendous amount of required friction and provocation to the *teleological and benevolent liberal judges* to do what they did in their dissenting opinions to develop and clarify *human rights law*, mainly the *principle of equality* and the *norm of non-discrimination*, centred around the then burning issue of *apartheid*. The overall contribution of the South West Africa cases, despite their multifarious judicial and jurisprudential tensions, to the development of human rights law may well be summarized in the following words: It is now well recorded in the history of the development of international law that the seven dissenting judges in the 1966 *South West Africa* cases judgment were in the right sense apostles of the promotion of human rights. They took upon them not to evade the substantive issues of equal treatment and racial discrimination. They went great length and took tremendous pains in writing their exhaustive dissenting opinions to untarnish the majority-judgment of the Court which had chosen to evade the human rights issues and stigmatise the Court with the *Dred Scott* label. Appreciating the *teleological or humanitarian approach* of the seven dissenting judges, and rejecting the *analytical-positivistic approach* adopted by the casting-vote-majority of seven judges Friedmann remarked: 'It is difficult to think of any contemporary jurisprudential treatise, many of them the work of eminent judges, and particularly of any modern study of the judicial process which has not rejected this approach as untenable in logic and disapproved by experience.'[104] They have demonstrated that the legal formalism and the tough conservatism do not go hand in hand with the progressive development of human rights law. On the contrary *benevolent liberalism* as judicial ideology and teleological-humanitarian interpretation are the orders of the day in the present era of human rights. They had insisted that international law cannot be treated as an outdated collection of dead rules from some bygone era of legal history, but law needs to be regarded as a process, a *process of legal decision making*. Mills of gods grind slow but they grind fine.

The Court's contribution to the development of human rights law is concerned the entire jurisprudence of the *South West Africa* joint cases which can

[103] AJ Pollock, 'The South West Africa Cases and the Jurisprudence of International Law' (1969) 23 *International Organization* Nr 1, 767–68.

[104] WG Friedmann, 'The Jurisprudencial Implications of the South West Africa Cases' (1967) 6 *Columbia Journal of Transnational Law* 1, 4–5.

in brief be compared to the two most important legal events in the United States of America where racial discrimination and violation of human rights against the black population formed a black page of legal history, the first one is the *Dread Scott* 1857 ruling of the US Supreme Court, which upheld the slavery in the United States, and the other is its outright repudiation by the US President Abraham Lincoln. The 1966 Judgement of the International Court of Justice is no less than the *Dread Scott v Stanford* case judgment and the dissenting opinions of seven judges, opposing the judgment and elaborating on the principle of equality and the concept of human rights, are in no less measure outright repudiation of the 1966 judgment. These dissenting judges had set trends for the future free from racial or any type of discrimination and violation of human rights. If the Civil War under the leadership of President Lincoln brought end to slavery in the United States with the passage of the Civil Rights Act of 1866 by the US Congress, the dissenting judges in the 1966 judgment not only '*marked the death-knell of the legal positivism and heralded a new, policy oriented approach to judicial decision-making of the Court*',[105] but equally highlighted the new trends and directions in the human rights law which resulted, like US Civil Rights Act 1866, in several international legislations outlawing apartheid and forbidding racial and several other types of discrimination. The utter disregard for the narrow majority judgment of *tough conservatism* and the greatest impact of the seven dissenting opinions of *benevolent liberalism* is evident from the fact that just three months after the delivery of 1966 judgment the UN *General Assembly adopted a Resolution on 26 October 1966 by which it terminated outright the Mandate* conferred on South Africa in respect of South West Africa, the historical victim of apartheid. Pollock has rightly remarked that 'by 1966, after the decision of the Court, the majority of the states in the United Nations could declare apartheid a crime against humanity and could unilaterally terminate the Mandate for South West Africa'.[106]

Further, it led to the signing of numerous international human rights instruments, such as two landmark Covenants of 1966 in general—1) International Covenant on Civil and Political Rights, 2) International Covenant on Economic, Social and Cultural Rights—and, concerning apartheid, the International Convention on the Suppression and Punishment of the Crime of Apartheid (1973) and the International Convention against Apartheid in Sports (1985) in particular. At last, on 17 June 1991 apartheid regime in the Republic of South Africa stood legally abolished with the repeal of the Population Registration Act of 1950, which was a cornerstone of apartheid. Today, it is widely accepted in all human rights law that the principle of equality and the norm of non-discrimination are forming part of customary international law. They are equally

[105] E McWhinney, *The International Court of Justice and the Western Tradition of International Law* (Dordrecht, Martinus Nijhoff, 1987) 129.

[106] AJ Pollock, 'The South West Africa Cases and the Jurisprudence of International Law' (1969) 23 *International Organization* Nr 1, 767, 785.

widely recognized as general principles of law. Several jurists, such as Schwelb, Brownlie and McKean, consider them as part of international *jus cogens.*[107] Therefore, if the 45 pages of the judgment of 1966 is a step backward in the history of the Court's human rights jurisprudence, its 291 pages of dissenting opinions stand as an extraordinary contribution to the development of human rights law, with its *stamp-mark influence on the international legislative process.* After all, the fact of the matter in jurisprudence is:

> Entre le législateur et le juge
> se noue une relation dynamique
> qui n'est pas à sens unique.[108]

[107] W McKean, *Equality and Discrimination under International Law* (Oxford, Clarendon Press, 1983) pp 227–84.

[108] F Rigaux, *La Loi des Juges* (Paris, Editions Odile Jacob, 1997) 246.

6

Barcelona Traction, Light and Power Co, Ltd (New Application: 1962) case (*Belgium v Spain*)[1] (1962–70)

I. Human Rights Run *Erga Omnes*

THIS CASE INVOLVED three States, Belgium, Spain and Canada. The Barcelona Traction, Light and Power Co Ltd, was incorporated in 1911 in Toronto (Canada) where it had its base. For the purpose of creating and developing an electric power production and distribution system in Catalonia (Spain) it formed a number of subsidiary companies, of which some had their registered offices in Canada and the others in Spain. In 1936 the subsidiary companies supplied the major of Catalonia's electricity requirements. According to the Belgian government, some years after the first world war Barcelona Traction's share capital came to be very largely held by Belgian nationals. The company was declared bankrupt subsequent to a proceeding company shareholders. On 23 September 1958, Belgium filed the case with the International Court of Justice against Spain in connection with the adjudication in Spain, in 1948. Belgium's Application stated that the company's share-capital belonged largely to Belgian nationals and claimed that the acts of organs of the Spanish State whereby the company had been declared bankrupt and liquidated were contrary to international law and that Spain, as responsible for the resultant damage, was under an obligation either to restore or to pay compensation for the liquidated assets.

[1] The composition of the Court in the Second Phase Judgment of Barcelona Traction case was: President Bustamante y Rivero; Vice-President Koretsky, Judges Sir Gerald Fitzmaurice, Tanaka, Jessup, Morelli, Padilla Nervo, Forster, Gros, Ammoun, Bengzon, Petrén, Lachs, Oneyama, Judghes *ad hoc* Armand-Ugon, and Riphagen (see ICJ Reports 1970, p 4).

Judges Petrén, Oneyama, and Lachs appended their Declarations to the Judgment of the Court (see ICJ Reports 1970, p 52); President Bustamante y Rivero, Judge Sir Gerald Fitzmaurice, Tanaka, Jessup, Morelli, Padilla Nervo, Gros and Ammoun appended their Separate Opinions to the Judgment of the Court; Judge *ad hoc* Riphagen appended a Dissenting Opinion to the Judgment of the Court (see ICJ Reports 1970, p 53).

Though Spain filed preliminary objections to the jurisdiction of the Court, Belgium voluntarily discontinued the first proceedings in 1961, hoping that the dispute could be settled by negotiations.

The negotiations bearing no results, Belgium filed a new Application on 19 June 1962. Belgium appeared before the Court to seek compensation for the damage claimed to have been caused to its nationals, shareholders in the Barcelona Traction. Spain was not the national State of the company; and submitted that the Belgian claim should be declared inadmissible or unfounded. Canada, though, had full legal right of protection in respect of the Barcelona Traction company but refused to appear before the Court. The Court, fully appreciating the importance of the legal problems raised by the allegation, which was at the root of the Belgian claim for reparation, concerning the *denial of justice* to its nationals allegedly by organs of Spanish State, stated in a Judgment delivered on 5 February 1970 that the possession by the Belgian Government of a right of protection is a prerequisite for the examination of these problems, and, found that Belgium had no *jus standi* to exercise diplomatic protection of its shareholders in a Canadian company in respect of measures taken against that company in Spain.[2]

The gist of the dispute in this case has been described by Judge Higgins in a capsule form: 'At issue, therefore, was the right of Belgium to exercise diplomatic protection of Belgian shareholders in a company which is a juristic entity incorporated in Canada'.[3]

Though the central issue in the Barcelona Traction case was the diplomatic protection of shareholders of a State's own nationals, the case became a landmark in the history of the development of human rights law by the revolutionizing concept of State obligations *erga omnes* developed by the Court, therewith strongly recognizing rights of human person in categorical terms[4] and putting human rights on the universal footing.

The Court in this case made important contribution to the development of human rights law by drawing distinction between a State's obligations towards another State and its obligations towards the international community. The Court argued:

> In particular, an essential distinction should be drawn between the obligations of a State towards the international community as a whole, and those arising *vis-a-vis* another State in the filed of diplomatic protection. By their very nature the former are the concern of all States. In view of the importance of the rights involved, all States can be held to have a legal interest in their protection; they are obligations *erga omnes*.[5]

By so making the State responsible towards the international community, the Court then defined what the obligations *erga omnes* might contain: 'Such obliga-

[2] *Barcelona Traction* case, ICJ Reports, 1970, p 51.

[3] R Higgins, 'Certain Aspects of the Barcelona Traction Case' (1971) 11 *Virginia Journal of International Law* 329.

[4] N Singh, *Enforcement of Human Rights in Peace and War and the Future of Humanity* (Dordrecht, Nijhoff, 1986) 29.

[5] *Barcelona Traction* case, ICJ Reports 1970, p 32.

tions derive, for example, in contemporary international law, from the outlawing of acts of aggression, and of genocide, as also from the principles and rules concerning the basic rights of the human person, including protection from slavery and racial discrimination.'[6]

The Court continued and further recognized that:

> Some of the corresponding rights of protection have entered into the body of general international law (*Reservations to the Convention on the Prevention and Punishment of the Crime of Genocide, Advisory Opinion, ICJ. Reports* 1951, p 23); others are conferred by international instruments of a universal or quasi-universal character.[7]

Furthermore, the Court declared that 'protection against *denial of justice*' should also be added to the above list of human rights.[8]

The concept of obligations *erga omnes* has became a popular *dictum* of the International Court of Justice.[9] The Court by developing the law in this case has clearly recognized three things: One, human rights are *erga omnes*; hence universal; [10] second, foreign nationals in a State are entitled for these rights; and third, a State may rightfully protest against another if the former's nationals are not getting rightful treatment in the latter's territory. Commenting on these contributions of the Court, Judge Schwebel writes:

> This is another holding of paramount importance for international law concerning human rights. By it, the Court has found that the rules concerning the basic rights of the human person are the concern of all States; that obligations flowing from these rights run *erga omnes*, that is, towards all States. Thus it follows that when one State protests that another is violating the basic human rights of the latter's own citizens the former State is not intervening in the latter's internal affairs; it rather is seeking to vindicate international obligations which run towards it as well as all other States.[11]

In his brilliant analytical study about the development of the International Covenant on Economic, Social, and Cultural Rights, Craven finds that in the

[6] *Ibid.*

[7] *Ibid.*

[8] *Ibid*, p 47.

[9] See two books: one by A de Hoogh, *Obligations Erga Omnes and International Crimes* (The Hague, Kluwer Law International, 1996); and the other by M Ragazzi, *The Concept of International Obligations Erga Omnes* (Oxford, OUP, 1997). Ragazzi provides an excellent work on the criteria for the identification of obligations *erga omnes*.

[10] Sieghart is of the opinion:

> The primary characteristic which distinguishes 'human' rights from other rights is their universality: according to the classic theory, they are said to 'inhere' in every human being by virtue of his humanity alone. It must necessarily follow that no particular feature or characteristic attaching to any individual, and which distinguishes him from others, can affecthis entitlement to his human rights, whether in degree or in kind, except where the instruments specifically provide for this for a clear and cogent reason—for example in restricting the right to vote to adults, or in requiring special protection for women and children.

P Siegart, *The International Law of Human Rights*, (1985) 75.

[11] SM Schwebel, 'Human Rights in the World Court' in RS Pathak and RP Dhokalia, (eds), *International Law in Transition: Essays in Memory of Judge Nagendra Singh* (Dordrecht, Martinus Nijhoff, 1992) 267, 285–86.

Barcelona Traction case the inclusion by the ICJ of 'the principles and rules concerning the basic rights of the human person including protection from slavery and racial discrimination' among the obligation of States *erga omnes*, is a clear development of Article 2, paragraph 2, of the Convention. Certainly, as a clear international test for discrimination in all fields, the Court's pronouncement provides a considerable relevance to the interpretation of this provision of the Convention.[12]

According to Professor Meron the quest for a hierarchy among international human rights continue unabated, despite the impressive challenge raised by Professor Weil to the notion of 'relative normativity' of international legal norms.[13] In answer to this quest and the question mark of Prof Weil, Prof Meron, referring to the Court's dictum of *erga omnes*, is of the view: 'The International Court of Justice gave currency to the idea of a hierarchy in the *Barcelona Traction* case in a famous dictum, by suggesting that "basic rights of the human person" ("droits fondamentaux de la personne humaine") create obligations *erga omnes*.'[14]

Given the emphasis that race, sex and religion have been accorded in the human rights law, it may be argued that in assessing the legitimacy of discriminatory treatment, actions based upon these grounds should be subject to a stricter scrutiny. The ICJ in this case has certainly, and appropriately, contributed by its *Barcelona Traction* case law that rules concerning racial discrimination have a force *erga omnes*.[15]

II. Enforcement of Human Rights

The Court in the *Barcelona Traction* case also dealt with the problem of enforcement of human rights. Pointing to a regional solution, the Court Stated:

> However, on the universal level, the instruments which embody human rights do not confer on States the capacity to protect the victim of infringements of such rights irrespective of their nationality. It is therefore still on the regional level that a solution to this problem had to be sought; thus, within the Council of Europe, of which Spain is not a member, the problem of admissibility encountered by the claim in the present case has been resolved by the European Convention on Human Rights, which entitles each State which is a party to the Convention to lodge a complaint against any other contracting State for violation of the Convention, irrespective of the nationality of the victim.[16]

[12] MCR Craven, *The International Covenant on Economic, Social, and Cultural Rights: A Perspective on its Development* (Oxford, Clarendon Press, 1995) 162–63.

[13] T Meron, *Human Rights Law-Making in the United Nations* (Oxford, Clarendon Press, 1986) 173. For Prof Weil's challenge Meron cites P Weil, 'Towards Relative Normativity in International Law' (1983) 77 *American Journal of International Law* 413.

[14] Meron, *ibid.*

[15] *Ibid*, p 176.

[16] *Barcelona Traction* Case, Judgment on Second Phase, ICJ Reports, 1970, p 47.

It is noteworthy here that some judges were not very happy with the regional solution provided by the Court. They were in favour of supporting the human rights more categorically than the Court has done in its judgement. Therefore, it evoked their separate opinions on this issue of the enforcement of human rights. Judge Morelli's own view, supporting human rights and their enforcement, reflected as follows:

> The conduct which international law renders incumbent upon a State with regard to the rights which the same State confers on foreign nationals within its own municipal order consists, in the first place, in the judicial protection of those rights. Any State which, having attributed certain rights to foreign nationals, prevents them from gaining access to the courts for the purpose of asserting those rights is guilty, in international law, of a *denial of justice.* In addition, international law lays upon a State, within certain limits and on certain conditions, the obligation to respect, in the conduct of its administrative or even legislative organs, the rights which the municipal legal order of the same State confers on foreign nationals. This is what is known as respecting the acquired rights of foreigners.[17]

Judge Morelli is here obviously subjecting the universal province of human rights and their enforceability. Judge Riphagen reflects the similar opinion, in a still stronger terms, recognizing the validity of human rights and their protection even in the customary law:

> . . . customary international law recognizes—in particular since the second world war—respect for fundamental human freedoms as an interest of the international community. In fact, even before and between the two World Wars the idea of the *protection of 'human rights'* by public international law was never absent from international decisions concerning the responsibility of States for the treatment of aliens. Here as in the protection of international commerce, it is not a matter of creating a common legal order determining the legal relationship between the public authorities and private persons or between private persons *inter se*, but of 'checking' the application of the municipal legal order in order to sanction the unlawful use of force, arbitrary *discrimination* and usurpation of jurisdiction, which violate a human being's *'right to existence'*. Here, as in the protection of international commerce, the different methods adopted by the municipal law of different countries are irrelevant to the attainment of the objectives of the rules of customary international law.[18]

In all clarity, Judge Riphagen has brought the idea of protection of human rights in retrospect and prospect therewith enhancing and enriching the notion.

[17] *Barcelona Traction* Case, Judgment on Second Phase, ICJ Reports, 1979, p 233.

[18] *Barcelona Traction* Case, Judgment on Second Phase, Dissenting Opinion of Judge Riphagen, ICJ Reports, 1970, p 338.

7

United States Diplomatic and Consular Staff in Tehran case (*USA v Iran*)[1] (1979–81)

I. Human Dignity and Diplomatic Immunity

MAN MUST TREAT man as befits man—be he or she a ruler or the ruled—for therein lies his human dignity. And similarly, sovereign State must treat sovereign State as befits sovereign State, for therein lies the stuff of its *superanus*, State dignity. The sense of cultivating and developing in oneself the value of human dignity and respecting the same of, and in, others is the greatest flower of human culture—be it a legal or political culture; be it a national or international culture; or be it a culture of East or the West. The innate worth of man is synonymous with his *superanus*; and the meaning of *superanus* in him individually as well as in State and international community collectively, of which he is an integral part, is unfolding day by day.

No matter how brute or vicious the type of culture in man or State at any given time, the awareness of at least some degree, occasionally even a tremendous display of it, of the value of human dignity has always remained alive in them is evident from the following old but very real story.

A historical military genius of antiquity, King Alexander the Great, at the end of his conquests reached India and fought with the army of the then king of Panjab, King Porus. It was only with great difficulty that the army of Alexander succeeded in defeating the army of Porus, who was captured. Porus was a very tall and majestic figure, whose courage and proud bearing made a great impression on the

[1] The composition of the Court in the Judgment of 24 May 1980 in the *Diplomatic and Consular Staff* case was: President Sir Humphrey Waldock; Vice-President Elias; Judges Forster, Gros, Lachs, Morozov, Nagendra Singh, Ruda, Mosler, Tarazi, Oda, Ago, El-Erian, Sette-Camara, and Baxter. (See ICJ Reports 1980, p 3).

Judge Lachs appended a Separate Opinion to the Judgment of the Court; Judges Morozov and Tarazi appended their Dissenting Opinions to the Judgment of the Court (see ICJ Reports 1980, p 46).

Macedonians; when brought before his conqueror he was found to have received nine wounds, and he could barely stand; but when Alexander asked him how he wished to be treated he boldly replied: '*As befits me—like a king!*' Alexander was so impressed by his captive that he restored him to his kingdom as a vassal and, on the retreat of his forces, left him in charge of the Panjab. Porus represented human dignity with dignity within the context of right of sovereign equality, and his wrongful conqueror, legislature, executive and judiciary all in one, even in those days of law-of-jungle, reciprocated a verdict of dignity based on the culture of human dignity.

This is a story of a dignified equal treatment of a king, for a king, and by a king; in other words: of a ruler, for a ruler and by a ruler. This is a manifestation of human dignity of the time, 326 BC, when the use of force was not only a great characteristic of the human culture of the day but was considered a great quality of the ruler. With the change of times change perceptions. The concept of Human dignity in the current legal culture of human rights not only declares the unauthorized use of force as illegal but also imposes a duty upon governments of all States to respect all human rights of all human beings irrespective of their race, sex, nationality, etc.

Was the treatment meted out to the United States' diplomatic and consular staff was a violation of their human rights and human dignity? It is deplorable for an act of a government of 20th century when not only for the national legal systems but for the entire international legal structure the legal culture rests mainly on the principles of human rights and human dignity.

The rules concerning respect for the dignity of diplomatic missions and staff had generally worked well. The most serious breakdown in the operation of the normal rules came when on 4 November 1979 some Iranian militants under the regime of Ayatollah Khomeini seized the US Embassy in Tehran and Consulates at Tabriz and Shiraz and took the diplomatic and consular staff as their hostages. At this, on 29 November 1979 the United States of America filed a case against Iran before the International Court of Justice.

Iran was notified by the Court accordingly but chose not to appear. Hence, the case was decided in the absence of the respondent.

At the very early stage in its Order on Provisional Measures the Court stressed at the cultural element of reciprocity of dignity in inviolability in the following words: '. . . there is no more fundamental prerequisite for the conduct of relations between States than the inviolability of diplomatic envoys and embassies so that throughout history nations of all creeds and cultures have observed reciprocal obligations for that purpose.'[2]

The Court later returned to the theme at the merits stage. During the course of examining the directly relevant law on the matter—1) Vienna Convention on Diplomatic Relations of 1961 and its Optional Protocol concerning compulsory

[2] *Case Concerning United States Diplomatic and Consular Staff in Tehran*, 15 December 1979 Order of the Court on Provisional Measures, ICJ Reports 1979, p 19, para 38.

settlement, 2) Vienna Convention on Consular Relations of 1963 and its Optional Protocol concerning compulsory settlement of disputes, and 3) Convention on the Prevention and Punishment of Crimes against Internationally Protected Persons, including Diplomatic Agents, of 1973—the Court in its Judgment of 24 May 1980 emphatically placed Iran under the most categorical obligations, as a receiving State, to take appropriate steps to ensure the protection of the US Embassy and Consulates, their staff, etc, by emphatic reference to the element of dignity in the following provisions:

> . . . after solemnly proclaiming the inviolability of the premises of a diplomatic mission, Article 22 of the 1961 Convention continues in paragraph 2:
>
> > *The receiving State is under a special duty to take all appropritae steps to protect the premises of the mission against any* intrusion or damage and to prevent any disturbance of the peace of the mission or impairment of its dignity. (Emphasis added)[3]

The Court continued:

> So, too, after proclaiming that the person of a diplomatic agent shall be inviolable, and that he shall not be liable to any form of arrest or detention, Article 29 provides:
>
> > The receiving State shall treat him with due respect and shall take all appropriate steps to prevent any attack on his person, freedom or dignity. (Emphasis added)[4]

The Court's emphasis on the principle of human dignity, while making determinations about the Vienna Convention on Diplomatic Relations, is obvious. But it is the historical and cultural perspective which highlights the setting of the mutual respect of States for each other's dignity.

II. 1948 Universal Declaration of Human Rights is Binding in Character

Further, within the given perspective of human dignity, stressing the fundamental nature of the Vienna Convention on Diplomatic Relations and its important role in facilitating respectful relations between States, and examining the merits of the case the Court observed:

> Wrongfully to deprive human beings of their freedom and to subject them to physical constraint in conditions of hardship is in itself manifestly incompatible with the principles of the Charter of the United Nations, as well as with the fundamental principles enunciated in the Universal Declaration of Human Rights.[5]

[3] Case Concerning United States Diplomatic and Consular Staff in Tehran, ICJ Reports 1980, p 30. para 62.

[4] *Ibid.*

[5] United States Diplomatic and Consular Staff in Tehran, ICJ Reports, 1980, p 42.

The binding nature of the UN Universal Declaration of Human Rights has always been in question, just like any other General Assembly resolution. The Declaration was signed in 1948 without any dissent. However, the years following the Declaration encountered diverging opinions as to its legal value. Even by Oppenheim, an eminent international jurist, the Declaration was seen as 'not an instrument which is legally binding either directly or indirectly'.[6] Such opinions about the said Declaration today appear as foregone dismal conclusions.

The impact and import of the Court's above observation made Judge Nagendra Singh to remark that:

> The point to emphasize is that, apart from the obligations created by the United Nations Charter, the Court does not hesitate to emphasize the legal importance of the Universal Declaration of Human Rights, 1948, when it specifically mentions that the said Declaration enunciates 'fundamental principles' of International Law.[7]

Categorizing the provisions of the declaration under 'fundamental principles' of International Law, the Court has developed the legal scope and status of the Declaration and brought the instrument in the class of full-fledged customary law to be respected and followed. Speaking about the reality of the Declaration today Judge Mbaye finds that: 'The Universal Declaration of Human Rights . . . which was considered at the time of its adoption simply as an ideal to be attained, has become as a whole . . . an element of customary law'.[8]

With such reasoning, promoting human rights and human dignity and clarifying the complementary nature of relation between human rights and international law, the Court decided:

> that the Islamic Republic of Iran, by the conduct which the Court has set out in this Judgment, has violated in several respects, and is still violating, obligations owed by it to the United States of America under international conventions in force between the two countries, as well as under long-established rules of general international law.[9]

[6] Oppenheim, *International Law*, 8th edn, vol I (Harlow, Longman) p 740.

[7] N Singh, *Enforcement of Human Rights in Peace and War and the Future of Humanity* (Dordrecht, Nijhoff, 1986) 29.

[8] KM Baye, 'Human Rights and Rights of Peoples: Introduction' in M Bedjaoui, (ed), *International Law: Achievements and Prospects* (Paris, UNESCO, 1991) 1054.

[9] United States Diplomatic and Consular Staff in Tehran, ICJ Reports, 1980, p 44, para 1.

8

Military and Paramilitary Activities in and Against Nicaragua case (*Nicaragua v USA*)[1] (1984–91)

I. The Use of Force not an Appropriate Method to Ensure Respect for Human Rights

IN DEFENDING ITS use of force against Nicaragua, the government of Nicaragua was accused by the 1985 finding of the United States Congress of violating human rights. The Court did not find this as a justification for the use of force.

The jurisdiction of the Court in this case was challenged by the respondent State. As basis for the jurisdiction of the Court Nicaragua invoked declarations, signed by Nicaragua and USA respectively, under Article 36 of the Statute of the Court. According to the government of the United States no required instrument of ratification of the Protocol of Signatures of the Permanent Court of International Justice was ever deposited by Nicaragua with the Secretary-General of the League of Nations. Hence, the declaration of Nicaragua, according to the United States, was not valid. The Court found that though at the provisional measures stage of the proceedings 'it has not so far been established to the Court's satisfaction that Nicaragua ever deposited an instrument of ratification of that Protocol', yet 'the Court finds that the two declarations do nevertheless appear to afford a basis on whih the jurisdiction of the Court might be founded'.[2] And later,

[1] The composition of the Court in the Judgment of 27 June 1986 (on Merits) in the *Nicaragua v USA* case was: President Nagendra Singh; Vice-President de Lacharrière; Judges Lachs, Ruda, Elias, Oda, Ago, Sette-Camara, Schwebel, Sir Robert Jennings, Mbaye, Bedjaoui, Ni, and Evensen. (see ICJ Reports 1986, p 15).

President Nagendra Singh, Judges Lachs, Ruda, Elias, Ago, Sette-Camara, and Ni appended their Separate Opinions to the Judgment of the Court; Judges Oda, Schwebel, and Sir Robert Jennings appended their Dissenting Opinion to the Judgment of the Court. (See ICJ Reports 1986, p 150).

[2] *Nicaragua v USA* case, Order of 10 May 1984 on Provisional Measures, ICJ Reports, 1984, pp 179–80.

after full examination of the matter in its judgment of 26 November 1984, the Court did find the declaration valid, together with another title of jurisdiction invoked by Nicaragua, despite its no trace of the deposit of the ratification with the Secretary-General of the United Nations.[3] This was again an anti-judicial restraint interpretation of an instrument applied by the Court. As a result of this, by clearing its path to adjudge on the merits of the case, the Court made a considerable contribution by developing and clarifying the law on matters relating human rights.

The Court studied this particular point independently of the question of a 'legal commitment' by Nicaragua towards the Organization of American States to respect these rights. This did not mean, according to the Court, that in the absence of such a commitment Nicaragua could with impunity violate human rights. The Court clarified the action of law here, in case of violations of human rights, in the following words: 'However, where human rights are protected by international conventions, the protection takes the form of such arrangements for monitoring or ensuring respect for human rights as are provided for in the conventions themselves.'[4]

All ambiguity of the law in question is removed here by laying down the rule that the alleged violation of human rights in a country cannot be used as a pretext for the use of force by another State in order to get such compliance.[5] The mechanism for such protection of human rights lies in the legal instruments themselves. To illustrate this further, the Court took notice of the fact that Nicaraguan government had in fact ratified a number of international instruments of human rights. And further, at the invitation of Nicaragua's government itself, the Inter-American Commission on Human Rights visited Nicaragua and compiled two reports: OEA/Ser.L/V/11.53 and OEA/Ser.L/V/11.62.[6] Nicaragua for this purpose was committed to the Organization of American States and the organs of that organization were consequently entitled to monitor the observance of human rights in Nicaragua. The Court noticed that the mechanism provided by the given international convention had functioned and, consequently, if the OAS so wished and found it proper it could have taken a decision on the basis of the two reports.

While condemning the use of force by America, the Court laid down a matter of principle in the following words:

> In any event, while the United States might form its own appraisal of the situation as to respect for human rights in Nicaragua, the use of force could not be the appropriate

[3] Military and Paramilitary Activities in and against Nicaragua *(Nicaragua v USA)*, Judgment on Jurisdiction and Admissibility, ICJ Reports, 1986, p 442.

[4] Military and Paramilitary Activities in and Against Nicaragua *(Nicaragua v USA)*, Judgment on Merits, ICJ Reports, 1986, p 134.

[5] Judge Azevedo also was of the opinion that: 'Respect for law must never constitute a reason for disturbing international harmony, nor cause an upheaval in the life of any society.' (Conditions of Admission of a State to Membership in the United Nations (Article 4 of the Charter), Individual Opinion of Judge Azevedo, ICJ Reprts, 1947–48, p 81).

[6] Military and ParaMilitary Activities in and Against Nicaragua *(Nicaragua v USA)*, Judgment on Merits, ICJ Report, 1986, p 90.

> method to monitor or ensure such respect. With regard to the steps actually taken, the protection of human rights, a strictly humanitarian objective, cannot be compatible with the mining of the ports, the destruction of oil installations, or again with the training, arming and equipping of the contras. The Court concludes that the argument derived from the preservation of human rights in Nicaragua cannot afford a legal justification for the conduct of the United States, and cannot in any event be reconciled with the legal strategy of the respondent State, which is based on the right of collective self-defence.[7]

This is establishing a firm guiding legal principle and a rule of human rights law that no State, or even a group of States, can, if not part of the decision taken by the human rights mechanism established by the relevant legal instrument, justify itself for the use of force in order to compel a State to respect human rights in its territory.

Seen in this light, for example, 'NATO Strike Against Yugoslavia', destruction of human life and property, would emerge utterly illegal. As far as the developed principle is concerned, it is clear enough in its logic and legality.

The Court's reasoning in developing this principle is very much in line with the universally established principle common to all legal systems, described by Kelsen as 'The Force Monopoly of the Community'.[8] Kelsen argues: 'The sanction as an act of coercion prescribed or permitted by the law is an act by which force is employed by one individual against another. Under national law the employment of force is delict unless it is prescribed or permitted by the legal order, and, as a rule, it is prescribed or permitted by the law only as a sanction.'[9] Kelsen further states:

> If a social order provides that coercive acts shall be performed only under certain conditions, determined by it, and only by certain individuals, likewise determined by it, and if we consider these individuals as organs of the community constituted by the social order, we may say that the social order reserves the employment of force to the community. Such a social order establishes a force monopoly of the community . . .. The force monopoly of the community is decentralized if the principle of self-help prevails, that is to say, if the legal order leaves these functions to the parties injured by the delict, as is the case in primitive society under primitive law and—as we shall presently see—in international society under general international law.[10]

The Court's developing the above principle, in this sense, is not only strengthening the international human rights law but is also indicative of the fact that the present system of international law has gained much more maturity than its primitive law stage and title. In a nutshell, 'human rights are universal'[11] and their monitoring and ensuring of respectability is the task of their related universal legal

[7] *Ibid*, pp 134–35.
[8] H Kelson, RT Tucker, (ed), *Principles of International Law*, 2nd edn, (New York, NY, Holt, Rinehart and Winston, 1967) 11.
[9] *Ibid.*
[10] *Ibid*, pp 11–12.
[11] Gibson, p 5.

instruments and established mechanism thereunder and not the use of force at will by any single State or a group of States.

II. The Principle of Self-Determination: Adherence to a Particular Doctrine Does not Violate Customary International Law

In the *Nicaragua v USA* case one of the arguments for using force against Nicaragua was that the Nicaragua's Governments had taken 'significant steps towards establishing a totalitarian Communist dictatorship'. Replying to this argument, the Court declared:

> However, the regime in Nicaragua be defined, adherence by a State to any particular doctrine does not constitute a violation of customary international law; to hold otherwise would make nonsense of the fundamental principle of State sovereignty, on which the whole of international law rests, and the freedom of choice of the political, social, economic and cultural system of a State. Consequently, Nicaragua's domestic policy options, even assuming that they correspond to the description given of them by the Congress finding, cannot justify on the legal plane the various actions of the respondent complained of. The Court cannot contemplate the creation of a new rule opening up a right of intervention by one State against another on the ground the latter has opted for some particular ideology or political system.[12]

The Court, however, made it explicit that in this context it was 'not here concerned with the process of decolonization'.[13]

[12] Military and Paramilitary Activities in and Against Nicaragua *(Nicaragua v USA)*, Judgment on Merits, ICJ Reports, 1986, p 133.

[13] *Ibid*, p 108.

9

East Timor (*Portugal v Australia*)[1] Human Rights Versus State Sovereignty

Indeed, it could be considered that the right of self-determination has changed the international legal system significantly as even the elements taken into consideration as to whether any entity is a State now include whether the entity complies with the right of self-determination.[2]

I. Some Preliminary Reflections

IT IS THE NON-COMPLIANCE of Australia with the right of self-determination of the people of East Timor which is challenged by Portugal, a UN recognized Administration Power, in this case. Hence, this case is one concerning human rights and human dignity of those very people whose rights and dignity were a 'sacred trust of civilization' kept in the hands of the peoples of the United Nations. *Portugal v Australia* may be seen as a case representing *human rights v State sovereignty.* Human rights is a normative school of thought seeking to define and apply standards of justice to human affairs in all their related aspects and dimensions. Human dignity is a symbiotic concept at the centre of the ethical system comprising the social values that are the essence of human rights. It may be defined as 'the fundamental innate worth of the human person'. All the values that give rise to specific concepts or principles of human rights emerge from this core concept. Global society, and all its individuals and institutions, particularly its judicial institutions, governed by the UN Charter and its ancillary documents, are committed to the values of human rights and human dignity. Human rights doctrine and human rights standards derive from the belief that certain forms of

[1] The composition of the Court in this case was as follows: President Judge Bedjaoui (Algeria), Vice-President Judge Schwebel (USA), Judges Oda (Japan), Sir Robert Jennings (UK), Guillaume (France), Shahabuddeen (Guyana), Aguillar-Mawdsley (Venezuela), Weeramantry (Sri Lanka), Ranjeva (Madagascar), Herczegh (Hungary), Shi (China), Fleischhauer (Germany), Koroma (Sierra Leone), Vereshchetin (Russia), and Judge *ad hoc* Skubiszewski (Poland). (See ICJ Reports 1995, p 90).

Judges Oda, Shahabuddeen, Ranjeva and Vereshchetin appended separate opinions to the Judgment of the Court. Judge Weeramantry and Judge *ad hoc* Skubiszewski appended dissenting opinions to the Judgment of the Court. (See ICJ Reports 1995, p 106).

[2] R McCorquodale, 'The Individual and the International Legal System' in MD Evans, (ed), *International Law* (Oxford, OUP, 2003) 300, 316.

human suffering and deprivation run counter to a society's notion of its values and purposes. The pre-human-rights international law derived its standards from the doctrine of sovereignty, leaving the individuals and peoples in a State to the mercy of its government. With the incorporation of human rights doctrine, international law has taken the individuals and peoples under their direct fold as far as their human rights, and human rights aspects of human affairs, are concerned. The same law has recognized the essential fact, with the blessings of the jurisprudence of the International Court, that human rights are *erga omnes.* Hence, the doctrine of sovereignty, which actually meant *we the governments*, as the fundamental basis of international law has been to that extent limited by the doctrine of human rights which actually means '*we the peoples*'. Given this perspective, a good government in a good society or State, committed as a Member to the purposes and principles of the United Nations, honours the dignity of all its persons and peoples and expects all its members to respect the dignity of others in their individual as well as group level capacities.[3] Any application and/or interpretation of rules and principles of contemporary international law which does not take into consideration this supervening change as a matter of fact still applies the old international law and takes the law backward to the pre-human-rights international law centred around the doctrine of absolute sovereignty, hence doing harm to the progressive development of international law, of international human rights law, and, therewith, also to the concept of human dignity which stands at the very centre of the doctrine of human rights.

'All argument and reasoning must be based upon certain perceptions. Without these, there cannot be any argument. Reasoning is the method of comparison between certain facts which we have already perceived. If these perceived facts are not there already, there cannot be any reasoning'.[4] Law is not in books, treaties and conventions alone. It is first and foremost an actual perception of *the way* we are organized in a given community, the way of human dignity. And, the way international community of peoples and nations is organized opens with the words '*We the peoples of the United Nations*'.[5] First time in the history of peoples and nations, this apex governing charter recognized at the very outset the fundamental innate worth of the human person. Remarkable of this perception is the fact that the word 'peoples' is mentioned first and the word 'Nations' later. This represents an ancient Indian perception '*Janata Janradhan*', meaning people are sovereign. Sovereignty of people and sovereignty of State indeed do not deny each other; one is actually the fulfilment of the other. The sad episode of the history of international law lies in the fact that from the time of Vattel to the end of the Second World War the perception of State sovereignty and State dignity, actually speak-

[3] BA Reardon, *Educating for Human Dignity: Learning About Rights and Responsibilities* (Philadelphia, PA, University of Pennsylvania Press, 1995) 5, 173.

[4] An extract from a lecture on the subject '*Realization*' delivered in London on 29 October 1896 by an Indian philosopher, S Vivekanda, *The Complete Works of Swami Vivekananda*, vol II, Mayavati Memorial edn, (Calcutta, Advaita Ashrama) 162.

[5] Opening words of the Charter of the United Nations.

ing government sovereignty and the government's dignity, remained the major characteristic of the international legal system and the perception of human dignity and peoples' sovereignty as such was not part of it. Governments were considered subjects of international law and the individuals its objects. When it did ultimately become part of the system in theory, its application through the process of interpretation and adjudication is rather slow to make home in the process of international legal reasoning. The UN Secretary-General, Kofi Annan, has aptly observed:

> . . . I have often recalled that the United Nations' Charter begins with the words: 'We the peoples'. What is not always recognized is that 'We the peoples' are made up of individuals whose claims to the most fundamental rights have too often been sacrificed in the supposed interests of the State or the nation . . . In this new century, we must start from the understanding that peace belongs not only to States or peoples but to each and every member of those communities. The sovereignty of States must no longer be used as a shield for gross violations of human rights. Peace must be made real and tangible in the daily existence of every individual in need. Peace must be sought, above all, because it is the condition for every member of the human family to live a life of dignity and security . . .. Throughout my term as Secretary-General, I have sought to place human beings at the centre of everything we do—from conflict prevention to development to human rights. Securing real and lasting improvement in the lives of individuals men and women is the measure of all we do at the United Nations'[6] (emphasis is mine).

Highlighting the human feeling of just treatment, Justice Frankfurter wrote:

> A judgment is not a technical conception with a fixed content unrelated to time, place and circumstance. Expressing as it does in its ultimate analysis respect enforced by law for that feeling of just treatment which has been evolved through centuries of . . . history and civilization, [it] cannot be imprisoned within the treacherous limits of any formula'.[7]

Disapproving the individual wrong by a Court of justice is as a matter of fact the universal disapprobation of his wrong conduct by the community of that individual. Sir Henry Maine has illustrated this fact in the following words: *'A person aggrieved complains not of an individual wrong but of the disturbance of the order of the entire little society . . . [and] the sole certain punishment would appear to be universal disapprobation.'*[8]

Not to apply this reasoning to individual wrong of an individual State is to uphold the absoluteness of its sovereignty which was true in the international community of 'the League of Nations' but not in the community of 'We the

[6] Kofi Annan, (UN Secretary-General), an extract from his speech on the award of the Nobel Peace Prize on 10 December 2001 (www.unhchr.ch).

[7] Justice Frankfurter in *Joint Anti-Fascist Refugee Comm v McGrath*, 341 US 123, 162–63 (Frankfurter, J, concurring); cited by Judge Manfred Lachs in his article M Lachs, 'Some Reflections on the Contribution of the International Court of Justice to the Development of International Law' (1983) 10(2) *Syracuse Journal of International Law and Commerce* Nr 1, 239, 240.

[8] H Maine, *Village Communities* (1872) 68; cited by Judge Manfred Lachs in his article M Lachs, 'Some Reflections on the Contribution of the International Court of Justice to the Development of International Law' (1983) 10(2) *Syracuse Journal of International Law and Commerce* Nr 1, 239, 240.

Peoples of the United Nations'. During his talk to the Third Committee (Social, Humanitarian and Cultural Committee) of the United Nations, Polish delegate to the United Nations, Marek Madej mentioned: *'State sovereignty is no more an absolute and untouchable principle in the contemporary world of globalization.'*[9] Agon Demjaha, of Kosovar Civil Society Foundation of Yugoslavia, observing himself the naked violation of human dignity by the power of the so-called State sovereignty, describes the reality of the UN Member States in the words: *'Member States should understand that the time of absolute and exclusive sovereignty has passed'*.[10]

II. Human Dignity Through Self-Determination v The Power of State Sovereignty

At the centre of this case are the people of East Timor, though earlier in principle a non-self-governing territory under Portugal as their Administrative Power yet later in reality under the forceful military occupation of Indonesia.[11] The central principle of international human rights law around which this case revolves is the principle of self-determination, together with its *adjunctus*, the principle of permanent sovereignty over natural resources. And the central principle around which the Court's entire reasoning in the judgment in this case revolves is the principle of State's consent, an *adjunctus* of the principle of State's sovereignty as described in the pre-human-rights international law.

Even cursorily seen through the ideological lenses of the human rights doctrine as a school of law based on the fundamental postulate of human dignity, and at the same time well aware of the still alive old ghost of State sovereignty intrinsically conspicuous to the legal system of the Court, the case concerning *East Timor* presents a classic equation as following: Human dignity through self-determination *v* the power of State sovereignty.

Timor is the largest and most easterly island of the lesser Sunda group in the Malay archipelago. The colonialism in the 16th century has given only one thing to the island; the division. East Timor was colonized by Portugal and the West Timor by the Netherlands. With the granting of independence to Indonesia the Netherlands ceded control over West Timor to Indonesia. In disregard to Article 1, paragraph 2, of the United Nations Charter[12] the government of Portugal,

[9] See (2003) XL(1) *UN Chronicle* 15.

[10] See (2000) XXXVIII(2) *UN Chronicle* 12.

[11] Just after seven years of the delivery of the Court' s Judgment (30 June 1995) in this case, the people of East Timor, despite years of bloodshed, oppression, subjugation, and occupation, succeeded in exercising their right of self-determination and attained their independence as a new State, called Timor Leste, on 20 May 2002.

[12] The provision, providing one of the purposes of the United Nations, reads as: 'To develop friendly relations among nations based on respect for the principle of equal rights and self-determination of peoples, and to take other appropriate measures to strengthen universal peace.'

however, refused to allow East Timor the right of self-determination. Consequently, in the 1970s a struggle for independence started in East Timor. The military government of Portugal ruling East Timor was overthrown. As a result, in mid 1975, Portugal withdrew from the island. Soon thereafter, wasting no time, Indonesian government sent in its army on 7 December 1975, invaded the island, and occupied it. This invasion and occupation, and the long trail of human rights violations in the territory, were deplored by the international community. It was estimated that within 20 years of this invasion 200,000 people, nearly one-third of pre-invasion population of East Timor had been killed.[13] Several resolutions were passed at the United Nations by the General Assembly and Security Council, condemning the invasion and calling for the withdrawal of Indonesia's military forces.[14] *These resolutions, however, reaffirmed* two things amply clear: first: that the status of the territory of East Timor was that of a non-self-governing territory, and the second, *that Portugal in principle was still its administering power.* Despite this background Australia and Indonesia signed a Treaty in 1989, called Timor Gap Treaty, providing for joint Australian and Indonesian exploitation of the off-shore oil and mineral resources of the maritime area called Timor Gap.

At this, the case was filed by Portugal against Australia, in 1991, instituting proceedings with the International Court of Justice to settle a dispute which concerned certain activities of Australia with regard to East Timor. As far as establishing the title of jurisdiction is concerned both these States had already accepted the compulsory jurisdiction of the Court by their declarations under Article 36, paragraph 2, of the Court's Statute. Portugal's Application made the following two submissions:

1) that by its conduct, Australia had failed to observe the obligation to respect the duties and powers of Portugal as Administering Power of East Timor;
2) that by its conduct, Australia had failed to observe the obligation to respect the right of the people of East Timor to self-determination.

The applicant, knowing well that Indonesia has not accepted the Court's jurisdiction in any form relating this case has filed the case *only* against Australia and *not* against Indonesia. Portugal's submissions have further made it amply clear that it is the behaviour of Australia in signing the Treaty of 1989 which is the issue and *not* that of Indonesia. The said declarations made by both the Parties were, however, in tact. Both the States, through the jurisdictional instrumentality of these declarations, had clearly consented to the compulsory jurisdiction of the Court and properly established the required bond of reciprocity.

[13] See the Editorial in *The Washington Post*, 12 November 1991.

[14] Security Council Resolution 384 dated 22 December 1975; Security Council Resolution 389 dated 22 April 1976; General Assembly Resolution 3485 dated 12 December 1975; General Assembly Resolution 31/53 dated 1 December 1976; General Assembly Resolution 32/34 dated 28 November 1977; General Assembly Resolution 33/39 dated 13 December 1978; General Assembly Resolution 34/40 dated 21 November 1979; General Assembly Resolution 35/27 dated 11 Noveember 1980; General Assembly Resolution 36/50 dated 24 November 1981; General Assembly Resolution 37/30 dated 23 November 1982.

Australia, though did recognize the right of self-determination for the people of East Timor, but, contrary to the UN resolutions, under the sovereignty of Indonesia and not under the administering power of Portugal, hence clearly recognizing the annexation of the territory of East Timor by the military force of Indonesia. In this light, the principle objection[15] which came from Australia was that: Portugal's Application would require the Court to determine the rights and obligations of Indonesia. Australia contended that the jurisdiction conferred upon the Court by the Parties' declarations under Article 36, paragraph 2, of the Statute would not enable the Court to act if, in order to do so, the Court were required to rule on the lawfulness of Indonesia's entry into and continuing presence in East Timor, on the validity of the 1989 Treaty between Australia and Indonesia, or on the rights and obligations of under that Treaty, even if the Court did not have to determine its validity. In support of its argument Australia referred to the Monetary Gold principle enunciated by the Court in its Judgment in the case concerning *Monetary Gold Removed from Rome in 1943*, requiring the consent of the *supposed* third party.

Australia objected to the second submission of Portugal in its Counter-Memorial and contended[16] that the Portuguese submission concerning Australia's violation of East Timor's right of self-determination is inadmissible *inter alia* because they could not be answered in the absence of Indonesia's consent. It is obvious that in order to escape Court's judgment on merits Australia applied the procedural strategy: the claim is inadmissible. And this procedural strategy is based on the narrowest and most conservative meaning of the concept of State sovereignty.

III. Court Upholds the State Sovereignty in the Face of Human Rights and Human Dignity

What was the Court's perception in the decision of this case? In the operative clause of the Judgment delivered on 30 June 1995, the Court found that: 'it cannot in the present case exercise the jurisdiction conferred upon it by the declarations made by the Parties under Article 36, paragraph 2, of its Statute to adjudicate upon the dispute referred to it by the Application of the Portuguese Republic'.[17] In other words the right of self-determination of the people of East Timor and the related discharge of the sacred trust of civilization through the administration of Portugal, on behalf of the international community, have become subject to the sovereign consent of Indonesia by the simple fact that East Timor has been annexed by Indonesia's use of military force. Still in other words the consent of the people of

[15] See paras 23–24 in the Judgment of 30 June 1995 concerning *East Timor*, ICJ Reports 1995, pp 100–1.

[16] See ICJ Pleadings, *East Timor (Portugal v Australia)*, Counter-Memorial of Australia, Part II.

[17] ICJ Reports, 1995, p 106.

East Timor which is represented by Portugal and international community has become conditional to the sovereign consent of Indonesia. After all what is at the heart of the principle of self-determination? The *consent of the people.* In general terms, the principle of self-determination refers to the right of persons living in a particular territory to determine the political and legal status of that territory. To put it in the theoretical framework of constitutional law the principle may be defined as: *those who govern draw their legitimacy from the consent of the people of the territory.*[18]

Every principle of human rights law, in fact of any law, has a long history of its origin. The history of the principle of self-determination, in this sense can go as far back as to the English Civil War and the political philosophy of John Lock. The echoes of self-determination were strongly heard during the American and French revolutions. History, both legal as well as political, provides evidence enough that in the ultimate analysis the right of self-determination prevails and the forces fighting against it, legal as well as political, give in.

It is beyond the aura of any doubt that the right of self-determination is widely recognized as an essential principle of contemporary international human rights law. Even the ICJ has recognized it as an *erga omnes* right evolved from the UN Charter and practice. What lacks, however, is the consensus on its meaning, content and scope. It was, therefore, very much hoped in the legal and academic circles that the Court in this case would pronounce on several aspects of the principle of self-determination.

What was behind such a reasoning of the Court which stopped it pronouncing on the right of self-determination and thereby from clarifying further its meaning, content and scope? And, when the jurisdiction was complete between the parties before the Court then why it is, one wonders, that the Court could not adjudicate upon the dispute! The following paragraphs in the *obiter dicta* of the Court answers this question.

'The Court has carefully considered the argument advanced by Portugal which seeks to separate Australia's behaviour from that of Indonesia. However, in the view of the Court, Australia's behaviour cannot be assessed without first entering into the question why it is that Indonesia could not lawfully have concluded the 1989 Treaty, while Portugal allegedly could have done so; the very subject-matter of the Court's decision would necessarily be a determination whether, having regard to the circumstances in which Indonesia entered and remained in East Timor, it could or could not have acquired the power to enter into treaties on behalf of East Timor relating to the resources of its continental self. The Court could not make such a determination in the absence of Indonesia'.[19] This reasoning of the Court touches upon only the first submission of Portugal and leaves aside the second. This approach of the Court not only overlooks the UN resolutions recognizing Portugal as East Timor's Administering Power but at the same

[18] J O'Brien, *International Law* (London, Cavendish, 2001) 162.
[19] ICJ Reports, 1995, p 102, para 28.

time gives recognition, implied recognition at least, to the forceful annexation of the *sacred trust* territory of East Timor by Indonesia. And by so doing, creates a barrier for itself, and therewith for the protection of human rights and human dignity, to protect the right of self-determination of the people of East Timor, equally a *sacred trust of civilization* and therefore also of the international legal system of which the Court is the apex legal guardian. Such a reasoning of the Court derives from the principle the Court itself formulated earlier in the case concerning *Monetary Gold Removed from Rome in 1943.* It is popularly known as Monetary Gold principle. The Court admits this in the following words: 'The Court recalls in this respect that one of the fundamental principles of its Statute is that it cannot decide a dispute between States without the consent of those States to its jurisdiction. This principle was reaffirmed in the Judgment given by the Court in the case concerning *Monetary Gold Removed from Romein 1943*'.[20] It is true that it is one of the fundamental principles of the Court's procedural law that the jurisdiction of the Court depends upon the consent, a rule derived from the doctrine of State sovereignty, given by the parties to dispute. But this rule of consent applies only to the parties to litigation and not necessarily to any supposedly third party. Any strict, narrow, literal, and conservative interpretation of this rule would prove counterproductive to the service of very preamble, purposes, and principles of the UN Charter of which the Court is the principal judicial organ and its Statute is the integral part. An eminent authority on the law and practice of the Court, Professor Rosenne, points to this direction in the following words: 'It is a matter of common sense that too rigid an attraction to that principle will paralyse any international tribunal'.[21] The legal interests, or the supposed legal interests, of a third party, or a supposedly third party are well protected by the procedural law of the Court in the following ways. First, Article 59 of the Statute provides that the decision of the Court in any contentious case has no binding force except between the parties and in respect of that particular case. Second, Article 62 of the Statute provides that should a State consider that it has an interest of a legal nature which may be affected by the decision in the case, it may submit a request to the Court to be permitted to intervene. The intervention under this provision has taken place several times in several cases decided by the Court. Thirdly, the Court itself has emphasized in its jurisprudence that 'no conclusion or inferences may legitimately be drawn from [its] findings or [its] reasoning with respect to rights or claims of other States not parties to the case'.[22]

Portugal, however, tried to put the matter in the framework of human rights and asserted that the right of peoples to self-determination, as evolved from the United Nations Charter and the UN practice, had an *erga omnes* character and was, hence, irreproachable. It further maintained that in effect the rights which

[20] ICJ Reports, 1995, p 101, para 26.

[21] S Rosenne, *The Law and Practice of the International Court of Justice 1920–1996*, 3rd edn, (The Hague, Martinus Nijhoff, 1997) 439.

[22] See the case concerning Continental Shelf (Tunisia/Libyan Arab Jamahiriya), Application for Permission to Intervene, Judgment, ICJ Reports 1981, p 20, para 35.

Australia allegedly breached were rights *erga omnes* and that accordingly Portugal could require it individually to respect them regardless of whether or not another State had conducted itself in a similarly unlawful manner. Seen the subject-matter in this human rights framework, Portugal put forward the argument to prove that the principle formulated in the *Monetary Gold* case is not applicable in the present case. One may however recall that the *Monetary Gold* case had nothing to do with human rights. To this assertion of Portugal the Court first reacted in a generally conservative way and soon in the last sentence of the following reasoning statement, a trinity of reasons, turned rather toughly conservative Court:

> However, the Court considers that the *erga omnes* character of a norm and the rule of consent to jurisdiction are two different things. Whatever the nature of the obligations invoked, *the Court could not rule on the lawfulness of the conduct of a State when its judgment would imply an evaluation of the lawfulness of the conduct of another State which is not a party to the case.* Where this is so, the Court cannot act, even if the right in question is a right *erga omnes.*[23] (emphasis is mine).

The tone and wording of this three-tier reasoning of the Court gives an impression of a triangular pronouncement born from the union of two ideologies: judicial restraint and legal conservatism, both the adored children of the doctrine of State sovereignty as understood in the pre-human-rights era of international law.

In the first arm of the triangle whereby the Court draws distinction between *erga omnes* character of a norm and the rule of consent, as a matter of fact the Court is drawing the theoretical distinction between the doctrine of State sovereignty and the doctrine of human rights. In practical terms, however, the distinction is being drawn between the element of State sovereignty relating the human rights character of the principle of *erga omnes* developed in its case concerning *Barcelona Traction* and the element of State sovereignty relating the rule of consent as old as the international law of Vattel and rooted in the arbitrational procedures as old as that of Jay Treaty. If, as Cicero pointed out, law cannot be different in Rome and Athens, then why the principle of sovereignty should be different in substantive law and the procedural law. If the meaning, nature and character of State sovereignty has changed with the time, place and circumstance, it has changed for all legal applications and not for only one. If 'we the peoples' conscience has changed the nature of contemporary international law in the sense that human rights character of law is prevailing over the State dominated character of law, and in that light the Court could develop principles like *'elementary considerations of humanity'* and *'human rights are erga omnes'*, then why, one wonders, the application of sovereignty should remain so conservative, and judicial restraint be exercised so narrowly, when it comes to the procedural matter such as jurisdiction and admissibility.

In the second arm of the triangle the procedural rule that the judgment cannot be made on the conduct of a State when it would imply an evaluation of the lawfulness of the conduct of another State, the rule is not sustainable by any logic

[23] ICJ Reports 1995, p 102, para 29.

of the concept of justice that was borne of the notions of human rights and human dignity as a result of the unprecedented violations of human dignity during the Second World War. To uphold the defence strategy of the respondent in this case is to give birth to a new anti-human rights principle which may be called as a *triple breach principle*, resulting from the situation: first Indonesia breaching international law by annexing East Timor by brutal force, the murder of the right of self-determination; secondly Australia breaching international law by recognising Indonesian sovereignty over the territory so brutally annexed, contributing and promoting the murder of the right to self-determination; thirdly, both entering, in violation of the UN Charter and several UN resolutions, into an international treaty, aiming at brutal exploitation of the territory and resources of East Timor, which are under the same Charter as much the 'sacred trust of civilization' for Australia and Indonesia as for Portugal and all other Members of the United Nations, demolishing the historical edifice of human rights based on human dignity. When one violation of human rights provides a shield to another violation of human rights, and the adjudication gives recognition to the reasoning of such a line of argument of defence, the foundations of the conscience of justice cannot remain unshaken. More and more human rights cases decided on the monetary gold principle type of sovereignty are enough to send the entire body of human rights to the judicial graveyard of history. Neither in the face of its own jurisprudence the rule is sustainable. Any interpretation of any concept or doctrine of international law, and the doctrine of State sovereignty must not remain an exception, has to take into consideration the developments in the supervening years. To this Professor Cassese concluded that self-determination has now become a fundamental standard of behaviour for States:

> The Court thus rightly emphasized that the principle of self-determination, which in the aftermath of the First World War had not yet acquired a foothold in the international community, became from 1945 an overarching principle of the international community . . . In other words, self determination, besides applying to current and future international relations, also constitute a fundamental standard of behaviour which, in a way, projects itself into the past.[24]

In the third arm of the triangle that 'Where this is so, the Court cannot act, even if the right in question is a right *erga omnes*' the Court in fact is formulating a rule which may not stand the test of time. Any development of law, be it substantive or procedural, if it does not reflect in the strongest measure the prevailing life current of legal culture, takes the law back to the pre-human-rights age. Human rights idea is the life current of the prevailing legal culture at every level of society, be it international, regional, or municipal, and to put it aside by the words such as 'even if the right in question is *erga omnes*' is to dive deep into the conservative waters at the risk of loosing sight of the liberal human rights fundamentals of the day. The

[24] A Cassese, 'The International Court of Justice and the Right of Peoples to Self-determination' in V Lowe and M Fitzmaurice, (eds), *Fifty Years of the International Court of Justice: Essays in Honour of Sir Robert Jennings* (Cambridge, CUP, 1996) 354.

words in the third arm are too strong and damaging the legal culture of human rights and human dignity. The judgment, even in its present form of pronouncement, could easily be delivered without making this sentence part thereof. It simply reflects the toughest conservatism and not so great regard to the sentiments of human dignity which has already suffered enough at the hands of State sovereignty prior to the birth of human rights in the post Second World War era.

Sometimes over concentration on the corollaries one risks loosing sight of the fundamentals. This is what seems resulting from the excessive emphasis on judicial restraint and tough conservatism of the State sovereignty based principle of consent. The case clearly is a case between Portugal and Australia and not between Portugal and Indonesia. And the matter at issue relates not to the peoples of either Portugal or Australia or Indonesia but the occupied, unable to govern themselves, people of East Timor.

Hence, by so doing, the Court upheld the objection of Australia, dismissed the claim of Portugal, and sacrificed the human dignity of the people of East Timor in the supposed interests of a third sovereign State, Indonesia, not a party to the case, and whose very supposedly legal interests stemmed from its very illegal act of annexing East Timor by means of military force.

Seen the people of East Timor in the image of the grand UN principle of '*We the people*' this judgment sounds a judgment in State sovereignty and not in human rights or human dignity; a blow to the progressive development of international human rights law, a blow to the principle of *sacred trust of civilization*, a blow to its principles of *self-determination*, and a blow to the principle of *permanent sovereignty over natural resources*. All because of its tough conservative judicial ideology upholding the doctrine of State sovereignty and rejecting the reality that sovereignty of States, actually of their governments, derives from the peoples and not peoples from their governments. Governments are made for the people and by the people and not the peoples for the governments and by the governments. History of human rights proves this and would prove it time and again, is the trend to be seriously taken into consideration by any court of law, be it national or international.

IV. Monetary Gold Principle v Human Rights

> The test enunciated in the Monetary Gold is dangerously uncertain.[25]

As already discussed, what prevented the Court from adjudicating upon the dispute was: 1) that the effects of the judgment requested by Portugal would amount to a determination that Indonesia's entry into and continued presence in East Timor are unlawful, and as a consequence, it does not have treaty-making power

[25] J Dugard, '1966 and All That: The South West Africa Judgment Revisited in the East Timor Case' (1996) 8 *African Journal of International and Comparative Law* 558.

in matters relating to continental shelf resources of East Timor, and 2) Indonesia's rights and obligations would thus constitute the very subject-matter of such a judgment made in the absence of that State's consent. Under the light of these two preventing factors, the Court foresaw that such a judgment would run directly counter to the 'well-established principle of international law', popularly know as Monetary Gold principle. The principle was well stated by the Court in its Judgment in the case concerning *Monetary Gold Removal from Rome* in the following words: 'To adjudicate upon the international responsibility of Albania without her consent would run counter to a well-established principle of international law embodied in the Court's Statute, namely, that the Court can only exercise jurisdiction over a State with its consent.'[26]

Even a cursory look at the language of this principle would reveal that the absent State in the given case was Albania and the link between the gold, a commodity, was a relation of subject-object dichotomy. Applying this principle to the situation of East Timor would amount to be treating the people of East Timor as a commodity and not human beings. It is true that East Timor in principle was subject to a subject of international law, namely Portugal, but by no means an object of international law, but a subject and participant in the form of a sacred trust of civilization. East Timor's right to self-determination, together with its *adjunctus* right to permanent sovereignty over its natural resources, rested in the hands of the United Nations and international community through the channel of Portuguese Government under the governing principle of the *sacred trust of civilization.*

Judicial self-restraint and the judicial ideology of conservatism are okay as long as they follow the holistic framework of law. But the moment the law starts following them it can do a tremendous damage to the dignity of human beings at the very core of the process of adjudication, particularly the human beings who are the sacred responsibility of the international community to make them stand on their own political legs. If one tiny stream, Indonesia in this case, becomes a theoretical block to the flow of entire jurisprudential river, the river should have the primacy and not a particular tiny stream. One falling star in the space cannot be allowed to make the entire sky dark and down, and more particularly so when human rights under the *sacred trust of civilization* are at stake.

Perhaps it is also in order here to recall how the principle of Monetary Gold, though appearing to be a jurisdictional principle turning around an object, a commodity actually, of international law in the first instance, was found for a good cause as a substantive principle of justice protecting the rights of an absent third state. The conception of the principle was not at the first instance of the Court itself but when the Applicant State, Italy, itself, which is very rare, raised the issue at a subsequent stage of the proceedings in the *Monetary Gold* case. The political background of the case lay in the following facts. First: a certain quantity of mon-

[26] Monetary Gold Removed from Rome in 1943(Preliminary Question) (*Italy v France, United Kingdom Great Britain and Northern Ireland and USA*), Judgment of 15 June 1954, ICJ Reports 1954, p 32.

etary gold was removed from Italy (Rome) in 1943. The same was later recovered in Germany and found belonging to Albania. Second: the 1946 agreement on reparation from Germany provided that the monetary gold recovered in Germany should be pooled for distribution among the countries entitled to receive a share of it. Third: the government of the United Kingdom however claimed that the gold should be given to it in partial satisfaction of the Court's Judgment of 15 December 1949 in the dispute concerning *Corfu Channel (United Kingdom v Albania)*. Fourth: Italian government at the same time claimed that the gold should be delivered to it in partial satisfaction for the damage which it alleged it had suffered as a result of an Albanian law of 13 January 1945. Fifth: in the face of such a situation a statement was issued in Washington on 25 April 1951 whereby the Governments of France, the United Kingdom and the United States, decided that the gold should be delivered to the United Kingdom unless, within a certain time-limit, Italy or Albania applied to the International Court of Justice requesting it to adjudicate on their respective rights. Albania kept silent over the matter but Italy applied to the Court. Later, doubting its own intentions to win the case, Italy, however raised the preliminary question, questioning the Court whether the Court had jurisdiction to adjudicate upon the validity of its claim against Albania. The Court, very rightly and conscientiously, respecting the sovereign dignity of Albania, found that without the consent of Albania, it could not deal with a dispute between that country and that it was therefore unable to decide the questions submitted. The gold was Albania's property. East Timor was not a property either of Indonesia or any other State.

It is absolutely true, and right, that whenever the jurisdictional issues come before the Court, the temper of caution exhibited by the Court in its formulation and exposition of the law manifests itself with some persistence in its attitude of restraint in relation to the question of its own jurisdiction.[27] However, when looking at the dispute concerning East Timor within this Monetary Gold framework, there is hardly any jurisdictional similarity. The central issue in the *Monetary Gold* case was monetary gold, a commodity, an object of international law based on traditional State sovereignty. The central issue in the *East Timor* case was a people, subjects of international law based on contemporary 'We the peoples' sovereignty of human rights (*erga omnes*) and human dignity. The dispute in the former case took a different turn when the applicant State itself raised a preliminary question which made the acceptance of the Court's jurisdiction by another State (Albania) necessary. In the later case, the jurisdictional link of consent between the applicant and the respondent was clearly established by their optional clause declarations. What the applicant in the *East Timor* case was asking was not the annexation of the territory or people of East Timor but the protection of human right of self-determination and respect for the human dignity of the people of East Timor and thereby respect for the UN Charter and its legislative spirit of 'We the peoples'.

[27] Sir H Lauterpacht, *The Development of International Law by the International Court of Justice* (London, Stevens & Sons, 1958) 91.

One of the striking characteristics by which the traditional international law differs from the contemporary international law is that traditional international law through its principles of respect for territorial integrity and non-interference in internal affairs aimed to protect only two elements of statehood, ie, territory and government. Its element of peoples, or population, was not taken care of.[28] However, it is that very element of statehood which is not only emphasized but is taken care of by the contemporary international law as it is well injected by the spirit and substance of the ideas of human rights and human dignity. And, the influence of the principles of human rights law over the principles of international law is so great that one cannot easily understand one without at the same time understanding the other. Certainly when the situation involved puts the traditional sovereignty face to face with the issues relating to human rights. It is in these particular cases, judges particularly cannot afford to overlook what Hersch Lauterpacht had to say: 'Fundamental human rights are rights superior to the law of the sovereign State'.[29] The extended reality may well be paraphrased in the words: Fundamental human rights are rights superior to the doctrine of State sovereignty. In this vein the peoples' right to self-determination is superior to the State right under the Monetary gold principle governed by State sovereignty. 'We the peoples' idea enshrined in the UN Charter is also nothing newer than the 'all humanity' idea of pre-Vattel days. Allott[30] has shown how the ideas of Vattel 'determined the course of history' as he propounded a sovereignty theory of the State, in contrast to the more inclusive 'all humanity' idea that had been expounded earlier, which now forms the basis of much of the dominant understanding of international law.[31]

However significant may be the occasional tendency of the Court to keep in check certain claims of State sovereignty, it would be misleading to assert that an account of that tendency gives a complete picture of the jurisprudence of the Court on the subject of sovereignty. It simply cannot be, for the concept of State sovereignty, like many other concepts of international law, is a dynamic, or perhaps more correctly, an evolutionary concept. Judge Hersch Lauterpacht, seeing contemporary international law in this light, mentions: '*the fact that sovereignty is in many respects part of international law does not always provide an automatic solution of the difficulty; for specific derogations from sovereignty may also be part of international law.*'[32]

[28] See R Mullerson, 'Sovereignty and Secession: Then and Now, Here and There' in J Dahlitz, (ed), *Secession and International Law: Conflict Avoidance—Regional Appraisals* (The Hague, TMC, 2003) 125, 127.

[29] H Lauterpacht, *International Law and Human Rights* (London, Stevens, 1950) 72.

[30] P Allott, *International Law and International Revolution: Reconceiving the World* (Hull, Hull University Press, 1989).

[31] R McCorquodale, 'The Individual and the International Legal System' in MD Evans, (ed), *International Law* (Oxford, OUP, 2003) 300, 320.

[32] Sir H Lauterpacht, *The Development of International Law by the International Court of Justice* (London, Stevens & Sons, 1958) 334.

The application of Monetary Gold principle is suitable to the strict situation of the *Monetary Gold case* issue, that is the situation of subject-object dichotomy, and not to the issues of human rights where the dichotomy is subject-subject, such as *East Timor.*

V. 'We the Peoples', Self-Determination and State Sovereignty

Nothing is so highlighted in the Charter of the United Nations as its very opening and crowning words: *'We the peoples of the United Nations'*. These words were the very first resolute collective and unanimous echo, a peoples-oriented echo, of the international community of the peoples, governing and governed alike, who had survived the Second World War to built upon its debris a better new world in which the dignity of human, individual as well as collective, would reign supreme as against the sovereignties of States. The very opening place those words were given is in itself the sounding core spirit of the Charter's legislative spirit: the spirit that speaks that sovereignty of peoples has primacy over the sovereignty of States. Every principle of international law, be it traditional international law or the law based on UN Charter, is subordinated to the Charter principle of 'We the Peoples'. If not, then neither the judges nor the jurists serving the Charter have upheld *the legislative spirit of the Charter.* Post-war drafting time of the Charter was a particular moment when *the repentance of the traditional State sovereignty and the forgiveness of the traditionally suffering humanity melted together* in one piece of paper, subordinating governing to the governed.

Three major conventional law corollaries of the principle We-the-peoples are the Universal Declaration of Human Rights and its resulting two covenants of 1966.[33] Article 1 of both these covenants provides that 'all peoples have the right of self-determination. By virtue of that right they freely determine their political status and freely pursue their economic, social and cultural development'. The wording clearly shows that the right is a human right of humans in their collectivity. And the people grouped as such form part and parcel as participants of international law and the international legal system mainly based on the UN Charter of the peoples, greatly highlighting the principle of self-determination in its Article 1(2), 55, and entire Chapter XI.

Assigning the pride of place for peoples, even a representative of the United Kingdom, supreme colonizers, to the United Nations Commission on Human Rights had to admit the importance of the UN Charter and two 1966 covenants and state that the right of self-determination is 'a right of peoples. Not States. Not

[33] 1) International Covenant on Civil and Political Rights of 1966; and 2) International Covenant on Economic, Social and Cultural Rights of 1966.

countries. Peoples'.[34] Judge Nagendra Singh in his declaration appended to the Advisory Opinion in *Western Sahara Case* could not fail to recognize that:

> the consultation of the people of a territory awaiting decolonisation is an inescapable imperative whether the method followed on decolonisation is integration or association or independence. Thus even if integration of territory was demanded by an interested State, as in this case, it could not be had without ascertaining the freely expressed will of the peoples—the very *sine qua non* of all decolonisation.[35]

One wonders, how could this strong *sine qua non* be brushed aside by Australia when signing a treaty like that of East Timor Gap. The signing of this treaty could be seen as a deliberate effort by two sovereignties to stop the growing political child of East Timor and to loot its economic heritage by betrayal of sacred trust of international society. Similarly, one may wonder how the light weight of a Monetary Gold could crush the same *sine qua non.* One liberal jurist of the day goes rightly as far as that that he sees the recognition of the principles of self-determination as one of the elements to be considered for achieving the status of statehood in the contemporary international law. Writing about the same principle in relation to a proper place of dignity for individuals in international law, Robert McCorquodale mentions: 'Indeed, it could be considered that the right of self-determination has changed the international legal system significantly as even the elements taken into consideration as to whether any entity is a State now include whether the entity complies with the right of self-determination'.[36]

Judge Ammoun, opining in an earlier case, seeing the right of self-determination as representing the contemporary humanity's conscience states: 'Indeed one is bound to recognize that the right of peoples to self-determination, before being written into charters that were not granted but won in bitter struggle, had first been written painfully, with the blood of the peoples, in the finally awakened *conscience of humanity*'.[37] (italics are mine).

Applying the parallel reasoning of the Court to the present 8 cases on the docket of the Court concerning the *Legality of the Use of Force* would reflect that if any or all of the 8 respondent parties follow the strategic path of Australia then the Court has no choice but to repeat the East Timor judgment in all these cases. History does not and will not hold this logic as consisting with the conscience of justice. It would leave to dangerous violations of human rights by groups of States, going escort-free. This would mean that any group of States forming a military alliance,

[34] See Statement of Mr H Steel, UK representative to the UN Commission on Human Rights, 9 February 1988, (1988) 59 *British Yearbook of International Law* 441.

[35] Western Sahara, Advisory Opinion of 16 October 1975, Judge Singh's Declaration, ICJ Reports 1975, p 81.

[36] R McCorquodale, 'The Individual and the International Legal System' in MD Evans, (ed), *International Law* (Oxford, OUP, 2003) 300, 316.

[37] Legal Consequences of States of the Continued Presence of South Africa in Namibia (South West Africa) Notwithstanding Security Council Resolution 276 (1970), Advisory Opinion of 21 June 1971, Separate Opinion of Judge Ammoun, p 74.

such as NATO, with one Indonesia-like State not having consented to the Court's jurisdiction, would be free to commit any number of human rights violations and shield behind, so to say, an *Indonesian Shield.* It is obvious that neither this carved out *Australian judicial strategy* nor its resultant Indonesian shield can stand the conformity test of the Court's most extraordinary judicial law making: the principle that human rights are *erga omnes.*

The reasoning part of the case is creating a situation wherein the Court's jurisprudence and judicial conscience is fighting against itself. Two principles are set against each other. The first, the principle formulated in the case concerning *Continental Shelf (Tunisia/Libyan Arab Jamahiriya), Application for Permission to Intervene*: *'no conclusions or inferences may legitimately be drawn from [its] findings or [its] reasoning with respect to rights or claims of other States not parties to the case'.*[38] The second formulated in the *Monetary Gold* case and further refined in language and narrowly applied in the present case: *'the Court could not rule on the lawfulness of the conduct of a State when its judgment would imply an evaluation of the lawfulness of the conduct of another State which is not a party to the case'.*[39]

The flow of the river of international legal culture of the day is towards its unalterable destination of the ocean of 'we the peoples' oriented human rights doctrine. The traditional doctrine of State sovereignty being just a part of this culture is bound to adjust to this flow and not to vainly go against its current.

VI. Sacred Trust of Civilization v State Sovereignty

In fact the expression 'sacred trust of civilization' was used in Article 22 of the Covenant of the League of Nations, as the first provision of its 'Mandatory System' The word 'sacred' was prefixed to the principle as a constant reminder to the potential of divine conscience of humanity in the minds of those sovereign States who were given the sacred duty by the international community to make the non-governing colonial territories stand on their own while meanwhile looking after their well-being at all times. Its activist application, benevolent liberal interpretation and respective development was made for the first time by the International Court of Justice in the *Namibia* advisory opinion of 1950. In the same case, for the proper discharge of those sovereign States, the ICJ established two paramount principles considered to be of paramount importance. The Court stated: 'When a decision was to be taken with regard to the future of these . . . territories . . . two principles were considered to be of paramount importance: the principle of non-annexation and the principle that the well-being and development of such peoples from "a sacred trust of civilization"'.[40]

[38] ICJ Reports 1981, p 20, para 35.

[39] ICJ Reports 1995, p 102, para 29.

[40] International Status of South West Africa, Advisory Opinion of 11 July 1950, ICJ Reports 1950, p 131.

Expounding on its universal sacredness in the face of any future development of law in any legal system, Judge McNair stated separately in his own separate opinion:

> Nearly every legal system possesses some institution whereby the property (and sometimes the persons) of those who are not *sui juris*, such as a minor or a lunatic, can be entrusted to some responsible person as a trustee or *tuteur* or *curateur*. . .. The trust has frequently been used to protect the weak and the dependent, in cases where there is 'great might on the one side and unmight on the other' . . .. I am convinced that in its future development the law governing the trust is a source from which much can be derived.[41]

The right of self-determination is an aspect of human dignity in its collective form. That collective aspect itself, as the fundamental principle of human dignity itself, is multifarious in nature—political, economic, social, cultural, etc. If the collectivity of human being in a given situation, such as East Timor, is not a sovereign State but a sovereign State in becoming, in this case non-governing territory of East Timor administered by Portugal, then the right of self-determination remains a 'sacred trust of civilization' in the hands of Portuguese Government and all States members of the United Nations. When Portugal finds that a certain member of the United Nations, in this case Australia, is trying to hinder the discharge of the duties relating the 'sacred trust', it is the right of Portugal to knock at the door of the principle judicial organ of the United Nations to protect the rights of the people of East Timor, that is protecting the human dignity of those people. Human dignity in such a situation is clamped between a rule and its parent principle. One must always draw a distinction between the concept of a rule and the concept of a principle. A rule needs to be seen as a specific, as a one of the specifics or corollaries, to its given universality, ie, the principle from which the rule is derived. Monetary Gold 'principle' in this sense is a rule derived from the principle of State sovereignty. Every principle which derives its existence from another higher principle to that extent ceases to be a principle and becomes a rule. The jurisdictional principle called Monetary Gold principle, being a rule derived from the principle of State sovereignty, and the State sovereignty of traditional international law in turn becoming a rule deriving its existence from the principle of 'We the People of the United Nations', and the same principle governing the principle of the 'sacred trust of civilization', and that in turn being turned into a rule derived from the principle of human dignity of the non-self-governing people, must play a principle role in any adjudication centred around the people of East Timor. The principles have no values if the people for which they are supposed to be established and applied are kept out of the picture. Generality must prevail over particularity. Universality must prevail over specificity. Rule must follow the law and not law the rule, according to the wisdom of Roman jurist Paulus. Even a majority judge, and the only judge among the majority voting in favour of the judgment in this case,

[41] International Status of South-West Africa, Separate Opinion of Judge McNair, ICJ Reports 1950, p 149.

Judge Vereshchetin, did not fail to point out that the rights of the peoples of East Timor have been overlooked.[42]

It is a fact that the evolution of the international human rights law and its further slow but steady progress is directly proportional to the gradual corresponding limitation of the powers of States under the traditional principle of State sovereignty. It is also a fact that to the extent that the Court has developed the substantive international law concerning human rights has direct bearing on the working of the principle of State sovereignty. Any process of application of law must begin with the related process of interpretation of law. And, the Court while progressively linking the principle of self-determination with the principle of sacred trust of civilization has clearly recognized a very liberal principle of interpretation in a previous case in the following words:

> . . . viewing the institutions of 1919, the Court must take into consideration the changes which have occurred in the *supervening half century*, and its interpretation cannot remain unaffected by the subsequent development of law, through the Charter of the United Nations and by way of customary law. Moreover, an international instrument has to be interpreted and applied within the framework of the *entire legal system* prevailing at the time of the interpretation. In the domain to which the present proceedings relate, the last fifty years, as indicated above, have brought important developments. These developments leave little doubt that the ultimate objective of the sacred trust was the self-determination and independence of the peoples concerned.'[43] (italics are mine).

Following its own extremely progressive principle concerning interpretation of any old instrument, and applying the concepts *ratione temporis* (half a century) and *entire legal system* in the interpretation of Monetary Gold principle based on the concept of consent corollary of the principle of State sovereignty, in an extremely facile consented jurisdictional situation such as between Portugal and Australia, and further strongly supported by the entire UN Charter and the human rights system of the time, the Court, had it so wished could have easily declared illegal the signing of East Timor Gap Treaty by Australia, as it amounted to violating the dignity of the people of East Timor. The humans whose dignity was raped repeatedly: first when colonized by Portugal, and later when neglected by the same administrative authority, consequently invaded, occupied and brutalized by Indonesian army, and now, as it was not degrading enough, Australia joining the joint exploitation of a people desperately struggling for independence and self-determination counting only on one power, the *power of the principle of sacred trust of civilization.* Is the juridical conscience of the Monetary Gold principle, a reincarnation of the doctrine of State sovereignty, higher in degree of human sacredness than the judicial conscience cultivated by history in the sacred trust of civilization principle? The answer is not at all difficult for this question: NO.

[42] ICJ Reports 1995, Separate Opinion of Judge Vereshchetin, pp 135–38.

[43] Legal Consequences for States of the Continued Presence of South Africa in Namibia (South-West Africa) Notwithstanding Security Council Resolution 276 (1970), Advisory Opinion of 21 June 1971, ICJ Reports, 1971, p 31.

The principle of sacred trust of civilization is by no means a static and limited concept meant only to be applied to the colonial or non-self-governing peoples. It is a dynamic concept making a constant and direct appeal to the divinity of mankind, be it a politician, a judge or a jurist of a sovereign State, that every human being, governed and protected by law, is the sacred trust of human civilization, which is divine and compassionate in its origin, in the hands of the governing and judging human beings in power.

Hence, the resulting perception: the principle of sacred trust of civilization seen in its universality is superior to the concept of State sovereignty.

VII. Dissent: Internal and Public

The Court's refusal to adjudicate upon the merits of the case made not only its own two judges dissent from the majority vote but drew strong public dissent too.

a) Judge Weeramantry: The Principle of Self-Determination is the Very Basis of Nationhood

To the Court's holding that it could not adjudicate on Portugal's claim in the absence of Indonesia, Judge Weeramantry set out in detail the reasons for his conclusion that the absence of Indonesia did not prevent the Court from considering Portugal's claim.

Judge Weeramantry in his Dissent finds that:

> ... the Court's Judgment stops, so to speak, 'at the threshold of the case'. It therefore does not examine such seminal issues as the duties flowing to Australia from the right to self-determination of the people of East Timor or from their right to permanent sovereignty over their natural resources. It does not examine the *jus standi* of Portugal to institute this action on behalf of the people of East Timor.[44]

Judge Weeramantry's disagreement with the majority view in the Judgment was in that that he could not accept 'that the Court cannot adjudicate on Portugal's claim in the absence of Indonesia.'[45] According to him: 'The central principle around which this case revolves is the principle of self-determination, and its ancillary, the principle of permanent sovereignty over natural resources. From those principles stem whatever rights are claimed for East Timor in this case.'[46]

[44] ICJ Reports 1995, p 142. Judge Weeramantry saw here the revisit of the *South West Africa* cases in the sense that the words 'at the threshold of the case' were an observation of Judge Jessup in the commencement of his dissenting opinion in *South West Africa, Second Phase*, Judgment, ICJ Reports 1966, p 325; the same words Judge Weeramantry found apt to be used here in his dissent to the *East Timor* case,

[45] ICJ Reports 1995, p 142.

[46] *Ibid*, p 193.

The issue was not, according to him, whether the Timor Gap Treaty was valid or whether the conduct of Indonesia was unlawful. *The issue was whether Australia had by signing that treaty breached obligations owed erga omnes.*

Observing that the respondent submits that it was not in breach of any international duty in signing the Timor Gap Treaty, Judge Weeramantry found it necessitating a consideration of State obligation implicit in the very principle of self-determination which he considers at 'the very basis of nationhood of the majority of Member States of the United Nations'. According to him, it 'raises also the important juristic question of the nature of international duties correlative to rights *erga omnes*.[47]

b) Judge Weeramantry: Practical Operation of Different Aspects of Right *erga omnes*

Judge Weeramantry, taking good note of the fact that the respondent in this case has well stated in its Rejoinder[48] that it did not dispute that the right to self-determination was an *erga omnes* principle, tried to elaborate two different aspects of the principle. According to him *erga omnes* right is equal to a series of separate rights *erga singulum*, including *inter alia* a separate right *erga singulum*. And further, these rights, according to him, are: 1) in no way dependent one upon the other, and 2) with the violation by any State of the obligation so lying upon it, the rights enjoyed *erga omnes* become opposable *erga singulum* to the State so acting.[49]

Applying this broad effectiveness of an *erga omnes* right and the independent effectiveness of its two *erga singulum* aspects against Australia as well as Indonesia, Judge Weeramantry presents the picture as: a separate right *erga singulum* against Australia and a separate right *erga singulum* against Indonesia.

With such *obiter dicta*, Judge Weeramantry arrives at the following persuasive but alarming conclusions: 1) to suggest that Indonesia is a necessary party to the adjudication of that breach of obligation by Australia is to hamper the practical operation of the erga omnes doctrine, and 2) it would mean that Indonesia could protect any country that has dealings with it in regard to East Timor from being pleaded before the Court, by Indonesia itself not consenting to the Court's jurisdiction. About the negative effect of a situation like this, Judge Weeramantry warns in the following words: 'In the judicial forum, the right erga omnes to that extant be substantially deprived of its effectiveness'[50]

Monetary Gold reasoning is not consistent with the concept of rights *erga omnes*. In other words traditional concept of State sovereignty is not consistent with the concept that human rights are *erga omnes*.

[47] *Ibid*, Dissenting Opinion of Judge Weeramantry, p 143.

[48] Rejoinder by Australia, para 78 (also cited by Judge Weeramantry in his dissenting opinion, ICJ Reports 1995, p 172).

[49] ICJ Reports 1995, Dissenting Opinion of Judge Weeramantry, p 172.

[50] *Ibid.*

> If self-determination is a right assertible *erga omnes*, and is thus a right opposable to Australia, and if Australia's action in entering into the Treaty is incompatible with that right, Australia's individual action, quite apart from any conduct of Indonesia, would not appear to be in conformity with the duties it owes to East Timor under International law.[51]

c) Judge Weeramantry: 'Principle of Self-Determination can itself be described as Central to the Charter'

According to Weeramantry the position of the right to self-determination is so central in the contemporary international law that any interpretation of that right which gives it less than a full and effective content of meaning would need careful scrutiny. And that scrutiny he bases on the two weighty and strongly persuasive facts.

In the first place, he finds that the principle receives confirmation from all the sources of international law, whether they are international conventions (such as the International Covenant on Civil and Political Rights and the International Covenant on Economic, Social and Cultural Rights), customary international law, the general principles of law, judicial decisions, or the teachings of publicists.

Secondly, the centrality of the right to self-determination he sees in the fact that Article 1, paragraph 2, of the UN Charter directs its Members that friendly relations among nations must be developed by the United Nations on the basis of equal rights and self-determination. Hence, developing such friendly relations is one of the purposes of the United Nations, central to its existence and mission. This way, Judge Weeramantry sees an inseparable link between a major purpose of the United Nations and the concept of self-determination. The same conceptual structure, he sees repeated in Article 55 which observes that respect for equal rights and self-determination is the basis on which are built the ideal of peaceful and friendly relations among nations. Article 55 recognizes that peaceful and friendly relations, though based on the principle of equal rights and self-determination, need conditions of stability and well-being, among which conditions of economic progress and development are specified. With such a broad human rights perspective, Judge Weeramantry makes his final point: 'Since the development of friendly relations among nations is central to the Charter, and since equal rights and self-determination are stated to be the basis of friendly relations, the principle of self-determination can itself be described as central to the Charter'.[52]

Judge Weeramantry thinks that the existence of a right is juristically incompatible with the absence of a corresponding duty. He thinks that while the right of self-determination has attracted much attention in contemporary international law, the notion of duties corresponding to that right has not received the same degree of analysis. Applying, hence, Hohfeld's theory of correlativity of rights and

[51] ICJ Reports 1995, p 202.
[52] *Ibid*, p 195.

duties to the field of international human rights law, the judge sees that if the people of East Timor have a right *erga omnes* to self-determination, there is a duty lying upon all Member States to recognize that right. In the absence of this factual acceptance it would be putting the horse before the cart. In his own words: 'To argue otherwise is to empty the right of its essential content and, thereby, to contradict the existence of the right itself'.[53] One cannot be in and out at the same time. Every freedom and respect for freedom is reciprocal. Enjoyment of one's rights is limited by the enjoyment of the rights of his counterpart or fellow beings, be it a man or the government of a State. Absolute right and absolute freedom do not exist. Enjoyment of any right in a given society is limited by the duty of recognizing similar right of others. After all, at the basis of right of self-determination is the concept of freedom. Although, this right in the history of international law reflects more as if it is a right only of the non-governing territories, yet it may equally be seen as a right for the full-fledged self-governing States as well. There is no talk about this because of the simple fact that the traditional sovereignty itself is based on the principle of freedom within a given territory. Yet the principle of sovereign equality is fully compact with the element of correlative duty to respect the freedom of other sovereign States. The distinction between the right of self-determination of the non-self-governing territory and the self-governing territory is that of the principle of *sacred trust of civilization*, meaning that the entire international community of the United Nations has a *sacred duty* towards any non-governing territory through the channel of its trustee or administering power, recognized by the law and practice of the UN Charter. Child is the father of man. Non-governing territory is a child-State in the making of a sovereign State. Hence, the corresponding duty is not just a duty towards its Administering Power but a *sacred duty* towards the people of the non-self-governing territory. To loot and exploit the resources of such a people and territory is to betray the *sacred trust of civilization*, the very core and compassion of humanity. Not recognizing this moral and legal duty by Australia, not to speak of Indonesia, and not to think of this *sacred trust* as an important ingredient of international legal culture by the International Court of Justice made the liberal benevolent judge, Weeramantry, to say: '*It is too late in the day*, having regard to the entrenched nature of the rights of self-determination and permanent sovereignty over natural resources in modern international law, for the accompanying duties to be kept at a level of non-recognition or semi-recognition.'[54] (italics are mine).

By this line of thinking, Judge Weeramantry clearly reflects that human rights as a school of law is establishing itself step by step and more and more an underlying doctrine to the development of international law based more and more on the human rights principles enshrined in the United Nations Charter, a form of world constitution.

[53] *Ibid*, p 209.
[54] *Ibid*.

d) Judge Skubiszewski: Four Elements Concerning Law, Justice and Human Dignity

Judge *ad hoc* Skubiszewski in his Dissenting Opinion finds that the judgment does not give sufficient expression to the present phase of international law where one of the finalities is to restore human dignity.[55] According to him this case created an opportunity for assessing the activities of a Member of the United Nations in the light of the Charter, whose very central core is the principle of 'we the people' and whose very highlight is the reflection of the values of human rights. This he saw as a capital issue at a time of crisis for the Organization and, more generally, in the present climate of the growing weakness of legality throughout the world.[56] Seen the issues in this holistic framework, his liberal reasoning suggests that the conduct of Australia, like that of any other Member State, can be assessed in the light of Australia's membership in the United Nations. Such an assessment, according to him, does not logically pre-suppose or requires that the lawfulness of the behaviour of another country should first be examined. Member States, he finds, have obligations towards the United Nations which in many instances are individual and do not depend on what another State has done or is doing.

Judge *ad hoc* Skubiszewski criticized the Court's approach as 'too cautious' and 'too narrow' in interpretation of the principles governing its competence. Such an overly legalistic approach of the Court, he finds, not only detrimental to the demands of justice but also to the concept of human dignity and people's right to self-determination.

There are four major elements characteristic to his liberal benevolent judicial ideology, each in turn strongly supported by reaffirming the relevant comments made by four prominent international legal authorities, three among them having sat on the bench of the ICJ and one even sitting as President, Judge Bedjaoui, in the given composition of the Court in this very case.

First element: The Court must use its discretion to decide a case very sparingly. He reaffirms what Professor Rosenne has argued, where the Court possesses 'a measure of discretion' . . . *to decline to decide a case, it should be 'sparingly used'*[57] (italics are mine)

The second element: there is, according to Skubiszewski, a real interest in maintaining and strengthening the Court's role in what Judge Sette-Camara described as the *'institutionalisation of the rule of law among nations'*.[58] (italics are mine)

The third element: restoring true dignity to peoples is one of the finalities of the present phase on international law. Because human dignity is at the centre of this he cites Judge Bedjaoui at length:

[55] ICJ Reports 1995, p 238, paras 44–45.

[56] *Ibid*, p 274, para 158.

[57] S Rosenne, *The Law and Practice of the International Court*, 2nd revised edn, (The Hague, Martinus Nijhoff, 1985) 305.

[58] J Sette-Camara, 'Methods of Obligatory Settlement of Disputes' in M Bedjaoui, (ed), *International Law: Achievements and Prospects* (Paris, UNESCO, 1991) 542.

> A few years ago President Bedjaoui wrote that 'it is through an awareness of the lines of force of [international] society, and of their articulation, that we can gain a better understanding . . . of [international law's] possible future conquests'. In the opinion of the President the present phase of international law is that of a transition '[f]rom a law of co-ordination to a law of finalities'. And the learned commentator states that 'one of the financial finalities' is development, 'true development, of a kind *which will restore dignity to [the] peoples* [of 'new States'] and put an end to relationships of domination'[59] (italics are mine)

And the fourth element: constructive application of law never ignores that the *ultimate beneficiaries of the legal system are individuals.* This element of his reasoning Judge Skubiszewski supports with the following equally weighty statement of Judge *ad hoc* Lauterpacht in the *Genocide case (Bosnia v Serbia and Montenegro)*:

> the Court should [not] approach it with anything other than its traditional impartiality and firm adherence to legal standards. At the same time, the circumstances call for a high degree of understanding of, and sensitivity to, the situation and must exclude any narrow or overly technical approach to the problems involved. While the demand of legal principle cannot be ignored, it has to be recalled that the rigid maintenance of principle is not an end in itself but only an element—albeit one of the greatest importance—in the constructive application of law to the needs of the ultimate beneficiaries of the legal system, individuals no less than the political structures in which they are organized.[60] (italics are mine)

His strong emphasis on human dignity reflects in his own words when he states: 'The subject-matter of the dispute and its wider ramifications would justify the adoption of the President's approach'. Observing that the over 'legal correctness' in the Judgment has sacrificed the other two postulates of justice and human dignity in the supposed interests of State sovereignty of a nation, Judge Skubiszewski remarked:

> East Timor has not been well served by the traditional interests and sovereignties of the strong, hence the importance of the Court's position on the territory and the rights of its people (para 2 above). But the position would be of more consequence if the holding was not silent on self-determination and on the status of the territory[61]

e) Judge Skubiszewski: Three Elementary Assumptions about Self-Determination

Aware of the fact that both parties invoked the interests and right of self-determination of the East Timorese people rather conveniently without presenting much solid evidence of what the actual wishes of that people were, Judge

[59] M Bedjaoui, (ed), *International Law: Achievements and Prospects* (Paris, UNESCO, 1991) pp 1, 14 and 15.

[60] Cited from the case concerning Application of the Convention on the Prevention and Punishment of the Crime of Genocide, Provisional Measures, ICJ Reports 1993, p 408, para 3.

[61] ICJ Reports 1995, p 238, para 45.

Skubiszewski expected the Court to base its thinking on certain elementary assumptions. There are three of these elementary assumptions[62] which he finds are part of the working of the *right of self-determination* of a non-self-governing people.

First: the interests of the people are enhanced when recourse is made to peaceful mechanisms, not to military intervention.

Second: When there is free choice, not incorporation into another State brought about essentially by the use of force.

And the third: when the active participation of the people is guaranteed, in contradistinction to arrangements arrived at by some States alone with the exclusion of the people and/or the United Nations Members who accepted *'the sacred trust'* under Chapter XI of the Charter.

These three assumptions, he finds as part of the right of self-determination. As the Judgment in this respect remained rather silent, in highlighting these elementary assumptions, Judge Skubiszewski adds considerable clarification to the principle of self-determination as applied to the non-self-governing peoples. This trilateral clarification and development of human rights law to that extent not only reaffirms the genuine *relation between the principles of self-determination and the sacred trust* of civilization but also emphasizes the incompatibility of the forcible incorporation of a non-self-governing territory with the requirement of self-determination.

Judge Skubiszewski advances the argument that the principle of non-recognition of acquisition by force protects the right to self-determination. The status of non-self-government implies, according to the judge, obviously the 'integrity' of the 'Territory'. Respecting the integrity of a territory is respecting human rights and human dignity of the people inhabiting that territory. To the application of the Monetary Gold principle reasoning of the Court as a reason, whereas the jurisdiction of the Court was accepted by both the litigants, did to decline to decide this case, Judge Skubiszewski provides a strong legal persuasiveness which is broadly human-rights-oriented approach killing two human wrongs—a) acquisition of territory by use of force, and b) giving recognition to the acquisition of territory by use of force—with one human right, ie, the correctness in observing the non-recognition principle in order to protect the right to self-determination.

The rule of non-recognition, which Sir Hersch Lauterpacht preferred to call[63] a principle, and Judge Skubiszewski himself sees it as a corollary of the principle of non-use of force, has by now become a part of general international law.

The Declaration on Principles of International Law concerning Friendly Relations and Co-operation among States in Accordance with the Charter of the United Nations states the principle in this way: 'No territorial acquisition result-

[62] See Judge *ad hoc* Skubiszewski's Dissenting Opinion, East Timor, ICJ Reports 1995, p 240, para 52.

[63] H Lauterpacht, *Recognition in International Law* (1947) ch XXI.

ing from the threat or use of force shall be recognized as legal'.[64] After the invasion and acquisition of the territory of East Timor by Indonesian army the UN Security Council called upon 'all States to respect the territorial integrity of East Timor'[65] Paragraph 5 of the UN General Assembly Resolution 3485, also referred to the territorial integrity of East Timor. It was further reaffirmed by the General Assembly in 1996–98. What else can this mean, says Judge Skubiszewski, but prohibition to do anything that would encroach upon the integrity of the Territory. The Rule is self-executory. Yet Australia recognized Indonesia's sovereignty over East Timor.

Skubiszewski is clear about the fact that the Court has not been asked to adjudicate or to make a declaration on non-recognition in regard to the Indonesian control over East Timor. But restating the question, he asks: can the Court avoid this issue when it states certain principles? At this, he promotes the cause of human rights and their ideological relation with international law in the following words: 'Non-recognition might protect or indeed does protect the rights to self-determination and to permanent sovereignty over natural resources. Any country has the corresponding duty to respect these rights and no act of recognition can release it from that duty'.[66]

This line of legal reasoning is developing a human-rights-oriented reasoning leading towards application and interpretation of the principles of international law within the perspectives of the principles of human rights law. Finding a link between Australia's attitude towards Indonesian annexation of East Timor and Australia's duty towards East Timor is not making a pronouncement on Indonesia. It is simply establishing a fact amounting to establishing the duty of a State, in this case Australia. Hence, Judge Skubiszewski concludes: 'Such a determination would not amount to delivering any judgment on Indonesia, for the Court would limit itself to passing upon a unilateral act of Australia'.[67]

It also shows that Monetary Gold principle was good in *Monetary Gold case* but not in the case of *East Timor.* Joint Human rights violations does not mean that an individual or an individual State cannot be judged individually. In the human rights issues, under the 'new international law'[68] in any issue actually, one cannot reduce peoples to the status of a commodity, an object of international law. East Timor's people were human beings and not a group of metals. In the age of human rights assessing the activities of a Member of the United Nations in the light of the principles of the Charter should be seen as a step forward towards the development of law protecting human dignity in all its aspects and dimensions. Applying and interpreting the rules derived from the traditional narrow doctrine of State sovereignty in isolation to its successor 'we the peoples' oriented principles is to

[64] This Declaration is annexed to UN General Assembly Resolution 2625(XXV). The principle is stated in the section dealing with the prohibition of use of force.

[65] See para 1 in each of the Security Council Resolutions 384 (1975) and 389 (1976).

[66] ICJ Reports 1995, p 264, para 131.

[67] *Ibid.*

[68] To use the language of Judge Alvarez. In several of his individual opinions appended to judgments and advisory opinions he used to describe post Second World War international law as 'new international law'.

undo the hard-won historical achievement of the human rights place in the international legal system and the international legal process.

Judge Skubiszewski is of the opinion that the *right of self-determination cannot be assessed in the abstract.* For him the balance between the concepts of law, justice, and human dignity was not very stable in the adjudication of this case. In dissenting with the majority of the Court, the judge *ad hoc* had observed that the Court in its ruling had given too narrow an interpretation to the rules governing its jurisdiction and matters of admissibility and had overlooked the element of the 'demands of justice'. The dichotomy between law and justice is perennial. The Court has constantly been looking for an answer to it. At the outset of writing his dissent he almost formulates a principle governing relation of rules of jurisdiction and admissibility and the demands of justice. His principle reads: 'The search for a solution becomes difficult, and the contours of the dichotomy gain in sharpness, when too narrow an interpretation of the principles governing competence restrains justice'.[69]

It may equally be added that the rules of law divorced from their broader principles of justice and human dignity take the law steps and steps backward and mars its further development perilously. What was overlooked in the judgment of this case was the vastly broad principles of human rights enshrined in the UN Charter and system whose very strength derives from the *Grundnorm* of 'we the people'. Judge *ad hoc* Skubiszewski reflects that the principle of State sovereignty is governed by these Charter principles and not the Charter principles by the State sovereignty.

The right of self-determination, according to Skubiszewski, is simply not to be reduced, as Australia did in this case, to the choice of the form of government, how they are governed, as he put it. The right is much broader in its meaning and scope. It is contradictory, the judge opines, that Australia on the one hand recognised the sovereignty of Indonesia over East Timor and on the other recognising the right of self-determination of the people of East Timor. In his own words: 'It may be observed that the parallelism represented by, on the one hand, recognition of sovereignty (no matter how its extension over a territory was achieved) on the other hand by support (albeit declaratory) for *self-determination cannot be assessed in the abstract*'.[70] (italics are mine). This way he finds that it puts the right of self-determination of East Timor in an imbalanced situation: recognition militating in favour of the permanency of incorporation, while self-determination is, in fact, suspended.

Analysing the legal phenomenon in terms of communication every judge does directly or indirectly. The judge in this way approaches 'law as a means of human interaction.' 'The concept', according to Prof Van Hoecke, 'allows a broad, pluralistic analysis, as communication can be found at different levels and under many different forms.'[71] Judge Skubiszewski's two prong 'pluralistic analysis' here

[69] ICJ Reports 1995, Dissenting Opinion of Judge *ad hoc* Skubiszewski, p 238.
[70] ICJ Reports 1995, p 268, para 141.
[71] M van Hoecke, *Law as Communication* (Oxford, Hart Publishing, 2002) 8.

clearly reflects *Human interaction and communication* at *different levels* and under *different forms.* Firstly, with his benevolent judicial ideology comprising four elements concerning law, justice and human dignity. And secondly, by his carving of three elementary assumptions about the right of self-determination—and then relating them to the quadruple interaction of the people of East Timor, the United Nations, Portugal, and Indonesia.

In this way Judge Skubiszewski has considerably enhanced the human value of the right of self-determination and therewith made a genuine contribution to the liberal approach to viewing the relation between human rights and international law.

So, the history of the development of the Court's human rights jurisprudence would certainly go on record that its two judges in this case, Judge Weeramantry and Judge *ad hoc* Skubiszewski, did not let the Court down and the human rights law was indeed developed and the human dignity was indeed promoted, though not in the *obiter dicta* or *dispositif* of the judgment but in their dissenting opinions. This is something very fortunate of the Court's system that sometimes what the majority fails to do the minority becomes extra responsible to do the same. After all, except for the two (rarely more) litigating States, the value of contribution to the development of law, as for as international law and international community of States is concerned, is the same, be it in the ruling proper or in its appended opinions.

f) Public Dissent

The most typical perhaps of all the strong public dissent was an article from Prof Dugard which stated in its title itself: '*The South West African Judgement Revisited in the East Timor Case*'.[72]

The Judgment in East Timor case made Prof Dugard comment that the ICJ is a conservative institution.

> Today it is generally believed that the 1966 decision in the *South West Africa Cases* is part of history; and that the judicial philosophy that led to that judgment is forgotten by a new breed of progressive judges. The judgment of the International Court of Justice in the East Timor Case raises doubts about this assumption.[73]

Having explored this question thoroughly in the light of the South West Africa judgment, Dugard arrives at the conclusion that: 'The East Timor Case confirms that the International Court of Justice is a conservative institution where matters of jurisdiction and admissibility are concerned.'[74]

According to Prof Fitzgerald the ICJ opts for State sovereignty over sovereign community of nations. He finds that: 'the Court remains wedded to conventional notions of sovereign autonomy and refuses the opportunity to add substance to

[72] J Dugard, '1966 and All That: The South West Africa Judgment Revisited in the East Timor Case' (1996) 8 *African Journal of International and Comparative Law* 549–63.

[73] *Ibid*, p 549.

[74] *Ibid*, p 563.

the *erga omnes* obligation by adjudicating Portugal's claim of breach by Australia'.[75]

Sensitive to the human dignity of the people of East Timor, and maintaining that Australia had a duty to respect the rights of East Timorese to self-determination, Fitzgerald opines that the judicial pronouncements made in this case are significant not only for their acceptance or rejection of *erga omnes* obligations owed by Australia to facilitate East Timor's right of self-determination, but more importantly for the fashion in which they deploy the potent missiles of sovereign autonomy of State and the sovereign community based on obligations owed *erga omnes*. The rhetorical structures that underpin these opinions tell us much more about this struggle than the legal doctrine. He derives the following conclusion from the entire *obiter dicta* of the judgment: 'These structures indicate that the conceptual tug-of-war between sovereign autonomy and sovereign community still rages in the jurisprudence of the ICJ—*even in an era where a more pragmatic vision of a substantive world order grows apace*' (emphasis is mine).[76] This way he shows that while the substantive law promoting sovereign community, the community of '*We the peoples of the United Nations*' expands, its implementation through judicial institutions, in this case the International Court of Justice, continues to be channelled through a process premised on sovereign autonomy. Disappointed, but not giving up his optimism towards the liberal human rights oriented development of law, particularly relating the Court's jurisdictional jurisprudence, Fitzgerald states: '*Portugal v Australia* demonstrates the extent to which international litigation before the ICJ continues to be plagued by the mounting conflicts between sovereign autonomy and sovereign community. This time sovereign autonomy reigned supreme—next time may be different'.[77] This was exactly the mood of public opinion in academic circles when the 1966 Second Phase Judgment[78] was delivered in the *South West Africa* cases concerning *apartheid*. This indeed proved true soon after when the ICJ delivered its Advisory Opinion of 21 June 1971 in the case concerning *Legal Consequences for States of the Continued Presence of South Africa in Namibia (South West Africa) Notwithstanding Security Council Resolution 276 (1970)* in which the Court showed its utmost sensitivity to human rights plight in Namibia.[79]

Kavanagh commented that the Court subordinated human rights to national interest of a single State. He saw the Judgment as 'a disheartening one in that it suggests that *the promise of 50 years ago embodied in the United Nations Charter—that the sovereign rights of states would be subordinated to the protection of human rights—is yet to be realized.*'[80] (italics are mine)

[75] BF Fitzgerald, '*Portugal v Australia*: Deploying the Missiles of Sovereign Autonomy and Sovereign Community' (1996) 37 *Harvard International Law Journal* 260.
[76] *Ibid*, p 271.
[77] *Ibid*.
[78] ICJ Reports 1966, p 6.
[79] ICJ Reports 1971, p 16.
[80] R Kavanagh, 'Oil in Troubled Waters: The International Court of Justice and East Timor: Case Concerning East Timor' (1996) 18 *Sydney Law Review* 87.

Kavanagh also found that the ruling shadowed by the Monetary Gold jurisdictional doctrine subordinated the principle of legal interest of the international community to the interest of an individual nation: 'In ignoring the legal interest of the international community in the protection of *erga omnes* rights and obligations, the Court has in effect subordinated the protection of fundamental human rights to the national interest of a single state.[81]

Dismayed by the still existing dominance of power politics, she concluded:

> The failure of the ICJ as illustrated in the *East Timor* case should not be the cause of much surprise. Indeed such outcome are perhaps inevitable when the high ideals on which international law is based conflict with the reality of power politics. Nevertheless the result is a disheartening one in that it suggests that the promise of 50 years ago embodied in the United Nations Charter—that the sovereign rights of states would be subordinated to the protection of human rights—is yet to be realised.[82]

Professor Scobbie and Drew reacted rather bitterly and found that in the judgment delivered by the ICJ the right to self-determination was disregarded. Their bitter reaction painted the decision of the Court as 'a bare judgment, denuded of the justification one would expect.'[83]

According to Professors Scobbie and Drew, the Court's judgment in this case has undermined the principle of Self-determination. Attaching high consideration to the human dignity of the people of East Timor and holding high their right to self-determination, the professors reflect their disappointment with the majority judgment in three respects.

Firstly, seeing the size and consideration given to a matter and principle of that magnitude they reacted:

> In seventeen pages, by fourteen votes to two, the Court dismissed the Portuguese case on the ground that it lacked jurisdiction, and yet managed to make observations on matters such as self-determination along the way. Surprise should only be magnified when one realizes that the Court spent only seven pages justifying its decision, once the factual account of the proceedings, statement of the parties' claims, and the like are subtracted from the total. This is a bare judgment, denuded of the justification one would expect.[84]

Secondly, considering the significant place the principle has in the modern international human rights world, they stated:

> In a Judgment in which the central issue was self-determination, 'one of the most essential principles of contemporary international law' which has 'evolved from the Charter and from United Nations practice', more could legitimately have been expected from the ICJ. Regardless of whether the decision favoured the Portuguese or Australian submissions, because of the importance of the issues at stake, such an impoverished and

[81] *Ibid*, p 93.

[82] *Ibid*, p 96.

[83] IGM Scobbie and CJ Drew, 'Self-Determination Undermined: The Case of East Timor' (1996) 9 *Leiden Journal of International Law* 185., 187.

[84] *Ibid*, p 187.

unreasoned judgment as this essentially amounts to a failure by the Court to discharge its functions as 'the principal judicial organ of the United Nations'.[85]

And thirdly, in the face of the given reality of the fact that neither Australia nor Portugal denied the entitlement of the right of self determination to the people of East Timor,[86] the Court's finding that any assessment of Australia's conduct in relation to East Timorese natural resources would require a prior determination of the lawfulness of Indonesian conduct in East Timor was difficult according to Professor Scobbie and Drew, to reconcile with any meaningful interpretation of the self-determination doctrine underlying the Portuguese submissions. Why was it difficult to reconcile? They gave very progressive and persuasive argument.

In their opinion there are two central tenets of the of the self-determination doctrine underlying the Portuguese submissions. First, they find, that 'the right of self-determination gives rise to a duty *erga omnes* opposable to all states (including Australia) to respect that right which exists independently of any express organizational directive to do so'. And the second, they continued, that 'the natural resources of a people of a non-self-governing territory form an integral core of the right of self-determination and cannot be disposed of without either their consent or that of administering power'.[87] Actually one would readily agree with them that the Judgment of the Court amounts to rejection of these two central tenets.

Professor Verma also finds that the East Timor case shows disrespect for the principle of self-determination.[88]

VIII. Nevertheless: The Court did Add Authority to the Various Areas of the Principle of Self-Determination which Needed Clarification

However, it was not as bad as that. Despite all this, though the Court, faithful to its jurisdictional judicial restraint, mainly resulting from the consent principle, a corollary of the concept of State sovereignty, could not pronounce in its operative part of the judgment its findings which could add some authority to the various areas of the principle of self-determination which needed clarification, yet, it has

[85] IGM Scobbie and CJ Drew, 'Self-Determination Undermined: The Case of East Timor' (1996) 9 *Leiden Journal of International Law*, p 210–11.

[86] Actually in its oral statements Australia unequivocally mentioned that, 'this case is not without whether the people of East Timor have the right to self-determination. They do. Portugal says they do. Australia says they do. There is no dispute on this metter.' (See G Griffith's statement made on 6 February 1995 recorded in the Court's document' *CR* 95/7, p 9).

[87] IGM Scobbie and CJ Drew, 'Self-Determination Undermined: The Case of East Timor' (1996) 9 *Leiden Journal of International Law* 185, 201.

[88] SK Verma, *An Introduction to Public International Law* (New Delhi, Prentice Hall of India, 1998) 77.

not failed altogether to do the same in its reasoning part of the Judgment. The Court is well known to be conservative when deciding its jurisdiction and admissibility related issues but it has often shown its extreme benevolent liberalism in dealing with the substantive law. The same was done by the Court in this case by observing as following.

Firstly, in answer to the Portugal's assertion that the right of peoples to self-determination, as it evolved from the Charter and from United Nations practice, has an *erga omnes* character, the Court replied that the assertion 'is irreproachable'.[89]

Secondly, not only the Court simply affirmed the Portuguese assertion but made an emphatic addition thereto in the following words: 'The principle of self-determination of peoples has been recognized by the United Nations Charter and in the jurisprudence of the Court'.[90]

And thirdly, citing its own jurisprudence in two previous advisory cases,[91] the Court reaffirmed the core value of the right of self-determination in the following words: 'it is one of the essential principles of contemporary international law'.[92]

Even though Judge Weeramantry, one of the two dissenting judges, did not agree with the Court that the absence of Indonesia prevented the Court from considering Portugal's claims, yet he fully agreed and supported the above observations of the Court in the following opening remarks of his dissenting opinion:

> I am . . . in agreement with the Court's observations in regard to the right to self-determination of the people of East Timor, their right to permanent sovereignty over their natural resources, and the *erga omnes* nature of these rights. The stress laid by the Court on self-determination as 'one of the essential principles of contemporary international law' (Judgment, para 29), has my complete and unqualified support[93].

Neither, despite its tough conservatism reasoning relating its jurisdiction, the Court failed in recognizing the true status of East Timor and their entitlement for the right of self-determination. That is obvious from the following words of the Court: 'The Court recalls in any event that it has taken note in the present Judgment (paragraph 31) that, for the two Parties, the territory of East Timor remains a non-self-governing territory and its people has the right to self-determination'.[94]

Taking clear note that 'for the two parties, the territory of East Timor remains a non-self-governing territory and its people has the right to self-determination', the Court added judicial cement to the facilitation of the ongoing East Timor's

[89] ICJ Reports 1995, p 102, para 29.

[90] *Ibid.*

[91] The one case was: Legal consequences for States of the Continued Presence of South Africa in Namibia (South West Africa) notwithstanding Security Council Resolution 276 (1970), Advisory Opinion, ICJ Reports 1971, pp 31–32, paras 52–53; the other case was: Western Sahara, Advisory Opinion, ICJ Reports 1975, pp 31–33, paras 54–59.

[92] ICJ Reports 1995, p 102, para 29.

[93] *Ibid*, p 142.

[94] *Ibid*, pp 105–6, para 37.

struggle for independence, hence recognizing that 'its people has the right to self-determination'.[95]

Even the other dissenting judge, Judge *ad hoc* Skubiszewski, did not fail to commend this restatement of the Court in the following words: 'The restatement in the Judgment is significant for an equitable settlement of the question of East Timor. I think that everybody who has the purposes and the principles of the United Nations at heart must commend the Court for this dictum.'[96]

Furthermore, Securing human dignity for the East-Timorese, the Court emphatically reminded the Parties in the case that the Security Council in its resolutions 384 (1975) and 389 (1976) has expressly called for the respect for 'the territorial integrity of East Timor as well as the inalienable right of its people to self-determination in accordance with General Assembly resolution 1514 (XV)'.[97]

In summary, the Court made a trinity of observations: 1) the people of East Timor has right to self-determination, 2) the people of East Timor has permanent sovereignty over their natural resources, and 3) and that these rights are characterized as *erga omnes*. Though these observations in the given case are centred around the people of East Timor, but taken in their generality this is a clarification, or at least further clarification in the form of reaffirmation, of the three different aspects of the principle of self-determination. The concept of State sovereignty is in the process of a rapid change and transformation. But these observations are stressing the aspect of peoples sovereignty in their general existential collectivity rather than State sovereignty in its political existence. It may not be adding new clarifications to the law in the developmental sense, yet it considerably solidifies the working of the principle of self-determination in all the four areas touched upon by Cassese.

IX. Conclusion

Having observed the judicial-ideological tug-of-war in the form of an equation drawn earlier—human dignity through self-determination v the doctrine of State sovereignty—one is bound to reach a bit of mixed conclusion in this case.

Seen within the framework of triangular criterion provided by 1) Kofi Annan—'We the peoples' at the centre of all we do at the UN, hence also at the ICJ—2) Justice J Frankfurter—a judgment cannot be imprisoned within the treacherous limits of any formula—and 3) Sir Henry Maine—the sole certain punishment would appear to be universal disapprobation—the operative clause of the Judgment is certainly a step backward in the development of human rights law and the promotion of the concept of human dignity.

[95] Western Sahara, Advisory Opinion, ICJ Reports 1975, pp 105–6, para 37.
[96] *Ibid*, p 226, para 2.
[97] *Ibid*, p 103, para 31.

In asking the Court to declare the Australia's signing of East Timor Gap Treaty as breaching its obligations under international law, Portugal was simply requesting the Court to enforce by law *the feeling of just treatment evolved through centuries of human history and civilization*, ie, respecting and protecting the rights and dignity of the people of East Timor through respecting and protecting the rights and dignity of the administration authority of Portugal, indeed representing international community of the United Nations, the institution the law whereof represents the feeling of just treatment evolved through centuries of human history and civilization. The '*treacherous formula*' in this case is that of the unjust application of the *Monetary Gold* principle, borne out of the out-of-date doctrine of State sovereignty, which by no means is a law binding on the Court, certainly not in the given case, time, place and circumstance. Had the Court not imprisoned its own process of judgment by this treacherous formula the Court would have pronounced the signing of East Timor Gap Treaty by Australia as an act violating: a) the principle of self-determination, b) the principle of permanent sovereignty over natural resources, c) the principle of 'sacred trust of civilization', and thereby violating the human dignity of the people of East Timor, the very dignity enshrined in their human right of self-determination and kept as 'sacred trust of civilization' in the hands of Portugal and 'we the peoples' international community of the United Nations. And, through the judicial guardianship of the International Court of Justice the Australian conduct would appear to be *universal disapprobation* by the international community.

Human dignity is the law and State sovereignty is secondary to it. The rule must follow the law and not law the rule. When rule follows the law the human dignity and justice blossom and get elevated. When law follows the rule, human dignity and justice wilt and get diminished. Human history, legal history included, is a story of trial and error. By making the human dignity follow the State sovereignty, the Court has certainly put the State sovereignty over and above human rights, hence '*fundamental rights . . . sacrificed in the supposed interests of the State*', as described by Kofi Annan.

However, the fact that through its *obiter dicta* the Court did add authority to the various areas of the principle of self-determination which needed clarification, and the same coupled with the most painstaking and extensive independent opinions of Judge Weeramantry and Judge *ad hoc* Skubiszewski, both establishing the primacy of sovereign international community over sovereign autonomy of a single State and at the same time providing considerable clarification to the principles of human rights law, the development of human rights law in the given Judgment is certainly an immense step forward. The dissenting opinions of two dissenting judges, strongly applauded in academic circles, would no doubt stand conspicuous as making their praiseworthy contributions to the development of human rights law and human dignity.

And finally, as the judgment of the Court is a majority vote judgment, hence reflective of the aggregate of the prevailing majority judicial ideology, sadly very conservative in this case, did not remain unchallenged by the healthy public dissent which strongly praised the dissenting opinions of two judges, provided plenty optimism in the sense that the Court cannot remain untouched by the fact that the concept of sovereignty cannot be interpreted in isolation to the prevailing human rights doctrine at the very basis of the UN Charter. Though the human dignity in this case lost to the state sovereignty, yet the hard and healthy criticism of the judgment in this case, on the one hand by its dissenting judges and on the other by the academic circles, flung the door wide open to the perceptions of judicial conscience of mankind. The same in turn not only facilitated the liberation of the people of East Timor from the military oppression of Indonesia but also condemned the joint economic and political loot of East Timor by Australia and Indonesia.

10

Application of the Convention on the Prevention and Punishment of the Crime of Genocide case (*Bosnia and Herzegovina v Yugoslavia*)[1] (1993–): Prohibition of Genocide as *Jus Cogens*

ON 20 MARCH 1993, the Republic of Bosnia and Herzegovina instituted proceedings against the Federal Republic of Yugoslavia in respect of a dispute concerning alleged violations of the Convention on the Prevention and Punishment of the Crime of Genocide as well as some other matters connected therewith. As the basis of jurisdiction Bosnia relied upon Article IX of the Genocide Convention. Among the major documents concerning human rights, Bosnia referred, in addition to the Genocide Convention, to several provisions of the United Nations Charter and to the 1948 Universal Declaration of Human Rights.

Immediately after the filing the Application instituting the proceedings, Bosnia also filed, the same day, a request for the indication of provisional measures, stating that: 'The overriding objective of this Request is to prevent further loss of *human life* in Bosnia and Herzegovina', and that: 'The very lives, well being, health, safety, physical, mental and bodily integrity, homes, property and personal possessions of hundreds of thousands of people in Bosnia and Herzegovina are right now at stake, hanging in the balance, awaiting the order of the Court'. Introducing the gravity of the situation in this way, Bosnia requested the Court to indicate the following provisional measures, among others:

> That Yugoslavia (Serbia and Montenegro), together with its agents and surrogates in Bosnia and elsewhere, must immediately cease and desist from all *acts of genocide* and

[1] At present official name of former Yugoslavia is *Serbia and Montenegro*. The composition of the Court in the Order of 8 April 1993 on Provision Measures in the *Bosnia v Yugoslavia* case was: President Sir Robert Jennings; Vice-President Oda; Judges Ago, Schwebel, Bedjaoui, Ni, Evensen, Tarassov, Guillaume, Shahabuddeen, Aguilar Mawdsley, Weeramantry, Ranjeva, and Ajibola. (see ICJ Reports, 1993, p 3).
Judge Tarassov appended a Declaration to the Order of the Court (see ICJ Reports, 1993, p 25).

> *genocidal acts* against People and State of Bosnia and Herzegovina, including but not limited to murder, summary executions; torture; rape; mayhem; so-called 'ethnic cleansing'; the wanton devastation of villages, towns, districts and cities; the siege of villages, towns, districts and cities; the starvation of the civilian population; the interruption of, interference with, or harassment of humanitarian relief supplies to the civilian population by the international community; the bombardment of civilian population centres; and the detention of civilians in concentration camps or otherwise.

On 1 April 1993, Yugoslavia submitted its written observations on Bosnia's request, in which it, in turn, recommended the Court to order the application of provisional measures to Bosnia and Herzegovina. After hearing the oral observations of both the parties, the Court issued an Order on 8 April 1993 indicating the following provisional measures:

> (a) The Government of the Federal Republic of Yugoslavia should immediately, in pursuance of its undertaking in the Convention on the Prevention and Punishment of the Crime of Genocide of 9 December 1948, take all measures within its power to prevent commission of the crime of genocide; and the Government of the Federal Republic of Yugoslavia should in particular ensure that any military, paramilitary or irregular armed units which may be directed or supported by it, as well as any organizations and persons which may be subject to its control, direction or influence, do not commit any acts of genocide, or conspiracy to commit genocide, of direct and public incitement to commit genocide, or of complicity in genocide, whether directed against the Muslim population of Bosnia and Herzegovina or against any other national, ethnical, racial or religious group.
> (b) The Government of Federal Republic of Yugoslavia and the Government of Bosnia and Herzegovina should not take any action and should ensure that no action is taken which may aggravate or extend the existing dispute over the prevention or punishment of the crime of genocide, or render it more difficult of solution.[2]

It may be noted that the Application of the Convention on the Prevention and Punishment of the Crime of Genocide falls under those cases where provisional measures to protect human rights are ordered just because the compliance with the human rights obligations is the subject matter of the dispute.[3] Yet, it is equally striking that other than taking notice of the facts and law mentioned in the Application and the Request for Provisional Measures by Bosnia, the Court did not make any particular effort to elaborate and interpret the law of genocide rigorously. Even when it came to the meaning of the term genocide, the Court simply reproduced the definition word by word given in the text of Article II of the Genocide Convention.[4] However, the Court did not fail to recall the gravity of the crime described in the following words of the General Assembly resolution 96(1)

[2] Application of the Convention on the Prevention and Punishment of the Crime of Genicide (*Bosnia and Herzegovina v Yugoslavia*), ICJ Reports, 1993, p 24.

[3] See R Higgins, 'The International Court of Justice and Human Rights' in K Wellens, (ed), *International Law: Theory and Practice: Essays in Honour of Eric Suy* (The Hague, Martinus Nijhoff, 1998) 694, 700.

[4] ICJ Reports, 1993, p 20.

of 11 December 1946 on the crime of Genocide: Whereas the crime of genocide 'shocks the conscience of mankind, results in great losses of humanity and is contrary to moral law and to the spirit and aims of the United Nations'.[5]

Not seeing any implementation on the part of Yugoslavia, Bosnia filed a second request on 27 July 1973, requesting the Court to indicate additional measures Two of these requested measures related to the possibility of 'partition and dismemberment', annexation or incorporation of the sovereign territory of Bosnia and Herzegovina. At this, on 5 August 1993, prior to issuing an Order on the second request the President of the Court called upon the parties and stated:

> I do now call upon the Parties so to act, and I stress that the provisional measures already indicated in the Order which the Court made after hearing the Parties, on 8 April 1993, still apply. Accordingly I call upon the Parties to take renewed note of the Court's Order and to take all and any measures that may be within their power to prevent any commission, continuance, or encouragement of the heinous international crime of genocide.[6]

In the light of the definition of Genocide provided in Article II of the Genocide Convention, the Court could not accept 'partition and dismemberment' constituting an act of genocide. The Court this time found it necessary to clarify the meaning of the crime of genocide and declared in its Order of 13 September 1993[7] as following:

> . . . it appears to the Court, from the definition of genocide in Article II of the Genocide Convention . . . that its essential characteristic is the intended destruction of 'a national, ethnical, racial or religious group', and not the disappearance of a State as a subject of international law or a change in its constitution or its territory. Accordingly, the Court is unable to accept for the purpose of the present request for the indication of provisional measures, that a 'partition and dismemberment', or annexation of a sovereign State, or its incorporation into another State, could in itself constitute an act of genocide.[8]

Judge Lauterpacht, the judge *ad hoc* for Bosnia in this case, while fully agreeing with the provisional measures indicated by the Court, found it necessary to append to the Order his Separate Opinion underlining that: 'Indeed, the prohibition of genocide has generally been accepted as having the status not of an ordinary rule of international law but of *jus cogens*. Indeed, prohibition of genocide long been regarded as one of the few undoubted examples of *jus cogens*.'[9]

[5] *Ibid*, p 23.

[6] *Ibid*, p 334.

[7] The composition of the Court in the Order of 13 September 1993 on Provisional Measures in *Bosnia v Yugoslavia* case was: President Sir Robert Jennings; Vice-President Oda; Judges Schwebel, Bedjaoui, Ni, Evensen, Tarassov, Guillaume, Shahabuddeen, Aguilar Mawdsley, Weeramantry, Ajibola, and Herczegh; Judges *ad hoc* Lauterpacht and Kreca (see ICJ Reports 1993, p 325).

Vice-President Oda appended a Declaration to the Order of the Court; Judges Shahabuddeen, Weeramantry, Ajibola, and Judge *ad hoc* Lauterpacht appended Separate Opinions to the Order of the Court; Judge Tarassov and Judge *ad hoc* Kreca appended their Dissenting Opinions to the Order of the Court (see ICJ Reports 1993, p 350).

[8] ICJ Reports, 1993, p 345.

[9] *Ibid*, p 440.

Judge Lauterpacht had also pointed to the possible limitations to Article 103 of the United Nations Charter[10] itself by operation of *jus cogens*, which he considered, as a matter of hierarchy of norms, to be superior to both customary international law and treaty.[11]

Unfortunately, the provisional measures indicated by the Court in its Order of 8 April 1993, and further recalled, stressed and renewed by a letter from the Court's President on 5 August 1993 addressed to the parties, and reaffirmed in its Order of 13 September 1993, went utterly unheeded, proving the traditional belief that justice without power cannot be effective.

The Court now moved to its jurisdictional phase to deal with the seven preliminary objections raised by the government of Yugoslavia against the jurisdiction of the Court and the admissibility of the application filed by Bosnia-Herzegovina. The Court in its judgment on jurisdiction and admissibility, delivered on 11 July 1996, considered, *inter alia*, the arguments of Yugoslavia according to which the Genocide Convention was not binding upon the two Parties or had not entered into force between them and the dispute submitted by Bosnia did not fall within the provisions of Article IX of the Convention, the principal basis of Court's jurisdiction in this case. The Court held that the proceedings instituted were between those two States whose territories were located within the former Socialist Federal Republic of Yugoslavia. At the time of the proclamation of the Federal Republic of Yugoslavia, on 27 April 1992, a formal declaration had been adopted on its behalf which expressed the intention of Yugoslavia to remain bound by the international treaties to which the former Yugoslavia was party. The Court also observed that it had not been contested that Yugoslavia was party to the Genocide Convention. Thus, according to the Court, Yugoslavia was bound by the provisions of the Convention on the date of 20 March 1993 when the application was filed by Bosnia.[12]

As far as Bosnia and Herzegovina is concerned, the Court observed that on 29 December 1992, Bosnia had transmitted to the UN Secretary-General, as depository of the Genocide Convention, a Notice of Succession. The validity of this Notice was contested by Yugoslavia. The Court noted that Bosnia and Herzegovina had become a Member of the United Nations following the decisions adopted on 22 May 1992 by the Security Council and the General Assembly, bodies competent under the UN Charter. Article XI of the Genocide Convention opened it to 'any Member of the United Nations'; from the time of its admission to the Organization, Bosnia and Herzegovina had thus been able to become a party to the Convention. The Court was of the view that the circumstances of Bosnia and Herzegovina's accession to independence, which Yugoslavia referred to in its third

[10] Article 103 of the Charter reads: 'In the event of a conflict between the obligations of the Members of the United Nations under the present Charter and their obligations under any other international agreement, their obligations under the present Charter shall prevail.'

[11] V Gowlland-Debbas, 'Judicial Insights into Fundamental Values and Interests of the International Community' (1997) *Leiden Journal of International Law* 335.

[12] ICJ Reports, 1996, p 610.

preliminary objection, were of little consequence. The Court concluded that it was clear from the foregoing that Bosnia was able to become a party to the Convention through the mechanism of State succession.[13]

Instead of adopting a progressive approach of automatic succession to human rights treaties, the Court in this case chose a rather conservative approach which is evident from its following words:

> Without prejudice as to whether or not the principle of 'automatic succession' applies in the case of certain types of international treaties or conventions, the Court does not consider it necessary, in order to decide on its jurisdiction in this case, to make a determination on the legal issues concerning State succession in respect to treaties which have been raised by the Parties. Whether Bosnia and Herzegovina automatically became party to the Genocide Convention on the date of its accession to independence on 6 March 1992, or whether it became a party as a result—retroactive or not—of its Notice of Succession of 29 December 1992, at all events it was a party to it on the date of the filing of its Application on 20 March 1993.[14]

Judge Higgins, who did not sit in this case, later observed in an essay that:

> The Court could have lent its weight to the emerging progressive doctrine on State succession to human rights treaties. But it chose to avoid taking a position, invoking grounds that, ironically, seem less rooted in established law . . . The retrospective application of jurisdictional clauses in treaties is in fact an extremely complex matter, representing perhaps a far greater legal minefield than support for the emerging doctrine of automatic succession to human rights treaties.[15]

The public hearings on the merits in the case were concluded on 9 May 2006. The Court is now deliberating in camera.

[13] *Ibid*, p 610–11.

[14] *Ibid*, p 612.

[15] R Higgins, 'The International Court of Justice and Human Rights' in K Wellens, (ed), *International Law: Theory and Practice: Essays in Honour of Eric Suy* (The Hague, Martinus Nijhoff, 1998) 694, 696–97.

11

Legality of Use of Force[1] (*Yugoslavia*[2] *v Belgium*; *Yugoslavia v Canada*; *Yugoslavia v France*; *Yugoslavia v Germany*; *Yugoslavia v Italy*; *Yugoslavia v Netherlands*; *Yugoslavia v Portugal*; *Yugoslavia v Spain*; *Yugoslavia v United Kingdom*; *Yugoslavia v USA*) (1999–2004)

To accept as lawful the deliberate terrorization of the enemy community by the infliction of large-scale destruction comes too close to rendering pointless all legal limitations on the exercise of violence.

(McDougal and Feliciano[3])

. . . genocidal behaviour cannot be shielded by claims of sovereignty, but neither can these claims be overridden by unauthorized uses of force delivered in an excessive and inappropriate manner.[4]

[1] The composition of the Court in the Orders on Provisional Measures made in these cases on 2 June 1999 was: Vice-President Weeramantry (as Acting President); President Schwebel; Judges Oda, Bedjaoui, Guillaume, Ranjeva, Herczegh, Shi, Fleischhauer, Koroma, Vereshchetin, Higgins, Parra-Aranguren, Kooijmans, Rezek; Judges *ad hoc* Gaja, Kreca, Duinslaeger.

[2] At present the new official name of former Yugoslavia is Serbia and Montenegro.

[3] MS McDougal and FP Feliciano, *Law and Minimum World Public Order: The Legal Regulation of International Coercion* (1961) 657.

[4] R Falk, 'Humanitarian Intervention after Kosovo' in L Boisson de Chazournes and V Gowlland-Debbas, *The International Legal System in Quest of Equity and Universality: Liber Amicorum Georges Abi-Saab* (2001) 179.

I. Yugoshima: Human Rights Issues of the Gravest Nature: Law Remained Silent When the Bombs Spoke

It is a matter of public knowledge that first the alleged ethnic cleansing by the government of Yugoslavia in Kosovo and then the alleged unauthorized and indiscriminate bombing of Yugoslavian people and premises by the NATO countries has put not only the entire Yugoslavia on fire but the entire edifice of the International Bill of Rights to burning. Ten cases filed by Yugoslavia on 29 April 1999 in the International Court of Justice against ten NATO States—Belgium, Canada, France, Germany, Italy, Portugal, Spain, the United Kingdom and the United States of America—raise human rights issues of the 'gravest nature',[5] as described by the Vice-President and Acting President of the ICJ, on both sides. The United Nations and international law were simply silenced and pushed to the corner. *'Zwijgt het Recht als de Wapens Spreken'* (Law Remains Silent When Weapons Speak), the self-explanatory title of a Dutch book written by Prof Kalshoven in the 70s became a painful reality once again. Innocent civilians were being killed by both sides. Neither the Yugoslavian leader nor the NATO authorities were being punished; it was the people who were being punished. When the entire population of a nation is in the grip of the fear of death at the hands of its own government at home and the military forces from abroad, this amounts to a mockery of human rights. As far as the population of Yugoslavia, Kosovo included, is concerned, after the atomic-bombing of Hiroshima and Nagasaki, Yugoslavia became the first country in the post second world war period to be the victim of 'might is right'. The phenomenon may therefore well be described as Yugoshima.

Viewing the law and the concept of human rights in its universality and the Yugoslavia crisis in its globality and the entire jurisprudence of the International Court in its totality, the issues involved and the jurisdictional hand-cuff of the Court in these cases put a great question mark on the very core of the international judicial conscience of the Human rights law. If 'each judgment is either a step forward or a step backward in the development of law', as Judge Lachs put it; then the Orders on Provisional Measures, not providing any relief, issued by the ICJ in these cases have no doubt taken the development, in the sense of protection, of human rights law 'a step backward'. It is in this light the following pages of this chapter intend to describe how the Court remained helpless to develop and enhance the human rights law and human dignity in the given cases.

As a result of the constant rain of NATO bombs for several weeks, it was as if lightning struck the premises of the International Court of Justice, when on 29 April 1999 the Government of Yugoslavia all of a sudden brought ten cases before the Court against the above mentioned ten NATO States. Never in the history of this Court, nor even during the time of its predecessor, the Permanent

[5] Legality of Use of Force (*Yugoslavia v Belgium*), Order of 2 June 1999, Dissenting Opinion of Vice-President Weeramantry, ICJ Reports 1999, p 502.

Court of International Justice, so many cases have been filed by one State against so many at one time, neither individually nor collectively. Among various titles of jurisdiction in each case, one common basis of jurisdiction in all the cases was Article IX of the 1948 Convention on the Prevention and Punishment of the Crime of Genocide. Equally, that Convention formed part of the Yugoslavia's statement of law in each case. Other than the Genocide Convention, the 'legal grounds on which the claim was based' in each case also included, among others, the provisions of the International Covenant on Civil and Political Rights (1966) and of the International Covenant on Economic, Social and Cultural Rights (1966). Included in its statement of claim in each case Yugoslavia's Applications mentioned, among other things, that

> by taking part in killing civilians, destroying enterprises, communications, health and cultural institutions, each respondent has acted against the Federal Republic of Yugoslavia in breach of its obligation *to respect the right to life*, the *right to work*, the *right to information*, the *right to health* care as well as other *basic human rights*.[6]

And further, in the statement of facts upon which the claim is based, the government of Yugoslavia stated: 'The use of weapons containing depleted uranium is having far-reaching consequences for *human life*. The above mentioned acts are deliberately creating conditions calculated at physical *destruction of an ethnic group*, in whole or in part.'[7]

Together with the ten Applications, ten Requests for the Indication of Provisional Measures were filed at the same time. Among the 'reasons' for the requesting the ordering of provisional measures by the Court were mentioned that the Federal Republic of Yugoslavia is exposed to acts of the use of force by each respondent. Each 'has violated its international obligations . . . to the *fundamental rights and liberties of the individual*, to the ban on the prohibited weapons and on deliberate *infliction on ethnic groups* conditions of life calculated to bring about physical *destruction of the group*.'[8] And further, it continued: 'The bombing of oil refineries and oil storage tanks as well as chemical plants is bound to produce massive pollution of the environment, posing a threat to *human life*, plants and animals. The use of weapons containing depleted uranium warheads is having far-reaching consequences for *human health*'.[9]

The Applications and the Requests were immediately transmitted to their respective respondents, the Secretary-General of the United Nations was informed, and a Circular Letter was accordingly sent to all States parties to the Statute of the International Court of Justice. The Court fixed the dates to hear the

[6] Legality of Use of Force (*Yugoslavia v Belgium*), Application of 29 April 1999, p 10. And similarly in other nine such Applications.

[7] Legality of Use of Force (*Yugoslavia v Belgium*), Application of 29 April 1999, p 12. And also in all other nine Applications.

[8] *Ibid*, Request for Provisional Measures of 29 April, p 3. And all other nine similar Requests.

[9] *Ibid*.

parties in connection with the proceedings on ordering the provisional measures by the Court.

After the Advisory Opinion of 28 May 1951 on the reservations to the Genocide Convention and the Genocide case filed by Bosnia against Yugoslavia on 20 March 1993, involving the questions relating the Genocide Convention, it is the first time that the Court was asked to apply and interpret the Genocide Convention, together with other laws governing human rights.

After hearing the statements of Yugoslavia and all respondents between 10 and 12 May, the Court gave its decisions on the requests for the indication of provisional measures submitted by Yugoslavia, refusing to indicate the measures. in any of the cases, for the lack of jurisdiction in all the cases.

In two of the ten cases (*Yugoslavia v Spain* and *Yugoslavia v USA*), the Court held that it manifestly lacked jurisdiction and ordered that the cases be removed from the General List of the Court.[10]

In the other eight cases (*Yugoslavia v Belgium*; *Yugoslavia v Canada*; *Yugoslavia v France*; *Yugoslavia v Germany*; *Yugoslavia v Italy*; *Yugoslavia v Netherlands*; *Yugoslavia v Portugal*; *Yugoslavia v United Kingdom*), the Court found that it lacked *prima facie* jurisdiction, which is a prerequisite for the issuing of provisional measures, and that it therefore could not indicate such measures.[11] A fuller consideration of the question of jurisdiction will take place at a later date in future. Hence, the Court accordingly remains seized of these eight cases and has reserved the subsequent procedure for further decision.[12]

II. *Grund* Case, *Grund* Subject, *Grund* Law and *Grund* Obligation

With minor differences on the 'basis of jurisdiction', all the cases, as far as the subject of the dispute, the claims submitted and the human rights law to be applied are concerned, are identical. Hence, for convenience sake the common references are made only to the documents in one case, *Yugoslavia v Belgium* (in view of the first country in alphabetic order).

In its Application bringing case against Belgium, Yugoslavia defines the subject of the dispute as follows:

> The subject-matter of the dispute are acts of the Kingdom of Belgium by which it has violated its international obligation banning the use of force against another State, the obligation not to intervene in internal affairs of another State, the obligation not to violate the sovereignty of another State, the obligation to protect the civilian population and civilian objects in wartime, the obligation to protect the environment, the obligation relating to free navigation on international rivers, the obligation regarding fundamental

[10] ICJ Comminique No 99/23 dated 2 June 1999, p 1.

[11] *Ibid.*

[12] *Ibid.*

human rights and freedoms, the obligation not to use prohibited weapons, the obligation not to deliberately inflict conditions of life calculated to cause the physical destruction of a national group.[13]

If at the core of the entire body of human rights law is the *right to life* then the respect for human life must be seen as the *Grundnorm* of the whole body of human rights law. The subject of the dispute summarized in the above paragraph in the Yugoslavia's Application(s) seems fundamentally related to every aspect of life of the Yugoslavian people, calling forth the help of every human rights law in order to stop violation of every related international obligation in question. In brief, in the human rights field this case is the case of cases, the '*Grund*' case, the subject of subjects, the '*Grund*' subject, the law of laws, the '*Grund*' law and the obligation of obligations, the '*Grund*' obligation. The right to life at the core of human rights law, irrespective of its jurisdiction *ratione personae*, *ratione temporis* and *ratione materiae*, is an obligation *erga omnes*, be it relating a State, government or an organization, national or international, and the International Court of Justice is no exception. Neither NATO States nor Yugoslavian government are immune to this obligation. When a dispute is brought by one State against another, and also requesting indication of provisional measures, it is up to the Court to examine the statements of facts and decide which laws to apply and to indicate which measures to which party. The Court in these cases have declined to indicate any provisional measures just on the basis that in the two cases (against Spain and USA) it has no jurisdiction at all and that in the other eight cases it has no *prima facie* jurisdiction which is as per the case law of the Court a prerequisite for the indication of provisional measures. The dispute in a nutshell is that human rights in Yugoslavia are violated by ten NATO States. But they were equally violated by the Yugoslavian government itself. At the stage of provisional measures nothing, if the jurisdiction existed, could stop the Court to indicate the required measures to all the Parties, including the Applicant. The claims of Yugoslavia in a nutshell are that the obligations *erga omnes* are violated. And the submission of Yugoslavia in nutshell is that NATO States stop violating the human rights in Yugoslavia. But this should not mean that the Yugoslavian government itself is not violating the human rights in its own territory. Whether the violator is the Applicant or the Respondents, it is up to the Court to decide when dealing with the merits of the case(s). But, at the provisional measures stage all that was asked, and even if not asked, the Court had the authority, nay even the duty, was that the Court indicate the required measures to stop the violation of human rights by any or all the parties involved, be it an applicant or a respondent. In other words an injunctive relief was not only asked by the applicant but was the need of the people victims of the violation of human rights. Judge Koroma (Sierra Leone) mentions that: 'These are perhaps the most serious cases to come before the Court for injunctive relief.'[14]

[13] Legality of Use of Force (*Yugoslavia v Belgium*), Provisional Measures, Order of 2 June 1999, ICJ Reports 1999, p 125.

[14] Legality of Use of Force (*Yugoslavia v Belgium*), Order of 2 June 1999, on Provisional Measures, Declaration of Judge Koroma, ICJ Reports 1999, p 142.

Judge Vereshchetin (Russia) also observed that:

> The extraordinary circumstances in which Yugoslavia made its request for protection imposed a need to react immediately. The Court should have promptly expressed its profound concern over the unfolding human misery, loss of life and serious violations of international law which by the time of the request were already a matter of public knowledge. It is unbecoming of the principal judicial organ of the United Nations, whose very *raison d'être* is the peaceful resolution of international disputes, to maintain silence in such a situation.[15]

But the 'judicial guardian' of the international community broke its silence on 2 June 1999 only to say that it can do nothing because it had no jurisdiction. Not all the judges agreed with this stance and conclusion of the Court.

III. *Obiter Dicta v Ratio Decidendi*: Human Rights Could Not Be Protected

In its Orders on Provisional Measures the Court refers to the following claims submitted by Yugoslavia to the Court and takes notice of the facts on which they are based:

> The Government of the Kingdom of Belgium, together with the Governments of other Member States of NATO, took part in the acts of use of force against the Federal Republic of Yugoslavia by taking part in the bombing targets in the Federal Republic of Yugoslavia. In bombing the Federal Republic of Yugoslavia military and civilian targets were attacked. Great number of people were killed, including a great many civilians. Residential houses came under attack. Numerous dwellings were destroyed. Enormous damage was caused to schools, hospitals, radio and television stations, cultural and health institutions and to places of worship. A large number of bridges, roads and railway lines were destroyed. Attacks on oil refineries and chemical plants have had serious environmental effects on cities, towns and villages in the Federal Republic of Yugoslavia. The use of weapons of containing depleted uranium is having far-reaching consequences for human life. The above mentioned acts are deliberately creating conditions calculated at the physical destruction of an ethnic group, in whole or in part. The Government of the Kingdom of Belgium is taking part in the training, arming, financing, equipping and supplying the so-called 'Kosovo Liberation Army'.[16]

It is clear enough that every single human person in Yugoslavia was living under the fear of death that any moment of the day or night a bomb or missile could end his or her life. And those who were still living at their work places were being destroyed, water-supplies cut, no gas to cook food, and the pregnant women dying while delivering their babies because hospitals were bombed, etc, etc. If this was to be seen in the light of the concepts of '*dignity of human person*' and the '*scourge of*

[15] Legality of Use of Force (*Yugoslavia v Belgium*), Order of 2 June 1999 on Provisional Measures, Dissenting Opinion of Judge Vereschetin, ICJ Reports 1999, p 209.

[16] *Ibid*, p 125.

war', then the human rights law in the Court this time had sunk to the middle ages. The Preamble of the UN Charter itself opens with the following words: 'We the people of the United Nations determined to save succeeding generations from the *scourge of war*, which twice in our life has brought untold sorrow to mankind, and to reaffirm faith in fundamental human rights, in the *dignity and worth of the human person* . . ..' The Court's Order has at no moment in its Orders made even the passing reference to these words. The very opening words of the Preamble of the 1948 Universal Declaration of Human Rights say: 'Whereas recognition of the *inherent dignity* and of the equal and inalienable rights of all members of the human family is the foundation of freedom, justice and peace in the world'. The Preamble of the 1966 International Covenant on Civil and Political Rights also mentions that:

> The States Parties to the present Covenant,
>
> Considering that, in accordance with the principles proclaimed in the Charter of the United Nations, recognition of the inherent dignity and of the equal and inalienable rights of all members of the human family is the foundation of freedom, justice and peace in the world . . ..

And these words are repeated in ditto in the preamble of the 1966 International Covenant on Economic, Social and Cultural Rights as well.

The last two instruments were also invoked by Yugoslavia in its statement of legal grounds as following:

> The above acts of the Government of Belgium represent a gross violation of the obligation not to use force against another State. By financing, arming, training and equipping the so-called 'Kosovo Liberation Army', support is given to terrorist groups and the secessionist movement in the territory of the Federal Republic of Yugoslavia in breach of the obligation not to intervene in the internal affairs of another State. In addition, the provisions of the Geneva Convention of 1949 and of the Additional Protocol No 1 of 1977 on the protection of civilians and civilian objects in time of war have been violated. The obligation to protect the environment has also been breached. The destruction of bridges on the Danube is in contravention of the provisions of Article 1 of the 1948 Convention on free navigation on the Danube. The provisions of the International Covenant on Civil and Political Rights and of the International Covenant on Economic, Social and Cultural Rights of 1966 have also been breached. Furthermore, the obligation contained in the Convention on the Prevention and Punishment of the Crime of Genocide not to impose deliberately on a national group conditions of life calculated to bring about physical destruction of the group has been breached. Furthermore, the activities in which the Kingdom of Belgium is taking part are contrary to Article 53, paragraph 1, of the Charter of the United Nations.[17]

In its *obiter dicta* part, the following preambulary paragraphs are of striking feature and certainly the guardians of human rights law:

[17] Legality of Use of Force (*Yugoslavia v Belgium*), Application of Yugoslavia, Printed Version, p 12.

16. Whereas the Court is deeply concerned with the human tragedy, the loss of life, and the enormous suffering in Kosovo which form the background of the present dispute, and with the continuing loss of life and human suffering in all parts of Yugoslavia;

17. Whereas the Court is profoundly concerned with the use of force in Yugoslavia; whereas under the present circumstances such use raises very serious issues of international law;

Whereas the Court is mindful of the purposes and principles of the United Nations Charter and of its own responsibilities in the maintenance of peace and security under the Charter and the Statute of the Court;

19. Whereas the Court deems it necessary to emphasize that all parties before it must act in conformity with their obligations under the United Nations Charter and other rules of international law, including humanitarian law.[18]

Despite all these concerns, the Court found itself helpless to stop this human tragedy and loss of life and mentioned in its operative part of the Orders that it could not indicate any provisional measures, for it lacked *prima facie* jurisdiction to do so.[19] Hence, to protect the human rights, to transfer the *obiter dicta* paragraphs to the operational part as *ratio decidendi* of the Order(s) on Provisional Measures, the hindrance was the self chosen ideology of judicial restraint exercised under the rule of *prima facie* jurisdiction. The Court in these cases has taken a strictly positivistic and formalistic approach overlooking the fact that human rights are mainly for the 'ruled,' devoid of human dignity for ages, and not for 'rulers,' the violators of human dignity for ages. The traditional separation between fact and value, and between form and content reflects here in strong measure. This 'binary thinking' such as fact/value, form/content, inside/outside, idealism/realism, political/legal, and political/humanitarian[20] is a pre-human-rights positivistic thinking which is devoid of social dimension of human rights and human dignity. Actually it is 'inner morality of law,' springing from the human rights provisions in the UN Charter, in the form of interaction between the citizen (a new subject of international law) and lawgiver which is at the basis of contemporary international law as against the narrow positivistic thinking in which only the rulers, sovereign States, were the subjects of international law. Lon Fuller, the author of Morality of Law, who distinguishes himself from positivists, rightly hits the point in his words:

. . . the positivist recognizes in the functioning of a legal system nothing that can truly be called a *social dimension.* The positivist sees the law at the point of its dispatch by the lawgiver and again at the point of its impact on the legal subject. He does not see the lawgiver and the citizen in interaction with one another, and by virtue of that failure he fails

[18] Legality of Use of Force (*Yugoslavia v Belgium*), Order of 2 June 1999 on Provisional Measures, ICJ Reports 1999, pp 131–32.

[19] . *Ibid*, pp 132–40.

[20] D Warner, 'Ethics, Law and Unethical Compassion in the Kosovo Intervention' in L Boisson de Chazournes and V Gowlland-Debbas, *The International Legal System in Quest of Equity and Universality: Liber Amicorum Georges Abi-Saab* (2001) 201.

to see that the creation of an effective interaction between them is an essential ingredient of the law itself.[21]

This interaction between the lawgiver and the individual human beings at the level of international law is the development as a result of the creation of human rights basis on human dignity, as a new branch of international law, which by all means reflect and asserts as human rights dimension of whole body of international law. Human dignity may also be seen as the 'inner morality' of international law. Human dignity is thus inevitably tied to any interpretation of international law, be it in form or content.

IV. *Prima Facie* Jurisdiction and Human Rights

It must be stated with added emphasis that the requirements of the jurisdiction, particularly its formula of *prima facie* jurisdiction are not the requirements mentioned either in the Statute of the Court or its Rules. The formula's origin does not go back farther than 1972. And it almost never was applied in a case where human tragedy and loss of life were involved comparable to the heart-rending situation of Yugoshima magnitude.

After reasoning the situation out the sole reason the Court gave in its Orders for not indicating the provisional measures, hence giving no relief to suffering and dying humanity, was in the following words:

> Whereas the Court has found above that it had no prima facie jurisdiction to entertain Yugoslavia's Application, either on the basis of Article 36, paragraph 2, of the Statute or of Article IX of the Genocide Convention; . . . and whereas it follows that the Court cannot indicate any provisional measures whatsoever in order to protect the rights claimed by Yugoslavia in its Application.[22]

The '*Grundnorm*' of the requirements for the indication of provisional measures by the Court is provided in Article 41 of its Statute which states:

> 1. The Court shall have the power to indicate, if it considers the circumstances so require, any provisional measures which ought to be taken to preserve rights of either party.
> 2. Pending the final decision, notice of the measures suggested shall forthwith be given to the parties and to the Security Council.

The provision, it is clear, does not put any requirements of jurisdiction to be established at the provisional measures stage. It leaves up to the Court to decide to indicate the measures 'if . . . circumstances so require'. However, even if Article 41 does not require the Court to satisfy itself at the provisional measures stage that it has

[21] LL Fuller, *The Morality of Law* (New Haven, CT, Yale University Press, 1969) 193.

[22] Legality of Use of Force (*Yugoslavia v Belgium*), Order of 2 June 1999 on Provisional Measures, ICJ Reports 1999, p 139.

jurisdiction on the merits of the case, yet the Court's own case law has developed the following *prima facie* formula:

> Whereas, on a request for the indication of provisional measures the Court need not, before deciding whether or not to indicate them, finally satisfy itself that it has jurisdiction on the merits of the case, but whereas it may not indicate them unless the provisions invoked by the Applicant appear, *prima facie*, to afford a basis on which the jurisdiction of the Court might be founded.[23]

However, seen the 'human rights issues of the gravest nature' at stake on both sides, one simply needs to recall that this *prima facie* formula is, though at present an established principle of the Court's jurisdictional jurisprudence, is of very recent origin. Just to mention one case of 1951, the *Anglo-Iranian Oil Company* case, in which not only the respondent (Iran) objected to the Court's jurisdiction before the date of making the Order on provisional measures, but also the Court even came to the conclusion in its later judgment[24] that it indeed had no jurisdiction to adjudicate on the merits of the case filed by the United Kingdom. And yet the Court did indicate the provisional measures in its Order of 5 July 1951. With no mention of the *prima facie* jurisdiction the Court had following to say about the jurisdictional questions:

> Whereas the indication of such measures in no way prejudges the question of the jurisdiction of the Court to deal with the merits of the case and leaves unaffected the right of the Respondent to submit arguments against such jurisdiction;
>
> Whereas the object of interim measures of protection provided for in the Statute is to preserve the respective rights of the Parties pending the decision of the Court, and whereas from the general terms of Article 41 of the Statute and from the power recognized by Article 61, paragraph 6, of the Rules of Court, to indicate interim measures of protection *proprio motu*, it follows that the Court must be concerned to preserve by such measures the rights which may be subsequently adjudged by the Court to belong either to the Applicant or to the Respondent;
>
> Whereas the existing state of affairs justifies the indication of interim measures of protection.[25]

One cannot understand that if the indication of provisional measures were justified without the requirement of *prima facie* jurisdiction in as simple a case as *Anglo-Iranian Oil Company*, why it was not justified in the cases involving gravest of human rights issues. It may also be added that the ICJ is not bound by the doctrine of *stare decisis* and the decisions given in all contentious cases are binding only on the parties involved.[26] The concept of provisional measures interpreted from the dimension of human rights and human dignity would, as a matter of fact

[23] *LeGrand* case (*Germany vUSA*), Order of 3 March 1999 on Provisional Measures, p 5.

[24] *Anglo-Iranian Oil Co*, Judgment of 22 July 1952, ICJ Reports 1952, p 115.

[25] *Anglo-Iranian Oil Co* Case (*UK v Iran*), Order of 5 July 1951 on Interim Measures, ICJ Reports, 1951, p 93.

[26] Article 59 of the Court's Statute provides: 'The decision of the Court has no binding force except between the parties and in respect of that partricular case.'

as well as value, not fail to find that there is inherent jurisdiction within the system of provisional measures to indicate the measures when life and dignity of the 'ruled,' new subject of and participant in international law, are in danger.

In view of the fact that in the present *Yugoslavia v NATO* cases, the President of the International Court of Justice has taken no action authorized under Article 74, paragraph 4, of the Court's Rules, it may also be observed that in the Anglo-Iranian Oil Co case, the gravity of which has no comparison with the present human rights violations in Yugoslavia, the then President did not fail to write a telegraphic message, under Article 61 of the Rules of Court, the equivalent Article 74, paragraph 4, of the present revised Rules, to the Iranian Prime Minister and to the Minister for Foreign Affairs. The President's message was in the following terms:

> Court being due to meet to consider Request for indication provisional measures of protection filed June 22nd by the United Kingdom Agent, it is my duty, in accordance with Article 61 of the Rules, to take such measures as appear necessary to me to enable the Court to give an effective decision. For this purpose I have honour suggest to your Excellencies that Imperial Government issue appropriate instructions to avoid all measures which might render impossible or difficult the execution of any judgment which the Court might subsequently give and to ensure that no action is taken which might aggravate the dispute submitted to the Court.[27]

This is indicative of the fact that in one of the simplest cases, the Court has been most benevolent liberal and on the contrary in one of the gravest of human rights cases it chose to be a tough conservative.

Even Judge Koroma (Sierra Leone) who voted in favour of the Orders of the Court does not fail to observe that:

> These are perhaps the most serious cases before the Court for injunctive relief. Under Article 41 of the Statute of the Court, a request for provisional measures should have its purpose the preservation of the respective rights of either party to a dispute pending the Court's decision. Jurisprudentially, the granting of such relief is designed to prevent violence, the use of force, to safeguard the peace, as well as serving as an important part of the dispute settlement process under the Charter. Where the risk of irreparable harm is said to exist or further action might aggravate or extend a dispute, the granting of the relief becomes all the more necessary.[28]

Judge Vereshchetin (Russia) was of the opinion that even if the Court cannot indicate fully fledged provisional measures in accordance with Article 41 of the Statute in relation to one or another of the respondent States, the Court is inherently empowered, at the very least, immediately to call upon the Parties neither to aggravate nor to extend the conflict and to act in accordance with their obligations under the Charter of the United Nations. This power he saw flowing from the Court's responsibility for the safeguarding of international law and from major

[27] *Anglo-Iranian Oil Co* Case (UK *v* Iran), ICJ Reports, 1951, p 91.
[28] *Ibid*, p 20.

considerations of public order not only under Article 41 of the Court's Statute, but also under Article 74, paragraph 4, and Article 75, paragraph 1, of its Rules.

Article 74, paragraph 4, of the Rules provide: 'Pending the meeting of the Court, the President may call upon the parties to act in such a way as will enable any order the Court may make on the request of provisional measures to have its appropriate effects.' And Article 75, paragraph 1, of the Rules mentions: 'The Court may at any time decide to examine *proprio motu* whether the circumstances of the case require the indication of provisional measures which ought to be taken or complied with by any or all of the parties.'

Furthermore, in his letter addressed to the President and the Members of the Court, the Agent of Yugoslavia had requested an action by the Court pursuant to Article 75, paragraph 1, of the Rules, in the following words:

> Considering the power conferred upon the Court by Article 75, paragraph 1, of the Rules of Court and having in mind the greatest urgency caused by the circumstances described in the Requests for provisional measures of protection I kindly ask the Court to decide on the submitted Requests *proprio motu* or to fix a date for a hearing at earliest possible time.[29]

In this connection Judge Shi (China) in his dissenting opinion drew attention of the Court to a recent case, *Le Grand* case (*Germany v USA*). Judge Shi mentioned that:

> In the recent *La Grand* case, the Court, at the request of the applicant State and despite the objection of the respondent State, decided to make use of its above-mentioned power under Article 75, paragraph 1, of the Rules of Court without hearing the respondent State in either written or oral form (*Order of 3 March 1999*, paragraphs 12 and 21). By contrast in the present case the Court failed to take any positive action in response to the similar request made by the Agent of Yugoslavia in a situation far more urgent[30] even than that in the former case.'[31]

In the Corfu Channel and *Nicaragua v USA* cases as well the Court had established its jurisdiction by adopting an activist approach.

It is a fact that *stare decisis* is not a doctrine in force with the Court. The Court is neither bound by its precedents, nor by any provision of its Statute or the Rules. And yet whereas it could protect people from being bombed day and night and save human lives from the jaws and claws of death just by relaxing its own *prima facie* formula of very young age, the Court chose not to override its own precedent. Whereas the Court could develop and enhance the prestige of human rights law, and therewith also its own, to the infinite heights.

[29] Legality of Use of Force (*Yugoslavia v Belgium*), Order of 2 June 1999 on Provisional Measures, Judge Shi's Dissenting Opinion, ICJ Reports 1999, p 208.

[30] In the LeGrand case, a German national, Mr LeGrand was on death row next day when the evening before his execution 2 March 1999 Germany filed its case against the United States and requested the Court to indicate provisional measures to protect Mr LaGrand's life. See the details in Legrand case mentioned in Part I of this book.

[31] Legality of Use of Force (*Yugoslavia v Belgium*), Order of 2 June 1999 on Provisional Measures, Dissenting Opinion of Judge Shi, ICJ Reports 1999, p 208.

V. The Development of Human Rights Law: An Analysis of Static Jurisdiction v Dynamic Law

At the very core of the development of human rights law by the ICJ lies the principle of 'elementary considerations of humanity'. In order to hold Albania responsible for the loss of human life, the Court developed this concept in its very first contentious case, the case concerning *Corfu Channel*, in 1949. Throughout its case law the entire development of human rights law in any contentious or advisory case, the Court has never failed to highlight the humanitarian considerations. Yet when the cases of the absolute humanitarian concern came and demanded to apply and adapt the law which the Court has been developing for the last five decades, the Court bound and judicially restrained itself with its own jurisdictional precedent. This is typical of a court reluctant to tread the path of judicial activism

Judge Alvarez, voting in favour of the judgment in the above case, further clarified in its individual opinion appended to the judgment that:

> The intervention of a State in the internal or external affairs of another—ie, action taken by a State with a view to compelling another State to do, or to refrain from doing, certain things—has long been condemned. It is expressly forbidden by the Charter of the United Nations. The same applies to other acts of force, and even to a threat of force.[32]

Seen in this light, the application of force by NATO States is, without the UN permission, an assault on the dignity of Yugoslavian State and people. The Court made no reference to this.

In the Barcelona Traction case the Court held that human rights are obligations *erga omnes.*[33] The concept became a popular *dictum* of the Court. If the substance of human rights law is obligation *erga omnes*, why not its procedural and jurisdictional side? The logic of obligation *erga omnes* implies a very dynamic and real interpretation of the substantive side of the human rights law. But to its jurisdictional side the Court applied a very traditional and static 19th century interpretation of the formula of consent based on sovereignty of States.

The jurisdictional principle of consent based on the concept of sovereignty was adopted by its predecessor, the Permanent Court of International Justice, in the early years of 1920s borrowed and adopted from the 18th and 19th century arbitration procedures in the settlement of international disputes. The formula has seen hardly any change or development of any sort so far, despite strong voices of some former judges of the Court, Judge Alvarez being always a strong advocate of this. While liberally, and innovatively, interpreting the mandatory institutions of 1919 in the *Namibia* advisory opinion of 1971 the Court affirmed once for all that the principle of 'self determination of peoples was a legal concept and not just a political talk. At the same time, in this case, the Court linked the principle of self

[32] *Corfu Channel* case, ICJ Reports, ICJ Reports, 1949, p 47.

[33] *Barcelon Traction* case, ICJ Reports, 1970, p 32.

determination with the concept of 'sacred trust' and interpreted the institutions of 1919 in the modern light and declared:

> That is why, viewing the institutions of 1919, the Court must take into consideration the changes which have occurred in the supervening half century, and its interpretation cannot remain unaffected by the subsequent development of law, through the Charter of the United Nations and by way of customary law. Moreover, an international instrument has to be interpreted and applied within the framework of the entire legal system prevailing at the time of the interpretation. In the domain to which the present proceedings relate, the last fifty years, as indicated above, have brought important developments. These developments leave little doubt that the ultimate objective of the sacred trust was the self-determination and independence of the peoples concerned.[34]

Seen in this light the ages old concepts of consent and sovereignty, often marring the contentious jurisdiction of the Court, within the framework of all the instruments governing the human rights law, the Court had all the reasons and necessity to give a fresh interpretation to its jurisdictional rules based on strict consent of sovereign States, particularly in the light that Human Rights are in the main, beyond the traditional display of sovereignty. The concept of sovereignty and its consequent jurisdictional corollaries, are both the products of 19th and earlier centuries time when the notion of 'human rights' in the modern legal sense of the term was not even born in the present sense of the term. The entire international legal system of human rights was at that time totally unknown. The Court could have taken these changes of supervening eight decades in general, since the PCIJ Statutes was enacted in 1919, and the last five decades in particular, the UN Charter being enacted in 1945 and the Universal Declaration of Human Rights was signed in 1948. Considering this, and the ultimate objective that the human rights run *erga omnes* and are a sacred trust in the hands of all States and such entities, the Court could well have established in the Yugoslavia cases that as far as enforcement and protection of human rights are concerned all States are bound by the instruments governing them even without their consent, and sovereignty offering no immunity from it, hence to decide disputes involving human rights matter the Court has jurisdiction *ipso facto, ratione personae* as well as *ratione materiae.* This could have been the best present from the Court to the present humanity of international community and its posterity at the occasion of the 50th anniversary of the Universal Declaration of Human Rights. Not only this, it could also have changed the entire history of the jurisdictional jurisprudence of the International Court of Justice.

Here, however, unfortunately the Court has missed a golden opportunity to develop the human rights international jurisdiction and protection. Undue judicial restraint and the undue tough conservatism of the Court has put second time,

[34] Legal Consequences for States of the Continued Presence of South Africa in Namibia (South-West Africa) Notwithstanding Security Council Resolution 276 (1970), Advisory Opinion of 21 June 1971, ICJ Reports, 1971, p 31.

after the 1966 Judgment in *South West Africa* cases, the pronouncements delivered in the *Legality of Use of Force* cases to be regarded as an 'aberration'.

The Court established a guiding principle in the *Nicaragua v USA* case that no State, or even a group of States, can, if not part of the decision taken by the human rights mechanism established by the relevant legal instrument, justify itself for the use of force in order to compel a State to respect human rights in its territory.[35] The Court did not recall this principle in its reasoning part of the Orders made in the cases filed by Yugoslavia.

In the *Reservations to the Genocide Convention* case the Court declared that: 'The Convention was manifestly adopted for a purely *humanitarian* and *civilizing porpose*.'[36] And the Court further held that: 'The first consequence arising from this conception is that the principles underlying the Convention are principles which are recognized by civilized nations as binding on States, even without any conventional obligations.'[37] If the underlying principles of the Convention are principles binding on all States, even if they have not signed the Convention, then at least they must have been considered binding at least on the ten NATO States who were actually parties to the Convention. It cannot be that the States are bound by the substantive principles and not by the jurisdictional principles. Yugoslavia invoked Article IX of the Convention as one of the jurisdictional titles. It was rejected either because a responded had reservation to this jurisdictional clause or the Court didn't see the NATO bombing as an act of Genocide. Though the Court was not supposed to judge on the merits of the case, and this amounts to doing the same, even then the gravity of the situation, actions of Yugoslavia taken into consideration, demanded the indication of provisional measures. The Court in these cases was given an opportunity to create and develop its own jurisdictional principles to decide disputes concerning human rights in general and genocide in particular. If human rights run *erga omnes* so must run the Court's jurisdiction to decide the human rights cases. But the Court preferred to take a step backward by declaring:

> Whereas there is a fundamental distinction between the question of the acceptance by a State of the Court's jurisdiction and the compatibility of particular acts with international law; the former requires consent; the latter question can only be reached when the Court deals with the merits after having established its jurisdiction and having heard full legal arguments by both parties.[38]

But, when indicating provisional measures, which in itself is an independent proceedings and require no consent of any party involved, the Court is neither dealing with the merits of the case nor supposed to establish any jurisdictional basis.

Considering the human rights law developed by the Court so far by eloquently following a benevolent liberalistic ideology, the majority of the judges of the Court

[35] Military and Paramilitary Activities in and against Nicaragua case, ICJ Reports, 1986, pp 134–35.

[36] Reservations to the Convention on the Prevention and Punishment of the Crime of Genocide, ICJ Reports, 1951, p 23.

[37] *Ibid*, p 38.

[38] Legality of Use of Force (*Yugoslavia v Belgium*), Order of 2 June 1999 on Provisional Measures, ICJ Reports, 1999, p 140.

in these cases have turned toughly conservative. It was not much of a question of either developing or clarifying the law but to adapt the law so consistently created in the past.

The cases, unfortunately, never reached the merits stage. In every case the Court found itself without jurisdiction, hence all the cases were removed from the General List of the Court.

12

Arrest Warrant of 11 April 2000 (*Democratic Republic of Congo v Belgium*)[1] An Analysis of Human Dignity of the People, for the People, by the People

I. Some Preliminary Reflections

HUMAN RIGHTS AND human dignity, together as aspects of war and peace, were face to face in this case when a sovereign State, namely Belgium, issued an arrest warrant against another State's (the Congo's) Foreign Minister, accusing him of war crimes and crimes against humanity. The Congo brought Belgium before the International Court of Justice accusing her of violating the immunity from prosecution granted by international law to the Congo's minister. Whereas, Belgium argued: immunity exists for official acts and not for private acts. The Court decided: in issuing the arrest warrant, Belgium failed to respect the immunity enjoyed by the minister, hence to remedy the situation the warrant must be cancelled. The Court was criticized for what it did, ie, deciding the case in the perspective of the doctrine of immunity; and was equally criticized for what it did not do, ie, to decide the question of immunity in without putting the doctrine within the framework of the principle of universal jurisdiction.

To frustrate grievances of the people in the name of State sovereignty and its resulting concept of immunity hardly contributes to the dignity of a government and its ministers. But, at the same time to obstruct the functioning of a government

[1] The composition of the Court delivering the Judgement of 14 February 2002 in the *Arrest Warrant* case was: President Guillaume; Vice-President Shi; Judges Oda, Ranjeva, Herczegh, Fleischhauer, Koroma, Vereshchetin, Higgins, Parra-Aranguren, Kooijmans, Rezek, Al-Khasawneh, Buergenthal; Judges *ad hoc* Bula-Bula, Van den Wyngaert. (See ICJ Reports 2002, p 4).

President Guillaume appended a separate opinion to the Judgment; Judge Oda appended a dissenting opinion; Judge Ranjeva appended a declaration; Judge Koroma appended a separate opinion; Judges Higgins, Kooijmans and Buergenthal appended a joint separate opinion; Judge Rezek appended a separate opinion; Judge Al-Khasawneh appended a dissenting opinion; Judge *ad hoc* Bula-Bula appended a separate opinion; Judge *ad hoc* Van den Wyngaert appended a dissenting opinion. (See ICJ Reports 2002, p 34).

and/or its ministers, particularly its minister for foreign affairs who needs to travel often for international functions and activities, in the name of human rights and human dignity is hardly elevating the cause of international human rights and human dignity. By conferring universal jurisdiction upon itself, without having derived that power from a clearly stated source of international law, a State, no matter how noble its intentions, amounts to taking international law in its own hands. This violates human dignity not only of the individuals and leaders of a sovereign State and immediate victims of such legislation but also that of all individuals and leaders of the States comprising the international community.

> While no general rule of positive international law can as yet be asserted which gives to states the right to punish foreign nations for crimes against humanity in the same way as they are, for instance, entitled to punish acts of piracy, there are clear indications pointing to the gradual evolution of a significant principle of international law to that effect.[2]
>
> It does not seem . . . that it has been shown that there is any State practice or general consensus let alone a widely supported convention that all crimes against international law should be justiciable in National Courts on the basis of the universality of jurisdiction . . .. That international law crimes should be tried before international tribunals or in the perpetrator's own state is one thing; that they should be pleaded without regard to a long established customary international law in the Courts of other states is another . . .. The fact even that an act is recognized as a crime under international law does not mean that the Courts of all States have jurisdiction to try it . . .. There is no universality of jurisdiction for crimes against international law . . ..[3]

Immunity if not impunity is the voice often heard in the international legal circles. There is a growing trend in the world of international relations that the immunity and the committal of core crimes do not go hand in hand.

Actually when a State accuses another State of committing an international wrong against it, in fact it accuses her of violating its dignity.

> One of the challenges of present international law is to provide for *stability of international relations* and effective international intercourse while at the same time guaranteeing respect for human rights. The difficult task that international law today faces is to provide that stability in international relations by a means other than the impunity of those *responsible for major human rights violations.*[4] (italics are mine)

Judges Higgins, Kooijmans and Buergenthal in these words are very clear about the fact that the greatest task of the international legal engineering is to establish a healthy balance between international relations and human rights, hence the legal

[2] See Jennings and Watts, *Oppenheim's International Law*, 9th edn (Harlow, Longman) p 998.

[3] Lord Slynn of Hadley, House of Lords, 25 November 1998, *R v Bartle; ex parte Pinochet.* These words from the first *Pinochet* case are also quoted by the President of the International Court of Justice in his Separate Opinion appended to the Judgement of 14 February 2002, Arrest Warrant of 11 April 2000, ICJ Reports 2002, p 42.

[4] See Joint Separate Opinion of three Judges, Higgins, Kooijmans and Buerganthal, appended to the Judgment of 14 February 2002 in the *Arrest Warrant* case, ICJ Reports 2002, p 63.

engineering of not only the concept of human dignity of individuals but also the dignity of their States and leaders.

The doctrine of human dignity is at the core of the doctrine of human rights. The doctrine of human rights is at the core of the Charter of the United Nations and its ancillary instruments. The Charter of the United Nations and its ancillary instruments is at the core of contemporary legal culture of international law. All put together is what we may call as the contemporary international legal system.

With all its dynamism and the rapidly developing principles and rules, international law is in the process of Global Law in the making.[5] Every *dispositif* of a ruling delivered by the principle judicial organ of the United Nations is on the one hand a contribution to the peaceful settlement of international disputes, and on the other, with its judicial sweat in the reasoning part thereof, an immense contribution to the development of Global Law in the making.

As a matter of fact when we talk of the strength of contemporary international law we talk about how much the legal culture of human rights and human dignity has become part of it, or more precisely, has been placed at the core of it. And, when we speak about the weakness of the same law we mean how much the culture of human rights and human dignity is still the prisoner of its old basis, the legal culture of State sovereignty.

Generally speaking, when a Court strictly adheres to the perception of the doctrine of traditional State sovereignty its judges are conservative in their judicial ideology. And, when the perception of human rights and human dignity is at the basis of their reasoning, its judges to that extent follow the judicial ideology of liberalism. However, a judge, like any thinker, is not always expected to be a conservative or strictly conservative or liberal or utmostly liberal. He/she might sometimes, or even most of the time, follow a judicial path which lies in the middle of these two judicial ideologies. In the reasoning of a judge sensitive to the concept of judicial restraint and more inclined to perceive international law based on the traditional concept of State sovereignty and yet have a somewhat liberal inclination towards the modern doctrine of human rights and human dignity, the middle path, a balancing path actually, which may also be called a conservo-liberal judicial ideology, this balancing ideology would play a decisive role in reaching a decision. Sometimes, this balancing judicial ideology of conservo-liberalism is not only a necessity of the time but also the only recipe to promote the rule of law and the concept of peaceful settlement of international disputes.

The principle of sovereign equality, and thereby State dignity, though in no way either superior or inferior to the doctrine of human rights and human dignity, is nonetheless still not only a determining factor of the contemporary international law but still is in the process of finding harmonious accommodation and cooperation with the rather new notion of human rights. Somewhere, somehow, a balance needs to be struck.

[5] See for instance a recent article by P Allott, 'The Emerging Universal Legal System' (2001) 3 *International Law Forum* 12.

Hence, the purpose of this chapter is to analyse the case of *Arrest Warrant* in the perspective of human dignity of the people, for the people, by the people.

II. The Factual Background of the *Yerodia* Case

On 11 April 2000 an investigating judge of the Brussels Tribunal de première instance issued 'an international arrest warrant *in absentia*' against Mr Abdulaye Yerodia Ndombasi, at the time the Minister for Foreign Affairs of the Democratic Republic of the Congo. The Belgian judge charged him, as perpetrator or co-perpetrator, with 1) offences constituting grave breaches of the Geneva Conventions of 1949 and their Additional Protocols, and 2) crimes against humanity. The complaints that initiated the proceedings with the Brussels Tribunals, as a result of which the arrest warrant was issued, emanated from 12 individuals residing in Belgium, five of whom had Belgian nationality.[6]

The arrest warrant was sent to the International Criminal Police Organization (abbreviated as Interpol) and to the Congolese authorities.

The warrant states that Mr Yerodia is accused of having made various speeches, during the month of August 1998, inciting racial hatred, particularly virulent remarks, allegedly having the effect of inciting the population to attack Tutsi residents in Kinshasa, dragnet searches, manhunts, and lynchings.

The crimes with which Mr Yerodia was charged were punishable under the Belgian Law of 16 June 1993 'concerning the Punishment of Grave Breaches of the International Geneva Conventions of 12 August 1949 and of Protocols I and II of 8 June 1977 Additional Thereto', as amended by the Law of 10 February 1999 'concerning the Punishment of Serious Violations of International Humanitarian Law'. The jurisdictional power of the Brussels Tribunal derives from Article 7 of the Belgian Law which stipulates: 'The Belgian courts shall have jurisdiction in respect of the offences provided for in the present Law, wheresoever they may have been committed'. Well conscious of any future impediment of immunity in the administration of justice, Article 5, paragraph 3, of the Belgian Law provides: '[i]mmunity attaching to the official capacity of a person shall not prevent the application of the present Law'. In a nutshell, seeing the arrest warrant in the framework of this Belgian legislation, Belgium conferred upon itself the right as against the Congo: 1) to exercise a universal criminal jurisdiction over the Foreign Minister of the Congo, and 2) to reject the immunity of the Foreign Minister as a defence strategy. Actually, the intention of Belgium in enacting this law is not an ill intention. It aims to promote the cause of human rights and human dignity by conferring upon itself the obligation to search, catch and punish the violators of

[6] This would though provide sufficient link for Belgium to convoke the principle of universal jurisdiction, yet it should be recalled that despite Belgium's assertion of this link at the Provisional Measures hearing the country did not appear to have argued the same in its written and oral proceedings on the Merits.

core human crimes. But, does international law permits Belgium to confer upon itself such a jurisdiction?

On 17 October 2000, the Congo feeling this as an attack on its State dignity and the dignity of its Foreign Minister filed in the Registry of the International Court an Application instating proceedings against Belgium. In that Application the Congo contented that in issuing the said warrant Belgium had violated the: '*principle that a State may not exercise its authority on the territory of another State, the principle of sovereign equality* among all Members of the United Nations, as laid down in Article 2, paragraph 1, of the Charter of the United Nations', as well as '*the diplomatic immunity* of the Minister for Foreign Affairs of a sovereign State, as recognized by the jurisprudence of the Court and following from Article 41, paragraph 2, of the Vienna Convention of 18 April 1961 on Diplomatic Relations'. In a nutshell, the Congo challenged the legality of the arrest warrant on two separate grounds: 1) Belgium's claim to exercise *universal jurisdiction*, and 2) alleged violation of the *immunities* of the Minister for Foreign Affairs.

Although, at the outset the Congo's Application advanced two separate grounds, yet in the submissions of its Memorial and also later in its final submissions made during the oral proceedings, it *dropped the ground of universal jurisdiction* and referred only to violation 'in regard to the . . . Congo of the rule of customary international law concerning the absolute inviolability and immunity from criminal process of incumbent foreign ministers'.[7]

This way the Applicant chose to fight the Respondent on only one front, that of immunity, and not on two fronts at a time. In its oral proceedings, the Congo's Counsel, Prof Rigaux, repeatedly stressed the withdrawal from the terrain of universal jurisdiction. First: 'In reality, that is an area of no interest to us. It was mentioned of course in the initial Application, but what interests the Democratic Republic of the Congo is a finding that its Minister for Foreign Affairs has been the victim of an internationally wrongful act'.[8] However, the Congo's counsel did give an impression that the Congo found the Belgian legislation somewhat far-fetched in the application and perception of the principle of universal jurisdiction. The counsel continued: 'Whether this occurred in the course of the exercise of an over-extensive universal jurisdiction seems to us to be an entirely secondary matter'.[9] Secondly, though the Congo would not mind the Court examining the issue of international law raised by universal jurisdiction, 'but', the Counsel added, 'it would not do so at the request of the Applicant'.[10] Thirdly, the Congo's great unwillingness of deciding the issue based on the universal jurisdiction reflected from the Counsel's words:

> it will, as it were, have the issue forced upon it as a result of the defence strategy adopted by the Respondent since the Respondent appears to contend not only that it is lawful to

[7] See ICJ Reports 2002, paras 11, 12, 17 and 21, on pages 7, 8, 10, and 11, respectively.
[8] CR 2001/10 dated 19 October 2001, p 7 (English translation by the Court's Registry).
[9] *Ibid.*
[10] *Ibid.*

> exercise such jurisdiction but that it is moreover obligatory to do so, and therefore that the exercise of such jurisdiction can represent a valid counterweight to the observance of immunities.[11]

And finally, the Counsel closed his statement with the final emphasis on the matter saying: 'I would stress that this is not at the request of the Applicant, which is not directly interested in the issue'.[12] It became clear that it was the dignity of Congo which it was seeking to redress and not the act of Belgium conferring upon itself the power of universal jurisdiction.

Belgium for its part maintained that while a Minister for Foreign Affairs in office generally enjoy an immunity from jurisdiction before the courts of a foreign State, such immunity applied only to acts carried out in the course of their official functions, and could not protect the minister in respect of his private acts. Belgium, hence, argued, that Mr Yerodia enjoyed no immunity at the time when he was alleged to have committed the violation of war crimes and the crimes against humanity. Hence, it observed, that the arrest warrant was issued against Mr Yerodia personally and not in his capacity as the Congo's Foreign Minister.[13]

The same day, as the Application was filed, the Congo also filed a Request, asking the Court to indicate provisional measures. The request was rejected by the Court in its Order of 8 December 2000.[14] Belgium raised objections to the jurisdiction of the Court and to the admissibility of the Application of the Congo. The same were also rejected by the Court.[15]

The decision on the merits of the case was given as under: 1) The Court

> *Finds* that the issue against Mr Abdulaye Yerodia Ndombasi of the arrest warrant of 11 April 2000, and its international circulation, constituted violations of a legal obligation of the Kingdom of Belgium towards the Democratic Republic of the Congo, in that they failed to respect the immunity from criminal jurisdiction and inviolability which the incumbent Minister for Foreign Affairs of the Democratic Republic of the Congo enjoyed under international law.

And further, to remedy the harm done to the Congo, the *dispositif* continues that the Court: '*Finds* that the Kingdom of Belgium must, by means of its own choosing, cancel the arrest warrant of 11 April 2000 and so inform the authorities to whom that warrant was circulated.'[16]

Hence, as the Congo did not challenge the self-conferred universal jurisdiction of Belgium, the Court did not rule, neither in the *obiter dicta* nor in the operative clause of its Judgement, on the question of whether the disputed arrest warrant fell under the universal jurisdiction. And with this exclusion, the Court concluded

[11] CR 2001/10 dated 19 October 2001, p 7 (English translation by the Court's Registry).

[12] *Ibid.*

[13] ICJ Reports 2002, p 20, paras 49–50.

[14] Arrest Warrant of 11 April 2000 (*Congo v Belgium*), *Provisional Measures* Order of 8 December 2000, *ICJ Reports 2000*, p 182.

[15] See ICJ Reports 2002, pp 11–19 (for the *obiter dicta*) and pp 32–33 for the decision in the *dispositif* of the Judgement in the case.

[16] *Ibid.*

that, for the purposes of this case, *it was only the immunity from criminal jurisdiction and the inviolability of an incumbent Minister for Foreign Affairs that stopped it being considered.*

III. Why Separate the Issues of Universal Jurisdiction and Immunity?

It is obvious that the issue was not the universal jurisdiction but the violation of the Congo's Foreign Minister, yet the Court was vehemently criticized not only for what it said but also for what it did not say. For instance, McLachlan saw the Pinochet episode revisiting in Mr.Yerodia, as the Judgment of the Court remained silent on the question of universal jurisdiction and took to only the issue of immunity.[17]

According to Judge Cassese, a former President of the Internal Tribunal for the former Yugoslavia, the Court has failed to pronounce on Belgium's assertion of absolute universal jurisdiction. He criticized the Court for separating the issues of universal jurisdiction and immunity in the following words: 'It would have been logical for the Court to first address the question of whether Belgium could legitimately invoke universal jurisdiction and, then in case of an affirmative answer to this question, decide upon the question of whether the Congolese foreign minister was entitled to immunity from prosecution and punishment.'[18] Aware of the dire need of the time to seek development and clarification of the principle of universal jurisdiction, Judge Cassese deplored that 'the Court has thus missed a golden opportunity to cast light on a difficult and topical legal issue.'[19]

Prof Wouters comments:

> The judgment makes it 'clear' that incumbent ministers for foreign affairs are, under customary international law, entitled to 'full' immunity of criminal jurisdiction and inviolability before the national courts of other states for acts performed both in an 'official capacity' and in a 'private capacity'. No exception to this rule is accepted for international crimes. The court thus favours the unhindered conduct of international relations above the interest the international community has in the persecution of international crimes.[20]

Though our international community of nations, ignited by the powerful notions of human rights and human dignity, is very much, very rapidly as compared to time measured in historical pace, in the process of becoming one global society of 'we the peoples', there is no magic wand shaping its destiny in a way that with the

[17] McLachla, 'Pinochet Revisited' (2000) 51 *International and Comparative Law Quarterly* 959.

[18] A Cassese, 'When May Senior State Officilas Be Tried for International Crimes? Some Comments on the *Congo v Belgium* Case' (2002) 13(4) *European Journal of International Law* 855.

[19] *Ibid*, p 856.

[20] J Wouters, 'The Judgment of the International Court of Justice in the Arrest Warrant Case: Some Critical Remarks' (2003) 16 *Leiden Journal of International Law* 267.

blink of an eye sovereign States are gone, their governmental authorities and institutions are nowhere to be seen, diplomatic immunities are things of the past, and in a nutshell, we are being governed by a ready-made centralized global government which has all the civil and criminal jurisdictions functioning immaculately according to the proper distribution of local and municipal powers of jurisdiction. The reality is that the nation-state system of Westphalia with its major actors and jurisdictions of State sovereignty, criminal jurisdiction included, is still the propellor of the system. The old man of sovereignty, no matter how weakened by age and burdened by asserted pressure of its newly born child of human rights, is still in charge.

What to say of the law concerning universal jurisdiction? Even the meaning of the concept is not only uncertain but equally unsettled. There is hardly one broadly accepted definition of the concept. Despite a massive literature available on the subject, there are as many views as the works of their authors. Feeble attempts, some quite serious though, have been made to build consensus on its meaning and definition. Not only is this true in the academic circle, one can equally glance and grasp the same differential of meaning in all the independent opinions appended to the judgement in this case.

In such a given situation of view, sometimes converging and sometimes diverging, of contemporary international law, it is simply an utmost judicial prudence of the Court to decide not to decide the case with such an uncertain and unsettled concept at the core of its reasoning, more particularly so when the Parties do not ask the Court to do the same in their final submissions. Yet, as a former President of the ICJ, Sir Robert Jennings, with all the insight of the internal working of the Court, seems making a very helpful and rightly guess: 'One can only suppose that the question of a universal national court jurisdiction must have led nevertheless so much discussion, for in the end some Judges, including the President, felt that something had to be said about this, even though it must be obiter.'[21]

Judge Oda, a Member of the Court in this case, sees the reason in the underdevelopment of the law on this matter: 'I believe . . . that the Court has shown wisdom in refraining from taking a definitive stance in this respect as the law is not sufficiently developed and, in fact, the Court is not requested in the present case to take a decision on this point.'[22]

Judge Koroma, also a Member of the Court, finds that it was not required: 'The Court did not rule on universal jurisdiction, because it was not indispensable to do so to reach its conclusion, nor was such submission before it.'[23]

Another academic and external opinion comes from Prof Wouters:

> The real reason may be that the judges were very much divided on this controversial issue. No fewer than ten judges found it necessary to address it in a separate or dissent-

[21] Sir Robert Jennings, 'Jurisdiction and Immunity in the ICJ Decision in the Yerodia case' (2002) 4(3) *International Law Forum* 103.

[22] Dissenting Opinion of Judge Oda, ICJ Reports 2002, p 51, para 11.

[23] See Separate Opinion by Judge Koroma, *Arrest Warrant of 11 April 2002*, Judgment of 14 February 2002, ICJ Reports 2002, p 62, para 9.

ing opinion, and although most of them were of the view that the Court should have ruled on the issue of jurisdiction, they did not agree on the way in which the Court should have pronounced itself.[24]

Taking all this into consideration, and on top of this that both Parties had relinquished the issue of universal jurisdiction, it was only wise for the Court to follow the rule of *non ultra petita*, well established in its own jurisprudence in the words: 'it is the duty of the Court not only to reply to the questions as stated in the final submissions of the parties, but also to abstain from deciding points not included in those submissions.'[25]

IV. Doctrine of Immunity and the Concept of Human Dignity

The dignity of the people and their leaders cannot be separated. In other words the concept of human dignity cannot be separated from the concept of State dignity. After all, as Kelsen expounded, in the ultimate analysis individual alone are the real subjects of international law. When we talk of human dignity we actually talk of every human being in the international community organized in the units of States. Mutual relations among States at international level are normally conducted through diplomats and other representatives of States, such as visiting leaders or authorities. The custom of sending an individual of a sovereign State to another sovereign State is as old as the history of international relations and international law. The person could be an ambassador, minister, or any representative of the State representing the sovereign of that State. The powers and immunities of such representatives grew up steadily and gradually during the 17th and 18th century when sea routes were discovered and the contacts between States started growing at a rapid pace. By the time the 1815 Congress of Vienna was held, the institution of immunity for the State's sovereign, in case of a visit to another State, and his representatives visiting for a short-term or long-term mission, was well known and well established. Actually at the base of the doctrine of immunity there are three theories: a) extra-territoriality theory, b) functional theory, and c) representational theory. It may be noted for practical reasons the extra-territorial theory is these days not in vogue. The functional theory as well as representational theory are at present very much at the basis of reasoning for giving immunities to diplomats and others. The dignity of a Foreign Minister, functionally speaking, derives from his right to perform unhindered, in freedom and without fear of any kind. And his dignity, representationally speaking derives from his right to equality in the sense of his State's right: *par in parem non habet imperium*. A State's

[24] J Wouters, 'The Judgment of the International Court of Justice in the Arrest Warrant Case: Some Critical Remarks' (2003) 16 *Leiden Journal of International Law* 263.

[25] The case concerning *Asylum*, Judgment, ICJ Reports 1950, p 402.

fundamental right is the right of its Foreign Minister. The principle of *parem non habet imperium* when applied to an individual is his human right of equality. And the human right of equality when applied to a State and its Foreign Minister is a fundamental right of the State and its minister.

About the personal inviolability of a diplomatic agent, Article 29 of the Vienna Convention lays down that: 'The person of a diplomatic agent shall be inviolable. He shall not be liable to any form of *arrest* or detention. The receiving State shall treat him with due respect and shall take all appropriate steps to prevent any attack on his person, freedom or *dignity*.' (italics are mine).

A Minister for Foreign Affairs is not only an *ad hoc* diplomatic agent abroad but also the head, during his term of office, of all the diplomatic agents abroad belonging to the State he represents. Hence, he is equally, if not more, inviolable; and deserves all steps to prevent any attack on his person, freedom or dignity.

One cannot talk of human dignity in abstract. And, one cannot violate dignity of one in order to redress the dignity of others. For the fairness of justice the concept of dignity, which indeed is the essence of fairness and justice itself, must be seen and applied in its holism.

In fact, neither can the principle of sovereign equality be separated from what we call human right of equality, nor human right of equality be defended and implemented without the machinery of State. It is an established principle of International law that one sovereign State is not permitted to determine the legal status of another sovereign State. International law, therefore confers certain immunities on certain persons who represent a certain State. Between 1815 and 1975 several international documents[26] were drawn to codify law of immunities, but the custom of immunity of a foreign minister did not take the conventional form until 1969 when the New York Convention on Special Missions was signed. The Congo and Belgium both cited this convention, to which they are not, however, parties. They recalled that under Article 21, paragraph 2, of that convention:

> The Head of the Government, the Minister for Foreign Affairs and other persons of high rank, when they take part in a special mission of the sending State, shall enjoy in the receiving State or in a third State, in addition to what is granted by the present Convention, the facilities, privileges and immunities accorded by international law.

Hence, other than in this Convention, his immunity remained rather obscure as far as conventional law was concerned, but the customary law never denied the same. Even in the given case the Respondent did not deny the necessary immunities for a Foreign Minister but it did challenge the immunity when the Minister was accused of war crimes and crimes against humanity. According to Belgium: 'such immunity applies only to acts carried out in the course of their official func-

[26] Regulation of Vienna by Congress of Vienna in 1815; 1961 Vienna Convention on Diplomatic Relations; 1963 Vienna Convention on Consular Relations; 1969 Convention on Special Missions, adopted by the UN General Assembly; 1973 Convention on Prevention and Punishment of Crimes Against Internationally Protected Persons, including Diplomats; 1975 Vienna Convention on Representation of States in their Relations with International Organizations of Universal Character.

tions, and cannot protect such persons in respect of private acts or when they are acting outside their official functions'.[27]

To this obscure area of international law, and to the uncertainty in the minds of States such as Belgium, the Court added the clarification, and seeing the frail position of the law of immunity in the treaty law, concluded the matter based on customary law as under:

> The Court accordingly concludes that the functions of a Minister for Foreign Affairs are such that, throughout the duration of his or her office, he or she when abroad enjoys full immunity from criminal jurisdiction and inviolability. That immunity and that inviolability protect the individual concerned against any act of authority of another State which would hinder him or her in the performance of his or her duties.[28]

The Court has here not only settled the uncertain law on this matter but by recognizing the fundamental right of equality of States and the right to perform in freedom and equality for its foreign minister, added equal dignity to the institution of State and to its foreign minister. In the words of 'immunity from criminal jurisdiction and inviolability' rests the right of freedom of the State and its minister; in the words of 'against an act of authority' rests the fundamental right of equality; and both these rights stem from the concept of sovereignty, synonymous with State dignity. In this, the Court has developed the scope and essence of the notion of human rights to the area of State and to the person of Foreign Minister. The concept of human dignity has been developed in its different dimensions and aspects. Seen from the aforementioned three theories about the diplomatic immunities, the Court has here reflected two theories in full balance, functional theory and the representational theory.

Because the respondent maintained that the immunities do not apply to the acts performed in private capacity. The Court settled the matter for good by stating:

> In this respect, no distinction can be drawn between acts performed by a Minister for Foreign Affairs in an 'official' capacity, and those claimed to have been performed in a 'private capacity', or, for that matter, between acts performed before the person concerned assumed office as Minister for Foreign Affairs and acts committed during the period of office.[29]

There was a considerable criticism of the Court on this unlimited immunity given to the Minister for Foreign Affairs.[30] The Court, seemingly well aware of this unavoidable criticism, and also aware of the uncertainty prevailing in the international relations of the day, clarified the matter in the following statement:

> . . . if a Minister for Foreign Affairs is arrested in another State on a criminal charge, he or she is clearly thereby prevented from exercising the functions of his or her office. The

[27] ICJ Reports 2002, p 20, para 49.

[28] *Ibid*, p 22, para 54.

[29] *Ibid*, p 22, para 54.

[30] See for instance C Schreur and Swittich, 'Immunity v Accountability: the ICJ's Judgment in the *Yerodia* case' (2002) 4(3) *International Law Forum* 117; and the Dissenting Opinion of Judge Al-Khasawneh appended to the Judgment in this case, ICJ Reports 2002, p 95.

> consequences of such impediment to the exercise of those official functions are equally serious, regardless of whether the Minister for Foreign Affairs was, at the time of arrest, present in the territory of the arresting State on an 'official' visit or a private visit, regardless of whether the arrest relates to acts allegedly performed before the person became the Minister for Foreign Affairs of to acts performed while in office, and regardless of whether arrest related to alleged acts performed in an 'official' capacity or a 'private' capacity, Further more even the mere risk that, by travelling to or transiting another State a Minister for Foreign Affairs might be exposing himself or herself to legal proceedings could deter the Minister from travelling internationally when required to do so for the purposes of the performance of his or her official functions.[31]

The Court made it clear that in the performance of smooth functioning of the minister it is not the question of 'official' or 'private', present or past, but the performance without fear from arrest or detention, enjoying the freedom of function, which is imperative when minister travels abroad. But that does not mean that Court has given a license to a Foreign Minister to commit violations of human rights and human dignity and to go free. Some critics commented in that vein. Prof Cassese for instance, commenting on this point, quoted the following words, though admittedly from a different context. From a Yugoslavia judgment:

'It would be a travesty of law and a betrayal of the universal need for justice, should the concept of state sovereignty be allowed to be raised successfully against human rights'.[32] Nothing is more true than what the Tribunal has mentioned in this statement. And, reflecting such thinking the critics of the judgment of the ICJ also reflect asking the question: should the doctrine of immunity, itself a corollary of the doctrine of State sovereignty, be allowed to serve as a procedural shield of defence against the crimes as grave as war crimes and crimes against humanity? The Court has answered this in an emphatic NO by stating: 'The Court emphasizes, however, that the *immunity* from jurisdiction enjoyed by incumbent Ministers for Foreign Affairs does not mean that they enjoy impunity in respect of any crimes they might have committed, irrespective of their gravity.'[33]

The words *'irrespective of their gravity'* cannot stand for anything else than for all the grave crimes, such as war crimes, crimes against humanity, and the crime against peace. For no crime more grave than these is known to international law. Hence, in clarifying and developing the law on granting immunity to a Minister for Foreign Affairs the Court has not given the minister a shield to escape the core international crimes.

The Court further clarifies the law by differentiating between 'jurisdictional immunity' and 'criminal responsibility' relating their respective characteristics to their respective fields of action:

> Immunity from criminal jurisdiction and individual criminal responsibility are quite separate concepts. While jurisdictional immunity is procedural in nature, criminal

[31] ICJ Reports 2002, p 22, para 54.

[32] ICTY, Appeals Chamber, Tadic (Interlocutory Appeal), judgment of 2 October 1995, p 32, para 58.

[33] 14 February 2002 Judgment, *Arrest Warrant of 11 April 2002*, ICJ Reports 2002, p 25, para 60.

> responsibility is a question of substantive law. Jurisdictional immunity may well bar prosecution for a certain period or for certain offences; it cannot exonerate the person to whom it applies from all criminal responsibility.[34]

The Court's reasoning on this issue of the right to immunity, deciding without linking it with the principle of universal jurisdiction, and yet seen in the broader framework of the international criminal jurisdiction, seems rather conservative. But, seen in the holistic understanding of the concept of human dignity, thinking of human rights of the people and leaders of a State in their entirety, the development of law on immunities in this case is an immense contribution to the law of human rights and human dignity. Dignity of the rulers and the ruled go hand in hand. Therein lies the culture of human rights and human dignity.

Sometimes, when saying so much about one subject and hardly anything about the other, it is to the other you actually make the contribution. Judge Al-Khasawneh in this judgment dissented with the Court on the issue of immunity and wrote his dissent with the central theme: *the concept of 'combating of grave crimes' prevails over the 'rules of immunity'.*

a) Judge Al-Khasawneh: The Concept of Combatting of Grave Crimes Prevails over the Rules of Immunity

Judge Al-Khasawneh dissented from the majority judgment because, in his opinion, while a foreign minister is undoubtedly an important personage of the State, yet, not being a Head of a State, he enjoys only limited immunity. Judge Al-Khasawneh suggests caution when the rules of immunity are to be applied to a minister for foreign affairs who is already accused of grave crimes and yet free from prosecution. In his opinion, a minister for foreign affairs, accused of war crimes and crimes against humanity—and for that matter: a) criminal conduct that infringes the interests of the community of States as a whole in terms of the gravity of the crimes he is alleged to have committed, b) the importance of the interests that the community seeks to protect, and c) and who is further more not prosecuted in his home State—'is hardly under the same conditions as a diplomatic representative granted immunity from criminal process'. He reminds that 'it should not be forgotten that immunity is by definition an exception from the general rule that man is responsible legally and morally for his actions'.[35] Hence, in his opinion, this exception in the face of grave crimes should be construed rather narrowly.

The Judge felt that when immunity becomes *de facto* impunity it is 'morally embarrassing' for the cause of human rights and human dignity. Therefore, he states: 'A more fundamental question is whether high State officials are entitled to benefit from immunity even when they are accused of having committed exceptionally grave crimes recognized as such by the international community'.

[34] *Ibid.*

[35] Dissenting Opinion of Judge Al-Khasawneh, *Arrest Warrant of 11 April 2002*, Judgment of 14 February 2002, ICJ Reports 2002, p 96, para 2.

According to Judge Al-Khasawneh the effective combatting of grave crimes has arguably assumed a *jus cogens* character. The same reflects recognition by the international community of the vital community interest and values. In order to protect and enhance those interests and values, the community needs to combat grave crimes, detrimental to those interests and values. 'Therefore', according to the Judge, 'when this hierarchically higher norm comes into conflict with the rules on immunity, it should prevail'.

These words of Judge El-Khasawney represents a liberal judicial ideology and serve as a reminder to the judicial minds that it was the horrible atrocities committed by nazi, fascist, and militaristic sovereignties of the East and West together in the wake of the Second World War which injected in the minds of the founding fathers of the UN Charter that it was necessity of placing human rights and universal criminal jurisdiction at the centre of international legal culture and system. Hence, in the wake of growing trend of restrictive immunities and prevailing trend of international criminal tribunals and courts, international law should be developed more in the direction of accountability rather than immunity, which in the ultimate analysis contributes to the legal culture of human dignity and curbs the old ghost of State sovereignty.

Obviously Judge Al-Khasawney is in favour of restricting the field of immunities and broadening the area of universal criminal jurisdiction. Yet, as is also clear from his opinion that he is not against the granting of the required immunity to a Minister for Foreign Affairs, as by custom and practice he/she already has, but his opinion reflects that he would have liked the Court to have developed the law more in the area universal jurisdiction rather than on immunity. By stressing the fact that combating the grave crimes prevails over rules of immunity and adding that grave crimes have assumed the character *jus cogens*, Judge Al-Khasawnew has added awareness, and showed concern of clarification and development, of urgency to that area of human rights and human dignity.

It is interesting to note here that even when the litigant—Congo, felt that its dignity has been violated by the Respondent by violating the immunity of its Minister for Foreign Affairs. The Court did not fail to take notice that the Applicant itself maintains that immunity is not impunity. The Court in this regard observed:

> The Congo states . . . that it does not deny the existence of a principle of international criminal law, deriving from the decisions of the Nuremberg and Tokyo international military tribunals, that the accused's official capacity at the times of the acts cannot, before any court, whether domestic or international, constitutes a 'ground of exemption from his criminal responsibility or a ground for mitigation of sentence'. The Congo then stresses that the fact that an immunity might bar prosecution before a specific court or over a specific period does not mean that the same prosecution cannot be brought, if appropriate, before another court which is not bound by that immunity, or at another time when the immunity need no longer be taken into account. *It concludes that immunity does not mean impunity*' (italics are mine).[36]

[36] ICJ Reports 2002, p 20, para 48.

One cannot fail to note from the above—by the Court, by the dissenting judge, by the Applicant, as well as by the Respondent—even on the issue of immunities it was a case of human dignity in its *ratione personae* of individual State, and its leaders, and in its *ratione materiae* of rights of equality and freedom, hence the human dignity in holism. The same was well clarified and developed by the Court, its dissenting judge, and well represented by both the Parties.

V. The Principle of Universal Jurisdiction and the Concept of Human Dignity

Though the principle of universal jurisdiction was first propounded in respect of the crime of piracy since pirates were considered as universal criminals, enemies of all mankind, its serious development emerged from the principles of Nüremberg and Tokyo international military tribunals.

Man's conscience, particularly his collective political and legal conscience, usually shakes only when the heart-rending drums of atrocities beat loud around him. Such was the case when people in the political and legal circles awoke to the reality during the Second World War. It was due to the appalling atrocities committed by German Nazism in the West and the Japanese militarism in the East that the world leaders awoke to the reality that international peace and security were not possible in the absence of a political and legal system for the protection of human rights and human dignity. Moreover, the atrocities were not committed only by States against certain people but also by States and against States. The idea gained momentum through the war time instruments such as Atlantic Charter of 1941 and the UN. Declaration of 1942. The constantly ringing note that the protection of human rights and respect for human dignity of all the peoples and nations everywhere brought to unite the peoples and nations of the world to proclaim in the very opening words of the UN Charter: 'WE, THE PEOPLES OF THE UNITED NATIONS'.

The determination for this global unity in a moment of refined human conscience aimed at only one thing to save the succeeding generations from the revisit of those atrocities of 'untold sorrow to mankind'. And, thereby, that determined and refined conscience resolved to set for itself *the path* enacting in the very international positive law: '. . . to reaffirm faith in fundamental human rights, in the dignity and worth of the human person, in the equal rights of men and women and of nations large and small . . .'.

The resolve reflected that human rights and human dignity would occupy a significant chapter in any story of the United Nations.[37] The Universal Declaration of Human Rights was adopted by the General Assembly of the United Nations in

[37] L Henkin, 'The UN and Human Rights' (1965) 21(3) *International Organisation* 504.

1948. Further to the stage of signing the Declaration, two stages were left to be worked out: a series of binding covenants and measures and machinery for the implementation. Human dignity remained all the way the legislative spirit of all the covenants, conventions or other documents signed thereafter. The stage of measures and implementation is an endless task which continues to this day and would continue forever.

Meanwhile, on 30 September 1946 the judgement of the Nuremberg Tribunal had already developed the international criminal law concepts and principles of war crimes, crimes against humanity, and crimes against peace.

All the walls of subject-object dichotomy of international law crumbled when the judges of international military tribunal of Nuremberg declared:

> 'The fact that a person who committed an act which constitutes a crime under International Law acted as the head of the State or responsible government official does not relieve him from responsibility under international law.'[38]

All war crimes, crimes against humanity and crimes against peace are now considered to be crimes against international public policy (*jus cogens*). They fall under the universal jurisdiction and they are treated as *delicts jure gentium*. Piracy and slave trade are old examples of such crimes. The law on the universal jurisdiction is though not very settled yet the field is now of rapid growth and urgency of concern. The principle of universality of war crimes has been embodied in the Geneva conventions of 1949 and their two Protocols of 1977. The principle also finds expression, though in a limited way, in a number of treaties such as genocide,[39] drug traffic,[40] trafficking in women and children, counterfeiting of currency, taking of hostages,[41] torture,[42] apartheid,[43] attacks on diplomats,[44] and hijacking.[45] All these treaties, state practice and several cases, such as *Lotus*,[46]

[38] The words of the Report of the International Law Commission, 1950. While delivering the judgment, the Neuremburg Tribunal laid down certain principle. This was one of the principles as recorded in the 1950 Report of the ILC.

[39] Article VI, Genocide Convention of 1948.

[40] Article 36(2)(iv), Single Convention on Narcotic Drugs, 1961.

[41] Article 8, 1979 International Convention against the Taking of Hostages.

[42] Article 5(2), 1984 UN Convention on Torture.

[43] Articles II-v, Convention on the Suppression and Punishment of Crime of Apartheid, 1973.

[44] Article 2, Convention on the Prevention and Punishment of Crimes against Internationally Protected Persons including Diplomats, 1973.

[45] Article 4, The Hague Convention for the Suppression of Unlawful Seizure of Aircraft, 1970, and Article 5, Montreal Convention for the Suppression of Unlawful Acts against the Safety of Civil Aviation, 1971.

[46] Those who draw support in favour of the universal jurisdiction from the precedent of piracy, Sir Robert Jennings have this to say: 'There is of course the precedent of piracy *jure gentium*, which long has been an international crime subject to a species of universal jurisdiction. But piracy takes place on the high seas or in a "place outside the jurisdiction of any State" (Article 101 of the 1982 Convention) which situation is practically the converse of what is being proposed in some quarters for these new crimes', Sir Robert Jennings, 'Jurisdiction and Immunity in the ICJ Decision in the Yerodia case' (2002) 4(3) *International Law Forum* 103.

Pinochet,[47] and *Eichmann*[48] were pleaded by Belgium and discussed by several judges in their individual opinions.

In the wake of the principle of universal jurisdiction some States have enacted their own national codes to deal with such crimes and criminals, Belgium is one of them. Judge Ranjeva observes that there are about 125 States having national legislation concerning punishment of war crimes and crimes against humanity. Of these only five provide that the presence of the accused in their territory is not required for initiating prosecution.[49] Of all these States, other than Belgium, only USA. and Israel seem to have taken the stance of universal jurisdiction *in absentia*. What has, however, been overlooked that there are certain principles for States to exercise universal jurisdiction. Those are: a) there should be a substantial and bona fide connection between the subject matter and the source of the jurisdiction, b) the principle of non-intervention in the domestic or territorial jurisdiction, and c) a principle based on elements of accommodation, mutuality and proportionality should be applied.[50]

The underlying rationale of punishing the core universal crimes is, like the rationale of human rights, is to uphold the principle of human dignity. But to confer upon itself (a State) the universal jurisdiction *in absentia* to try a Foreign Minister of a State, in disregard to the principles of non-intervention in domestic jurisdiction and that of mutuality and proportionality is to violate the dignity not only of the minister in question, but also of the State and the people which that minister represents. To issue an arrest warrant to an incumbent Foreign Minister in violation of his immunity, which may be considered *his* basic right by way of his office and function, is to violate his human right through his being. Just as essence behind the entire notion of human rights and human dignity is that of 'elementary human needs', similarly in discharge of a high function, as a matter of fact any function, there is 'elementary human need' for sheer survival and performance. A Minister for Foreign Affairs when travelling to other States has the 'elementary need of immunity from local jurisdiction'. Human rights and human dignity

[47] See the Statement by Lord Slynn of Hadley at the outset of this chapter in the section Some Preliminary Reflections. Lord Slynn of Hadley, House of Lords, 25 November 1998, *R v Bartle; ex parte Pinichet*. These words from the first *Pinochet* case are also quoted by the President of the International Court of Justice in his Separate Opinion appended to the Judgement of 14 February 2002, Arrest Warrant of 11 April 2000, ICJ Reports 2002, p 42.

[48] *Adolf Eichmann v Attorney-General of the Government of Israel*, Supreme Court of Israel, (1962) 136 ILR 277. There is no doubt that the principles laid by the Israeli Court in the Eichmann case is a great contribution to the development of the international criminal law, yet one must never overlook the fact that Mr Eichmann was abducted by Israeli spies in an irregular way to present him before the Israeli Court. This abduction is hardly contributing to the concept of human dignity and the dignity of a State. The universal jurisdiction exercised in this irregular way is contrary to the spirit of law, justice and human dignity.

[49] See Declaration of Judge Ranjeva appended to the Judgement of 14 February 2002 in this case, ICJ Reports 2002, p 57, para 8. See also the Counter-Memorial of Belgium, pp 98–99, para 3.3.57.

[50] HO Agarwal, *International Law* (Fridabad, India, Allahabad Law Agency, 1997) 187.

are not abstract terms. They are holistic concepts of international legal system and culture. Hence, without the settled authority deriving from an international code, a State conferring upon itself the power of jurisdiction to try a Foreign Minister of another State, acts counter to the culture and principles of human rights and human dignity.

The concept of human dignity and the principle of universal jurisdiction found there place in the positive international law almost at the same time. The idea of human dignity first found its settled place in the United Nations Charter. The principle of universality of war crimes was affirmed by the Geneva Conventions of 1949 and the principle of human dignity was equally affirmed in the International Bill of Rights. Both the concepts are in constant evolution since then. What would be the most universal common element governing relations between them? It depends from which angle of human rights we like to approach the relation. When it comes, for instance, to the question of immunity for a Foreign Minister the principle of equality, appears as right of equality at the individual level and the right of sovereign equality at the State and inter-State level. After all, when Vattel laid down the rule that since men were by nature equal, so States, composed of men, were also by nature equal, it was the reasoning of equality behind his entire theory of international law. Though the Court chose to decide the case within the perspective of the doctrine of immunity without linking it with the principle of universal jurisdiction, and did thereby missed the opportunity of developing the law of the very field whereof the law is very unsettled, yet the following judges have compensated for the same by doing several times more so than otherwise would have been the case in the one *obiter dicta* of the majority. Their individual and joint opinions reveal a myriad of views which is not only shedding the light on the topic in question but are going to prove a great contribution to any future code on the principle of universal jurisdiction.

a) Judge Guillaume: The Clarity of the Principle of Universal Jurisdiction

President Guillaume draws distinction between the terms *universal jurisdiction* and *universal jurisdiction in absentia*. According to him, traditionally, customary international law did, however, recognize one case of universal jurisdiction, that of piracy. Reviewing the related provisions from the international conventions, relating various crimes, between 1958 and 1999, Judge Guillaume arrives at the following two conclusions, concerning universal jurisdiction and universal jurisdiction *in absentia*, respectively.

First:

> . . . a system corresponding to the doctrines espoused long ago by Grotius was set up by treaty. Whenever the perpetrator of any of the offences covered by these conventions is found in the territory of a State, that State is under an obligation to arrest him, and then extradite him or prosecute. It must have first conferred jurisdiction on its courts to try

> him if he is not extradited. Thus, universal punishment of the offences in question is assured, as the perpetrators are denied refuge in all States.[51]

Secondly: 'By contrast, none of these texts has contemplated establishing jurisdiction over offences committed abroad by foreigners against foreigners when the perpetrator is not present in the territory of the State in question'. In his view: 'Universal jurisdiction *in absentia* is unknown to international conventional law.'[52]

International law, according to President Guillaume, knows only one true case of universal jurisdiction, that is piracy.

The principle of territoriality is not only a firm traditional element of any universal jurisdiction, maintains President Guillaume, but: 'The adoption of the United Nations Charter proclaiming the sovereign equality of States, and the appearance on the international scene of new States, born of decolonisation, have strengthened the territorial principle.'[53]

Throughout his opinion the reasoning of President Guillaume even when stressing a great deal the principle of territoriality actually rests on the principle of *par in parem non habet imperium*, promoting the dignity of State's people and leaders, stemming from the State's fundamental right of equality.

> . . . at no time has it been envisaged that jurisdiction should be conferred upon the courts of every State in the world to prosecute such crimes, whoever their authors and victims and irrespective of the place where the offender is to be found. To do this would, moreover, risk creating total judicial chaos. It would also be to encourage the arbitrary for the benefit of the powerful, purportedly acting as agent for an ill-defined 'international community'. Contrary to what is advocated by certain publicists, such a development would represent not an advance in the law but a step backward[54]

Having studied the judgment and all its appended individual opinions, In strong support of the President Guillaume's clarification of the principle, the former President of the Court, Sir Robert Jennings commented: '. . . the writer must be allowed simply to express his strongly held agreement with the President's view, and also to express extreme disquiet at the claim to some kind of universal national jurisdiction for the category of international law crimes.'[55]

[51] See Separate Opinion by President Guillaume, *Arrest Warrant of 11 April 2002*, Judgment of 14 February 2002, ICJ Reports 2002, p 39, para 9.

[52] *Ibid*, p 39–40, para 9.

[53] *Ibid*, p 43, para 15.

[54] *Ibid*, p 43, para 15.

[55] Sir Robert Jennings, 'Jurisdiction and Immunity in the ICJ Decision in the Yerodia case' (2002) 4(3) *International Law Forum* 103.

b) Judge Ranjeva: Territoriality as the Basis of Entitlement to Jurisdiction Remains at the Core of Contemporary Positive International Law

Though Judge Ranjeva subscribed to the majority decision in the *dispositif* of the Judgment, yet he found himself in a rather 'awkward position'[56] as the Court remained utterly silent on the question of universal jurisdiction even in its *obiter dicta*.

The principle of universal jurisdiction and the crimes covered, or to be covered, under the given category of jurisdiction have direct bearing on the protection as well as promotion of human rights and human dignity. Hence, the principle provides a strong link of relation between human rights and international law. The very preambulary statement of Judge Ranjeva commencing his opinion on the subject reflects human rights and human dignity at the core of his undertaking:

> Expressing an opinion on the subject would be an unusual exercise, because it would involve reasoning in the realm of hypothesis, whereas the problem is real one, not only in the present case but also in the light of developments in international criminal law aimed at preventing and punishing heinous crimes violating human rights and dignity under international law.[57]

The problem is real in the sense that the fully developed notion of human rights and human dignity are face to face with the State sovereignty carrying a weapon of immunity in its hands in a deplorable state of international law which is very much under-developed as far as the principle of universal jurisdiction is concerned.

In this vein Judge Ranjeva, aware of the fact that Mr Yerodia was accused of serious violations of humanitarian law and of crimes against humanity, and to that extent the charges were laid under the 'Belgian Law', observed that the Belgian legislation establishing universal jurisdiction *in absentia* for serious violations of international humanitarian law had '*adopted the broadest possible interpretation of such jurisdiction*'[58] which he found unprecedented. The problem of adjudication, in the process of application and interpretation of international law, results from the reality that the broadest possible interpretation of the principle of universal jurisdiction has been drawn by Belgium from the law whose conventional limits are still very narrow.

Allowing the ordinary Belgian Courts with jurisdiction over crimes such as war crimes, crimes against humanity and genocide by non-Belgians outside Belgium, and going as far as issuing arrest warrant of a person as high as a Foreign Minister of a sovereign State, without seriously taking into consideration the concept of the 'territorial connection', which is at the core of whatever universal jurisdiction

[56] See Separate Opinion of Judge Ranjeva, *Arrest Warrant of 11 April 2002*, Judgment of 14 February 2002, ICJ Reports 2002, p 54, para 3.

[57] See Separate Opinion of Judge Ranjeva, *ibid*, p 55, para 3.

[58] *Ibid*, p 55, para 5.

there is, such as for the crime of piracy, is, according to the Judge not consistent with the existing international law. Viewing the complete development of international law since the maritime piracy, Judge Ranjeva arrives at the conclusion that: 'These legal developments did not result in the recognition of jurisdiction *in absentia*.'[59] Answering to the Belgium's strong reliance on the Permanent Court of International Justice's decision in the '*Lotus*' case[60] to justify the scope of Belgian national legislation to expand its criminal jurisdiction beyond its own territory, Judge Ranjeva opines: 'Doubtless, evolving opinion and political conditions in the contemporary world can be seen as favouring the retreat from territory-based conception of jurisdiction and the emergence of a more functional approach in the service of higher common ends.' He continues: 'Acknowledging such a trend cannot however justify the sacrifice of cardinal principles of law in the name of a particular kind of modernity.'[61]

Judge Ranjeva also finds that the scholarly acceptance of the principle laid down in the '*Lotus*' case relating international crimes has not yet found expression in a consequential development of the positive law concerning criminal jurisdiction. Hence, Judge Ranjeva's final conclusion on the principle of universal jurisdiction is: '*Territoriality as the basis of entitlement to jurisdiction remains a given, the core of contemporary positive international law.*'[62] And this is where, he makes it clear, that the law concerning universal jurisdiction stands. Judge Ranjeva presents a perfect balance of: a) sovereignty and human rights, and b) judicial conservatism and judicial liberalism.

c) Judge Koroma: Concepts of Jurisdiction and Immunity are not the Same

In Judge Koroma's view, although immunity is predicated upon jurisdiction, whether national or international, 'it must be emphasized that the concepts are not the same'.[63] Jurisdiction, according to him, relates to the power of a State to affect the rights of a person or persons by legislative, executive or judicial means. Whereas, immunity represents independence and the exemption from the jurisdiction or competence of the courts and tribunals of a foreign State. And both, in his opinion must be in conformity with international law.

[59] *Ibid*, p 57, para 7.

[60] It is of interest to note here that the facts of the case were confined to the issue of the Turkish criminal courts' jurisdiction as a result of the arrest in Turkish territorial waters of Lieutenant Demons, the second-in-command of a vessel flying French flag. The judgment states, *inter alia*: '[All] that can be required of a State is that it should not overstep the limits which international law places upon its jurisdiction; ... The territoriality of criminal law, therefore, is not an absolute principle of international law and by no means coincides with territorial sovereignty.' (See PCIJ Series A, No 10, p 19–20).

[61] See Separate Opinion of Judge Ranjeva, *ibid*, p 57, para 8.

[62] *Ibid*, p 58, para 9.

[63] See Separate Opinion by Judge Koroma, *Arrest Warrant of 11 April 2002*, Judgment of 14 February 2002, ICJ Reports 2002, p 60, para 5.

He further clarifies the working of immunity by stating: 'It is not, however, that immunity represents freedom from legal liability as such, but rather it represents exemption from legal process.'[64]

In this way, coming directly to the question of immunity of a Foreign Minister, Judge Koroma states: 'The paramount justification for this, in my opinion, is that immunity of the Foreign Minister is not only of functional necessity but increasingly these days the Foreign Minister represents the State, even though his or her position is not assimilable to that of Head of State.'[65] Judge Koroma supports the immunity of a Foreign Minister on two theories: the theory of functional necessity and the theory of State's representation. One finds its source in the practicalities of international life and the other in the dignity of the people of a State. To respect both, he states: 'International law imposes a limit on Belgium's jurisdiction where the Foreign Minister in office of a foreign State is concerned.'[66] However, it is not very clear what is the general view of Judge Koroma, except in case of a Foreign Minister and that too only in office. On the face of it one is bound to draw the following conclusion: if the Foreign Minister is not in office, he may fall under the Belgian jurisdiction. The conclusion seems even more correct if one read the sentence preceding to the above: 'The Judgment implies that while Belgium can initiate criminal proceedings *in its jurisdiction* against *anyone*, an incumbent Minister for Foreign Affairs of a foreign State is immune from Belgian jurisdiction.'[67] This again clears the exemption for a Foreign Minister. What about others: ordinary people and other dignitaries with or without immunity. '*Anyone*' actually would mean anyone except the Foreign Minister *in office*. The words '*in its jurisdiction*' if understood as *in its territory* would have made the picture clear that Belgium could exercise its criminal jurisdiction on all in its territory; but then there are others too on the same territory, such as diplomatic staff, etc. Further paragraph makes the situation even more doubtful:

> On the other hand, in my view, the issue and circulation of the arrest warrant show how seriously Belgium views its international obligations to combat international crimes. *Belgium is entitled to invoke its criminal jurisdiction against anyone, save a Foreign Minister in office.* It is unfortunate that the wrong case would appear to have been chosen in attempting to carry out what Belgium considers its international obligation.(italics are mine).

This clearly means what it means: *Belgium is entitled to invoke its criminal jurisdiction against anyone, save a Foreign Minister in office.* If so, the reader is bound to draw two conclusions from Judge Koroma's separate opinion: 1) Universal jurisdiction in absentia is permissible except in case of a Foreign Minister in office, and 2) Belgian courts can prosecute anyone on its territory, except a Foreign Minister in office.

[64] See Separate Opinion by Judge Koroma, *Arrest Warrant of 11 April 2002*, Judgment of 14 February 2002, ICJ Reports 2002, p 60, para 5.

[65] *Ibid*, p 61, para 6.

[66] *Ibid*, p 61, para 7.

[67] *Ibid*, p 61, para 7.

However, Judge Koroma is very clear about the general universal jurisdiction when he states: 'In my considered opinion, today, together with piracy, universal jurisdiction is available for certain crimes, such as war crimes and crimes against humanity, including the slave trade and genocide.'[68]

d) Judges Higgins, Kooijmans, and Buergenthal: Universal Jurisdiction *in absentia* for the most Heinous International Crimes is Permitted under Certain Safeguards

Judges Higgins, Kooijmans and Buergenthal agree with the Court on the issues of jurisdiction and admissibility and also with the conclusions it reached. However, they did have their reservations on: a) what the Court said, and b) what the Court did not say. For them, even if the Court chose to arrive at its decision based on the doctrine of immunity yet it was necessary for the Court to state its position on the principle of universal jurisdiction. According to them: 'Immunity' for them 'is the common shorthand phrase' for 'immunity from jurisdiction'.[69] They opined that passing the question of jurisdiction the Court gave an impression that the subject of 'immunity' is a free standing topic, which they do not find.

In dealing with this topic they first conceptualised the broadest possible framework of relation between human rights and international law. Seeing the current situation of international law they see two distinct norms in action: the norm of 'immunity' and the norm of 'jurisdiction'. And, they state, that immunity can arise only if the jurisdiction exists. The larger picture can only be seen when both the norms are fully appreciated and the diagnosis from the larger picture reveals the problem:

> One of the challenges of present international law is to provide for stability of international relations and effective international intercourse while at the same time guaranteeing respect for human rights. The difficult task that international law today faces is to provide that stability in international relations by a means other than the impunity of those responsible for major human rights violations.[70]

Three judges describe the universal jurisdiction as of two different types: 1) '*universal jurisdiction properly so called*', and 2) '*territorial jurisdiction over persons for extraterritorial events*'. The underlying idea of universal jurisdiction properly so-called . . . is, according to them, a common endeavour in the face of atrocities. This is the type of jurisdiction covering where: a) crimes are committed abroad by foreigners over foreigners, and b) the accused is not present on the territory of the forum State. The second type of jurisdiction covers the persons who are present on

[68] *Ibid*, p 61, para 9.

[69] See Joint Separate Opinion by Judges Higgins, Kooijmans, and Buergenthal, *Arrest Warrant of 11 April 2002*, Judgment of 14 February 2002, ICJ Reports 2002, p 64, para 3.

[70] *Ibid*, p 63.

the territory of the forum State and who have allegedly committed crimes abroad.[71]

Whether the permission to exercise universal jurisdiction *in absentia* is permitted under international law is a question which has no clear answer. The topic is surrounded with great confusion. Having reasoned the State practice, international convention, and the *Lotus* case decided by the Permanent Court of International Justice the three judges arrive at a conclusion that the universal jurisdiction *in absentia* is permitted under the following three safeguards[72]:

> First: no exercise of criminal jurisdiction may occur which fails to respect the inviolability or infringes the immunity of the person concerned.
>
> Second: a State contemplating bringing criminal charges based on universal jurisdiction must first offer to the national State of the prospective accused person the opportunity itself to act upon the charges concerned[73];
>
> Third: such charges may only be laid by a prosecutor or *juge d'instruction* who acts in full independence, without links to or control by the government of that State.

The conclusion of the three judges is prescriptive rather than descriptive. It is a guiding contribution for those who would ever engage in drafting the law on the principle of universal jurisdiction *in absentia.* The approach of the three ICJ judges, all well known in the filed of human rights, and forming part of the composition in the present case is, is clearly seeking: 1) to take the relationship between human rights and international law in the broadest possible perspective, and 2) to suggest that the doctrines of State sovereignty and human rights are not to conflict with each other but to complement each other. This is an exemplary clarification of the fact that you cannot separate human dignity of the State from the human dignity of the individual as the concept is comprehensive and holistic.

e) Judge Rezek: Judicial Restraint Going Hand in Hand with Political Restraint is Good for the Health of Human Rights

Judge Rezek is more concerned with the existing reality between the contemporary function of the international legal system still mainly based on the old sovereignty of States and yet without an unsettled law on the subject of universal jurisdiction, particularly the jurisdiction *in absentia.* 'It is essential', he states:

> that all States ask themselves, before attempting to steer public international law in a direction conflicting with certain principles which still govern contemporary international relation, what the consequences would be should other States, and possibly a large number of other States, adopt such a practice. Thus it was apt for the Parties to discuss before the Court what the reaction of some European countries would be if a judge

[71] See Joint Separate Opinion by Judges Higgins, Kooijmans, and Buergenthal, *Arrest Warrant of 11 April 2002*, Judgment of 14 February 2002, ICJ Reports 2002, pp 71–79, paras 31–52.

[72] *Ibid*, pp 79–80, paras 53–59.

[73] The three Judges also observed that the Court made reference to these elements in the context of this case at p 10, para 16 of the Judgment, ICJ Reports 2002.

> in the Congo had accused their leaders of crimes purportedly committed in Africa by them on their orders.[74]

In his opinion, one State cannot be allowed, and should not be allowed, and the existing law does not allow to exercise criminal jurisdiction of another sovereign and equal State.

Turning to the political reality of international relation on his own continent, the judge boldly states:

> An even more pertinent scenario could serve as counterpoint to the present case. There are many judges in the southern hemisphere, no less qualified that Mr Vandermeersch, and, like him, imbued with good faith and a deep attachment to human rights and peoples' rights, who would not hesitate for one instant to launch criminal proceedings against various leaders in the northern hemisphere in relation to recent military episodes, all of which have occurred north of the equator. There knowledge of the facts is no less complete, or less impartial, than the knowledge which the Court in Brussels thinks it possesses about events in Kinshasa.

Judge Rezek poses a pertinent question. 'Why do these judges show restraint?'[75] and he facilitates the situation of human rights and human dignity in answering the question himself: 'Because they are aware that international law does not permit the assertion of criminal jurisdiction in such circumstances. Because they know that their national Governments, in light of this legal reality, would never support such action at international level.'[76]

With profound emphasis on the reality that the universal jurisdiction *in abtentia* does not exist in international law, Judge Rezek states: 'If the application of the principle of universal jurisdiction does not presuppose that the accused be present on the territory of the forum State, co-ordination becomes totally impossible, leading to the collapse of the international system of co-operation for the prosecution of crime.'[77] Judge Rezek finds it important that the domestic treatment of issues of the kind, and the related conduct of the legal and political authorities of

[74] See Separate Opinion of Judge Rezek, *Arrest Warrant of 11 April 2002*, Judgment of 14 February 2002, ICJ Reports 2002, p 93, para 8.

[75] *Ibid*, p 93, para 9.

[76] *Ibid*, p 93, para 9. It is also interesting to note here that in the similar vein Sir Robert Jennings comments on the subject in these words:

> Where does one stop in this national jurisdiction campaign against just some of those who have undertaken the burdens and risks of office? At the time of this writing either or both Mr Arafat or Mr Sharon might be thought possible candidates for being subjected to some national jurisdiction after they cease to hold their present offices, which could be fairly soon in both cases. One does not need a good case against either. The universal jurisdiction idea would give the green light to any national judge equipped with a sufficient measure of self-righteousness. But what could such action contribute to the pacification of the most turbulent area of the globe.

Sir Robert Jennings, 'Jurisdiction and Immunity in the ICJ Decision in the *Yerodia* Case' (2002) 4(3) *International Law Forum* 103.

[77] See Separate Opinion of Judge Rezek, *ibid*, p 93, para 9. NB Judge Rezek adds here a footnote especially pointing out: 'As regards the current status of the principle of universal jurisdiction, note that the States which negotiated the Rome Treaty avoided extending this principle to the jurisdiction of the future International Criminal Court'.

each State should remain in balance with the existing decentralized characteristic of international community, the community which rests on the principle of equality of all its members and necessarily requires every co-ordination of their efforts.

Balancing both the pillars, legal as well as political, on which stands the entire edifice of human rights and human dignity, Judge Rezek contrives a directive principle for the States comprising international community and given to the cause of human rights: 'Any policy adopted in the name of human rights but not in keeping with that discipline threatens to harm rather than serve that cause.'[78]

Judge Rezek is suggesting to balance human rights with human rights. In other words, based on the biblical second command, appealing to the innermost morality of law and politics together in all human conduct: *do to others as you would like to be done by.*

f) Judge *ad hoc* Bula-Bula: Universal Jurisdiction in Absentia Runs Counter to the Dignity of People

Dignity, the State dignity and people's dignity, is great concern of Judge Bula-Bula.

One must recognize the reality that behind the convocation of a legal principle or the adoption of a certain litigation strategy, the foremost for a litigating party is the dignity of State and people. First to convoke and then to withdraw from the principle of universal jurisdiction was a litigation strategy of the Congo, appears clearly from the following words of Judge *ad hoc* Bula-Bula, appointed by the Congo: 'What is at stake here is a debt owed to the Congolese people, freely organized in a sovereign State calling for its dignity to be respected'.[79] He continues:

> But dignity has no price. It is one of those intangible assets, on which it is impossible to put a price in money terms. When a person whether legal or natural, gives up his dignity, he loses the essence of his natural or legal personality. The dignity of the Congolese people, victim of the neo-colonial chaos imposed upon it on the morrow of decolonisation, of which the current tragic events largely represent the continued expression, is a dignity of this kind.[80]

What strikes here is that he does not speak here of the dignity of the State but the dignity of the people. And, in a sense, be it the dignity of the State, people, or a single human, it belongs in its essence with the concept of human dignity in its individual as well as group level. The principle which under the label of justice would violate human dignity would run counter to the very notion of human dignity. Based on this rationale when cannot altogether sweep away the notion of State sovereignty if it proves detrimental to the notion of human dignity. Hence, the doctrine of human rights, even when it comes to apply to the rights of nations, if

[78] See Separate Opinion of Judge Rezek, *ibid*, p 94, para 9.

[79] Separate Opinion of Judge *ad hoc* Bula-Bula, 14 February 2002 Judgment, *Arrest Warrant of 11 April 2002*, ICJ Reports 2002, p 109, para 24.

[80] *Ibid*, p 109, para 25.

it violates the dignity of the people of that nation, or any representative of those people, runs counter to the very essence of human rights and human dignity.

Therefore, imagining the working of the principle of universal jurisdiction *in absentia*, Judge Bula-Bula takes the following stand: 'The idea that a State could have the legal power to try offences committed abroad, by foreigners against foreigners, while the suspect himself is on foreign territory, runs counter to the very notion of international law.'[81]

g) Judge *ad hoc* Van Den Wyngaert: Universal Jurisdiction in Absentia is Permissible

Judge *ad hoc* Van Den Wyngaert maintains all the way that universal jurisdiction *in absentia* is permissible for States. On the subject of immunities, she finds that there is no legal basis in international law, neither conventional nor customary, to grant immunity to a Foreign Minister in office.

Judge Van Den Wyngaert bases her reasoning by thinking of the case in a more principled way. According to her, there are, today, two diverging interests in modern international criminal law: 1) the need of international accountability for such crimes as torture, terrorism, war crimes and crimes against humanity, and 2) the principle of sovereign equality of States which presupposes a system of immunities. This way she thinks that the case was about the question of what international law requires or allows States to do as 'agents' of international community when they are confronted with complaints of victims of such crimes, given the fact that international criminal courts will not be able to judge *all* international crimes.[82]

A careful analysis of this would reveal that the Judge thinks that there are so many international crimes and not many international courts, hence, States should confer upon themselves the task of administering international criminal justice. And further, citing the examples, *inter alia*, of *Lotus* case decided by the PCIJ she opines that since international law does not prohibit such powers to States, hence, allows them to do so as Belgium has done.

VI. Belgian Reaction after the Judgment

It is interesting to note the following positive developments in Belgium just a short while after the delivery of the Judgement. Brussels Court of Appeal in three recent cases concerning *Yerodia* (on 16 April 2002), *Sharon* (on 26 June 2002) and *Gbagbo* (26 June 2002), respectively decided in favour of conditional universal

[81] *Ibid*, p 124, para 74.

[82] See Dissenting Opinion by Judge *ad hoc* Van Den Wyngaert, *Arrest Warrant of 11 April 2002*, Judgment of 14 February 2002, ICJ Reports 2002, p 141, para 5.

jurisdiction: only if the alleged perpetrator can be found on Belgian territory can a criminal prosecution take place in Belgium. Article 7 of Belgian Law has meanwhile been replaced by the Law of 23 April 2003. In its original version, the Article did not contain any filter and the law was further made very 'user-friendly' by the combination of its progressive features with the procedural instrument of *constitution de partie civile* (which enables individuals to put the criminal procedure in motion). Under the new Article 7(1), the possibility of a complaint with *constitution de partie civile* will no longer be available for those international crimes which have no connection at all with Belgium. If the crime has not been committed in Belgium, the suspect is not a Belgian or is not found on Belgian territory, or the victim is not a Belgian or does not reside in Belgium for at least three years, only the federal public prosecutor will be able to launch the criminal procedure.[83]

These actions of Belgian political as well as judicial authorities is a clear recognition and respect to the Court's extremely balanced judgment and the painstaking clarification and development of law on the principle of universal jurisdiction in the independent opinions appended thereto by its judges.

VII. Conclusion

The concept of human dignity, both at the individual level as well as at State level was present at every inch in this case. Belgium enacted its law to confer upon its courts the power of universal jurisdiction in order to try criminals violating core human crimes, hence the underlying principle was the concept of human dignity. It issued a warrant of arrest against a Minister of Foreign Affairs because the victims of his alleged crimes complained against him. It was again the concept of human dignity in action. The Congo filed a case before the Court because the dignity of that State and its Foreign Minister was violated. It was again a litigation based on human dignity. The Court developed the law on immunity for a Foreign Minister. It actually developed the law on the dignity of a State, the dignity of a Foreign Minister of a State, and the dignity of the people of a State. The Court decided not to decide the matter based on the principle of universal jurisdiction as the Parties did not ask for it, the law was not very certain and settled on that subject, and its judges seemingly had different views on the principle. It is again a dignified approach of the Court not to turn activist. The Court showed its dignity by taking to a dignified judicial restraint. Judges develop law *only* when there already *is* a law to be developed. Several judges clarified and developed the law on the principle of universal jurisdiction, some favouring jurisdiction *in absentia*, with others against it. One judge even took it upon himself to write only on the subject of immunity for a Foreign Minister but did not remain untouched with the

[83] The above three judgments have not yet been published. I owe gratitude to Prof Jan J Wouters, 'The Judgment of the International Court of Justice in the Arrest Warrant Case: Some Critical Remarks' (2003) 16 *Leiden Journal of International Law* 265–67.

issue of combating grave crimes. The concept of human dignity, however, remained at the basis of their thinking in one way or another. The most conspicuous of this case and its judgment is that the Respondent having fully respected the Judgment and enlightened by the individual opinions of its several judges decided to make changes in its municipal law which was at the root of this case.

The Judgment of the Court, taken in conjunction with the individual opinions of eleven judges, including two *ad hocs*, is an immense contribution to the clarification and development of international law concerning the doctrine of immunity as well as the principle of universal jurisdiction. The immunity from jurisdiction and the inviolability of a Minister for Foreign Affairs was an obscure area of the law to which the Court put a seal of certainty and clarity, adding emphatically that immunity is no impunity, hence the Minister remains answerable to law despite his/her functionally necessary immunities. Judge Al-Khasawneh stressing the need of restrictive immunities equally stressed the importance and priory of dealing with the question of crimes against international public policy (*jus cogens*). President Guillaume, judges Ranjeva, Rezek, and judge *ad hoc* Bula-Bula clarifying that that international law does not permit universal jurisdiction *in absentia*. Judges Higgins, Kooijmans, Buergenthal and Koroma though see a degree of permissibility of jurisdiction in absentia, according to international law, maintain that it can prevail over the immunity of an incumbent Foreign Minister. Judge *ad hoc* Van Den Wyngaert though asserts strongly in favour of this jurisdiction *in absentia* even in the face of the given immunities, she sees it out of a dire necessity of the international society.

On the subject of immunity for a Minister of Foreign Affairs, Wickremasinghe has this to say: 'In so far as the *ratio decidendi* of the case is confined to the immunity from criminal jurisdiction, and inviolability of serving Ministers of Foreign Affairs *(ratione personae)*, the judgment may be welcomed as clarifying a previously uncertain law on which state practice is very limited.'[84]

Prof Cassese commented as: 'The Court must be commended for elucidating and spelling out an obscure issue of existing law. In so doing it has considerably expanded the protection afforded by international law to foreign ministers. It has thus given priority to the need for foreign relations to be conducted unimpaired.'[85]

It is to be observed that even though Judges Higgins, Kooijmans and Buergenthal conclude that there is an element in international law permitting universal jurisdiction in absentia, that element is just *indicative* and not sufficient, hence they also subscribe to the following view:

> While no general rule of positive international law can as yet be asserted which gives to states the right to punish foreign nations for crimes against humanity in the same way as

[84] C Wickremasinghe, 'Arrest Warrant of 11 April 2000 (*Democratic Republic of the Congo v Belgium*), Preliminary Objections and Merits, Judgment of 14 February 2002' 52(3) *International and Comparative Law Quarterly* 781.

[85] A Cassese, 'When May Senior State Officilas Be Tried for International Crimes? Some Comments on the *Congo v Belgium* Case' (2002) 13(4) *European Journal of International Law* 855.

> they are, for instance, entitled to punish acts of piracy, there are clear indications pointing to the gradual evolution of a significant principle of international law to that effect.[86] (emphasis is mine)

In view of this they prescribe an ingenious scheme of 'safeguards'. On this step forward contribution made by Judges Higgins, Kooijmans and Buergenthal to the principle of universal jurisdiction, Prof Cassese remarked:

> Judges Higgins, Kooijmans and Buergenthal maintain that international customary law, in addition to authorizing 'universal jurisdiction properly so called' over piracy, does not prohibit such jurisdiction for other offences, subject to a set of conditions they carefully set out. The enunciation of these conditions—whether or not one can fully subscribe to all of them—indubitably constitutes a commendable contribution to the careful delineation of general legal principles on the question of universal jurisdiction.[87]

Hence, the Court's silence and all the individual opinions of judges taken together proclaim to the international community that there is 'no general rule' of international law on the subject of universal jurisdiction and it is high time to take steps to meet that need of international society.

The ingenuity of the perception, conception, and balancing of two old and new, respectively, doctrines of State sovereignty and human rights, two notions of State dignity and human dignity, two adjudicational approaches of judicial restraint and judicial activism, two ideologies of judicial conservatism and judicial liberalism, in the face of two conflicting trends of smooth running of international relations on the old pattern of sovereignty and safeguarding the new international values of human rights, is the hallmark of the judgment on merits in this case concerning the *Arrest Warrant of 11 April 2000.* The balance could not better be achieved without the risk of one prevailing over the other. In the ultimate analysis it is the smooth running of both the doctrinal wheels of State sovereignty and human rights that the evolving bicycle of international legal culture and a system of human dignity of the people, for the people, and by the people will move forward.

[86] ICJ Reports 2002, p 79, para 52. Quoted from Jennings and Watts, *Oppenheim's International Law*, 9th edn (Harlow, Longman) p 998.

[87] A Cassese, 'When May Senior State Officilas Be Tried for International Crimes? Some Comments on the *Congo v Belgium* Case' (2002) 13(4) *European Journal of International Law* 855, 856–57.

13

Vienna Convention on Consular Relations cases: the Convention Does Create Individual Rights (1998–2004)

I. Some Preliminary Observations

THE STRUGGLE FOR rights by the ruled against the ruler is centuries old and is still far from over. Persons to whom law attributes rights and duties are the subjects of law. The law commands its subjects but it merely regulates the use and disposition of its objects.[1] Based on this sovereignty oriented traditional criterion it has long been maintained that States alone are subjects of international law. The issue of the rights and legal status of the individual in international law has long been a subject of debate. Whenever there has been in issue the question of acquisition of individual rights under treaty the judges and jurists have usually resorted, directly or indirectly, to one of the three prevailing theories concerning rights and duties of individuals under customary international law, all approaching the issue in the context of subjects of international law and the place of the individual in international law. The first and the most conservative theory, the *object theory*, advocates: *States alone are subjects of international law*, hence, individual is an object of international law. This theory was developed by Heilborn in 1896.[2] Its chief exponent was Lassa Oppenheim.[3] The second, the benevolent liberal *subject theory*, maintains: *Individuals alone are the subjects of international law*. Westlake[4] and Kelson[5] were its chief advocates. And the third, *beneficiary theory*, also called the midway theory, stands for:,: individual is neither an object nor a subject but *a beneficiary of the rules of international law*. Borchard developed

[1] DP O'Connell, *International Law*, 2nd edn, (London, Stevens & Sons, 1970) vol 1, p 234.

[2] *Ibid*, p 106.

[3] L Oppenhiem, *International Law*, 1st edn, (1905).

[4] Westlake had remarked: 'the duties and rights of States are only the duties and rights of men who compose them;' *Collected Papers of Westlake*, vol 1 (1914) p 78, quoted by in JG Satrke, *Introduction to International Law*, 10th edn, (1989), p 59.

[5] H Kelson, RT Tucker, (ed), *Principles of International Law*, 2nd edn, (New York, NY, Holt, Rinehart and Winston, 1967) 221–30.

this theory in 1928.[6] The beneficiary theory is no less conservative and traditional than the object theory, for it neither authorizes a beneficiary of rights to take independent steps in his own name to enforce his individual rights.

The support for a less conservative approach was adopted by the Permanent Court of International Justice in its Judgment in the case concerning *Danzig Railway Officials* where the Court ruled that a treaty could in certain circumstances confer rights directly on individuals.[7] Since the days of Heilborn (1896) and the first edition of Oppenhein (1905) the situation of individual in international law has considerably changed. The principle that certain provisions of a treaty may be invoked by individuals in national courts is a central doctrine of European Union law today. Article 34 of the ICJ Statute may bar individuals from bringing their claims but the development of international and regional human rights instruments has certainly enabled them to pursue cases before international tribunals. European Union law has very liberally developed the doctrine that treaty provisions are capable of conferring rights directly upon European citizens[8]

Do as I say not as I do. A human person betrays its own dignity and that of its fellow human being when he does not treat others as it likes to be treated by them, and groups of humans such as States have no exception to this contradictory conduct. The United States of America is the State which invokes more than any other State the provisions of 1963 Vienna Convention on Consular Relations to protect its own citizens abroad from the laws of those states. The United States also invoked the same Convention before the International Court of Justice in the case concerning *United States Diplomatic and Consular Staff in Tehran (USA v Iran)* (see chapter 6). Yet, its double standard is well revealed by one of its editorials:

> The Protections, however, have less currency within the United States, which employs a 'Do as I say not as I do' application of the treaty provisions—to the deprivation of international law. The much was clear from the International Court of Justice ruling last week that the United States had violated the rights of 51 Mexicans on death row in this country by not advising them of their right to get help from their government.[9]

The task for the ICJ in the given cases was the interpretation and application of the 1963 Vienna Convention on Consular Relations. Which approach the Court adopted and promoted, liberal or conservative, remains to be seen.

[6] This was Borchard's theory in *Diplomatic Protection of Citizens Abroad* (1928), cited in DP O'Connell, *International Law*, 2nd edn, (London, Stevens & Sons, 1970) vol 1, pp 106–12.

[7] Advisory Opinion on the Jurisdiction of the Courts of Danzig (1928), PCIJ Series B, No 15.

[8] J O'Brien, *International Law* (London, Cavendish, 2001) 153–55.

[9] Editorial: 'Double Standard Revealed', *The Journal News.com* (an online newspaper), 4 April 2004.

II. Three Cases with One Common Fact: Vienna Convention on Consular Relations Creates Human Rights

All the three applicants—Paraguay, Germany and Mexico, respectively—have separately sued the United States to prevent execution of their citizens on death row in the United States who according to these States were not informed of their individual rights under the Vienna Convention on Consular Relations to seek help from their consulates. In bringing these cases the applicants sought to assert their own rights as States which they claimed to have been violated by the respondent, as well as their right to diplomatic protection of their nationals whose *individual rights* according to the applicants were also alleged to have been violated by the respondent State.[10]

It is not the issue of the legality or illegality of the death penalty as such which is at the centre of these cases. But the *issue whether Article 36 of the Vienna Convention on Consular Relations creates individual rights.* According to the applicants *it does* and according to the respondent *it does not.*

Neither the consulates of these countries nor their citizens on death row were informed by the competent United States of their rights under Article 36 of the 1963 Vienna Convention.

Article 36 of the Vienna Convention on Consular Relations reads:

> 1. With a view to facilitating the exercise of consular functions relating to nationals of the sending State:
>
> (a) consular officers shall be free to communicate with nationals of the sending State and to have access to them. Nationals of the sending State shall have the same freedom with respect to communication with and access to consular officers of the sending State;
>
> (b) if he so requests, the competent authorities of the receiving States shall, without delay, inform the consular post of the sending State if within its consular district, a national of that State is arrested or committed to prison or to custody pending trial or is detained in any other manner.
>
> Any communication addressed to the consular post by the person arrested, in prison, custody or detention shall also be forwarded by the said authorities without delay. The said authorities shall inform the person concerned without delay of his rights under this sub-paragraph;

[10] It is interesting to note that Mexico had already sought an advisory opinion from the Inter-American Court of Human Rights in 1997, following the execution of two Mexican nationals in the United States who were, after their arrest, not informed of the individual right to seek consular assistance. In its decision, the Court unanimously held that Article 36 of the Vienna Convention on Consular Relations confers specific legal and human rights in individual foreign nationals. The Court's most important holding (voting 6–1) was that the execution of an individual whose VCCR rights have been violated is an 'arbitrary' deprivation of life, and violates international law. (See IACHR's Advisory Opinion OC–16/1999).

(c) consular officers shall have the rights to visit a national of the sending State who is in prison, custody or detention, to converse and correspond with him and to arrange for his legal representation. They shall also have the right to visit any national of the sending State who is in prison, custody or detention in their district in pursuance of a judgment. Nevertheless, consular officers shall refrain from taking action on behalf of a national who is in prison, custody or detention if he expressly opposes such action.

2. The rights referred to in paragraph 1 of this Article shall be exercised in conformity with the laws and regulations of the receiving State, subject to the proviso, however, that the said laws and regulations must enable full effect to be given to the purposes for which the rights accorded under this Article are intended.

III. Case Concerning the Vienna Convention on Consular Relations (*Paraguay v USA*)[11]: Individual Rights Remained Undecided

On 3 April 1998 Paraguay filed its case before the ICJ instituting proceedings against the United States in a dispute concerning alleged violations of the 1963 Vienna Convention on Consular Relations. The Application stated that in 1992 the authorities of Virginia had arrested Mr Angel Francisco Breard, a Paraguayan national; he had been charged, tried, convicted of culpable homicide and sentenced to death in 1993, the execution date being 14 April 1998, without having been informed that he had rights under Article 36, paragraph 1(b) of the Vienna Convention to be informed to communicate with his consulate in the United States to seek assistance. It was further alleged that authorities of Virginia had also failed to inform Paraguayan Consulate of Mr Breard's detention. Paraguay at the same day also requested the Court to indicate provisional measures. The *rationale* of indicating the provisional measures is well described by Judge Koroma in his declaration appended to the Court's Order of 9 April 1998: 'The purpose of a request for provisional measures is to preserve as well as to safeguard the rights of the parties that are in dispute, especially when such rights or subject-matter of the dispute could be irretrievably or irreparably destroyed thereby rendering the Court's decision ineffective or without object.'[12]

[11] The composition of the Court in the Order of 9 April 1998 on Provisional Measures in the case concerning the Vienna Convention on Consular Relations *(Paraguay v USA)* was: Vice-President Weeramantry, Acting President; President Schwebel; Judges Oda, Bedjaoui, Guillaume, Ranjeva, Herczegh, Shi, Fleischhauer, Koroma, Vereshchetin, Higgins, Parra-Aranguren, Kooijmans, Rezek. (See ICJ Reports 1998, p 248).

President Schwebel and Judge Oda and Koroma appended declarations to the Order of the Court. (See ICJ Reports, pp 259–64).

[12] Declaration of Judge Koroma appended to the Provisional Measures Order in the case concerning Vienna Convention on Consular Relations *(Paraguay v USA)*, ICJ Report 1998, p 263.

In its Order on Provisional Measure, the ICJ ordered unanimously that: 'The United States should take all measures at its disposal to ensure that Angel Francisco Breard is not executed pending the final decision in these proceedings'.[13] The Order was disregarded by Virginia authorities and Bread nonetheless was executed on 14 April 1998, clearly rendering the right of Paraguay to render consular assistance to is citizen as well as Angel Breard's right to life irretrievable and irreparable. Thereafter, Paraguay withdrew its case.[14] Hence, the Court did not have the opportunity to deal whether the Convention creates individual rights or not.

IV. LaGrand Case (*Germany v USA*)[15]: Vienna Convention Does Create Individual Rights

Germany picked it up where Paraguay left it. Germany filed a similar case against the United States on 2 March 1999 concerning two German nationals, La Grand brothers. *LaGrand* case has its roots in a 1982 bank robbery committed in an Arizona bank (USA) by Walter and Karl LaGrand brothers. During this robbery the two brothers stabbed the 63-year-old bank manager to death. For this they were tried, convicted and sentenced to death. Despite all appeals for clemency and numerous diplomatic efforts by the German Government Karl LaGrand was executed by lethal injection on 24 February 1999. The execution of Walter LaGrand had been set for 3 March 1999. In order to save the life of Walter, Germany filed a case on 2 March 1999 against the United States, just hours before the scheduled execution of Walter, and also at the same time requested the ICJ to issue an Order on Provisional Measures. The Order similar to the one in the *Breard case* was issued[16] by the Court on the same day. However, the Order had the same fate and the Order in the *Breard* case. Walter LaGrand was executed in utter disregard to the Court's Order. But Germany did not give up like Paraguay did and went ahead with the case.

[13] Vienna Convention on Consular Relations (*Paraguay v USA*), Provisional Measures Order of 9 April 1998, ICJ Reports 1998, para 41(I), p 258.

[14] For the details see the Court's discontinuance Order of 10 November 1998, *Vienna Convention on Consular Relations (Paraguay v USA)*, ICJ Report 1998, p 426.

[15] The composition of the Court in its Judgment in the case concerning *LaGrand (Germany v USA)* was: President Guillaume; Vice-President Shi; Judges Oda, Bedjaoui, Ranjeva, Herczegh, Fleischhauer, Koroma, Vereshchetin, Higgins, Parra-Aranguren, Kooijmans, Rezel, Al-Khasawneh, Buergenthal. (see ICJ Reports 2001, p 468).

Vice-President Shi appended a separate opinion to the Judgment of the Court; Judge Oda appended a dissenting opinion to the Judgment of the Court; Judges Koroma and Parra-Aranguren appended separate opinion to the Judgment of the Court; Judge Buergenthal appended a dissenting opinion to the Judgment of the Court (see ICJ Reports 2001, pp 518–57).

[16] See the Court's Order of 3 March 1999, *LaGrand (Germany v USA)*, ICJ Reports 1999.

Germany claimed in its written pleadings that:

> the right to be informed upon arrest of the rights under Article 36(1)(b) of the Vienna Convention does not only reflect a right of the sending State (and home State of the individuals involved) towards the receiving State but also is an individual right of every national of a foreign State party to the Vienna Convention entering the territory of another State party.[17]

Germany's contention is obviously following a liberal approach and endeavouring to promote acquisition of individual rights under treaties and therewith adding legal weight to the standing of individual as a subject of international law.

Germany, during its oral proceedings on the merits, made a 'most crucial' argument concerning the relation between the Vienna Convention and human rights. Germany maintained: 'that the right to be informed of the rights under Article 36, paragraph 1(b), of the Vienna Convention, is an individual right of every national of a State party to the Convention who enters the territory of another State party.'[18] Further, Germany submitted that:

> the 'United Nations Declaration on the human rights of individuals who are not nationals of the country in which they live', adopted by General assembly resolution 40/144 on 13 December 1985, confirms the view that the right of access to the consulate of the home State, as well as the information on this right, constitute individual rights of foreign national and are to be regarded as human rights of aliens.[19]

Whereas the United States contended that: 'rights of consular notification and access under the Vienna Convention in any event are rights of States, not individuals. Clearly they can benefit individuals by permitting—not requiring—States to offer them consular assistance, but the Convention's role is not to articulate or confer individual rights.'[20]

Obviously, the US approach is very narrow and conservative, vehemently questioning this liberal argument of Germany and trying to restrict the scope of the Vienna Convention only to conferring rights on the States and not individuals. Its contention that rights of consular notification and access under the Vienna Convention are *rights of States, and not of individuals*, even though these rights *may benefit individuals* by permitting States to offer them consular assistance subscribes to the beneficiary theory of Brochard, dragging the place of human back to the pre-human rights era.

Professor Simma, counsel for Germany at that time (and now a judge at the ICJ), found this line of US thinking to be extremely narrow and not in line with contemporary rules on interpretation. In his view the understanding of the rights under Article 36 of the Vienna Convention on Consular Relations as individual rights is in conformity with all rules on interpretation of international treaties that

[17] Memorial of Germany, vol 1, para 4.91, p 116.

[18] Judgement of 27 June 2001 in the case concerning *LaGrand (Germany v USA)*, ICJ Reports 2001, para 75, pp 492–93.

[19] *Ibid*, para 75, p 493.

[20] Counter-Memorial of the United States of America, para 97, p 81.

one can find in Article 31 of the Vienna Convention on the Law of Treaties. He supported this view with two forceful arguments. First, according to him it is clear enough that the words 'ordinary meaning' of the words 'his rights' in Article 36, paragraph 1(b) refers to an individual. Secondly, he argued that the context of Article 36 relates to both the concerns of sending and receiving States and those of individuals. Arguing in this vein and refuting the narrow interpretation of the United States, Professor Simma made a profoundly convincing statement giving four strong reasons in favour of the individual rights character of the rights under Article 36: 1) 'It is individuals who are accorded freedom with respect to communication in subparagraph 1(a), 2) 'it is individual who have the right to request or not request the notification of the consulate pursuant to subparagraph 1(b)', 3) 'it is individuals who are to be informed of that right', and lastly 4) 'it is individuals who have the right to oppose a prison visit according to paragraph 1(c)'.[21] He questioned the human rights judicial conscience of the legal minds: 'Can there be a clearer indication of an individual than the placing of its exercise squarely into the hands of the individual?' This is a great tribute to individual human dignity and a reminder to the State sovereignty oriented interpreters of international law to wake up to the realities of the legal age of human rights and human dignity. As if the tide of human spirit of an international jurist surged to the highest ebb in service of the cause of human rights, Simma loudly wondered and spoke his judicial conscience: 'Why something which looks like an individual right, feels like an individual right and smells like an individual right should be anything else but an individual right?'[22] This clearly is a wake-up call for all legal and judicial minds to realize that it is an era of human rights and every individual should be accorded his/her proper place of dignity in interpreting any instrument of international law. It is obvious from these arguments that Germany stands for liberal view of human rights and the United States defends itself with a conservative view of looking at international law as between States and sovereignty based.

From the globality of Article 36 the Court noted that it establishes an *'interrelated regime'* designed to facilitate the implementation of the system of consular relations. First and foremost it noted that the provision begins with a *'basic principle'* governing consular protection: the right of communication and access (Article 36, paragraph 1(a)). The clause is followed by the provision which spells out 'the modalities' of consular relation (Article 36, paragraph 1(b)). And finally, the paragraph 1(c) of Article 36 sets out 'the measures' consular officers may take in rendering consular assistance to their nationals in the custody of the receiving State.

The contents in paragraph 77 of the Court's Judgment in the LaGrand case are most historic in the development of international human rights law as it gave a human rights character to the 1963 Consular Convention. In taking notice, though in a plain textual meaning way of treaty interpretation, the Court's

[21] ICJ Verbatim Record, *CR* [2000] para 3, p 57.
[22] *Ibid.*

reasoning slowly and gradually moved towards further clarifying the modalities spelled out in Article 36, paragraph 1(b). It follows that when the sending State is unaware of the detention of its nationals due to the failure of the receiving State to provide the requisite consular notification without delay, 'which was true in the present case', the sending State has been prevented for all practical purposes from exercising its rights under Article 36, paragraph 1. In cementing the creation of individual rights, though together with the rights of the State, the Court forcefully mentioned:

> It is immaterial for the purposes of the present case whether the LaGrands would have sought consular assistance from Germany, whether Germany would have rendered such assistance, or whether a different verdict would have been rendered. *It is sufficient that the Convention conferred these rights*, and that Germany *and the LaGrands were in effect prevented* by the breach of the United States from exercising them, had they so chosen.[23] (emphasis added)

Further, striving to establish the independent character of these individual rights from the Article 36 of the Consular Convention and adding clarification to the said provision the Court analysed Article 36, paragraph 1(b) step by step in the context of their modalities. The first thing the Court notes is that Article 36, paragraph 1(b) spells out *twofold obligations of the receiving State:* 1) *obligations towards the detained persons*, and 2) the *obligations towards the sending State.*

Secondly, the Court takes due note that the provision provides: 1) at the request of the detained person, the receiving State must inform the consular post of the sending State of the individual's detention 'without delay', and 2) any communication by the detained person addressed to the consular post of the sending State must be forwarded to it by authorities of the receiving State 'without delay'.

And finally, the Court finds it most significant that the subparagraph ends with the following language: 'The said authorities shall inform the person concerned without delay of *his rights* under this subparagraph. (emphasis added).'

The Court had no doubt about the clarity of these provisions. Based on that clear and step by step textual interpretation, the Court concluded that: '*Article 36, paragraph1, creates individual rights*'[24] (italics are mine).

The Court further added that by virtue of Article 1 of the Optional Protocol to the said Convention these individual rights 'may be invoked in this Court by the national State of the detained person'. Hence, the Court decided: 'These rights were violated in the present case.'[25]

As a local rule of the '*procedural default*' prevented LaGrands from effectively challenging their convictions and sentences, Germany argued that, under Article 36, paragraph 2, of the Vienna Convention:

[23] ICJ Reports 2001, para 74, p 492.

[24] Judgment of 27 June 2001 in the case concerning *La Grand (Germany v USA)*, ICJ Reports 2001, para 77, p 494.

[25] *Ibid*, para 77, p 494.

> the United States is under an obligation to ensure that its municipal 'laws and regulations ... enable full effect to be given to the purposes for which the rights accorded under this article are intended' [and that it] is in breach of its obligations by upholding rules of domestic law which make it impossible to successfully raise a violation of the right to consular notification in proceedings subsequent to a conviction of a defendant by a jury.[26]

To this US argued that: '[t]he Vienna Convention does not require States party to create a national law remedy permitting individuals to assert claims involving the Convention in criminal proceedings',[27] and, the United States further argued that German interpretation of Article 36, paragraph 2, of the Convention 'is premised on a misinterpretation'[28] of the provision. The Court reacted rather sharply by stating: 'The Court cannot accept the argument of the United States which proceeds, in part, on the assumption that paragraph 2 of Article 36 applies only to the rights of the sending State and not also to those of the detained individual.' Adding even more clarity and authority to what the Court already mentioned in its paragraph 77 of the Judgment, it stated:

> The Court has already determined that Article 36, paragraph 1, *creates individual rights for the detained person in addition to the rights accorded the sending State*, and that consequently the reference to 'rights' in paragraph 2 must be read as applying not only to the rights of the sending State, but also to the rights of the detained individual.[29] (emphasis added).

The Court found that under the circumstances of the present case the local *'procedural default'* rule had the effect of preventing 'full effect [from being] given to the purposes for which the rights accorded under this article are intended',[30] and thus United States violated paragraph 2 of Article 36. In so doing the Court also settled that a municipal rule of *'procedural default'* may not under international law bar a claim by an individual unaware of his rights at trial.

This is, up to a degree, an effective combination between the traditional doctrine of State sovereignty with the legitimate force of human dignity developed by the Court thorough its liberal judicial ideology. This is a progressive circumvention of municipal law by international human rights law. This broad and human dignity oriented interpretation of the Court puts individual human more on the footing in international law as an actor and legal personality.

By fourteen votes to one, the Court decided in its *dispositif* that:

> by not informing Karl and Walter LaGrand without delay following their arrest of *their rights* under Article 36 1(b), of the Convention, and by thereby depriving the Federal Republic of Germany of the possibility, in timely fashion, to render the assistance

[26] ICJ Reports 2001, para 80, p 495.

[27] *Ibid*, para 85, p 496.

[28] *Ibid*, para 83, p 496.

[29] Judgment of 27 June 2001 in the case concerning *LaGrand (Germany v USA)*, ICJ Reports 2001, para 89, p 497.

[30] ICJ Reports 2001, para 91, p 498.

> provided for by the Convention *to the individuals* concerned, the United States of America breached its obligations to the Federal Republic of Germany *and to the LaGrand brothers* under Article 36, para 1.[31] (emphasis added).

The Court also noted that, at the hearings, 'Germany further contended that the right of the individual to be informed without delay under Article 36, paragraph 1, of the Vienna Convention was not only an individual right but has today assumed the character of a human right.' To this contention of Germany the Court reacted: 'The Court having found that the United States violated the rights accorded by Article 36, paragraph 1, to the LaGrand brothers, it does not appear necessary to consider the additional argument developed by Germany in this regard.'[32] It is obvious that the Court in this case applied the essence and not the terminology of the doctrine of human rights. Indeed, to use the word 'human' repeatedly and showing reluctance to use its synonyms as 'individual' and 'people,' in their singular and plural sense, is also blocking the essence of human rights from its further development. It is the *human treatment* of the human which is at the core of the doctrine and not just the word human. Even if the Court uses the words individual right and not human right it comes to the same. For instance, commenting on the judgment delivered by the Court in this case, Meyer, an eminent American jurist, liberally uses the word human as synonym to individual when mentioning that the Court settled the following point, *inter alia*, in deciding this case: 'A country's treaty right of consular access to its nationals may be enforced not only on behalf of the state, but by the state for its national as the latter's human right.'[33] In the ultimate analysis it is the humanization of international law and the recognition of human being as being the ultimate addressee of that law which matters. Hence, the befitting comment of Martin Mennecke: 'the *LaGrand* judgment may well be considered to have contributed both to the humanization of the Consular Convention and to the humanization of international law as a whole. Doing so, the international legal order returns to the final and ultimate addressee of juridical norms: the human being.'[34]

The question of the binding force of the Court's orders on provisional measures, in fact of any international tribunal, has long been a matter of debate and had remained unsettled.

The rationale of the indication of provisional measures lies in Article 41 of the Court's Statute which states that the Court shall have the power to indicate, if it considers the circumstances so require, any provisional measures which ought to be taken to preserve rights of either party to a dispute, pending the Court's deci-

[31] Judgment of 27 June 2001 in the case concerning *LaGrand (Germany v USA)*, ICJ Reports 2001, para 128(3), p 515.

[32] ICJ Reports 2001, para 78, p 494.

[33] HN Meyer, *The World Court in Action: Judging among Nations* (Lanban, Rowman & Littlefield) 226.

[34] M Mennecke, 'Towards the Humanization of the Vienna Convention of Consular Rights—The *LaGrand* Case Before the International Court of Justice' (2001) 44 *German Yearbook of International Law* 445, 468.

sion. Beyond the aura of any doubt preservation of no material right is more important than human right of right to life. And, the right to life is more at stake when it is faced with death penalty. And, the order on provisional measures may not serve better in any situation than saving the life of an individual who may perhaps in the pending judgment be found not guilty.

The Court took note of the unfortunate fact that despite its stay Orders in *Breard* and *LaGrand* cases the detainees were executed nevertheless. And, more so the US Government took the stance that orders on provisional measures were not of binding character. In its written pleadings Germany claimed that by executing Walter LaGrand the United States has violated the Court's Order of 3 March 1999. German Counsel Prof Dupuy had, during the course of the oral proceedings in this case, also argued that irrespective of the general position that the orders on provisional measures are not binding, the orders should be interpreted as binding where they seek to protect human lives from irreparable harm.[35] The Court dealt with this matter in its Judgment most comprehensively and after having thoroughly analysed Article 41 of the Statute reached the conclusion that *orders on provisional measures have binding effect.*[36]

Without treating either the issue of death penalty—which is popularly considered as anti-human rights—or treating individual rights created by the Vienna Convention as human rights, the Court's judgment has done a great service to the cause of human rights, for it is there where the institution of provisional measures would save more lives than in any other situation.

This way, in addition to the most important aspect of this case that Article 36 of the Vienna Convention creates individual rights, the judgment is also known for making history in international adjudication by settling two more points in international law: One, local rule of 'procedural default' may not under international law bar a claim by one unaware of her right at trial. And the other that an indication of provisional measures temporarily issued to keep a case from being futile is 'binding' and enforceable when disobeyed. 'Looking at international law in general, the most spectacular aspect of the Court's decision is certainly to have declared provisional measures to be binding', is the opinion of Mennecke.[37]

[35] CR 2000/26, Statement by German Counsel Professor Pierre-Marie Dupuy, para IX, p 51.

[36] ICJ Reports 2001, paras 92–116, pp 498–508.

[37] M Mennecke, 'Towards the Humanization of the Vienna Convention of Consular Rights—The *LaGrand* Case Before the International Court of Justice' (2001) 44 *German Yearbook of International Law* 445.

V. The Case Concerning Avena and Other Mexican Nationals (*Mexico v USA*)[38]: Individual Rights Further Clarified

V-A. United States Must Provide 'Review and Reconsideration of Convictions and Sentences'

Though the holding in *LaGrand* case came too late to save the German national, Walter LaGrand, it did save lives of Mexican nationals. *La Grand* gave to *Avena* and others what *Breard* failed to achieve itself and pass it on to *LaGrand*, means to protect life through the individual rights churned by the International Court of Justice's human dignity oriented approach to treaty interpretation.

On 9 January 2003, Mexico filed a case similar to the *LaGrand* case instituting proceedings against the United States for violations of 1963 Vienna Convention on Consular Relations in respect of 52 Mexican nationals on death row in the Unites States who were not informed of their right to consular assistance under Article 36 of the Convention. Neither Mexican consular officers were informed about their detention. Mexico also requested the Court to indicate provisional measures to stay their execution, pending the judgment on merits. The order was issued by the Court[39] and was duly complied with by the United States. Heavily relying on its findings in the *LaGrand* case the Court ruled that the United States had denied 51[40] Mexican nationals on death row of their individual rights under the Vienna Convention, hence, as a remedy, must provide effective 'review and reconsideration of convictions and sentences.'[41]

As the case was mainly decided on the basis of the *LaGrand* judgment ruling that the Vienna Convention on Consular Relations does create individual rights, there were few more aspects of those rights to which the Court added more clarity and development in the *Avena* case.

[38] The composition of the Court in its Judgment in the case concerning Avena and Other Mexican Nationals *(Mexico v USA)* was: President Shi; Vice-President Ranjeva; Judges Guillaume, Koroma, Vereshchetin, Higgins, Parra-Aranguren, Kooijmans, Rezek, Al-Khasawneh, Buergenthal, Elaraby, Owada, Tomka; Judge *ad hoc* Sepulveda. (See ICJ Reports 2004, p 14).

President Shi and Vice-President Ranjeva appended declarations to the Judgment of the Court; Judge Vereshchetin, Parra-Aranguren and Tomka and Judge *ad hoc* Sepulveda appended separate opinions to the Judgment of the Court. (See ICJ Reports 2004, pp 74–128).

[39] Order of 5 February 2003 on Provisional Measures, Avena and Other Mexican Nationals *(Mexico v USA)*, ICJ Reports 2003, p.

[40] As the Court found that in one of the 52 Mexican nationals one indeed 'was informed of his consular rights' under Article 36, para 1(b) of the Vienna Convention but he had declined to have his consular post notified. See ICJ Reports 2004, para 93, p 50.

[41] ICJ Reports 2004, para 153, pp 72–73.

V-B. Interdependence of the Rights of the State and Individual Rights

In its final submissions Mexico has asked the Court to adjudge and declare that the United States, in failing to comply with Article 36, paragraph 1, of the Vienna Convention, has 'violated its international legal obligations to Mexico, in its own right and in the exercise of its right of diplomatic protection of its nationals'.

When dealing with this situation of the rights of the State and the rights of the individual going hand in hand, both ensuing from the same Convention, the Court recalled its own ruling in the *LaGrand* case recognizing that: 'Article 36, paragraph 1, [of the Vienna Convention], creates individual rights [for the national concerned], which . . . may be invoked in this court by the national State of the detained person' (ICJ. Reports 2001 2000, para 77, p 494)'.[42] To this interdependence of the rights already clarified and emphasized in the *LaGrand* case the Court added more judicial weight by observing that: '. . . *violations of the rights of the individual under Article 36 may entail a violation of the rights of the sending State, and that violations of the rights of the latter may entail a violation of the rights of the individual.*' The Court continued and found that these are '*special circumstances of interdependence of the rights of the State and of individual rights.*'[43] This is an immense enhancement of the human dignity of the individual which has in the traditional international law been often treated only as an 'object' as against the State and not a 'subject' of that law. This goes beyond the beneficiary theory and far beyond the outdated object theory. This makes individual as much an actor and person in international law as the State, despite individual's grossly deficient procedural capacity to enforce the observance of his rights.

V-C. Right of an Arrested Person to Information and Time Factor

Further, in interpreting Article 36, paragraph 1(b) the Court analyzed that it contained 'three separate but interrelated elements': 1) the right of the individual concerned to be informed without delay of his rights under Article 36, paragraph 1(b), 2) the right of the consular post to be notified without delay of the individual's detention, if he so requests, and 3) the obligation of the receiving State to forward without delay any communication addressed to the consular post by the detained person.[44] As the third element had not been raised on the facts before the Court thus it began with the right of an arrested or detained individual to information.

But when does the obligation to provide Article 36, paragraph 1(b) information to alien detainees arise? Based on its analysis the Court found two *ratione temporis* circumstances when the detaining authorities in a State become bound to give

42 *Ibid*, para 40, p 36.
43 *Ibid*, para 40, p 36.
44 *Ibid*, para 61, p 43.

Article 36, paragraph 1(b) information to the arrested or detainees: 1) once it is realized that the person is a foreign national, or 2) once there are grounds to think that the person is probably a foreign national.[45]

There is no doubt that this interpretation of the Court secures and enhances the protection of alien individuals and safeguards their human rights. However, it limits providing information by State authorities to *when they know* about foreign nationality of the arrested persons. This limitation was well detected by Judge Tomka.

V-D. Judge Tomka: State authorities must show due diligence in the exercise of their powers

Not very satisfied with such an interpretation of the Court, Judge Tomka found it necessary to develop the provision a bit more in his separate opinion. According to him: 'Were such an approach to the interpretation of the norms of international law to be applied more widely, there is a danger that it might weaken the protection accorded to certain subjects (for example, children) under the procedures for safeguarding human rights or under international humanitarian law.'[46]

Judge Tomka's concern was that time factor may bring in an element of 'ignorance' that the foreign nationality of the arrested was not known to the arresting authorities. Judge Tomka did not want that the obligation of the receiving State should depend on its authorities knowing that the person arrested was a foreigner. Therefore, he pressed on: 'The obligation to provide information arises as soon as a foreigner is detained. Such an arrest constitutes an objective fact sufficient in itself to activate the receiving State's obligations.'[47] Knowledge of facts, according to Judge Tomka, plays no role, either in respect of the existence of applicability of the obligation to provide information under Article 36, paragraph 1(b), or in respect of the violation of that obligation. Ignorance is not a circumstance precluding wrongfulness, he maintained. His *ratione temporis* concern, avoiding any element of 'ignorance,' aimed at promoting human dignity at the hands of State authorities and developing the precept safeguarding human rights and respecting human dignity, is obvious from his following words:

> The State authorities must show due diligence in the exercise of their powers, and there is nothing to prevent them from making enquiry, as soon as the arrest is made, in regard to the nationality of the person detained . . .. Informing a person in custody that the Vienna Convention accords him certain rights if he is a national of another State is undoubtedly the best way of avoiding any breach of the obligations incumbent upon the authorities of the receiving State under Article 36 of the Convention.[48]

[45] ICJ Reports 2004, para 63, p 43.
[46] *Ibid*, para 14, p 97.
[47] *Ibid*, para 15, p 97.
[48] *Ibid*, para 16, p 97.

V-E. Judge Tomka: Individual First Element not the State

According to Judge Tomka it is just because of the procedural deficiency in international law for individual Mexican nationals to bring their own claims to the ICJ that the Mexican State has brought their claims to the Court for the violations of their individual rights. 'In my view, it is the violation of the rights of an individual and the wrong done to that individual, rather than the violation of a right of Mexico and the resulting injury to that State, that may have a certain role to play in the context of criminal proceedings in the United States.'[49]

VI. General Conclusion

Even much earlier than the Judgment of the ICJ in the Avena case, ruling on 24 September 2002 in the death penalty case concerning *Gregory Madej* (a Polish national), US District Judge David H Coar found that the ICJ Judgment in *LaGrand case* 'conclusively determines that Article 36 of the Vienna Convention creates individually enforceable rights, resolving the question most American courts have left open.'[50]

Accepting and respecting the Court's judgment in the *Avena* case, US President Bush notified his Attorney General Alberto Gonzales of his determination 'that the United States will discharge its international obligations under the decision of the International Court of Justice'[51]

Just days before the scheduled execution of Osvaldo Torres, a Mexican national on Oklahoma's death row, and one of the 51 Mexican nationals for whom the ICJ ordered the United States to review cases because they were denied to seek consular assistance, Oklahoma's Governor, Brad Henry, had granted clemency. In his statement, Governor Henry said that the International Court of Justice ruling is binding on US Courts, and that the US State Department had contacted his office to urge that he give careful consideration to the fact that the US signed the 1963 Vienna Convention Consular Relations, which ensures access to consular assistance for foreign nationals who are arrested. 'The treaty is also important to protecting the rights of American citizens abroad,' Henry added.[52]

California has become the first US State to pass legislation requiring full compliance with the notification under Article 36 of the Vienna Convention. Senate Bill 287 requires: 1) all California law enforcement agencies to ensure that policy

[49] *Ibid*, Separate Opinion of Judge Tomka, Judgment of 31 March 2004 in the case concerning Avena and Other Mexican Nationals (*Mexico v USA*), ICJ 2004, p 95.

[50] Online paper: Death Penaly Information: DPIC: Foreign Nationals: Current Issues and News, 21 December 2004, p 16, http://www.deathpenaltyinfo.org/article.php?scid=31&did+579.

[51] See Bush and the ICJ: Executive Obligation and International Law in FORUM, http://jurist.law.pitt.edu/forumy/2005/3/bush-and-icj-executive obligation-and.php.

[52] Foreign Nationals: Current Issues and News, 21 December 2004, p 2, http://www.deathpenaltyinfo.org/article.php?scid=31&did+579.

or procedure and training manuals incorporate language based on the provisions of 1963 Vienna Convention on Consular Relation, 2) every peace officer, upon the arrest and booking or detaining of a foreign national, to advise the foreign national that he or she has a right to communicate with a consular representative, and 2) the notification of consular rights must take place within two hours of the detention. Several other US States have taken similar measures.[53]

Jaimie Fellner, Director of the US. Program at Human Rights Watch, reacted to the *Avena* Judgment of the ICJ in the following words: 'Today's decision could make the difference between life and death for foreigners prosecuted in the United States . . . Giving defendants access to consular officials means that they can get good defence lawyers—the surest way to avoid the death penalty . . . Today's ruling puts teeth in the Vienna Convention by requiring effective legal review of convictions when defendants were not notified that they could contact their consulate'.[54]

The judicial reasoning of the Court in these cases shows that human rights doctrine first and foremost is a school of law and later only a normative branch of public international law. By adopting this humanization approach in interpreting the 1963 Vienna Convention on Consular Relations the Court has rejected the *object* and *beneficiary* theories concerning the status of individuals in international law and has contributed to the ever unleashing reality that in the ultimate analysis individual is a subject of international law and not an object as believed by sovereignty intoxicated thinkers.

The significance of these judgments of the Court lies not so much in deciding that the United States has breached its obligations under a treaty as against Germany and Mexico as in the recognition that treaties create enforceable individuals rights and the United States has violated the individual rights of those German and Mexican individuals.

In the end, one cannot draw a conclusion better than already drawn by Martin Mennecke in the the *LaGrand* case but to paraphrase it a bit: in deciding the three cases centred around the question of violation of rights under 1963 Vienna Convention on Consular Relations the International Court of Justice may well be said to have contributed to the humanization of the Consular Convention and to the humanization of international law as a whole. In doing so, the international legal order returns to the final and ultimate addressee of juridical norms: the human being.

[53] Online paper: Death Penaly Information: DPIC: Foreign Nationals: Current Issues and News, 21 December 2004, p 29, http://www.deathpenaltyinfo.org/article.php?scid=31&did+579.

[54] Human Rights Watch, New York, 31 March 2004, 'US Violated Rights of Mexicans on Death Row: International Court of Justice Orders Judicial Review of US Convictions', pp 1–2, http://www.hrw.org/english/docs/2004/03/31/usdom8331_txt.htm.

Part III

The Development of Human Rights Law by the International Court of Justice:

Advisory Cases

Introduction to the Advisory Procedure of the Court

Advisory Opinions offer the Court a much greater potential to further develop the law than do judgments in contentious proceedings: the former, unlike the latter, are not limited to a strict analysis of the facts and submissions that are presented to the Court.[1]

[1] M Lachs, 'Some Reflections on the Contribution of the International Court of Justice to the Development of International Law' (1983) 10(2) *Syracuse Journal of International Law and Commerce* Nr 1, 239, 249.

Introduction to the Advisory Procedure of the Court

In addition to the jurisdiction to decide disputes between States, the International Court also has the jurisdiction to give advisory opinions to public international organizations, and to them alone.

Certain UN organs and agencies, at present 22 in number,[2] including the General Assembly and the Security Council, are entitled to request such opinions from the Court.

Three conditions, however, are required to be satisfied to found the advisory jurisdiction of the Court when a request for an advisory opinion is submitted to the Court by a specialized agency. First: the agency requesting the opinion must be duly authorized under the United Nations Charter to request opinions from the Court. Second: the opinion requested must be on a legal question. Third: this question must be one arising within the scope of the activities of the requesting agency.[3]

A request for an advisory opinion usually gives rise to written proceedings followed by oral proceedings.[4] On receiving a request, the Court decides which States and organizations might provide useful information and gives them an opportunity of presenting written and/or oral statements.[5] The Court's advisory procedure is otherwise not much different from its contentious procedure, and the sources of law are also the same.

There are two major differences between the advisory cases and the contentious cases. First, the Opinions given by the Court are purely non-binding[6] recommendations,[7] whereas judgments in contentious cases are of binding force between the parties. And the second, only authorized international organisations may request an opinion of the Court. Contentious cases may be brought before the Court by any State party to the Court's Statute, and also to other States, under certain conditions. Hence, an advisory opinion cannot be asked by a State, and, a contentious case cannot be filed by an international organization. Since its inception in 1946,

[2] The International Court of Justice: 1946–96, (Court's Handbook), 1996, p 78.

[3] ICJ Reports, 1998, pp 71–72.

[4] Article 66 of the Court's Statute; Articles 105 and 106 of the Rules of Court.

[5] Article 66, paras 2–4 of the Court's Statute.

[6] Certain instruments can, however, provide in advance that the advisory opinion shall be binding.

[2] The International Court of Justice: 1946–96, (Court's Handbook), 1996, p 78.

[3] ICJ Reports, 1998, pp 71–72.

[4] Article 66 of the Court's Statute; Articles 105 and 106 of the Rules of Court.

[5] Article 66, paras 2–4 of the Court's Statute.

[6] Certain instruments can, however, provide in advance that the advisory opinion shall be binding.

[7] The body requesting the opinion may however be committed to accepting it as binding by the terms of the instrument under which it is authorized to request advisory opinions of the Court. In three cases it was so stipulated beforehand: 1) *Applicability of the Obligation to Arbitrate under Section 21 of the United Nations Headquarters Agreement of 26 June 1947*; 2) *Applicability of Article VI, Section 22, of the Convention on Privileges and Immunities of the United Nations*; and 3) *Difference Relating to Immunity from Legal Process of a Special Rapporteur of the Commission on Human Rights.*

the ICJ has so far given some 24 Advisory Opinions[8] to various UN organs and Agencies, including, among others, the General Assembly, Security Council and Economic and Social Council. Thus, advisory opinions have become an integral and important part of the Court's jurisdiction. According to Judge Lachs, it is also often argued rather forcefully that 'advisory opinions are sometimes more important than judgments, in international relations, because the persuasive nature of advice is frequently superior to force and coercion'.[9]

The following account relating the development of human rights law by means of advisory opinions delivered by the Court would testify thereto.

[8] See the list under section b of the Bibliography.

[9] Lachs, *ibid.*

14

International Status of South-West Africa[1] (1949–50)

The Principle of Sacred Trust of Civilization

THE PRINCIPLE OF sacred trust of civilization clarified and developed by the Court in this advisory case, within the framework of the Mandates System, highlighting the responsibility of the international system in general and of the mandatory State in particular, towards the inhabitants of the territory in question, is in fact touching the very core of the legal system and the legal theory of human rights. There is no doubt that human beings and their related human rights can and should be seen as a sacred trust of civilization in the hands of the United Nations, as a governing international organization, and its 191 States, as its governing national organizations. The very definition of human rights that 'human rights can best be defined as those rights which human beings have simply because they are human beings'[2] links the concept of human rights with the principle of sacred trust of civilization in retrospect as well as prospect.

In fact the expression 'sacred trust of civilization' was used in Article 22 of the Covenant of the League of Nations, as the first provision of its 'Mandatory System'. Its activist application, benevolent liberal interpretation and respective development was made for the first time by the International Court of Justice in the *Namibia* advisory opinion of 1950.

The request by the UN General Assembly, in 1949, asking the advisory opinion of the Court concerning the *International Status of South-West Africa*, known as *Namibia*, became necessary due to defiant attitude of the government of South Africa, a mandatory State for Namibia.

[1] The composition of the Court in the Advisory Opinion delivered on 11 July 1950 in the case concerning *International Status of South-West Africa* was: President Basdevant; Vice-President Guerrero; Judges Alvarez, Hackworth, Winiarski, Zoricic, De Visscher, Sir Arnold McNair, Klaestad, Badawi Pasha, Krylov, Read, Hsu Mo, and Azevedo. (See ICJ Reports 1950, p 128).

Vice-President Guerrero appended a declaration to the Advisory Opinion. Judges Zoricic and Badawi Pasha appended their joint declaration. Judge Sir Arnold McNair and Judge Read appended their separate opinions. Judges Alvarez, De Visscher and Krylov appended their dissenting opinions. (See ICJ Reports 1950 pp 144–45).

[2] M Palumbo, *Human Rights: Meaning and History* (Malabar FL, Krieger, 1982) 9.

By virtue of its resolution of 18 April 1946 the League of Nations dissolved itself as an International Organization and consequently also its Mandatory System. At the first Assembly of the United Nations in 1946 the former League Mandatory States of Great Britain, Australia, New Zealand, Belgium and, with some qualifications, France, made their declarations announcing their intention to place their mandated territories under the Trusteeship System of the United Nations. The government of South Africa, however, refused to do so reasoning that as the League had ceased to exist resulting in the Mandate's lapse, and, therewith claimed the right to incorporate the mandated territory, known as South-West Africa. Having taken such stand, South Africa discontinued sending reports and petitions from the inhabitants of South-West Africa to the United Nations. Therefore, the UN General Assembly, by its resolution of 6 December 1949, decided to submit the following questions to the ICJ with a request for an advisory opinion:

> What is the international status of the Territory of South-West Africa and what are the international obligations of the Union of South Africa arising therefrom, in particular:
>
> (a) Does the Union of South Africa continue to have international obligations under the mandate for South-West Africa and, if so, what are those obligations?
> (b) Are the provisions of Chapter XII of the Charter applicable and, if so, in what manner, to the territory of South-West Africa?
> (c) Has the Union of South Africa the competence to modify the international
>
> Status of the Territory of South-West Africa, or, in the event of a negative reply, where does competence rest to determine and modify the international status of the Territory?[3]

Beginning with question (a) the Court at once put the wording of Article 22 of the Covenant of the League of Nations in its historical objective and perspective. The Court recalled that the territory of South-West Africa was one of the German overseas possessions in respect of which Germany, by Article 119 of the Treaty of Versailles, renounced all her rights and titles in favour of the Principal Allied and Associated Powers. When a decision was to be taken with regard to the future of these possessions as well as of other territories which, as a consequence of war of 1914–18, had ceased to be under the sovereignty of the States which formerly governed them, and which were inhabited by peoples not yet able to assume a full measure of self-government, two principles were considered to be of paramount importance. According to the Court, these two principles were:

> a) the principle of non-annexation,
> b) the principle that the well-being and development of such peoples forms 'a sacred trust of civilization'.[4]

It was to give practical effect to these two principles that the international regime of Mandates System was created by Article 22 of the Covenant, the Court declared.

[3] International Status of South-West Africa, Advisory Opinion of 11 July 1950, ICJ Reports, 1950, p 129.
[4] *Ibid*, p 131.

It is no doubt a clear positivistic interpretation of the Court, yet as a specific ideology of the subject matter in question there at the same time is an obvious benevolent liberalism reflecting if we see how the Court took it further to bring South Africa in the fold of her responsibilities as a Mandatory Power. The Court further held: 'The Mandate was created, in the interest of the inhabitants of the territory, and of humanity in general, as an international institution with an international object—a sacred trust of civilization.'[5]

This is the most liberal, universal and humanitarian interpretation of a positive law provision conductive to the entire generality of the notion of human rights which may also be understood as liberal positivistic-naturalistic interpretation, promoting human dignity in the face of a traditional monster of State sovereignty.

The Court rejected the contention of South Africa that with the demise of the League of Nations the Mandate also lapsed. The Court's answer to this contention was: 'If the Mandate lapsed, as the Union Government contends, the latter's authority would equally have lapsed. To retain the rights derived from the Mandate and deny the obligations thereunder could not be justified.'[6] This correlation of the rights and obligations, Hohfeldian theory in action, indeed correlated rights and duties of a sovereign State in the image of human dignity and human rights which echoed throughout the findings of this advisory opinion. With this the positivistic theory of Hohfeld also found its right place in the school of human rights.

Hence, according to the Court, the international obligations, assumed by South Africa, were of two kinds: The first kind was directly related to the administration of the territory, and corresponded to the sacred trust of civilization referred to in Article 22 of the Covenant. The second kind related to the machinery for implementation, and was closely linked to the supervision and control of the League. Referring to the relevant provisions of the Covenant and of the Mandate, the Court elaborated the first-mentioned group of obligations of South Africa as following:

> The Union undertook the general obligation to promote to the utmost the material and moral well-being and the social progress of the inhabitants. It assumed particular obligations relating to slave trade, forced labour, traffic in arms and ammunition, intoxicating spirits and beverages, military training and establishments, as well as obligations relating to freedom of conscience and free exercise of worship, including special obligations with regard to missionaries.[7]

Considering the above-mentioned second group of obligations resulting from the Mandate System the Court held:

> When the authors of the Covenant created this system, they considered that the effective performance of the sacred trust of civilization by the mandatory Powers required that the administration of mandated territories should be subject to international supervision.

[5] *Ibid*, p 132.

[6] *Ibid*, p 133.

[7] *Ibid.*

> The authors of the Charter had in mind the same necessity when they organized an International Trusteeship System.[8]

Hence, the Court could not accept that South Africa's obligation to submit to the United Nations' supervision has disappeared. The Court further held that:

> These general considerations are confirmed by Article 80, paragraph 1, of the Charter, ... It purports to safeguard, not only the rights of States, but also the rights of the peoples of mandated territories until Trusteeship Agreements are concluded. The purpose must have been to provide a real protection for those rights; but no such rights of the peoples could be effectively safeguarded without international supervision and a duty to render reports to a supervisory organ.[9]

Describing the importance of this conclusion of the International Court of Justice, Judge Schwebel (USA) writes:

> In its advisory opinion on the *International Status of South-West Africa*, the International Court of Justice carried the conclusion . . . of the PCIJ in *Jurisdiction of the Courts of Danzig* further, holding that, as a result of resolutions adopted by the Council of the League of Nations in 1923, the inhabitants of the mandated territories acquired the international right of petition, a right maintained by Article 80, paragraph 1, of the United Nations Charter . . .. Once again, individuals are treated by the World Court as invested by an international instrument with an international right.[10]

With these findings the Court has almost prepared a capsule of all obligations which a governing body, be it a mandatory State or any other State responsible for the well-being and human rights of its subjects. The Court further declared that:

> These obligations represent the very essence of the sacred trust of civilization. Their *raison d'être* and original object remain. Since their fulfilment did not depend on the existence of the League of Nations, they could not be brought to an end merely because this supervisory organ ceased to exist. Nor could the right of the population to have the Territory administered in accordance with these rules depend thereon.[11]

Seen in a broader and general context, the Court herewith has established a general guideline for any State or organization, irrespective of its national, regional or international character, and irrespective of its *ratione temporis*, *ratione materiae* or *ratione personae* jurisdiction, that material and moral well-being and social development are the collective human rights everywhere and it is the duty of the authorities governing the populations in question to promote these rights. Hence, the development of the principle of sacred trust of civilization can be seen as the early

[8] International Status of South-West Africa, Advisory Opinion of 11 July 1950, ICJ Reports, 1950, p 136.

[9] *Ibid*, pp 136–37.

[10] SM Schwebel, 'Human Rights in the World Court' in RS Pathak and RP Dhokalia, (eds), *International Law in Transition: Essays in Memory of Judge Nagendra Singh* (Dordrecht, Martinus Nijhoff, 1992) 267, 279–80.

[11] International Status of South-West Africa, ICJ Reports, 1950, p 133.

version of the interpretation by the Court of the later developed concept of obligation *erga omnes*, establishing therewith that human rights run *erga omnes*.

Further within the framework of two principles, no annexation and the sacred trust of civilization, and combined with the rights and obligations bonded together for a mandatory State, the Court further came to conclusion to give its opinion to the General Assembly's three questions as follows.

On the general question, the Court unanimously declared: 'that South-West Africa is a territory under the international Mandate assumed by the Union of South Africa on 17 December 1920'.[12] On Question (a), the Court, by twelve votes to two, was of the opinion:

> that the Union of South Africa continues to have the international obligations stated in Article 22 of the Covenant of the League of Nations and in the Mandate for South-West Africa as well as the obligation to transmit petitions from the inhabitants of that territory, the supervisory functions to be exercised by the United Nations, to which the annual reports and the petitions are to be submitted, and the reference to the Permanent Court of International Justice to be replaced by a reference to the International Court of Justice, in accordance with Article 7 of the Mandate and Article 37 of the Statute of the Court.[13]

The question (b) was unanimously answered as: 'that the provisions of Chapter XII of the Charter are applicable to the Territory of South-West Africa in the sense that they provide a means by which the Territory may be brought under the Trusteeship System'; and by eight votes to six: 'that the provisions of Chapter XII of the Charter do not impose on the Union of South Africa a legal obligation to place the Territory under the Trusteeship System'.[14] On Question (c) again the Court was unanimous and answered: 'that the Union of South Africa acting alone has not the competence to modify the international status of the Territory of South-West Africa, and that the competence to determine and modify the international status of the Territory rests with the Union of South Africa with the consent of the United Nations'.[15]

The questions asked of the Court, and the answers provided by the Court in this advisory opinion are of great importance not only from the point of view of international law concerning a mandatory territory, its governing authority and its inhabitants, but also from the human rights point of view relating to its social, economic, political and international aspects. Speaking about its social aspect, Judge Alvarez mentions in its individual opinion: 'From the social point of view, for the first time in the history of mankind, States, through a great change in their international outlook, have proclaimed . . . that the well-being and the development of peoples not yet able to govern themselves form, for the civilized countries, a sacred trust of civilization.'[16] This is a contribution to the right of development in the

[12] *Ibid*, p 143.
[13] *Ibid*.
[14] *Ibid*, p 144.
[15] *Ibid*, p 144.
[16] *Ibid*, p 174.

jurisprudence of human rights. The same can be said about the economic and political aspects of international human rights. Technical aid and financial aid programmes at the international level, between developed and developing countries, are the obvious examples in that direction. In applying, elaborating and developing the law, the Court in this advisory opinion has provided, provides guidelines for States to promote human rights in its various aspects at almost every level of their existence.

It is true that it is said in the text of a mandatory power governing a non-self-governing people. But who can deny that people in every State are in a way non-self-governing and their governments are mandatories for them, as far as their well-being is concerned? What is of crucial significance here is that the well-being, in the form of promotion of protection of human rights, of all the governed human beings is the sacred trust of civilization in the hands of the governing human beings, at every level of governance.

Seeking to discover, in his separate opinion, the underlying policy and principles of Article 22 of the League's Covenant and the Mandates, Judge McNair (UK) states: 'No technical significance can be attached to the words "sacred trust of civilization", but they are an apt description of the policy of the authors of the Mandates System'.[17]

Seeking the generality and universality of the principle of sacred trust of civilization Judge McNair further mentions:

> Nearly every legal system possesses some institution whereby the property (and sometimes the persons) of those who are not *sui juris*, such as a minor or a lunatic, can be entrusted to some responsible person as a trustee or *tuteur* or *curateur* . . . The trust has frequently been used to protect the weak and the dependent, in cases where there is 'great might on the one side and unmight on the other' . . .. I am convinced that in its future development the law governing the trust is a source from which much can be derived.[18]

The importance of this would certainly mark the fact that human rights are a sacred trust of civilization in the hands of States and their governing bodies.

It may, however, be mentioned here that three judges of the ICJ—Alvarez (Chile), De Visscher (Belgium) and Krylov (Russia)—appended their dissenting opinions holding that South Africa was legally obliged to place South-West Africa under the United Nations Trusteeship System, in as much as all the mandatory powers, except South Africa, had consented to the conversion from Mandatory to the Trusteeship System. Judge Alvarez in particular was not happy with the Court's system of 'textual interpretations', which he found too positivistic, of articles 75 and 77 of the UN Charter in reaching its negative conclusion on Question (b). He preferred a more natural law system of interpretation, in the light of the principle of effectiveness. In his own words: 'Our starting point must be the existence of the sacred trust of civilization. The ideas and aims contained in this expres-

[17] International Status of South-West Africa, ICJ Reports, 1950, Separate Opinion of Judge Sir Arnold Mcnair, p 148.

[18] *Ibid*, Separate Opinion of Judge McNair, p 149.

sion and the general principles of the new international law must be our compass in our quest for the answers to the questions put to the Court.'[19] It is also interesting to note that on this point, contrary to the opinion of the Court, and in accordance with the dissents of the above three judges, the United Nations Trusteeship Committee decided on 6 December 1950 to recommend South Africa to place South-West Africa under United Nations Trusteeship System.

Apart from the genuine criticism and dissent of the above three judges concerning the 'textual interpretation' system of the Court in reaching its conclusion on Question (b), the Court without doubt has been considerably radical in clarifying and developing the law in question. Judge Higgins's appraisal seems to be just the right appreciation of the Court's work in this case. According to her:

> . . . the Court observed that the fact that South Africa held a 'C Class' mandate did not mean that, upon the demise of the League of nations, it could annex South West Africa. South Africa had no territorial entitlements. Rather, it had—in a celebrated phrase that caught the imagination—a 'sacred trust for civilization' . . . the Court found that the Mandate system presupposed an international scrutiny and, in the face of the demise of the League, that function was now to be performed by the UN General Assembly. There can be no doubting that this represented a certain judicial radicalism, with final findings directed to the securing of desired objectives.[20]

This was a clear victory of the principle of human dignity over the principle of State sovereignty, bringing the traditional rules of international law in line with the contemporary international law with human rights orientation.

[19] *Ibid*, Dissenting Opinion of Judge Alvarez, p 179.

[20] R Higgins, 'The International Court of Justice and Africa' in E Yakpo and T Boumedra, (eds), *Liber Amicorum: Judge Mohammed Bedjaoui* (The Hague, Kluwer International Law, 1999) 343, 359.

15

Reservations to the Convention on the Prevention and Punishment of the Crime of Genocide case[1]

(1950–51)

Genocide is Supremely Unlawful and its Principles are Binding on all States Irrespective of Being Party to a Convention

IN THE ABOVE mentioned case the question concerning reservations to the Convention on the Prevention and Punishment of the Crime of Genocide had been referred for an advisory opinion to the International Court of Justice by the General Assembly of the United Nations. The General Assembly Resolution of 16 November 1950 requested the opinion of the Court on the following threefold question:

> In so far as concerns the Convention on the Prevention and Punishment of the Crime of Genocide in the event of a State ratifying or acceding to the Convention subject to a reservation made either on ratification or accession, or on signature followed by ratification:
>
> I. Can the reserving State be regarded as being a party to the Convention while still maintaining its reservation if the reservation is objected to by one or more of the parties to the Convention but not by others?
>
> II. If the answer to question I is in the affirmative, what is the effect of the reservation as between the reserving State and:
>
> (a) The parties which object to the reservation?
> (b) Those which accept it?

[1] The composition of the Court in the Advisory Opinion of 28 May 1951 in the case concerning *Reservation to the Convention on the Prevention and Punishment of the Crime of Genocide* was: President Basdevant; Vice-President Guerrero; Judges Alvarez, Hackworth, Winiarski, Zoricic, De Visscher, Sir Arnold McNair, Klaestad, Badawi Pasha, Read, an Hsu Mo. (See ICJ Reports 1951, p 15).
Vice-President Guerrero, Judge Sir Arnold McNair, Read, and Hsu, appended their joint dissenting opinion to the Advisory Opinion. Judge Alvarez appended his dissenting opinion. (See ICJ Reports 1951, p 30).

III. What would be the legal effect as regards the answer to question I if an objection to a reserving State is made:

(a) By a signatory which has not yet ratified?
(b) By a State entitled to sign or accede but which has not yet done so?[2]

By 7 votes to 5 the Court gave the following answers to the above questions:

On Question I:

a State which has made and maintained a reservation which has been objected to by one of the parties to the convention but not by others, can be regarded as being a party to the Convention if the reservation is compatible with the object and purpose of the Convention; otherwise, that State cannot be regarded as being a party to the Convention.

On Question II:

(a) if a party to the Convention objects to a reservation which it considers to be incompatible with the *object and purpose* of the Convention, it can in fact consider that the reserving State is not a party to the Convention;
(b) if, on the other hand, a party accepts the reservation as being compatible with the *object and purpose* of the Convention, it can in fact consider that the reserving State is a party to the Convention;

On Question III:

(a) an objection to a reservation made by a signatory State which has not yet ratified the Convention can have the legal effect indicated in the reply to Question I only upon ratification. Until that moment it merely serves as a notice to the other State of the eventual attitude of the signatory State;
(b) an objection to a reservation made by a State which is entitled to sign or accede but which has not yet done is without legal effect.[3]

What is striking of this advisory opinion is that while examining all the three questions the Court focused and took to the key elements of the *object and purpose* of the Convention. The Court declared:

The *object* of such a Convention must also be considered. The Convention was manifestly adopted for a purely *humanitarian* and civilizing *purpose*. It is indeed difficult to imagine a Convention that might have this dual character to a greater degree, since its *object* on the one hand is to safeguard the very existence of certain human groups and on the other to confirm and endorse the most elementary principles of morality. In such a Convention the contracting States do not have any interests of their own; they merely have, one and all, a common interest, namely, the accomplishment of those high *purposes* which are *raison d'être*of the Convention.[4]

[2] Reservation to the Convention on the Prevention and Punishment of the Crime of Genocide, ICJ Reports, 1951, p 16.
[3] *Ibid*, pp 29–30.
[4] *Ibid*, p 23.

This way, while highlighting the 'high ideals' and the 'common will of the parties', and noting the universal character of the United Nations under whose auspices the Convention was concluded, the Court declared:

> The origin of the Convention show that it was the intention of the United Nations to condemn and punish genocide as 'a crime under international law involving a denial of the right of existence of entire human groups, a denial which shocks the conscience of mankind and results in great losses to humanity, and which is contrary to moral law and to the spirit and aims of the United Nations (Resolution 96(1) of the General Assembly, 11 December 1946).[5]

With this reasoning, in one stroke, the Court developed the international human rights law in the following words in such a way that whether a State is party to a Convention such as Genocide Convention or not, the law and principles of genocide are binding on all and sundry:

> The first consequence arising from this conception is that *the principles underlying the Convention are* principles which are recognized by civilized nations as *binding on States, even without any conventional obligations.* A second consequence is the universal character both of the condemnation of genocide and of the co-operation required 'in order to liberate mankind from such an odious scourge' (Preamble to the Convention). The Genocide Convention was therefore intended by the General Assembly and by the contracting parties to be definitely universal in scope.[6]

This has led Judge Schwebel to conclude that: 'The Court thus recognized that *genocide is supremely unlawful under international law,* customary as well as convention, and foreshadowed its later holdings on international obligations *erga omnes.*'[7]

Traditionally, a predominant rule meant that a reservation not expressly provided for in the treaty, was in effect a new offer; and accordingly a reserving State could not become a party unless the reservation received the express or tacit approval of every other State party.[8] In the course of its advisory opinion on the *Genocide Convention,* the Court rejected the view that a reservation to the Genocide Convention needed the assent of all other parties to the Convention. The traditional doctrine, said the Court, had undisputed value but had not been 'transformed into a rule of international law'; and that 'the appraisal of a reservation and the effect of objections that might be made to it depend upon the particular circumstances of each individual case'. Therefore, for the individual case of Genocide Convention, the Court advised, keeping in view the *object and purpose*

[5] *Ibid.*

[6] *Ibid.*

[7] SM Schwebel, 'Human Rights in the World Court' in RS Pathak and RP Dhokalia, (eds), *International Law in Transition: Essays in Memory of Judge Nagendra Singh* (Dordrecht, Martinus Nijhoff, 1992) 267, 279. About the Court's holdings on international obligations erga omnes see under Barcelona Traction case, ICJ Reports, 1970, p 3.

[8] RY Jennings, 'Treaties' in M Bedjaoui, (ed), *International Law: Achievements and Prospects* (Paris, UNESCO, 1991) 140.

of the Convention, that a State can be regarded to be a party to the Convention if its reservation is compatible with the object and purpose, despite objection to the reservation by one or more States.[9] This obviously contributes to the development of international human rights law.

In its Resolution of 16 November 1950, the General Assembly of the United Nations also invited the International Law Commission, to study, in the course of its work on the codification of the law of treaties, the question of reservations to multilateral conventions both from the point of view of codification and from that of the progressive development of international law; to give priority to this study and to report thereon, especially as regards multilateral conventions of which the Secretary-General is the depositary, this report to be considered by the General Assembly at its sixth session. The General Assembly in the same Resolution instructed the Secretary-General, pending the rendering of the Advisory Opinion of the International Court of Justice, the receipt of a report from the International Law Commission and further action by the General Assembly, to follow its prior practice with respect to the receipt of reservations to conventions and with respect to the notification and solicitation of approvals thereof, all without prejudice to the legal effect of objections to reservations to conventions as it may be recommended by the General Assembly at its sixth session.[10] This Advisory Opinion of the Court on Genocide Convention had a 'determinative influence' on the content of the subsequent Vienna Convention on the Law of Treaties in respect of reservations.

Judge Schwebel, a former President of the International Court of Justice, has indeed marked the opinion as a 'landmark opinion'.[11]

[9] RY Jennings, 'Treaties' in M Bedjaoui, (ed), *International Law: Achievements and Prospects* (Paris, UNESCO, 1991); for the details of this see also ICJ Reports, 1951, pp 24, 26 and 29.

[10] Reservations to the Convention on the Prevention and Punishment of the Crime of Genocide, ICJ Reports, 1951, pp 5–6.

[11] S Schwebel, 'The Role of the Security Council and the International Court of Justice in the Application of International Humanitarian Law' (1995) 27 *NYU J Int'l L & Pol* 731, 734 cited by GS DeWeese, 'The Failure of the International Court of Justice to Effectively Enforce the Genocide Convention' (1998) 26 *Denver Journal of International Law and Policy* Nr 4 633.

16

Legal Consequences for States of the Continued Presence of South Africa in Namibia (South West Africa) Notwithstanding Security Council Resolution 276 (1970)[1]

(1970–71)

I. Introduction

AFTER THE MOST criticized 1966 judgment of the Court this advisory case brought to the Court by the UN Security Council provided an opportunity to the Court to clear its bad name of being insensitive to human rights plight in Namibia. The Court welcomed it with both arms and grabbed it tightly with both hands and all of its might. No doubt the advisory opinion delivered by the Court on 21 June 1971 proved a boon for the development of human rights law. This made a former President of the International Court of Justice, Judge Nagendra Singh, remark that: 'The most celebrated advisory opinion which deals with the concept of human rights in more ways than one is the advisory opinion of the Court in the *Namibia* case'.[2]

Following the 1966 judgment in the *South West Africa* cases, in which the Court decided that Ethiopia and Liberia have no right or legal interest to ask the Court if

[1] The composition of the Court in the Advisory Opinion of 21 June 1971 in the case concerning Legal Consequences for States of the Continued Presence of South Africa in Namibia (South West Africa) Notwithstanding Securiy Council Resolution 276 (1970) was: President Sir Muhammad Zafrulla Khan; Vice-President Ammoun; Judges Sir Gerald Fitzmaurice, Padilla Nervo, Forster, Gros, Bengzon, Petrén, Lachs, Oneyeama, Dillard, Ignacio-Pinto, De Castro, Morozov, and Jiménez de Aréchaga. (See ICJ Reports 1971, p 16). President Sir Muhammad Zafrulla Khan appended his declaration to the advisory opinion. Vice-President Ammoun and Judges Padilla Nervo, Petrén, Onyeama, Dillard, and de Castro, appended their separate opinions. Judges Sir Gerald Fritzmaurice and Gros appended their dissenting opinions. (See ICJ Reports, pp 59–323).

[2] N Singh, *Enforcement of Human Rights in Peace and War and the Future of Humanity* (Dordrecht, Nijhoff, 1986) 31.

South Africa had violated the obligations arising from the Mandate on South West Africa, the General Assembly of the United Nations, sharply criticizing the judgment of the Court, passed the resolution 2145(XXI) and therewith terminated South Africa's Mandate over Namibia and assumed direct control over the territory in question. South Africa was asked, in 1969, to withdraw her administration from the territory of South West Africa. South African government defied the resolution and refused to withdraw. At this, the following year, the Security Council of the United Nations adopted its Resolution No 276, declaring that 'the continued presence of the South African authorities in Namibia is illegal'. The resolution also declared that as a result of this illegality all acts performed by South African government 'on behalf of or concerning Namibia after the termination of the Mandate are illegal and invalid'.

The resolution further called upon all States to refrain from any dealings with the South African Government that were incompatible with that declaration. On 29 July 1970, the Security Council decided to request of the Court an advisory opinion on the following question: 'What are the legal consequences for States of the continued presence of South Africa in Namibia, notwithstanding Security Council resolution 276 (1970)?'[3]

By this question from the UN Security Council, the Court has been called upon to pronounce in regard to certain fundamental principles of human rights law, namely the right of peoples to self-determination, racial discrimination and equality between nations and between individuals.

II. Self-Determination in Retrospect and Prospect

In arriving at its deliverance of the opinion—opining that the continued presence of South Africa in Namibia is illegal[4]—the Court at the very outset adopted a very progressive and active approach. It first recalled its own finding in its Advisory Opinion of 1950 in the International Status of South West Africa that: 'The Mandate was created, in the interest of the inhabitants of the territory, and of humanity in general, as an international institution with an international object—a sacred trust of civilization.'[5] The Court, enunciating an exceedingly important legal principle of international law,[6] added:

> Mindful as it is of the primary necessity of interpreting an instrument in accordance with the intentions of the parties, at the time of its conclusion, the Court is bound to take into account the fact that the concepts embodied in Article 22 of the Covenant—'the strenu-

[3] Legal Consequences for States of the Continued Presence of South Africa in Namibia (South West Africa) Nothwithstanding Security Council Resolution 276 (1970), ICJ Reports, 1971, p 17.

[4] ICJ Reports, 1971, p 58.

[5] *Ibid*, p 29. For the quote from the 1950 Advisory Opinion see ICJ Reports, 1950, p 132.

[6] A Cassese, 'The International Court of Justice and the Right of Peoples to Self-determination' in V Lowe and M Fitzmaurice, (eds), *Fifty Years of the International Court of Justice: Essays in Honour of Sir Robert Jennings* (Cambridge, CUP, 1996) 353.

ous conditions of the modern world' and 'the well-being and development' of the peoples concerned—were not static, but were by definition evolutionary, as also, therefore, was the concept of the 'sacred trust'.[7]

Further, the Court linked the principle of sacred trust of civilization with the principle of self-determination in the following manner: 'In the domain to which the present proceedings relate, the last fifty years, as indicated above, have brought important developments. These developments have little doubt that the ultimate objective of the sacred trust was the self-determination and independence of the peoples concerned.'[8]

This is a clear development of the application of the principle of self-determination in retrospect and prospect. Cassese also appraised the foregone as:

> The Court thus rightly emphasized that the principle of self-determination, which in the aftermath of the First World War had not yet acquired a foothold in the international community, became from 1945 an overarching principle of the international community; hence, it must of necessity apply to pre-existing legal institutions as well. In other words, self determination, besides applying to current and future international relations, also constitute a fundamental standard of behaviour which, in a way, projects itself into the past.[9]

Further, it may be recalled that in 1945 the UN Charter envisaged self-determination only for territories falling under the system of international trusteeship. However, as a result of further awareness and evolution of the aspiration for self-determination, the UN General Assembly declared in 1960 that the right to self-determination is a right meant for all dependent territories. The Court at once endorsed this in its Advisory Opinion and gave it a stamp of judicial recognition in the following words:

> Furthermore, the subsequent development of international law in regard to non-self governing territories, as enshrined in the Charter of the United Nations, made the principle of self-determination applicable to all of them.[10]. A further important stage in this development was the Declaration on the Granting of Independence to Colonial Countries and Peoples (General Assembly resolution 1514(XV) of 14 December 1960), which embraces all peoples and territories which 'have not yet attained independence'.[11]

Fully agreeing with the Court's progressive and developmental opinion, Judge Ammoun mentioned that the Opinion is not lacking in persuasive force, but it would have possessed still more if it had retraced the path whereby the people's right of self-determination has made its entry into positive international law and had determined exactly what were the factors which have gone into its making. He was here referring to the fight of peoples for freedom and independence, which has been going on ever since there have been conquering and dominating peoples, and

[7] ICJ Reports, 1971, p 31.
[8] *Ibid.*
[9] A Cassese, *ibid*, p 354.
[10] Referring here to the non-self-governing territories.
[11] ICJ Reports, 1971, p 31.

the resulting charters and covenants, for instance Atlantic Charter, UN Charter, Pact of Bogota, declarations of Bandung, Belgrade and Cairo, declarations in UN resolutions, etc.[12] Further, he emphasized:

> As for the 'general practice' of States to which one traditionally refers when seeking to ascertain the emergence of customary law, it has, in the case of the right of peoples to self-determination, become so widespread as to be not merely 'general' but universal, since it has been enshrined in the Charter of the United Nations (Article 1, paragraph 2, and Article 55) and confirmed by the texts that have just been mentioned: pacts, declarations and resolutions, which taken as a whole, epitomize the unanimity of States in favour of the imperative right of peoples to self-determination.[13]

Of the above observation of the Court, Cassese comments: 'The Court authoritatively confirmed this legal evolution by endorsement with its formal seal.'[14]

III. Apartheid as a Policy Constitutes a Denial of Fundamental Human Rights

What is *apartheid*? The briefest possible definition is given by Judge Ammoun: it is the negation of equality.[15] As currently as in 1965, the then Minister of Justice of South Africa, Mr Vorster, proudly spoke the shamelessly uncivilized language of racial discrimination in the country's parliament in the following words: 'In this Parliament, whose business it is to decide the destiny of the Republic of South Africa, Whites, and Whites only, will have the right to sit.'[16] The words suffice to show what was meant by the policy of *apartheid.*

In its written as well as oral statements to the Court, South Africa had expressed its readiness to supply the Court with further factual information concerning the purposes and objectives of its policy of *apartheid,* contending that to establish a breach of its international obligations under the Mandate it would be necessary to prove that South Africa had failed to exercise its powers with a view to promoting the well-being and progress of the inhabitants.[17] To this the Court found that:

> no factual evidence is needed for the purpose of determining whether the policy of *apartheid* as applied by South Africa in Namibia is in conformity with the international obligations assumed by South Africa under the Charter of the United Nations. In order to determine whether the laws and decrees applied by South Africa in Namibia, which are a matter of public record, constitute a violation of the purposes and principles of the Charter of the United Nations, the question of intent or governmental discretion is not

[12] ICJ Reports, 1971, p 74.
[13] *Ibid,* p 74–75.
[14] A Cassese, *ibid.*
[15] ICJ Reports, 1971, p 81.
[16] Cited by Judge Ammoun in his Separate Opinion appended to the Advisory Opinion of 21 June 1971, ICJ Reports, 1971, p 82.
[17] *Ibid,* p 56.

relevant; nor is it necessary to investigate or determine the effects of those measures upon the welfare of the inhabitants.[18]

Giving great weight to the matter of public record concerning *apartheid* as a State policy, and finding it to be a breach of international law, the Court declared that: 'It is undisputed, and is amply supported by documents annexed to South Africa's written statement in these proceedings, that the official governmental policy pursued by South Africa in Namibia is to achieve a complete physical separation of races and ethnic groups in separate areas within the territory.'[19]

Condemning apartheid as a policy of a State, looking at it as a gross breach of human rights, the Court declared a guiding norm:

> Under the Charter of the United Nations, the former mandatory had pledged itself to observe and respect, in a territory having an international status, human rights and fundamental freedoms for all without distinction as to race. To establish instead, and to enforce, distinctions, exclusions, restrictions and limitations exclusively based on grounds of race, colour, descent or national or ethnic origin which constitute a denial of fundamental human rights is a flagrant violation of the purposes and principles of the Charter.[20]

IV. People as Such Can Become Holder of Rights

Referring to, and elaborating on, article 80, paragraph 1,[21] of the UN Charter, the Court pointed out: 'A striking feature of this provision is the stipulation in favour of the rights of "any people", thus clearly including the inhabitants of the mandate territories and, in particular, their indigenous populations. These rights were thus confirmed to have an existence independent of that of the League of Nations.'

Herewith, the Court seems to have been departing from the traditional theory of international law, still advocated by some States, which maintains that rights and duties are conferred on States and States alone and not on individuals or international organizations. Concerning this Cassese is of the view: 'Arguably, by emphasizing the "rights" of dependent peoples, the Court took the view that in international law people as such can become holders of rights and obligations.'[22]

[18] *Ibid*, p 57.
[19] *Ibid*, p 57.
[20] *Ibid*, p 57.
[21] Article 80, para 1, Chapet XII on International Trusteeship System, of the UN Charter reads:
Except as may be agreed upon in individual trusteeship agreements, made under Articles 77, 79, and 81, placing each territory under the trusteeship system, and until such arrangements have been concluded, nothing in this Chaper shall be construed in or of itself to alter in any manner the rights whatsoever of any States or any peoples or the terms of existing international instruments to which Members of the United Nations may respectively be parties.
[22] A Cassese, *ibid*, p 355.

17

Western Sahara case[1] (1974–75) The Principle of Self-determination

IN THE *WESTERN Sahara* case the Court carried forward the principle of self-determination. On 13 December 1974, the UN General Assembly requested an advisory opinion of the Court on the following questions:

> I. Was Western Sahara (Rio de Oro and Sakiet El Hamra) at the time of colonization by Spain a territory belonging to no one (*terra nullius*)?
>
> If the answer to the first question is in the negative,
>
> II. What were the legal ties between this territory and the Kingdom of Morocco and the Mauritanian entity?[2]

In its Advisory Opinion delivered on 16 October 1975, the Court replied to Question I in the negative. With regard to Question II, it was of the opinion that the materials and information presented to it showed the existence, at the time of Spanish colonization, of legal ties of allegiance between the Sultan of Morocco and some of the tribes living in the territory of Western Sahara. They equally showed the existence of rights, including some rights relating to the land, which constituted legal ties between the Mauritanian entity, as understood by the Court, and the territory of Western Sahara.

But what have these questions and answers to do with the principle of self-determination? At the background of this request was the reason that the General Assembly had asked the Court for an Opinion so as to be in a position to decide on the choice of a policy designed to accelerate the decolonization process in Western Sahara in application of the General Assembly's 1960 resolution—

[1] The composition of the Court in its Advisory Opinion in the case concerning *Western Sahara* was: President Lachs; Vice-President Ammoun; Judges Forster, Gros, Bengzon, Petrén, Onyeama, Dillard, Ignacio-Pinto, de Castro, Morozov, Jiménez de Aréchaga, Sir Humphrey Waldock, Nagendra Singh, and Ruda; Judge *ad hoc* Boni. (ICJ Reports 1975, p 12).

Judges Gros, Ignacio-Pinto and Nagendra Singh appended their declaration to the Advisory Opinion. Vice-President Ammoun and Judges Forster, Petrén, Dillard, and de Castro appended their separate opinions. Judge *ad hoc* Boni appended appended his separate opinion. Judge Ruda appended his dessinting opinion. (See ICJ Reports, pp 69–175).

[2] Western Sahara, ICJ Reports, 1975, p 14.

containing the Declaration on the Granting of Independence to Colonial Countries and Peoples. Though none of the questions put to the Court were directly related to the principle of self-determination, yet the four States directly concerned—Algeria, Mauritania, Morocco and Spain—made references to, *inter alia*, self-determination. Extensive arguments and divergent views were presented to the Court regarding the principle of self-determination governing decolonization. Faced with this wide range, the Court stated that although the matter was not directly the subject of question, yet it was bound to deal with it.

At the outset of its *obiter* the Court while referring, and adding weight, to its own previous pronouncements in the *Namibia* case stated that by the 1970s the principle of self-determination was firmly established and applicable to all dependent peoples and that all of them were free to choose for independence.[3] To this Judge Cassese opined: 'The authoritative nature of such pronouncements irrefutably establishes that the granting of such a right to all non-self-governing territories has become part of customary international law. Clearly, in this process of formation of a general rule on the matter, the Court's contribution has been of the utmost importance.'[4]

Further, adding more life to the principle and giving dignity to the dependent people the Court mentioned 'the need to pay regard to the freely expressed will of the people'.[5] Commenting on this Judge Cassese of the International Criminal Tribunal for former Yugoslavia mentioned that by doing so 'the Court brought to the forefront the very essence of the principle of self-determination'.[6] As a matter of fact, the law on self-determination, prior to this pronouncement of the Court, was not clear on the point whether the freely expressed will of the dependent people was always needed. Neither the General Assembly resolutions nor the practice of colonial states and the UN were definitive on this matter. Again, Judge Cassese evaluated this development by the Court in this way: 'The Court definitively settled the matter by prescribing a free and genuine expression of the will of the population concerning any instance of exercise of self-determination by a colonial people, subject to two exceptions. These apply when one is not faced with a "people" proper and when "special circumstances" make a plebiscite or referendum unnecessary'.[7] According to Cassese the aforementioned dictum of the Court is a contribution to the law relating self-determination not only within the context of colonial dimension but also outside of it, for instance in the case of territorial sovereignty by one state to another by bilateral agreement.[8] It is interesting to note that the British Government, which formerly opposed the principle, has in recent years adopted it and applied it 'in self-defence' in relations to questions concerning the status of Gibraltar and the Falklands (or Malvinas).[9]

[3] Western Sahara, ICJ Reports, 1975, p 31.
[4] A Cassese, *ibid*, p 357–58.
[5] Western Sahara, ICJ Reports, 1971, p 33.
[6] A Cassese, *ibid*, 358.
[7] *Ibid*, p 359.
[8] *Ibid*.
[9] I Brownlie, *Principles of Public International Law*, 5th edn (Oxford, OUP), 601.

Judge Higgins of the International Court of Justice is of the view that:

> The Concept of self-determination was, of course, carried forward in the *Western Sahara* case, in the sense that having found no sovereign legal ties to either Mauritania or Morocco, there was nothing to stand in the way of 'the principle of self-determination through the free and genuine expression of will of the peoples of the Territory'.[10]

This is how, by placing the two questions of the General Assembly within the context of the principle of self-determination, the Court considerably developed this one of the most important principles of human rights of peoples. The Court stated:

> The right of self-determination leaves the General Assembly a measure of discretion with respect to the forms and procedures by which that right is to be realized . . .. As to the future action of the General Assembly, various possibilities exist, for instance with regard to consultations between the interested States, and the procedures and guarantees required for ensuring a free and genuine expression of the will of the people.[11]

Again, reacting on this statement of the Court, the very best comment comes from Judge Cassese when he says:

> One should not underestimate the importance of the statement, in spite of its expression in such terse terms. The Court clearly implied that, whenever self-determination is at issue, the states concerned should be consulted, at least to the extent that such consultations may facilitate the implementation of self-determination and do not tend to negate or pre-empt the expression of popular will.[12]

It seems that the Court's humanism, liberalism, benevolence and activism have all come to play their best role in this case to give dignity, freedom and due right of self-determination to the dependent and non-governing people whether they are for the independence or the free association or integration with any other sovereign state. This case and the progressive development of the principle of self-determination in this case have earned a great praise for the Court's contribution to the international law in general and the human rights law in particular. There are few international law text books which do not speak about this contribution of the Court. For instance, Prof Brownlie's popular textbook has this to say about the principle of self-determination: 'Until recently the majority of Western jurists assumed or asserted that the principle had no legal content, being an ill-defined concept of policy and morality. Since 1945 developments in the United Nations have changed the position, and Western jurists now generally admit that self-determination is a legal principle . . . The Advisory Opinion of the Western Sahara confirms the validity of the principle of self-determination in the context of international law.'[13]

[10] R Higgins, 'The International Court of Justice and Africa' in E Yakpo and T Boumedra, (eds), *Liber Amicorum: Judge Mohammed Bedjaoui* (The Hague, Kluwer International Law, 1999) 343, 360.
[11] Western Sahara, ICJ Reports, 1971, pp 36–37.
[12] A Cassese, 'The International Court of Justice and the Right of Peoples to Self-determination' in V Lowe and M Fitzmaurice, (eds), *Fifty Years of the International Court of Justice: Essays in Honour of Sir Robert Jennings* (Cambridge, CUP, 1996) 353, 360.
[13] I Brownlie, *Principles of Public International Law*, 5th edn, 599–601.

18

Applicability of Article VI, Section 22, of the Convention on the Privileges and Immunities of the United Nations case[1]

(1989)

I. Special Rapporteur of UN Human Rights Commission Entitled to Privileges and Immunities of a UN Expert on Mission

ON 13 MARCH 1984 the Commission on Human Rights, a subsidiary organ of the Economic and Council (ECOSOC) of the United Nations, elected Mr Dumitru Mazilu, a Romanian national, to serve as a member of the Sub-Commission on Prevention of Discrimination and Protection of Minorities to pay due attention to the role of youth in the field of human rights. Mr Mazilu had been entrusted, by a resolution of the Sub-Commission, with the task of drawing up a report on 'Human Rights and Youth' in connection with which the Secretary-General of the United Nations was asked to provide him with all the assistance he might need. Mr Mazilu was absent from the 1987 session of the Sub-Commission, during which he was supposed to file his report. Romanian government let it be known that he had been taken into hospital. Mr Mazilu's mandate actually expired on 31 December 1987, but without his being relieved of the task of Rapporteur that had been assigned to him. In a letter of 19 April 1988 to the Chairman of the Sub-Commision Mr Mazilu complained that his government 'did everything possible to discourage him from preparing the said report. The travel permit was refused to him. In an other letter of 8 May 1988, Mr Mazilu mentioned that: 'Since February 1988 more than twenty policemen are following me, my wife and my son day and night.' In his further letters he stated that his

[1] The composition of the Court in the Advisory Opinion of 15 December 1989 in the Case Concerning Applicability of Article VI, S 22 of the Convention of the Privileges and Immunities of the United Nations was: President Ruda; Judges Lachs, Elias, Oda, Ago, Schwebel, Sir Robert Jennings, Bedjaoui, Ni, Evensen, Tarassov, Guillaume, Shahabuddeen, and Pathak. (ICJ Reports 1989, p 177).
Judges Oda, Evensen, and Shahabuddeen appended their separate opinions to the Advisory Opinion.

'access to the UN Information Centre in Bucharest was blocked'. His 'telephone has been disconnected', etc. The Romanian authorities subsequently made it clear to the United Nations Secretariat with regard to the applicability to Mr Mazilu of the Convention on the Privileges and Immunities of the United Nations, and, that any intervention of the United Nations would be considered as interference in Romania's internal affairs.

With the above background, the Economic and Social Council of the United Nations, by its resolution 1989/37 dated 24 May 1989, concluded that: 'a difference has arisen between the United Nations and the Government of Romania as to the applicability of the Convention on the Privileges and Immunities of the United Nations . . . to Mr.Dumitru Mazilu as Special Rapporteur of the Sub-Commision on Prevention of Discrimination and Protection of Minorities.'[2] And, accordingly, the ECOSOC requested the International Court of Justice to give an advisory opinion on the legal question of the applicability of the Convention in the case of Mr Mazilu as Special Rapporteur of the Sub-Commission.[3]

The Court examined the applicability of the Section 22 of the Convention *ratione personae*, *ratione temporis* and *ratione loci*. The operational part of its Advisory Opinion of 15 December 1989 read as following

> The Court,
>
> Unanimously,
>
> *Is of the opinion* that Article VI of the Convention on the Privileges and Immunities of the United Nations is applicable in the case of Mr Dumitru Mazilu as a special rapporteur of the Sub-Commission on the Prevention of the Discrimination and Protection of Minorities.'[4] '

II. Judge Evensen: Integrity of a Person's Family and Family Life is A Basic Human Right

While fully agreeing with the Advisory Opinion of the Court, Judge Evensen had some additional views to express concerning one special aspect thereof. In his Separate Opinion appended thereto, he drew attention to the principle of the integrity of a person's family and family life.

Recounting the special incidents of pressures Mr Mazilu was subject to by the Romanian Government, Judge Evensen mentioned:

> . . . it seems evident that the pressures exerted have caused concern and hardship not only to Mr.Mazilu but also to his family. It seems obvious that the protection provided for in

[2] Applicability of Article VI, Section 22, of the Convention on the Privileges and Immunities of the United Nations, ICJ Reports, 1989, p 178.

[3] *Ibid.*

[4] *Ibid*, p 198.

> Article VI, Section 22, of the 1946 Convention cannot be confined only to the 'expert Mazilu' but must apply to a reasonable extent to his family.[5]

To Judge Evensen, it seemed self-evident and he recalled that it had been touched upon on one special relation in Article V, Section 18(d) of the Convention, stating that officials of the United Nations shall 'be immune, together with their spouses and relatives dependent on the immigration restrictions and alien registration'. He saw this provision as one concrete expression of a basic general principle and stated:

> The integrity of a person's family and family life is a basic human right protected by prevailing principles of international law which derive not only from conventional international law or customary international law but from 'general principles of law recognized by civilized nations.[6]

Thus bringing the family into international human rights under the universal jurisdiction. Judge Evensen greatly facilitates the progress towards harmonization of various conflicting municipal human rights concerning family relations with the international human rights law. Referring first to Article 16, paragraph 3, of the 1948 Family, as an international human rights, first found its place in the Universal Declaration of Human Rights. Referring to its Article 16, paragraph 3, which provides: 'The family life is the natural and fundamental group unit of society and is entitled to protection by society and the State', Judge Evensen finds that the integrity of family and family life was laid down, by the Universal Declarations, as a basic human right. Stretching it further he maintains that:

> This principle, which is concrete expression of an established principle of human rights in modern law of nations, has been similarly expressed in other international law instruments. Thus the European Convention on Human Rights (the Rome Convention) of 4 November 1950 provides in Article 8, paragraph 1: 'Everyone has the right to respect for his private and family life, his home and his correspondence.[7]

III. Judge Evensen: Rights of Family and Family Life are Integral Parts of Privileges and Immunities

First by firmly establishing the principle of integrity of family and family life within the context of the Convention on the Privileges and Immunities of the United Nations, and simultaneously recognizing its universal validity under the general principles of law by all civilized nations, Judge Evensen finally concluded the solid link with the given Convention: 'The respect for a person's family and family life

[5] Applicability of Article VI, Section 22, of the Convention on the Privileges and Immunities of the United Nations, Separate Opinion of Judge Evensen, ICJ Reports, 1989, p 210.

[6] *Ibid*, pp 210–11.

[7] Applicability of Article VI, Section 22, of the Convention on the Privileges and Immunities of the United Nations, Separate Opinion of Judge Evensen, ICJ Reports, 1989, p 211.

must be considered as integral parts of the "privileges and immunities" that are necessary for "the independence exercise of their functions" under Article VI, Section 22, of the 1946 Convention on the Privileges and Immunities of the United Nations.'[8]

It is not that he sees the rights of family and family life of a person as a matter secondary to the Convention but as basic human rights forming integral parts of the privileges and immunities springing from the relevant Convention. Therewith enriching the principles of the integrity of family and family life on the one hand and the Convention on the Privileges and Immunities of the United Nations on the other hand. It is equally an indicator that the prospects of the development of international human rights law on the one hand and its link with various other branches of international law on the other hand is indeed considerable.

This may be seen as a twofold contribution of Judge Evensen to the development of the international human rights law.

[8] Applicability of Article VI, Section 22, of the Convention on the Privileges and Immunities of the United Nations, Separate Opinion of Judge Evensen, ICJ Reports, 1989, p 211.

19

Legality of the Use by a State of Nuclear Weapons in Armed Conflict[1] (Request for Advisory Opinion by World Health Organization) (1993–96)

. . . enjoyment of the highest attainable standard of health is one of the fundamental rights of every human being.

(Preamble to the WHO Constitution)

I. Human Right to Health v Use of Power: Separation of Powers is the Answer

PROF CHANDAN BALA has said of the International Court of Justice that it is a court but without natural authority towards its subjects. And, also that this court has a law to administer without any agency handing it ready-made for adopting or administering.[2] Further, she has stated about the law development role of the International Court: 'It has to pick something in a lump-form, cut it, carve it, chisel it, give it the shape, dress it, educate it, train it and breathe life into it, give an identity, a name and call it a rule of international law; such that one should not be persuaded to agree with it'.[3] That the ICJ judges have developed

[1] The composition of the Court in the Advisory Opinion of 8 July 1996 in the case concerning *Legality of the Use by a State of Nuclear Weapons in Armed Conflict* (requested by WHO) was: President Bedjaoui; Vice-President Schwebel; Judges Oda, Guillaume, Shahabuddeen, Weeramantry, Ranjeva, Herczegh, Shi, Fleischhauer, Koroma, Vereshchetin, Ferrari Bravo, and Higgins. (See ICJ Reports 1996, p 66).

Judges Ranjeva and Ferrari Bravo appended their declaration to the Advisory Opinion. Judge Oda appended a separate opinion. Judges Shahabuddeen, Weeramantry, and Koroma, appended their dissenting opinion. (See ICJ Reports 1996, p 85).

[2] C Bala, *International Court of Justice: Its Functioning and Settlement of International Disputes* (New Delhi, Deep & Deep, 1997) vii.

[3] *Ibid.*

human rights law even in the cases which could by civil law countries standard simply be disposed off by a brief ruling of a page or two is exemplified in the advisory case filed by the World Health Organization in 1993.

By its resolution No WHA 46.40 dated 14 May 1993, the World Health Assembly of the World Health Organization requested the International Court of Justice to give an advisory opinion on the following question: 'In view of the health and environmental effects, would the use of nuclear weapons by a State in war or other armed conflict be a breach of its obligations under international law including the WHO Constitution?'

In its Advisory Opinion delivered on 8 July 1996,[4] the Court found, by 11 votes to 3, that the request for an advisory opinion submitted by the WHO does not relate to a question which arises 'within the scope of [the] activities' of that Organization in accordance with Article 96, paragraph 2, of the Charter of the United Nations, and, therefore, it was not able to give the advisory opinion requested of it.[5]

It is obviously a case concerning the question of the health aspect of human dignity, human right to health. But can an international organization responsible for human health encroach on the responsibilities of other parts of the United Nations system responsible for the questions concerning the use of force, the regulation of armaments and disarmaments, is the corollary of this question. It is also true that the notion and the principles of human rights are getting very much interwoven with other branches of law as are the activities of institutions and organizations, national and international alike, promoting and preventing human rights are beginning to touch upon, and even intersecting, the jurisdictions of other specialized institutions and organizations. The separation of powers, though very traditional and ancient in nature and character, is not just a principle of governance at the national levels. With the evolution and the march of time (though certainly with the required differentiation and modification according to the time), the situation and nature of the governance, with its need and practicality is beginning to be felt at the international level of governance. By declining the request of the WHO to deliver an advisory opinion it may seem that the Court has missed the opportunity to develop the human rights law concerning right to health, but the farsighted reasoning of the Court in its reasoning part of the Advisory Opinion has clarified and developed the concept of separation of powers by elucidating 'the powers conferred on international organizations'.[6]

The right to health had long been recognized as fundamental human right, even before the United Nations' Universal Declaration of Human Rights came into being in 1948. The Constitution of the World Health Organization which was signed in 1946 and has at present been accepted by more than 180 States declares,

[4] ICJ Reports 1996, p 66.

[5] *Ibid*, p 84.

[6] *Ibid*, p 79.

inter alia, that: 'The enjoyment of the highest attainable standard of health is one of the fundamental rights of every human being'. However, the Court found that although according to the Constitution of the World Health Organization the Organization is authorized to deal with the effects on health of the use of nuclear weapons, or of any other hazardous activity, and to take preventive measures aimed at protecting the health of populations in the event of such weapons being used, but the question asked by the WHO relates 'not to the effects' of the use of nuclear weapons on health, 'but to the legality' of the use of such weapons in view of their health and environmental effects. And, in the Court's opinion, the competence to address the 'legality' of the use of nuclear weapons cannot be ascribed to the World Health Organization because it would be tantamount to disregarding the '*principle of speciality*' by which the WHO and all international organizations are governed.

The Court pointed out:

> . . . international organizations are subjects of international law which did not, unlike States, possess a general competence. International organizations were governed by the 'principal of speciality', that is to say, they were invested by the States which create them with powers, the limits of which are a function of the common interests whose promotion those States entrust to them.[7]

Specifying the relation between the United Nations and the World Health Organization and clearly attempting to separate the powers of the two organizations, the Court pointed out:

> The World Health Organization is, . . . an international organization of a particular kind. As indicated in the Preamble and confirmed by Article 69 of its Constitution, 'the Organization shall be brought into relation with the United Nations as one of the specialized agencies referred to in Article 57 of the Charter of the United Nations.'[8]

In other words, the Court found that the promotion of health and the human right to health are within the competence of the WHO and the competence of WHO to deal with them is not dependent on the legality of the acts that caused them.

[7] *Ibid*, p 78. The Court's reasoning in this matter relied heavily on the reasoning of the Permanent Court of International Justice in the Advisory Opinion in the case concerning *Jurisdiction of the European Commission of the Danube* where the PCIJ referred to the principle of speciality in the following words: 'As the European Commission is not a State, but an international institution with a special purpose, it only has the functions bestowed upon it by the Definitive Statute with a view to the fulfilment of that purpose, but it has power to exercise these functions to their full extent in so far as the Statute does not impose restrictions upon it' (see *PCIJ* Series B, No 14, p 64).

[8] ICJ Reports 1996, p 79, para 26.

II. Judge Weeramantry: to Find Law on Nuclear Weapons is Not to Legislate on the Subject

One of the reasons adduced by those who opposed the delivery of the advisory opinion by the Court was that the Court by doing so would be involving itself in a law-making function. Though it was not on these terms that the Court declined for the first time to render an advisory opinion, yet Judge Weeramantry (Sri Lanka) found it necessary to touch upon this subject in his individual opinion appended to the advisory opinion.

Weeramantry stated: 'This objection covers well-trodden jurisprudential ground. Do judges, in deciding cases, make law undercover of merely applying pre-existing law?' In answer to this question he observed that 'the law has always relied for its development on the ability of the judiciary to apply the general principles to the specific instance. Out of the resulting clarification comes further development'. He further stated that: 'If the law were all embracing, self-evident and specifically tailored to cover every situation, the judicial function would be reduced to a merely mechanical application of rules'.[9] Hence, Judge Weeramantry was not satisfied with such a passive role of the Court. According to him international law is not such a system any more than any domestic system. Inherent principles of international law, and therewith international human rights law, infuse it with vitality, enabling it to apply them to new situations as they arise and give them a specificity they lacked before. How in the given case a new situation has arisen he reasoned in retrospect when a hundred or so years ago humanitarian law, the war situation component of human rights, had begun to evolve, and certainly no specific rule banning nuclear weapons as such could have been formulated at that time. As the nuclear weapons had come into being only half a century later, the Court, according to him, in the given advisory case, is being invited to exercise its classic judicial function. The International Court, in his opinion, 'is being asked to pronounce whether general principles already existing in the body of international law are comprehensive enough to cover the specific instance.'[10] In concluding answer to the objection that the Court would be involved in a law-making exercise by the act of delivering the requested opinion, he remarked: 'To suggest that this is to invite the Court to legislate is to lose sight of the essence of the judicial function.'[11]

III. Judge Koroma: Right to Health is a Pillar of Peace

Judge Koroma (Sierra Leone), dissenting with the Court's refusal to give the advisory opinion to the WHO, criticized the Court's 'restrictive and narrow' view. His

[9] Legality of the Use by a State of Nuclear Weapons in Armed Conflict, Advisory Opinion of 8 July 1996, Dissenting Opinion of Judge Weeramantry, ICJ Reports 1996, p 164.

[10] *Ibid*, p 165.

[11] *Ibid*, p 165.

liberal judicial ideology not only empowers the Court with the jurisdictional power to give the advisory opinion to the WHO but also stands to protect and promote the right to health as one of the fundamental rights of every human being. All through his 52 pages long dissenting opinion, nearly three times in size to the advisory opinion itself (19 pages actually), he firmly opposes the Court's unusually 'narrow' approach in interpreting its advisory jurisdiction, argues in favour of right to health, and right to clean environment. Judge Koroma, having thoroughly reviewed the Court's jurisprudence, concludes:

> The Court has accordingly always taken a liberal view of its advisory jurisdiction and, while not abandoning its judicial character, it has not taken as unduly *restrictive and narrow a view* of that jurisdiction as the Court appears to have done in the present case, even though the question put by the WHO is not only of cardinal importance to the WHO in terms of its constitutional functions, but is also of significance for the attainment of one of its objectives, namely, that 'the enjoyment of the highest attainable standard of *health is one of the fundamental rights of every human being.*[12]

With this human rights approach of interpretation, Judge Koroma establishes one solid fact that right to health is not simply a right to be found in human rights documents only, the same right can be seen and protected from an other dimension as well, the dimension of human welfare. Not agreeing with the Court's interpretation based on the principle of 'speciality,' hence reflecting the narrow working of the principle of 'separation of powers,' at international level, Judge Koroma develops the fields of health and human rights while by countering the narrow separation of powers by the theory of checks and balances at the same time. In his opinion:

> . . . while the principle of 'speciality' governing international organizations is to be respected for reasons of effectiveness and co-ordination and to prevent duplication, it is wrong in my view to give an unduly restricted and narrow interpretation to that concept in relation to health matters and humanitarian affairs . . .. These matters would involve not only the efforts of the WHO but those of the other functional agencies as well, with a common purpose of protecting human welfare and saving the lives of human beings.[13]

Refuting the Court's view that the request by the WHO is encroaching on the competence of other UN organs, Judge Koroma argued that:

> Not only can such co-operation not be regarded as an encroachment on the competence of the other organs or agencies of the United Nations system, but the case before the Court relates to the health and environmental effects of the use of nuclear weapons, matters which fall within the domain of the WHO and which would require such consideration for effective action.[14]

[12] Koroma, Judge, Dissenting Opinion, Legality of the Use by a State of Nuclear Weapons in Armed Conflict, Advisory Opinion of 8 July 1996, ICJ Reports 1996, p 193.
[13] *Ibid*, p 197.
[14] *Ibid*, p 197.

Laying first the ground by demonstrating the restricted application by the Court of the principle of 'speciality', Judge Koroma prepared the ground for the simultaneous positive application of the principle of checks and balances in an imaginary situation of Security Council versus World Health Organization. In his words:

> However, the WHO is the only specialized agency that is assigned the study of public health. If too narrow an interpretation is given to the scope of activities, then because of its activities, even the Security Council could be regarded as encroaching in the fields of health and humanitarian affairs. It cannot, therefore, be sustained that the request violated the principle of 'speciality' which also seemed to have inspired its rejection.[15]

This innovative and liberal thinking of Judge Koroma seems to be contributing to the development of international constitutional law in which right to health and other matters relating human welfare, such as right to clean environment, would remain inescapably linked not only to other fields of international law but also to other international institutions within the system of United Nations.

After having reasoned the place of right to health within the international constitutional ambits of separation of powers and checks and balances within the framework of the principle of 'speciality', Judge Koroma gave the befitting place to this right in the international substantive law in the following words: 'It has been said that "medicine is one of the pillars of peace"; it can equally be said that "health is a pillar of peace" or as is stated in the Constitution of the WHO "the health of all peoples is fundamental to the attainment of peace and security" '.[16]

[15] Koroma, Judge, Dissenting Opinion, Legality of the Use by a State of Nuclear Weapons in Armed Conflict, Advisory Opinion of 8 July 1996, ICJ Reports 1996, p 197.

[16] *Ibid*, p 223.

20

Legality of the Threat or Use of Nuclear Threat[1] (Request for Advisory Opinion by UN General Assembly) (1994–96)

'No weapon ever invented in the long history of man's inhumanity to man has so negatived the dignity and worth of the human person as has the nuclear bomb'.[2]

'The law is not to be deduced from the rule,
but the rule from the law'.[3]

(Roman jurist Paulus)

ON 6 JANUARY 1996, the General Assembly of the United Nations requested, with reference to its resolution 49/75 K adopted on 15 December 1994, an advisory opinion of the International Court of Justice[4] on the following question: '*Is the threat or use of nuclear weapons in any circumstance permitted under international law?*'[5]

[1] The composition of the Court in the Advisory Opinion of 8 July 1996 in the case concerning *Legality of the Threat or Use of Nuclear Weapons* (requested by the UN General Assembly) was: President Bedjaoui; Vice-President Schwebel; Judges Oda, Guillaume, Shahabuddeen, Weeramantry, Ranjeva, Herczegh, Shi, Fleischhauer, Koroma, Vereshchetin, Ferrari Bravo, and Higgins. (See ICJ Reports 1996, p 227).

President Bedjaoui and Judges Herczegh, Shi, Vereshchetin, and Ferrari Bravo appended their declarations to the Advisory Opinion. Judges Guillaume, Ranjeva, and Fleischhauer, appended their separate opinions. Vice-President Schwebel and Judges Oda, Shahabuddeen, Weeramantry, Koroma and Higgins, appended their dissenting opinions. (See ICJ Reports 1996, p 267).

[2] Judge Weeramantry, Dissenting Opinion, Advisor Opinion of 8 July 1996 in the case concerning Legality of the Threat or Use of Nuclear Weapons, ICJ Reports 1996, p 507.

[3] Quoted by BN Mani Tripathi, *Jurisprudence (Legal Theory)*, 11th edn, (Allahabad, Allahabad Law Agency, 1988) 2.

[4] The composition of the Court in this case was as follows: President Bedjaoui (Algeria), Vice-President Schwebel (USA), Judges Oda (Japan), Guillaume (France), Shahabuddeen (Guyana), Weeramantry (Sri Lanka), Ranjeva (Madagascar), Herczegh (Hungary), Shi (China), Fleischhauer (Germany), Koroma (Sierra Leone), Vereshchetin (Russia), Ferrari Bravo (Italy), Higgin (United Kingdom). Remark worthy is also the fact that in this case the crucial part of whose *dispositif* (2E) was decided by the casting vote of the President, all the fourteen participating judges, including the

By an Order of 1 February 1995, the Court decided that the States entitled to appear before the Court and the United Nations were likely to be able to furnish information on the question, in accordance with Article 66, paragraph 2, of the Court's Statute. Written statements on the question of nuclear weapons were filed by 28 States,[6] and subsequently written observations were filed by 2 States.[7] In the course of the oral proceedings held in this case, from 30 October 1995 to 15 November 1995, 22 States[8] presented their oral statements on the legality or illegality of the of the threat or use of nuclear weapons. Having held its closed deliberations, and having considered a great corpus of international law norms, and then applying the Charter law on the use of force and the law of armed conflict, in particular humanitarian law, the Court delivered its Advisory Opinion to the General Assembly in the culminating part, paragraph 2E of the *dispositif*, in the following words:

> It follows from the above-mentioned that the threat or use of nuclear weapons would generally be contrary to the rules applicable in armed conflict, and in particular the principles and rules of humanitarian law;
>
> However, in view of the current state of international law, and of the elements of fact at its disposal, the Court cannot conclude definitely whether the threat or use of nuclear weapons would be lawful in an extreme circumstances of self-defence, in which the very survival of a State would be at stake.[9]

What can one say of the reaction to this in the outside world? Even the Court's own impression to its own opinion reflected as follows:

> I. Human Rights are not Hostage to Military Activities:
>
> The Court is obviously aware that, at first sight, its reply to the General Assembly is unsatisfactory. However, while the Court may leave some people with the impression that it has left the task assigned to it half completed, I am on the contrary persuaded that it has discharged its duty by going as far, in its reply to the question put to it, as the elements at its disposal would permit.[10]

President and the Vice-President, have appended either their declarations or their separate or dissenting opinions. (See ICJ Reports 1996, p 227 and p 267).

[5] Legality of the Threat or Use of Nuclear Weapons, Advisory Opinion of 8 July 1996, ICJ Reports, 1996, p 228.

[6] The 28 States which filed the written statements were: Bosnia and Herzegovina, Burundi, Democratic People's Republic of Korea, Ecuador, Egypt, Finland, France, Germany, India, Ireland, Iran, Italy, Japan, Lesotho, Malaysia, Marshall Islands, Mexico, Nauru, Netherlands, New Zealand, Qatar, Russia, Samoa, San Marino, Solomon Islands, Sweden, United Kingdom and the United States of America; see ICJ Reports, 1996, p 229.

[7] These two States were Egypt and Solomon Islands. Actually Nauru had also earlier filed its written observations but at a later date had requested the Court's permission to withdraw the same; the permission was granted. (See ICJ Reports, 1996, pp 229–30).

[8] 22 States which made oral statements were: Australia, Costa Rica, Egypt, France, Germany, Indonesia, Mexico, Iran, Italy, Japan, Malaysia, New Zealand, Philippines, Qatar, Russia, San Marino, Samoa, Marshall Islands, Solomon Islands, United Kingdom, United States of America and Zimbabwe. (See ICJ Reports, 1996, pp 230–32).

[9] ICJ Reports 1996, p 266, para 2E.

[10] President Bedjaoui's Declaration appended to the Advisory Opinion of 8 July 1996 in the case concerning *Legality of the Threat or Use of Nuclear Weapons*, ICJ Reports 1996, p 272, para 17.

These are the words of the then President of the International Court of Justice, Judge Mohammed Bedjaoui, with whose casting vote the opinion of the seven against seven judges the Advisory Opinion received the stamp of the Court's authority. No doubt when the entire Court itself was unsatisfied, being split seven against seven; when the President of the Court, using his casting vote under Article 55(2) of the Court's Statute, was not satisfied; when the Vice-President of the Court was not satisfied, being a dissenting judge[11]; there certainly is something seriously amiss either with the international law as it exists in substance or with the doctrine at the basis of judges' reasoning and interpretation, or both.

At the very face of it, this case is like a hat (international law) which fits every shape (interpretation of law) or size of head (of judge and/or jurist). But what is inside (the doctrine) the head of the wearer (judge and/or jurist)! The day after the advisory opinion in this case was delivered, together with the refusal of similar opinion to the WHO's request, the headlines in three widely read English news papers were as different as these: 1) 'International Court Fudges Nuclear Arms Ruling; No Ban',[12] 2) 'Use or Threat of Nuclear Arms Unlawful',[13] 3) 'Hague Court Declines to Give Ruling'.[14] A triangular tension in the press, a perfect example for the saying 'law is as you interpret it'. This case presents many tensions: 1) the tension between State based international law and human-being based international law, 2) the tension between State sovereignty based international law and human dignity based international law, 3) the tension between positivist thinking of international law and naturalistic thinking of international law, etc. An amalgam of all these, and others, results in a titanic tension between human rights and nuclear weapons on the one hand and between the ideology of judicial restraint and the ideology of judicial activism on the other hand. This advisory case, together with the one separately filed by the World Health Organization, has raised a storm of different opinions, mainly by criticizing the Court for having failed to declare the illegality of the threat or use of nuclear weapons[15] and also for 'The Court's dismissal of the relevance of the human rights framework',[16] as Professor Vera Gowlland-Debbas put it. But there were also voices of praise, for instance international jurist Falk mentioned:

> The International Court of Justice has issued an advisory opinion of great weight on the legality of nuclear weapons . . .. The Court lived up to its historical challenge . . . the conclusions reached by the Court represent a large step forward with respect to doctrinal clarification . . .. As with other normative projects, such as the abolition of slavery and the repudiation of apartheid, perseverance, struggle and historical circumstances will shape

[11] Vice-President Schwebel's Dissenting Opinion, ICJ Reports 1996, pp 311–29.

[12] *The Guardian*, 9 July 1996.

[13] *The Financial Times*, 9 July 1996.

[14] *The Times*, 9 July 1996.

[15] See VP Nanda and D Krieger, *Nuclear Weapons and the World Court* (New York, NY, Transnational Publishers, 1998).

[16] V Gowlland-Debbas, 'The Right to Life and Genocide: The Court and an International Public Policy' in L Boisson de Chazourzounes and P Sands, (eds), *International Law, The International Court of Justice and Nuclear Weapons* (Cambridge, CUP, 1999) 318.

> the future with respect to nuclear weaponry, but this process has been pushed forward in a mainly beneficial direction by this milestone decision of the World Court.[17]

Matheson is of the opinion that in making this request for advisory opinion, the UN General Assembly has put the Court in a difficult situation, yet he thinks that 'it is to the Court's credit that it found a way to avoid giving an incorrect categorical answer to the question posed without appearing to be indifferent to the potential horrors of nuclear war'.[18] In the same vein his view on the Court's conclusions relevant to human rights in this case is:

> In my view, these conclusions of the Court on the relevance of human rights and environmental principles are correct . . .. If the Court had yielded to the temptation of undiscriminating application to armed conflict of peacetime norms, then the negotiation and ratification of environmental, human rights and similar instruments would have become hostage to the need to agree on express exemptions and special rules for military activities.[19]

But where do we stand? Has the Court made any contribution to the development of human rights in this case or not. Was it a step forward or a step backward as far as the doctrine of human rights is concerned? These are the enquiries to be made in the following analysis.

Not just close but even a quick analysis of paragraph 2E of the *dispositif* reveals that what has characterized the Advisory Opinion as 'unsatisfactory' and 'half completed' are the elements of 'humanitarian law' and 'survival of a State'. It is in plain words the equation of humanitarian law versus survival of a State. But does humanitarian law exist in isolation to human rights law? Professor Buergental (now the United States Judge at the ICJ), for instance, is of the opinion that: humanitarian law can be defined as the human rights component of the law of war. Thus perceived, for him it is that *branch of human rights law* which applies in international armed conflicts, not only that, but in certain limited circumstances, also in internal armed conflicts.[20] Judge Nagendra Singh (India), a former President of the ICJ, sees humanitarian laws as one of the four aspects of human rights. He writes: 'humanitarian laws are all based on the concept of human rights projected to cover the vital field of armed conflicts and it is in this special sphere that the future of the world hinges'.[21] Humanitarian law is an aspect of human rights derived from the principle of human dignity, irrespective of the military or civilian status of a human being. Survival of a State is an aspect of the lingering old

[17] RA Falk, 'Nuclear Weapons, International Law and World Court: An Historic Encounter' (1997) 91 *American Journal of International Law* 64–75.

[18] MJ Matheson, 'The Opinions of the International Court of Justice on the Threat or Use of Nuclear Weapons' (1997) 91 *American Journal of International Law* 417, 435.

[19] *Ibid*, p 423.

[20] T Buergenthal, *International Human Rights Law* (St Paul, MN, West Publishing, 1995) 249; see also AH Robertson and JG Merrills, *Human Rights in the World* (1989) 277; L Boisson de Chazourzounes, 'The Collective responsibility of States to Ensure Respect for Humanitarian Principles' in A Bloed, *et al*, (eds), *Monitoring Human Rights in Europe* (1993) 247.

[21] N Singh, *Human Rights and the Future of Mankind* (Dordrecht, Nijhoff, 1982) 86.

principle of State sovereignty. It is the old ghost of State sovereignty again which is face to face with the emerging and rapidly surging new legal thinking based on human rights and human dignity.

However, a close analysis of the entire operative part of the Advisory Opinion would reveal that even though those voting in favour of the 'survival of a State' were not altogether missing in their reasoning the human rights aspect of the opinion. The operative part was divided into two paragraphs. The second paragraph itself was divided into 5 sub-paragraphs, 2A to 2F respectively.

I. Judge Oda: Judges Do Not Legislate

In paragraph No 1 the Court simply decided, by thirteen votes to one, to comply with the request of the General Assembly of the United Nations. It may be observed that in this decision the only dissenting judge was Judge Oda (Japan). And his dissent was not based on either the legality or illegality of nuclear weapons or the primacy of human rights over the survival of a State; for him his opposition was simply based on the reason of 'judicial economy' and the 'political' nature of the question. Judge Oda was of the opinion that the Request of the General Assembly should have been simply dismissed on the basis of 'judicial economy' in the sense that the question was without any practical dispute or need of seeking solution. And, he saw the request as a hypothetical case the compliance to which opens flood-gates for hypothetical questions. Irrespective of its human rights or any other aspect of the question, Judge Oda mentioned:

> I would like to explain why I consider that the request should have been dismissed in the present case, on account of considerations of judicial economy. There are any number of questions which could be brought to the Court as requiring legal interpretation or the application of international law in general terms in fields such as the law of the sea, law of humanitarian and human rights, environmental law, etc. If the Court were to decide to render an opinion—as in the present case—by giving a response to a legal question of a general nature as to which a specific action would not be in conformity with the application of treaty law or of customary law—a question raised in the absence of any practical need—this could in the long run mean that the Court could be seized of a number of hypothetical cases of a general nature and would eventually risk its main function—to settlement international disputes on the basis of law—to become a consultative or even a legislative organ.[22]

It is hard to disagree with this strongly persuasive opinion of Judge Oda. However, in the body of General Assembly it is the international legislator, responsible for any would be legislation on the legality or illegality of the use of nuclear weapon, and their impact on human rights, such as right to life, which is asking the opinion. And it is not unusual to ask legal opinion on a point of law relating the subject which is already in the process of legislation for the last several decades, mainly

[22] Judge Oda's Dissenting Opinion, ICJ Reports 1996, p 372, para 53.

under the heading of 'nuclear disarmament' as the Court has also noted in its paragraph 2F of the operative part.[23]

While Judge Oda took the position that the Court should have dismissed the request of the General Assembly, he proceeded nonetheless to cast his vote on all of the subparagraphs of paragraph 2, apart from paragraph 2E. Nevertheless, he clarified his personal opposition to nuclear weapons, and therewith their violating nature of human rights, in the following words:

> *(My personal appeal.)* In concluding this exposition of my position against the Court's rendering an opinion in the present case, *I would emphasize that I am among the first to hope that nuclear weapons can be totally eliminated* as proposed in General Assembly resolutions 49/75H and 50/70C, which were adopted at the General Assembly without there being one single objection.

Reflecting his tough conservatism and judicial restraint ideology, hence strictly against any legislative role of the judge, Judge Oda made it more clear in his words: 'However, a decision on this matter is a function of *political* negotiations among States in Geneva or New York and is not one which concerns our judicial institution here at The Hague, where an interpretation of *existing international law* can only be given in response to a genuine need.'[24] One might point out that Judge Oda, being a staunch positivist, would not think much of the application of general principles[25] of law, enshrined in Article 38, paragraph c, of the ICJ Statute, as a source of international law to be applied by the Court. Several dissenting judges have relied upon that source when interpreting the humanitarian law in the process of their application on nuclear weapons and the implications of their use on human rights and environment.

II. Right to Life and The Human Rights Component of the Law of War

'*Thou shall not kill*'[26] is an ancient affirmation of the right to life. René Cassin described the right to life as '*the right of human beings to exist*'.[27] The linkage between right to life and nuclear weapons has been well highlighted by the General Assembly of the United Nations when it condemned the nuclear war '*as a violation of the foremost human right—the right to life*'.[28]

[23] ICJ Reports 1996, p 267.

[24] Judge Oda's Dissenting Opinion, ICJ Reports 1996, p 373, para 54.

[25] It might be interesting here to note that a former Japanese Judge, Judge Tanaka, was a staunch advocate of Natural Law approach to international law; and in the contentious cases concerning *South West Africa (Second Phase)*, he has attributed general principles of law 'the primary position vis-à-vis the other two' sources. (see ICJ Reports 1966, p 300).

[26] Exodus, XX–13.

[27] See CR 95/32, p 64, including n 20.

[28] General Assembly Resolution 38/75 dated 15 December 1983, 'Condemnation of Nuclear War', operative para 1.

In seeking to answer the question asked by the General Assembly the Court considered that it must decide, after consideration of the great corpus of international law norms available to it, what might be the relevant applicable law. In doing so the Court also took notice of the fact that some of the States, proponents[29] of the illegality of the use of nuclear weapons, have argued that such use would violate the right to life as guaranteed in Article 6 of the International Covenant of Civil and Political Rights, as well as in certain regional instruments for the protection of human rights. Article 6, paragraph 1, of the International Covenant provides as follows: 'Every human being has the inherent right to life. This right shall be protected by law. No one shall be arbitrarily deprived of his life.'[30]

In reply to the view of those proponent States, other States[31] contended that the International Covenant on Civil and Political Rights made no mention of war or weapons, and it had never been envisaged that the legality of nuclear weapons was regulated by the instrument. It was suggested that the Covenant was directed to the protection of human rights in peacetime, but that questions relating to unlawful loss of life in hostilities were governed by the law applicable in armed conflict.[32]

Taking into account these conflicting and opposing opinions of two camps of States, the Court observed: '*the protection of the International Covenant of Civil and Political Rights does not cease in time of war*, except by operation of Article 4 of the Covenant whereby certain provisions may be derogated from in a time of national emergency.'[33] Those who think that the Court has limited the scope of right to life with the word 'except', need only to be reminded of the wording of Article 4 of the Covenant which reads:

> In time of public emergency which threatens the life of the nation and the existence of which is officially proclaimed, the State Parties to the present Covenant may take measures derogating from their obligations under the present Covenant to the extent strictly required by the exigencies of the situation, provided that such measures are not inconsistent with their obligations under international law and do not involve solely on the ground of race, colour, sex language, religion or social origin.

The wording simply provides that the right to life is not an absolute right. Hence, the limitation provided by the word 'except', from its becoming an absolute right, is not the limitation provided by the Court but by the Covenant itself. As a matter of fact the Court clarified the law here by stating that '*In principle, the right not arbitrarily to be deprived of one's life applies also in hostilities.*' In so clearly stating

[29] Egypt (Written Statement, June 1995, pp 15–16), Malaysia (Written Statement, June 1995, pp 13–14), Samoa (Written Statement, June 1995, pp 20–22), Solomon Islands (Written Statement, June 1995, pp 91–92), and Indonesia (Oral Statement, CR 95/25, p 3).

[30] ICJ Reports 1996, p 239, para 23.

[31] France (Written Statement, June 1995, p 20, and also CR 95/24), Netherlands (Written Statement, June 1995, pp 10–11), Russia (Written Statement, June 1995, pp 9–10), United Kingdom (Written Statement, June 1995, pp 64–68), and the United States (Written Statement, June 1995, pp 43–46).

[32] ICJ Reports 1996, p 239, para 24.

[33] Legality of the Threat or Use of Nuclear Weapons, Advisory Opinion of 8 July 1996, ICJ Reports, 1996, p 240.

the law, bringing the arguments of States face to face with the right to life enshrined in the Covenant, the Court concluded that the existing human rights law provide a test for determining what is an arbitrary deprivation of life. The Court continued and further observed that: 'The test of what is an arbitrary deprivation of life, however, then falls to be determined by the applicable *lex specialis*, namely, the law applicable in armed conflict which is destined to regulate the conduct of hostilities.[34] The right to life in peace is brought face to face with the right to life in war. The Covenant is here brought face to face with the law of armed conflict. It is also an answer to those who disagree about humanitarian law being integral part of the international human rights law. That the right to life has its 'human rights component of the law of war' is clarified by the way the Court chose to examine this right. In the Court's own words: 'Thus whether a particular loss of life, through the use of certain weapon in warfare, is to be considered an arbitrary deprivation of life contrary to Article 6 of the Covenant, can only be decided by reference to the law applicable in armed conflict and not deduced from the terms of the Covenant itself.'[35] Hence, whether the use of nuclear weapons violates the right to life or not, the Court's answer is that it is not up to the International Covenant on Civil and Political Rights to regulate the legality or the illegality of the recourse to nuclear weapons.

III. Judge Bedjaoui: Nuclear Weapons v Right to Life:

However, Judge Bedjaoui, the President of the ICJ at the time of this case, in his Declaration, showed the adverse relationship between the use of nuclear weapons on the one side and the humanitarian law and right to life on the other side:

> By its very nature, the nuclear weapons, a blind weapon, therefore has a destabilizing effect on humanitarian law, the law of discrimination which regulates discernment in the use of weapons. Nuclear weapons, the ultimate evil, destabilize humanitarian law which is the law of the lesser evil. The existence of nuclear weapons is therefore a major challenge to the very existence of humanitarian law . . . in respecting which the right to life may be exercised.[36] (italics are original).

We may recall here that there has, for a long time been an extensive discussion over the question of the relation between international humanitarian law and the law of human rights. And, at the 1968 Teheran Conference on Human Rights the four 1949 Geneva Conventions were included by the United Nations as part of the list of instruments protecting human rights. Subsequently, the General Assembly of the United Nations had also endeavoured by a series of resolutions under the title 'Respect for Human Rights in Armed Conflict' to establish a link of responsibility

[34] Legality of the Threat or Use of Nuclear Weapons, Advisory Opinion of 8 July 1996, ICJ Reports, 1996, p 240.

[35] ICJ Reports 1996, p 240.

[36] M Bedjaoui, Declaration of President Bedjaoui, ICJ Reports, 1996, p 272, para 20.

and accountability between the international humanitarian law and the international human rights law. The Court's aforementioned statement has established an inescapable link between the two branches of international law, though not bringing outright both the fields of law under a single field but certainly reflecting international humanitarian law as an integral part of the broader concept of human rights law. This brings the relation of human rights law with the international law governing the conduct of war in the lime light in such a way, that the Court, by means of providing a doctrinal clarification, leaves it up to the international legislator to think that that there is a close link between the principle of State sovereignty's corollary of the right to self-defence of the State and the principle of human dignity's corollary of the right to life of the individual. None of them are absolute rights. Both are conditioned by each other.

How far these conditioning factors may develop the relation between human rights law and international law when it really comes to the conscious international legislation, by means of a treaty or so, bearing upon the relationship between the right to life in the face of use of nuclear weapons, may well be gleaned through the declarations, dissents and separate opinions appended every single judge composing the Court in this advisory case. The very fact that every judge irrespective of voting in favour or against any part of the *dispositif* found it necessary to append its additional views to the advisory opinion in itself is fact of great weight which cannot be easily overlooked in this regard.

Those who see the *dispositif* as legalizing the threat or use of nuclear weapons need only to give thought to the fact that even the casting President of Court saw the relationship between humanity and nuclear weapons as that of a 'blackmail'. In his own words: 'Man is subjecting itself to a perverse and unremitting nuclear blackmail'.[37] But one may wonder, why the President, Judge Bedjaoui, first voted in favour of the *dispositif* which itself was neither clear nor complete and then even let it be ultimately decided by his own casting vote? He did it with a hope that someday the international legislature would correct the imperfections of international law. Again, in his own words:

> It is to be hoped that that the international community will give the Court credit for having carried out its mission—even if its reply may seem unsatisfactory—and will endeavour as quickly as possible to correct the imperfections of an international law which is ultimately no more than the creation of the States themselves.[38]

This is clearly a judicial self-restraint of a judge who is conscious enough of not stepping into the field of legislation. Judge Bedjaoui, though acting with judicial self-restraint ideology did not for a second hesitate to describe the nuclear weapons as 'the ultimate evil' and in that vein clarified and promoted the war component of human rights law in the following words: 'atomic warfare and humanitarian law therefore appear to be mutually exclusive; the existence of the

[37] *Ibid*, p 269, para 6.
[38] *Ibid*, p 269, para 8.

one automatically implies the non-existence of the other'. Further, portraying the use of nuclear weapons as 'terror', Judge Bedjaoui indicated to the international legislature that the survival of a State (representing the principle of State sovereignty) is not above the survival of mankind (representing the principle of human dignity, particularly the right to life). The superiority of the principle of human dignity, particularly the right to life, over the principle of sovereignty, in the guise of self-defence and State survival, he recognized in this way:

> The fact remains that the use of nuclear weapons by a State in circumstances in which its survival is at stake risks in its turn endangering the survival of all mankind, precisely because of the inextricable link between terror and escalation in the use of such weapons. It would thus be quite foolhardy unhesitatingly to set the survival of a State above all considerations, in particular above the survival of mankind itself.

IV. Judge Weeramantry: Nuclear Weapons Totally Belie Human Dignity

All human rights, maintains Judge Weeramantry, follow from one central right, and that is the right to life. He finds this right as the foundation on which stands the entire structure of human rights. Therefore, he rates the right to life as an absolute right and identifies it with the human dignity itself, at the very basis of the entire system of human rights. Those who think that the right to life is not an absolute right and that the taking of life in armed hostilities is a necessary exception to this principle, Judge Weeramantry's answer to them is:

> . . . when a weapon has the potential to kill between one million and one billion people, as WHO has told the Court, human life becomes reduced to a level of worthlessness that totally belies human dignity as understood in any culture. Such a deliberate action by any State is, in any circumstances whatever, incompatible with a recognition by it of that respect for basic human dignity on which world peace depends, and respect for which is assumed on the part of all Member States of the United Nations.[39]

Such a forceful and penetrating language at once, first, sees nuclear weapons as an insult to human dignity, and then, elevates the right to life to that status of respect that without respect to dignity of human beings, his right to life is devoid of the very word *life*. Further, referring to the Universal Declaration of Human Rights and other human rights instruments, particularly the United Nations Charter's one of the aims 'to reaffirm faith in fundamental human rights, in the *dignity and worth* of the human person (his own emphasis), Judge Weeramantry finds nuclear weapons as utterly nullifying the principle of human dignity: 'No weapon ever invented in the long history of man's inhumanity to man has so negatived the dignity and worth of human person as has the nuclear bomb.'[40]

[39] C Weeramantry, Dissenting Opinion of Judge Weeramantry, ICJ Reports 1996, p 507.
[40] *Ibid*, p 507.

V. Judge Koroma: Both Human Rights Law and International Humanitarian Law Have as their *Raison d'être* the Protection of the Individual as well as the Worth and Dignity of the Human Person

As to question whether recourse to nuclear weapons violates the right to human life or not and the Court's answer that the International Covenant on Civil and Political Rights never envisaged the need to regulate lawfulness or otherwise of such weapons, found by Judge Koroma as '*too narrow a view*'[41] taken by the Court on this matter.

Judge Koroma reminded the Court that '... both human rights law and international humanitarian law have as their *raison d'être* the protection of the individual as well as the worth and dignity of the human person, both during peacetime or in armed conflict.'[42] According to Judge Koroma one only need to recall that what were the circumstances which gave birth to the UN Charter and other relevant international legal instruments. He observed that it was the serious and grave human rights violations during the Second World War, and also the use of atomic weapons in Hiroshima and Nagasaki, which were the background for the signing of the UN Charter and other instruments. Therefore, according to Judge Koroma: 'The possibility that the human rights of citizens, in particular their right to life, would be violated during a nuclear conflagration, is a matter which falls within the purview of the Charter and other relevant international instruments.'[43]

Judge Koroma's approach here is obviously developing international law based on UN Charter and related human rights instruments, particularly its provisions concerning human rights and human dignity, and putting limitations on the classical international law based on the principle of State sovereignty. Demonstrating the actual development of international human rights law in that direction, Judge Koroma observed that:

> Any activity which involves a terrible violation of the principles of the Charter deserves to be considered in the context of both the Charter and the other applicable rules. It is evidently in this context that Human Rights Committee under the International Covenant on Civil and Political Rights adopted, in November 1984, 'a general comment' on Article 6 of the Covenant (Right to Life), according to which the production, testing, possession, deployment and use of nuclear weapons ought to be prohibited and recognized as crimes against humanity.[44]

[41] A Koroma, Dissenting Opinion of Judge Koroma, ICJ Reports 1996, p 577.
[42] *Ibid*, p 577.
[43] *Ibid*, p 577.
[44] *Ibid*, p 578.

VI. Genocide and Nuclear Weapons

The term 'genocide' was first coined by Professor Raphael Lemkin in 1944. According to an Indian scholar, Professor Agarwal, the term has been derived from the Greek word '*genos*' (meaning race) and the Latin word '*cidium*' (substantive, meaning killing).[45] But according to Professor Gibson the word genocide comes from 'genus' (meaning group) and '*caedere*' (verb, meaning to kill). Raphael Lemkin survived the Holocaust, which destroyed about fifty members of his family, by fleeing his native Poland and gaining asylum in the United States.[46] A legal scholar, he became a member of the law faculties of Duke and Yale Universities and authored a remarkable book, *Axis Rule in Occupied Europe*,[47] in which he coined the term 'genocide'.

Actually, genocide is also considered as a form of arbitrary deprivation of life. Some States in the given advisory case made arguments that the prohibition against genocide,[48] referred to in the 1948 Convention on the Prevention and Punishment of the Crime of Genocide, is a relevant rule of customary international law and, therefore, must be applied by the Court in deciding about the delivery of opinion in the case. The Court took notice that it was maintained before the Court that the number of deaths occasioned by the use of nuclear weapons would be enormous in the sense that the victims could, in certain cases, include persons of a particular national, ethnic, racial, or religious groups; and the intention to destroy such groups could be inferred from the fact that the user of the nuclear weapon would have omitted to take account of the well-known effects of the use of such weapons. In this regard, the Court recalled Article II of the Genocide Convention and relied on the definition of genocide given therein in the following words:

> any of the following acts committed with intent to destroy, in the whole or in part, a national, ethnical, racial or religious group, as such: (a) Killing members of the group; (b) Causing serious bodily or mental harm to members of the group; (c) Deliberately inflicting on the group conditions of life calculated to bring about its physical destruction in whole or in part; (d) Imposing measures intended to prevent births within the group; (e) Forcibly transferring children of the group to another group.[49]

For anyone who was looking forward from the Court's opinion that it will develop, in the wake of nuclear perils of the age, a human-rights-oriented international law, drawing distinction between intent to destroy and extent of destruction, the approach taken by the Court must be very disappointing. The Court quoted such

[45] HO Agarwal, *International Law* (Fridabad, India, Allahabad Law Agency, 1997) 610.

[46] JS Gibson, *Dictionary of International Human Rights* Law (1996) 178–79.

[47] R Lemkin, *Axix Rule in Occupied Europe* (New York, NY, Carnegie Endowment for International Peace, 1944); see also Lemkin's article, 'Genicide as a Crime in International Law' (1947) 41 *American Journal of International Law* 145.

[48] Fllowing States made references to genocide: Egypt (Written Statement, June 1995, pp 16–17); Russia (Written Statement, June 1995, p 9); United States (Written Statement, June 1995, pp 33–34); and New Zealand (Written Statement, June 1995, p 20).

[49] Quoted in full in the ICJ Reports 1996, p 240.

an extensive definition to fish out just one single word of '*intent*' to draw the conclusion just in one short sentence: 'The Court would point out in that regard that the prohibition of genocide would be pertinent in this case if the recourse to nuclear weapons did indeed entail the element of intent, towards a *group* as such, required by the provision quoted above.'[50]

In the age of human rights and the era of law based on human dignity, when the risk of a presumable self-defence of a State goes beyond the extent that the lines of the element of 'intent' are easily and certainly blurred then you do look for a new legal reasoning which limits the extent of intent by developing the dimensions of extent in such a way that the law moves from its analytical limits to its pristine natural principle of justice based on human dignity seen in the extent of loss of life. In order to develop the meaning and spirit of human rights and human dignity the new elements of a new legal ideology in a new era, born in contrast to the traditional era of State as the only subject and the individual as only an object, one needs to move from the thinking of rule based law of Austin and Hart to the principle based law of Dworkin and Fuller. The element of intent is only a rule of law which can go only to a certain extent, but beyond that when a given rule is in haze then you look for the underlying principle, ie, the right to life must be respected (even the positivist school recognizes that) because human body is the living temple of God (the natural law school provides the underlying principle for the analytical rule). Three following elements—1) a gigantic and uncontrollable loss of civilian life, 2) unnecessary suffering by the military and civilian populations alike, and 3) resulting unclean air to breath—could have provided a new legal reasoning for setting limits to the element of intent. We may yet be very far from the inner spirituality of law, yet the age of '*The Morality of Law*,' as advocated by Lon L. Fuller, and the age of '*Taking Rights Seriously*', as advocated by Ronald Dworkin has certainly begun. The Court in its dealings with the issues of right to life and the questions of genocide related to the problems of the use or threat of use of nuclear weapons could easily have drawn the limits to the rule of 'intent' and clarify its meaning by developing the definition of Genocide under a broader interpretation of the right to life based on human dignity, and not State sovereignty, though both are equally the principles of international law. Which should prevail, is not difficult to guess, in the light of havoc created by the latter throughout the recorded history of law, politics, and mankind.

VII. Judge Higgins: Intent Approximates to Legal Doctrine of Foreseeability

In order to clarify the meaning of 'intent', Judge Higgins first selects an aptly particular definition of intent given by Finnis, Boyle and Grisez:: 'One's intent is

[50] ICJ Reports 1996, p 240, para 26.

defined by what one chooses to do, or seeks to achieve through what one chooses to do.'[51]

Judge Higgins continues and observes: 'This closely approximates to the legal doctrine of foreseeability, by which one is assumed to intend the consequences of one's actions'. In order to elaborate this she poses the following question: 'Does it follow that knowledge that in concrete circumstances civilians will be killed by the use of nuclear weapons is tantamount to an intention to attack civilians? At once bringing the relevance of 'intent' to nuclear weapons, as to conventional weapons, Judge Higgins answered the question in the broadest possible way: 'In law, analysis must always be contextual and the philosophical question here put is no different for nuclear weapons than for other weapons'.[52]

The core of the matter is firmly established that the element of 'intent' amounts to 'foreseeability'.

VIII. Judge Weeramantry: Nuclear Weapons are Instruments of Genocide and their Use is Plainly Genocide

Judge Weeramantry (Sri Lanka) found the Court's treatment of the relevance of genocide to the nuclear weapons as inadequate.

In his view, the nuclear weapons used in response to a nuclear attack, especially in the event of an all-out nuclear response, would be likely to cause genocide by triggering off an all-out nuclear exchange. Judging from the number of deaths they are known to have caused, Judge Weeramantry finds that even single 'small' nuclear weapons, such as those used in Japan, could be '*instruments of genocide*'. By the sheer massive scale of loss of life Judge Weeramantry identifies the use of nuclear weapons with acts of genocide:

> If cities are targeted, a single bomb could cause a death tall exceeding a million. If the retaliatory weapons are more numerous, on WHO's estimates of the effects of nuclear war, even a billion people, both of the attacking State and of others, could be killed. *This is plainly genocide* and, whatever the circumstances, cannot be within the law.[53] (italics are mine).

Judge Weeramantry, identifying nuclear weapons as 'instruments of Genocide' and judging the resulting death toll as a consequence of a nuclear war, questions the very definition of genocide. According to him: 'In discussions on the definition of genocide in the Genocide Convention, much play is made upon the words "*as such*". The argument offered is that there must be an *intention to target* a particu-

[51] Finnis, Boyle and Grisez, *Nuclear Deterrence, Morality and Idealism* (Oxford, Clarendon Press, 1987) 92–93.

[52] R Higgins, Dissenting Opinion of Judge Higgins, ICJ Reports 1996, p 588.

[53] C Weeramantry, Dissenting Opinion of Judge Weeramantry, ICJ Reports 1996, p 501.

lar national, ethical, racial or religious group qua such group, and not incidentally to some other act.' This is how, in his opinion, the Court has used the meaning of the definition of genocide. In this reasoning, he continues and states: 'However, having regard to the ability of nuclear weapons to wipe out *blocks of population* ranging from hundreds of thousands to millions, *there can be no doubt that the weapon targets*, in whole or in part, the national group of the State at which it is directed'.[54] By so clarifying the definition of genocide, Judge Weeramantry has introduced a new legal element to its meaning that simple '*intention to target*' a particular group loses it meaning when the extent of destruction is so massive as to wipe out groups and groups of population. This scientifically verified knowledge of the ability of nuclear weapons would make any decision to use such weapons to be interpreted as having intention to target a particular group or groups, as the element of 'incidentally' would have lost its meaning by the possible resulting scale of destruction of life.

Judge Weeramantry develops the genocide law to the extent that it is time when the fate genocide (killing a particular group or groups), keeping in view the extent of common destruction of all, is common to a particular group or groups 'as such' and other groups (blocks of population) then the lines of distinction between particular groups and groups disappear. The situation is similar to the pre-human rights law that in the classical international law States could enter into treaties with each other about the protection of ethnic, national, or religious groups of one State who were resident in the territory of the other State.[55] In this system States provided protection and obligation to foreign groups and not to such groups of its own nationality. Paraphrasing Professor Higgins' words[56]: there is no reason or logic why the Genocide Convention protection should be provided to certain groups, groups 'as such', and not to other groups, the blocks of populations. The criterion for protection under the Convention for groups 'as such' is their *vulnerability and victimization* at the hands of majority government and majority population. But when it comes to the effects of the use of nuclear weapons the *vulnerability and victimization* is without any distinction or discrimination. Therefore, Judge Weeramantry's clarifies the status of nuclear weapons to that extent that it gives them the apt title: 'instruments of genocide'. It commits genocide not of a particular group or groups but of all groups subjected. And when the States intending to use it, irrespective of its use either as first strike or in self defence, know this scientific fact, the element of 'intent to destroy' is manifested as a matter of course.

[54] *Ibid*, p 502.

[55] This was essentially the system adopted by the Inter-War Minority treaties; See J Fouques-Duparc, *La Protection des minorities de race, de langue et de religion* (1922); P de Azcarate, *The League of Nations and National Minorities* (1945); R Jennings and A Watts, (eds), *Oppenheim's International Law*, 9th edn, (1992) vol I, Parts 2–4, pp 973–75.

[56] R Higgins, *Problems and Process: International Law and How We Use It* (Oxford, OUP, 1994) 96; Prof Higgins (now Judge at the ICJ), speaking about extending the same writes to natives under human rights system which were earlier available only to foreign nationals, wrote: 'there is no reason of logic why the obligations should be owed only to foreign individuals, and not to nationals'.

Not even in self-defence, according to Judge Weeramantry, the use of nuclear weapons can escape being categorized as 'instruments of genocide'. Self-defence, resulting in all probability in all-out nuclear war, as he put it, is even more likely to cause genocide than the act of launching an initial strike. In his opinion the fact of human beings killed in millions deserves a solid consideration when it comes to the definition of genocide and its relevance to nuclear weapons: 'If the killing of human beings, in numbers ranging from a million to a billion, does not fall within the definition of genocide, one may well ask what will.'[57] By this emphatic statement, Judge Weeramantry gives an additional criterion and an element to the existing definition of genocide.[58] The element of 'intent' is clearly 'State sovereignty' oriented. But the element of 'killing of human beings in millions' is 'human dignity' oriented.

If 'WE THE PEOPLES OF THE UNITED NATIONS'[59] (human dignity in collectivity) have given recognition to the customary right of self defence of the institution of sovereign State and if 'WE THE PEOPLES OF THE UNITED NATIONS' (human dignity in collectivity) are going to be the victimized in millions and billions by the exercise of that very right—the right of the peoples, for the peoples, and by the peoples—then the element of 'killing in millions' should be seen as amounting to genocide, states Judge Weeramantry. It brings international law in line with the 'DETERMINED' aims of 'WE THE PEOPLE OF THE UNITED NATIONS', *inter alia*: 1) 'to save succeeding generations from scourge of war', the constant history of 'untold sorrow to mankind' a legacy of the traditional right of self defence under the flag of principle of State sovereignty, and 2) 'to reaffirm faith in fundamental human rights, in the dignity and worth of the human person'.[60]

[57] C Weeramantry, Dissenting Opinion of Judge Weermantry, ICJ Reports 1996, p 517.

[58] N Singh, *Human Rights and the Future of Mankind* (Dordrecht, Nijhoff, 1982). In this book Judge Nagendra Singh (India), a former President and the International Court of Justice (1985–88) and its Vice-President (1976–79), also sees 'the wholesale destruction of human beings' as 'the essence of the crime of genicide'. The relevance of genocide to nuclear weapons was well described by him in his following words. Refering to Article 1 of the Genocide Convention he wrote:

> it declares genocide which is defined as 'the killing or causing serious bodily or mental harm to members of a group, the deliberate infliction of conditions of life calculated physically to destroy the group wholly or partially, the imposition of measures to prevent births within the group, or the forcible transfer of children from one group to another group—whether committed in peace or war' to be a crime under international law. It is said by jurists that taking into consideration the known effects of nuclear weapons, both generic and immediate, their use would undoubtedly involve one if not all the first three acts detailed above. What it is sought to prohibit is the wholesale destruction of human beings classified as a group on racial, ethnical or national basis which is the essence of the crime of genocide . . . *The present day weapons of mass destruction that annihilate the entire citizen body of not one but several states en bloc no matter whether neutral or belligerent, would appear to run contrary to the basic idea of human rights in an armed conflict.* (pp 93–94).

[59] The opening words (capitals are original) of the preamble of the Charter of the United Nations, the very constitution of the United Nations and the basis of International Law.

[60] See the preamble of the Charter of the United Nations.

IX. Judge Koroma: Quantum of the People Killed by Nuclear Weapons Could be Tantamount to Genocide

Judge Koroma vehemently disagreed with the Court's view that no intent to kill means no genocide. According to him: 'The Court cannot . . . view with equanimity the killing of thousands, if not millions, of innocent civilians which the use of nuclear weapons would make inevitable, and conclude that genocide has not been committed because the State using such weapons has not manifested any intent to kill so many thousands or millions of people.'[61]

Judge Koroma was not happy that the Court so detachedly simply recalled Article II of the Genocide Convention to point out the element of 'an intent to destroy' to conclude that the use of nuclear weapons used in self defence would not amount to genocide. He expected the Court to be mindful of the special characteristics of the Convention, its object and purpose, to which the Court itself has earlier referred in the *Reservations* advisory case.[62] Having briefly emphasized on various previous finding findings of the Court in the same case, Judge Koroma arrived at a conclusion: 'Indeed, under the Convention, the quantum of the people killed is comprehended as well.'[63]

Judge Koroma, criticizing the Court of its 'extreme form of positivism'[64] in this case, which is out of keeping with the international jurisprudence, including that of the ICJ itself, remarked: 'It does not appear to me that judicial detachment requires the Court from expressing itself on the abhorrent shocking consequences that a whole population could be wiped out by the use of nuclear weapons during an armed conflict, and the fact that this could tantamount to genocide'.[65]

X. Human Rights Component of the Law of War

In view of the questions relating the right to life, the prohibition of genocide, and the protection and safeguarding of the environment, the Court noted that the

[61] A Koroma, Dissenting Opinion of Judge Koroma, ICJ Reports 1996, p 577.

[62] In the Reservations case the Court stated:

> The origins of the Convention show that it was the intention of the United Nations to condemn and punish genocide as 'a crime under international law' involving a denial of the right of existence of entire human groups, a denial which shocks the conscience of mankind and results in great losses to humanity, and which is contrary to moral law and to the spirit and aims of the United Nations.

Reservations to the Convention on the Prevention and Punishment of the Crime of Genocide, ICJ Reports 1951, p 23.

[63] A Koroma, Dissenting Opinion of Judge Koroma, ICJ Reports 1966, p 577.

[64] *Ibid*, p 575.

[65] *Ibid*, p 577.

most directly relevant applicable law governing the question asked by the General Assembly is that relating to: a) the use of force enshrined in the United Nations Charter, and b) the law applicable in armed conflict that law regulates the conduct of hostilities together with any specific treaties on nuclear weapons that the Court might determine to be relevant.

Those who maintain that the Court has declared the legality of the use or threat of nuclear weapons, only need read the paragraph 2A of the operative part wherein the Court was unanimous in saying that: '*There is in neither customary nor conventional international law any specific authorization of the threat or use of nuclear weapons*'.

The Court perhaps would have done a great service to the development of international law in general, and international human rights law in particular, by not adding the next paragraph, 2B, to the operative part which states, by eleven votes to three: '*There is in neither customary nor conventional international law any comprehensive and universal prohibition of the threat or use of nuclear weapons as such*'.

Why? Swaying between two doctrines, the old ghost doctrine of State sovereignty and the new doctrine of human rights. As a result the Court revives the *Lotus* case thinking that what is not prohibited by law is permitted. Not only that, but 2B wording also gives an obvious impression that the Court did not give any weight to its own third source of law, the general principles of law, mentioned in Article 38, paragraph 1(c), Statute of the Court. Since the general principles of law are considered as victory of natural law in entering the statute, it also suggests that the seven judges, including the casting voter President, gave a primacy to the positive law, mainly based on the principle of State sovereignty and the theory of consent, over the natural law. Despite all this, paragraph 2C shows that the operative part is not all together silent on the questions of human rights. The Court finds here, unanimously: 'A threat or *use of force by means of nuclear weapons that is contrary to Article 2, paragraph 4, of the United Nations Charter* and that fails to meet all the requirements of Article 51, *is unlawful*' (italics added). In order to grasp the significance of these italicised words, within the human rights framework, we may recall here the words of Article 2, paragraph 4, of the Charter: '*All Members shall refrain* in their international relations *from the threat or use of force* against the territorial integrity or political independence of any State, or in any other manner *inconsistent with the Purposes of the United Nations.*' And what are the *purposes* of the United Nations? The purposes of the United Nations are mentioned in Article 1 of the Charter. And, paragraph 3 thereof reads: 'To achieve international co-operation in solving international problems of an economic, social, cultural, or humanitarian character, and in *promoting and encouraging respect for human rights and fundamental freedoms of all without distinction as to race, sex, language, or religion*'. This is indicative of the fact that the Court does recognize the limit provided by human rights law on the use or threat of nuclear weapons. The failure of States to take this into account will meet with the legitimate consequences. In the same vein, the Court further decided with unanimous voice:

> A threat or use of nuclear weapons should also be compatible with the requirements of the international law applicable in armed conflict, particularly those of the principles and rules of international humanitarian law, as well as with specific obligations under treaties and other undertakings which expressly deal with nuclear weapons.

This provision too circumscribes the threat or use of nuclear weapons with every aspect of human rights. All these paragraphs from 2A to 2D culminated in the paragraph of the operative part, the paragraph 2E, quoted in full above, which raised a storm of different opinions.

XI. Conclusion

The opinion should be seen as a step forward and not as a step backward towards the development of the doctrine of human rights.

With their lengthy clarifications and development of law all dissenting judges seem to convey one conclusion that in their opinions the Court knew perfectly well, or could decide perfectly well, what the precise answer regarding the legality or illegality of nuclear weapons should be and yet it remained reluctant to choose one precise answer, legality or illegality. Why? Because the Court chose not to go legislating and let the UN legislature do the job of legislation. In the absence of a settled customary and conventional international law, and reluctance to decide an issue of such a grave importance upon the basis of the general principles of law, the Court chose to reflect the reality of *Yes and No* of the legality and illegality. Reading the *obiter dicta* between the two poles of its *dispositif* 2E—use of nuclear weapons 'generally [are] contrary' to law 'but cannot conclude definitely . . . lawful or unlawful'[66]—and 2F—'There exists an obligation' for States to pursue in good faith and bring to a conclusion negotiations leading to nuclear disarmament in all its aspects under strict and effective international control'[67]—the Court's advice to the UN General Assembly is most clearly stating: may use; may not use; but do not use; hence, do legislate: MAY NOT USE.

The conclusions reached by the Court represent a large step forward with respect to doctrinal clarification. In addition to this the individual opinions of judges immensely clarified and developed the law to the extent that is well summarized by Judge Weeramantry: '*No weapon ever invented in the long history of man's inhumanity to man has so negatived the dignity and worth of the human person as has the nuclear bomb.*'[68]

[66] ICJ Reports 1996, 266.
[67] *Ibid*, p 267.
[68] C Weeramantry, Dissenting Opinion, Advisor Opinion of 8 July 1996 in the case concerning Legality of the Threat or Use of Nuclear Weapons, ICJ Reports 1996, p 507.

21

Difference Relating to Immunity from Legal Process of a Special Rapporteur of the Commission on Human Rights[1]

(1998–99)

LEGAL OBLIGATIONS OF a Sovereign State in the Wake of Discharge of Duties by a Special Rapporteur of the Commission on Human Rights: Court Sets New Principles:

Even if it is an advisory case, its nature is by no means less contentious than the proceedings in a contentious case when it comes to the conditioning of State sovereignty in the face of an aspect of human rights. Although, advisory opinion as such has no binding force, yet the basis (Article VIII, Section 30 of the Convention on the Privileges and Immunities of the United Nations (1946), signed by 137 UN member States, including Malaysia) on which the present case was filed makes the Advisory Opinion as 'decisive'[2] for the Parties. There is a triangle of three international actors involved in this case: An individual human being (Mr Comaraswamy), an international organization (the United Nations), and a sovereign State (Malaysia). It appears as a tug-of-war between two human rights actors on the one side and a sovereign State actor on the other side.

The case revolves around one Malaysian jurist, Mr Dato' Param Comaraswamy, who was an international civil servant of the United Nations, appointed in 1994 as Special Rapporteur on the Independence of Judges and Lawyers by the United

[1] The composition of the Court in the Advisory Opinion of 29 April 1999 in the case concerning *Difference Relating to Immunity from Legal Process of a Special Rapporteur of the Commission on Human Rights* was: President Schwebel; Vice-President Weeramantry; Judges Oda, Bedjaoui, Guillaume, Ranjeva, Herczegh, Shi, Fleischhauer, Koroma, Vereshchetin, Higgins, Parra-Aranguren, Kooijmans, and Rezek. (See ICJ Reports 1999, p 63).

Vice-President Weeramantry and Judges Oda and Rezek appended their separate opinions to the Advisory Opinion. Judge Koroma appended his dissenting opinion. (see ICJ Reports 1999, p 91).

[2] Section 30 of the Convention provides as follows:

All differences arising out of the interpretation or application of the present convention shall be referred to the International Court of Justice, unless in any case it is agreed by the parties to have recourse to another mode of settlement. If a difference arises between the United States on the one hand and a Member on the other hand, a request shall be made for an advisory opinion on any legal question involved in accordance with Article 96 of the Charter and Article 65 of the Statute of the Court. *The opinion given by the Court shall be accepted as decisive by the parties.* (Italics added).

Nations Commission of Human Rights, a subsidiary organ of the Economic and Social Council. His global mandate consisted of tasks including, *inter alia*, to enquire into substantial allegations concerning, and to identify and record attacks on, the independence of the judiciary, lawyers and court officials. On the basis of an interview which Mr Comaraswamy gave to a magazine, *International Commercial Litigation*, there appeared an article, *Malaysian Justice on Trial*, in the November 1995 issue of the journal. As a result of this he faced several lawsuits filed in Malaysian courts by plaintiffs who asserted that he used defamatory language during the course of his interview and they sought damages in several million dollars. However, the United Nations Secretary-General, Mr Kofi Annan, made several efforts to explain the matter to Malaysian authorities that Mr Comaraswamy had spoken in his official capacity of Special Rapporteur and was thus immune from legal process by virtue of Article VI, Section 22, of the Convention on the Privileges and Immunities of the United Nations. However, these efforts by the Secretary-General to ensure respect for Mr Comaraswamy's immunity had not achieved the desired result. At this on 5 August 1998, the Economic and Social Council of the United Nations, filed a request with the International Court of Justice asking an Advisory Opinion on the issue.

In order to pinpoint the issues involved in this case the Court began by recalling the question on which the advisory opinion had been requested is set forth in decision 1998/297 adopted by the United Nations Economic and Social Council on 5 August 1998. The decision read, *inter alia*, as follows:

> The Economic and Social Council, . . . Requests on priority basis, pursuant to Article 96, paragraph 2, of the Charter of the United Nations and in accordance with General Assembly resolution 89(1), an advisory opinion from the International Court of Justice on the legal question of the applicability of Article VI, Section 22, of the Convention on the Privileges and Immunities of the United Nations in the case of Dato' Param Cumaraswamy as Special Rapporteur of the Commission on Human Rights on the independence of judges and lawyers, taking into account the circumstances set out in paragraphs 1 to 15 of the note by the Secretary-General, and on *the legal obligations of Malaysia in this case.* (italics added)

The Court also observed in the request that the ECOSOC at the same time 'Calls upon the Government of Malaysia to ensure that all judgments and proceedings in this matter in the Malaysian courts are stayed pending receipt of the *advisory opinion of the International Court of Justice, which shall be accepted as decisive by the parties*'. (italics added).

The words '*the legal obligations of Malaysia*' read together with the 'note of the Secretary-General on the privileges and immunities of the Special Rapporteur of the Commission on Human Rights on the independence of judges and lawyers', annexed to the Request, brings in the light that issue to be considered by the Court is not just whether Mr Cumaraswamy is entitled to immunity from legal process for the words spoken by him during an interview, but related to that issue is the conduct of a sovereign State, Malaysia, together with the conduct of its courts and Foreign Secretary, which the Court has to consider. In other words an international organization, the United Nations, a machinery of international law, committed to promote and protect international human rights, is questioning the conduct of a sovereign State who has allegedly failed in carrying out its obligations under an international law instrument and whose executive and judicial authorities have allegedly denied a Special Rapporteur of the Commission on Human Rights immunity from legal process.

And, the words that '*the advisory opinion of the International Court of Justice, which shall be accepted as decisive by the parties*' not only carries a considerable weight as if a judgment in a contentious case is binding on the parties, but provides profound potential for the International Court to set an international precedent concerning the sovereign authority of a State in the face of a human rights matter.

The decision of the Court, in its *dispositif*, reflected six decisions as corollaries of the decision concerning the main equation of issue, *a Special Rapporteur of the Commission on Human Rights versus a sovereign State.* Three decisions pertained the special Rapporteur and the other three concerned the sovereign State. Regarding the Rapporteur the Court decided: 1) 'That Article VI, Section 22, of the Convention on the Privileges and Immunities of the United Nations is applicable in the case of Dato' Param Comaraswamy as Special Rapporteur of the Commission on Human Rights on the Independence of Judges and Lawyers. '2) "That Dato" Param Cumaraswamy is entitled to immunity from legal process of every kind for the words spoken by him during an interview as published in an article in the November 1995 issue of International Commercial Litigation.' 3) That Dato 'Param Cumaraswamy shall be held financially harmless for any costs imposed upon him by the Malaysian courts, in particular taxed costs.'

Judging on the legal obligations of Malaysia and its legal authorities, the Court decided: 1) 'That the Government of Malaysia had the obligation to inform the Malaysian courts of the finding of the Secretary-General that Dato' Param Cumaraswamy was entitled to immunity from legal process.' 2) 'That the Malaysian courts had the obligation to deal with the question of immunity from legal process as a preliminary issue to be expeditiously decided in limine litis.' 3) 'That the Government of Malaysia has the obligation to communicate this advisory opinion to the Malaysian courts, in order that Malaysia's international obligations be given effect and Dato' Param Cumaraswamy's immunity be respected.'

Human rights in contemporary international law occupy a place of no trivial importance. And, perhaps this is the only branch of international law which not only cuts across all domestic jurisdictions but also effects several principles of law governing other branches of international law. In the present case it is obvious that the issue of claims to immunity of a Special Rapporteur of the Commission on Human Rights has not only questioned the legal obligations of a sovereign State but also the conduct of national courts of that State. Viewing the independent discharge of human rights activities by a United Nations functionary the International Court of Justice did not fail to develop the law in such a way that a new development was brought to light that there is a difference between claims to immunity of a State functionary and claims to immunity by a United Nations functionary. The former functions in the interest of a sovereign State and the latter in the interest of the international community. Human rights are *erga omnes*, so must be seen their activities in various aspects. In this Advisory Opinion, which is of binding character as far as parties involved are concerned, the Court certainly has set two principles out: 1) it is the duty of a sovereign State to notify its national courts without delay of any finding by the Secretary-General concerning the immunity of a United Nations agent, and 2) the Secretary-General's finding carries a presumption of immunity which can only be set aside for the most compelling reasons.

Judge Weeramantry (Sri Lanka), the Vice-President of the Court when this case was decided, a born natural law subscriber with an exceptional commitment to the promotion of human rights, while fully agreeing with the conclusions of the Court set out in its Advisory Opinion wished to add a few observations stemming from the issues involved in the Opinion. One of these issues was the conceptual antecedents of the system of immunity for the United Nations officials who are engaged in their official duties. In view of the international legal system which draws upon its past experience of the international system of immunity evolved in regard to diplomats, consuls, members of armed forces, particularly under the sway of the principle of domestic autonomy, setting different degrees of immunity. Judge Weeramantry first stated the fact that there is a distinction between the immunities of the State officials and the immunities of the functionaries of the United Nations and then expressed the need for uniformity in the jurisprudence relating this matter. Particularly mindful of the sensitivity of this problem concerning the functions relating human rights he stated: 'In so sensitive a field as human rights, the freedom and independence of rapporteurs would be gravely affected if there should be varying standards and hence a resulting uncertainty regarding the principles applicable to this matter'.[3]

Judge Higgins, who voted in favour of all parts of the *dispositif* of the Advisory Opinion, in her article '*The Concept of' The State: 'Variable Geometry and Dualist Perception*', published after the delivery of the Opinion, found the opinion breaking new ground in several respects. In reality it is still the case that most international courts and *quasi* judicial bodies can deal only with 'states'. Also recalling that: Article 2(1) of the International Covenant on Civil and Political Rights provides that each state party to the Covenant undertakes to respect and ensure to all individuals within its jurisdiction the rights recognized therein. Further, Article 50 of the Covenant stipulates that its provisions extend to 'all parts' of federal states without limitation or exception; and also noticing that international courts, including the International Court of Justice, face comparable problems in its relations with particular states; Judge Higgins sees the contribution of the International Court to the development of international law by means of this Advisory Opinion in the following words: 'In a dispositif which broke new ground

[3] ICJ Reports 1999, Separate Opinion of Judge Weeramantry, p 96.

in going behind "the unitary veil of the State", the International Court determined, *inter alia*: "2(a). That the Government of Malaysia had the obligation to inform the Malaysian courts of the finding of the Secretary-General that Dato' Param Cumaraswamy was entitled to immunity from legal process; (b) that the Malaysian courts had the obligation to deal with the question of immunity from legal process as a preliminary issue to be expeditiously decided in *limine litis*... 4. That the Government of Malaysia has the obligation to communicate this Advisory Opinion to the Malaysian Courts, in order that Malaysia's international obligations be given effect and Dato' Param Cummaraswamy's immunity be respected."[4]

Judge Higgins continues and points out:

> the International Court for the first time made determinations directly on the conduct of the courts of a state.... This Advisory Opinion breaks new ground in advising a state as to its legal obligations, but recognizing also that various State organs comprise 'the state', and may indeed be required constitutionally to act independently of each other[5] (emphasis added).

It reflects drastic conditioning of the working of the principle of State sovereignty in international law, which in turn may make frequent determinations directly on the conduct of a sovereign state and its organs, judicial, executive, and legislative. This is conductive to achieve the aims and objectives of the United Nations, one of which is to promote and protect human rights.

[4] R Higgins, 'The Concept of "The State": Variable Geometry and Dualist Perceptions' in L Boisson de Chazournes and V Gowlland-Debbas, *The International Legal System in Quest of Equity and Universality: Liber Amicorum Georges Abi-Saab* (2001) 560.

[5] Higgins, *ibid.*

22

Legal Consequences of the Construction of a Wall in the Occupied Palestinian Territory (2003–04)[1]

Belligerent Occupation and Human Rights

I. Some Preliminary Observations

THE FIRST THING which this case brings to mind is that it is the law of belligerent occupation around which the whole problem evolves.

As far back as in 1992, two prominent professors, Richard Falk and Burns Weston, grasped the problems of occupation of Palestinian territories by Israel in the following words:

> . . . the occupier is confronted by threats to its security that arise . . . primarily, and especially in the most recent period, from a pronounced and sustained failure to restrict the character and terminate its occupation so as to restore the sovereign rights of the inhabitants. Israeli occupation, by its substantial violation of Palestinian rights, has itself operated as an inflaming agent that threatens the security of its administration of the territory, inducing reliance on more and more brutal practices to restore stability which in turn provokes the Palestinians even more. In effect, the illegality of the Israeli occupation regime itself set off an escalatory spiral of resistance and repression, and under these conditions all considerations of morality and reason establish a right of resistance inherent in the population. This right of resistance is an implicit legal corollary of the fundamental legal rights associated with the primacy of sovereign identity and assuring the humane protection of the inhabitants.[2]

[1] The composition of the Court in the Advisory Opinion of 9 July 2004 in the Wall case was: President Shi; Vice-President Ranjeva; Judges Guillaume, Koroma, Vereshchetin, Higgins, Parra-Aranguren, Kooijmans, Rezek, Al-Khasawneh, Buergenthal, Elaraby, Owada, Simma and Tomka (see ICJ Reports 2004, p 4).

Judges Koroma, Higgins, Kkoijmans, Al-Khasawneh, Elaraby and Owada appended separate opinions to the Advisory Opinion of the Court; Judge Buergenthal appended a declaration to the Advisory Opinion of the Court.

[2] R Falk and B Weston, 'The Relevance of International Law to Israeli and Palestinian Rights in the West Bank and Gaza' in E Playfair, (ed), *International Law and Administration of Occupied Territories* (Oxford, Claredon Press, 1992) ch 3, pp 146–47; also cited by Judge Elaraby in his Separate Opinion appended to the ICJ Advisory Opinion of 9 July 2004 in the case concerning *Legal Consequences of the construction of a Wall in the Occupied Palestinian Territory*, pp 8–9.

In violating human rights and human dignity of others you cannot expect that they will respect yours. Moses's second commandment—*do to others as you will be done by*—is neither simply Jewish nor simply biblical or theological. It is undeniably that voice of refined universal human conscience which in its essence is simply constant in human nature. Take it or leave it but you cannot change it, for you are bound to face its corollary principle: *as you sow so shall you reap.* Given a profound thought, one would find that in these two interrelated principles lies the essential core of any system of law and justice, including the international legal system and justice.

'Even in the present international environment, in which anti-terrorism measures challenge old liberties and freedoms, it is not denied that a balance must be struck between respect for basic human rights and the interests of security'.[3] (John Dugard)

II. Facts of the Case in a Nutshell

This advisory case revolves around a *'wall'* being built by Israel *in the 'Occupied Palestinian Territory.'* Israel as the 'Occupying Power' contends that: a) the Court lacks jurisdiction to consider the case, b) if the Court finds that it has jurisdiction, as a matter of judicial propriety it should decline to answer the request, c) the construction of the wall is an action under right of self-defence to counter terrorist attacks from the West Bank and it is a temporary measure, and d) greater parts of international humanitarian law and human rights law do not apply in the occupied Palestinian territories. Palestine, being in the process of achieving its status of an independent State and claiming its *right to self-determination*, contends that a) the construction of the wall in the Occupied Palestinian Territory is 'the *de facto* annexation of land' which interferes with the territorial sovereignty and consequently with the right of the Palestinian people to self-determination, and b) the occupation and the construction of the wall violates numerous rules under international humanitarian law and human rights law. With regard to this Israeli occupation the UN *General Assembly* has referred to the two salient points. First: the principle of *'the inadmissibility of the acquisition of territory by war'* must be respected by the belligerent occupier. And the second: its concern about human rights violations by the belligerent Israel in the Occupied Palestinian Territory reflected in one of the documents forming part of the Secretary-General's dossier stating:

[3] J Dugard in Report of the Special Rapporteur of the Commission on Human Rights; J Dugard, on the situation of human rights in the Palestinian territories occupied by Israel since 1967, submitted in accordance with Commission resolution 1993/2 A, United Nations Economic and Social Council Distribution No E/CN4/2004/6, dated 8 September 2003, p 6. The document also formed part of the United Nations Secretary-General's dossier to the International Court of Justice in this advisory case.

> Many of the rights contained in the International Covenant on Civil and Political Rights and the International Covenant on Economic, Social and Cultural Rights have been violated by the Israel Defence Forces (IDF) in their actions against the Palestinian People. Many of the obligations of international humanitarian law have likewise been violated. . . . There must be some limit to the extent to which human rights may be violated in the name of counter-terrorism.[4]

With this background, the General Assembly decided on 8 December 2003 vide its resolution ES–10/14 to ask the advisory opinion of the Court on the *following question*:

> What are the legal consequences arising from the construction of the wall being built by Israel, the occupying power, in the Occupied Palestinian Territory, including in and around East Jerusalem, as described in the report of the Secretary-General, considering the rules and principles of international law, including the Fourth Geneva Convention of 1949, and relevant Security Council and General Assembly resolutions.[5]

III. Historical Analysis of the Occupied Territory

Finding unanimously that it has jurisdiction to give the advisory opinion to the United Nations General Assembly, the Court decided by fourteen votes to one that there was no compelling reason precluding it from giving the requested opinion.

Having decided these preliminary questions of jurisdiction and propriety, and before proceeding to address the legal consequences of the construction of the wall, the Court considered whether the construction of the wall is legal or illegal. To this end it first made a brief historical analysis of the territory in question. The Court noted that having been part of the Ottomon Empire, Palestine, after the First World War, was an 'A' class mandate entrusted by the League of Nations to Great Britain. The United Kingdom evacuated the mandated territory on 29 November 1947. Meanwhile, on 29 November 1947, the General Assembly of the United Nations adopted resolution 181(II) on the future of Palestine. The resolution recommended to the United Kingdom and to all other Members of the United Nations a partition of the territory in three parts: 1) One Arab State, 2) One Jewish State, and 3) the creation of a special international regime for the City of Jerusalem. The Arab population of Palestine and the Arab States rejected this plan, but Israel, on 14 May 1948 proclaimed its independence on the strength of this resolution. After the hostilities of 1948–49 between Arab and Israeli forces a general armistice agreement was signed between Jordan and Israel fixing the demarcation line, popularly known as 'Green Line' for the colour of this line on the map was green, between Arab and Israeli forces. Article III, paragraph 2, of the agreement

[4] United Nations Economic and Social Councils document E/CN4/2004/6 dated 8 September 2003: J Dugard, Report of the Special Rapporteur on Human Rights, on the situation of human rights in the Palestinian territories occupied by Israel since 1967, submitted in accordance with Commission resolution 1993/2 A, p 6.

[5] ICJ Reports 2004, p 7.

provided that 'No element of the . . . military or para-military forces of either Party . . . shall advance beyond or pass over for any purpose whatsoever the Armistice Demarcation Lines . . .'. The war erupted again in 1967. At the close of its analysis, the Court noted that the territories situated between the Green Line and the former eastern boundary of Palestine under the Mandate were *occupied* by Israel in 1967 during the armed conflict between Israel and Jordan. Under customary international law, Court observed these were therefore *occupied territories* in which Israel had the status of *occupying power*. After a thorough historical analysis the Court concluded: 'All these territories (including East Jerusalem) remain occupied territories and Israel has continued to have the status of occupying Power.'[6]

In 2002, Israel began constructing a wall which ran not only across its own territory but also across the West Bank territory of Palestine, which forms part of the '*occupied Palestinian territory*'. The argument for constructing this wall was to *combat terrorist attacks* coming from the Palestinians in the West Bank. According to Palestinian authorities the construction constituted a form of *illegal annexation* of their territory, undermining their *right to self-determination*. The question put by the General Assembly concerns the legal consequences of the construction of that wall. In order to indicate those consequences the Court must first determine whether or not the construction of the wall breaches international law. In determining the rules and principles of international law relevant in assessing the legality of the wall, the Court observed that such rules and principles are to be found in the following: the United Nations Charter, treaty and customary international humanitarian law and human rights law, and relevant resolutions adopted by General Assembly and Security Council pursuant to the Charter.

IV. Human Rights Law Does Apply in the Occupied Territories

Human Rights as a legal doctrine may also be defined as a comprehensive term comprising all the human values the law of human rights provides to be observed as rules and principles in relation to our fellow human beings. And, human dignity lies in knowing and rightly reflecting those values, rules and principles when dealing with our fellow human beings, irrespective of their nationality, political, social, economic and cultural background. There hardly is a legal principle which does not have its corresponding underlying principle of universal moral or religious principle. For a particular State of Israel, mainly a Jewish State, the underlying principle to aforementioned is the second commandment of Moses: do to others as you will be done by. The principle certainly bears the authority of Moses but none can deny the existence of its equivalent human virtue in all other legal, political, religious, moral, etc systems. Hence, the principle is a common univer-

[6] ICJ Reports 2004, para 78, p 167. For a detailed historical analysis made by the Court see paras 70–78, pp 165–67.

sal human virtue, and, as far as international law of human rights is concerned it is the principle of respecting human dignity of others as we would like them to respect ours, be it at individual or State level.

Whereas the construction of the wall was considered as a temporary measure by Israel to combat terrorism, Palestinian authorities saw it as *illegal annexation* of their territory, undermining their *right to self-determination.* Putting the *right of self-determination* in its historical perspective, the starting point for the Court was that after the First World War Palestine was entrusted to Great Britain as class 'A' mandate Article 22, paragraph 4, of the League of Nations Covenant which provided that: 'Certain communities, formerly belonging to the Turkish Empire have reached a stage of development where their existence as independent nations can be provisionally recognized subject to the rendering of administrative advice and assistance by a Mandatory until such time as they are able to stand alone'. Observing mandates in general, the Court then recalled its own ruling in the Advisory Opinion on the *International Status of South West Africa:* 'The Mandate was created, in the interest of the inhabitants of the territory, and of humanity in general, as an international institution with an international object—a *sacred trust of civilization.*' The Court also recalled that it held in the same ruling that two principles were considered to be of 'paramount importance': 1) 'the principle of *non-annexation,* and 2) the *principle that the well being* of the people not yet able to govern themselves is a sacred trust of civilization.'

In the course of assessing the applicability of international humanitarian law and human rights law to the Occupied Palestinian Territory, the Court also recalled Article 2, paragraph 4, of the United Nations Charter providing: 'All Members shall refrain in their international relations from the *threat or use of force* against the territorial integrity or political independence of any State, or in any other manner inconsistent with the Purposes of the United Nations.' The Court also noted that the UN General Assembly adopted a resolution in 1970 declaring: '*No territorial acquisition resulting from the threat or use of force shall be recognized as legal.*'[7] Recalling its own case law in the case concerning *Military and Paramilitary Activities in and against Nicaragua* (see chapter 8) stating that the *principles as to the use of force* incorporated in the Charter reflects customary international law, the Court added that 'the same is true of its corollary entailing the illegality of territorial acquisition resulting from the threat or use of force.'[8]

Further, the Court also noted that the principle of self-determination of peoples has been enshrined in the United Nations Charter and in the Article 1 common to the International Covenant on Civil and Political Rights and the International Covenant on Economic, Social and Cultural Rights. In order first to emphasize that the principle of *self determination* was born out of the grand human principle of the sacred trust of civilization the Court again recalled its law developed in

[7] *Ibid,* para 87, p 171; United Nations General Assembly Resolution 2625(XXV) entitled 'Declaration on Principles of International Law concerning Friendly Relations and Co-operation among States.

[8] ICJ Reports 2004, para 87, p 171.

Namibia[9] (see chapter 16) and *Western Sahara*[10] (see chapter 14) advisory cases, and then, to make it clear that the right of self-determination is *'today a right erga omnes'*[11] it cited its own case law from the case concerning *East Timor.*[12] (See chapter 9). The Court observed that the position of Israel that the construction of the wall was temporary and did not amount to annexation actually which creating a *'fait accompli'* on the ground that it could well become permanent, in which case it would be tantamount to *de facto annexation.* Hence, the Court concluded that the construction 'severely impedes the exercise by the Palestinian people of its right to self-determination, and therefore a breach of Israel's obligation to respect that right.'[13]

By putting these heavy weight *humane elements* around the principle of self-determination at stake in such a volatile situation as the belligerent occupation of Palestinian territory where the international political equation of the day appears as *human rights v terrorism* the Court has added an immense sacredness of law to the right of self-determination and to the process leading towards its achievement by the Palestinian people. It emphasizes the human dignity of the occupied Palestinian people as against belligerent occupier, the sovereign State of Israel. By reaffirming its *erga omnes* character it reminds the international community that people anywhere struggling for their right to self-determination are the sacred trust of the civilization and to protect their human dignity is the sacred legal duty of the community as a whole and to respect their human dignity is the sole responsibility of the States governing them.

Israel, however, denied that the International Covenant on Civil and Political Rights and the International Covenant on Economic, Social and Cultural Rights, whereas to both of which it actually is a party, are applicable to the occupied Palestinian territory. Its assertion was based on the reasoning that 'humanitarian law is the protection granted in a conflict situation such as the one in the West Bank and Gaza Strip, whereas human rights were intended for the protection from their own Government in times of peace'.[14]

This assertion of Israel considerably narrows the scope of human rights by meaning: 1) human rights can be claimed only in peace times and not in times of war or any conflict situation, and 2) human rights are meant only for the protection from individuals' own government, ie, only on the territory of a State's own territory. Actually, the Court took notice of the fact that in its communications to the United Nations Human Rights Committee and the Committee on Economic,

[9] Legal Consequences for States of the Continued Presence of South Africa in Namibia (South West Africa) nothwithstanding Security Council Resolution 276(1970), Advisory Opinion, ICJ Reports 1971, paras 52–53, p 31.

[10] Western Sahara, Advisory Opinion, ICJ Reports 1975, para 162, p 68.

[11] It may again be recalled here that this revolutionary concept that human rights are *erga omnes* was developed by the Court in its *Barcelona Traction (Belgium v Spain)* case (see ch 6).

[12] *East Timor* (*Portugal v Australia*), Judgment, ICJ Reports 1995, para 29, p 102.

[13] ICJ Reports 2004, para 122, p 184.

[14] *Ibid*, para 102, p 177.

Social and Cultural Rights Israel has consistently maintained that both the Covenants do not apply to the areas that are not subject to its sovereign territory and jurisdiction, hence to the occupied Palestinian territories.

In order to determine this the Court first addressed the issue of the relationship between international humanitarian law and human rights law and the applicability of human rights instruments outside national territory. In rejecting the Israeli argument, of splitting the applicability *ratione temporis* of these two fields of international law the Court at once recalled its own case law developed in the advisory case of *Legality of the Threat or Use of Nuclear Weapons* (see chapter 20) citing:

> the protection of the International Covenant of Civil and Political Rights does not cease in times of war, except by operation of Article 4 of the Covenant whereby certain provisions may be derogated from in a time of national emergency. Respect for the right to life is not, however, such a provision. In principle, the right not to arbitrarily be deprived of one's life applies also in hostilities. The test of what is an arbitrary deprivation of life, however, then falls to be determined by the applicable *lex specialis*, namely, the law applicable in armed conflict which is designed to regulate the conduct of hostilities.[15]

More generally, the Court considered that the protection offered by human rights conventions does not cease in case of armed conflict, except through the effect of provisions for derogation of the kind stated in Article 4 of the International Covenant on Civil and Political Rights. In further clarifying the law as regards the relationship between international humanitarian law and human rights law, the Court described three situations: 1) some rights may be exclusively matters of international humanitarian law, 2) others may be exclusively matters of human rights law, and 3) yet others may be matters of both these branches of international law.[16] This proves that international humanitarian law and human rights law are two different sides of the same coin we may call human dignity, the currency of the school of human rights. Hence, in order to answer the question put to it the Court found it necessary to take into consideration both these branches of international law.

After a thorough examination of the scope of the International Covenant on Civil and Political Rights the Court observed that:

> while the jurisdiction of States is primarily territorial, it may sometimes be exercised outside its national territory. Considering the *object and purpose* of the International Covenant on Civil and Political Rights, it would seem natural that, even when such is the case, States parties to the Covenant should be bound to comply with its provisions.[17] (italics are mine).

What carries to the humanization of international law in this statement of the Court are the words *'object and purpose,'* indicative of broad and liberal interpretation in the text of the word *'natural,'* indicative of the natural law approach

[15] Advisory Opinion of 8 July 1996 on the case *Legality of the Threat or Use of NuclearWeapons*, ICJ Reports 1996, para 25, p 240.

[16] ICJ Reports 2004, para 106, p 178.

[17] *Ibid*, para 109, p 179.

of human rights, Judge Tanaka's strongly advocated approach in the 1966 Judgment in the *South West Africa* cases (see chapter 5). Hence, the Court concluded: 'the International Covenant on Civil and Political Rights is applicable in respect of acts done by a State in the exercise of its jurisdiction outside its own territory,'[18] hence also in the occupied territory of Palestine.

Examining in the same legal vein the scope of the International Covenant on Economic, Social and Cultural Rights, the Court noted that no doubt that 'this Covenant guarantees rights which are essentially territorial'. 'However, it is not to be excluded that it applies *both* to territories over which a State party has sovereignty *and* to those over which that State exercises territorial jurisdiction.'[19] The Court further observed that: '. . . the territories occupied by Israel have for over 37 years been subject to its territorial jurisdiction as occupying Power. In the exercise of the powers available to it on this basis, Israel is bound by the provisions of the International Covenant on Economic, Social and Cultural Rights.'[20]

As regards the Convention on the Rights of the Child, making a brief mention that the instrument containing Article 2 according to which 'States Parties shall respect and ensure the rights set forth in the . . . Convention to each child within their jurisdiction . . .', the Court found therefore that the Convention is applicable within the Occupied Palestinian Territory.[21]

By reaching a conclusion, based on a thorough analysis, that the instruments of International Covenant on Civil and Political Rights, International Covenant on Economic, Social and Cultural Rights, and the Convention on the Rights of the Child are applicable in the occupied territory, the Court has considerably broadened the scope of these major human rights instruments. Noteworthy of the Court's reasoning and interpretation of the human rights instruments in this case is that by highlighting the concept of territorial jurisdiction of State into two distinct jurisdictions, 1) territories over which a State party has sovereignty, and 2) territories over which that State exercises territorial jurisdiction, the Court has universalised the territorial applicability of human rights law and circumvented the traditional sovereign power of States in depriving individuals, irrespective of their nationality, of their human rights and respect for human dignity. This is a step forward for the cause of human dignity and a step backward for the traditional narrow meaning of State sovereignty

[18] *Ibid*, para 111, p 180.
[19] *Ibid*, para 112, p 180.
[20] *Ibid*, para 112, p 181.
[21] *Ibid*, para 113, p 181.

V. International Humanitarian Law Does Apply in the Occupied Territory: The Rules of International Humanitarian Law are Binding on All Nations and the Law is *Erga Omnes*

International humanitarian law, according to Professor Buergenthal (now a Judge at the ICJ) can be defined as 'the human rights component of the law of war'.[22] Other than the customary international law, the principal treaty sources of this law are four Geneva Conventions of 1949 and Hague Conventions of 1899 and 1907. Pertinent to this case, as the treatment of civilians in the Occupied Palestinian Territory by Israeli authorities is in question, are the Hague Regulations annexed to Hague Convention of 1907 and the Fourth Geneva Convention of 1949.

As the military authority of Israel over the Occupied Palestinian Territory is of great relevance in this case, and Section III of the Hague Regulations concerns the 'Military authority over the territory of the hostile State,' the Court found those regulations 'particularly pertinent in the present case.' The Court noticed the first difficulty that Israel is not a party to the Fourth Hague Convention of 1907, to which Hague Regulations are annexed. It considered, however, the following three important elements: 1) those regulations were prepared 'to revise the general laws and customs of war', 2) later, the International Military Tribunal of Nuremburg has found that 'the rules laid down in the Convention were recognized by all civilized nations, and were regarded as being declaratory of the laws and customs of war', and 3) The Court itself reached the same conclusion when examining the rights and duties of belligerents in their conduct of military operations in the case concerning *Legality of the Threat or Use of Nuclear Weapons* (see chapter 20). Hence, the Court observed that: 'the provisions of the Hague Regulations have become part of customary law, as in fact recognized by all the participants before the Court.'[23] The Court also observed that, pursuant to Article 154, of the Fourth Geneva Convention, that Convention is supplementary to Section II and III of the Hague Regulations.

By so interpreting the Regulations, the Court reaffirmed that the rules of Hague Regulations have become customary international law and they are binding on all States, including Israel, irrespective of their being parties or non-parties to them.

Generally speaking, four Geneva Conventions of 1949 are the principal sources of international humanitarian law. The Fourth Geneva Convention, relative to the Protection of Civilian Persons in Time of War, is however of particular concern in this case. Though Israel is a party to this instrument, yet, contrary to the great majority of other participants, it disputed the applicability *de jure* of the Convention to the Occupied Palestinian Territory contending that under Article

[22] T Buergenthal, *Public International Law in a Nutshell*, 2nd edn, (St Paul, MN, West Publishing, 1990) 142.

[23] ICJ Reports 2004, para 89, p 172.

2, paragraph 2, of the Convention it applies only in the case of occupied territories falling under the sovereignty of a High Contracting Party involved in an armed conflict. Relying on this provision Israel mentioned two main reasons in support of its position: 1) the lack of recognition of the territory as sovereign prior to its annexation by Jordan and Egypt, and 2) inferring that it was not a territory of a High Contracting Party as required by the Conventions.[24]

The Court examined the intentions of the Convention drafters, related *travaux préparatoires*, and the statements made by States parties. The Court noted that, according to the first paragraph of Article 2 of the Fourth Geneva Convention, that Convention applies when *two conditions* are met: 1) when there exists an armed conflict (whether or not a state of war has been recognized, and 2) when the conflict has arisen between two contracting parties. If these two conditions are fulfilled, the Convention applies, *in particular in any territory occupied in the course of the conflict by one of the contracting parties.*[25] The *object* of the second paragraph of Article 2, which refers to 'occupation of the territory of a High Contracting Party', is, according to the Court, *not to restrict the scope* of the application of the Convention, as defined by the first paragraph, by excluding there from territories not falling under the sovereignty of one of the contracting parties. On the contrary, it simply aims at making it clear that, even if occupation effected during the conflict met no armed resistance, the Convention is still applicable.[26]

Further, in examining the consequences for all State parties to the Fourth Geneva Convention, the Court first emphatically recalled the text of Article 1 of the Fourth Geneva Convention, a provision common to all four Geneva Conventions, that 'The High Contracting Parties undertake to respect and to ensure respect for the present Convention in all circumstances.'[27] Later, it reminded signatories to the Fourth Convention that: '*every State party to that Convention, whether or not it is a party to a specific conflict, is under an obligation to ensure that the requirements of the instruments in question are complied with*'.[28] Though the Court does not indicate how, and leaves it up to the States, but implies for any individual or collective action and approach to protect human rights ensuing from the Geneva Conventions.

Hence, the Court reaffirmed that not being a party to a specific conflict does not relieve a State from the obligations resulting from the Fourth Geneva Convention. To this Araujo commented: 'Of particular significance in this advisory opinion is the fact that the *Fourth Geneva Convention applies to all cases of occupation* of the territory of a High Contracting Party, *regardless of whether the occupation is accompanied by armed resistance.*'[29] (emphasis added).

[24] ICJ Reports 2004, para 90, p 173.

[25] *Ibid*, para 95, pp 174–75.

[26] *Ibid*, para 95, pp 175.

[27] *Ibid*, para 158, p 199.

[28] *Ibid*, para 158, pp 199–200.

[29] RJ Araujo, 'Implementation of the ICJ Advisory Opinion: Legal Consequences of the Construction of a Wall in the Occupied Palestinian Territory: Fences (Do Not) Make Good Neighbours' (2004) 22(2) *Boston University International Law Journal* 370.

The Court recalled its own statement in the *Advisory Opinion on the Legality of the Threat or Use of Nuclear Weapons*: 'a great many rules of humanitarian law applicable in armed conflict are so fundamental to the respect of the human person and "elementary considerations of humanity" . . .', that they are 'to be observed by all States whether or not they have ratified the conventions that contain them, because they constitute intransgressible principles of international customary law. . . . In the Court's view, these rules incorporate obligations which are essentially of an *erga omnes* character.'[30]

It must be recalled that the principle of *elementary considerations of humanity* was developed by the ICJ in its very first contentious case of *Corfu Channel* (see chapter 4). And, the principle of *human rights are erga omnes* was formulated by the Court in dealing with the *Barcelona Traction* case (see chapter 6). The Court went a step further in this case by characterizing a great many rules of international humanitarian law as *erga omnes.*

VI. Terrorism v Self-Defence: Grave Infringement of Human Rights cannot be Justified by Military Exigencies and National Security

Israeli government has justified the construction of the wall and the actions related thereto by its defence forces as steps taken in *self-defence* and to counter *terrorist attacks.* Israel based this argument on three legal grounds: 1) its inherent right of self-defence under Article 51 of the United Nations Charter; 2) Security Council resolutions 1368 (2001) and 1373 (2001), passed after 9/11,[31] which provide support for certain claims made by States exercising the right of self-defence against terrorist activities; and 3) that a state of necessity existed for the erection and maintenance of the security wall.

The Court stated that Article 51 of the Charter undoubtedly recognizes the existence of an inherent right of self-defence in the case of an armed attack. *But* it does so when the attack is by one State against another State. The Court also observed that Israel does not claim that the attacks against it are imputable to a *foreign State.*

Regarding the Israeli argument based on Security Council resolutions, the Court also noted that Israel exercised control in the Occupied Palestinian Territory and that, as Israel itself stated, the threat which it regarded as justifying the construction of the wall originated within, and *not outside*, that territory. Consequently, the Court concluded: 'The situation is thus different from that contemplated by Security Council resolutions 1368 (2001) and 1373 (2001), and therefore Israel could not in any event invoke those resolutions in support of its claim to be exercising a right of self-defence.'

[30] ICJ Reports 2004, para 157, p 199.

[31] 9/11 has become a short form to describe the 11 September 2001 terrorist attack on World Trade Centre building in the United States.

By emphasizing the *'foreign'* and *'outside'* elements in interpreting the right of self-defence as a measure to counter terrorism the Court has greatly contributed to oblige States not to use the right of self-defence as a justification to use force unilaterally in the name of terrorism. The clarification has been added to the law that the right to self-defence under Article 51 of the United Nations Charter applies *only* when an armed attack is made by one *State* against another *State.* As far as the Security Council resolutions are concerned, Gray commenting in this context also stated: 'The situation was thus different from that contemplated by Security Council resolutions 1368 and 1372 which had recognized *a wide right of self-defence against global terrorism*[32] (emphasis added).

Turning to the Israeli claim to state of necessity, the Court again relied on its own case law in the case concerning the *Gabcikovo-Nagymaros Project* (Hungary/Slovakia) in which it ruled: 'the state of necessity is a ground recognized by customary international law' that 'can only be accepted on an exceptional basis'; it 'can only be invoked under certain strictly defined conditions which must be cumulatively satisfied; and the State concerned is not the sole judge of whether conditions have been met'[33] It further added that one of these conditions was stated by the Court in terms used by the International Law Commission, in a text which in its present form requires that the act being challenged be 'the only way for the State to safeguard an essential interest against a grave and imminent peril'.[34] Hence, the Court was not convinced that the construction of the wall along the route chosen was the *only* means to safeguard the interests of Israel against the peril invoked by it as justification for the construction.

Hence, the Court considered that 'Israel cannot rely on a right of self-defence or on a state of necessity in order to preclude the wrongfulness of the construction of the wall . . .. The Court accordingly finds that the construction of the wall, and its associated regime, are contrary to international law.'[35]

The Court also observed that:

> The Court . . . is not convinced that the specific course Israel has chosen for the wall was necessary to maintain its security objectives. The wall, along the route chosen, and its associated régime a number of rights of Palestinians residing in the territory occupied by Israel, and the infringements resulting from that route cannot be justified by *military exigencies* or by the requirements of *national security* or public order.[36]

[32] C Gray, 'The ICJ Advisory Opinion on Legal Consequences of the Construction of a Wall in the Occupied Palestinian Territory' (2004) 63 *Cambridge Law Journal* 531.

[33] ICJ Reports 1997, para 51, p 40.

[34] The Court here referred to Article 25 of the International Law Commission's Articles on Responsibility of States for Internationally Wrongful Acts; ICJ Reports 2004, para 140, p 195.

[35] *Ibid*, para 142, p 195.

[36] *Ibid*, para 137, p 193.

VII. The Court's Advice to the General Assembly: Human Rights are Violated by Israel and They Must be Enforced by All States

Having concluded that by constructing the wall Israel has violated certain international obligations, the Court held Israel responsible for *not respecting* the Palestinian people's *right to self-determination* and for *violating* its obligations under *international humanitarian law and human rights law*.[37] *In sum*, the Court found, that the construction of the wall has resulted in the destruction or requisition of Palestinian properties under conditions which *contravened the Fourth Geneva Convention*, impeded the freedom of movement of inhabitants and breached their right to work, to health and to education.[38]

Having examined the legal consequences of those violations,[39] the Court announced its final ruling as follows:

Wall is Illegal:

'The construction of the wall being built by Israel, the occupying Power, in the occupied Palestinian Territory, including in and around East Jerusalem, and its associate régime, are contrary to international law.'[40] This is a ruling to the effect that the act of constructing a wall by an occupying power in the territory of the people occupied is violating human rights and human dignity of those people.

Israel Must Undo the Illegal Construction:

The Court required Israel to undo the illegal construction in the following manner declaring: 1) Israel is under an obligation to terminate its breaches of international law, 2) to cease forthwith the works of the construction of the wall being built, 3) to dismantle forthwith the structure therein situated, 4) to repeal and render ineffective forthwith all legislative and regulatory acts relating thereto, in accordance with paragraph 151 of the Court's Opinion.[41] This is asking the occupying power to restore human rights and human dignity of the people occupied.

Israel Must Make Reparations for Damages:

The Court declared that: 'Israel is under an obligation to make reparation for all damage caused by the construction of the wall in the Occupied Palestinian

[37] Advisory Opinion of 9 July 2004 in the case concerning *Legal Consequences of the Construction of a Wall in the Occupied Palestinian Territory*, ICJ Reports 2004, paras 114–42, pp 181–95.

[38] *Ibid*, paras 123–37, pp 184–94.

[39] *Ibid*, paras 143–60, pp 195–200.

[40] *Ibid*, para 163, 3A, p 201.

[41] *Ibid*, para 163, 3B, p 201–2.

Territory, including in and around East Jerusalem.'[42] This is a remedy that restores human dignity of the occupied Palestinians and directs Israel to behave according to the dignity of an occupying power.

All States Must Ensure Compliance by Israel:

All States are under an obligation: 1) not to recognize the illegal situation resulting from the construction of the wall, 2) not to render aid or assistance in maintaining the situation created by such construction.[43]

> . . . all States parties to the Fourth Geneva Convention relative to the Protection of Civilian Persons in Time of War of 12 August 1949 have in addition the obligation, while respecting the United Nations Charter and international law, to ensure compliance by Israel with international humanitarian law as embodied in that Convention.[44]

The Court here promotes the concept of collective responsibility of the international community and the principle of international rule of law in the face of a situation in which an occupying power has violated human rights and human dignity of the very people considered to be a sacred trust of civilization.

The United Nations Must Consider Further Action:

'The United Nations, and especially the General Assembly and the Security Council, should consider what further action is required to bring to an end the illegal situation resulting from the construction of the wall and associated regime, taking due account of the present Advisory Opinion'.[45] By directly urging and directing the two key institutions of the United Nations, the General Assembly and Security Council, *the Court as the guardian of international law is reminding the world's legislature and executive, respectively, in the making* that it is high time that they act as the UN Charter obliges the world's governing institutions to act in order to protect human rights and human dignity of a people victimized by an occupying power.

VIII. Conclusion

It is true that according to the provisions of the UN Charter and the ICJ Statute, advisory opinions rendered by the ICJ are non-binding in character, however, as observed by Peter Bekker, they are not altogether without any legal effect.[46]

[42] Advisory Opinion of 9 July 2004 in the case concerning *Legal Consequences of the Construction of a Wall in the Occupied Palestinian Territory*, ICJ Reports 2004, para 163, 3C, p 202.

[43] *Ibid*, para 163, 3D, p 202.

[44] *Ibid.*

[45] *Ibid*, para 163, 3E, p 202.

[46] PHF Bekker *ASIL Insights*, 'The World Court Rules that Israel's West Bank Barrier Violates International Law', http://www.asil.org/insights/insigh 141.htm, p 4. Bekker States: 'This non-binding charcter does not mean that such opinions are without legal effect, because the legal reasoning embodied in them reflect authoraitative views on important issues of international law'.

Christine Gray also commented on this Advisory Opinion in a similar manner: 'The Court issued a clear and unequivocal opinion which, although technically not binding, represents an authoritative statement of the legal position.'[47]

Four conclusions from this authoritative statement of the International Court of Justice seem very obvious. 1) Belligerent occupation is not immune to human rights. 2) The people not yet able to govern themselves, be they under a belligerent occupation, are a sacred trust of civilization; the principle of non-annexation and the principle of their well-being remain to be strictly observed by their occupying power. 3) By recalling, applying and further developing almost every major human rights principle developed by the Court throughout its adjudicational career and supporting its reasoning by citing from almost every principal case in which those principles were developed, the Court's reasoning in this advisory opinion has presented an ocean of human rights in a drop of human dignity. 4) The Court in this case—first, by limiting the scope of the use of force under the right to self defence, secondly by developing the scope of collective measures at the international community level, certainly implying the right to collective use of force by the international community, and finally by adopting the broadest possible human rights approach through the application of the rules of international humanitarian law and human rights—has presented to the international community an adequate model of global governance based on the legal culture of human rights whose greatest characteristic reflects the respect for human dignity, of human dignity and by human dignity in all its forms and aspects.

If there was any case in which the Court rigorously applied every inch the approach of human rights to its judicial decision making process it was this.

[47] C Gray, 'The ICJ Advisory Opinion on Legal Consequences of the Construction of a Wall in the Occupied Palestinian Territory' (2004) 63 *Cambridge Law Journal* 528.

23

Summary and General Conclusion

IT IS IMPORTANT to recall in full that the inspiration to write this book came from the words: 'There are no limits to the heights that a human being can attain, nor to the depths that he can sink. It is for you to choose between the heights of bliss and happiness or the depths of pain and agony.'[1]

We discussed that 'you' for us is *'We, the peoples of the United Nations.'* The choice of heights to be attained by us was made by choosing the path of human rights at the core of the international legislative conscience of the United Nations Charter. The depths to which the perverted human conscience sank was identified with the scourge of terrorism in two World Wars. The choice of the path of human rights was made by *'we, the peoples of the United Nations'* having suffered the *pain and agony* at the hands of *fascist terrorism* between 1939 and 1945. The resolve was to save succeeding generations from revisiting that scourge of terrorism.

Respect for human dignity and protection of human rights are the two great hall-marks of any ideal democratic society worth its name. With the growing 'pluralization' of society at every level (national, regional or international) and the evolving human interaction and communication (involving legal actors from all walks of life, such as legislators, judges, jurists, etc) in all forms is it still proper to view the traditional relation between the legislator and the judge as: one making the law and the other simply applying it? Setting the perspective at the outset of this book, aiming to find the contribution of the International Court of Justice to the development of human rights law, two questions were asked[2] from the theoretical point of view: First, what is the legislative role of the judge?,[3] and the second, what is the relationship between human rights and international law?[4]

The answer to the first question sounded in the following three voices of three prominent judges: first, the following famous expression—which has truly become a cardinal point in the philosophy of judicial legislation—of American celebrity Judge Oliver Holmes: 'I recognize without hesitation that judges do and must legislate, but they can do so only interstitially; they are confined from molar to molecule.'[5]

[1] MC Singh, *Quest for Light*, 4th edn, (Panjab, India, Radha Soami Satsang Beas, 1988) 54.

[2] In Part I.

[3] In ch 2.

[4] In ch 3.

[5] *Southern Pacific Co v Jensen*, 244 US 205 (1917) p 221.see also in the F Rigaux, *La Loi des Juges* (Paris, Editions Odile Jacob, 1997) 247; and also in E Bodenheimer, *Jurisprudence: The Philosophy and the Method of the Law* (1974) 442. Neil MacCormick provides a good commentary on the Holmes'

The Second, the voice of a former Chief Justice of Indian Supreme Court, Justice Bhagwati: 'Law-making is an inherent and inevitable part of the judicial process. Even where a Judge is concerned with interpretation of a statute, there is ample scope for him to develop and mould the law. It is he, who infuses life and blood into the dry skeleton provided by the Legislature and creates a living organism appropriate and adequate to meet the needs of the society and by *thus making and moulding the law, he takes part in the work of creation.* A Judge is not a mimic. Greatness on the bench lies in creativity. The process of judging is a phase of a never ending movement and something more is expected of a Judge than mere imitative reproduction, lifeless repetition of a mechanical routine. It is for this reason that when a law comes before a Judge, he has to invest it with meaning and content and in this process of interpretation he makes law.'[6] (italics are mine) And the third, the voice of a former President of the International Court of Justice, Judge Lachs:

> Judgment is a process of mind that some claim to know and others continue to discover. Each judgment is either a step forward or a step backward in the development of law. As a result, since each judgment is the product of the minds of several individuals—*how each understands and interprets the law*—judges *cannot avoid being vital force in the life of the law.*[7] (italics are mine)

Hence, we settled with the conclusion that judges do legislate in the sense that they clarify and develop the law in the process of applying and interpreting the law. And, by this process they further refine the legislative spirit, the common legislative conscience of 'we the peoples.'

As a corollary of the first question we also examined the view of Prof Merrills that: the extent to which the decisions of an international tribunal develop the law depends in large measure on which of two general judicial ideologies.—1) the ideology of judicial restraint and 2) the ideology of judicial activism—the members of the Court subscribe to.[8] And further we found that when an international court develops the law, the direction, the subject matter, in which it does so is again influenced by two of the specific ideologies—1) tough conservatism and 2) benevolent liberalism.[9] Hence, how a judge *understands and interprets* law depends in large measure also on which doctrine or school of law, such as positivist school of State sovereignty and the human rights school of human dignity, the judge bases his reasoning. The ideologies of judicial restraint and tough conservatism were identified with the school of State sovereignty and the ideologies of

expression 'interstitially' in his book N MacCormick, *Legal Reasoning and Legal Theory* (Oxford, Clarendon Press, 1978) pp 122 and 187–88.

[6] Cited by Justice RP Sethi in KL Bhatia, (ed), *Judicial Activism and Social Change* (1990) 40.

[7] M Lachs, 'Some Reflections on the Contribution of the International Court of Justice to the Development of International Law' (1983) 10(2) *Syracuse Journal of International Law and Commerce* Nr 1, 239.

[8] JG Merrills, *The Development of International Law by the European Court of Human Rights* (Manchester, MUP, 1993) 229.

[9] *Ibid.*

judicial activism and benevolent liberalism were identified with the school of human rights and human dignity.

In answer to the second question we observed that: *the relation of human rights to international law depends not upon what law is treated but how law is treated*, meaning to which school of law and judicial ideologies the judges subscribe, or in other words as Judge Lachs put it how each judge *'understands and interprets the law.'* State sovereignty in its unperverted sense of the term is inseparable from the individual human sovereignty, as described by Judge Hersch Lauterpacht in the following words:

> For fundamental human rights are rights superior to the law of the sovereign State. The hope expressed by Emerson, that 'man shall treat with man as a sovereign state with a sovereign state' may be brought nearer to fruition by sovereign States recognizing the duty to treat man with the respect which traditional law exacted from them in relation to other States.[10]

State sovereignty is identical with State dignity and the individual sovereignty with individual human dignity. Former is the earlier version of the latter in its singular and unified form. The latter is the continued version of the former in its pluralized diversified form.

Our analysis also revealed that: under the new ideological trends set by the human rights school the entire body of international law must conform to the human rights law which stands for the human dignity in all its civil, political, economic, and cultural aspects; nationally, regionally as well as internationally. The principle of human dignity seems to be possessing and unleashing such a tremendous legal force that no rules of international law, even under the authority of State sovereignty, will be considered having any validity if they purport to contradict with the principles of human rights. It is as if a new school of law resting on the principle of human dignity, a synthesis of State sovereignty and individual human sovereignty, and a synthesis of positive law school and natural law school, is born. In other words: we concluded that there is an indissoluble ideological link between human rights and international law which may be described as follows: Human rights as an ideology of law, with the concept of human dignity at its core, is the legislative spirit of the body of international law. And, the international law, with human rights ideology at its core, is the manifestation of that legislative spirit.

In order to appreciate how this human rights legislative spirit manifested through the vast jurisprudence churned out by the judges of the International Court of Justice, it needs to have a brief glance of the cases discussed in Part II and Part III.

With the fresh memories of a) the human rights path adopted by the allied nations and the opposite path of terrorism adopted by the fascist nations, b) the resulting UN Charter and the Universal Declaration of Human Rights, the Court put the wheel in motion with its very first contentious case. The development of the founding *principle of elementary considerations of humanity* in the *Corfu*

[10] H Lauterpacht, *International Law and Human Rights* (London, Stevens, 1950) 70.

Channel case[11] is an original contribution to the jurisprudence of human rights. The dispute which arose out of the explosions of mines by which some British warships suffered damage and members of crew were killed while passing through the Corfu Channel, in a part of Albanian waters, was not simply judged by the traditional use of the language of international law based on the doctrine of State sovereignty and State responsibility but the same was put on the firm foundation of a new human rights language: *the elementary considerations of humanity*. This was the first contentious case ever decided by the International Court of Justice. It reflects that in the judicial reasoning of the Court any principle of international law has its underlying human rights and human dignity dimension.

In the joint cases of *South West Africa*,[12] despite the most criticized judgment in the Second Phase, the dissenting opinions of seven judges not only thoroughly elaborated the *principles of equal rights and self-determination* but added tremendous legal weight to the principle of human dignity by condemning the *concept of apartheid*, a concept which generated tremendous mental agony and suffering without visible use of armed terrorism. In the same case, the extraordinary quality of the dissenting opinion of Judge Tanaka and the endless development of the principles and philosophy of the human rights makes the opinion as a vast human rights jurisprudence in itself. The technique to custom-legislate the greater part of the human rights law is also considerably developed in these cases by the dissenting judges, particularly Judges Tanaka and Jessup.

In the *Barcelona Traction* case,[13] the case though related to the bankruptcy of the Barcelona Traction Company and the consequent problem of shares held in it by Belgian nationals, the International Court developed a revolutionizing concept of State obligations *erga omnes*. The obligations of States *erga omnes* included: the principles and rules concerning the basic rights of the human person including protection from slavery and racial discrimination. To stamp that human rights run *erga omnes*, while dealing with as traditional a subject as international financial transactions, is a great contribution to characterize international law with its human rights perspective which though slowly and steadily is bound to guide international community to the direction of realizing the international rule of law based on collective security.

In its *Hostages* case,[14] the Court greatly emphasized the legal importance of the 1948 *Universal Declaration of Human Rights*, often considered as not a legally binding document, by mentioning that the Declaration enunciates '*fundamental principles*' of international law. The same was preceded, during the process of examining the law on diplomatic immunities, by stressing the elements of dignity as related to diplomatic immunities and State relations. Here again human dignity was affirmed in the face of human terrorism.

[11] See ch 4.
[12] See ch 5.
[13] See ch 6.
[14] See ch 7.

In the *Nicaragua v USA* case[15]—relating to United States' responsibility for military and paramilitary activities in and against Nicaragua—not only the *principle of self-determination*—adherence to a particular doctrine does not violate customary international law—was developed but a guiding principle was established that the *use of force is not an appropriate method to ensure respect for human rights.* This was the case in which not only the Court's *benevolent* liberalism interpreted and applied general principles of international law with human rights school of thought, but, at the same time, the *bold* liberalism stood for a small nation (Nicaragua) in the face of a super military and political giant (USA) of the world, holding the respondent responsible for as sensitive a matter as military and paramilitary activities.

The benevolent liberalism and the bold activism of the Court has often reflected in developing the principle of *self-determination* in more cases, ie, contentious case of *Nicaragua v USA*,[16] two advisory cases of *Namibia*[17] and *Western Sahara.*[18] *Namibia* and *Western Sahara* Advisory Opinions in the 1970s stand conspicuous to the fact that the benevolent liberal ideology and the promotion of broadest possible human values, particularly human rights and humanitarian values, play a predominant role in shaping the *obiter dicta* of the Court when it deals with the advisory cases.

The international community of '*we the peoples*', including legal academics, have hardly forgiven (actually only after the benevolent liberalism of the Court in *Nicaragua v USA* case) the Court for its insensitivity towards so sensitive an issue as *apartheid* in the *South West Africa* cases that the Court, unfortunately, once again turned to its 'tough conservatism' in the case concerning *East Timor.*[19] At the centre of this case were *the people* of East Timor, though earlier in principle a non-self-governing territory under Portugal as their Administrative Power yet later in reality under the forceful *military occupation* of Indonesia.[20] The central principle of international human rights law around which this case revolved was the *principle of self-determination*, together with its *adjunctus*, *the principle of permanent sovereignty over natural resources.* And the central principle around which the Court's entire reasoning in the judgment in this case revolved was *the principle of State's consent*, an *adjunctus* of the principle of State's sovereignty as described in the pre-human-rights international law. Hence, State sovereignty in this case prevailed over human rights. Nevertheless, as the Court's benevolent tradition would have it, two of its judges did not let the Court down for its sacred undertaking of colouring international law with the colour of human rights and

[15] See ch 8.

[16] See ch 8.

[17] See chs 15 and 16.

[18] See ch 16.

[19] See ch 9.

[20] Just after seven years of the delivery of the Court' s Judgment (30 June 1995) in this case, the people of East Timor, despite years of bloodshed, oppression, subjugation, and occupation, succeeded in exercising their right of self-determination and attained their independence as a new State, called Timor Leste, on 20 May 2002.

human dignity. Judge Weeramantry elevated the human rights status of the principle of self-determination by clarifying: a) the practical operation of the right of self-determinations as right *erga omnes*, and b) that *principle of self-determination can itself be described as central to the UN Charter*. Judge *ad hoc* Skubiszewski shed a new light on the right first by developing four elements concerning law, justice and human dignity and then highlighting within this quadruple context a trinity of elementary assumptions about the right of self-determination.

In the *Legality of Use of Force*[21] cases, the preambular paragraphs to the Orders on Provisional Measures could considerably enhance the cause and protection of human rights if the same were parts of its *dispositif*. As there was no legal impediments provided by the provisions of the Statute or the Rules of the Court to do so, the Court simply has shown its judicial restraint and tough conservatism which is unfortunate not only to the development and progress of human rights and human dignity but also to their protection.

The case concerning *Arrest Warrant*[22] though mainly resting on two issues—doctrine of immunities applied to a Foreign Minister and the principle of universal jurisdiction—not only settled the long uncertain law on the immunities to a Foreign Minister but made amply clear, in the majority judgment as well as several individual opinions of judges, that the concept of *human dignity is a holistic term*; hence a new perception of human dignity of the people, for the people, by the people.

Every branch of international law has its one or other human rights aspect, directly or indirectly, we discussed in Part I of this book. The rules of consular relations and principles of human rights may at first glance seem strange bedfellows, but the three cases decided by the ICJ between 1998 and 2004—1) *Vienna Convention on Consular Relations* (*Paraguay v United States of America*), 2) *LaGrand* (*Germany v United States of America*), and 3) *Avena and Other Mexican Nationals* (*Mexico v United States of America*)—in the human rights legislative spirit prove that even the law of consular relations, like all law, cannot be interpreted in disregard to the school of human rights and human dignity.

In these cases centred around the application and interpretation of 1963 *Vienna Convention on Consular Relations*,[23] the Court, by ruling that the convention does create individual, has settled three points in international law, as observed by Meyer.[24] First: a country's treaty right of consular access to its nationals may be enforced not only on behalf of the State, but by the State for its national as the latter's human right. Second: a local rule of 'procedural default' may not under international law bar a claim by one unaware of her right at trial. Third: an indication of provisional measures temporarily issued to keep a case from being futile is 'binding' and enforceable when disobeyed. The significance of the judgments in

[21] See ch 11.

[22] See ch 12.

[23] See ch 13.

[24] HN Meyer, *The World Court in Action: Judging among Nations* (Lanban, Rowman & Littlefield) 226.

these cases lies not so much in deciding that the United States has breached its obligations under a treaty as against Germany and Mexico as in the recognition that *treaties create enforceable individuals rights* and the United States has *violated the individual rights* of those German and Mexican individuals as well. Without treating either the issue of death penalty—which is popularly considered as anti-human rights—or labelling individual rights created by the Vienna Convention as human rights, the Court's judgment has done a great service to the cause of human rights, for it is there where the institution of provisional measures would save more lives than in any other situation. The Court's pronouncements in the given cases bring the international legal order to the final and ultimate addressee of juridical norms: the human being.

In the advisory case concerning *International Status of West Africa*,[25] having extensively examined South African Government's responsibility for the well-being and human rights of its subjects, the Court clarified the very essence of the *principle of sacred trust of civilization* by declaring: 'These obligations represent the very essence of the sacred trust of civilization.'[26]

Seen in a broader and general context, the Court herewith has established a general guideline for any State or organization, irrespective of its national, regional or international character, and irrespective of its *ratione temporis*, *ratione materiae* or *ratione personae* jurisdiction, that material and moral well-being and social development are the collective human rights everywhere and it is the duty of the authorities governing the populations in question to promote these rights. Hence, the development of the principle of *sacred trust of civilization* can be seen as the early version of the interpretation by the Court of the later developed concept of obligation *erga omnes*, establishing therewith that human rights run *erga omnes*.

The act of Genocide in modern times is the invention of the perverted mind of Nazi terrorism. The advisory case of *Genocide*[27] represents a full scale activism of the Court by declaring that the principles underlying the Genocide Convention are binding on *all* States whether they are parties to the Convention or not. This is an anti-terrorism contribution to the law of human rights. Although the Court adopted a slightly conservative approach on the question of automatic succession to human rights treaties, Judge Lauterpacht did not fail to emphasize that the prohibition of genocide has generally been accepted as having the status not of an ordinary rule of international law but of *jus cogens*. This penetrates to the deepest depths to build unshakable mechanism against human terror.

In the advisory case concerning *Applicability of Article VI, Section 22, of the Convention on the Privileges and Immunities of the United Nations*,[28] the Court on the one hand ensured the independence of human rights operations by advising that a special rapporteur of the UN Human Rights Commission is entitled to privileges and immunities of a UN Expert on Mission under Article VI, Section 22,

[25] See ch 14.
[26] International Status of South-West Africa, ICJ Reports, 1950, pp 133.
[27] See ch 15.
[28] See ch 18.

of the Convention on the Privileges and Immunities of the United Nations, on the other, one of its judges, Judge Evensen added more to the field of human rights and human dignity by stating that: '*The integrity of a person's family and family life is a basic human right* protected by prevailing principles of international law which derive not only from conventional international law or customary international law but from "general principles of law recognized by civilized nations".'[29] (emphasis is added).

Legality of the Use by a State of Nuclear Weapons in Armed Conflict case[30] is the only advisory case in which the Court declined to give opinion. Notable of the case is not its conservative thinking. Even in declining to give the opinion, the Court liberally *developed the international constitutional law* of the very institution, the United Nations, which is the sole guardian of human rights. In not answering to the question asked by the World Health Organization—whether, in view of the health and environmental effects, the use of nuclear weapons by States in armed conflict is legal or illegal—the Court for the first time found the reason in the international constitutional framework by stating: the competence to address the 'legality' of the use of nuclear weapons cannot be ascribed to the WHO because it would be tantamount to disregarding the *'principle of speciality'* by which the WHO and all international organizations are governed.

It is obviously a case concerning the question of health aspect of human dignity, human right to health. But can an international organization responsible for human health encroach on the responsibilities of other parts of the United Nations system responsible for the questions concerning the use of force, the regulation of armaments and disarmaments, is the corollary of this question. It is also true that the notion and the principles of human rights are getting very much interwoven with other branches of law. It is equally true that as the notion and principles of human rights are getting interwoven with other branches of law so are the activities of institutions and organizations, national and international alike, promoting and preventing human rights are beginning to touch upon, and even intersecting, the jurisdictions of other specialized institutions and organizations. Has the Court then missed the opportunity to develop the human rights law concerning right to health? No. While the farsighted reasoning of the Court in its reasoning part of the Advisory Opinion has clarified and developed *the concept of separation of powers* by elucidating 'the powers conferred on international organizations', some of its judges undertook the substantive responsibility relating right to health, for instance, Judge Koroma elucidating and concluding that *'right to health is a pillar to peace'*.

In the *Legality of the Threat or Use of Nuclear Weapons* advisory case[31] in which the right to life itself was at the very centre of the case, the Court was criticized to be unnecessarily conservative on a matter which could have great impact on human rights and human dignity. Yet that is one side of the story. Though the

[29] See ch 18, pp 210–11.
[30] See ch 19.
[31] See ch 20.

Court confined itself to the conservative judicial ideology based on the doctrine of State sovereignty as far as its *dispositif* was concerned but it followed a very liberal approach based on the doctrine of human rights and human dignity when it was in the field of its reasoning part. What was the reason? Because neither the customary nor conventional international law stood settled on as serious a matter as threat or use of nuclear weapons. In the absence of a settled international law, customary and conventional law, and reluctant to rely on the general principles when there already was in progress every effort of States for the solid written law on such a serious issue, the Court chose to reflect the reality of *Yes and No* of the legality and illegality. Reading the reasoning part between the two poles of its *dispositif* 2E—use of nuclear weapons *'generally be contrary' to law* 'but cannot conclude definitely . . . lawful or unlawful'[32]—and 2F—'There exists an obligation' for States to pursue in good faith and bring to a conclusion negotiations leading to nuclear disarmament in all its aspects under strict and effective international control'[33]—the Court's advice to the UN General Assembly in reality reads: may use; may not use; but do not use; hence, do legislate: MAY NOT USE. The conclusions reached by the Court represent a large step forward with respect to doctrinal clarification. In addition to this the individual opinions of judges immensely clarified and developed the law to the extent that is well summarized by Judge Weeramantry: *'No weapon ever invented in the long history of man's inhumanity to man has so negatived the dignity and worth of the human person as has the nuclear bomb.'*[34]

In the *Differnce relating to Immunity from Legal Process of a Special Rapporteur of the Commission on Human Rights* case[35] the Court clarified the legal obligations of a sovereign State in the wake of discharge of duties by a Special Rapporteur of the Commission on Human Rights and set new principles which Judge Higgins found as breaking new grounds. In her own words:

> In a *dispositif* which broke new ground in going behind 'the unitary veil of the State', the International Court determined, *inter alia*: '2(a). That the Government of Malaysia had the obligation to inform the Malaysian courts of the finding of the Secretary-General that Dato' Param Cumaraswamy was entitled to immunity from legal process; (b) that the Malaysian courts had the obligation to deal with the question of immunity from legal process as a preliminary issue to be expeditiously decided in *limine litis* . . . 4. That the Government of Malaysia has the obligation to communicate this Advisory Opinion to the Malaysian Courts, in order that Malaysia's international obligations be given effect and Dato Param Cummaraswamy' immunity be respected.[36]

[32] ICJ Reports 1996, 266.

[33] *Ibid*, p 267.

[34] Judge Weeramantry, Dissenting Opinion, Advisor Opinion of 8 July 1996 in the case concerning Legality of the Threat or Use of Nuclear Weapons, ICJ Reports 1996, p 507.

[35] See ch 21.

[36] R Higgins, 'The Concept of "The State": Variable Geometry and Dualist Perceptions' in L Boisson de Chazournes and V Gowlland-Debbas, *The International Legal System in Quest of Equity and Universality: Liber Amicorum Georges Abi-Saab* (2001) 560.

Judge Higgins continues and points out:

> the International Court for the first time made determinations directly on the conduct of the courts of a state . . . This Advisory Opinion breaks new ground in advising a state as to its legal obligations, but recognizing also that various State organs comprise 'the state', and may indeed be required constitutionally to act independently of each other[37] (emphasis added).

It reflects drastic conditioning of the working of the principle of State sovereignty in international law, which in turn may make frequent determinations directly on the conduct of a sovereign state and its organs, judicial, executive, and legislative. This is conductive to achieve the aims and objectives of the United Nations, one of which is to promote and protect human rights. This is certainly a victory of new actors in international law against the sole old international actor, sovereign State.

In the very recent advisory case concerning *Legal Consequences of the Construction of a Wall in the Occupied Palestinian Territory*[38] the Court has dealt with a problem involving terrorism, but without even mentioning the word terrorism.

Four conclusions from the authoritative statement of the International Court of Justice seem very obvious. 1) Belligerent occupation is not immune to human rights, 2) The people not yet able to govern themselves, be they under a belligerent occupation, are a sacred trust of civilization; the principle of non-annexation and the principle of their well-being remain to be strictly observed by their occupier. 3) By recalling, applying and further developing almost every major human rights principle developed by the Court throughout its adjudicational career and supporting its reasoning by citing from almost every principal case in which those principles were developed, the Court's reasoning in this advisory opinion has presented an ocean of human rights in a drop of human dignity. 4) The Court in this case—first, by limiting the scope of the use of force under the right to self defence, secondly by developing the scope of collective measures at the international community level, certainly implying the right to collective use of force, and finally by adopting the broadest possible human rights approach through the application of the rules of international humanitarian law and human rights—has presented to the international community an adequate model of global governance based on the legal culture of human rights whose greatest characteristic reflects the respect for human dignity, of human dignity and by human dignity in all its forms and aspects. If there was any case in which the Court rigorously applied every inch the approach of human rights to its judicial decision making process it was this.

In the light of the cases discussed and some large generalizations provided by them, it can safely be concluded that the ample evidence points out that the Court mainly has been articulating the *ideology of moderate activism guided by benevolent*

[37] R Higgins, 'The Concept of "The State": Variable Geometry and Dualist Perceptions' in L Boisson de Chazournes and V Gowlland-Debbas, *The International Legal System in Quest of Equity and Universality: Liber Amicorum Georges Abi-Saab* (2001) 560.

[38] See ch 22.

liberalism. However, while being sufficiently careful to keep its pronouncements in accordance with international law, as required by its Statute, the Court has *occasionally been activist enough* in striking out a path towards new developments in the human rights law. The tendency to go radically activist in human rights cases is certainly not to be detected. But the *benevolent liberalism as a dominant character of the Court's human rights thinking*, with few exceptions—first in the second phase judgment in the *South West Africa* cases,[39] the second in the 1995 judgment in the *East Timor* case, the third in the jurisdictional judgment of 1996 in the case concerning *Application of the Convention on the Prevention and Punishment of the Crime of Genocide*,[40] and the fourth its declining to indicate provisional measures in the ten *Legality of Use of Force* cases[41]—has been reflecting throughout the Court's human rights jurisprudence.

As the concepts of human rights and human dignity enshrined in the UN Charter have profoundly influenced the post-war development of international law, the jurisprudence of the International Court of Justice have constantly developed and strengthened the law of human rights by making pertinent references to the general principles of human rights whenever the occasions arose. If the Court has ever omitted to refer to the concept of human rights or failed fully to deal with it, as one of its former President[42] put it, the Members of the Court have at no point failed to elaborate that aspect in their independent or separate supporting opinions, or even give vent to their thinking in dissenting opinions which in fact is quite remarkable.

When a head-on collision between general ideologies of judicial restraint and judicial activism on the one hand and between the tough conservatism and benevolent liberalism in the matter pertaining *apartheid* on the other had taken place in the second phase of the *South West Africa* cases[43] the decision was taken by the casting vote of the President, the votes being equally divided. In the total composition of 14 judges, two being *ad hoc*, there were seven dissenting opinions appended rigorously criticizing the decision of the Court and clarifying the law. Of all these dissents, the opinion of Judge Tanaka (Japan) certainly stands conspicuous and has become a classic document of human rights law, cited and appraised frequently. The most prominent work on the collected documents on Human Rights by Prof Brownlie of Oxford University, *Basic Documents on Human Rights*, includes only one individual opinion from the ICJ Judges, that of Judge Tanaka alone. In the legal circles it is seen as an extraordinary opinion about the clarification and development of human rights law. Speaking about human rights in their generality, Judge Tanaka mentioned: 'A State or States are not capable of creating human rights by law or by convention; they can only confirm their

[39] See ch 5.

[40] See ch 10.

[41] See ch 11.

[42] N Singh, *Enforcement of Human Rights in Peace and War and the Future of Humanity* (Dordrecht, Nijhoff, 1986) 29.

[43] See ch 5.

existence and give them protection. The role of the State is no more than declaratory.'[44] The hallmark of a liberal that authority is pernicious but necessary is what Tanaka here speaks about. Concerning particularly about human rights protection, Tanaka says:

> The principal of the protection of human rights is derived from the concept of man as a *person* and his relationship with society which cannot be separated from universal human nature. The existence of human rights does not depend on the will of a State; neither internally on its law or any other legislative measure, nor internationally on treaty or custom, in which the express or tacit will of a State constitutes the essential element.[45]

Further, he continues:

> Human rights have always existed with the human being. They existed independently of, and before, the State. Alien and even Stateless persons must not be deprived of them. Belonging to diverse kinds of communities and societies—ranging from family, club, corporation, to State and international community, the human rights of man must be protected everywhere in this social hierarchy, just as copyright is protected domestically and internationally. There must be no legal vacuum in the protection of human rights.[46]

Tanaka's individual opinion is a perfect blend of judicial activism and benevolent liberalism.

The Court in the *Legality of Use of Force cases*,[47] strongly under the sway of the ideologies of judicial restraint and tough conservatism could not recall Tanaka's opinion that there must be no legal vacuum in the protection of human rights, not even provided by its creation of the rule of *prima facie* jurisdiction. In those cases too the individual opinions of several judges, but particularly of the four—Weeramantry (Sri Lanka), Acting President in all the ten cases, Shi (China), Vereshchetin (Russia) and Kreca (Yugoslavia), an *ad hoc* judge appointed by Yugoslavia in all these cases, did what the Court failed to do. All these judges in most of these cases vehemently disagreed with the majority of judges who advocated judicial restraint in saying that the Court has no *prima facie* jurisdiction to indicate provisional measures in these cases. Though the expositions of these four dissenting judges by no means can be considered as activist approach, but the benevolent liberalism reflecting in their individual opinions, every inch highlighting the *elementary considerations of humanity* and the severity of human rights violations, stood for human rights and human dignity. Judge Weeramanty, showing that the human rights issues involved on both sides are of the gravest nature stated that:

> If the allegations made are substantiated, this would constitute one of the severest violations of human rights and dignity that have occurred since the conclusion of World War II. Human Rights violations on this scale are such as to throw upon the world community

[44] South West Africa cases, Second Phase Judgment, Dissenting Opinion of Judge Tanaka, ICJ Reports, 1966, p 297.
[45] *Ibid.*
[46] *Ibid*, pp 297–98.
[47] See ch 11.

> a grave responsibility to intervene for their prevention and it is well-established legal doctrine that such gross denials of human rights anywhere are everyone's concern everywhere. The concept of sovereignty is no protection against action by the world community to prevent such violations if they be of the scale and nature alleged.[48]

This is a committed and forceful voice of benevolent liberalism ideology giving proper direction to the ICJ with a hope that the right direction concerning human rights law would be followed by the Court in future. It does not reflect any undue judicial restraint but does show an approach of a healthy and required bit of activism.

The majority of the Court, often subscribing to the judicial ideology of benevolent liberalism, as far the development of substantive human rights law is concerned, has left a highlighted mark that as far as the development of its jurisdictional law is concerned the Court hardly has moved an inch towards its progressive development of law in favour of dealing with the contentious cases, hence not giving up the old judicial restraint ideology. The Court has been always generous enough in dealing with the merits of cases, ceaselessly understanding and interpreting general principles of international law through the principles of human rights, but seldom kind to itself when it came to deal with its jurisdiction. Hence, in few cases where the Court failed to develop the human rights law and to strengthen the human dignity link between human rights and international it was not that the Court failed but its own jurisdictional obstacles failed it, but because of jurisdictional judicial restraint ideology. Some judges have been constantly reminding the Court that the formula of consent based on the ages old concept of sovereignty is out of date and must be brought in line with the present international conditions and circumstances. Judge Alvarez has been a leading advocate of this interpretation of international law. As early as 1948, he mentioned in one of his individual opinions:

> As a result of the increasingly closer relations between States, which has led to their ever greater interdependence, the old *community* of nations has been transformed into a veritable international *society*, though it has neither an executive power, nor a legislative power, nor yet a judicial power, which are the characteristics of a national society, but not of international society. This society comprises all States throughout the world, without there being any need for consent on their part or on that of other States; it has aims and interests of its own; States no longer have an absolute sovereignty but are interdependent.[49]

Despite these few exceptions the International Court of Justice, though not even a human rights court in the contemporary sense of the term, has yet availed itself of every possible opportunity to refer in its cases to the general doctrine of human rights, and to deal in great depth with the questions of human rights as and when

[48] Legality of Use of Force (*Yugoslavia v Belgium*), Order on Provisional Measures, Dissenting Opinion of Judge Weeramantry, ICJ Reports, 199, p.

[49] Conditions of Admission of a State to Membership in the United Nations (Article 4 of the Charter), Advisory Opinion of 28 May 1948, Individual Opinion of Judge Alvarez, ICJ Reports 1947–48, p 8.

the occasion arose. And, its resulting contribution has indeed been 'progressive, developmental and helpful' to the cause of human rights and human dignity.

There is not a single case in the history of the Court's adjudication, involving human rights and human dignity aspects, in which if the Court had failed and its individual judges had not taken upon themselves to clarify and develop human rights law. Whenever the Court followed the judicial ideology of tough conservatism, for instance in the *South West Africa*[50] contentious cases, the period following thereafter witnessed the most benevolent approach in its judicial process, for instance in the *Namibia*[51] and *Western Sahara*[52] advisory cases. Seen in that trait, in the post *East Timor* case,[53] in which the Court was sharply criticized to visit literally the *South West Africa* cases,[54] the Court turned immensely liberal and activist in the *Differnce relating to Immunity from Legal Process of a Special Rapporteur of the Commission on Human Rights* case[55] to the extent of first time making determinations directly on the conduct of national courts, hence not only breaking new grounds in advising a state as to its legal obligations, but recognizing also that 'various State organs comprise "the state", and may indeed be required constitutionally to act independently of each other.'[56] In the very recent advisory case concerning *Legal Consequences of the Construction of a Wall in the Occupied Palestinian Territory*[57] the Court's reasoning every inch has been liberal and human rights oriented. Declaring not only human rights law as *erga omnes* and customary but also characterizing a greater part of international humanitarian law equally *erga omnes* and customary. Putting 'all States' under an obligation to ensure compliance by Israel of the relevant human rights law and advising in particular the prominent organs of the United Nations, General Assembly and Security Council, to consider taking required action to undo the illegality, the Court has openly, liberally and boldly aroused the international enforcement mechanism of the world's governing body.

In a nutshell, and highlighting only the pillars of human rights strength on which international law is being moulded to stand: with the founding principle of *elementary considerations of humanity* in the *Corfu Channel* case the Court established a firm link of common essence between human rights and international law, the spirit of which permeates through the common Article 3 of the four Geneva Conventions. Its views regarding the *scope of reservations to the Genocide Convention* in the *Genocide case*, made an immense impact on the drafting of Article 199 *et seq* of the 1969 Vienna Convention on the Law of Treaties. Its devel-

[50] See ch 5.
[51] See ch 16.
[52] See ch 17.
[53] See ch 9.
[54] See ch 5.
[55] See ch 21.
[56] R Higgins, 'The Concept of "The State": Variable Geometry and Dualist Perceptions' in L Boisson de Chazournes and V Gowlland-Debbas, *The International Legal System in Quest of Equity and Universality: Liber Amicorum Georges Abi-Saab* (2001) 560.
[57] See ch 22.

opment of the concept of obligations *erga omnes* in the *Barcelona Traction* case, and declaring thereby that human rights run *erga omnes*, was another expression of its fundamental principle of *elementary considerations of humanity*, which has not failed in becoming an integral part of the positive international law, another human rights colour added to the substance of international law. In the *Hostages case*, earlier 1948 Universal Declaration of Human Rights known to be unbinding received its binding character. Liberal and flexible interpretation of law has been compassionately and toughly advocated and applied by the Court in the *Namibia cases* and the *Western Sahara* case, thereby creating universal acceptance for its opinions on *apartheid* and on the *right of peoples to self-determination*, respectively. The contributions made individually by the ICJ judges, through appending their individual opinions, too numerous to narrate here, are equally immense. The survey of the development of human rights law—through the judgments, advisory opinions, orders, and the individual opinion appended to them by individual judges of the International Court of Justice—demonstrates a continual process of the enrichment of the international legal culture and system by taking into consideration values and principles of human rights and human dignity which had previously been excluded from the international legal order. The jurisprudence thus produced by the Court, amply reflect that the notion of human rights and human dignity being an integral part of the UN Charter law and system, and the promotion of human rights being one of the main purposes of the United Nations, no treaty or custom, irrespective of its particular human rights character or any other character, can be interpreted in disregard to the ideology and principles of human rights. In other words it demonstrates that all international law, customary as well as conventional, has its innate elements of human rights as an integral part of its very letter and spirit, thereby making the principle of human dignity as an integral part of all international law mentioned in Article 38, paragraph 1 of the Court's Statute. This brings the doctrine of human rights and its core principle of human dignity at the very basis of entire international law, thereby establishing a cultural link of human and humanitarian thought—highlighted by the Court in the words: '*elementary considerations of humanity, even more exacting in peace than in war*'—irrespective of the working of traditional doctrine of State sovereignty, between the systems of human rights and international law.

What has been the human rights value of all this in relation to international law as far as its binding character is concerned? And 'how can we legitimate such judicial decisions'? It is well described by no one less than the then President of the International Court of Justice, Judge Gilbert Guillaume, when he addressed the Sixth Committee (Legal Committee) of the UN General Assembly on, *inter alia*, the development of human rights jurisprudence by the ICJ, in the following words:

> . . . the Court, by characterizing certain conventional obligations as customary ones and then treating such obligations as obligations erga omnes, has sought to impose on all States minimum norms deriving from the elementary considerations of humanity already invoked by it in the Corfu Channel case. It has thus given those considerations a

specific content. In so doing, it has laid the foundations for a universal customary law which, without challenging conventional law, is binding.[58]

This answer by President Guillaume matches perfectly the answer provided by Prof Van Hoecke in *Law as Communication* approach: 'The answer is: through deliberative communication'.[59] The process of characterization of 'Conventional obligations' (legislative aspect) as 'customary ones' (one combined aspect of plurality comprising international legislature of States and the international community at large) is tantamount to the process of interpretation (teleological) by means of deliberative communication of the legislative purpose (respect for human dignity) of human rights in two forms: written (treaties) and unwritten (principles). This way, the judges of the International Court first created the *erga omnes*[60] human rights obligations from within the conventional law and then sought to impose them on States as norms derived from the fundamental minimum norms derived from the fundamental principle of *the elementary considerations of humanity*[61] (considerations of human dignity). Hence, in giving a specific content to the considerations of humanity the Court has given a specific content to the principle of human dignity and therewith created a universal customary human rights law which is binding without challenging conventional law (legislature).

From the systematic analysis of the development of human rights law by the ICJ it transpires that:

> . . . law is not something which is (completely) made at one point in time, and afterwards simply 'applied' by officials, by citizens and by judges to concrete cases. *Law is constantly made, adapted and developed in legal practice*, and most prominently by judges. If a court adapts, and even changes, the content of a legislative rule, it is not, in so doing, usurping its role, but in most cases rather fully assuming its tasks and duties. Legislators cannot foresee everything, nor can they constantly adapt every statute to changed circumstances. It is precisely the task and the duty of the judges to fill in the gaps which every legislator must inevitably leave.[62]

The precise nature and direction of the development of human rights law (like all law) by judges depends on which ideological lines (conservative or liberal) they choose to communicate with the legislator. Since pluralization of the international community (based on the *Grundnorm* of human dignity) is the greatest characteristic of the contemporary legal culture, judges of the International Court of Justice have in general enhanced human dignity (by their liberal and human rights

[58] An extract from the Speech given by Judge Gilbert Guillame, President of the International Court of Justice, to the Sixth Committee of the UN General Assembly on 30 October 2002.

[59] M van Hoecke, *Law as Communication* (Oxford, Hart Publishing, 2002) 176.

[60] The revolutionizing concept of State obligations *erga omnes* was developed by the Court in the *Barcelona Traction* case (see ch 6) and since then it has become a popular dictum of the ICJ.

[61] The most fundamental principle of the Court's entire case law developed in its very first contentious case of *Corfu Channel* (see ch 4).

[62] M van Hoecke, *Law as Communication* (Oxford, Hart Publishing, 2002) 176.

approach to the involved deliberative communication) considerably and thereby contributed substantially to the development of human rights law.

Returning to the opening postulate, completing the circle, in a nutshell it can be said: There are no limits to the heights of human rights path that the clear human conscience can attain, nor to the depths of the rampage terrorism that the perverted human conscience can sink. It is for us, the peoples of the United Nations to choose between the peace and happiness generating from the path of human rights or the depths of horror and terror of terrorism. The human rights law developed by the judges of the International Court of Justice has an immense treasury of refined legal wisdom to offer to the post 9/11 world, it is up to the world—'*we the people of the United Nations*', rulers and ruled alike—*to choose* which way to go. But, as the law of human rights developed by the Court is in fact the clarified and refined version of the legislative spirit of the UN Charter, to ignore this in the face of revisiting and ever growing terrorism is to deviate from the very path of human rights which was at a time of resolution made to counter the revisit of the very scourge, hence an invitation thereto. International human rights legislation of the United Nations looked and studied in the mirror of international adjudication by the International Court of Justice may reflect back the realization embedded every inch in the vast jurisprudence produced by its judges: the story of mankind is a story of trial and error but by no means hopeless; all we need is the determined strengthening of international human rights enforcement mechanism, indeed the enforcement mechanism in its entirety.

Man is half angel and half demon. If he overcomes his vicious nature and other destructive tendencies, he rises higher than the angels; if vicious nature overcomes him, he falls below the level of the beasts. 'We, the peoples of the United Nations', can, if we will, rise to the infinite heights of human dignity or sink to the depths of terrorism. The path of the world peace through world law, with the respect for human rights and human dignity at its core, may not be the best path humans know but there is none better than that so far known to mankind. In this age of growing terrorism we need to set our priorities and the Court's human rights jurisprudence indeed provides a legal bible for 'We, the peoples of the United Nations', including its leaders and governing institutions.

GENERAL BIBLIOGRAPHY

Aghahosseini, M, 'The Claims of Dual Nationals before the Iran-United States Claims Tribunal: Some Reflections' (1997) 10 *Leiden Journal of International Law* 21.

Agarwal, HO, *International Law* (Fridabad, India, Allahabad Law Agency, 1997).

—— *Human Rights* (Allahabad, India, Central Law, 1999).

Akande, D, 'Nuclear Weapons: Unclear Law? Deciphering the Nuclear Weapons Advisory Opinion of the International Court' (1997) *The British Year Book of International Law*, 68th edn, p 165.

Akhavan, P, 'Enforcement of the Genocide Convention through the Advisory Opinion Jurisdiction of the International Court of Justice', *Human Rights Law Journal*, 30 September 1991.

Allott, P, *International Law and International Revolution: Reconceiving the World* (Hull, Hull University Press, 1989).

Alston, P (ed), *The United Nations and Human Rights: A Critical Appraisal* (Oxford, OUP, 1995).

Bala, C, *International Court of Justice* (New Delhi, Deep & Deep, 1997).

Bedi, SRS, 'African Participation in the International Court of Justice: A Statistical Appraisal (1946–1998)' (1998) 6 *African Yearbook of International Law* 181.

Bekker, PHF, *Commentaries on World Court Decisions (1987–1996)* (The Hague, Martinus Nijhoff, 1998).

Boisson de Chazourzounes, L, and Sands, P (eds), *International Law, The International Court of Justice and Nuclear Weapons* (Cambridge, CUP,1999).

Brownlie, I, *Public International Law*, 4th edn, (Oxford, Clarendon Press, 1990).

Bulterman, MK, and Kuijer, M (eds), *Compliance with Judgments of International Courts* (The Hague, Nijhoff, 1996).

Carrithers, DW (ed), *The Spirit of Laws by Montesquieu* (Berkeley, University of California Press, 1977).

Cassese, A, *Self-Determination of Peoples* (Cambridge, CUP, 1998).

Chen, L, *An Introduction to Contemporary International Law: A Policy Oriented Perspective* (New Haven, CT, Yale University Press, 1989).

Cheng, B, *General Principles of Law as Applied by International Courts and Tribunals* (Cambridge, Grotius, 1987).

Chimini, BS, *International Law and World Order: A Critique of Contemporary Approaches* (New Delhi, Sage, 1993).

Cosgrove, RA, *Scholars of the Law: English Jurisprudence from Blackstone to Hart* (New York, NY, NYU Press).

Cotterrell, R, *The Politics of Jurisprudence* (Philadelphia, University of Pennsylvania Press,1989).

Crawford, J, and Sands, P, 'Legal Aspects of a Nuclear Weapons Convention' (1998) 6 *African Yearbook of International Law* 153.

Crawford, JF, 'South West Africa: Mandate Termination in Historical Perspective' (1967) 6(1) *Columbia Journal of International Law* 91.

Dahlitz, J (ed), *Secession and International Law: Conflict Avoidance—Regional Appraisals*, (The Hague, TMC Asser, 2003).
Devlin, P, *The Judge* (Oxford, OUP, 1979).
Dewese, GS, 'The Failure of the International Court of Justice to Effectively Enforce the Genocide Convention' (1998) 26 *Denver Journal of International Law and Policy* 625.
Dhayani, SN, *Fundamental of Jurisprudence: The Indian Approach* (Allahabad, India, Central Law Agency, 1997).
Dhokalia, RP, and Nirmal, BC (eds), *International Court in Transition: Essays in Memory of Professor Dharam Pratap*, (1994).
Diwan, P, and Diwan, P *Human Rights and the Law: Universal and Indian* (New Delhi, Deep & Deep, 1998).
Dixon, M, *Textbook on International Law*, 3rd edn, (London, Blackstone, 1996).
Duursma, J, 'Justifying NATO's Use of Force in Kosovo?' (1999) 12(2) *Leiden Journal of International Law* 287.
Dwivedi, SP, *Jurisprudence and Legal Theory*, 3rd edn, (Allahabad, India, Central Law Agency, 1994).
Dworkin, R, *Taking Rights Seriously* (Cambridge, MA, Harvard University Press, 1977).
Eichelberber, CM, *UN: The First Twenty Years* (Delhi, Sterling, 1966).
Eide, A, 'Human Rights Require Responsibilities and Duties' in K Vasak, *Amicorum Liber: Human Rights at the Dawn of the Twenty-First Century* (Bruxelles, UNESCO, 1999) 581.
Evans, MD (ed), *International Law* (Oxford, OUP, 2003).
Falk, RA, 'The South West Africa Cases: An Appraisal' in XXI *International Organization*, No 11967, 1.
—— 'Nuclear Weapons, International Law and World Court: An Historic Encounter' (1997) 91 *American Journal of International Law*.
Fitzgerald, BF, '*Portugal v Australia*: Deploying the Missiles of Sovereign Autonomy and Sovereign Community' (1996) 37 *Harvard International Law Journal* 260.
Fitzgerald, PJ, *Salmond on Jurisprudence*, 12th edn, (Bombay, NM Tripathi Private Ltd, Indian reprint edn, 1997).
Flemming, B, 'South West Africa Cases: *Ethiopia v South Africa*; *Liberia v South Africa: Second Phase*' (1967) 5 *Canadian Yearbook of International Law* 241.
Foque, R, 'Global Governance and the Rule of Law: Human Rights and General Principles of Good Global Governance' in K Wellens, (ed), *International Law: Theory and Practice: Essays in Honour of Eric Suy* (The Hague, Nijhoff, 1998) 25.
Friedmann, W, *Law in a Changing Society* (Sweet & Maxwell, 1972; 2nd edn, New Delhi, Universal Book Traders, 1996).
—— *The Changing Structure of International Law* (New York, NY, Feffer & Simons, 1964).
—— 'The Jurisprudential Implications of the South West Africa Case' (1967) 6 *Columbia Journal of International Law* 1.
Fuller, LL, *The Morality of Law* (New Haven, CT, Yale University Press, 1969).
Gilson, B, *The Conceptual System of Sovereign Equality* (Peeter, Leuven, 1984).
Goodman, E, *The Origins of The Western Legal Tradition* (Sydney, Federation Press, 1995).
Govindraj, VC, *Judge Nagendra Singh of the World Court: His Contribution to the Development of Contemporary International Law* (New Delhi, Deep & Deep, 1999).
Gowlland-Debbas, V, 'Judicial Insights into Fundamental Values and Interests of the International Community' (1997) *Leiden Journal of International Law*.
Goy, R, *La Cour Internationale de Justice et les Droits de l'homme* (Brussels, Nemesis Bruylant, 2002)

Gross, L, 'Review of the Role of the International Court of Justice' (1972) 66 *American Journal of International Law* 479.

Hambro, E (1959–63) IV–a *The Case Law of the International Court*, (Leiden, AW Sijthoff, 1966).

—— and AW Rovine, (1964–66) V–b *The Case Law of the International Court*, (Leiden, AW Sijthoff-Leyden, 1968).

—— ——, (1973–74) VIII *The Case Law of the International Court*, (Leiden, AW Sijthoff-Leyden, 1979).

Harris, JW, *Legal Philosophies*, 2nd edn, (London, Butterworths, 1997).

DJ Harris, *Cases and Materials on International Law*, 5th edn, (London, Sweet & Maxwell, 1995).

Hart, HLA, *The Concept of Law*, 2nd edn, (Oxford, Clarendon Press, 1994).

Holland, KM, *Judicial Activism in Comparative Perspective* (London, MacMillan, 1991).

De Hoogh, A, *Obligations Erga Omnes and International Crimes* (The Hague, Kluwer Law International, 1996).

Huaraka, T, 'International Protection of Human Rights and Rights of Peoples: Civil and Political Rights' in M Bedjaoui, (ed), *International Law: Achievements and Prospects* (UNESCO, Martinus Nijhoff, 1991) 1061.

Hubbard, HK, 'Separation of Powers within the United Nations: A Revised Role for the International Court of Justice' (1985–86) 38 *Stanford Law Review* 165.

Hussain, I, *Dissenting and Separate Opinions at the World Court* (Dordrecht, Martinus Nijhoff, 1984).

Iwe, NSS, *The History and Contents of Human Rights* (1986).

Jackson, BS, *Making Sense in Jurisprudence* (Liverpool, Deborah Charles Publications, 1996).

Jacquart, M, 'International Protection of Human Rights: Economic, Social and Cultural Rights' in M Bedjaoui, (ed), *International Law: Achievements and Prospects*, (UNESCO, Martinus Nijhoff, 1991) 1083.

Janis, MW, 'Judicial Insights into Fundamental Values and Interests of the International Community' (1997) *Leiden Journal of International Law*.

Johnson, JP, *The Path of the Masters*, 12th edn, (Radha Soami Satsang Beas Beas, India, 1980)

Johnson, MG, and Synmonides, J, *The Universal Declaration of Human Rights: A History of its Creation and Implementation: 1948—1998*, (Paris, UNESCO, 1998).

Kalshoven, F, and Sandoz, Y, (eds), *Implementation of International Humanitarian Law* (Martinus Nijhoff Publishers, Dordrecht, 1989).

Kapoor, SK, *International Law* (Allahabad, India, Central Law Agency, 1987).

Kaul, J (ed), *Human Rights: Issues and Perspectives* (New Delhi, Regency, 1995).

Kavanagh, R, 'Oil in Troubled Waters: The International Court of Justice and East Timor: Case Concerning East Timor' (1996) 18 *Sydney Law Review* 87.

Kelly, JM, *A Short History of Western Legal Theory* (Oxford, Clarendon Press, 1992).

Kelson, H, Tucker, RT (ed), *Principles of International Law*, 2nd edn, (New York, NY, Holt, Rinehart and Winston, 1967).

Kent, P, *Law of the European Union*, 2nd edn, (London, Pitman, 1986).

Koskenniemi, M, 'Lauterpacht: The Victorian Tradition in International Law' (1997) 2 *European Journal of International Law* 215.

—— (ed), *International Law* (Aldershot, Dartmouth, 1992).

Krishna, VR, *Human Rights and Human Wrongs* (Delhi, BR, 1997).

Krishna, VR, *Human Rights: A Judge's Miscellany* (Delhi, BR, 1997).
Lammers, JG, 'General Principles of Law Recognized by Civilized Nations' in *Essays on the Development of the International Legal Order in Memory of Haro F van Panhuys* (Alphen aan den Rijn, Sijthoff & Noordhoff, 1980) 53.
Lauterpacht, H, *International Law: A Treatise by L Oppenheim*, 7th edn, (London, Longmans, Green and Co).
Lowe, V, and Fitzmaurice, M, *Fifty Years of the International Court of Justice: Essays in Honour of Sir Robert Jennings* (Cambridge, CUP, 1996).
Lowe, V, 'Jurisdiction' in MD Evans, (ed), *International Law* (Oxford, OUP, 2003) 329.
MacCormick, N, *Legal Reasoning and Legal Theory* (Oxford, Clarendon Press, 1978).
McDonell, Sir J, and Manson, E, *Great Jurists of the World* (London, 1913).
Malanczuk, P, *Akehurst's Modern Introduction to International Law*, 7th edn, (London, Routledge, 1997).
Mani, VS, *International Adjudication: Procedural Aspects: Developments in International Law* (New Delhi, Radiant, 1980).
Mani Tripathi, BN, *Jurisprudence (Legal Theory)*, 11th edn, (Allahabad, Allahabad Law Agency, 1988).
Mapel, DR, and Nardin, T, *International Society: Diverse Ethical Perspectives* (Princeton, NJ, Princeton University Press, 1998).
Matheson, MJ, 'The Opinions of the International Court of Justice on the Threat or Use of Nuclear Weapons' (1997) 91 *American Journal of International Law* 417.
Mazour, AG, and Peoples, JM, *Men and Nations: A World History* (New York, NY, Harcourt Brace Jovanovich, 1975).
McCorquodale, R, 'The Individual and the International Legal System' in MD Evans, (ed), *International Law* (Oxford, OUP, 2003) 300.
Mehta, PL, and Verma, N, *Human Rights under the Indian Constitution: The Philosophy and Judicial Gerrymandering* (New Delhi, Deep & Deep, 1999).
McWhinney, E, *The International Court of Justice and the Western Tradition of International Law* (Dordrecht, Martinus Nijhoff, 1987).
—— 'The Changing United Nations Constitutionalism: New Arenas and New Techniques for International Law Making' (1967) 5 *Canadian Yearbook of International Law* 68.
—— 'Self-Determination of Peoples in Contemporary Constitutional and International Law' in *Liber Amicorum Mohammed Bedjaoui* (1999) 725.
—— 'The Legislative Role of the World Court in an Era of Transition' in R Bernhardt, *et al*, (eds), *Volkerrecht als Rechtsordnung Internationale Gerichtsbarkeit Menschenrechte: Festschrift fur Hermann Mosler* (1983) 568.
—— *The World Court and the Contemporary International Law-Making Process* (Alphen aan den Rijn, Netherlands, Sijthoff & Noordhoff, 1979).
Mehartaj Begum, S (ed), *Human Rights in India: Issues and Perspectives* (New Delhi, APH).
Meron, T, 'On the Inadequate Reach of Humanitarian and Human Rights Law and the Need for a New Instrument' (1983) 77 *American Journal of International Law* 589.
—— (ed), *Human Rights in International Law: Legal and Policy Issues*, vol I–II, (Oxford, Clarendon Press, 1984).
—— 'On the Inadequate Reach of Humanitarian and Human Rights Law and the Need for a New Instrument' (1983) 77 *American Journal of International Law* 589.
Merrills, JG, *The Development of International Law by the European Court of Human Rights* (Manchester, MUP, 1993).
Muller, R, *My Testament to the UN* (Washington, World Happiness and Cooperation, 1995).

Mullerson, R, 'Sovereignty and Secession: Then and Now, Here and There' in J Dahlitz, (ed), *Secession and International Law: Conflict Avoidance—Regional Appraisals* (The Hague, TMC, 2003) 125.

Murphy, JG, and Coleman, JL, *Philosophy of Law: An Introduction to Jurisprudence* (Delhi, OUP, 1997).

Musgrave, TD, *Self-Determination and National Minorities* (Oxford, OUP, 1997).

Nafziger, JAR, 'The General Admission of Aliens under International Law' (1983) 77 *American Journal of International Law* 804.

Nanda, VP, and Krieger, D, *Nuclear Weapons and the World Court* (New York, Transnational Publishers, 1998).

Newman, F, and Weissbrodt, D, *International Human Rights* (Cincinnati, OH, Anderson, 1990).

—— ——, *Selected International Human Rights Instruments* (Cincinnati, OH, Anderson, 1990).

Nirmal, CJ (ed), *Human Rights in India: Historical, Social and Political Perspectives* (Oxford, OUP, 1999).

O'Brien, J, *International Law* (London, Cavendish, 2001).

O'Connell, DP, *International Law*, vols 1–2, (London, Stevens & Sons, 1970).

OST Francois and M van de Kerchove, *Legal System between Order and Disorder* (Oxford, OUP, 1994).

Palmer, ND, and Perkins, HC, *International Relations: The World Community in Transition*, 3rd edn, (Delhi, CBS, 1985).

Palmer, RR, *History of the Modern World* (New York, NY, Alfred A Knopf, 1953).

Palumbo, M, *Human Rights: Meaning and History* (Malabar FL, Krieger, 1982).

Paranjape, NV, *Jurisprudence and Legal Theory*, 2nd edn, (Allahabad, India, Central Law Agency).

Pathak, RS, and Dhokalia, RP (eds), *International Law in Transition: Essays in Memory of Judge Nagendra Singh* (Dordrecht, Martinus Nijhoff, 1992).

Patrnogic, J, 'International Humanitarian Law and Peace' (1998) 1 *Boutros Boutros-Ghali Amicorum Discipulorumque Liber* 571.

Perry, MJ, *The Idea of Human Rights: Four Inquiries* (Oxford, OUP, 1998).

Pound, R, *An Introduction to the Philosophy of Law* (Delhi, Universal Law, 1998).

Ragazzi, M, *The Concept of International Obligations Erga Omnes* (Oxford, OUP, 1997).

Rajan, MS (ed), *United Nations at 50 and Beyond* (New Delhi, Lancers Books 1996).

Ramacharan, BG, *The Concept and Present Status of the International Protection of Human Rights: Forty Years after the Universal Declaration* (The Hague, Martinus Nijhoff, 1989).

Reardon, BA, *Educating for Human Dignity: Learning About Rights and Responsibilities* (Philadelphia, University of Pennsylvania Press, 1995).

Rosenne, S, *The Law and Practice of the International Court of Justice 1920–1996* (The Hague, Martinus Nijhoff, 1997).

Saxena, KP (ed), *Human Rights: Perspectives and Challenges* (New Delhi, Lancers Books, 1995).

Saxena, M, and Chandra, H (eds), *Law and Changing Society* (New Delhi, Deep & Deep, 1995).

Schachter, O, 'Human Dignity as a Normative Concept' (1983) 77 *American Journal of International Law* 848.

Schermers, HG, *International Institutional Law*, vol III, (Leyden, AW Sijthoff, 1974).

Schwarzenberger, G, *Power Politics: A Study of International Society* (London, Stevens & Sons, 1951).

Schwelb, E, 'The International Court of Justice and the Human Rights Clauses of the Charter' (1972) 66 *American Journal of International Law* 337.
Scobbie, IGM, 'The Theorist as Judge: Hersch Lauterpacht's Concept of the International Judicial Function' (1997) 2 *European Journal of International Law* 264.
—— and CJ Drew, 'Self-Determination Undermined: The Case of East Timor' (1996) 9 *Leiden Journal of International Law* 185.
Seidl-Hohenveldem, I, 'Judicial Insights into Fundamental Values and Interests of the International Community' (1997) *Leiden Journal of International Law*, special issue: AS Muller, D Raic and Thuranszky, (eds), *The International Court of Justice: Its Future Role after Fifty Years.*
Sharma, G, *Human Rights and Social Justice* (New Delhi, Deep & Deep, 1997).
—— *Human Rights and Legal Remedies* (New Delhi, Deep & Deep, 2000).
Shaw, MN, *International Law*, 4th edn, (Grotius Publications, CUP, 1997).
Singh, JS, *Science of the Soul* (Radha Soami Satsang Beas, India).
Skouteris, T, and Korhonen, O, 'Under Rhodes' Eyes: The "Old" and the "New" International Law at Looking Distance' (1998) 11 *Leiden Journal of International Law* 429.
Skouteris, T, 'Fin the NAIL: New Approaches to International Law and its Impact on Contemporary International Legal Scholarship' (1997) 10 *Leiden Journal of International Law* 415.
Steiner, HJ, and Alston, P, *International Human Rights in Context: Law, Politics, Morals* (Oxford, Clarendon Press, 1996).
Stern, B, 'A Propos de la Competence Universelle . . .' in *Liber Amicorum M Bedjaoui*, (The Hague, Kluwer Law International, 1999). YDM
Szasz, PC, 'Judicial Insights into Fundamental Values and Interests of the International Community' (1997) *Leiden Journal of International Law*, special issue: AS Muller, D Raic and Thuranszky, (eds), *The International Court of Justice: Its Future Role after Fifty Years.*
Sztucki, J, 'Judicial Insights into Fundamental Values and Interests of the International Community' (1997) *Leiden Journal of International Law*, special issue: AS Muller, D Raic and Thuranszky, (eds), *The International Court of Justice: Its Future Role after Fifty Years.*
Tandon, MP, *International Relations*, 4th edn, (Allahabad, India, Allahabad Law Agency).
—— and R Tandon, *Cases on International Law* (Faridabad, India, Allahabad Law Agency, 1998).
Thirlway, H, 'International Court of Justice' in MD Evans, (ed), *International Law* (Oxford, OUP, 2003) 559.
Thee, M, 'The Right of Peoples to Peace' in K Vasak, *Amicorum Liber: Human Rights at the Dawn of the Twenty-First Century* (Bruylant, Bruxelles, UNESCO, 1999).
Trachtman, J, 'The South-West Africa Cases and the Development of International Law' (1976) 5(3) *LSE Journal of International Studies* 292.
Turner, R, (ed), *Thinkers of the Twentieth Century*, 2nd edn, (Chicago, IL, St James' Press, 1988).
van Hoecke, M, *Law as Communication* (Oxford, Hart Publishing, 2002).
—— and F Ost, (eds), *The Harmonization of European Private Law* (Oxford, Hart Publishing, 2000).
—— *What is Legal Theory?* (Leuven/Amersfoort, Acco, 1985).
Venkataraman, S, 'South West Africa: The Contentious Case (Phase I)' (1969) 1(3) *Eastern Journal of International Law* 270.
—— 'South West Africa: The Contentious Case (Phase II)' (1970) 1(4) *Eastern Journal of International Law* 344.

Vijapur, AP, *The United Nations at Fifty: Studies in Human Rights* (New Delhi, South Asian Publishers, 1996).

Verma, SK, *An Introduction to Public International Law* (New Delhi, Prentice Hall of India, 1998).

Wallace, RMM, *International Law: A Student Introduction* (London, Sweet & Maxwell, 1997).

Weil, P, 'Towards Relative Normativity in International Law' (1983) 77 *American Journal of International Law* 413.

Wellens, K (ed), *International Law: Theory and Practice: Essays in Honour of Eric Suy* (The Hague, Martinus Nijhoff, 1998).

—— 'La Cour internationale de justice et la protection des droit de l'homme' in *Les incidences des jurisprudences internationale sur les droits Néderlandais et Français notamment sur les Droits de l'Homme* (Paris, Presses Universitaires de France) 41.

Wiechers, M, 'South West Africa: The Decision of 16 July 1966 and its Aftermath' (1968) 1(3) *Comparative and International Law Journal of Southern Africa* 408.

BIBLIOGRAPHY OF WORKS BY JUDGES OF THE COURT

ABI-SAAB, G.

Abi-Saab, G, 'International Criminal Tribunals and the Development of International Humanitarian and Human Rights Law' in E Yakpo and T Boumedra, (eds), *Liber Amicorum: Judge Mohammed Bedjaoui* (The Hague, Kluwer International Law, 1999) 649.

Aghahosseini, M, 'The Claims of Dual Nationals before the Iran-United States Claims Tribunal: Some Reflections' (1997) 10 *Leiden Journal of International Law* 21.

ABRAHAM, R.

Abrahams, R, *Les Procédures Incidents devant la Cour Internationale de Justice* (Paris, Pedone, 2001).

BAXTER, R. R.

Draper, G, 'Judge Baxter on the Law of War' (1980) 21 *Havard International Law Journal* 623.

BEDJAOUI, M.

Bedjaoui, M, 'À Propos de la Place des Droits de la Personne Humaine dans la Jurisprudence de la Cour Internationale de Justice' in P Mahoney, *et al*, (eds), *Protecting Human Rights: The European Perspective* (Köln) 87.

—— *International Law: Achievements and Prospects* (Paris, UNESCO, 1991).

—— *The New World Order and the Security Council: Testing the Legality of its Acts* (Dordrecht, Nijhoff, 1994).

—— 'The Réception by National Courts of Decisions of International Tribunals' in TM Franck and GH Fox, (eds), *International Law Decisions in National Courts* (New York, Transnational, 1996).

BENNOUNA, M.

'La délimitation des espaces maritimes en Méditerranée', in *The Law and the Sea. Essays in Memory of Jean Carroz* (Rome, 1987) pages 13–20.

BROWNLIE, I.

Brownlie, I, V Lowe and M Fitzmaurice, (eds), *Remedies in the International Court of Justice in Fifty Years of the International Court of Justice* (Essays in Honour of Sir Robert Jennings) (Cambridge, 1996) 557.

BUERGENTHAL, T.

Buergenthal, T, *Public International Law* (St Paul, MN, West Publishing, 1990).

—— *International Human Rights Law* (St Paul, MN, West Publishing, 1995).

COHEN, M. (Canada)

Cohen, M, Dinstein, Y (ed), *Impartiality, Realism and International Process, in International Law at a Time of Perplexity* (Essays in Honour of Shabtai Rosenne) (Dordrecht, 1989) 91.

COLLIARD, C.A. (France)

Colliard, CA, *Institutions Internationales*, 3rd edn, (Paris, Dalloz, 1996).

DUGARD, C. J. R.

Dugard, CJR, 'Terrorism and International Law: Consensus at Last' in E Yakpo and T Boumedra, (eds), *Liber Amicorum: Judge Mohammed Bedjaoui* (The Hague, Kluwer International Law, 1999) 159.

EL-ERIAN, A.

El-erian, A, 'The International Court of Justice and the Concept of Universality' (1981) 19 *Columbia Journal of Transnational Law* 197.

FABELA, I.

Neutralité, Paris, Pedone, 1949.

FRANCK, T. M

Franck, TM, 'Constructing the Self: the Right to One's Name' in E Yakpo and T Boumedra, (eds), *Liber Amicorum: Judge Mohammed Bedjaoui* (The Hague, Kluwer International Law, 1999) 691.

Franck, TM, and Fox, GH (eds), *International Law Decisions in National Courts* (New York, Transnational, 1996).

GANSHOF VDMEERSCH, WJ. (Belgium)

De Belgische rechter tegenover het internationaal recht en het gemeenschapssrecht (Rechtskundig Weekblad, 33e jaargang, Nr. 5, 1969, zondag 5 Oktober, pages 194–238.

GOLUNSKY, S.A.

Golunsky, SA, *Election of a Member of the International Court of Justice to Fill the Vacancy Caused by Resignation of Judge SA Golunsky* (Official Records of the General Assembly of the UN, 8th Session, New York, 1953: 48th Plenary Meeting) 27 November, 1953.

GUILLAUME, G.

Guillaume, G, 'La 'Cause Commune'devant la Cour Internationale de Justice' in E Yakpo and T Boumedra, (eds), *Liber Amicorum: Judge Mohammed Bedjaoui* (The Hague, Kluwer International Law, 1999) 325.

HIGGINS, R.

Higgins, R, *The Development of International Law through the Political Organs of the United Nations* (London, OUP, 1963).

—— *Conflict of Interests: International Law in a Divided World* (London, Bodley Head, 1965).

—— and Fawcett, J (eds), *Law in Movement—Essays in Memory of John McMahon* (London, OUP for RIIA, 1974).

—— *Problems and Process: International Law and How We Use It* (Oxford, OUP, 1994).

—— and Flory, M (eds), *Terrorism and International Law* (London, Routledge, 1997).

—— *Authority and Control—Trends in the Literature of International Law and International Relations in Towards World Control and Human Dignity*, in B Weston and M Reisman (eds) *Essays in Honour of Myres McDougal* (Philadelphia, Pennsylvania University Press, 1978).
—— *The Advisory Opinion on Namibia: Which UN Resolutions are Binding Under Article 25 of the Charter?* (1972) *International and Comparative Law Quarterly.*
—— 'Legal Limits to the Use of Force by States: UN Practice' (1961) 37 *British Yearbook of International Law* 269.
—— 'Intervention in International Law' in H Bull, (ed), *Intervention in World Politics* (Oxford, OUP, 1984).
—— 'The Death Throes of Absolute Immunity' (1979) 73 *American Journal of International Law* 465.
—— 'Damages for Violations of Human Rights' in Sims, (ed), *Explorations in Ethics and International Relations.*
—— 'The Right in International Law of an Individual to Enter, Stay in and Leave a Country' in (1973) *International Affairs*, July.
—— 'Reality and Hope in International Human Rights: A critique' (1981) 9 *Hofstra Law Review* 265.
—— *Human Rights: Some Questions of Integrity* (Chorley Lecture) (1989) *Modern Law Review.*
—— *Human Rights as General Norms and a State's Right to Opt Out, Reservations and Objections to Human Rights Conventions* (Gardner, 1997).
—— 'The International Court of Justice and Human Rights' in *International Law: Theory and Practice: Essays in Honour of Eric Suy* (The Hague, Nijhoff, 1998).
—— 'Human Rights' in *The Social Science Encyclopedia*, 2nd edn, (London, Routledge, 1995).
—— 'Interim Measures for the Protection of Human Rights' (1997) 36 *Columbia Journal of Transnational Law.*
—— 'The International Court and South West Africa: The Implications of the Judgment' in (1966) *International Affairs*, October.
—— 'Certain Aspects of the Barcelona Traction Case' (1971) *Virginia Journal of International Law.*
—— 'Judge Dillard and the Right to Self-Determination' (1983) *Virginia Journal of International Law* 387.
—— *International Law at the Threshold of the 21st Century—Essays in Honour of Krzystof Skubiszewski* (1997).
—— 'The International Court of Justice and Africa' in E Yakpo and T Boumedra, (eds), Liber Amicorum: Judge Mohammed Bedjaoui (The Hague, Kluwer International Law, 1999) 343.
—— 'Conceptual Thinking about the Individual in International Law' (1978) 4 British Journal of International Studies.
—— 'Reflections from the International Court' in MD Evans, (ed), *International Law* (Oxford, OUP, 2003) 3.

JESSUP, P. C.

Jessup, PC, 'A Half Century of Efforts to Substitute Law for War' (1960) 99 *Recueil des Cours* 1.
—— 'To Form a More Perfect United Nations' (1970) 129 *Recueil des Cours* 1.

LACHS, M.

Lachs, M, 'The Decision-Making Powers and the Judiciary within the United Nation' in P Fischer, HF Kock and A Verdross, (eds), *Volkerrecht und Rechtsphilosophie* (1980) 389.

—— 'Some Reflections on the Contribution of the International Court of Justice to the Development of International Law' (1983) 10(2) *Syracuse Journal of International Law and Commerce* 239.

—— *The Development and General Trends of International Law in Our Time* (the text of his General Course given at the Hague Academy of International Law, Extract from the *Recueil des cours*, vol 169, for private circulation) (Hague, Martinus Nijhoff, 1984).

—— 'The Revised Procedure of the International Court of Justice' *in Essays on the Development of the International Legal Order in Memory of Haro F van Panhuys*, (Alphen aan den Rijn, Sijthoff & Noordhoff, 1980) 21.

—— 'Thoughts on the Recent Jurisprudence of the International Court of Justice' (1990) 4(1) *Emory International Law Review.*

LAUTERPACHT, H. Sir

Lauterpacht, Sir H, *The Development of International Law by the International Court of Justice* (London, Stevens & Sons, 1958).

MBAYE, K.

MBaye K 'Human Rights and Rights of Peoples: Introduction' in M Bedjaoui, (ed) *International Law: Achievements and Prospects* (Dordrecht, Nijhoff, 1991).

PATHAK, R. S.

Pathak, RS, and Dhokalia, RP (eds), *International Law in Transition: Essays in Memory of Judge Nagendra Singh* (Dordrecht, Martinus Nijhoff, 1992).

RAO, S.P.

Rao, S.P, 'The United Nations and International Peace and Security: An Indian Perspective', in C Tomuschat (ed) *The United Nations at Age Fifty: A Legal Perspective* (The Hague (etc.), 1995, pages 143–184.

RIGAUX, F.

Rigaux, F, *La Loi des Juges* (Paris, Editions Odile Jacob, 1997).

—— *Les attributs du Droit de la Personnalité de la Dignité Humaine, Schriften der Ernst von Caemmerer-Gedächtnisstiftung*, No 4, (Nomos, Baden-Baden)

SCHWEBEL, S. M.

Schwebel, SM, 'Human Rights in the World Court' in RS Pathak and RP Dhokalia, (eds), *International Law in Transition, Essays in Memory of Judge Nagendra Singh*, (New Delhi, Lancer Books, 1992) 267

—— 'The Treatment of Human Rights and Aliens in the International Court of Justice' in V Lowe and M Fitzmaurice, (eds), *Fifty Years of the International Court of Justice* 327.

SHAHABUDDEEN, M.

Shahabuddeen, M, 'The International Court of Justice: The Integrity of an Idea' in RS Pathak and RP Dhokalia, (eds), *International Law in Transition* (New Delhi, Lancer Books, 1992).

SINGH, N. (India)

Singh, N, The Role and Record of the International Court of Justice (Dordrecht, Nijhoff, 1989).
—— *Nuclear Weapons and International Law* (Dordrecht, Nijhoff, 1959).
—— Human Rights and International Co-operation (Dordrecht, Nijhoff, 1969).
—— *Human Rights and the Future of Mankind* (Dordrecht, Nijhoff, 1982).
—— Enforcement of Human Rights in Peace & War and the Future of Humanity (Dordrecht, Nijhoff, 1986).

VALTICOS, N.

Valticos, N, 'D'une Cour Europeen des Droits de l'homme a l'autre, Pavane pour une Cour Bientot Defune' in E Yakpo and T Boumedra, (eds), Liber Amicorum: Judge Mohammed Bedjaoui (The Hague, Kluwer International Law, 1999) 755.

VERESHCHETIN, V. S.

Vereshchetin, VS, 'Is "Deceptive Clarity" better than "Apparent Indecision" in an Advisory Opinion' in E Yakpo and T Boumedra, (eds), *Liber Amicorum: Judge Mohammed Bedjaoui* (The Hague, Kluwer International Law, 1999) 531.

VIRALLY, M.

Virally, M, 'Unilateral Acts of International Organizations' in M Bedjaoui, (ed), *International Law: Achievements and Prospects* (Paris, UNESCO, 1991) 241.

VUKAS, B.

Vukas, B, 'The International Tribunal of the Law of the Sea: Some Features of the New International Judicial Institution' (1997) 37 *Indian Journal of International Law* 372.

WEERAMANTRY, C. G.

Weeramantry, CG, 'An Appreciation of Judge Nagendra Singh' in RS Pathak and RP Dhokalia, (eds), *International Law in Transition* (New Delhi, Lancer Books, 1992.
—— *The Lord' Prayer: Bridge to a Better World* (Liguori, Missouri, Triumph, 1998).

BIBLIOGRAPHICAL ANNEXES

Annex 1

Judgments of the International Court of Justice

1. Corfu Channel (*United Kingdom v Albania*), Judgment of 25 March 1948, on Preliminary Objections, ICJ Reports 1948, page15.
2. Corfu Channel, Judgment of 9 April 1949, on Merits, ICJ Reports 1949, 4.
3. Corfu Channel, Judgment of 15 December 1949, on assessment of amount of compensation, ICJ Reports 1949, 244.
4. Asylum (Colombia/Peru), Judgment of 20 November 1950, ICJ Reports 1950, 266.
5. Request for Interpretation of the Judgment 20 November 1950, Judgment of 27 November 1950, ICJ Reports 1950, 395.
6. Haya de la Torre (*Colombia v Peru*), Judgment of 13 June 1951, ICJ Reports 1951, 71.
7. Fisheries (*United Kingdom v Norway*), Judgment of 18 December 1951, ICJ Reports 1951, 116.
8. Ambatielos (*Greece v United Kingdom*), Judgment of 1 July 1952, on Preliminary Objections, ICJ Reports 1952, 28.
9. Anglo- Iranian Oil Co (*United Kingdom v France*), Judgment of 22 July 1952, ICJ Reports 1952, 93.
10. Rights of Nationals of the United States of America in Morocco (*France v United States of America*), Judgment of 27 August 1952, ICJ Reports 1952, 176.
11. Ambatielos (*Greece v United Kingdom*), Judgment of 19 May 1953, on Merits, ICJ Reports 1953, 10.
12. Minquiers and Ecrehos (*France v United Kingdom*), Judgment of 17 November 1953, ICJ Reports 1953, 47.
13. Nottebohm (*Liechtenstein v Guatemala*), Judgment of 18 November 1953, on Preliminary Objections, ICJ Reports 1953, 111.
14. Monetary Gold Removed from Rome in 1943 (*Italy v France, United Kingdom and United States of America*), Judgment of 15 June 1954, ICJ Reports 1954, 19.
15. Nottebohm, Second Phase, Judgment of 6 April 1955, ICJ Reports 1955, 4.
16. Certain Norwegian Loans (*France v Norway*), Judgment of 6 July 1957, ICJ Reports 1957, 9.
17. Right of Passage over Indian Territory (*Portugal v India*), Judgment of 26 November 1957, on Preliminary Objections, ICJ Reports 1957, 125.
18. Application of the Convention of 1902 Governing the Guardianship of Infants (*Netherlands v Sweden*), Judgment of 28 November 1958, ICJ Reports 1958, 55.
19. Interhandel (*Switzerland v USA*), Judgment of 21 March 1959, on Preliminary Objections, ICJ Reports 1959, 6.
20. Aerial Incident of 27 July 1955 (*Israel v Bulgaria*), Judgment of 26 May 1959, on Preliminary Objections, ICJ Reports 1959, 127.

21. Sovereignty over Certain Frontier Land (Belgium/Netherlands), Judgment of 20 June 1959, ICJ Reports 1959, 209.
22. Right of passage over Indian Territory (*Portugal v India*), Judgment of 12 April 1960, on Merits, ICJ Reports 1960, 6.
23. Arbitral Award made by the King of Spain on 23 December 1906 (*Honduras v Nicaragua*), Judgment of 18 November 1960, ICJ Reports 1960, 192.
24. Temple of Preah Vihear (*Cambodia v Thailand*), Judgment of 26 May 1961, on Preliminary Objections, ICJ Reports 1961, 17.
25. Temple of Preah Vihear (*Cambodia v Thailand*), Judgment of 15 June 1962, on Merits, ICJ Reports 1962, 6.
26. South West Africa (*Ethiopia v South Africa; Liberia v South Africa*), Judgment of 21 December 1962, on Preliminary Objections, ICJ Reports 1962, 319.
27. Northern Cameroons (*Cameron v UK*), Judgment of 2 December 1963, ICJ Reports 1963, 15.
28. Barcelona Traction, Light and Power Company, *Ltd* (New Application: 1962) (*Belgium v Spain*), Judgment of 24 July 1964, on Preliminary Objections, ICJ Reports 1964, 6.
29. South West Africa (*Ethiopia v South Africa; Liberia v South Africa*), Second Phase, Judgment of 18 July 1966, ICJ Reports 1966, 6.
30. North Sea Continental Shelf (Federal Republic of Germany/Denmark; Federal Republic of Germany/Netherlands), Judgment of 20 February 1969, ICJ Reports 1969, 3.
31. Barcelona Traction, Light and Power Company, Ltd (New Application: 1962) (*Belgium v Spain*), Second Phase, Judgment of 5 February 1970, ICJ Reports 1970, 3.
32. Appeal Relating to the Jurisdiction of the ICAO Council (*India v Pakistan*), Judgment of 18 August 1972, ICJ Reports 1972, 46.
33. Fisheries Jurisdiction (*UK v Iceland*), Jurisdiction of the Court, Judgment of 2 February 1973, ICJ Reports 1973, 3.
34. Fisheries Jurisdiction (*Federal Republic of Germany v Iceland*), Judgment of 2 February 1973, ICJ Reports 1973, 49.
35. Fisheries Jurisdiction (*UK v Iceland*), Judgment of 25 July 1974, on merits, ICJ Reports 1974, 3.
36. Fisheries Jurisdiction (*Federal Republic of Germany v Iceland*), Judgment of 25 July 1974, on merits, ICJ Reports 1974, 175.
37. Nuclear Tests (*Australia v France*), Judgment of 20 December 1974, ICJ Reports 1974, 253.
38. Nuclear Tests (*New Zealand v France*), Judgment of 20 December 1974, ICJ Reports 1974, 457.
39. Aegean Sea Continental Shelf (*Greece v Turkey*), Judgment of 19 December 1978, ICJ Reports 1978, 3.
40. United States Diplomatic and Consular Staff in Tehran (*USA v Iran*), Judgment of 24 May 1980, ICJ Reports 1980, 3.
41. Continental Shelf (Tunisia/Libyan Arab Jamahiriya), Application by Malta for permission to intervene, Judgment of 14 April 1981, ICJ Reports 1981, 3.
42. Continental Shelf (Tunisia/Libyan Arab Jamahiriya), 24 February 1982, ICJ Reports 1982, 18.
43. Continental Shelf (Tunisia/Libyan Arab Jamahiriya), Application by Italy for permission to intervene, 21 March 1984, ICJ Reports 1984, 3.
44. Delimitation of the Maritime Boundary in the Gulf of Maine Area (*Canada v USA*) [Case referred to a Chamber], 12 October 1984, ICJ Reports 1984, 246.

45. Military and Paramilitary Activities in and against Nicaragua (*Nicaragua v USA*), Judgment of 26 November 1984, ICJ Reports 1984, 392.
46. Continental Shelf (Libyan Arab Jamahiriya/Malta), Judgment of 3 June 1985, ICJ Reoprts 1985, 13.
47. Application for Revision and Interpretation of the Judgment of 24 February 1982 in the case concerning the Continental Shelf (Tunisia/Libyan Arab Jamahiriya) (*Tunisia v Libyan Arab Jamahiriya*), Judgment of 10 December 1985, ICJ Reports 1985, 14.
48. Military and Paramilitary Activities in and against Nicaragua (*Nicaragua v USA*), Judgment of 27 June 1986 on merits, ICJ Reports 1986, 14.
49. Frontier Dispute (Burkina Faso/Mali) [case referred to a Chamber], Judgment of 22 December 1986, ICJ Reports 1986, 554.
50. Border and Transborder Armed Actions (*Nicaragua v Honduras*) (Jurisdiction and Admissibility), Judgment of 20 December 1988, ICJ Reports 1988, 69.
51. Elettronica Sicula Sp.A (ELSI) (Italy *v* USA) (Admissibility and Merits), Judgment of 20 July 1989, ICJ Reports 1989, 15.
52. Land, Island and Maritime Frontier Dispute (El Salvador/Honduras) (Intervention), Judgment of 13 September 1990, ICJ Reports 1990, 92.
53. Arbitral Award of 31 July 1989 (*Guinea- Bissau v Senegal*), Judgment of 12 November 1991, ICJ Reports 1991, 53.
54. Certain Phosphate Lands in Nauru (*Nauru v Australia*), Judgment of 26 June 1992 on Preliminary Objections, ICJ Reports 1992, 240.
55. Land, Island and Maritime Frontier Dispute (El Salvador/Honduras), Judgment of 11 September 1992, ICJ Reports 1992, 351.
56. Maritime Delimitation in the Area between Greenland and Jan Mayen (*Denmark v Norway*), Judgment of 14 June 1993, ICJ Reports 1993, 38.
57. Territorial Dispute (Libyan Arab Jamahiriya/Chad), Judgment of 3 February 1994, ICJ Reports 1994, 6.
58. Maritime Delimitation and Territorial Questions between Qatar and Bahrain (*Qatar v Bahrain*) (Jurisdiction and Admissibility), Judgment of 1 July 1994, ICJ Reports 1994, 112.
59. Maritime Delimitation and Territorial Questions between Qatar and Bahrain (*Qatar v Bahrain*) (Jurisdiction and Admissibility), Judgment of 15 February 1995, ICJ Reports 1995, 6.
60. East Timor (*Portugal v Australia*) (POs were linked to merits), Judgment of 30 June 1995, ICJ Reports 1995, 90.
61. Application of the Convention on the Prevention and Punishment of the Crime of Genocide (*Bosnia and Herzegovina v Yugoslavia*), Judgment of 11 July 1996 on Preliminary Objections, ICJ Reports 1996, 595.
62. Oil Platforms (*Islamic Republic of Iran v USA*), Judgment of 12 December 1996 on Preliminary Objections, ICJ Reports 1996, 803.
63. The Gabcikovo- Nagymaros Project (Hungary/Slovakia), Judgment of 25 September 1997, ICJ Reports 1997, 7.
64. Questions of Interpretation and Application of the 1971 Montreal Convention arising from the Aerial Incident at Lockerbie (*Libya v United Kingdom*), Judgment of 27 February 1998 on Preliminary Objections, ICJ Reports 1998, 6.
65. Questions of Interpretation and Application of the 1971 Montreal Convention arising from the Aerial Incident at Lockerbie (*Libya v USA*), Judgment of 27 February 1998 on Preliminary Objections, ICJ Reports 1998, 115.

66. Land and Maritime Boundary between Cameroon and Nigeria (*Cameroon v Nigeria*), Judgment of 11 June 1998 on Preliminary Objections, ICJ Reports 1998, 275.
67. Fisheries Jurisdiction (*Spain v Canada*), Judgment of 4 December 1998 on Jurisdiction, ICJ Reports 1998, 432.
68. Request for Interpretation of the Judgment of 11 June 1998 in the Case concerning the Land and Maritime Boundary between Cameroon and Nigeria (*Cameroon v Nigeria*), Preliminary Objections (*Nigeria v Cameroon*), Judgment of 25 March 1999 on Preliminary Jurisdiction, ICJ Reports 1999, 31.
69. Kasikili/Sedudu Island (Botswana/Namibia), Judgment of 13 December 1999, ICJ Reports 1999, 1045.
70. Aerial Incident of 10 August 1999 (*Pakistan v India*), Judgment of 21 June 2000 on Jurisdiction, ICJ Reports 2000, 12.
    12.
71. Arrest Warrant of 11 April 2000 (*Democratic Republic of the Congo v Belgium*), Judgment of 14 February 2002, ICJ Reports 2002, 3.
72. LaGrand (*Germany v United States of America*), Judgment of 27 June 2001, ICJ Reports 2001, 466.
73. Sovereignty over Pulau Ligitan and Pulau Sipadan (Indonesia-Malaysia) (on request Intervention by Philippines: not granted), Judgment of 23 October 2001, ICJ Reports 2001, 575.
74. Arrest Warrant of 11 April 2000 (*Dem Rep of Congo v Belgium*), Judgment of 14 February 2002, ICJ Reports 2002, 3.
75. Land and Maritime Boundary Dispute between Cameroon and Nigeria (Cameroon v Nigeria: Equatorial Guinea Intervening), Judgment of 10 October 2002 (on merits), ICJ Reports 2002, 303.
76. Sovereignty over Pulau Ligitan and Pulau Sipadan (Indonesia-Malaysia), Judgment of 17 December 2002, ICJ Reports 2002, 625.
77. Application for Revision of the Judgment of 11 July 1996 in the case concerning Application of the Convention on the Prevention and Punishment of the Crime of Genocide (*Bosnia and Herzegovina v Yugoslavia*), Preliminary Objections (*Yugoslavia v Bosnia and Herzegovina*), Judgment of 3 February 2003, ICJ Reports 2003, 7.
78. Oil Platforms (*Iran v USA*), Judgment of 6 November 2003, ICJ Reports 2003, 161.
79. Application for Revision of the Judgment of 11 September 1992 in the Case Concerning the Land, Island and Maritime Frontier Dispute (El Salvador/Honduras: Nicaragua Intervening) (*El Salvador v Honduras*), Judgment of 18 December 2003, ICJ Reports 2003, 392.
80. Avena and Other Mexican Nations (*Mexico v United States of America*), Judgment of 31 March 2004, ICJ Reports 2004 (still at press).
81. Legality of Use of Force (*Serbia and Montenegro v Belgium*) (Preliminary Objections), Judgment of 15 December 2004, ICJ Reports 2004 (still at press).
82. Legality of Use of Force (*Serbia and Montenegro v Canada*) (Preliminary Objections), Judgment of 15 December 2004, ICJ Reports 2004 (still at press).
83. Legality of Use of Force (*Serbia and Montenegro v France*) (Preliminary Objections), Judgment of 15 December 2004, ICJ Reports 2004 (still at press).
84. Legality of Use of Force (*Serbia and Montenegro v Germany*) (Preliminary Objections), Judgment of 15 December 2004, ICJ Reports 2004 (still at press).
85. Legality of Use of Force (*Serbia and Montenegro v Italy*) (Preliminary Objections), Judgment of 15 December 2004, ICJ Reports 2004 (still at press).

86. Legality of Use of Force (*Serbia and Montenegro v Netherlands*) (Preliminary Objections), Judgment of 15 December 2004, ICJ Reports 2004 (still at press).
87. Legality of Use of Force (*Serbia and Montenegro v Portugal*) (Preliminary Objections), Judgment of 15 December 2004, ICJ Reports 2004 (still at press).
88. Legality of Use of Force (*Serbia and Montenegro v United Kingdom*) (Preliminary Objections), Judgment of 15 December 2004, ICJ Reports 2004 (still at press).
89. Certain Properties (*Liechtenstein v Germany*) (Preliminary Objections), Judgment of 10 February 2005, ICJ Reports 2005 (still at press).

Annex 2

Advisory Opinions of the International Court of Justice

1. Conditions of Admission of a State to Membership in the United Nations (Article 4 of Charter), Advisory Opinion of 28 May 1948, ICJ Reports 1948, 57.
2. Reparation for injuries suffered in the Service of the United Nations, Advisory Opinion of 11 April 1949, ICJ Reports 1949, 174.
3. Interpretation of Peace Treaties with Bulgaria, Hungary and Romania, First Phase, Advisory Opinion of 30 March 1950, ICJ Reports 1950, 65.
4. Interpretation of Peace Treaties with Bulgaria, Hungary and Romania, Second Phase, Advisory Opinion of 18 July 1950, ICJ Reports 1950, 221.
5. Competence of the General Assembly for the Admission of a Sate to the United Nations, Advisory Opinion of 3 March 1950, ICJ Reports 1950, 4.
6. International Status of South West Africa, Advisory Opinion of 11 July 1950, ICJ Reports 1950, 128.
7. Reservations to the Convention on the Prevention and Punishment of the Crime of Genocide, Advisory Opinion of 28 May 1951, ICJ Reports 1951, 15.
8. Effect of Awards of Compensation Made by the United Nations Administrative Tribunal, Advisory Opinion of 13 July 1954, ICJ Reports 1954, 47.
9. Voting Procedure on Questions relating to Reports and Petitions concerning the Territory of South West Africa, Advisory Opinion of 7 June 1955, ICJ Reports 1955, 67.
10. Judgments of the Administrative Tribunal of the ILO upon complaints made against UNESCO, Advisory Opinion of 23 October 1956, ICJ Reports 1956, 77.
11. Admissibility of Hearings of Petitioners by the Committee on South West Africa, Advisory Opinion of 1 June 1956, ICJ Reports 1956, 23.
12. Constitution of the Maritime Safety Committee of the Inter-Governmental Maritime Consultative Organization, Advisory Opinion of 8 June 1960, ICJ Reports 1960, 150.
13. Certain Expenses of the United Nations (Article 17, Paragraph 2 of the Charter), Advisory Opinion of 20 July 1962, ICJ Reports 1962, 151.
14. Legal Consequences for States of the Continued Presence of South Africa in Namibia (South West Africa) notwithstanding Security Council Resolution 276 (!970), Advisory Opinion of 21 June 1971, ICJ Reports 1971, 16.
15. Application for Review of Judgment No 158 of the United Nations Administrative Tribunal, Advisory Opinion of 12 July 1953, ICJ Reports 1953, 166.
16. Western Sahara, Advisory Opinion of 16 October 1975, ICJ Reports 1975, 12.
17. Interpretation of the Agreement of 25 March 1951 between the World Health Organization and Egypt, Advisory Opinion of 20 December 1980, ICJ Reports 1980, 73.

18. Application for Review of Judgment No 273 of the United Nations Administrative Tribunal, Advisory Opinion of 20 July 1982, ICJ Reports 1982, 325.
19. Application for Review of Judgment No 333 of the United Nations Administrative Tribunal, Advisory Opinion of 27 May 1987, ICJ Reports 1987, 18.
20. Applicability of the Obligation to Arbitrate under Section 21 of the United Nations Agreement of 26 June 1947, Advisory Opinion of 26 April 1988, ICJ Reports 1988, 12.
21. Applicability of Article VI, Section 22, of the Convention on the Privileges and Immunities of the United Nations, Advisory Opinion of 15 December 1989, ICJ Reports 1989, 177.
22. Legality of the Use by a State of Nuclear Weapons in Armed Conflict (requested by WHO), Advisory Opinion of 8 July 1996, ICJ Reports 1996, 68.
    Legality of the Threat or Use of Nuclear Weapons (requested by UN General Assembly), Advisory Opinion of 8 July 1996, ICJ Reports 1996, 226.
    Difference relating to Immunity from Legal Process of a Special Rapporteur of the Commission on Human Rights, Advisory Opinion of 29 April 1999, ICJ Reports 1999, 60.
    Legal Consequences of the Construction of a Wall in the Occupied Plaestinian Territory (Request for Advisory Opinion), Advisory Opinion of 9 July 2004, ICJ Reports 2004, 136.

Annex 3

Orders on Provisional Measures of the International Court of Justice

Anglo Iranian Oil Co (*United Kingdom v Iran*), Provisional Measures Order of 5 July 1951, ICJ Reports 1951, 89.

Interhandel (*Switzerland v United States of America*), Provisional Measures Order of 24 October 1957, ICJ Reports 1957, 105.

Fisheries Jurisdiction (*UK v Iceland*), Provisional Measures Order of 17 August 1972, ICJ Reports 1972, 17.

Fisheries Jurisdiction (*Federal Republic of Germany v Iceland*), Provisional Measures Order of 17 August 1972, ICJ Reports1972, 35.

Nuclear Tests (*Australia v France*), Provisional Measures Order of 22 June 1973, ICJ Reports 1973, 99–105.

Nuclear Tests (*New Zealand v France*), Provisional Measures Order of 22 June 1973, ICJ Reports 1973, 135

Fisheries Jurisdiction (*United Kingdom v Iceland*), Provisional Measures Order of 12 July 1973, ICJ Reports 1973, 302.

Fisheries Jurisdiction (*Fed Rep of Germany v Iceland*), Provisional Measures Order of 12 July 1973, ICJ Reports 1973, 313.

Trial of Pakistani Prisoners of War (*Pakistan v India*), Provisional Measures Order of 13 July 1973, ICJ Reports1973, 328–31.

Aegean Sea Continental Shelf (*Greece v Turkey*), Provisional Measures Order of 11 September 1976, ICJ Reports1976, 3–14.

Us Diplomatic and Consular Staff in Tehran (*United States of America v Iran*), Provisional Measures Order of 15 December 1979, ICJ Reports1979, 7.

Military and Paramilitary Activities in and against Nicaragua (*Nicaragua v United States*), Provisional Measures Order of 10 May 1984, ICJ Reports 1984, 169.

Frontier Dispute (Burkina Faso/Mali), Provisional Measures Order of 10–Jan–1986, ICJ Reports 1986, 3.

Border and Transborder Armed Actions (*Nicaragua v Honduras*), Provisional Measures Order of 31 March 1988, ICJ Reports1988, 9.

Arbitral Award 31 Jul 1989 (*Guinea-Bissau v Senegal*), Provisional Measures Order of 2 March 1990, ICJ Reports 1990, 64.

Passage through the Great Belt (*Finland v Denmark*), Provisional Measures Order of 29 July 1991, ICJ Reports 1991, 12.

Question of Interpretation and Application of the 1971 Montreal Convention arising from the Aerial Incident at Lockerbie (*Libya v UK*), Provisional Measures Order of 14 April 1992, ICJ Reports 1992, 3.

Question of Interpretation and Application of the 1971 Montreal Convention arising from the Aerial Incident at Lockerbie (*Libya v United States*), Provisional Measures Order of 14 April 1992, ICJ Reports1992, 114.

Application of the Convention on the Prevention and Punishment of the Crime of Genocide (*Bosnia and Herzegovina v Yugoslavia*), Provisional Measures Order of 8 April 1993, ICJ Reports1993, 3.

Application of the Convention on the Prevention and Punishment of the Crime of Genocide (*Bosnia Herzegovina v Yugoslavia*), Provisional Measures Order of 13 September 1993, ICJ Reports 1993, 325.

Request for an Examination of the Situation in Accordance with Paragraph 63 of the Court's Judgment of 20 December 1974 in the Nuclear Tests (*New Zealand v France*), Provisional Measures Order of 22 September 1995, ICJ Reports 1995, 288. NB It was a general Order for the entire case which also referred to the request for provisional measures.

Land and Maritime Boundary between Cameroon and Nigeria (*Cameroon v Nigeria*), Provisional Measures Order of 15 March 1996, ICJ Reports 1996, 13.

Vienna Convention on Consular Relations (*Paraguay v United States*), Provisional Measures Order of 9 April 1998, ICJ Reports 1998, 248.

La Grand Case (*Germany v United States*), Provisional Measures Order of 3 March 1999, ICJ Reports 1999, 9.

Legality of Use of Force (*Yugoslavia v Belgium*), Provisional Measures Order of 2 June 1999, ICJ Reports1999, 124.

Legality of Use of Force (*Yugoslavia v Canada*), Provisional Measures Order of 2 June 1999, ICJ Reports 1999, 259.

Legality of Use of Force (*Yugoslavia v France*), Provisional Measures Order of 2 June 1999, ICJ Reports 1999, 363.

Legality of Use of Force (*Yugoslavia v Germany*), Provisional Measures Order of 2 June 1999, ICJ Reports 1999, 422.

Legality of Use of Force (*Yugoslavia v Italy*), Provisional Measures Order of 2 June 1999, ICJ Reports 1999, 481.

Legality of Use of Force (*Yugoslavia v Netherlands*), Provisional Measures Order of 2 June 1999, ICJ Reports 1999, 542.

Legality of Use of Force (*Yugoslavia v Portugal*), Provisional Measures Order of 2 June 1999, ICJ Reports 1999, 656.

Legality of Use of Force (*Yugoslavia v Spain*), Provisional Measures Order of 2 June 1999, ICJ Reports 1999, 761.

Legality of Use of Force (*Yugoslavia v United Kingdom*), Provisional Measures Order of 2 June 1999, ICJ Reports 1999, 826.

Legality of Use of Force (*Yugoslavia v United States*), Provisional Measures Order of 2 June 1999, ICJ Reports 1999, 916.

Armed Activities on Territory of Congo (*Congo v Uganda*), Provisional Measures Order of 1 July 2000, ICJ Reports 2000, 111.

Arrest Warrant of 11 April 2000 (*Congo v Belgium*), Provisional Measures Order of 8 December 2000, ICJ Reports 2000, 182.

Armed Activities on the Territory of Congo (*Democratic Republic of the Congo v Rwanda*) (New Application: 2002), Provisional Measures Order of 10 July 2002, ICJ Reports 2002, 219.

Avena and Other Mexican Nations (*Mexico v United Staes of America*) Provisional Measures Order of 5 February 2003, ICJ Reports 2003, 77.

39. Certain Criminal Proceedings in France (*Republic of the Congo v France*), Order of 17 June 2003, on Provisional Measures (not indicated), ICJ Reports 2003, 102.

Annex 4

Judges of the International Court of Justice

AGO, R (Italy): 1979–95.

In Judgments.

Separate Opinion of Judge Ago, Continental Shelf (Tunisia/Libyan Arab Jamahiriya), Judgment of 24 February 1982, ICJ Reports 1982 95–98.

Separate Opinion of Judge Ago, Military and Paramilitary Activities in and against Nicaragua (*Nicaragua v USA*), Judgment of 26 November 1984, ICJ Reports 1984 514–32.

Separate Opinion of Judge Ago, Military and Paramilitary Activities in and against Nicaragua (*Nicaragua v USA*), Judgment of 27 June 1986 on merits, ICJ Reports 1986 181–91.

Dissenting Opinion of Judge Ago, Certain Phosphate Lands in Nauru (*Nauru v Australia*), Judgment of 26 June 1992 on Preliminary Objections, ICJ Reports 1992 326–28.

Declaration of Judge Ago, Territorial Dispute (Libyan Arab Jamahiriya/Chad), Judgment of 3 February 1994, ICJ Reports 1994 43.

Separate Opinion of Judge Ago, Questions of Interpretation and Application of the 1971 Montreal Convention arising from the Aerial Incident at Lockerbie (*Libya v USA*), Judgment of 27 February 1998 on Preliminary Objections, ICJ Reports 1998 328–41.

In Advisory Opinions.

Separate Opinion of Judge Ago, Interpretation of the Agreement of 25 March 1951 between the World Health Organization and Egypt, Advisory Opinion of 20 December 1980, ICJ Reports 1980 155–62.

Separate Opinion of Judge Ago, Interpretation of the Agreement of 25 March 1951 between the World Health Organization and Egypt, Advisory Opinion of 20 December 1980, ICJ Reports 1980 108.

In Orders.

Joint Separate Opinion of Judges Ruda, Mosler, Ago, Sir Robert Jennings, and De Lachaarriere, Order of 4 October 1984 on Declaration of Intervention of El Salvador in the case concerning Military and Paramilitary Activities in and against Nicaragua (*Nicaragua v USA*), ICJ Report 1984, 219.

AGUILARD-MAWDSLEY, A (Venezuela): 1991–1995.

In Judgments.

Joint Dissenting Opinion of Judge Aguilard-Mawdsley, Arbitral Award of 31 July 1989 (Guinea- Bissau v Senegal), Judgment of 12 November 1991, ICJ Reports 1991 120–129.

Declaration of Judge Aguilard-Mawdsley, Maritime Delimitation in the Area between Greenland and Jan Mayen (*Denmark v Norway*), Judgment of 14 June 1993, ICJ Reports 1993 86.

In Orders Relating Provisional Measures.

Joint Declaration of Judge Aguilard-Mawdsley, Question of Interpretation and Application of the 1971 Montreal Convention arising from the Aerial Incident at Lockerbie (*Libya v UK*), Provisional Measures Order of 14 April 1992, ICJ Reports1992, 24.

Joint Declaration of Judge Aguillard-Mawdsley, Question of Interpretation and Application of the 1971 Montreal Convention arising from the Aerial Incident at Lockerbie (*Libya v United States*), Provisional Measures Order of 14 April 1992, ICJ Reports1992, 136.

AJIBOLA, Prince B A (Nigeria): 1991–94.

In Judgments.

Separate Opinion of Judge Ajibola, Maritime Delimitation in the Area between Greenland and Jan Mayen (*Denmark v Norway*), Judgment of 14 June 1993, ICJ Reports 1993 280–303.

Separate Opinion of Judge Ajibola, Territorial Dispute (Libyan Arab Jamahiriya/Chad), Judgment of 3 February 1994, ICJ Reports 1994 51–92.

In Orders Relating Provisional Measures.

Dissenting Opinion of Judge Ajibola, Question of Interpretation and Application of the 1971 Montreal Convention arising from the Aerial Incident at Lockerbie (*Libya v UK*), Provisional Measures Order of 14 April 1992, ICJ Reports1992, 78–93.

Dissenting Opinion of Judge Ajibola, Question of Interpretation and Application of the 1971 Montreal Convention arising from the Aerial Incident at Lockerbie (*Libya v United States*), Provisional Measures Order of 14 April 1992, ICJ Reports1992, 183–98.

Separate Opinion of Judge Ajibola, Application of the Convention on the Prevention and Punishment of the Crime of Genocide (*Bosnia Herzegovina v Yugoslavia*), Provisional Measures Order of 13 September 1993, ICJ Reports1992, 390–406.

ALFARO, R J (Panama): 1959–64.

In Judgments.

Declaration of Vice-President Alfaro, Temple of Preah Vihear (*Cambodia v Thailand*), Judgment of 26 May 1961 on Preliminary Objections, ICJ Reports 1961 35.

Separate Opinion of Vice-President Alfaro, Temple of Preah Vihear (*Cambodia v Thailand*), Judgment of 15 June 1962 on Merits, ICJ Reports 1962 39–42.

AL-KHASAWNEH, A S (Jordan): 2000-

In Judgments.

Dissenting Opinion of Judge Al-Khasawneh, Aerial Incident of 10 August 1999 (*Pakistan v India*), Judgment of 21 June 2000 on Jurisdiction, ICJ Reports 2000 48–59.

Separate Opinion of Judge Al-Khasawneh, Maritime Delimitation and Territorial questions between Qatar and Bahrain (*Qatar v Bahrain*), Judgment of 16 March 2001 (merits), ICJ Reports 2001, 248.

Dissenting Opinion of Judge Al-Khasawneh, Arrest Warrant of 11 April 2000, Judgment of 14 February 2002, ICJ Reports 2002, 95.

Separate Opinion of Judge Al-Khasawneh, Land and Maritime Boundary between Cameroon and Nigeria (*Cameroon v Nigeria: Equatorial Guinea Intervening*), Judgment of 10 October 2002, ICJ Reports 2002, 492.

Dissenting Opinion of Judge Al-Khasawneh, Oil Platforms (*Iran v USA*), Judgment of 6 November 2003, ICJ Reports 2003, 266.

Joint Declaration of Judge Al-Khasawneh, Legality of Use of Force, (*Serbia and Montenegro v Belgium*), Preliminary Objections, Judgment of 15 December 2004, ICJ Reports 2004 (still at press).

Joint Declaration of Judge Al-Khasawneh, Legality of Use of Force, (*Serbia and Montenegro v Canada*), Preliminary Objections, Judgment of 15 December 2004, ICJ Reports 2004 (still at press).

Joint Declaration of Judge Al-Khasawneh, Legality of Use of Force, (*Serbia and Montenegro v France*), Preliminary Objections, Judgment of 15 December 2004, ICJ Reports 2004 (still at press).

Joint Declaration of Judge Al-Khasawneh, Legality of Use of Force, (*Serbia and Montenegro v Germany*), Preliminary Objections, Judgment of 15 December 2004, ICJ Reports 2004 (still at press).

Joint Declaration of Judge Al-Khasawneh, Legality of Use of Force, (*Serbia and Montenegro v Italy*), Preliminary Objections, Judgment of 15 December 2004, ICJ Reports 2004 (still at press).

Joint Declaration of Judge Al-Khasawneh, Legality of Use of Force, (*Serbia and Montenegro v Netherlands*), Preliminary Objections, Judgment of 15 December 2004, ICJ Reports 2004 (still at press).

Joint Declaration of Judge Al-Khasawneh, Legality of Use of Force, (*Serbia and Montenegro v Portugal*), Preliminary Objections, Judgment of 15 December 2004, ICJ Reports 2004 (still at press).

Joint Declaration of Judge Al-Khasawneh, Legality of Use of Force, (*Serbia and Montenegro v United KIngdom*), Preliminary Objections, Judgment of 15 December 2004, ICJ Reports 2004 (still at press).

In Advisory Opinions.

Separate Opinion of Judge Al-Khasawneh, Legal Consequences of the Construction of a Wall in the Occupied Palestinian Territory, Advisory Opinion of 9 July 2004, ICJ Reports 2004, 235.

ALVAREZ, A (Chile): 1946–55.

In Judgments.

Joint Separate Opinion of Judge Alvarez, Corfu Channel (*United Kingdom v Albania*), Judgment of 25 March 1948 on Preliminary Objections, ICJ Reports 1948, 31–32.

Separate Opinion of Judge Alvarez, Corfu Channel, Judgment of 9 April 1949 on Merits, ICJ Reports 1949, 39–48.

Dissenting Opinion of Judge Alvarez, Asylum (Colombia/Peru), Judgment of 20 November 1950, ICJ Reports 1950, 290–302.

Separate Opinion of Judge Alvarez, Fisheries (*United Kingdom v Norway*), Judgment of 18 December 1951, ICJ Reports 1951. 145–53.
Declaration of Judge Alvarez, Ambatielos (*Greece v United Kingdom*), Judgment of 1 July 1952 on Preliminary Objections, ICJ Reports 1952, 47.
Dissenting Opinion of Judge Alvarez, Anglo- Iranian Oil Co (*United Kingdom v France*), Judgment of 22 July 1952, ICJ Reports 1952, 124–135.
Declaration of Judge Alvarez, Minquiers and Ecrehos (*France v United Kingdom*), Judgment of 17 November 1953, ICJ Reports 1953, 73.

In Advisory Opinions.
Separate Opinion of Judge Alvarez, Conditions of Admission of a State to Membership in the United Nations (Article 4 of Charter), Advisory Opinion of 28 May 1948, ICJ Reports 194867.
Separate Opinion of Judge Alvarez, Reparation for injuries suffered in the Service of the United Nations, Advisory Opinion of 11 April 1949, ICJ Reports 1949 190.
Dissenting Opinion of Judge Alvarez, Competence of the General Assembly for the Admission of a Sate to the United Nations, Advisory Opinion of 3 March 1950, ICJ Reports 1950 12.
Dissenting Opinion of Judge Alvarez, International Status of South West Africa, Advisory Opinion of 11 July 1950, ICJ Reports 1950 174.
Dissenting Opinion of Judge Alvarez, Reservations to the Convention on the Prevention and Punishment of the Crime of Genocide, Advisory Opinion of 28 May 1951, ICJ Reports 1951 49.
Dissenting Opinion of Judge Alvarez, Effect of Awards of Compensation Made by the United Nations Administrative Tribunal, Advisory Opinion of 13 July 1954, ICJ Reports 1954 67.

AMMOUN, F (Lebanon): 1965–76.

In Judgments.
Separate Opinion of Judge Ammoun, North Sea Continental Shelf (Federal Republic of Germany/Denmark; Federal Republic of Germany/Netherlands), Judgment of 20 February 1969, ICJ Reports 1969 100–53.
Separate Opinion of Judge Ammoun, Barcelona Traction, Light and Power Company, Ltd (New Application: 1962) (*Belgium v Spain*), Second Phase, Judgment of 5 February 1970, ICJ Reports 1970 286–333.

In Advisory Opinions.
Separate Opinion of Vice-President Ammoun, Legal Consequences for States of the Continued Presence of South Africa in Namibia (South West Africa) notwithstanding Security Council Resolution 276 (!970), Advisory Opinion of 21 June 1971, ICJ Reports 1971 67–100.
Dissenting Opinion of Vice-President Ammoun, Application for Review of Judgment No 158 of the United Nations Administrative Tribunal, Advisory Opinion of 12 July 1953, ICJ Reports 1953 246–251.
Separate Opinion of Vice-President Ammoun, Western Sahara, Advisory Opinion of 16 October 1975, ICJ Reports 1975 83–102.

In Orders.

Joint Declaration of Vice-President Ammoun, Fisheries Jurisdiction (*UK v Iceland*), Provisional Measures Order of 17 August 1972, ICJ Reports1972, 18–20.

Joint Declaration of Vice-President Ammoun, Fisheries Jurisdiction (*Federal Republic of Germany v Iceland*), Provisional Measures Order of 17 August 1972, ICJ Reports1972, 36.

ARMAND-UGON, E C (Uruguay): 1952–1961.

In Judgments.

Dissenting Opinion of Judge Armand Ugon, Interhandel (*Switzerland v USA*), Judgment of 21 March 1959 on Preliminary Objections, ICJ Reports 1959, 85–94.

Separate Opinion of Judge Armand-Ugon, Aerial Incident of 27 July 1955 (*Israel v Bulgaria*), Judgment of 26 May 1959 on Preliminary Objections, ICJ Reports 1959, 152–155.

Dissenting Opinion of Judge Armand-Ugon, Sovereignty over Certain Frontier Land (Belgium/Netherlands), Judgment of 20 June 1959, ICJ Reports 1959, 233–251.

Dissenting Opinion of Judge Armand-Ugon, Right of passage over Indian Territory (*Portugal v India*), Judgment of 12 April 1960 on Merits, ICJ Reports 1960, 76–87.

Dissenting Opinion of Judge Armand-Ugon, Barcelona Traction, Light and Power Company, Ltd (New Application: 1962) (*Belgium v Spain*), Judgment of 24 July 1964 on Preliminary Objections, ICJ Reports 1964 116–166.

In Advisory Opinion.

Joint Dissenting Opinion of Judge Armand-Ugon, Admissibility of Hearings of Petitioners by the Committee on South West Africa, Advisory Opinion of 1 June 1956, ICJ Reports 1956 60.

AZEVEDO Ph. (Brazil): 1946–51.

In Judgments.

Dissenting Opinion of Judge Azevedo, Corfu Channel, Judgment of 9 April 1949 on Merits, ICJ Reports 1949, 78–114.

Dissenting Opinion of Judge Azevedo, Asylum (Colombia/Peru), Judgment of 20 November 1950, ICJ Reports 1950, 332–58.

Dissenting Opinion of Judge Azevedo, Interpretation of Peace Treaties with Bulgaria, Hungary and Romania, Second Phase, Advisory Opinion of 18 July 1950, ICJ Reports 1950 248.

In Advisory Opinion.

Separate Opinion of Judge Azevedo, Conditions of Admission of a State to Membership in the United Nations (Article 4 of Charter), Advisory Opinion of 28 May 1948, ICJ Reports 1948 73.

Separate Opinion of Judge Asevedo, Reparation for injuries suffered in the Service of the United Nations, Advisory Opinion of 11 April 1949, ICJ Reports 1949 193.

Separate Opinion of Judge Azevedo, Interpretation of Peace Treaties with Bulgaria, Hungary and Romania, First Phase, Advisory Opinion of 30 March 1950, ICJ Reports 1950 79.

Dissenting Opinion of Judge Azevedo, Competence of the General Assembly for the Admission of a Sate to the United Nations, Advisory Opinion of 3 March 1950, ICJ Reports 1950 22.

BADAWI, A H (Egypt): 1946–65.

In Judgments.

Separate Opinion of Judge Badawi (Vice-President), Certain Norwegian Loans (*France v Norway*), Judgment of 6 July 1957, ICJ Reports 1957, 29–34.

Joint Separate Opinion of Judge Badawi, Corfu Channel (*United Kingdom v Albania*), Judgment of 25 March 1948 on Preliminary Objections, ICJ Reports 1948, 31–32.

Dissenting Opinion of Judge Badawi, Corfu Channel, Judgment of 9 April 1949 on Merits, ICJ Reports 1949, 58–67.

Dissenting Opinion of Judge Badawi, Asylum (Colombia/Peru), Judgment of 20 November 1950, ICJ Reports 1950, 303–15.

Joint Dissenting Opinion of Judge Badawi, Rights of Nationals of the United States of America in Morocco (*France v United States of America*), Judgment of 27 August 1952, ICJ Reports 1952, 215–33.

Dissenting Opinion of Judge Badawi (Vice-President), Right of Passage Over Indian Territory (*Portugal v India*), Judgment of 26 November 1957 on Preliminary Objections, ICJ Reports 1957, 154–164.

Separate Opinion of Judge Badawi, Application of the Convention of 1902 Governing the Guardianship of Infants (*Netherlands v Sweden*), Judgment of 28 November 1958, ICJ Reports 1958, 74–78.

Separate Opinion of Judge Badawi, Aerial Incident of 27 July 1955 (*Israel v Bulgaria*), Judgment of 26 May 1959 on Preliminary Objections, ICJ Reports 1959, 148–51.

Declaration of Judge Badawi, Right of passage over Indian Territory (*Portugal v India*), Judgment of 12 April 1960 on Merits, ICJ Reports 1960, 50–51.

Dissenting Opinion of Judge Badawi, Northern Cameroons (*Cameron v UK*), Judgment of 2 December 1963, ICJ Reports 1963 150–54.

In Advisory Opinion.

Dissenting Opinion of Judge Badawi Pasha, Reparation for injuries suffered in the Service of the United Nations, Advisory Opinion of 11 April 1949, ICJ Reports 1949 205.

Joint Declaration of Judge Badawi Pasha, International Status of South West Africa, Advisory Opinion of 11 July 1950, ICJ Reports 1950 145.

Dissenting Opinion of Vice-President Badawi, Judgments of the Administrative Tribunal of the ILO upon complaints made against UNESCO, Advisory Opinion of 23 October 1956, ICJ Reports 1956 123.

Declaration of Vice-President Badawi, Admissibility of Hearings of Petitioners by the Committee on South West Africa, Advisory Opinion of 1 June 1956, ICJ Reports 1956 71.

Joint Dissenting Opinion of Vice-President Badawi, Admissibility of Hearings of Petitioners by the Committee on South West Africa, Advisory Opinion of 1 June 1956, ICJ Reports 1956 60.

In Orders.

Joint Dissenting Opinion of Judge Badawi, Anglo Iranian Oil Co (*United Kingdom v Iran*), Provisional Measures Order of 5 July 1951, ICJ Reports 1951, 96–98.

BASDEVANT, J (France): 1946–64.

In Judgments.

Joint Separate Opinion of Judge Basdevant, Corfu Channel (*United Kingdom v Albania*), Judgment of 25 March 1948 on Preliminary Objections, ICJ Reports 1948, 31–32.

Dissenting Opinion of Judge Basdevant, Ambatielos (*Greece v United Kingdom*), Judgment of 1 July 1952 on Preliminary Objections, ICJ Reports 1952, 66–73.

Joint Dissenting Opinion of Judge Basdevant, Ambatielos (*Greece v United Kingdom*), Judgment of 19 May 1953 on Merits, ICJ Reports 1953, 25–35.

Separate Opinion of Judge Basdevant, Minquiers and Ecrehos (*France v United Kingdom*), Judgment of 17 November 1953, ICJ Reports 1953, 74–84.

Dissenting Opinion of Judge Basdevant, Certain Norwegian Loans (*France v Norway*), Judgment of 6 July 1957, ICJ Reports 1957, 71–78.

Declaration of Judge Basdevant, Interhandel (*Switzerland v USA*), Judgment of 21 March 1959 on Preliminary Objections, ICJ Reports 1959, 30.

Declaration of Judge Basdevant, Right of passage over Indian Territory (*Portugal v India*), Judgment of 12 April 1960 on Merits, ICJ Reports 1960, 48–49.

Dissenting Opinion of Judge Basdevant, South West Africa (*Ethiopia v South Africa*; *Liberia v South Africa*), Judgment of 21 December 1962 on Preliminary Objections, ICJ Reports 1962 459–64.

In Advisory Opinions.

Joint Dissenting Opinion of Judge Basdevant, Conditions of Admission of a State to Membership in the United Nations (Article 4 of Charter), Advisory Opinion of 28 May 1948, ICJ Reports 1948 82.

Separate Opinion of Judge Basdevant, Voting Procedure on Questions relating to Reports and Petitions concerning the Territory of South West Africa, Advisory Opinion of 7 June 1955, ICJ Reports 1955 80.

Joint Dissenting Opinion of Judge Basdevant, Admissibility of Hearings of Petitioners by the Committee on South West Africa, Advisory Opinion of 1 June 1956, ICJ Reports 1956 60.

Dissenting Opinion of Judge Basdevant, Certain Expenses of the United Nations (Article 17, Paragraph 2 of the Charter), Advisory Opinion of 20 July 1962, ICJ Reports 1962 235–38.

BEDJAOUI, M (Algeria): 1982–2001.

In Judgments.

Joint Separate Opinion of Judge Bedjaoui, Continental Shelf (Libyan Arab Jamahiriya/Malta), Judgment of 3 June 1985, ICJ Reports 1985 76–92.

Separate Opinion of Judge Bedjaoui, The Gabcikovo- Nagymaros Project (Hungary/Slovakia), Judgment of 25 September 1997, ICJ Reports 1997 120–141.

Joint Declaration of Judge Bedjaoui, Questions of Interpretation and Application of the 1971 Montreal Convention arising from the Aerial Incident at Lockerbie (*Libya v United Kingdom*), Judgment of 27 February 1998 on Preliminary Objections, ICJ Reports 1998, 32–45.

Joint Declaration of Judge Bedjaoui, Questions of Interpretation and Application of the 1971 Montreal Convention arising from the Aerial Incident at Lockerbie (*Libya v United Kingdom*), Judgment of 27 February 1998 on Preliminary Objections, ICJ Reports 1998 46.

Joint Declaration of Judge Bedjaoui, Questions of Interpretation and Application of the 1971 Montreal Convention arising from the Aerial Incident at Lockerbie (*Libya v USA*), Judgment of 27 February 1998 on Preliminary Objections, ICJ Reports 1998 138.

Dissenting Opinion of Judge Bedjaoui, Fisheries Jurisdiction (*Spain v Canada*), Judgment of 4 December 1998 on Jurisdiction, ICJ Reports 1998 516–52.

Joint Separate Opinion of Judge Bedjaoui, Maritime Delimitation and Territorial questions between Qatar and Bahrain (*Qatar v Bahrain*), Judgment of 16 March 2001 (merits), ICJ Reports 2001, 145.

In Advisory Opinions.

Declaration of President Bedjaoui, Legality of the Threat or Use of Nuclear Weapons (requested by UN General Assembly), Advisory Opinion of 8 July 1996, ICJ Reports 1996 268.

In Orders Relating Provisional Measures.

Dissenting Opinion of Judge Bedjaoui, Question of Interpretation and Application of the 1971 Montreal Convention arising from the Aerial Incident at Lockerbie (*Libya v UK*), Provisional Measures Order of 14 April 1992, ICJ Reports1992, 33–49.

Dissenting Opinion of Judge Bedjaoui, Question of Interpretation and Application of the 1971 Montreal Convention arising from the Aerial Incident at Lockerbie (*Libya v United States*), Provisional Measures Order of 14 April 1992, ICJ Reports1992, 143–59.

BENGZON, C **(Philippines): 1967–76.**

In Judgments.

Declaration of Judge Bengzon, North Sea Continental Shelf (Federal Republic of Germany/Denmark; Federal Republic of Germany/Netherlands), Judgment of 20 February 1969, ICJ Reports 1969 56.

Joint Separate Opinion of Judge Bengzon, Fisheries Jurisdiction (*UK v Iceland*), Judgment of 25 July 1974 on merits, ICJ Reports 1974 45.

Joint Separate Opinion of Judge Bengzon, Fisheries Jurisdiction (*Federal Republic of Germany v Iceland*), Judgment of 25 July 1974 on merits, ICJ Reports 1974 217–24.

Joint Declaration of Judge Bengzon, Nuclear Tests (*Australia v France*), Judgment of 20 December 1974, ICJ Reports 1974 273.

In Orders Relating Provisional Measures.

Joint Dissenting Opinion of Judge Bengzon, Fisheries Jurisdiction (*Federal Republic of Germany v Iceland*), Order of 18 August 1972, ICJ Reports 1972, 184.

Dissenting Opinion of Judge Bengzon, Fisheries Jurisdiction (*United Kingdom v Iceland*), Order of 18 August 1972, ICJ Reports 1972, 191.

BUERGENTHAL, T **(United States): 2000–6.**

In Judgments.

Dissentin Opinion of Judge Buerngenthal, LaGrand (*Germany v USA*), Judgment of 27 June 2001, ICJ Reports 2001, 548.

Joint Separate Opinion of Judge Buerengenthal, Arrest Warrant of 11 April 2000, Judgment of 14 February 2002, ICJ Reports 2002, 63.

Separate Opinion of Judge Buergenthal, Oil Platforms (*Iran v USA*), Judgment of 6 November 2003, ICJ Reports 2003, 270.

Joint Declaration of Judge Buergenthal, Legality of Use of Force, (*Serbia and Montenegro v Belgium*), Preliminary Objections, Judgment of 15 December 2004, ICJ Reports 2004 (still at press).

Joint Declaration of Judge Buergenthal, Legality of Use of Force, (*Serbia and Montenegro v Canada*), Preliminary Objections, Judgment of 15 December 2004, ICJ Reports 2004 (still at press).

Joint Declaration of Judge Buergenthal, Legality of Use of Force, (*Serbia and Montenegro v France*), Preliminary Objections, Judgment of 15 December 2004, ICJ Reports 2004 (still at press).

Joint Declaration of Judge Buergenthal, Legality of Use of Force, (*Serbia and Montenegro v Germany*), Preliminary Objections, Judgment of 15 December 2004, ICJ Reports 2004 (still at press).

Joint Declaration of Judge Buergenthal, Legality of Use of Force, (*Serbia and Montenegro v Italy*), Preliminary Objections, Judgment of 15 December 2004, ICJ Reports 2004 (still at press).

Joint Declaration of Judge Buergenthal, Legality of Use of Force, (*Serbia and Montenegro v Netherlands*), Preliminary Objections, Judgment of 15 December 2004, ICJ Reports 2004 (still at press).

Joint Declaration of Judge Buergenthal, Legality of Use of Force, (*Serbia and Montenegro v Portugal*), Preliminary Objections, Judgment of 15 December 2004, ICJ Reports 2004 (still at press).

Joint Declaration of Judge Buergenthal, Legality of Use of Force, (*Serbia and Montenegro v United KIngdom*), Preliminary Objections, Judgment of 15 December 2004, ICJ Reports 2004 (still at press).

In Advisory Opinions.

Dissenting Opinion of Judge Buergenthal, Legal Consequences of the Construction of a Wall in the Occupied Palestinian Territory, Advisory Opinion of 9 July 2004, ICJ Reports 2004, 240.

In Orders Relating Provisional Measures.

Declaration of Judge Buergenthal, Armed Activities on the Territory of Congo (New Application: 2002) (*Democratic Republic of Congo v Rwanda*), Provisional Measures Order of 10 July 2002, ICJ Reports 2002, 257–59.

BUSTAMANTE Y RIVERO, J L (Peru) **: 1961–70.**

In Judgments.

Separate Opinion of Judge Bustamante, South West Africa (*Ethiopia v South Africa; Liberia v South Africa*), Judgment of 21 December 1962 on Preliminary Objections, ICJ Reports 1962 349–86.

Separate Opinion of Judge Bustamante, Northern Cameroons (*Cameron v UK*), Judgment of 2 December 1963, ICJ Reports 1963 155–83.

Separate Opinion of Judge Bustamante, Barcelona Traction, Light and Power Company, Ltd (New Application: 1962)(*Belgium v Spain*), Judgment of 24 July 1964 on Preliminary Objections, ICJ Reports 1964 78–84.

Separate Opinion of President Bustamante, North Sea Continental Shelf (Federal Republic of Germany/Denmark; Federal Republic of Germany/Netherlands), Judgment of 20 February 1969, ICJ Reports 1969 57–65.

Separate Opinion of President Bustamante, Barcelona Traction, Light and Power Company, Ltd (New Application: 1962)(*Belgium v Spain*), Second Phase, Judgment of 5 February 1970, ICJ Reports 1970, 54–63.

In Advisory Opinion.

Dissenting Opinion of Judge Bustamante, Certain Expenses of the United Nations (Article 17, Paragraph 2 of the Charter), Advisory Opinion of 20 July 1962, ICJ Reports 1962 188–308.

CARNEIRO, L F (Brazil): **1951–55.**

In Judgments.

Separate Opinion of Judge Carneiro, Ambatielos (*Greece v United Kingdom*), Judgment of 1 July 1952 on Preliminary Objections, ICJ Reports 1952, 48–54.

Dissenting Opinion of Judge Carneiro, Anglo- Iranian Oil Co (*United Kingdom v France*), Judgment of 22 July 1952, ICJ Reports 1952, 151–171.

Joint Dissenting Opinion of Judge Carneiro, Rights of Nationals of the United States of America in Morocco (*France v United States of America*), Judgment of 27 August 1952, ICJ Reports 1952, 215–33.

Separate Opinion of Judge Carneiro, Minquiers and Ecrehos (*France v United Kingdom*), Judgment of 17 November 1953, ICJ Reports 1953, 85–109.

Dissenting Opinion of Judge Carneiro, Monetary Gold Removed from Rome in 1943 (*Italy v France, United Kingdom and United States of America*), Judgment of 15 June 1954, ICJ Reports 1954, 39–45.

In Advisory Opinions.

Dissenting Opinion of Judge Carniero, Effect of Awards of Compensation Made by the United Nations Administrative Tribunal, Advisory Opinion of 13 July 1954, ICJ Reports 1954 92.

CASTRO, F De (Spain): **1970–79.**

In Judgments.

Separate Opinion of Judge De Castro, Appeal Relating to the Jurisdiction of the ICAO Council (*India v Pakistan*), Judgment of 18 August 1972, ICJ Reports 1972 116–39.

Separate Opinion of Judge De Castro, Fisheries Jurisdiction (*UK v Iceland*), Judgment of 25 July 1974 on merits, ICJ Reports 1974 72–101.

Separate Opinion of Judge De Castro, Fisheries Jurisdiction (*Federal Republic of Germany v Iceland*), Judgment of 25 July 1974 on merits, ICJ Reports 1974 225–26.

Dissenting Opinion of Judge De Castro, Nuclear Tests (*Australia v France*), Judgment of 20 December 1974, ICJ Reports 1974 372.

Dissenting Opinion of Judge De Castro, Nuclear Tests (*New Zealand v France*), Judgment of 20 December 1974, ICJ Reports 1974 524.

Dissenting Opinion of Judge De Castro, Aegean Sea Continental Shelf (*Greece v Turkey*), Judgment of 19 December 1978, ICJ Reports 1978 62–71.

In Advisory Opinion.

Separate Opinion of Judge De Castro, Legal Consequences for States of the Continued Presence of South Africa in Namibia (South West Africa) notwithstanding Security Council Resolution 276 (!970), Advisory Opinion of 21 June 1971, ICJ Reports 1971 170–219.

Dissenting Opinion of Judge De Castro, Application for Review of Judgment No 158 of the United Nations Administrative Tribunal, Advisory Opinion of 12 July 1953, ICJ Reports 1953 274–95.

Separate Opinion of Judge De Castro, Western Sahara, Advisory Opinion of 16 October 1975, ICJ Reports 1975 127–72.

CORDOVA, R (Mexico): 1955–64.

In Judgments.

Dissenting Opinion of Judge Cordova, Application of the Convention of 1902 Governing the Guardianship of Infants (*Netherlands v Sweden*), Judgment of 28 November 1958, ICJ Reports 1958, 139–45.

Separate Opinion of Judge Cordova, Interhandel (*Switzerland v USA*), Judgment of 21 March 1959 on Preliminary Objections, ICJ Reports 1959, 41–47.

In Advisory Opinion.

Dissenting Opinion of Judge Cordova, Judgments of the Administrative Tribunal of the ILO upon complaints made against UNESCO, Advisory Opinion of 23 October 1956, ICJ Reports 1956 155.

DE LACHARRIERE, Ladreit G (France): 1982–87.

In Orders.

Joint Separate Opinion of Judges Ruda, Mosler, Ago, Sir Robert Jennings, and De Lachaarriere, Order of 4 October 1984 on Declaration of Intervention of El Salvador in the case concerning Military and Paramilitary Activities in and against Nicaragua (*Nicaragua v USA*), ICJ Report 1984, 219.

DE VISSCHER, Ch. (Belgium): 1946–52.

In Judgments.

Joint Separate Opinion of Judge De Visscher, Corfu Channel (*United Kingdom v Albania*), Judgment of 25 March 1948 on Preliminary Objections, ICJ Reports 1948, 31–32.

In Advisory Opinion.

Dissenting Opinion of Judge De Visscher, International Status of South West Africa, Advisory Opinion of 11 July 1950, ICJ Reports 1950 186.

DILLARD, H C (United States): 1970–79.

In Judgments.

Separate Opinion of Judge Dillard, Appeal Relating to the Jurisdiction of the ICAO Council (*India v Pakistan*), Judgment of 18 August 1972, ICJ Reports 1972 92–115.

Separate Opinion of Judge Dillard, Fisheries Jurisdiction (*UK v Iceland*), Judgment of 25 July 1974 on merits, ICJ Reports 1974 53–71.

Declaration of Judge Dillard, Fisheries Jurisdiction (*Federal Republic of Germany v Iceland*), Judgment of 25 July 1974 on merits, ICJ Reports 1974 207–8.

Joint Declaration of Judge Dillard, Nuclear Tests (*Australia v France*), Judgment of 20 December 1974, ICJ Reports 1974 273.

Joint Dissenting Opinion of Judge Dillard, Nuclear Tests (*Australia v France*), Judgment of 20 December 1974, ICJ Reports 1974 312.

Joint Dissenting Opinion of Judge Dillard, Nuclear Tests (*New Zealand v France*), Judgment of 20 December 1974, ICJ Reports 1974 494.

In Advisory Opinion.

Separate Opinion of Judge Dillard, Legal Consequences for States of the Continued Presence of South Africa in Namibia (South West Africa) notwithstanding Security Council Resolution 276 (!970), Advisory Opinion of 21 June 1971, ICJ Reports 1971 150–69.

Separate Opinion of Judge Dillard, Application for Review of Judgment No 158 of the United Nations Administrative Tribunal, Advisory Opinion of 12 July 1953, ICJ Reports 1953 230–41.

Separate Opinion of Judge Dillard, Western Sahara, Advisory Opinion of 16 October 1975, ICJ Reports 1975 116–26.

In Orders.

Joint Declaration of Judge Dillard, Legal Consequences for States of the Continued Presence of South Africa in Namibia (South West Africa) notwithstanding Security Council Resolution 276(1970), Order of 29 January 1971, ICJ Reports 1971, P 14.

ELARABY, N (Egypt): 2001–

In Judgments.

Dissenting Opinion of Judge Elaraby, Oil Platforms (Iran v USA), Judgment of 6 November 2003, ICJ Reports 2003, 290.

Joint Declaration of Judge Elaraby, Legality of Use of Force, (*Serbia and Montenegro v Belgium*), Preliminary Objections, Judgment of 15 December 2004, ICJ Reports 2004 (still at press).

Joint Declaration of Judge Elaraby, Legality of Use of Force, (*Serbia and Montenegro v Canada*), Preliminary Objections, Judgment of 15 December 2004, ICJ Reports 2004 (still at press).

Joint Declaration of Judge Elaraby, Legality of Use of Force, (*Serbia and Montenegro v France*), Preliminary Objections, Judgment of 15 December 2004, ICJ Reports 2004 (still at press).

Joint Declaration of Judge Elaraby, Legality of Use of Force, (*Serbia and Montenegro v Germany*), Preliminary Objections, Judgment of 15 December 2004, ICJ Reports 2004 (still at press).

Joint Declaration of Judge Elaraby, Legality of Use of Force, (*Serbia and Montenegro v Italy*), Preliminary Objections, Judgment of 15 December 2004, ICJ Reports 2004 (still at press).

Joint Declaration of Judge Elaraby, Legality of Use of Force, (*Serbia and Montenegro v Netherlands*), Preliminary Objections, Judgment of 15 December 2004, ICJ Reports 2004 (still at press).

Joint Declaration of Judge Elaraby, Legality of Use of Force, (*Serbia and Montenegro v Portugal*), Preliminary Objections, Judgment of 15 December 2004, ICJ Reports 2004 (still at press).

Joint Declaration of Judge Elaraby, Legality of Use of Force, (*Serbia and Montenegro v United KIngdom*), Preliminary Objections, Judgment of 15 December 2004, ICJ Reports 2004 (still at press).

Separate Opinion of Judge Elaraby, Legality of Use of Force, (*Serbia and Montenegro v Belgium*), Preliminary Objections, Judgment of 15 December 2004, ICJ Reports 2004 (still at press).

Separate Opinion of Judge Elaraby, Legality of Use of Force, (*Serbia and Montenegro v Canada*), Preliminary Objections, Judgment of 15 December 2004, ICJ Reports 2004 (still at press).

Separate Opinion of Judge Elaraby, Legality of Use of Force, (*Serbia and Montenegro v France*), Preliminary Objections, Judgment of 15 December 2004, ICJ Reports 2004 (still at press).

Separate Opinion of Judge Elaraby, Legality of Use of Force, (*Serbia and Montenegro v Germany*), Preliminary Objections, Judgment of 15 December 2004, ICJ Reports 2004 (still at press).

Separate Opinion of Judge Elaraby, Legality of Use of Force, (*Serbia and Montenegro v Italy*), Preliminary Objections, Judgment of 15 December 2004, ICJ Reports 2004 (still at press).

Separate Opinion of Judge Elaraby, Legality of Use of Force, (*Serbia and Montenegro v Netherlands*), Preliminary Objections, Judgment of 15 December 2004, ICJ Reports 2004 (still at press).

Separate Opinion of Judge Elaraby, Legality of Use of Force, (*Serbia and Montenegro v Portugal*), Preliminary Objections, Judgment of 15 December 2004, ICJ Reports 2004 (still at press).

Separate Opinion of Judge Elaraby, Legality of Use of Force, (*Serbia and Montenegro v United KIngdom*), Preliminary Objections, Judgment of 15 December 2004, ICJ Reports 2004 (still at press).

Dissenting Opinion of Judge Elaraby, Certain Property (*Liechtenstein v Germany*) (Preliminary Objections), Judgment of 10 February 2005, ICJ Reports 2005 (still at press).

In Advisory Opinions.

Separate Opinion of Judge Elaraby, Legal Consequences of the Construction of a Wall in the Occupied Palestinian Territory, Advisory Opinion of 9 July 2004, ICJ Reports 2004, 235.

In Orders on Provisional Measures.

Declaration of Judge Elaraby, Armed Activities on the Territory of Congo (New Application: 2002) (*Democratic Republic of Congo v Rwanda*), Provisional Measures Order of 10 July 2002, ICJ Reports 2002, 260–64.

EL-ERIAN, A (Egypt): **1979–1981.**

In Advisory Opinion.

Separate Opinion of Judge El-Erian, Interpretation of the Agreement of 25 March 1951 between the World Health Organization and Egypt, Advisory Opinion of 20 December 1980, ICJ Reports 1980 163–177.

ELIAS, T O **(Nigeria): 1976–91.**

In Judgments.

Separate Opinion of Judge Elias, Military and Paramilitary Activities in and against Nicaragua (*Nicaragua v USA*), Judgment of 27 June 1986 on merits, ICJ Reports 1986 178–80.

In Advisory Opinion.

Separate Opinion of Judge Elias, Interpretation of the Agreement of 25 March 1951 between the World Health Organization and Egypt, Advisory Opinion of 20 December 1980, ICJ Reports 1980 76.

Declaration of Judge Elias, Applicability of the Obligation to Arbitrate under Section 21 of the United Nations Agreement of 26 June 1947, Advisory Opinion of 26 April 1988, ICJ Reports 1988 38.

In Orders Relating Provisional Measures.

Separate Opinion of Judge Elias, Aegean Sea Continental Shelf (*Greece v Turkey*), Provisional Measures Order of 11 September 1976, ICJ Reports1976, 27–30.

EL-KHANI, A (Syria): 1981–1985.

In Judgments.

Declaration of Judge El-Khani, Continental Shelf (Libyan Arab Jamahiriya/Malta), Judgment of 3 June 1985, ICJ Reoprts 1985 59.

In Advisory Opinion.

Dissenting Opinion of Judge El-Khani, Application for Review of Judgment No 273 of the United Nations Administrative Tribunal, Advisory Opinion of 20 July 1982, ICJ Reports 1982 446.

EVENSEN, J **(Norway): 1985–94.**

In Judgments.

Declaration of Judge Evensen, Maritime Delimitation in the Area between Greenland and Jan Mayen (*Denmark v Norway*), Judgment of 14 June 1993, ICJ Reports 1993 84–85.

In Advisory Opinion.

Dissenting Opinion of Judge Evensen, Interpretation of the Agreement of 25 March 1951 between the World Health Organization and Egypt, Advisory Opinion of 20 December 1980, ICJ Reports 1980 159.

Separate Opinion of Judge Evensen, Applicability of Article VI, Section 22, of the Convention on the Privileges and Immunities of the United Nations, Advisory Opinion of 15 December 1989, ICJ Reports 1989 210.

In Orders Relating Provisional Measures.

Separate Opinion of Judge Evensen, Arbitral Award 31 Jul 1989 (*Guinea-Bissau v Senegal*), Provisional Measures Order of 2 March 1990, ICJ Reports1990, 72–73.

FERRARI BRAVO, L **(Italy) : 1995–97.**

In Advisory Opinion.

Declaration of Judge Ferrari Bravo, Legality of the Use by a State of Nuclear Weapons in Armed Conflict (requested by WHO), Advisory Opinion of 8 July 1996, ICJ Reports 1996 87.

Declaration of Judge Ferrari Bravo, Legality of the Threat or Use of Nuclear Weapons (requested by UN General Assembly), Advisory Opinion of 8 July 1996, ICJ Reports 1996 282.

FITZMAURICE, G Sir (United Kingdom): 1960–73.

In Judgments.

Joint Declaration of Judge Fitzmaurice, Arbitral Award made by the King of Spain on 23 December 1906 (*Honduras v Nicaragua*), Judgment of 18 November 1960, ICJ Reports 1960 36–38.

Separate Opinion of Judge Fitzmaurice, Temple of Preah Vihear (*Cambodia v Thailand*), Judgment of 15 June 1962 on Merits, ICJ Reports 1962 52–66.

Joint Dissenting Opinion of Judge Fitzmaurice, South West Africa (*Ethiopia v South Africa; Liberia v South Africa*), Judgment of 21 December 1962 on Preliminary Objections, ICJ Reports 1962 465–563.

Separate Opinion of Judge Fitzmaurice, Northern Cameroons (*Cameron v UK*), Judgment of 2 December 1963, ICJ Reports 1963 97–130.

Separate Opinion of Judge Fitzmaurice, Barcelona Traction, Light and Power Company, Ltd (New Application: 1962) (*Belgium v Spain*), Second Phase, Judgment of 5 February 1970, ICJ Reports 1970 64–113.

Separate Opinion of Judge Fitzmaurice, Fisheries Jurisdiction (*UK v Iceland*), Jurisdiction of the Court, Judgment of 2 February 1973, ICJ Reports 1973 24–35.

Separate Opinion of Judge Fitzmaurice, Fisheries Jurisdiction (*Federal Republic of Germany v Iceland*), Judgment of 2 February 1973, ICJ Reports 1973 68–80.

In Advisory Opinion.

Separate Opinion of Judge Fitzmaurice, Certain Expenses of the United Nations (Article 17, Paragraph 2 of the Charter), Advisory Opinion of 20 July 1962, ICJ Reports 1962 198–215.

Dissenting Opinion of Judge Fitzmaurice, Legal Consequences for States of the Continued Presence of South Africa in Namibia (South West Africa) notwithstanding Security Council Resolution 276(1970), Advisory Opinion of 21 June 1971, ICJ Reports 1971 220–322.

In Orders.

Joint Declaration of Judge Fitzmaurice, Legal Consequences for States of the Continued Presence of South Africa in Namibia (South West Africa) notwithstanding Security Council Resolution 276(1970), Order of 29 January 1971, ICJ Reports 1971, 13.

FLEISCHHAUER, C-A (Germany): **1994–2003.**

In Judgments.

Dissenting Opinion of Judge Fleishhauer, The Gabcikovo- Nagymaros Project (Hungary/Slovakia), Judgment of 25 September 1997, ICJ Reports 1997 204–218.

Joint Declaration of Judge Fleishhauer, Questions of Interpretation and Application of the 1971 Montreal Convention arising from the Aerial Incident at Lockerbie (*Libya v United Kingdom*), Judgment of 27 February 1998 on Preliminary Objections, ICJ Reports 1998 47–50.

Joint Declaration of Judge Fleishhauer, Questions of Interpretation and Application of the 1971 Montreal Convention arising from the Aerial Incident at Lockerbie (*Libya v USA*), Judgment of 27 February 1998 on Preliminary Objections, ICJ Reports 1998 139.

Dissenting Opinion of Judge Fleishhauer, Kasikili/Sedudu Island (Botswana/Namibia), Judgment of 13 December 1999, ICJ Reports 1999 1196–207.

Declaration of Judge ad hoc Fleischhauer, Certain Property (*Liechtenstein v Germany*) (Preliminary Objections), Judgment of 10 February 2005, ICJ Reports 2005 (still at press).

In Advisory Opinion.

Separate Opinion of Judge Fleishhauer, Legality of the Threat or Use of Nuclear Weapons (requested by UN General Assembly), Advisory Opinion of 8 July 1996, ICJ Reports 1996 305.

FORSTER, I (Senegal): 1964–82.

In Judgments.

Dissenting Opinion of Judge Forster, South West Africa (*Ethiopia v South Africa; Liberia v South Africa*), Second Phase, Judgment of 18 July 1966, ICJ Reports 1966 474–83.

Joint Separate Opinion of Judge Forster, Fisheries Jurisdiction (*UK v Iceland*), Judgment of 25 July 1974 on merits, ICJ Reports 1974 45.

Joint Separate Opinion of Judge Forster, Fisheries Jurisdiction (*Federal Republic of Germany v Iceland*), Judgment of 25 July 1974 on merits, ICJ Reports 1974 217–24.

Separate Opinion of Judge Forster, Nuclear Tests (*Australia v France*), Judgment of 20 December 1974, ICJ Reports 1974 275.

Joint Separate Opinion of Judge Forster, Nuclear Tests (*New Zealand v France*), Judgment of 20 December 1974, ICJ Reports 1974 479.

In Advisory Opinion.

Joint Declaration of Judge Forster, Application for Review of Judgment No 158 of the United Nations Administrative Tribunal, Advisory Opinion of 12 July 1953, ICJ Reports 1953 214–22.

Separate Opinion of Judge Forster, Western Sahara, Advisory Opinion of 16 October 1975, ICJ Reports 1975 103.

In Orders.

Joint Declaration of Judge Forster, Fisheries Jurisdiction (*UK v Iceland*), Provisional Measures Order of 17 August 1972, ICJ Reports1972, 18–20.

Joint Declaration of Judge Forster, Fisheries Jurisdiction (*Federal Republic of Germany v Iceland*), Provisional Measures Order of 17 August 1972, ICJ Reports 1972, 36.

Dissenting Opinion of Judge Forster, Nuclear Tests (*Australia v France*), Provisional Measures Order of 22 June 1973, ICJ Reports 1973, 111–14.

Dissenting Opinion of Judge Forster, Nuclear Tests (*New Zealand v France*), Provisional Measures Order of 22 June 1973, ICJ Reports 1973, 148.

GROS, A (France): 1964–84.

In Judgments.

Separate Opinion of Judge Gros, Barcelona Traction, Light and Power Company, Ltd (New Application: 1962)(*Belgium v Spain*), Second Phase, Judgment of 5 February 1970, ICJ Reports 1970 267–85.

Dissenting Opinion of Judge Gros, Fisheries Jurisdiction (*UK v Iceland*), Judgment of 25 July 1974 on merits, ICJ Reports 1974 126–49.

Dissenting Opinion of Judge Gros, Fisheries Jurisdiction (*Federal Republic of Germany v Iceland*), Judgment of 25 July 1974 on merits, ICJ Reports 1974 234–39.

Separate Opinion of Judge Gros, Nuclear Tests (*Australia v France*), Judgment of 20 December 1974, ICJ Reports 1974 276.

Joint Separate Opinion of Judge Gros, Nuclear Tests (*New Zealand v France*), Judgment of 20 December 1974, ICJ.

Reports 1974 480–82.

Declaration of Judge Gros, Aegean Sea Continental Shelf (*Greece v Turkey*), Judgment of 19 December 1978, ICJ Reports 1978 49.

Dissenting Opinion of Judge Gros, Continental Shelf (Tunisia/Libyan Arab Jamahiriya), Judgment of 24 February 1982, ICJ Reports 1982 143–56.

Dissenting Opinion of Judge Gros, Delimitation of the Maritime Boundary in the Gulf of Maine Area (*Canada v USA*) [Case referred to a Chamber], Judgment of 12 October 1984, ICJ Reports 1984 360–90.

In Advisory Opinion.

Dissenting Opinion of Judge Gros, Legal Consequences for States of the Continued Presence of South Africa in Namibia (South West Africa) notwithstanding Security Council Resolution 276 (!970), Advisory Opinion of 21 June 1971, ICJ Reports 1971 323–45.

Dissenting Opinion of Judge Gros, Application for Review of Judgment No 158 of the United Nations Administrative Tribunal, Advisory Opinion of 12 July 1953, ICJ Reports 1953 252–73.

Declaration of Judge Gros, Western Sahara, Advisory Opinion of 16 October 1975, ICJ Reports 1975 69–77.

Separate Opinion of Judge Gros, Interpretation of the Agreement of 25 March 1951 between the World Health Organization and Egypt, Advisory Opinion of 20 December 1980, ICJ Reports 1980 99–107.

In Orders.

Joint Declaration of Judge Gros, Legal Consequences for States of the Continued Presence of South Africa in Namibia (South West Africa) notwithstanding Security Council Resolution 276(1970), Order of 29 January 1971, ICJ Reports 1971, 13.

Dissenting Opinion of Judge Gros, Nuclear Tests (Australia v France), Provisional Measures Order of 22 June 1973, ICJ Reports1973, 115–23.

Dissenting Opinion of Judge Gros, Nuclear Tests (*New Zealand v France*), Provisional Measures Order of 22 June 1973, ICJ Reports 1973, 149–58.

Dissenting Opinion of Judge Gros, Fisheries Jurisdiction (*United Kingdom v Iceland*), Provisional Measures Order of 12 July 1973, ICJ Reports1973, 306–9.

Dissenting Opinion of Judge Gros, Fisheries Jurisdiction (*Fed Rep of Germany v Iceland*), Provisional Measures Order of 12 July 1973, ICJ Reports1973, 317.

Dissenting Opinion of Judge Gros, Nuclear Tests (*Australia v France*), Provisional Measures Order of 22 June 1973, ICJ Reports 1973, 115.

Dissenting Opinion of Judge Gros, Nuclear Tests (*New Zealand v France*), Provisional Measures Order of 22 June 1973, ICJ Reports, 149.

GUERRERO, JH (El Salvador) : 1946–58.

In Judgments.

Dissenting Opinion of Judge Guerrero, Certain Norwegian Loans (*France v Norway*), Judgment of 6 July 1957, ICJ Reports 1957, 67–70.

In Advisory Opinion.

Declaration of Vice-President Guerrero, International Status of South West Africa, Advisory Opinion of 11 July 1950, ICJ Reports 1950 144–145.

Joint Dissenting Opinion of Vice-President Guerrero, Reservations to the Convention on the Prevention and Punishment of the Crime of Genocide, Advisory Opinion of 28 May 1951, ICJ Reports 1951 31.

GUILLAUME, G (France): 1987–2009.

In Judgments.

Joint Declaration of Judge Guillaume, Questions of Interpretation and Application of the 1971 Montreal Convention arising from the Aerial Incident at Lockerbie (*Libya v United Kingdom*), Judgment of 27 February 1998 on Preliminary Objections, ICJ Reports 1998 32–45.

Joint Declaration of Judge Guillaume, Questions of Interpretation and Application of the 1971 Montreal Convention arising from the Aerial Incident at Lockerbie (*Libya v United Kingdom*), Judgment of 27 February 1998 on Preliminary Objections, ICJ Reports 1998 47–50.

Joint Declaration of Judge Guillaume, Questions of Interpretation and Application of the 1971 Montreal Convention arising from the Aerial Incident at Lockerbie (*Libya v USA*), Judgment of 27 February 1998 on Preliminary Objections, ICJ Reports 1998 138.

Declaration of President Guillaume, LaGrand (*Germany v USA*), Judgment of 27 June 2001, ICJ Reports 2001, 517.

Separate Opinion of President Guillaume, Arrest Warrant of 11 April 2000, Judgment of 14 February 2002, ICJ Reports 2002, 35.

Joint Declaration of Judge Guillaume, Legality of Use of Force, (*Serbia and Montenegro v Belgium*), Preliminary Objections, Judgment of 15 December 2004, ICJ Reports 2004 (still at press).

Joint Declaration of Judge Guillaume, Legality of Use of Force, (*Serbia and Montenegro v Canada*), Preliminary Objections, Judgment of 15 December 2004, ICJ Reports 2004 (still at press).

Joint Declaration of Judge Guillaume, Legality of Use of Force, (*Serbia and Montenegro v France*), Preliminary Objections, Judgment of 15 December 2004, ICJ Reports 2004 (still at press).

Joint Declaration of Judge Guillaume, Legality of Use of Force, (*Serbia and Montenegro v Germany*), Preliminary Objections, Judgment of 15 December 2004, ICJ Reports 2004 (still at press).

Joint Declaration of Judge Guillaume, Legality of Use of Force, (*Serbia and Montenegro v Italy*), Preliminary Objections, Judgment of 15 December 2004, ICJ Reports 2004 (still at press).

Joint Declaration of Judge Guillaume, Legality of Use of Force, (*Serbia and Montenegro v Netherlands*), Preliminary Objections, Judgment of 15 December 2004, ICJ Reports 2004 (still at press).

Joint Declaration of Judge Guillaume, Legality of Use of Force, (*Serbia and Montenegro v Portugal*), Preliminary Objections, Judgment of 15 December 2004, ICJ Reports 2004 (still at press).

Joint Declaration of Judge Guillaume, Legality of Use of Force, (*Serbia and Montenegro v United Kingdom*), Preliminary Objections, Judgment of 15 December 2004, ICJ Reports 2004 (still at press).

In Advisory Opinion.

Separate Opinion of Judge Guillaume, Legality of the Threat or Use of Nuclear Weapons (requested by UN General Assembly), Advisory Opinion of 8 July 1996, ICJ Reports 1996 287.

In Orders Relating Provisional Measures.

Joint Declaration of Judge Guillaume, Question of Interpretation and Application of the 1971 Montreal Convention arising from the Aerial Incident at Lockerbie (*Libya v UK*), Provisional Measures Order of 14 April 1992, ICJ Reports1992, 24.

Joint Declaration of Judge Guillaume, Question of Interpretation and Application of the 1971 Montreal Convention arising from the Aerial Incident at Lockerbie (*Libya v United States*), Provisional Measures Order of 14 April 1992, ICJ Reports 1992, 136.

HACKWORTH GH (United States) **: 1946–61.**

In Judgments.

Declaration of Judge Hackworth, Fisheries (*United Kingdom v Norway*), Judgment of 18 December 1951, ICJ Reports 1951. 144.

Dissenting Opinion of Judge Hackworth, Anglo- Iranian Oil Co (*United Kingdom v France*), Judgment of 22 July 1952, ICJ Reports 1952, 136–141.

Joint Dissenting Opinion of Judge Hackworth, Rights of Nationals of the United States of America in Morocco (*France v United States of America*), Judgment of 27 August 1952, ICJ Reports 1952, 215–33.

Separate Opinion of Judge Hackworth, Interhandel (*Switzerland v USA*), Judgment of 21 March 1959 on Preliminary Objections, ICJ Reports 1959, 33–40.

In Advisory Opinion.

Dissenting Opinion of Judge Hackworth, Reparation for injuries suffered in the Service of the United Nations, Advisory Opinion of 11 April 1949, ICJ Reports 1949 196.

Dissenting Opinion of Judge Hackworth, Effect of Awards of Compensation Made by the United Nations Administrative Tribunal, Advisory Opinion of 13 July 1954, ICJ Reports 1954 76.

Dissenting Opinion of President Hackworth, Judgments of the Administrative Tribunal of the ILO upon complaints made against UNESCO, Advisory Opinion of 23 October 1956, ICJ Reports 1956 116.

In Orders Relating Provisional Measures.

Joint Declaration of President Hackworth, Interhandel (*Switzerland v United States of America*), Provisional Measures Order of 24 October 1957, ICJ Reports 1957, 113.

HERCZEGH, G (Hungary): **1993–2003.**

In Judgments.

Dissenting Opinion of Judge Herczegh, The Gabcikovo- Nagymaros Project (Hungary/ Slovakia), Judgment of 25 September 1997, ICJ Reports 1997 176–203.

Declaration of Judge Herczegh, Questions of Interpretation and Application of the 1971 Montreal Convention arising from the Aerial Incident at Lockerbie (*Libya v United Kingdom*), Judgment of 27 February 1998 on Preliminary Objections, ICJ Reports 1998 51–53.

Declaration of Judge Herczegh, Questions of Interpretation and Application of the 1971 Montreal Convention arising from the Aerial Incident at Lockerbie (*Libya v USA*), Judgment of 27 February 1998 on Preliminary Objections, ICJ Reports 1998 143.

Declaration of Judge Herczegh, Maritime Delimitation and Territorial questions between Qatar and Bahrain (*Qatar v Bahrain*), Judgment of 16 March 2001 (merits), ICJ Reports 2001, 216.

Declararion of Judge Herczegh, Land and Maritime Boundary between Cameroon and Nigeria (*Cameroon v Nigeria: Equatorial Guinea Intervening*), Judgment of 10 October 2002, ICJ Reports 2002, 472.

In Advisory Opinion.

Declaration of Judge Herczegh, Legality of the Threat or Use of Nuclear Weapons (requested by UN General Assembly), Advisory Opinion of 8 July 1996, ICJ Reports 1996 275.

HIGGINS, R (United Kingdom): **1995–2009.**

In Judgments.

Separate Opinion of Judge Higgins, Oil Platforms (*Islamic Republic of Iran v USA*), Judgment of 12 December 1996 on Preliminary Objections, ICJ Reports 1996 847–61.

Separate Opinion of Judge Higgins, Questions of Interpretation and Application of the 1971 Montreal Convention arising from the Aerial Incident at Lockerbie (*Libya v USA*), Judgment of 27 February 1998 on Preliminary Objections, ICJ Reports 1998 345–49.

Declaration of Judge Higgins, Kasikili/Sedudu Island (Botswana/Namibia), Judgment of 13 December 1999, ICJ Reports 1999 1113–15.

Declaration of Judge Higgins, Maritime Delimitation and Territorial questions between Qatar and Bahrain (*Qatar v Bahrain*), Judgment of 16 March 2001 (merits), ICJ Reports 2001, 222.

Joint Separate Opinion of Judge Higgins, Arrest Warrant of 11 April 2000, Judgment of 14 February 2002, ICJ Reports 2002, 63.

Separate Opinion of Judge Higgins, Oil Platforms (*Iran v USA*), Judgment of 6 November 2003, ICJ Reports 2003, 225.

Joint Declaration of Judge Higgins, Legality of Use of Force, (*Serbia and Montenegro v Belgium*), Preliminary Objections, Judgment of 15 December 2004, ICJ Reports 2004 (still at press).

Joint Declaration of Judge Higgins, Legality of Use of Force, (*Serbia and Montenegro v Canada*), Preliminary Objections, Judgment of 15 December 2004, ICJ Reports 2004 (still at press).

Joint Declaration of Judge Higgins, Legality of Use of Force, (*Serbia and Montenegro v France*), Preliminary Objections, Judgment of 15 December 2004, ICJ Reports 2004 (still at press).

Joint Declaration of Judge Higgins, Legality of Use of Force, (*Serbia and Montenegro v Germany*), Preliminary Objections, Judgment of 15 December 2004, ICJ Reports 2004 (still at press).

Joint Declaration of Judge Higgins, Legality of Use of Force, (*Serbia and Montenegro v Italy*), Preliminary Objections, Judgment of 15 December 2004, ICJ Reports 2004 (still at press).

Joint Declaration of Judge Higgins, Legality of Use of Force, (*Serbia and Montenegro v Netherlands*), Preliminary Objections, Judgment of 15 December 2004, ICJ Reports 2004 (still at press).

Joint Declaration of Judge Higgins, Legality of Use of Force, (*Serbia and Montenegro v Portugal*), Preliminary Objections, Judgment of 15 December 2004, ICJ Reports 2004 (still at press).

Joint Declaration of Judge Higgins, Legality of Use of Force, (*Serbia and Montenegro v United Kingdom*), Preliminary Objections, Judgment of 15 December 2004, ICJ Reports 2004 (still at press).

Separate Opinion of Judge Higgins, Legality of Use of Force, (*Serbia and Montenegro v Belgium*), Preliminary Objections, Judgment of 15 December 2004, ICJ Reports 2004 (still at press).

Separate Opinion of Judge Higgins, Legality of Use of Force, (*Serbia and Montenegro v Canada*), Preliminary Objections, Judgment of 15 December 2004, ICJ Reports 2004 (still at press).

Separate Opinion of Judge Higgins, Legality of Use of Force, (*Serbia and Montenegro v France*), Preliminary Objections, Judgment of 15 December 2004, ICJ Reports 2004 (still at press).

Separate Opinion of Judge Higgins, Legality of Use of Force, (*Serbia and Montenegro v Germany*), Preliminary Objections, Judgment of 15 December 2004, ICJ Reports 2004 (still at press).

Separate Opinion of Judge Higgins, Legality of Use of Force, (*Serbia and Montenegro v Italy*), Preliminary Objections, Judgment of 15 December 2004, ICJ Reports 2004 (still at press).

Separate Opinion of Judge Higgins, Legality of Use of Force, (*Serbia and Montenegro v Netherlands*), Preliminary Objections, Judgment of 15 December 2004, ICJ Reports 2004 (still at press).

Separate Opinion of Judge Higgins, Legality of Use of Force, (*Serbia and Montenegro v Portugal*), Preliminary Objections, Judgment of 15 December 2004, ICJ Reports 2004 (still at press).

Separate Opinion of Judge Higgins, Legality of Use of Force, (*Serbia and Montenegro v United KIngdom*), Preliminary Objections, Judgment of 15 December 2004, ICJ Reports 2004 (still at press).

In Advisory Opinion.

Dissenting Opinion of Judge Higgins, Legality of the Threat or Use of Nuclear Weapons (requested by UN General Assembly), Advisory Opinion of 8 July 1996, ICJ Reports 1996 583.

Separate Opinion of Judge Higgins, Legal Consequences of the Construction of a Wall in the Occupied Palestinian Territory, Advisory Opinion of 9 July 2004, ICJ Reports 2004, 207.

In Orders Relating Provisional Measures.

Separate Opinion of Judge Higgins, Legality of Use of Force (*Yugoslavia v Belgium*), Provisional Measures Order of 2 June 1999, ICJ Reports1999, 161–70.

Separate Opinion of Judge Higgins, Legality of Use of Force (*Yugoslavia v Canada*), Provisional Measures Order of 2 June 1999, ICJ Reports1999, 295–304.

Separate Opinion of Judge Higgins, Legality of Use of Force (*Yugoslavia v Netherlands*), Provisional Measures Order of 2 June 1999, ICJ Reports 579–88.

Separate Opinion of Judge Higgins, Legality of Use of Force (*Yugoslavia v Portugal*), Provisional Measures Order of 2 June 1999, ICJ Reports1999, 693–702.

Separate Opinion of Judge Higgins, Legality of Use of Force (*Yugoslavia v Spain*), Provisional Measures Order of 2 June 1999, ICJ Reports1999, 798–807.

Separate Opinion of Judge Higgins, Legality of Use of Force (*Yugoslavia v United Kingdom*), Provisional Measures Order of 2 June 1999, ICJ Reports1999, 866–75.

Declaration of Judge Higgins, Armed Activities on the Territory of Congo (New Application: 2002)(*Democratic Republic of Congo v Rwanda*), Provisional Measures Order of 10 July 2002, ICJ Reports 2002, 256.

HSU MO (China): 1946–56.

In Judgments.

Separate Opinion of Judge Hsu Mo, Fisheries (*United Kingdom v Norway*), Judgment of 18 December 1951, ICJ Reports 1951. 154–57.

Dissenting Opinion of Judge Hsu Mo, Ambatielos (*Greece v United Kingdom*), Judgment of 1 July 1952 on Preliminary Objections, ICJ Reports 1952, 85–88.

Declaration of Judge Hsu Mo, Rights of Nationals of the United States of America in Morocco (*France v United States of America*), Judgment of 27 August 1952, ICJ Reports 1952, 214.

In Advisory Opinion.

Joint Dissenting Opinion of Judge Hsu Mo, Reservations to the Convention on the Prevention and Punishment of the Crime of Genocide, Advisory Opinion of 28 May 1951, ICJ Reports 1951 31.

Joint Dissenting Opinion of Judge Hsu Mo, Admissibility of Hearings of Petitioners by the Committee on South West Africa, Advisory Opinion of 1 June 1956, ICJ Reports 1956 60.

IGNACIO-PINTO (Benin): 1970–1979.

In Judgments.

Declaration of Judge Ignacio-Pinto, Fisheries Jurisdiction (*UK v Iceland*), Judgment of 25 July 1974 on merits, ICJ Reports 1974 35–37.

Declaration of Judge Ignacio-Pinto, Fisheries Jurisdiction (*Federal Republic of Germany v Iceland*), Judgment of 25 July 1974 on merits, ICJ Reports 1974 208.

Separate Opinion of Judge Ignacio-Pinto, Nuclear Tests (*Australia v France*), Judgment of 20 December 1974, ICJ Reports 1974 308.

Joint Separate Opinion of Judge Ignacio-Pinto, Nuclear Tests (*New Zealand v France*), Judgment of 20 December 1974, ICJ Reports 1974 493.

In Advisory Opinion.

Declaration of Judge Ignacio-Pinto, Western Sahara, Advisory Opinion of 16 October 1975, ICJ Reports 1975 78.

In Orders Relating Provisional Measures.

Dissenting Opinion of Judge Ignacio-Pinto, Nuclear Tests (*Australia v France*), Provisional Measures Order of 22 June 1973, ICJ Reports1973, 128–133.

Dissenting Opinion of Judge Ignacio-Pinto, Nuclear Tests (*New Zealand v France*), Provisional Measures Order of 22 June 1973, ICJ Reports1973, 163–164.

Declaration of Judge Ignacio-Pinto, Fisheries Jurisdiction (*United Kingdom v Iceland*), Provisional Measures Order of 12 July 1973, ICJ Reports1973, 304–305.

Declaration of Judge Ignacio-Pinto, Fisheries Jurisdiction (*Fed Rep of Germany v Iceland*), Provisional Measures Order of 12 July 1973, ICJ Reports1973, 315–316.

JENNINGS, RY Sir (United Kingdom): 1982–95.

In Judgments.

Dissenting Opinion of Judge Jennings, Continental Shelf (Tunisia/Libyan Arab Jamahiriya), Application by Italy for permission to intervene, Judgment of 21 March 1984, ICJ Reports 1984 148–60.

Separate Opinion of Judge Jennings, Military and Paramilitary Activities in and against Nicaragua (*Nicaragua v USA*), Judgment of 26 November 1984, ICJ Reports 1984 533–57.

Dissenting Opinion of Judge Jennings, Military and Paramilitary Activities in and against Nicaragua (*Nicaragua v USA*), Judgment of 27 June 1986 on merits, ICJ Reports 1986 528–46.

Dissenting Opinion of President Jennings, Certain Phosphate Lands in Nauru (*Nauru v Australia*), Judgment of 26 June 1992 on Preliminary Objections, ICJ Reports 1992 301–2.

In Advisory Opinion.

Dissenting Opinion of Judge Jennings, Interpretation of the Agreement of 25 March 1951 between the World Health Organization and Egypt, Advisory Opinion of 20 December 1980, ICJ Reports 1980 134.

In Orders.

Joint Separate Opinion of Judge Jennings, Military and Paramilitary Activities in and against Nicaragua (*Nicaragua v United States*), Provisional Measures Order of 10 May 1984, ICJ Reports 1984, 189.

Joint Separate Opinion of Judges Ruda, Mosler, Ago, Sir Robert Jennings, and De Lachaarriere, Order of 4 October 1984 on Declaration of Intervention of El Salvador in the case concerning Military and Paramilitary Activities in and against Nicaragua (*Nicaragua v USA*), ICJ Report 1984, 219.

JESSUP, P. C. (United States): **1961–70.**

In Judgments.

Separate Opinion of Judge Jessup, South West Africa (*Ethiopia v South Africa; Liberia v South Africa*), Judgment of 21 December 1962 on Preliminary Objections, ICJ Reports 1962 357–436.

Declaration of Judge Jessup, Northern Cameroons (*Cameron v UK*), Judgment of 2 December 1963, ICJ Reports 1963 40.

Declaration of Judge Jessup, Barcelona Traction, Light and Power Company, Ltd (New Application: 1962)(*Belgium v Spain*), Judgment of 24 July 1964 on Preliminary Objections, ICJ Reports 1964 49–50.

Separate Opinion of Judge Jessup, South West Africa (*Ethiopia v South Africa; Liberia v South Africa*), Second Phase, Judgment of 18 July 1966, ICJ Reports 1966 325–442.

Separate Opinion of Judge Jessup, North Sea Continental Shelf (Federal Republic of Germany/Denmark; Federal Republic of Germany/Netherlands), Judgment of 20 February 1969, ICJ Reports 1969 66–84.

Separate Opinion of Judge Jessup, Barcelona Traction, Light and Power Company, Ltd (New Application: 1962) (*Belgium v Spain*), Second Phase, Judgment of 5 February 1970, ICJ Reports 1970 161–221.

JIMENEZ DE ARECHAGA, E (Uruguay): 1970–79.

In Judgments.

Separate Opinion of Judge Jimenez De Arechaga, Appeal Relating to the Jurisdiction of the ICAO Council (*India v Pakistan*), Judgment of 18 August 1972, ICJ Reports 1972 140–56.

Joint Separate Opinion of Judge Jimenez De Arechaga, Fisheries Jurisdiction (*UK v Iceland*), Judgment of 25 July 1974 on merits, ICJ Reports 1974 45.

Joint Separate Opinion of Judge Jimenez De Arechaga, Fisheries Jurisdiction (*Federal Republic of Germany v Iceland*), Judgment of 25 July 1974 on merits, ICJ Reports 1974 217–24.

Joint Declaration of Judge Jimenez De Arechaga, Nuclear Tests (*Australia v France*), Judgment of 20 December 1974, ICJ Reports 1974 273.

Joint Dissenting Opinion of Judge Jimenez De Arechaga, Nuclear Tests (*Australia v France*), Judgment of 20 December 1974, ICJ Reports 1974 312.

Joint Dissenting Opinion of Judge Jimenez De Arechaga, Nuclear Tests (*New Zealand v France*), Judgment of 20 December 1974, ICJ Reports 1974 494.

Joint Separate Opinion of Vice-President Jimenez De Arechaga, Continental Shelf (Libyan Arab Jamahiriya/Malta), Judgment of 3 June 1985, ICJ Reports 1985 76–92.

In Advisory Opinion.

Separate Opinion of Judge Jimenez De Arechaga, Application for Review of Judgment No 158 of the United Nations Administrative Tribunal, Advisory Opinion of 12 July 1953, ICJ Reports 1953 242–45.

In Orders.

Joint Declaration of Judge Jimenez De Arechaga, Fisheries Jurisdiction (*UK v Iceland*), Provisional Measures Order of 17 August 1972, ICJ Reports1972, 18–20.

Joint Declaration of Judge Jimenez De Arechaga, Fisheries Jurisdiction (*Federal Republic of Germany v Iceland*), Provisional Measures Order of 17 August 1972, ICJ Reports1972, 36.

Joint Dissenting Opinion of Judge Jemenez De Arechaga, Fisheries Jurisdiction (*Federal Republic of Germany v Iceland*), Order of 18 August 1972, ICJ Reports 1972, 184.

Joint Dissenting Opinion of Judge Jemenez De Arechaga, Fisheries Jurisdiction (*United Kingdom v Iceland*), Order of 18 August 1972, ICJ Reports 1972, 191.

Declaration of Judge Jimenez De Arechaga, Nuclear Tests (*Australia v France*), Provisional Measures Order of 22 June 1973, ICJ Reports1973, 106–7.

Declaration of Judge Jimenez De Arechaga, Nuclear Tests (*New Zealand v France*), Provisional Measures Order of 22 June 1973, ICJ Reports1973, 143.

Separate Opinion of President Jimenez De Arechaga, Aegean Sea Continental Shelf (*Greece v Turkey*), Provisional Measures Order of 11 September 1976, ICJ Reports1976, 15–16.

KLAESTAD, H (Norway): **1946–61.**

In Judgments.

Dissenting Opinion of Judge Klaestad, Ambatielos (*Greece v United Kingdom*), Judgment of 1 July 1952 on Preliminary Objections, ICJ Reports 1952, 80–84.

Joint Dissenting Opinion of Judge Klaestad, Ambatielos (*Greece v United Kingdom*), Judgment of 19 May 1953 on Merits, ICJ Reports 1953, 25–35.

Declaration of Judge Klaestad, Nottebohm (*Liechtenstein v Guatemala*), Judgment of 18 November 1953 on Preliminary Objections, ICJ Reports 1953, 125.

Dissenting Opinion of Judge Klaestad, Nottebohm, Second Phase, Judgment of 6 April 1955, ICJ Reports 1955, 28–33.

Dissenting Opinion of Judge Klaestadt, Right of Passage Over Indian Territory (*Portugal v India*), Judgment of 26 November 1957 on Preliminary Objections, ICJ Reports 1957, 164–65.

Dissenting Opinion of Judge Klaestadt (President), Interhandel (*Switzerland v USA*), Judgment of 21 March 1959 on Preliminary Objections, ICJ Reports 1959, 75–82.
Declaration of President Klaestadt, Right of passage over Indian Territory (*Portugal v India*), Judgment of 12 April 1960 on Merits, ICJ Reports 1960, 47.

In Advisory Opinion.
Separate Opinion of Judge Klaestad, Voting Procedure on Questions relating to Reports and Petitions concerning the Territory of South West Africa, Advisory Opinion of 7 June 1955, ICJ Reports 1955 84.
Separate Opinion of Judge Klaestad, Judgments of the Administrative Tribunal of the ILO upon complaints made against UNESCO, Advisory Opinion of 23 October 1956, ICJ Reports 1956 109.
Dissenting Opinion of President Klaestad, Constitution of the Maritime Safety Committee of the Inter-Governmental Maritime Consultative Organization, Advisory Opinion of 8 June 1960, ICJ Reports 1960 173.

In Orders.
Separate Opinion of Judge Klaestad, Interhandel (*Switzerland v United States of America*), Provisional Measures Order of 24 October 1957, ICJ Reports1957, 115–16.

KOJEVNIKOV, FI (USSR): **1953–61.**

In Judgments.
Declaration of Judge Kojevkinov, Right of Passage Over Indian Territory (*Portugal v India*), Judgment of 26 November 1957 on Preliminary Objections, ICJ Reports 1957, 153.
Declaration of Judge Kojevnikov, Application of the Convention of 1902 Governing the Guardianship of Infants (*Netherlands v Sweden*), Judgment of 28 November 1958, ICJ Reports 1958, 72.
Declaration of Judge Kojevnikov, Interhandel (*Switzerland v USA*), Judgment of 21 March 1959 on Preliminary Objections, ICJ Reports 1959, 31.
Declaration of Judge Kojevnikov, Right of passage over Indian Territory (*Portugal v India*), Judgment of 12 April 1960 on Merits, ICJ Reports 1960, 52.

In Advisory Opinion.
Declaration of Judge Kojevnikov, Voting Procedure on Questions relating to Reports and Petitions concerning the Territory of South West Africa, Advisory Opinion of 7 June 1955, ICJ Reports 1955 72.
Declaration of Judge Kojevnikov, Judgments of the Administrative Tribunal of the ILO upon complaints made against UNESCO, Advisory Opinion of 23 October 1956, ICJ Reports 1956 2.
Declaration of Judge Kojevnikov, Admissibility of Hearings of Petitioners by the Committee on South West Africa, Advisory Opinion of 1 June 1956, ICJ Reports 1956 33.

In Orders.
Dissenting Opinion of Judge Kojevnikov, Interhandel (*Switzerland v United States of America*), Provisional Measures Order of 24 October 1957, ICJ Reports1957, 114–15.

KOOIJMANS, P H (Netherlands): 1997–2006.

In Judgments.

Separate Opinion of Judge Kooijmans, Questions of Interpretation and Application of the 1971 Montreal Convention arising from the Aerial Incident at Lockerbie (*Libya v USA*), Judgment of 27 February 1998 on Preliminary Objections, ICJ Reports 1998 144–51.

Separate Opinion of Judge Kooijmans, Land and Maritime Boundary between Cameroon and Nigeria (*Cameroon v Nigeria*), Judgment of 11 June 1998 on Preliminary Objections, ICJ Reports 1998 354–61.

Separate Opinion of Judge Kooijmans, Fisheries Jurisdiction (*Spain v Canada*), Judgment of 4 December 1998 on Jurisdiction, ICJ Reports 1998 489–95.

Separate Opinion of Judge Kooijmans, Kasikili/Sedudu Island (Botswana/Namibia), Judgment of 13 December 1999, ICJ Reports 1999 1144–52.

Separate Opinion of Judge Kooijmans, Maritime Delimitation and Territorial questions between Qatar and Bahrain (*Qatar v Bahrain*), Judgment of 16 March 2001 (merits), ICJ Reports 2001, 225.

Declaration of Judge Kooijmans, Sovereignty over Pulau Ligitan and Pulau Sipadan (Indonesia/Malaysia), Judgment of 23 October 2001 (Application by the Philippines for Permission to Intervene), ICJ Reports 2001, 626.

Joint Separate Opinion of Judge Kooijmans, Arrest Warrant of 11 April 2000, Judgment of 14 February 2002, ICJ Reports 2002, 63.

Separate Opinion of Judge Kooijmans, Oil Platforms (*Iran v USA*), Judgment of 6 November 2003, ICJ Reports 2003, 246.

Joint Declaration of Judge Kooijmans, Legality of Use of Force, (*Serbia and Montenegro v Belgium*), Preliminary Objections, Judgment of 15 December 2004, ICJ Reports 2004 (still at press).

Joint Declaration of Judge Kooijmans, Legality of Use of Force, (*Serbia and Montenegro v Canada*), Preliminary Objections, Judgment of 15 December 2004, ICJ Reports 2004 (still at press).

Joint Declaration of Judge Kooijmans, Legality of Use of Force, (*Serbia and Montenegro v France*), Preliminary Objections, Judgment of 15 December 2004, ICJ Reports 2004 (still at press).

Joint Declaration of Judge Kooijmans, Legality of Use of Force, (*Serbia and Montenegro v Germany*), Preliminary Objections, Judgment of 15 December 2004, ICJ Reports 2004 (still at press).

Joint Declaration of Judge Kooijmans, Legality of Use of Force, (*Serbia and Montenegro v Italy*), Preliminary Objections, Judgment of 15 December 2004, ICJ Reports 2004 (still at press).

Joint Declaration of Judge Kooijmans, Legality of Use of Force, (*Serbia and Montenegro v Netherlands*), Preliminary Objections, Judgment of 15 December 2004, ICJ Reports 2004 (still at press).

Joint Declaration of Judge Kooijmans, Legality of Use of Force, (*Serbia and Montenegro v Portugal*), Preliminary Objections, Judgment of 15 December 2004, ICJ Reports 2004 (still at press).

Joint Declaration of Judge Kooijmans, Legality of Use of Force, (*Serbia and Montenegro v United Kingdom*), Preliminary Objections, Judgment of 15 December 2004, ICJ Reports 2004 (still at press).

Separate Opinion of Judge Kooijmans, Legality of Use of Force, (*Serbia and Montenegro v Belgium*), Preliminary Objections, Judgment of 15 December 2004, ICJ Reports 2004 (still at press).

Separate Opinion of Judge Kooijmans, Legality of Use of Force, (*Serbia and Montenegro v Canada*), Preliminary Objections, Judgment of 15 December 2004, ICJ Reports 2004 (still at press).

Separate Opinion of Judge Kooijmans, Legality of Use of Force, (*Serbia and Montenegro v France*), Preliminary Objections, Judgment of 15 December 2004, ICJ Reports 2004 (still at press).

Separate Opinion of Judge Kooijmans, Legality of Use of Force, (*Serbia and Montenegro v Germany*), Preliminary Objections, Judgment of 15 December 2004, ICJ Reports 2004 (still at press).

Separate Opinion of Judge Kooijmans, Legality of Use of Force, (*Serbia and Montenegro v Italy*), Preliminary Objections, Judgment of 15 December 2004, ICJ Reports 2004 (still at press).

Separate Opinion of Judge Kooijmans, Legality of Use of Force, (*Serbia and Montenegro v Netherlands*), Preliminary Objections, Judgment of 15 December 2004, ICJ Reports 2004 (still at press).

Separate Opinion of Judge Kooijmans, Legality of Use of Force, (*Serbia and Montenegro v Portugal*), Preliminary Objections, Judgment of 15 December 2004, ICJ Reports 2004 (still at press).

Separate Opinion of Judge Kooijmans, Legality of Use of Force, (*Serbia and Montenegro v United KIngdom*), Preliminary Objections, Judgment of 15 December 2004, ICJ Reports 2004 (still at press).

Dissenting Opinion of Judge Kooijmans, Certain Property (*Liechtenstein v Germany*) (Preliminary Objections), Judgment of 10 February 2005, ICJ Reports 2005 (still at press).

In Advisory Opinions.

Separate Opinion of Judge Kooijmans, Legal Consequences of the Construction of a Wall in the Occupied Palestinian Territory, Advisory Opinion of 9 July 2004, ICJ Reports 2004, 219.

In Orders Relating Provisional Measures.

Separate Opinion of Judge Kooijmans, Legality of Use of Force (*Yugoslavia v Belgium*), Provisional Measures Order of 2 June 1999, ICJ Reports1999, 173–80.

Separate Opinion of Judge Kooijmans, Legality of Use of Force (*Yugoslavia v Canada*), Provisional Measures Order of 2 June 1999, ICJ Reports1999, 307–14.

Separate Opinion of Judge Kooijmans, Legality of Use of Force (*Yugoslavia v Netherlands*), Provisional Measures Order of 2 June 1999, ICJ Reports1999, 591–98.

Separate Opinion of Judge Kooijmans, Legality of Use of Force (*Yugoslavia v Portugal*), Provisional Measures Order of 2 June 1999, ICJ Reports1999, 705–12.

Separate Opinion of Judge Kooijmans, Legality of Use of Force (*Yugoslavia v Spain*), Provisional Measures Order of 2 June 1999, ICJ Reports1999, 809–16.

Separate Opinion of Judge Kooijmans, Legality of Use of Force (*Yugoslavia v United Kingdom*), Provisional Measures Order of 2 June 1999, ICJ Reports1999, 878–87.

KORETSKY:

In Judgments.

Declaration of Judge Koretsky, Northern Cameroons (*Cameron v UK*), Judgment of 2 December 1963, ICJ Reports 1963 39–40.

Declaration of Judge Koretsky, Barcelona Traction, Light and Power Company, Ltd (New Application: 1962) (*Belgium v Spain*), Judgment of 24 July 1964 on Preliminary Objections, ICJ Reports 1964 48–49.

Dissenting Opinion of Judge Koretsky, South West Africa (*Ethiopia v South Africa*; *Liberia v South Africa*), Second Phase, Judgment of 18 July 1966, ICJ Reports 1966 239–49.

Dissenting Opinion of Vice-President Koretsky, North Sea Continental Shelf (Federal Republic of Germany/Denmark; Federal Republic of Germany/Netherlands), Judgment of 20 February 1969, ICJ Reports 1969 154–170.

In Advisory Opinion.

Dissenting Opinion of Judge Koretsky, Certain Expenses of the United Nations (Article 17, Paragraph 2 of the Charter), Advisory Opinion of 20 July 1962, ICJ Reports 1962 254–87.

KOROMA, A G (Sierra Leone): **1994–2003.**

In Judgments.

Dissenting Opinion of Judge Koroma, Maritime Delimitation and Territorial Questions between Qatar and Bahrain (*Qatar v Bahrain*) (Jurisdiction and Admissibility), Judgment of 15 February 1995, ICJ Reports 1995 67–73.

Separate Opinion of Judge Koroma, The Gabcikovo- Nagymaros Project (Hungary/ Slovakia), Judgment of 25 September 1997, ICJ Reports 1997 142–152.

Joint Declaration of Judge Koroma, Questions of Interpretation and Application of the 1971 Montreal Convention arising from the Aerial Incident at Lockerbie (*Libya v United Kingdom*), Judgment of 27 February 1998 on Preliminary Objections, ICJ Reports 1998 46.

Joint Declaration of Judge Koroma, Questions of Interpretation and Application of the 1971 Montreal Convention arising from the Aerial Incident at Lockerbie (*Libya v USA*), Judgment of 27 February 1998 on Preliminary Objections, ICJ Reports 1998 138.

Dissenting Opinion of Judge Koroma, Land and Maritime Boundary between Cameroon and Nigeria (*Cameroon v Nigeria*), Judgment of 11 June 1998 on Preliminary Objections, ICJ Reports 1998 377–91.

Separate Opinion of Judge Koroma, Fisheries Jurisdiction (*Spain v Canada*), Judgment of 4 December 1998 on Jurisdiction, ICJ Reports 1998 486–88.

Dissenting Opinion of Judge Koroma, Request for Interpretation of the Judgment of 11 June 1998 in the Case concerning the Land and Maritime Boundary between Cameroon and Nigeria (*Cameroon v Nigeria*), Preliminary Objections (*Nigeria v Cameroon*), Judgment of 25 March 1999 on Preliminary Jurisdiction, ICJ Reports 1999 49–53.

Declaration of Judge Koroma, Kasikili/Sedudu Island (Botswana/Namibia), Judgment of 13 December 1999, ICJ Reports 1999 1111–12.

Separate Opinion of Judge Koroma, Aerial Incident of 10 August 1999 (*Pakistan v India*), Judgment of 21 June 2000 on Jurisdiction, ICJ Reports 2000 45–46.

Joint Separate Opinion of Judge Koroma, Maritime Delimitation and Territorial questions between Qatar and Bahrain (*Qatar v Bahrain*), Judgment of 16 March 2001 (merits), ICJ Reports, 145.

Separate Opinion of Judge Koroma, LaGrand (*Germany v USA*), Judgment of 27 June 2001, ICJ Reports 2001, 541.

Separate Opinion of Judge Koroma, Sovereignty over Pulau Ligitan and Pulau Sipadan (Indonesia/Malaysia), Judgment of 23 October 2001 (Application by the Philippines for Permission to Intervene), ICJ Reports 2001, 622.

Separate Opinion of Judge Koroma, Arrest Warrant of 11 April 2000, Judgment of 14 February 2002, ICJ Reports 2002, 59.

Dissenting Opinion of Judge Koroma, Land and Maritime Boundary between Cameroon and Nigeria (*Cameroon v Nigeria: Equatorial Guinea Intervening*), Judgment of 10 October 2002, ICJ Reports 2002, 474.

Separate Opinion of Judge KOroma, Application for Revision of the Judgment of 11 July 1996 in the case Concerning Application of the Convention on the Prevention and Punishment of the Crime of Genocide (*Bosnia and Herzegovina v Yugoslavia*). Preliminary Objections (*Yugoslavia v Bosnia and Herzegovina*), Judgment of 3 February 2003, ICJ Reports 2003, 34.

Declaration of Judge Koroma, Oil Platforms (*Iran v USA*), Judgment of 6 November 2003, ICJ Reports 2003, 223.

Declaration of Judge Koroma, Legality of Use of Force, (*Serbia and Montenegro v Belgium*), Preliminary Objections, Judgment of 15 December 2004, ICJ Reports 2004 (still at press).

Declaration of Judge Koroma, Legality of Use of Force, (*Serbia and Montenegro v Canada*), Preliminary Objections, Judgment of 15 December 2004, ICJ Reports 2004 (still at press).

Declaration of Judge Koroma, Legality of Use of Force, (*Serbia and Montenegro v France*), Preliminary Objections, Judgment of 15 December 2004, ICJ Reports 2004 (still at press).

Declaration of Judge Koroma, Legality of Use of Force, (*Serbia and Montenegro v Germany*), Preliminary Objections, Judgment of 15 December 2004, ICJ Reports 2004 (still at press).

Declaration of Judge Koroma, Legality of Use of Force, (*Serbia and Montenegro v Italy*), Preliminary Objections, Judgment of 15 December 2004, ICJ Reports 2004 (still at press).

Declaration of Judge Koroma, Legality of Use of Force, (*Serbia and Montenegro v Netherlands*), Preliminary Objections, Judgment of 15 December 2004, ICJ Reports 2004 (still at press).

Declaration of Judge Koroma, Legality of Use of Force, (*Serbia and Montenegro v Portugal*), Preliminary Objections, Judgment of 15 December 2004, ICJ Reports 2004 (still at press).

Declaration of Judge Koroma, Legality of Use of Force, (*Serbia and Montenegro v United KIngdom*), Preliminary Objections, Judgment of 15 December 2004, ICJ Reports 2004 (still at press).

In Advisory Opinion.

Dissenting Opinion of Judge Koroma, Legality of the Use by a State of Nuclear Weapons in Armed Conflict (requested by WHO), Advisory Opinion of 8 July 1996, ICJ Reports 1996 172.

Dissenting Opinion of Judge Koroma, Legality of the Threat or Use of Nuclear Weapons (requested by UN General Assembly), Advisory Opinion of 8 July 1996, ICJ Reports 1996 556.

Dissenting Opinion of Judge Koroma, Difference relating to Immunity from Legal Process of a Special Rapporteur of the Commission on Human Rights, Advisory Opinion of 29 April 1999, ICJ Reports 1999 111.

Separate Opinion of Judge Koroma, Legal Consequences of the Construction of a Wall in the Occupied Palestinian Territory, Advisory Opinion of 9 July 2004, ICJ Reports 2004, 204.

In Orders Relating Provisional Measures.

Dissenting Opinion of Judge Koroma, Request for an Examination of the Situation in Accordance with Paragraph 63 of the Court's Judgment of 20 December 1974 in the

Nuclear Tests (*New Zealand v France*), Provisional Measures Order of 22 September 1995, ICJ Reports1995, 363–80.

Declaration of Judge Koroma, Land and Maritime Boundary between Cameroon and Nigeria (*Cameroon v Nigeria*), Provisional Measures Order of 15 March 1996, ICJ Reports1996, 30.

Declaration of Judge Koroma, Vienna Convention on Consular Relations (*Paraguay v United States*), Provisional Measures Order of 9 April 1998, ICJ Reports 1998, 263–64.

Declaration of Judge Koroma, Legality of Use of Force (*Yugoslavia v Belgium*), Provisional Measures Order of 2 June 1999, ICJ Reports1999, 142–43.

Declaration of Judge Koroma, Legality of Use of Force (*Yugoslavia v Canada*), Provisional Measures Order of 2 June 1999, ICJ Reports 1999, 276–77.

Declaration of Judge Koroma, Legality of Use of Force (*Yugoslavia v France*), Provisional Measures Order of 2 June 1999, ICJ Reports 1999, 379–80.

Declaration of Judge Koroma, Legality of Use of Force (*Yugoslavia v Germany*), Provisional Measures Order of 2 June 1999, ICJ Reports 1999, 438.

Declaration of Judge Koroma, Legality of Use of Force (*Yugoslavia v Italy*), Provisional Measures Order of 2 June 1999, ICJ Reports 1999, 498–99.

Declaration of Judge Koroma, Legality of Use of Force (*Yugoslavia v Netherlands*), Provisional Measures Order of 2 June 1999, ICJ Reports 1999, 560–61.

Declaration of Judge Koroma, Legality of Use of Force (*Yugoslavia v Portugal*), Provisional Measures Order of 2 June 1999, ICJ Reports 1999, 674–75.

Declaration of Judge Koroma, Legality of Use of Force (*Yugoslavia v Spain*), Provisional Measures Order of 2 June 1999, ICJ Reports1999, 777–78.

Declaration of Judge Koroma, Legality of Use of Force (*Yugoslavia v United Kingdom*), Provisional Measures Order of 2 June 1999, ICJ Reports1999, 845–46.

Declaration of Judge Koroma, Legality of Use of Force (*Yugoslavia v United States of America*), Provisional Measures Order of 2 June 1999, ICJ Reports1999, 929–30.

Declaration of Judge Koroma, Armed Activities on Territory of Congo (*Congo v Uganda*), Provisional Measures Order of 1 July 2000, ICJ Reports2000, 134–35.

Separate Opinion of Judge Koroma, Arrest Warrant of 11 April 2000 (*Congo v Belgium*), Provisional Measures Order of 8–Dec–2000, ICJ Reports2000, 209–210.

Declaration of Judge Koroma, Armed Activities on the Territory of Congo (New Application: 2002) (*Democratic Republic of Congo v Rwanda*), Provisional Measures Order of 10 July 2002, ICJ Reports 2002, 252–55.

Joint Declaration of Judge Koroma, Certain Criminal Proceedings in France, Provisional Measures Order of 17 June 2003, ICJ Reports 2003, 113.

KRYLOV, S B (USSR): 1946–52.

In Judgments.

Joint Separate Opinion of Judge Krylov, Corfu Channel (*United Kingdom v Albania*), Judgment of 25 March 1948 on Preliminary Objections, ICJ Reports 1948, 31–32.

Dissenting Opinion of Judge Krylov, Corfu Channel, Judgment of 9 April 1949 on Merits, ICJ Reports 1949, 68–77.

Declaration of Judge Krylov, Corfu Channel, Judgment of 15 December 1949 on assessment of amount of compensation, ICJ Reports 1949, 251.

Declaration of Judge Krylov, Interpretation of Peace Treaties with Bulgaria, Hungary and Romania, Second Phase, Advisory Opinion of 18 July 1950, ICJ Reports 1950 230.

In Advisory Opinion.

Dissenting Opinion of Judge Krylov, Conditions of Admission of a State to Membership in the United Nations (Article 4 of Charter), Advisory Opinion of 28 May 1948, ICJ Reports 1948 107.

Dissenting Opinion of Judge Krylov, Reparation for injuries suffered in the Service of the United Nations, Advisory Opinion of 11 April 1949, ICJ Reports 1949 217.

Dissenting Opinion of Judge Krylov, Interpretation of Peace Treaties with Bulgaria, Hungary and Romania, First Phase, Advisory Opinion of 30 March 1950, ICJ Reports 1950 105.

Dissenting Opinion of Judge Krylov, International Status of South West Africa, Advisory Opinion of 11 July 1950, ICJ Reports 1950 191.

LACHS, M (Poland): **1967–93.**

In Judgments.

Dissenting Opinion of Judge Lachs, North Sea Continental Shelf (Federal Republic of Germany/Denmark; Federal Republic of Germany/Netherlands), Judgment of 20 February 1969, ICJ Reports 1969 218–40.

Declaration of Judge Lachs, Barcelona Traction, Light and Power Company, Ltd (New Application: 1962)(*Belgium v Spain*), Second Phase, Judgment of 5 February 1970, ICJ Reports 1970 52–53.

Declaration of Judge Lachs, Appeal Relating to the Jurisdiction of the ICAO Council (*India v Pakistan*), Judgment of 18 August 1972, ICJ Reports 1972 72–75.

Declaration of President Lachs, Fisheries Jurisdiction (*UK v Iceland*), Judgment of 25 July 1974 on merits, ICJ Reports 1974 35.

Declaration of President Lachs, Fisheries Jurisdiction (*Federal Republic of Germany v Iceland*), Judgment of 25 July 1974 on merits, ICJ Reports 1974 206–7.

Declaration of President Lachs, Nuclear Tests (*Australia v France*), Judgment of 20 December 1974, ICJ Reports 1974 273.

Separate Opinion of Judge Lachs, Aegean Sea Continental Shelf (*Greece v Turkey*), Judgment of 19 December 1978, ICJ Reports 1978 50–53.

Separate Opinion of Judge Lachs, United States Diplomatic and Consular Staff in Tehran (*USA v Iran*), Judgment of 24 May 1980, ICJ Reports 1980 47–50.

Separate Opinion of Judge Lachs, Continental Shelf (Libyan Arab Jamahiriya/Malta), Judgment of 3 June 1985, ICJ Reports 1985 158–73.

Separate Opinion of Judge Lachs, Military and Paramilitary Activities in and against Nicaragua (*Nicaragua v USA*), Judgment of 27 June 1986 on merits, ICJ Reports 1986 158–73.

Declaration of Judge Lachs, Border and Transborder Armed Actions (*Nicaragua v Honduras*) (Jurisdiction and Admissibility), Judgment of 20 December 1988, ICJ Reports 1988 108.

Separate Opinion of Judge Lachs, Arbitral Award of 31 July 1989 (*Guinea- Bissau v Senegal*), Judgment of 12 November 1991, ICJ Reports 1991 92.

In Advisory Opinion.

Declaration of President Lachs, Application for Review of Judgment No 158 of the United Nations Administrative Tribunal, Advisory Opinion of 12 July 1953, ICJ Reports 1953 214.

Separate Opinion of Judge Lachs, Interpretation of the Agreement of 25 March 1951 between the World Health Organization and Egypt, Advisory Opinion of 20 December 1980, ICJ Reports 1980 108–13.

Dissenting Opinion of Judge Lachs, Application for Review of Judgment No 273 of the United Nations Administrative Tribunal, Advisory Opinion of 20 July 1982, ICJ Reports 1982 411.

Declaration of Judge Lachs, Interpretation of the Agreement of 25 March 1951 between the World Health Organization and Egypt, Advisory Opinion of 20 December 1980, ICJ Reports 1980 74.

In Orders Relating Provisional Measures.

Separate Opinion of Judge Lachs, Aegean Sea Continental Shelf (*Greece v Turkey*), Provisional Measures Order of 11 September 1976, ICJ Reports1976, 19–20.

Separate Opinion of Judge Lachs, Question of Interpretation and Application of the 1971 Montreal Convention arising from the Aerial Incident at Lockerbie (*Libya v UK*), Provisional Measures Order of 14 April 1992, ICJ Reports1992, 26–27.

Separate Opinion of Judge Lachs, Question of Interpretation and Application of the 1971 Montreal Convention arising from the Aerial Incident at Lockerbie (*Libya v United States*), Provisional Measures Order of 14 April 1992, ICJ Reports1992, 138–39.

LAUTERPACHT, H Sir (United Kingdom): **1955–60.**

In Judgments.

Separate Opinion of Judge Lauterpacht Certain Norwegian Loans (*France v Norway*), Judgment of 6 July 1957, ICJ Reports 1957, 34–66.

Separate Opinion of Judge Lauterpacht, Application of the Convention of 1902 Governing the Guardianship of Infants (*Netherlands v Sweden*), Judgment of 28 November 1958, ICJ Reports 1958, 79–101.

Dissenting Opinion of Judge Lauterpacht, Interhandel (*Switzerland v USA*), Judgment of 21 March 1959 on Preliminary Objections, ICJ Reports 1959, 95–122.

Joint Dissenting Opinion of Judge Lauterpacht (together with Judges Wellington Koo and Spender), Aerial Incident of 27 July 1955 (*Israel v Bulgaria*), Judgment of 26 May 1959 on Preliminary Objections, ICJ Reports 1959, 156–94.

Declaration of Judge Lauterpacht, Sovereignty over Certain Frontier Land (Belgium/Netherlands), Judgment of 20 June 1959, ICJ Reports 1959, 230–32.

In Advisory Opinion.

Separate Opinion of Judge Lauterpacht, Voting Procedure on Questions relating to Reports and Petitions concerning the Territory of South West Africa, Advisory Opinion of 7 June 1955, ICJ Reports 1955 90.

Separate Opinion of Judge Lauterpacht, Admissibility of Hearings of Petitioners by the Committee on South West Africa, Advisory Opinion of 1 June 1956, ICJ Reports 1956 35.

In Orders.

Separate Opinion of Judge Lauterpacht, Interhandel (*Switzerland v United States of America*), Provisional Measures Order of 24 October 1957, ICJ Reports1957, 117–20.

MCNAIR, A Sir (United Kingdom): 1946–55.

In Judgments.

Dissenting Opinion of Judge McNair, Fisheries (*United Kingdom v Norway*), Judgment of 18 December 1951, ICJ Reports 1951. 158–85.

Separate Opinion of President McNair, Anglo- Iranian Oil Co (*United Kingdom v France*), Judgment of 22 July 1952, ICJ Reports 1952, 116–123.

Dissenting Opinion of President McNair, Ambatielos (*Greece v United Kingdom*), Judgment of 1 July 1952 on Preliminary Objections, ICJ Reports 1952, 58–65.

Joint Dissenting Opinion of President McNair, Ambatielos (*Greece v United Kingdom*), Judgment of 19 May 1953 on Merits, ICJ Reports 1953, 25–35.

Declaration of President McNair, Monetary Gold Removed from Rome in 1943 (*Italy v France, United Kingdom and United States of America*), Judgment of 15 June 1954, ICJ Reports 1954, 35.

In Advisory Opinion.

Separate Opinion of Judge McNair, International Status of South West Africa, Advisory Opinion of 11 July 1950, ICJ Reports 1950 146.

Joint Dissenting Opinion of Judge McNair, Reservations to the Convention on the Prevention and Punishment of the Crime of Genocide, Advisory Opinion of 28 May 1951, ICJ Reports 1951 31.

Joint Dissenting Opinion of Judge McNair, Conditions of Admission of a State to Membership in the United Nations (Article 4 of Charter), Advisory Opinion of 28 May 1948, ICJ Reports 1948 82.

MBAYE, K (Senegal): 1982–91.

In Judgments.

Separate Opinion of Judge Mbaye, Continental Shelf (Tunisia/Libyan Arab Jamahiriya), Application by Italy for permission to intervene, Judgment of 21 March 1984, ICJ Reports 1984 35–54.

Separate Opinion of Judge Mbaye, Continental Shelf (Libyan Arab Jamahiriya/Malta), Judgment of 3 June 1985, ICJ Reoprts 1985 93–103.

MORELLI, G (Italy): 1961–70.

In Judgments.

Separate Opinion of Judge Morelli, Arbitral Award made by the King of Spain on 23 December 1906 (*Honduras v Nicaragua*), Judgment of 18 November 1960, ICJ Reports 1960 43–50.

Joint Declaration of Judge Morelli, Temple of Preah Vihear (*Cambodia v Thailand*), Judgment of 15 June 1962 on Merits, ICJ Reports 1962 37–38.

Dissenting Opinion of Judge Morelli, South West Africa (*Ethiopia v South Africa*; *Liberia v South Africa*), Judgment of 21 December 1962 on Preliminary Objections, ICJ Reports 1962 564–74.

Separate Opinion of Judge Morelli, Northern Cameroons (*Cameron v UK*), Judgment of 2 December 1963, ICJ Reports 1963 131–49.

Dissenting Opinion of Judge Morelli, Barcelona Traction, Light and Power Company, Ltd (New Application: 1962) (*Belgium v Spain*), Judgment of 24 July 1964 on Preliminary Objections, ICJ Reports 1964 85–115.

Separate Opinion of Judge Morelli, South West Africa (*Ethiopia v South Africa*; *Liberia v South Africa*), Second Phase, Judgment of 18 July 1966, ICJ Reports 1966 59–66.

Dissenting Opinion of Judge Morelli, North Sea Continental Shelf (Federal Republic of Germany/Denmark; Federal Republic of Germany/Netherlands), Judgment of 20 February 1969, ICJ Reports 1969 197–217.

Separate Opinion of Judge Morelli, Barcelona Traction, Light and Power Company, Ltd (New Application: 1962) (*Belgium v Spain*), Second Phase, Judgment of 5 February 1970, ICJ Reports 1970 222–42.

In Advisory Opinion.

Separate Opinion of Judge Morelli, Certain Expenses of the United Nations (Article 17, Paragraph 2 of the Charter), Advisory Opinion of 20 July 1962, ICJ Reports 1962 216–26.

MORENO QUINTANA, LM (Argentina): 1955–64.

In Judgments.

Declaration of Judge Moreno Quintana, Certain Norwegian Loans (France v Norway), Judgment of 6 July 1957, ICJ Reports 1957, 28.

Separate Opinion of Judge Moreno Quintana, Application of the Convention of 1902 Governing the Guardianship of Infants (*Netherlands v Sweden*), Judgment of 28 November 1958, ICJ Reports 1958, 102–9.

Dissenting Opinion of Judge Moreno Quintana, Sovereignty over Certain Frontier Land (Belgium/Netherlands), Judgment of 20 June 1959, ICJ Reports 1959, 252–58.

Dissenting Opinion of Judge Moreno Quintana, Right of passage over Indian Territory (*Portugal v India*), Judgment of 12 April 1960 on Merits, ICJ Reports 1960, 88–96.

Declaration of Judge Moreno Quintana, Arbitral Award made by the King of Spain on 23 December 1906 (*Honduras v Nicaragua*), Judgment of 18 November 1960, ICJ Reports 1960 217–18.

Dissenting Opinion of Judge Moreno Quintana, Temple of Preah Vihear (*Cambodia v Thailand*), Judgment of 15 June 1962 on Merits, ICJ Reports 1962 67–74.

In Advisory Opinion.

Joint Dissenting Opinion of Judge Moreno Quintana, Admissibility of Hearings of Petitioners by the Committee on South West Africa, Advisory Opinion of 1 June 1956, ICJ Reports 1956 60.

Dissenting Opinion of Judge Moreno Quintana, Constitution of the Maritime Safety Committee of the Inter-Governmental Maritime Consultative Organization, Advisory Opinion of 8 June 1960, ICJ Reports 1960 177.

Dissenting Opinion of Judge Moreno Quintana, Certain Expenses of the United Nations (Article 17, Paragraph 2 of the Charter), Advisory Opinion of 20 July 1962, ICJ Reports 1962 239–52.

MOROZOV, PD (USSR): **1970–85.**

In Judgments.

Dissenting Opinion of Judge Morozov, Appeal Relating to the Jurisdiction of the ICAO Council (*India v Pakistan*), Judgment of 18 August 1972, ICJ Reports 1972 157–63.

Declaration of Judge Morozov, Aegean Sea Continental Shelf (*Greece v Turkey*), Judgment of 19 December 1978, ICJ Reports 1978 54.

Separate Opinion of Judge Morozov, United States Diplomatic and Consular Staff in Tehran (USA v Iran), Judgment of 24 May 1980, ICJ Reports 1980 51–57.

Separate Opinion of Judge Morozov, Continental Shelf (Tunisia/Libyan Arab Jamahiriya), Application by Malta for permission to intervene, Judgment of 14 April 1981, ICJ Reports 1981 22.

Separate Opinion of Judge Morozov, Continental Shelf (Tunisia/Libyan Arab Jamahiriya), Application by Italy for permission to intervene, Judgment of 21 March 1984, ICJ Reports 1984 30.

In Advisory Opinion.

Dissenting Opinion of Judge Morozov, Application for Review of Judgment No 158 of the United Nations Administrative Tribunal, Advisory Opinion of 12 July 1953, ICJ Reports 1953 296–300.

Dissenting Opinion of Judge Morozov, Interpretation of the Agreement of 25 March 1951 between the World Health Organization and Egypt, Advisory Opinion of 20 December 1980, ICJ Reports 1980 190–97.

Dissenting Opinion of Judge Morozov, Application for Review of Judgment No 273 of the United Nations Administrative Tribunal, Advisory Opinion of 20 July 1982, ICJ Reports 1982 435.

In Orders Relating Provisional Measures.

Separate Opinion of Judge Morozov, Aegean Sea Continental Shelf (*Greece v Turkey*), Provisional Measures Order of 11 September 1976, ICJ Reports1976, 21–22.

MOSLER, H (Federal Republic of Germany): 1976–85.

In Judgments.

Separate Opinion of Judge Mosler, Military and Paramilitary Activities in and against Nicaragua (*Nicaragua v USA*), Judgment of 26 November 1984, ICJ Reports 1984 461–70.

Dissenting Opinion of Judge Mosler, Continental Shelf (Libyan Arab Jamahiriya/Malta), Judgment of 3 June 1985, ICJ Reoprts 1985 114–22.

In Advisory Opinion.

Separate Opinion of Judge Mosler, Interpretation of the Agreement of 25 March 1951 between the World Health Organization and Egypt, Advisory Opinion of 20 December 1980, ICJ Reports 1980 125–30.

Separate Opinion of Judge Mosler, Application for Review of Judgment No 273 of the United Nations Administrative Tribunal, Advisory Opinion of 20 July 1982, ICJ Reports 1982 379.

In Orders.

Separate Opinion of Judge Mosler, Aegean Sea Continental Shelf (*Greece v Turkey*), Provisional Measures Order of 11 September 1976, ICJ Reports1976, 24–26.

Joint Separate Opinion of Judge Mosler, Military and Paramilitary Activities in and against Nicaragua (*Nicaragua v United States*), Provisional Measures Order of 10 May 1984, ICJ Reports1984, 189.

Joint Separate Opinion of Judges Ruda, Mosler, Ago, Sir Robert Jennings, and De Lachaarriere, Order of 4 October 1984 on Declaration of Intervention of El Salvador in the case concerning Military and Paramilitary Activities in and against Nicaragua (*Nicaragua v USA*), ICJ Report 1984, 219.

NI ZHENGYU (China): **1985–94.**

In Judgments.

Separate Opinion of Judge Ni Zhengyu, Military and Paramilitary Activities in and against Nicaragua (*Nicaragua v USA*), Judgment of 27 June 1986 on merits, ICJ Reports 1986 201–11.

Separate Opinion of Judge Ni Zhengyu, Arbitral Award of 31 July 1989 (*Guinea- Bissau v Senegal*), Judgment of 12 November 1991, ICJ Reports 1991 96.

In Orders Relating Provisional Measures.

Declaration of Judge Ni Zhengyu, Question of Interpretation and Application of the 1971 Montreal Convention arising from the Aerial Incident at Lockerbie (*Libya v UK*), Provisional Measures Order of 14 April 1992, ICJ Reports1992, 20–23.

Declaration of Judge Ni Zhengyu, Question of Interpretation and Application of the 1971 Montreal Convention arising from the Aerial Incident at Lockerbie (*Libya v United States*), Provisional Measures Order of 14 April 1992, ICJ Reports1992, 132–35.

ODA, S (Japan): **1976–2003.**

In Judgment.

Separate Opinion of Judge Oda, Continental Shelf (Tunisia/Libyan Arab Jamahiriya), Application by Malta for permission to intervene, Judgment of 14 April 1981, ICJ Reports 1981 23–34.

Dissenting Opinion of Judge Oda, Continental Shelf (Tunisia/Libyan Arab Jamahiriya), Judgment of 24 February 1982, ICJ Reports 1982 157–277.

Dissenting Opinion of Judge Oda, Continental Shelf (Tunisia/Libyan Arab Jamahiriya), Application by Italy for permission to intervene, Judgment of 21 March 1984, ICJ Reports 1984 90–114.

Separate Opinion of Judge Oda, Military and Paramilitary Activities in and against Nicaragua (*Nicaragua v USA*), Judgment of 26 November 1984, ICJ Reports 1984 471–513.

Dissenting Opinion of Judge Oda, Continental Shelf (Libyan Arab Jamahiriya/Malta), Judgment of 3 June 1985, ICJ Reoprts 1985 123–71.

Separate Opinion of Judge Oda, Application for Revision and Interpretation of the Judgment of 24 February 1982 in the case concerning the Continental Shelf (Tunisia/Libyan Arab Jamahiriya) (*Tunisia v Libyan Arab Jamahiriya*), Judgment of 10 December 1985, ICJ Reports 1985 236–45.

Dissenting Opinion of Judge Oda, Military and Paramilitary Activities in and against Nicaragua (*Nicaragua v USA*), Judgment of 27 June 1986 on merits, ICJ Reports 1986 212–58.

Separate Opinion of Judge Oda, Border and Transborder Armed Actions (*Nicaragua v Honduras*) (Jurisdiction and Admissibility), Judgment of 20 December 1988, ICJ Reports 1988 109–25.

Separate Opinion of Judge Oda, Elettronica Sicula Sp.A (ELSI) (*Italy v USA*) (Admissibility and Merits), Judgment of 20 July 1989, ICJ Reports 1989 83–93.

Separate Opinion of Judge Oda, Land, Island and Maritime Frontier Dispute (El Salvador/Honduras) (Intervention), Judgment of 13 September 1990, ICJ Reports 1990 138–44.

Separate Opinion of Vice-President Oda, Arbitral Award of 31 July 1989 (*Guinea- Bissau v Senegal*), Judgment of 12 November 1991, ICJ Reports 1991 81.

Dissenting Opinion of Vice-President Oda, Certain Phosphate Lands in Nauru (*Nauru v Australia*), Judgment of 26 June 1992 on Preliminary Objections, ICJ Reports 1992 303–325.

Declaration pf Vice-President Oda, Land, Island and Maritime Frontier Dispute (El Salvador/Honduras), Judgment of 11 September 1992, ICJ Reports 1992 619.

Dissenting Opinion of Vice-President Oda, Land, Island and Maritime Frontier Dispute (El Salvador/Honduras), Judgment of 11 September 1992, ICJ Reports 1992 732–761.

Declaration of Vice-President Oda, Maritime Delimitation in the Area between Greenland and Jan Mayen (*Denmark v Norway*), Judgment of 14 June 1993, ICJ Reports 1993 83.

Separate Opinion of Vice-President Oda, Maritime Delimitation in the Area between Greenland and Jan Mayen (*Denmark v Norway*), Judgment of 14 June 1993, ICJ Reports 1993 89–117.

Dissenting Opinion of Judge Oda, Maritime Delimitation and Territorial Questions between Qatar and Bahrain (*Qatar v Bahrain*) (Jurisdiction and Admissibility), Judgment of 1 July 1994, ICJ Reports 1994 131–49.

Dissenting Opinion of Judge Oda, Maritime Delimitation and Territorial Questions between Qatar and Bahrain (*Qatar v Bahrain*) (Jurisdiction and Admissibility), Judgment of 15 February 1995, ICJ Reports 1995 40–50.

Declaration of Judge Oda, Application of the Convention on the Prevention and Punishment of the Crime of Genocide (*Bosnia and Herzegovina v Yugoslavia*), Judgment of 11 July 1996 on Preliminary Objections, ICJ Reports 1996 625–30.

Dissenting Opinion of Judge Oda, Oil Platforms (*Islamic Republic of Iran v USA*), Judgment of 12 December 1996 on Preliminary Objections, ICJ Reports 1996 890–900.

Dissenting Opinion of Judge Oda, The Gabcikovo- Nagymaros Project (Hungary/Slovakia), Judgment of 25 September 1997, ICJ Reports 1997 153–169.

Dissenting Opinion of Judge Oda, Questions of Interpretation and Application of the 1971 Montreal Convention arising from the Aerial Incident at Lockerbie (*Libya v United Kingdom*), Judgment of 27 February 1998 on Preliminary Objections, ICJ Reports 1998 82–98.

Dissenting Opinion of Judge Oda, Questions of Interpretation and Application of the 1971 Montreal Convention arising from the Aerial Incident at Lockerbie (*Libya v USA*), Judgment of 27 February 1998 on Preliminary Objections, ICJ Reports 1998 173–88.

Separate Opinion of Judge Oda, Fisheries Jurisdiction (*Spain v Canada*), Judgment of 4 December 1998 on Jurisdiction, ICJ Reports 1998 474–85.

Separate Opinion of Judge Oda, Kasikili/Sedudu Island (Botswana/Namibia), Judgment of 13 December 1999, ICJ Reports 1999 1116–43.

Separate Opinion of Judge Oda, Aerial Incident of 10 August 1999 (*Pakistan v India*), Judgment of 21 June 2000 on Jurisdiction, ICJ Reports 2000 36–44.

Separate Opinion of Judge Oda, Maritime Delimitation and Territorial questions between Qatar and Bahrain (*Qatar v Bahrain*), Judgment of 16 March 2001 (merits), ICJ Reports 2001, 119.

Dissenting Opinion of Judge Oda, LaGrand (*Germany v USA*), Judgment of 27 June 2001, ICJ Reports 2001, 525.

Dissenting Opinion of Judge Oda, Sovereignty over Pulau Ligitan and Pulau Sipadan (Indonesia/Malaysia), Judgment of 23 October 2001 (Application by the Philippines for Permission to Intervene), ICJ Reports 2001, 609.

Dissenting Opinion of Judge Oda, Arrest Warrant of 11 April 2000, Judgment of 14 February 2002, ICJ Reports 2002, 46.

Declararion of Judge Oda, Land and Maritime Boundary between Cameroon and Nigeria (*Cameroon v Nigeria: Equatorial Guinea Intervening*), Judgment of 10 October 2002, ICJ Reports 2002, 459.

Declaration of Judge Oda, Sovereignty over Pulau Ligitan and Pulau Sipadan (Indonesia/ Malaysia), Judgment of 17 December 2002, ICJ Reports 2002, 687.

In Advisory Opinion.

Separate Opinion of Judge Oda, Interpretation of the Agreement of 25 March 1951 between the World Health Organization and Egypt, Advisory Opinion of 20 December 1980, ICJ Reports 1980 155–62.

Separate Opinion of Judge Oda, Application for Review of Judgment No 273 of the United Nations Administrative Tribunal, Advisory Opinion of 20 July 1982, ICJ Reports 1982 389.

Separate Opinion of Judge Oda, Interpretation of the Agreement of 25 March 1951 between the World Health Organization and Egypt, Advisory Opinion of 20 December 1980, ICJ Reports 1980 83.

Separate Opinion of Judge Oda, Applicability of the Obligation to Arbitrate under Section 21 of the United Nations Agreement of 26 June 1947, Advisory Opinion of 26 April 1988, ICJ Reports 1988 83.

Separate Opinion of Judge Oda, Applicability of the Obligation to Arbitrate under Section 21 of the United Nations Agreement of 26 June 1947, Advisory Opinion of 26 April 1988, ICJ Reports 1988 37.

Separate Opinion of Judge Oda, Applicability of Article VI, Section 22, of the Convention on the Privileges and Immunities of the United Nations, Advisory Opinion of 15 December 1989, ICJ Reports 1989 200.

Separate Opinion of Judge Oda, Legality of the Use by a State of Nuclear Weapons in Armed Conflict (requested by WHO), Advisory Opinion of 8 July 1996, ICJ Reports 1996 88.

Dissenting Opinion of Judge Oda, Legality of the Threat or Use of Nuclear Weapons (requested by UN General Assembly), Advisory Opinion of 8 July 1996, ICJ Reports 1996 330.

Separate Opinion of Judge Oda, Difference relating to Immunity from Legal Process of a Special Rapporteur of the Commission on Human Rights, Advisory Opinion of 29 April 1999, ICJ Reports 1999 99.

In Orders Relating Provisional Measures.

Separate Opinion of Vice-President Oda, Passage through the Great Belt (*Finland v Denmark*), Provisional Measures Order of 29 July 1991, ICJ Reports1991, 25–27.

Declaration of Vice-President Acting President Oda, Question of Interpretation and Application of the 1971 Montreal Convention arising from the Aerial Incident at Lockerbie (*Libya v UK*), Provisional Measures Order of 14 April 1992, ICJ Reports1992, 17–19

Declaration of Vice-President Acting President Oda, Question of Interpretation and

Application of the 1971 Montreal Convention arising from the Aerial Incident at Lockerbie (*Libya v United States*), Provisional Measures Order of 14 April 1992, ICJ Reports1992, 129–131

Declaration of Vice-President Oda, Application of the Convention on the Prevention and Punishment of the Crime of Genocide (*Bosnia Herzegovina v Yugoslavia*), Provisional Measures Order of 13 September 1993, ICJ Reports1993, 351

Declaration of Judge Oda, Request for an Examination of the Situation in Accordance with Paragraph 63 of the Court's Judgment of 20 December 1974 in the Nuclear Tests (*New Zealand v France*), Provisional Measures Order of 22 September 1995, ICJ Reports1995, 310

Declaration of Judge Oda, Land and Maritime Boundary between Cameroon and Nigeria (*Cameroon v Nigeria*), Provisional Measures Order of 15 March 1996, ICJ Reports 199627

Declaration of Judge Oda, Vienna Convention on Consular Relations (*Paraguay v United States*), Provisional Measures Order of 9 April 1998, ICJ Reports1998, 260–262

Declaration of Judge Oda, La Grand Case (*Germany v United States*), Provisional Measures Order of 3 March 1999, ICJ Reports1999, 18–20.

Separate Opinion of Judge Oda, Legality of Use of Force (*Yugoslavia v Belgium*), Provisional Measures Order of 2 June 1999, ICJ Reports1999, 144–160

Separate Opinion of Judge Oda, Legality of Use of Force (*Yugoslavia v Canada*), Provisional Measures Order of 2 June 1999, ICJ Reports 1999, 278–294

Separate Opinion of Judge Oda, Legality of Use of Force (*Yugoslavia v France*), Provisional Measures Order of 2 June 1999, ICJ Reports1999, 383–399

Separate Opinion of Judge Oda, Legality of Use of Force (*Yugoslavia v Germany*), Provisional Measures Order of 2 June 1999, ICJ Reports1999, 442–458

Separate Opinion of Judge Oda, Legality of Use of Force (*Yugoslavia v Italy*), Provisional Measures Order of 2 June 1999, ICJ Reports 1999, 503–519

Separate Opinion of Judge Oda, Legality of Use of Force (*Yugoslavia v Netherlands*), Provisional Measures Order of 2 June 1999, ICJ Reports1999, 562–578

Separate Opinion of Judge Oda, Legality of Use of Force (*Yugoslavia v Portugal*), Provisional Measures Order of 2 June 1999, ICJ Reports1999, 676–692

Separate Opinion of Judge Oda, Legality of Use of Force (*Yugoslavia v Spain*), Provisional Measures Order of 2 June 1999, ICJ Reports 1999, 781–797

Separate Opinion of Judge Oda, Legality of Use of Force (*Yugoslavia v United Kingdom*), Provisional Measures Order of 2 June 1999, ICJ Reports1999, 849–865

Separate Opinion of Judge Oda, Legality of Use of Force (*Yugoslavia v United States of America*), Provisional Measures Order of 2 June 1999, ICJ Reports1999, 933–949

Declaration of Judge Oda, Armed Activities on Territory of Congo (*Congo v Uganda*), Provisional Measures Order of 1 July 2000, ICJ Reports1999, 131–133

Declaration of Judge Oda, Arrest Warrant of 11 April 2000 (*Congo v Belgium*), Provisional Measures Order of 8–Dec–2000, ICJ Reports 2000, 204–207

Declaration of Judge Oda, Avena and Others Mexican Nationals (*Mexico v USA*), Provisional Measures Order of 5 February 2003, ICJ Reports 2003, 93.

ONYEAMA, CD. (Nigeria): 1967–1976

In Judgments

Joint Declaration of Judge Onyeama, Barcelona Traction, Light and Power Company, Ltd (New Application: 1962) (*Belgium v Spain*), Second Phase, Judgment of 5 February 1970, ICJ Reports 1970 52–53.

Separate Opinion of Judge Onyeama, Appeal Relating to the Jurisdiction of the ICAO Council (*India v Pakistan*), Judgment of 18 August 1972, ICJ Reports 1972 86–91.

Dissenting Opinion of Judge Onyeama, Fisheries Jurisdiction (*UK v Iceland*), Judgment of 25 July 1974 on merits, ICJ Reports 1974 164–173.

Dissenting Opinion of Judge Onyeama, Fisheries Jurisdiction (*Federal Republic of Germany v Iceland*), Judgment of 25 July 1974 on merits, ICJ Reports 1974 244–251

Joint Declaration of Judge Onyeama, Nuclear Tests (*Australia v France*), Judgment of 20 December 1974, ICJ Reports 1974 273.

Joint Dissenting Opinion of Judge Onyeama, Nuclear Tests (*Australia v France*), Judgment of 20 December 1974, ICJ Reports 1974 312.

Joint Dissenting Opinion of Judge Onyeama, Nuclear Tests (*New Zealand v France*), Judgment of 20 December 1974, ICJ Reports 1974 494.

In Advisory Opinion

Separate Opinion of Judge Onyeama, Legal Consequences for States of the Continued Presence of South Africa in Namibia (South West Africa) notwithstanding Security Council Resolution 276(1970), Advisory Opinion of 21 June 1971, ICJ Reports 1971 138–149.

Separate Opinion of Judge Onyeama, Application for Review of Judgment No 158 of the United Nations Administrative Tribunal, Advisory Opinion of 12 July 1953, ICJ Reports 1953 223–229.

In Orders

Joint Declaration of Judge Onyeama, Legal Consequences for States of the Continued Presence of South Africa in Namibia (South West Africa) notwithstanding Security Council Resolution 276(1970), Order of 29 January 1971, ICJ Reports 1971, 14.

OWADA, H. (JAPAN): 2003

In Judgments

Separate Opinion of Judge Owada, Oil Platforms (*Iran v USA*), Judgment of 6 November 2003, ICJ Reports 2003, 306.

Dissenting Opinion of Judge Owarda, Certain Property (*Liechtenstein v Germany*) (Preliminary Objections), Judgment of 10 February 2005, ICJ Reports 2005 (still at press).

In Advisory Opinions

Separate Opinion of Judge Owada, Legal Consequences of the Construction of a Wall in the Occupied Palestinian Territory, Advisory Opinion of 9 July 2004, ICJ Reports 2004, 260.

PADILLA NERVO, L. (Mexico): 1964–1973

In Judgments

Dissenting Opinion of Judge Padilla Nervo, South West Africa (*Ethiopia v South Africa; Liberia v South Africa*), Second Phase, Judgment of 18 July 1966, ICJ Reports 1966 443–473.

Separate Opinion of Judge Padilla Nervo, North Sea Continental Shelf (Federal Republic of Germany/Denmark; Federal Republic of Germany/Netherlands), Judgment of 20 February 1969, ICJ Reports 1969 85–99.

Separate Opinion of Judge Padilla Nervo, Barcelona Traction, Light and Power Company, Ltd (New Application: 1962) (*Belgium v Spain*), Second Phase, Judgment of 5 February 1970, ICJ Reports 1970 243–266.

Dissenting Opinion of Judge Padilla Nervo, Fisheries Jurisdiction (*UK v Iceland*), Jurisdiction of the Court, Judgment of 2 February 1973, ICJ Reports 1973 36–47.

Dissenting Opinion of Judge Padilla Nervo, Fisheries Jurisdiction (*Federal Republic of Germany v Iceland*), Judgment of 2 February 1973, ICJ Reports 1973 81–91.

In Advisory Opinion

Separate Opinion of Judge Padilla Nervo, Legal Consequences for States of the Continued Presence of South Africa in Namibia (South West Africa) notwithstanding Security Council Resolution 276 (!970), Advisory Opinion of 21 June 1971, ICJ Reports 1971 101–126.

In Orders

Dissenting Opinion of Judge Padilla Nervo, Fisheries Jurisdiction (*UK v Iceland*), Provisional Measures Order of 17 August 1972, ICJ Reports1972, 20–28.

Dissenting Opinion of Judge Padilla Nervo, Fisheries Jurisdiction (Federal Republic of Germany v Iceland), Provisional Measures Order of 17 August 1972, ICJ Reports1972, 37–44.

PARRA-ARANGUREN, G. (Venezuela) : 1996–2009

In Judgments

Separate Opinion of Judge Parra-Aranguren, Application of the Convention on the Prevention and Punishment of the Crime of Genocide (*Bosnia and Herzegovina v Yugoslavia*), Judgment of 11 July 1996 on Preliminary Objections, ICJ Reports 1996 656–657.

Separate Opinion of Judge Parra-Aranguren, Oil Platforms (*Islamic Republic of Iran v USA*), Judgment of 12 December 1996 on Preliminary Objections, ICJ Reports 1996 862–863.

Dissenting Opinion of Judge Parra-Aranguren, The Gabcikovo- Nagymaros Project (Hungary/Slovakia), Judgment of 25 September 1997, ICJ Reports 1997 227–231.

Separate Opinion of Judge Parra-Aranguren, Questions of Interpretation and Application of the 1971 Montreal Convention arising from the Aerial Incident at Lockerbie (*Libya v USA*), Judgment of 27 February 1998 on Preliminary Objections, ICJ Reports 1998 350–353.

Dissenting Opinion of Judge Parra-Aranguren, Kasikili/Sedudu Island (Botswana/ Namibia), Judgment of 13 December 1999, ICJ Reports 1999 1208–1232.

Separate Opinion of Judge Parra-Aranguren, Maritime Delimitation and Territorial questions between Qatar and Bahrain (*Qatar v Bahrain*), Judgment of 16 March 2001 (merits), ICJ Reports 2001, 223.

Separate Opinion of Judge Parra-Aranguren, LaGrand (*Germany v USA*), Judgment of 27 June 2001, ICJ Reports 2001, 544.

Declaration of Judge Parra-Aranguren, Sovereignty over Pulau Ligitan and Pulau Sipadan (Indonesia/Malaysia), Judgment of 23 October 2001 (Application by the Philippines for Permission to Intervene), ICJ Reports 2001, 625.

Separate Opinion of Judge Parra-Aranguren, Land and Maritime Boundary between Cameroon and Nigeria (*Cameroon v Nigeria: Equatorial Guinea Intervening*), Judgment of 10 October 2002, ICJ Reports 2002, 488.

Separate Opinion of Judge Parra-Aranguren, Oil Platforms (*Iran v USA*), Judgment of 6 November 2003, ICJ Reports 2003, 241.

Separate Opinionof Judge Parra-Aranguren, Avena and Other Mexican Nationals (*Mexico v USA*), Judgment of 31 March 2004, ICJ Reports 2004, 84

In Orders Relating Provisional Measures

Separate Opinion of Judge Parra-Aranguren, Legality of Use of Force (*Yugoslavia v Belgium*), Provisional Measures Order of 2 June 1999, ICJ Reports 1999, 171–172

Separate opinion of Judge Parra-Aranguren, Legality of Use of Force (*Yugoslavia v Canada*), Provisional Measures Order of 2 June 1999, ICJ Reports 1999, 305–306

Separate Opinion of Judge Parra-Aranguren, Legality of Use of Force (*Yugoslavia v France*), Provisional Measures Order of 2 June 1999, ICJ Reports 1999, 400–401

Separate Opinion of Judge Parra-Aranguren, Legality of Use of Force (*Yugoslavia v Germany*), Provisional Measures Order of 2 June 1999, ICJ Reports 1999, 459

Separate Opinion of Judge Parra-Aranguren, Legality of Use of Force (*Yugoslavia v Italy*), Provisional Measures Order of 2 June 1999, ICJ Reports1999, 520–521

Separate Opinion of Judge Parra-Aranguren, Legality of Use of Force (*Yugoslavia v Netherlands*), Provisional Measures Order of 2 June 1999, ICJ Reports1999, 589–590

Separate Opinion of Judge Parra-Aranguren, Legality of Use of Force (*Yugoslavia v Portugal*), Provisional Measures Order of 2 June 1999, ICJ Reports1999, 703–704

Separate Opinion of Judge Parra-Aranguren, Legality of Use of Force (*Yugoslavia v Spain*), Provisional Measures Order of 2 June 1999, ICJ Reports1999, 808

Separate Opinion of Judge Parra-Aranguren, Legality of Use of Force (*Yugoslavia v United Kingdom*), Provisional Measures Order of 2 June 1999, ICJ Reports1999, 866–875

Separate Opinion of Judge Parra-Aranguren, Legality of Use of Force (*Yugoslavia v United States of America*), Provisional Measures Order of 2 June 1999, ICJ Reports1999, 876–877

Separate Opinion of Judge Parra-Aranguren, Arrest Warrant of 11 April 2000 (*Congo v Belgium*), Provisional Measures Order of 8–Dec–2000, ICJ Reports2000, 211–215

PATHAK, R. S. (India): **1989–1991**

(Judge Pathak wrote no individual opinions)

PETREN, S. (Sweden): **1967–1976**

In Judgments

Joint Declaration of Judge Petren, Barcelona Traction, Light and Power Company, Ltd (New Application: 1962) (*Belgium v Spain*), Second Phase, Judgment of 5 February 1970, ICJ Reports 1970 52–53.

Separate Opinion of Judge Petren, Appeal Relating to the Jurisdiction of the ICAO Council (*India v Pakistan*), Judgment of 18 August 1972, ICJ Reports 1972 76–85.

Dissenting Opinion of Judge Petren, Fisheries Jurisdiction (*UK v Iceland*), Judgment of 25 July 1974 on merits, ICJ Reports 1974 150–163.

Dissenting Opinion of Judge Petren, Fisheries Jurisdiction (*Federal Republic of Germany v Iceland*), Judgment of 25 July 1974 on merits, ICJ Reports 1974 240–243.

Separate Opinion of Judge Petren, Nuclear Tests (*Australia v France*), Judgment of 20 December 1974, ICJ Reports 1974 298.

Joint Separate Opinion of Judge Petren, Nuclear Tests (*New Zealand v France*), Judgment of 20 December 1974, ICJ Reports 1974 483–492.

In Advisory Opinion

Separate Opinion of Judge Petren, Legal Consequences for States of the Continued Presence of South Africa in Namibia (South West Africa) notwithstanding Security Council Resolution 276 (!970), Advisory Opinion of 21 June 1971, ICJ Reports 1971 127–137.

Separate Opinion of Judge Petren, Western Sahara, Advisory Opinion of 16 October 1975, ICJ Reports 1975 104–115.

In Orders

Joint Declaration of Judge Petren, Legal Consequences for States of the Continued Presence of South Africa in Namibia (South West Africa) notwithstanding Security Council Resolution 276(1970), Order of 29January 1971, ICJ Reports 1971, 13.

Dissenting Opinion of Judge Petren, Nuclear Tests (*Australia v France*), Provisional Measures Order of 22 June 1973, ICJ Reports 1973, 124–127.

Dissenting Opinion of Judge Petren, Nuclear Tests (*New Zealand v France*), Provisional Measures Order of 22 June 1973, ICJ Reports 1973, 159–162.

Dissenting Opinion of Judge Petren, Fisheries Jurisdiction (*United Kingdom v Iceland*), Provisional Measures Order of 12 July 1973, ICJ Reports1973, 310–311.

Dissenting Opinion of Judge Petren, Fisheries Jurisdiction (*Fed Rep of Germany v Iceland*), Provisional Measures Order of 12 July 1973, ICJ Reports1973, 318

Dissenting Opinion of Judge Petren, Trial of Pakistani Prisoners of War (*Pakistan v India*), Provisional Measures Order of 13 July 1973, ICJ Reports1973, 334–336

Dissenting Opinion of Judge Petren, Nuclear Tests (*Australia v France*), Provisional Measures Order of 12 July 1973, ICJ Reports1973, 124.

Dissenting Opinion of Judge Petren, Nuclear Tests (*New Zealand v France*), Provisional Measures Order of 12 July 1973, ICJ Reports, 159.

RANJEVA, R. (Madagascar): 1991–2009

In Judgments

Joint Dissenting Opinion of Judge Ranjeva, Arbitral Award of 31 July 1989 (*Guinea- Bissau v Senegal*), Judgment of 12 November 1991, ICJ Reports 1991 120–129.

Declaration of Judge Ranjeva, Maritime Delimitation in the Area between Greenland and Jan Mayen (*Denmark v Norway*), Judgment of 14 June 1993, ICJ Reports 1993 87.

Separate Opinion of Judge Ranjeva, East Timor (*Portugal v Australia*) (POs were linked to merits), Judgment of 30 June 1995, ICJ Reports 1995 129–134.

Separate Opinion of Judge Ranjeva, Oil Platforms (*Islamic Republic of Iran v USA*), Judgment of 12 December 1996 on Preliminary Objections, ICJ Reports 1996 842–846.

Dissenting Opinion of Judge Ranjeva, The Gabcikovo- Nagymaros Project (Hungary/ Slovakia), Judgment of 25 September 1997, ICJ Reports 1997 170–175.

Joint Declaration of Judge Ranjeva, Questions of Interpretation and Application of the 1971 Montreal Convention arising from the Aerial Incident at Lockerbie (*Libya v United Kingdom*), Judgment of 27 February 1998 on Preliminary Objections, ICJ Reports 1998 32–45.

Joint Declaration of Judge Ranjeva, Questions of Interpretation and Application of the 1971 Montreal Convention arising from the Aerial Incident at Lockerbie (*Libya v United Kingdom*), Judgment of 27 February 1998 on Preliminary Objections, ICJ Reports 1998 46.

Joint Declaration of Judge Ranjeva, Questions of Interpretation and Application of the 1971 Montreal Convention arising from the Aerial Incident at Lockerbie (*Libya v USA*), Judgment of 27 February 1998 on Preliminary Objections, ICJ Reports 1998 138.

Dissenting Opinion of Judge Ranjeva, Fisheries Jurisdiction (*Spain v Canada*), Judgment of 4 December 1998 on Jurisdiction, ICJ Reports 1998 553–569.

Declaration of Judge Ranjeva, Kasikili/Sedudu Island (Botswana/Namibia), Judgment of 13 December 1999, ICJ Reports 1999 1110.

Joint Separate Opinion of Judge Ranjeva, Maritime Delimitation and Territorial questions between Qatar and Bahrain (*Qatar v Bahrain*), Judgment of 16 March 2001 (merits), ICJ Reports 2001, 145.

Declaration of Judge Ranjeva, Arrest Warrant of 11 April 2000, Judgment of 14 February 2002, ICJ Reports 2002, 54.

Separate Opinion of Judge Ranjeva, Land and Maritime Boundary between Cameroon and Nigeria (*Cameroon v Nigeria: Equatorial Guinea Intervening*), Judgment of 10 October 2002, ICJ Reports 2002, 469.

Declaration of Vice-President Ranjeva, Avena and Other Mexican Nationals (*Mexico v USA*), Judgment of 31 March 2004, ICJ Reports 2004, 75.

Declaration of Vice-President Ranjeva, Oil Platforms (*Iran v USA*), Judgment of 6 November 2003, ICJ Reports 2003, 220.

Joint Declaration of Vice-President Ranjeva, Legality of Use of Force, (*Serbia and Montenegro v Belgium*), Preliminary Objections, Judgment of 15 December 2004, ICJ Reports 2004 (still at press).

Joint Declaration of Vice-President Ranjeva, Legality of Use of Force, (*Serbia and Montenegro v Canada*), Preliminary Objections, Judgment of 15 December 2004, ICJ Reports 2004 (still at press).

Joint Declaration of Vice-President Ranjeva, Legality of Use of Force, (*Serbia and Montenegro v France*), Preliminary Objections, Judgment of 15 December 2004, ICJ Reports 2004 (still at press).

Joint Declaration of Vice-President Ranjeva, Legality of Use of Force, (*Serbia and Montenegro v Germany*), Preliminary Objections, Judgment of 15 December 2004, ICJ Reports 2004 (still at press).

Joint Declaration of Vice-President Ranjeva, Legality of Use of Force, (*Serbia and Montenegro v Italy*), Preliminary Objections, Judgment of 15 December 2004, ICJ Reports 2004 (still at press).

Joint Declaration of Vice-President Ranjeva, Legality of Use of Force, (*Serbia and Montenegro v Netherlands*), Preliminary Objections, Judgment of 15 December 2004, ICJ Reports 2004 (still at press).

Joint Declaration of Vice-President Ranjeva, Legality of Use of Force, (*Serbia and Montenegro v Portugal*), Preliminary Objections, Judgment of 15 December 2004, ICJ Reports 2004 (still at press).

Joint Declaration of Vice-President Ranjeva, Legality of Use of Force, (*Serbia and Montenegro v United KIngdom*), Preliminary Objections, Judgment of 15 December 2004, ICJ Reports 2004 (still at press).

In Advisory Opinion

Declaration of Judge Ranjeva, Legality of the Use by a State of Nuclear Weapons in Armed Conflict (requested by WHO), Advisory Opinion of 8 July 1996, ICJ Reports 1996 86.

Separate Opinion of Judge Ranjeva, Legality of the Threat or Use of Nuclear Weapons (requested by UN General Assembly), Advisory Opinion of 8 July 1996, ICJ Reports 1996 294.

In Orders Relating Provisional Measures

Dissenting Opinion of Judge Ranjeva, Question of Interpretation and Application of the 1971 Montreal Convention arising from the Aerial Incident at Lockerbie (Libya v UK), Provisional Measures Order of 14 April 1992, ICJ Reports1992, 72–77

Dissenting Opinion of Judge Ranjeva, Question of Interpretation and Application of the 1971 Montreal Convention arising from the Aerial Incident at Lockerbie (*Libya v United States*), Provisional Measures Order of 14 April 1992, ICJ Reports1992, 182

Declaration of Judge Ranjeva, Request for an Examination of the Situation in Accordance with Paragraph 63 of the Court's Judgment of 20 December 1974 in the Nuclear Tests (*New Zealand v France*), Provisional Measures Order of 22 September 1995, ICJ Reports 311

Declaration of Judge Ranjeva, Land and Maritime Boundary between Cameroon and Nigeria (*Cameroon v Nigeria*), Provisional Measures Order of 15 March 1996, ICJ Reports1996, 29

Declaration of Judge Ranjeva, Arrest Warrant of 11 April 2000 (*Congo v Belgium*), Provisional Measures Order of 8–Dec–2000, ICJ Reports 2000, 208.

RAU, B. Sir (India): **1952–1953**

In Judgments

Joint Dissenting Opinion of Judge Rau, Rights of Nationals of the United States of America in Morocco (*France v United States of America*), Judgment of 27 August 1952, ICJ Reports 1952, 215–233.

READ, J E. (Canada): **1946–1958**

In Judgments

Dissenting Opinion of Judge Read, Asylum (Colombia/Peru), Judgment of 20 November 1950, ICJ Reports 1950, 316–331.

Dissenting Opinion of Judge Read, Fisheries (*United Kingdom v Norway*), Judgment of 18 December 1951, ICJ Reports 1951. pp.. 186–206.

Dissenting Opinion of Judge Read, Anglo- Iranian Oil Co. (*United Kingdom v France*), Judgment of 22 July 1952, ICJ Reports 1952, 142–150.

Joint Dissenting Opinion of Judge Read, Ambatielos (*Greece v United Kingdom*), Judgment of 19 May 1953 on Merits, ICJ Reports 1953, 25–35.

Separate Opinion of Judge Read, Monetary Gold Removed from Rome in 1943 (*Italy v France, United Kingdom and United States of America*), Judgment of 15 June 1954, ICJ Reports 1954, 37–38.

Dissenting Opinion of Judge Read, Nottebohm, Second Phase, Judgment of 6 April 1955, ICJ Reports 1955, 34–49.

Dissenting Opinion of Judge Read, Certain Norwegian Loans (*France v Norway*), Judgment of 6 July 1957, ICJ Reports 1957, 79–100.

In Advisory Opinion

Joint Dissenting Opinion of Judge Read, Conditions of Admission of a State to Membership in the United Nations (Article 4 of Charter), Advisory Opinion of 28 May 1948, ICJ Reports 1948 82.

Dissenting Opinion of Judge Read, Interpretation of Peace Treaties with Bulgaria, Hungary and Romania, Second Phase, Advisory Opinion of 18 July 1950, ICJ Reports 1950 231.

Separate Opinion of Judge Read, International Status of South West Africa, Advisory Opinion of 11 July 1950, ICJ Reports 1950 164.

Joint Dissenting Opinion of Judge Read, Reservations to the Convention on the Prevention and Punishment of the Crime of Genocide, Advisory Opinion of 28 May 1951, ICJ Reports 1951 31.

Dissenting Opinion of Judge Read, Judgments of the Administrative Tribunal of the ILO upon complaints made against UNESCO, Advisory Opinion of 23 October 1956, ICJ Reports 1956

In Orders Relating Provisional Measures

Joint Declaration of Judge Read, Interhandel (*Switzerland v United States of America*), Provisional Measures Order of 24 October 1957, ICJ Reports1957, 113.

REZEK, F. (Brazil): **1997–2006**

In Judgments

Declaration of Judge Rezek, The Gabcikovo- Nagymaros Project (Hungary/Slovakia), Judgment of 25 September 1997, ICJ Reports 1997 86–87.

Separate Opinion of Judge Rezek, Questions of Interpretation and Application of the 1971 Montreal Convention arising from the Aerial Incident at Lockerbie (*Libya v USA*), Judgment of 27 February 1998 on Preliminary Objections, ICJ Reports 1998 152–154.

Dissenting Opinion of Judge Rezek, Kasikili/Sedudu Island (Botswana/Namibia), Judgment of 13 December 1999, ICJ Reports 1999 1233–1237.

Separate Opinion of Judge Rezek, Arrest Warrant of 11 April 2000, Judgment of 14 February 2002, ICJ Reports 2002, 91.

Declararion of Judge Rezek, Land and Maritime Boundary between Cameroon and Nigeria (*Cameroon v Nigeria: Equatorial Guinea Intervening*), Judgment of 10 October 2002, ICJ Reports 2002, 489.

Declaration of Judge Rezek, Application for Revision of the Judgment of 11 July 1996 in the case Concerning Application of the Convention on the Prevention and Punishment of the Crime of Genocide (*Bosnia and Herzegovina v Yugoslavia*). Preliminary Objections (*Yugoslavia v Bosnia and Herzegovina*), Judgment of 3 February 2003, ICJ Reports 2003, 51.

In Advisory Opinion

Separate Opinion of Judge Rezek, Difference relating to Immunity from Legal Process of a Special Rapporteur of the Commission on Human Rights, Advisory Opinion of 29 April 1999, ICJ Reports 1999 109.

In Orders Relating Provisional Measures

Dissenting Opinion of Judge Rezek, Arrest Warrant of 11 April 2000 (*Congo v Belgium*), Provisional Measures Order of 8–Dec–2000, ICJ Reports2000, 216–217

RUDA, J M. (Argentina): **1973–1991**

In Judgments

Joint Separate Opinion of Judge Ruda, Fisheries Jurisdiction (*UK v Iceland*), Judgment of 25 July 1974 on merits, ICJ Reports 1974 45.

Joint Separate Opinion of Judge Ruda, Fisheries Jurisdiction (*Federal Republic of Germany v Iceland*), Judgment of 25 July 1974 on merits, ICJ Reports 1974 217–224.

Separate Opinion of Judge Ruda, Military and Paramilitary Activities in and against Nicaragua (*Nicaragua v USA*), Judgment of 26 November 1984, ICJ Reports 1984 452–460.

Separate Opinion of Judge Ruda, Continental Shelf (Libyan Arab Jamahiriya/Malta), Judgment of 3 June 1985, ICJ Reoprts 1985 174–177.

Joint Separate Opinion of Judge Ruda, Continental Shelf (Libyan Arab Jamahiriya/Malta), Judgment of 3 June 1985, ICJ Reoprts 1985 76–92.

Separate Opinion of Judge Ruda, Application for Revision and Interpretation of the Judgment of 24 February 1982 in the case concerning the Continental Shelf (Tunisia/Libyan Arab Jamahiriya) (*Tunisia v Libyan Arab Jamahiriya*), Judgment of 10 December 1985, ICJ Reports 1985 232–235.

Separate Opinion of Judge Ruda, Military and Paramilitary Activities in and against Nicaragua (*Nicaragua v USA*), Judgment of 27 June 1986 on merits, ICJ Reports 1986 174–177.

In Advisory Opinion

Dissenting Opinion of Judge Ruda, Western Sahara, Advisory Opinion of 16 October 1975, ICJ Reports 1975 175–176.

Separate Opinion of Judge Ruda, Interpretation of the Agreement of 25 March 1951 between the World Health Organization and Egypt, Advisory Opinion of 20 December 1980, ICJ Reports 1980 114–124.

Separate Opinion of Judge Ruda, Application for Review of Judgment No 273 of the United Nations Administrative Tribunal, Advisory Opinion of 20 July 1982, ICJ Reports 1982 373.

In Orders

Separate Opinion of Judge Ruda, Aegean Sea Continental Shelf (*Greece v Turkey*), Provisional Measures Order of 11 September 1976, ICJ Reports1976, 23.

Joint Separate Opinion of Judges Ruda, Mosler, Ago, Sir Robert Jennings, and De Lachaarriere, Order of 4 October 1984 on Declaration of Intervention of El Salvador in the case concerning Military and Paramilitary Activities in and against Nicaragua (*Nicaragua v USA*), ICJ Report 1984, 219.

SCHWEBEL, S. M. (United States): 1981–2000

In Judgments

Separate Opinion of Judge Schwebel, Continental Shelf (Tunisia/Libyan Arab Jamahiriya), Application by Malta for permission to intervene, Judgment of 14 April 1981, ICJ Reports 1981 35–40.

Separate Opinion of Judge Schwebel, Continental Shelf (Tunisia/Libyan Arab Jamahiriya), Judgment of 24 February 1982, ICJ Reports 1982 99.

Dissenting Opinion of Judge Schwebel, Continental Shelf (Tunisia/Libyan Arab Jamahiriya), Application by Italy for permission to intervene, Judgment of 21 March 1984, ICJ Reports 1984 131–147.

Separate Opinion of Judge Schwebel, Delimitation of the Maritime Boundary in the Gulf of Maine Area (*Canada v USA*) [Case referred to a Chamber], Judgment of 12 October 1984, ICJ Reports 1984 353–359.

Dissenting Opinion of Judge Schwebel, Military and Paramilitary Activities in and against Nicaragua (*Nicaragua v USA*), Judgment of 26 November 1984, ICJ Reports 1984 558–637.

Separate Opinion of Judge Schwebel, Application for Revision and Interpretation of the Judgment of 24 February 1982 in the case concerning the Continental Shelf (Tunisia/Libyan Arab Jamahiriya) (*Tunisia v Libyan Arab Jamahiriya*), Judgment of 10 December 1985, ICJ Reports 1985 246.

Dissenting Opinion of Judge Schwebel, Military and Paramilitary Activities in and against Nicaragua (*Nicaragua v USA*), Judgment of 27 June 1986 on merits, ICJ Reports 1986 259–527.

Dissenting Opinion of Judge Schwebel, Continental Shelf (Libyan Arab Jamahiriya/Malta), Judgment of 3 June 1985, ICJ Reports 1985 172–190.

Separate Opinion of Judge Shwebel, Border and Transborder Armed Actions (*Nicaragua v Honduras*) (Jurisdiction and Admissibility), Judgment of 20 December 1988, ICJ Reports 1988 126–132.

Dissenting Opinion of Judge Schwebel, Elettronica Sicula S.p.A. (ELSI) (*Italy v USA*) (Admissibility and Merits), Judgment of 20 July 1989, ICJ Reports 1989 94–121.

Dissenting Opinion of Judge Schwebel, Certain Phosphate Lands in Nauru (*Nauru v Australia*), Judgment of 26 June 1992 on Preliminary Objections, ICJ Reports 1992 329–343.

Separate Opinion of Judge Schwebel, Maritime Delimitation in the Area between Greenland and Jan Mayen (*Denmark v Norway*), Judgment of 14 June 1993, ICJ Reports 1993 118–129.

Separate Opinion of Vice-President Schwebel, Maritime Delimitation and Territorial Questions between Qatar and Bahrain (*Qatar v Bahrain*) (Jurisdiction and Admissibility), Judgment of 1 July 1994, ICJ Reports 1994 130–131.

Dissenting Opinion of Vice-President Schwebel, Maritime Delimitation and Territorial Questions between Qatar and Bahrain (*Qatar v Bahrain*) (Jurisdiction and Admissibility), Judgment of 15 February 1995, ICJ Reports 1995 27–39.

Dissenting Opinion of Vice-President Schwebel, Oil Platforms (*Islamic Republic of Iran v USA*), Judgment of 12 December 1996 on Preliminary Objections, ICJ Reports 1996 874–889.

Declaration of President Schwebel, The Gabcikovo- Nagymaros Project (Hungary/ Slovakia), Judgment of 25 September 1997, ICJ Reports 1997 85.

Joint Declaration of President Schwebel, Questions of Interpretation and Application of the 1971 Montreal Convention arising from the Aerial Incident at Lockerbie (*Libya v United Kingdom*), Judgment of 27 February 1998 on Preliminary Objections, ICJ Reports 1998 64–81.

Dissenting Opinion of President Schwebel, Questions of Interpretation and Application of the 1971 Montreal Convention arising from the Aerial Incident at Lockerbie (*Libya v USA*), Judgment of 27 February 1998 on Preliminary Objections, ICJ Reports 1998 155–172.

Separate Opinion of President Schwebel, Fisheries Jurisdiction (*Spain v Canada*), Judgment of 4 December 1998 on Jurisdiction, ICJ Reports 1998 470–473.

In Advisory Opinion

Dissenting Opinion of Judge Schwebel, Application for Review of Judgment No 273 of the United Nations Administrative Tribunal, Advisory Opinion of 20 July 1982, ICJ Reports 1982 454.

Dissenting Opinion of Judge Schwebel, Interpretation of the Agreement of 25 March 1951 between the World Health Organization and Egypt, Advisory Opinion of 20 December 1980, ICJ Reports 1980 110.

Separate Opinion of Judge Schwebel, Applicability of the Obligation to Arbitrate under Section 21 of the United Nations Agreement of 26 June 1947, Advisory Opinion of 26 April 1988, ICJ Reports 1988 42.

Dissenting Opinion of Vice-President Schwebel, Legality of the Threat or Use of Nuclear Weapons (requested by UN General Assembly), Advisory Opinion of 8 July 1996, ICJ Reports 1996 311.

In Orders Relating Provisional Measures

Dissenting Opinion of Judge Schwebel, Military and Paramilitary Activities in and against Nicaragua (*Nicaragua v United States*), Provisional Measures Order of 10 May 1984, ICJ Reports 1984, 190

Declaration of Vice-President Schwebel, Request for an Examination of the Situation in Accordance with Paragraph 63 of the Court's Judgment of 20 December 1974 in the Nuclear Tests (*New Zealand v France*), Provisional Measures Order of 22 September 1995, ICJ Reports1995, 309

Declaration of President Schwebel, Vienna Convention on Consular Relations (*Paraguay v United States*), Provisional Measures Order of 9 April 1998, ICJ Reports1998, 259

Separate Opinion of President Schwebel, La Grand Case (*Germany v United States*), Provisional Measures Order of 3 March 1999, ICJ Reports1999, 21–22

SETTE-CAMARA, J (Brazil) : 1979–1988

In Judgments

Dissenting Opinion of Vice-President Sette-Camara, Continental Shelf (Tunisia/Libyan Arab Jamahiriya), Application by Italy for permission to intervene, Judgment of 21 March 1984, ICJ Reports 1984 71–89.

Separate Opinion of Vice-President Sette-Camara, Continental Shelf (Libyan Arab Jamahiriya/Malta), Judgment of 3 June 1985, ICJ Reoprts 1985 60–75.

Separate Opinion of Judge Sette-Camara, Military and Paramilitary Activities in and against Nicaragua (*Nicaragua v USA*), Judgment of 27 June 1986 on merits, ICJ Reports 1986 192–200.

In Advisory Opinion

Separate Opinion of Judge Sette-Camara, Interpretation of the Agreement of 25 March 1951 between the World Health Organization and Egypt, Advisory Opinion of 20 December 1980, ICJ Reports 1980 178–189.

SHAHABUDDEEN, M. (Guyana): 1988–1997

In Judgments

Separate Opinion of Judge Shahabudden, Border and Transborder Armed Actions (*Nicaragua v Honduras*) (Jurisdiction and Admissibility), Judgment of 20 December 1988, ICJ Reports 1988 133–156.

Separate Opinion of Judge Shahabudden, Arbitral Award of 31 July 1989 (*Guinea- Bissau v Senegal*), Judgment of 12 November 1991, ICJ Reports 1991 106.

Separate Opinion of Judge Shahabudden, Certain Phosphate Lands in Nauru (*Nauru v Australia*), Judgment of 26 June 1992 on Preliminary Objections, ICJ Reports 1992 270–300.

Separate Opinion of Judge Shahabudden, Maritime Delimitation in the Area between Greenland and Jan Mayen (*Denmark v Norway*), Judgment of 14 June 1993, ICJ Reports 1993 130–210.

Separate Opinion of Judge Shahabudden, Territorial Dispute (Libyan Arab Jamahiriya/Chad), Judgment of 3 February 1994, ICJ Reports 1994 44–50.

Declaration of Judge Shahabudden, Maritime Delimitation and Territorial Questions between Qatar and Bahrain (*Qatar v Bahrain*) (Jurisdiction and Admissibility), Judgment of 1 July 1994, ICJ Reports 1994 129.

Dissenting Opinion of Judge Shahabudden, Maritime Delimitation and Territorial Questions between Qatar and Bahrain (*Qatar v Bahrain*) (Jurisdiction and Admissibility), Judgment of 15 February 1995, ICJ Reports 1995 51–66.

Separate Opinion of Judge Shahabudden East Timor (*Portugal v Australia*) (POs were linked to merits), Judgment of 30 June 1995, ICJ Reports 1995 119–128.

Separate Opinion of Judge Shahabudden, Application of the Convention on the Prevention and Punishment of the Crime of Genocide (*Bosnia and Herzegovina v Yugoslavia*), Judgment of 11 July 1996 on Preliminary Objections, ICJ Reports 1996 634–639.

Separate Opinion of Judge Shahabudden, Oil Platforms (*Islamic Republic of Iran v USA*), Judgment of 12 December 1996 on Preliminary Objections, ICJ Reports 1996 822–841.

In Advisory Opinion

Separate Opinion of Judge Shahabudden, Applicability of the Obligation to Arbitrate under Section 21 of the United Nations Agreement of 26 June 1947, Advisory Opinion of 26 April 1988, ICJ Reports 1988 57.

Separate Opinion of Judge Shahabudden, Applicability of Article VI, Section 22, of the Convention on the Privileges and Immunities of the United Nations, Advisory Opinion of 15 December 1989, ICJ Reports 1989 212.

Dissenting Opinion of Judge Shahabudden, Legality of the Use by a State of Nuclear Weapons in Armed Conflict (requested by WHO), Advisory Opinion of 8 July 1996, ICJ Reports 1996 97.

Dissenting Opinion of Judge Shahabudden, Legality of the Threat or Use of Nuclear Weapons (requested by UN General Assembly), Advisory Opinion of 8 July 1996, ICJ Reports 1996 375.

In Orders Relating Provisional Measures

Separate Opinion of Judge Shahabudden, Arbitral Award 31 Jul 1989 (*Guinea-Bissau v Senegal*), Provisional Measures Order of 2 March 1990, ICJ Reports1990, 74–78

Separate Opinion of Judge Shahabudden, Passage through the Great Belt (*Finland v Denmark*), Provisional Measures Order of 29 July 1991, ICJ Reports1991 28–36

Separate Opinion of Judge Shahabudden, Question of Interpretation and Application of the 1971 Montreal Convention arising from the Aerial Incident at Lockerbie (*Libya v UK*), Provisional Measures Order of 14 April 1992, ICJ Reports1992, 28–32

Separate Opinion of Judge Shahabudden, Question of Interpretation and Application of the 1971 Montreal Convention arising from the Aerial Incident at Lockerbie (*Libya v United States*), Provisional Measures Order of 14 April 1992, ICJ Reports1992, 140–142

Separate Opinion of Judge Shahabudden, Application of the Convention on the Prevention and Punishment of the Crime of Genocide (*Bosnia Herzegovina v Yugoslavia*), Provisional Measures Order of 13 September 1993, ICJ Reports 1993 353–369

Separate Opinion of Judge Shahabudden, Request for an Examination of the Situation in Accordance with Paragraph 63 of the Court's Judgment of 20 December 1974 in the Nuclear Tests (*New Zealand v France*), Provisional Measures Order of 22 September 1995, ICJ Reports1995, 312–316

Declaration of Judge Shahabudden, Land and Maritime Boundary between Cameroon and Nigeria (*Cameroon v Nigeria*), Provisional Measures Order of 15 March 1996, ICJ Reports1996, 28

SHI JIUYONG (China): **1994–2003**

In Judgments

Joint Declaration of Judge Shi, Application of the Convention on the Prevention and Punishment of the Crime of Genocide (*Bosnia and Herzegovina v Yugoslavia*), Judgment of 11 July 1996 on Preliminary Objections, ICJ Reports 1996 631–632.

Separate Opinion of Vice-President Shi, LaGrand (*Germany v USA*), Judgment of 27 June 2001, ICJ Reports 2001, 518.

Declaration of President Shi, Avena and Other Mexican Nationals (*Mexico v USA*), Judgment of 31 March 2004, ICJ Reports 2004, 74.

In Advisory Opinion

Declaration of Judge Shi, Legality of the Threat or Use of Nuclear Weapons (requested by UN General Assembly), Advisory Opinion of 8 July 1996, ICJ Reports 1996 277.

In Orders Relating Provisional Measures

Joint Declaration of Judge Shi, Land and Maritime Boundary between Cameroon and Nigeria (*Cameroon v Nigeria*), Provisional Measures Order of 15 March 1996, ICJ Reports1996 31

Dissenting Opinion of Judge Shi, Legality of Use of Force (*Yugoslavia v Belgium*), Provisional Measures Order of 2 June 1999, ICJ Reports1999, 209–215

Dissenting Opinion of Judge Shi, Legality of Use of Force (*Yugoslavia v Canada*), Provisional Measures Order of 2 June 1999, ICJ Reports1999, 316–319.

Declaration of Judge Shi, Legality of Use of Force (*Yugoslavia v France*), Provisional Measures Order of 2 June 1999, ICJ Reports 377–378

Declaration of Judge Shi, Legality of Use of Force (*Yugoslavia v Germany*), Provisional Measures Order of 2 June 1999, ICJ Reports1999, 436

Declaration of Judge Shi, Legality of Use of Force (*Yugoslavia v Italy*), Provisional Measures Order of 2 June 1999, ICJ Reports 496–497

Dissenting Opinion of Judge Shi, Legality of Use of Force (*Yugoslavia v Netherlands*), Provisional Measures Order of 2 June 1999, ICJ Reports1999, 600–603

Dissenting Opinion of Judge Shi, Legality of Use of Force (*Yugoslavia v Portugal*), Provisional Measures Order of 2 June 1999, ICJ Reports 1999, 714–717

Declaration of Judge Shi, Legality of Use of Force (*Yugoslavia v Spain*), Provisional Measures Order of 2 June 1999, ICJ Reports 1999, 775–776

Declaration of Judge Shi, Legality of Use of Force (*Yugoslavia v United Kingdom*), Provisional Measures Order of 2 June 1999, ICJ Reports1999, 843–844

Declaration of Judge Shi, Legality of Use of Force (*Yugoslavia v United States of America*), Provisional Measures Order of 2 June 1999, ICJ Reports1999, 927–928

SIMMA, B. (Germany): **2003**

In Judgments

Separate Opinion of Judge Simma, Oil Platforms (*Iran v USA*), Judgment of 6 November 2003, ICJ Reports 2003, 324.

SINGH, N. (India): **1973–1988**

In Judgments

Declaration of Judge Singh, Fisheries Jurisdiction (*UK v Iceland*), Judgment of 25 July 1974 on merits, ICJ Reports 1974 38–44.

Joint Separate Opinion of Judge Singh, Fisheries Jurisdiction (*UK v Iceland*), Judgment of 25 July 1974 on merits, ICJ Reports 1974 45.

Declaration of Judge Singh, Fisheries Jurisdiction (*Federal Republic of Germany v Iceland*), Judgment of 25 July 1974 on merits, ICJ Reports 1974 211–216.

Joint Separate Opinion of Judge Singh, Fisheries Jurisdiction (*Federal Republic of Germany v Iceland*), Judgment of 25 July 1974 on merits, ICJ Reports 1974 217–224.

Separate Opinion of Vice-President Singh, Aegean Sea Continental Shelf (*Greece v Turkey*), Judgment of 19 December 1978, ICJ Reports 1978 46–48.

Separate Opinion of Judge Singh, Continental Shelf (Tunisia/Libyan Arab Jamahiriya), Application by Italy for permission to intervene, Judgment of 21 March 1984, ICJ Reports 1984 31–34.

Separate Opinion of Judge Singh, Military and Paramilitary Activities in and against Nicaragua (*Nicaragua v USA*), Judgment of 26 November 1984, ICJ Reports 1984 444–451.

Separate Opinion of President Singh, Continental Shelf (Libyan Arab Jamahiriya/Malta), Judgment of 3 June 1985, ICJ Reoprts 1985 151–157.

Separate Opinion of President Singh, Military and Paramilitary Activities in and against Nicaragua (*Nicaragua v USA*), Judgment of 27 June 1986 on merits, ICJ Reports 1986 151–157.

In Advisory Opinion

Joint Declaration of Judge Singh, Application for Review of Judgment No 158 of the United Nations Administrative Tribunal, Advisory Opinion of 12 July 1953, ICJ Reports 1953 214–222.

Declaration of Judge Singh, Western Sahara, Advisory Opinion of 16 October 1975, ICJ Reports 1975 78–82.

Separate Opinion of Judge Singh, Application for Review of Judgment No 273 of the United Nations Administrative Tribunal, Advisory Opinion of 20 July 1982, ICJ Reports 1982 388.

In Orders

Declaration of Judge Singh, Nuclear Tests (*Australia v France*), Provisional Measures Order of 22 June 1973, ICJ Reports1973, 108–109.

Declaration of Judge Singh, Nuclear Tests (*New Zealand v France*), Provisional Measures Order of 22 June 1973, ICJ Reports 1973, 145.

Separate Opinion of Judge Singh, Trial of Pakistani Prisoners of War (*Pakistan v India*), Provisional Measures Order of 13 July 1973, ICJ Reports1973, 332–333.

Separate Opinion of Vice-President Singh, Aegean Sea Continental Shelf (*Greece v Turkey*), Provisional Measures Order of 11 September 1976, ICJ Reports1976 17–18.

SPENDER, P. C. Sir (Australia): **1958–1967**

In Judgments

Separate Opinion of Judge Spender, Application of the Convention of 1902 Governing the Guardianship of Infants (*Netherlands v Sweden*), Judgment of 28 November 1958, ICJ Reports 1958, 116–131.

Separate Opinion of Judge Spender, Interhandel (*Switzerland v USA*), Judgment of 21 March 1959 on Preliminary Objections, ICJ Reports 1959, 54–74.

Joint Dissenting Opinion of Judge Spender (together with Judges Wellington Koo and Lauterpacht), Aerial Incident of 27 July 1955 (*Israel v Bulgaria*), Judgment of 26 May 1959 on Preliminary Objections, ICJ Reports 1959, 156–194.

Dissenting Opinion of Judge Spender, Right of passage over Indian Territory (*Portugal v India*), Judgment of 12 April 1960 on Merits, ICJ Reports 1960, 97–115.

Separate Opinion of Judge Spender, Arbitral Award made by the King of Spain on 23 December 1906 (*Honduras v Nicaragua*), Judgment of 18 November 1960, ICJ Reports 1960 219–220.

Separate Opinion of Judge Spender, Arbitral Award made by the King of Spain on 23 December 1906 (*Honduras v Nicaragua*), Judgment of 18 November 1960, ICJ Reports 1960 39–42.

Dissenting Opinion of Judge Spender, Temple of Preah Vihear (*Cambodia v Thailand*), Judgment of 15 June 1962 on Merits, ICJ Reports 1962 101–146.

Dissenting Opinion of Judge Spender, South West Africa (*Ethiopia v South Africa*; *Liberia v South Africa*), Judgment of 21 December 1962 on Preliminary Objections, ICJ Reports 1962 465–563.

Separate Opinion of Judge Spender, Northern Cameroons (*Cameron v UK*), Judgment of 2 December 1963, ICJ Reports 1963 65–96.

Declaration of President Spender, Barcelona Traction, Light and Power Company, Ltd (New Application: 1962)(*Belgium v Spain*), Judgment of 24 July 1964 on Preliminary Objections, ICJ Reports 1964 47–48.

Declaration of President Spender, South West Africa (*Ethiopia v South Africa*; *Liberia v South Africa*), Second Phase, Judgment of 18 July 1966, ICJ Reports 1966 51–58.

Separate Opinion of Judge Spender, Certain Expenses of the United Nations (Article 17, Paragraph 2 of the Charter), Advisory Opinion of 20 July 1962, ICJ Reports 1962 182–197.

SPIROPOULOS, J (Greece): 1958–1967

In Judgments

Declaration of Judge Spiropoulos, Application of the Convention of 1902 Governing the Guardianship of Infants (*Netherlands v Sweden*), Judgment of 28 November 1958, ICJ Reports 1958, 72.

Dissenting Opinion of Judge Spiropoulos, Interhandel (*Switzerland v USA*), Judgment of 21 March 1959 on Preliminary Objections, ICJ Reports 1959, 123–125.

Declaration of Judge Spiropoulos, Sovereignty over Certain Frontier Land (Belgium/ Netherlands), Judgment of 20 June 1959, ICJ Reports 1959, 232.

Declaration of Judge Spiropoulos, Right of passage over Indian Territory (*Portugal v India*), Judgment of 12 April 1960 on Merits, ICJ Reports 1960, 53.

Declaration of Judge Spiropoulos, South West Africa (*Ethiopia v South Africa*; *Liberia v South Africa*), Judgment of 21 December 1962 on Preliminary Objections, ICJ Reports 1962 347–348.

Declaration of Judge Spiropoulos, Northern Cameroons (*Cameron v UK*), Judgment of 2 December 1963, ICJ Reports 1963 39.

Declaration of Judge Spiropoulos, Barcelona Traction, Light and Power Company, Ltd (New Application: 1962)(*Belgium v Spain*), Judgment of 24 July 1964 on Preliminary Objections, ICJ Reports 1964 48.

In Advisory Opinion

Declaration of Judge Spiropoulos, Certain Expenses of the United Nations (Article 17, Paragraph 2 of the Charter), Advisory Opinion of 20 July 1962, ICJ Reports 1962 180–181.

TANAKA, K. (Japan): **1961–1970**

In Judgments

Joint Declaration of Judge Tanaka, Arbitral Award made by the King of Spain on 23 December 1906 (*Honduras v Nicaragua*), Judgment of 18 November 1960, ICJ Reports 1960 36–38.

Joint Declaration of Judge Tanaka, Temple of Preah Vihear (*Cambodia v Thailand*), Judgment of 15 June 1962 on Merits, ICJ Reports 1962 37–38.

Separate Opinion of Judge Tanaka, Barcelona Traction, Light and Power Company, Ltd (New Application: 1962) (*Belgium v Spain*), Judgment of 24 July 1964 on Preliminary Objections, ICJ Reports 1964 65–77.

Dissenting Opinion of Judge Tanaka, South West Africa (*Ethiopia v South Africa; Liberia v South Africa*), Second Phase, Judgment of 18 July 1966, ICJ Reports 1966 250–324.

Dissenting Opinion of Judge Tanaka, North Sea Continental Shelf (Federal Republic of Germany/Denmark; Federal Republic of Germany/Netherlands), Judgment of 20 February 1969, ICJ Reports 1969 171–196.

Separate Opinion of Judge Tanaka, Barcelona Traction, Light and Power Company, Ltd (New Application: 1962)(*Belgium v Spain*), Second Phase, Judgment of 5 February 1970, ICJ Reports 1970 114–160.

TARRASOV, N. K. **(Russian Federation): 1985–1995**

In Judgments

Declaration of Judge Tarassov, Arbitral Award of 31 July 1989 (*Guinea- Bissau v Senegal*), Judgment of 12 November 1991, ICJ Reports 1991 77–79.

In Orders Relating Provisional Measures

Declaration of Judge Tarassov, Passage through the Great Belt (*Finland v Denmark*), Provisional Measures Order of 29 July 1991, ICJ Reports 1991, 22–24

Joint Declaration of Judge Tarassov, Question of Interpretation and Application of the 1971 Montreal Convention arising from the Aerial Incident at Lockerbie (*Libya v UK*), Provisional Measures Order of 14 April 1992, ICJ Reports1992, 24

Joint Declaration of Judge Tarassov, Question of Interpretation and Application of the 1971 Montreal Convention arising from the Aerial Incident at Lockerbie (*Libya v United States*), Provisional Measures Order of 14 April 1992, ICJ Reports1992, 136

Declaration of Judge Tarassov, Application of the Convention on the Prevention and Punishment of the Crime of Genocide (*Bosnia and Herzegovina v Yugoslavia*), Provisional Measures Order of 8 April 1993, ICJ Reports 1993, 26–28

Dissenting Opinion of Judge Tarassov, Application of the Convention on the Prevention and Punishment of the Crime of Genocide (*Bosnia Herzegovina v Yugoslavia*), Provisional Measures Order of 13 September 1993, ICJ Reports1993, 449–452.

TARAZI, S. **(Syria): 1976–1980**

In Judgments

Separate Opinion of Judge Tarazi, Aegean Sea Continental Shelf (*Greece v Turkey*), Judgment of 19 December 1978, ICJ Reports 1978 55–61.

Dissenting Opinion of Judge Tarazi, United States Diplomatic and Consular Staff in Tehran (*USA v Iran*), Judgment of 24 May 1980, ICJ Reports 1980 58–68.

In Orders Relating Provisional Measures

Separate Opinion of Judge Tarazi, Aegean Sea Continental Shelf (*Greece v Turkey*), Provisional Measures Order of 11 September 1976, ICJ Reports1976, 31–34

TOMKA, P (Slovakia): 2003-

In Judgments

Separate Opinionof Judge Tomka, Avena and Other Mexican Nationals (*Mexico v USA*), Judgment of 31 March 2004, ICJ Reports 2004, 94

VERESHCHETIN, V. S. (**Russian Federation**): **1995–2006**

In Judgments

Separate Opinion of Judge Vereshchetin, East Timor (*Portugal v Australia*) (POs were linked to merits), Judgment of 30 June 1995, ICJ Reports 1995 135–138.

Joint Declaration of Judge Vereshchetin, Application of the Convention on the Prevention and Punishment of the Crime of Genocide (*Bosnia and Herzegovina v Yugoslavia*), Judgment of 11 July 1996 on Preliminary Objections, ICJ Reports 1996 631–632.

Dissenting Opinion of Judge Vereshchetin, The Gabcikovo- Nagymaros Project (Hungary/Slovakia), Judgment of 25 September 1997, ICJ Reports 1997 219–226.

Separate Opinion of Judge Vereshchetin, Questions of Interpretation and Application of the 1971 Montreal Convention arising from the Aerial Incident at Lockerbie (*Libya v USA*), Judgment of 27 February 1998 on Preliminary Objections, ICJ Reports 1998 342–344.

Dissenting Opinion of Judge Vereshchetin, Fisheries Jurisdiction (*Spain v Canada*), Judgment of 4 December 1998 on Jurisdiction, ICJ Reports 1998 570–581.

Declaration of Judge Vereshchetin, Maritime Delimitation and Territorial questions between Qatar and Bahrain (**Qatar v Bahrain**), Judgment of 16 March 2001 (merits), ICJ Reports 2001, 217.

Dissenting Opinion of Judge Vereshchetin, Application for Revision of the Judgment of 11 July 1996 in the case Concerning Application of the Convention on the Prevention and Punishment of the Crime of Genocide (*Bosnia and Herzegovina v Yugoslavia*). Preliminary Objections (*Yugoslavia v Bosnia and Herzegovina*), Judgment of 3 February 2003, ICJ Reports 2003, 39.

Separate Opinionof Judge Vereshchetin, Avena and Other Mexican Nationals (*Mexico v USA*), Judgment of 31 March 2004, ICJ Reports 2004, 79

In Advisory Opinion

Declaration of Judge Vereshchetin, Legality of the Threat or Use of Nuclear Weapons (requested by UN General Assembly), Advisory Opinion of 8 July 1996, ICJ Reports 1996 279.

In Orders Relating Provisional Measures

Joint Declaration of Judge Vereshchetin, Land and Maritime Boundary between Cameroon and Nigeria (*Cameroon v Nigeria*), Provisional Measures Order of 15 March 1996, ICJ Reports1996, 31

Dissenting Opinion of Judge Vereshchetin, Legality of Use of Force (*Yugoslavia v Belgium*), Provisional Measures Order of 2 June 1999, ICJ Reports1999, 209–215

Dissenting Opinion of Judge Vereshchetin, Legality of Use of Force (*Yugoslavia v Canada*), Provisional Measures Order of 2 June 1999, ICJ Reports1999, 320–326

Declaration of Judge Vereshchetin, Legality of Use of Force (*Yugoslavia v France*), Provisional Measures Order of 2 June 1999, ICJ Reports1999, 381–382

Declaration of Judge Vereshchetin, Legality of Use of Force (*Yugoslavia v Germany*), Provisional Measures Order of 2 June 1999, ICJ Reports1999, 440–441

Declaration of Judge Vereshchetin, Legality of Use of Force (*Yugoslavia v Italy*), Provisional Measures Order of 2 June 1999, ICJ Reports1999, 500–501

Dissenting Opinion of Judge Vereshchetin, Legality of Use of Force (*Yugoslavia v Netherlands*), Provisional Measures Order of 2 June 1999, ICJ Reports1999, 604–610

Dissenting Opinion of Judge Vereshchetin, Legality of Use of Force (*Yugoslavia v Portugal*), Provisional Measures Order of 2 June 1999, ICJ Reports1999, 718–724

Declaration of Judge Vereshchetin, Legality of Use of Force (*Yugoslavia v Spain*), Provisional Measures Order of 2 June 1999, ICJ Reports1999, 779–780

Declaration of Judge Vereshchetin, Legality of Use of Force (*Yugoslavia v United Kingdom*), Provisional Measures Order of 2 June 1999, ICJ Reports1999, 847–848

Declaration of Judge Vereshchetin, Legality of Use of Force (*Yugoslavia v United States of America*), Provisional Measures Order of 2 June 1999, ICJ Reports1999, 931–932

Joint Declaration of Judge Vereshchetin, Certain Criminal Proceedings in France, Provisional Measures Order of 17 June 2003, ICJ Reports 2003, 113.

WALDOCK, H. Sir (United Kingdom): **1973–1981**

In Judgments

Separate Opinion of Judge Waldock, Fisheries Jurisdiction (*UK v Iceland*), Judgment of 25 July 1974 on merits, ICJ Reports 1974 105.

Separate opinion of Judge Waldock, Fisheries Jurisdiction (*Federal Republic of Germany v Iceland*), Judgment of 25 July 1974 on merits, ICJ Reports 1974 227.

Joint Declaration of Judge Waldock, Nuclear Tests (*Australia v France*), Judgment of 20 December 1974, ICJ Reports 1974 273.

Joint Dissenting Opinion of Judge Waldock, Nuclear Tests (*Australia v France*), Judgment of 20 December 1974, ICJ Reports 1974 312.

Joint Dissenting Opinion of Judge Waldock, Nuclear Tests (*New Zealand v France*), Judgment of 20 December 1974, ICJ Reports 1974 494.

In Orders

Declaration of Judge Waldock, Nuclear Tests (*Australia v France*), Provisional Measures Order of 22 June 1973, ICJ Reports 1973, 108.

Declaration of Judge Waldock, Nuclear Tests (*New Zealand v France*), Provisional Measures Order of 22 June 1973, ICJ Reports1973, 144.

WEERAMANTRY, C. G. (Sri Lanka): **1991–2000**

In Judgments

Dissenting Opinion of Judge Weeramantry, Arbitral Award of 31 July 1989 (*Guinea- Bissau v Senegal*), Judgment of 12 November 1991, ICJ Reports 1991 130–174.

Separate Opinion of Judge Weeramantry, Maritime Delimitation in the Area between Greenland and Jan Mayen (*Denmark v Norway*), Judgment of 14 June 1993, ICJ Reports 1993 211–279.

Dissenting Opinion of Judge Weeramantry, East Timor (*Portugal v Australia*) (POs were linked to merits), Judgment of 30 June 1995, ICJ Reports 1995 139–223.

Separate Opinion of Judge Weeramantry, Application of the Convention on the Prevention and Punishment of the Crime of Genocide (*Bosnia and Herzegovina v Yugoslavia*), Judgment of 11 July 1996 on Preliminary Objections, ICJ Reports 1996 640–655.

Separate Opinion of Vice-President Weeramantry, The Gabcikovo- Nagymaros Project (Hungary/Slovakia), Judgment of 25 September 1997, ICJ Reports 1997 88–119

Dissenting Opinion of Vice-President Weeramantry, Land and Maritime Boundary between Cameroon and Nigeria (*Cameroon v Nigeria*), Judgment of 11 June 1998 on Preliminary Objections, ICJ Reports 1998 362–376.

Dissenting Opinion of Vice-President Weeramantry, Fisheries Jurisdiction (*Spain v Canada*), Judgment of 4 December 1998 on Jurisdiction, ICJ Reports 1998 496–515.

Dissenting Opinion of Vice-President Weeramantry, Request for Interpretation of the Judgment of 11 June 1998 in the Case concerning the Land and Maritime Boundary between Cameroon and Nigeria (*Cameroon v Nigeria*), Preliminary Objections (*Nigeria v Cameroon*), Judgment of 25 March 1999 on Preliminary Jurisdiction, ICJ Reports 1999 42–48.

Dissenting Opinion of Vice-President Weeramantry, Kasikili/Sedudu Island (Botswana/ Namibia), Judgment of 13 December 1999, ICJ Reports 1999 1153–1195.

Separate Opinion of Judge ad hoc Weeramantry, Sovereignty over Pulau Ligitan and Pulau Sipadan (Indonesia/Malaysia), Judgment of 23 October 2001 (Application by the Philippines for Permission to Intervene), ICJ Reports 2001, 630.

In Advisory Opinion

Dissenting Opinion of Judge Weearamantry, Legality of the Use by a State of Nuclear Weapons in Armed Conflict (requested by WHO), Advisory Opinion of 8 July 1996, ICJ Reports 1996 101.

Dissenting Opinion of Judge Weearamantry, Legality of the Threat or Use of Nuclear Weapons (requested by UN General Assembly), Advisory Opinion of 8 July 1996, ICJ Reports 1996 429.

Separate Opinion of Vice-President Weearamantry, Difference relating to Immunity from Legal Process of a Special Rapporteur of the Commission on Human Rights, Advisory Opinion of 29 April 1999, ICJ Reports 1999 92.

In Orders Relating Provisional Measures

Dissenting Opinion of Judge Weeramantry, Question of Interpretation and Application of the 1971 Montreal Convention arising from the Aerial Incident at Lockerbie (*Libya v UK*), Provisional Measures Order of 14 April 1992, ICJ Reports1992, 50–71

Dissenting Opinion of Judge Weeramantry, Question of Interpretation and Application of the 1971 Montreal Convention arising from the Aerial Incident at Lockerbie (*Libya v United States*), Provisional Measures Order of 14 April 1992, ICJ Reports1992, 160–181

Separate Opinion of Judge Weeramantry, Application of the Convention on the Prevention and Punishment of the Crime of Genocide (*Bosnia Herzegovina v Yugoslavia*), Provisional Measures Order of 13 September 1993, ICJ Reports19993, 370–389

Dissenting Opinion of Judge Weeramantry. Request for an Examination of the Situation in Accordance with Paragraph 63 of the Court's Judgment of 20 December 1974 in the Nuclear Tests (*New Zealand v France*), Provisional Measures Order of 22 September 1995, ICJ Reports1995, 317–362

Joint Declaration of Judge Weeramantry, Land and Maritime Boundary between Cameroon and Nigeria (*Cameroon v Nigeria*), Provisional Measures Order of 15 March 1996, ICJ Reports1996, 31

Dissenting Opinion of Vice-President Weeramantry, Legality of Use of Force (*Yugoslavia v Belgium*), Provisional Measures Order of 2 June 1999, ICJ Reports1999, 181–204

Dissenting Opinion of Vice-President Weeramantry, Legality of Use of Force (*Yugoslavia v Canada*), Provisional Measures Order of 2 June 1999, ICJ Reports1999, 315

Declaration of Vice-President Weeramantry, Legality of Use of Force (*Yugoslavia v France*), Provisional Measures Order of 2 June 1999, ICJ Reports 1999, 376

Declaration of Vice-President Weeramantry, Legality of Use of Force (*Yugoslavia v Germany*), Provisional Measures Order of 2 June 1999, ICJ Reports1999, 435

Declaration of Vice-President Weeramantry, Legality of Use of Force (*Yugoslavia v Italy*), Provisional Measures Order of 2 June 1999, ICJ Reports 1999, 495

Dissenting Opinion of Vice-President Weeramantry, Legality of Use of Force (*Yugoslavia v Netherlands*), Provisional Measures Order of 2 June 1999, ICJ Reports1999, 599

Dissenting Opinion of Vice-President Weeramantry, Legality of Use of Force (*Yugoslavia v Portugal*), Provisional Measures Order of 2 June 1999, ICJ Reports1999, 713

Declaration of Vice-President Weeramantry, Legality of Use of Force (*Yugoslavia v United Kingdom*), Provisional Measures Order of 2 June 1999, ICJ Reports 1999, 842

WELLINGTON KOO, V. K. (China): 1957–1967

In Judgments

Separate Opinion of Judge Wellington Koo, Application of the Convention of 1902 Governing the Guardianship of Infants (*Netherlands v Sweden*), Judgment of 28 November 1958, ICJ Reports 1958, 110–115.

Separate Opinion of Judge Wellington Koo, Interhandel (*Switzerland v USA*), Judgment of 21 March 1959 on Preliminary Objections, ICJ Reports 1959, 48–53.

Joint Dissenting Opinion of Judge Wellington Koo (together with Judges Lauterpacht and Spender), Aerial Incident of 27 July 1955 (*Israel v Bulgaria*), Judgment of 26 May 1959 on Preliminary Objections, ICJ Reports 1959, 156–194.

Separate Opinion of Judge Wellington Koo, Right of passage over Indian Territory (*Portugal v India*), Judgment of 12 April 1960 on Merits, ICJ Reports 1960, 54–68.

Declaration of Judge Wellington Koo, Temple of Preah Vihear (*Cambodia v Thailand*), Judgment of 26 May 1961 on Preliminary Objections, ICJ Reports 1961 36.

Dissenting Opinion of Judge Wellington Koo, Temple of Preah Vihear (*Cambodia v Thailand*), Judgment of 15 June 1962 on Merits, ICJ Reports 1962 75–100.

Separate Opinion of Judge Wellington Koo, Northern Cameroons (*Cameron v UK*), Judgment of 2 December 1963, ICJ Reports 1963 41–64.

Separate Opinion Vice-President Wellington Koo, Barcelona Traction, Light and Power Company, Ltd (New Application: 1962) (*Belgium v Spain*), Judgment of 24 July 1964 on Preliminary Objections, ICJ Reports 1964 51–64.

Dissenting Opinion of Vice-President Wellington Koo, South West Africa (*Ethiopia v South Africa; Liberia v South Africa*), Second Phase, Judgment of 18 July 1966, ICJ Reports 1966 216–238.

In Orders Relating Provisional Measures

Declaration of Judge Wellington Koo, Interhandel (*Switzerland v United States of America*), Provisional Measures Order of 24 October 1957, ICJ Reports1957, 113–114.

WINIARSKI, B. (Poland): 1946–1967

In Judgments

Dissenting Opinion of Judge Winiarski, Application of the Convention of 1902 Governing the Guardianship of Infants (*Netherlands v Sweden*), Judgment of 28 November 1958, ICJ Reports 1958, 132–138.

Joint Separate Opinion of Judge Winiarski, Corfu Channel (*United Kingdom v Albania*), Judgment of 25 March 1948 on Preliminary Objections, ICJ Reports 1948, 31–32.

Dissenting Opinion of Judge Winiarski, Corfu Channel, Judgment of 9 April 1949 on Merits, ICJ Reports 1949, 49–57.

Dissenting Opinion of Judge Winiarski, Interhandel (*Switzerland v USA*), Judgment of 21 March 1959 on Preliminary Objections, ICJ Reports 1959, 83–84.

Dissenting Opinion of President Winiarski, South West Africa (*Ethiopia v South Africa; Liberia v South Africa*), Judgment of 21 December 1962 on Preliminary Objections, ICJ Reports 1962 449–458.

In Advisory Opinion

Joint Dissenting Opinion of Judge Winiarski, Conditions of Admission of a State to Membership in the United Nations (Article 4 of Charter), Advisory Opinion of 28 May 1948, ICJ Reports 1948 82.

Declaration of Judge Winiarski, Reparation for injuries suffered in the Service of the United Nations, Advisory Opinion of 11 April 1949, ICJ Reports 1949 189.

Dissenting Opinion of Judge Winiarski, Interpretation of Peace Treaties with Bulgaria, Hungary and Romania, First Phase, Advisory Opinion of 30 March 1950, ICJ Reports 1950 89.

Separate Opinion of Judge Winiarski, Effect of Awards of Compensation Made by the United Nations Administrative Tribunal, Advisory Opinion of 13 July 1954, ICJ Reports 1954 64.

Separate Opinion of Judge Winiarski, Judgments of the Administrative Tribunal of the ILO upon complaints made against UNESCO, Advisory Opinion of 23 October 1956, ICJ Reports 1956 104.

Dissenting Opinion of Judge Winiarski, Certain Expenses of the United Nations (Article 17, Paragraph 2 of the Charter), Advisory Opinion of 20 July 1962, ICJ Reports 1962 227–234.

In Orders

Joint Dissenting Opinion of Judge Winiarski, Anglo Iranian Oil Co. (United Kingdom v Iran), Provisional Measures Order of 5 July 1951, ICJ Reports1951, 96–98.

ZAFRULLA KHAN, M. Sir (Pakistan): 1954–1961 and 1964–1973

In Judgments

Declaration of Judge Zafrulla Khan (Vice-President), Application of the Convention of 1902 Governing the Guardianship of Infants (*Netherlands v Sweden*), Judgment of 28 November 1958, ICJ Reports 1958, 73.

Declaration of Judge Zafrulla Khan (Vice-President), Interhandel (*Switzerland v USA*), Judgment of 21 March 1959 on Preliminary Objections, ICJ Reports 1959, 32.

Declaration of Vice-President Zafrulla Khan, Aerial Incident of 27 July 1955 (*Israel v Bulgaria*), Judgment of 26 May 1959 on Preliminary Objections, ICJ Reports 1959, 146.

Declaration of Judge Zafrulla Khan, North Sea Continental Shelf (Federal Republic of Germany/Denmark; Federal Republic of Germany/Netherlands), Judgment of 20 February 1969, ICJ Reports 1969 54–56.
Declaration of President Zafrulla Khan, Appeal Relating to the Jurisdiction of the ICAO Council (*India v Pakistan*), Judgment of 18 August 1972, ICJ Reports 1972 71.
Declaration of President Zafrulla Khan, Fisheries Jurisdiction (*UK v Iceland*), Jurisdiction of the Court, Judgment of 2 February 1973, ICJ Reports 1973 22–23.
Declaration of Judge Zafrulla Kahn, Fisheries Jurisdiction (*Federal Republic of Germany v Iceland*), Judgment of 2 February 1973, ICJ Reports 1973 66–67.

In Advisory Opinion
Separate Opinion of Judge Zafrulla Khan, Judgments of the Administrative Tribunal of the ILO upon complaints made against UNESCO, Advisory Opinion of 23 October 1956, ICJ Reports 1956 114.
Declaration of President Zafrulla Khan, Legal Consequences for States of the Continued Presence of South Africa in Namibia (South West Africa) notwithstanding Security Council Resolution 276 (!970), Advisory Opinion of 21 June 1971, ICJ Reports 1971 59–66.

ZORICIC, M. (Yugoslavia): 1946–1958

In Judgments
Joint Separate Opinion of Judge Zoricic, Corfu Channel (*United Kingdom v Albania*), Judgment of 25 March 1948 on Preliminary Objections, ICJ Reports 1948, 31–32.
Declaration of Judge Zoricic, Asylum (Colombia/Peru), Judgment of 20 November 1950, ICJ Reports 1950, 289.
Dissenting Opinion of Judge Zoricic, Ambatielos (*Greece v United Kingdom*), Judgment of 1 July 1952 on Preliminary Objections, ICJ Reports 1952, 74–79.

In Advisory Opinion
Joint Dissenting Opinion of Judge Zoricic, Conditions of Admission of a State to Membership in the United Nations (Article 4 of Charter), Advisory Opinion of 28 May 1948, ICJ Reports 1948 82.
Dissenting Opinion of Judge Zoricic, Interpretation of Peace Treaties with Bulgaria, Hungary and Romania, First Phase, Advisory Opinion of 30 March 1950, ICJ Reports 1950 98.
Joint Declaration of Judge Zoricic, International Status of South West Africa, Advisory Opinion of 11 July 1950, ICJ Reports 1950 145.

Annex 5

Judges ad hoc at the International Court of Justice

ABI-SAAB, G. (Egypt)

In Judgments
Separate Opinion of Judge ad hoc Abi-Saab, Frontier Dispute (Burkina Faso/Mali) [case referred to a Chamber], Judgment of 22 December 1986, ICJ Reports 1986 659–663.

AGO, R. (Italy)
See under Bibliography: Judges of the International Court of Justice.

AJIBOLA, Prince B. A. (Nigeria)

In Judgments

Dissenting Opinion of Judge ad hoc Ajibola, Land and Maritime Boundary between Cameroon and Nigeria (*Cameroon v Nigeria*), Judgment of 11 June 1998 on Preliminary Objections, ICJ Reports 1998 392–418.

Dissenting Opinion of Judge ad hoc Ajibola, Request for Interpretation of the Judgment of 11 June 1998 in the Case concerning the Land and Maritime Boundary between Cameroon and Nigeria (*Cameroon v Nigeria*), Preliminary Objections (*Nigeria v Cameroon*), Judgment of 25 March 1999 on Preliminary Jurisdiction, ICJ Reports 1999 54–60.

Dissenting Opinion of Judge ad hoc Ajibola, Land and Maritime Boundary between Cameroon and Nigeria (*Cameroon v Nigeria: Equatorial Guinea Intervening*), Judgment of 10 October 2002, ICJ Reports 2002, 538.

In Orders Relating Provisional Measures

Separate Opinion of Judge ad hoc Ajibola, Land and Maritime Boundary between Cameroon and Nigeria (*Cameroon v Nigeria*), Provisional Measures Order of 15 March 1996, ICJ Reports1996, 31

see also under Biobliogrpahy: Judge of the International Court of Justice

ALAYZA Y PAZ SOLDAN (Peru)

In Judgments

Declaration of Judge ad hoc Alayza Y Paz Soldan, Haya de la Torre (*Colombia v Peru*), Judgment of 13 June 1951, ICJ Reports 1951, 84.

ARMAND-UGON, EC. (Uruguay)
See under Bibliography: Judges of the International Court of Justice.

ARRUDA FERRER-CORREIA, A. de (Portugal)
Mr Arrudfa Ferrer-Correia was chosen by Portugal in the case concerning East Timor (*Portugal v Australia*). But the judge resigned before the case was decided.

BARWICK, Sir Garfield (Australia)

In Judgments

Dissenting Opinion of Judge ad hoc Barwick, Nuclear Tests (*Australia v France*), Judgment of 20 December 1974, ICJ Reports 1974 391.

Dissenting Opinion of Judge ad hoc Barwick, Nuclear Tests (*New Zealand v France*), Judgment of 20 December 1974, ICJ Reports 1974 525–528.

In Orders

Declaration of Judge ad hoc Barwick, Nuclear Tests (*Australia v France*), Provisional Measures Order of 22 June 1973, ICJ Reports1973, 110.

Declaration of Judge ad hoc Barwick, Nuclear Tests (*New Zealand v France*), Provisional Measures Order of 22 June 1973, ICJ Reports 1973, 146–147.

BASTID, S. (France)

In Judgments

Separate Opinion of Judge ad hoc Bastid, Application for Revision and Interpretation of the Judgment of 24 February 1982 in the case concerning the Continental Shelf (Tunisia/ Libyan Arab Jamahiriya) (Tunisia v Libyan Arab Jamahiriya), Judgment of 10 December 1985, ICJ Reports 1985 247.

BEB A DON, P. (Cameroon)

In Judgments

Separate Opinion of Judge ad hoc Beb A Don, Northern Cameroons (*Cameron v UK*), Judgment of 2 December 1963, ICJ Reports 1963 184–196

BEDJAOUI, M (Algeria)

See under Bibliography: Judges of the International Court of Justice.

BENNOUNA, M. (Morocco)

(Judg ad hoc in the case concerning Frontier Dispute (Benin/Niger); the case is in the deliberation stage as on 23 April 2005)

BERMAN, F. (United Kingdom)

Dissenting Opinion of Judge ad hoc Berman, Certain Property (*Liechtenstein v Germany*) (Preliminary Objections), Judgment of 10 February 2005, ICJ Reports 2005 (still at press).

BONI, A. (Ivory Coast)

In Advisory Opinion

Separate Opinion of Judge ad hoc Boni, Western Sahara, Advisory Opinion of 16 October 1975, ICJ Reports 1975 173–174.

BROMS, B. (Finland)

In Orders Relating Provisional Measures

Separate Opinion of Judge ad hoc Broms, Passage through the Great Belt (*Finland v Denmark*), Provisional Measures Order of 29 July 1991, ICJ Reports 1991, 37–39

BROWNLIE, I. (United Kingdom)

(Mr Brownlie was Judge ad hoc in the case concerning Certain Property (*Liechtenstein v Germany*) but resigned before the case was decided.)

BULA-BULA, S. (Congo)

In Judgment

Dissenting Opinion of Judge ad hoc Bula-Bula, Arrest Warrant of 11 April 2000 (*Congo v Belgium*), Judgment of 14 February 2002, ICJ Reports 2002, 100–136.

In Orders Relating Provisional Measures

Dissenting Opinion of Judge ad hoc Bula-Bula, Arrest Warrant of 11 April 2000 (*Congo v Belgium*), Provisional Measures Order of 8–Dec–2000, ICJ Reports 2000, 218–228

CAICEDO CASTILLA, J J (Colombia)

In Judgments

Dissenting Opinion of Judge ad hoc Caicedo Castilla, Asylum (Colombia/Peru), Judgment of 20 November 1950, ICJ Reports 1950, 359–381.

Declaration of Judge ad hoc Cicedo Castilla, Request for Interpretation of the Judgment of 20 November 1950, Judgment of 27 November 1950, ICJ Reports 1950, 404.

CARRY, P. (Switzerland)

In Judgments

Declaration of Judge ad hoc Carry, Interhandel (*Switzerland v USA*), Judgment of 21 March 1959 on Preliminary Objections, ICJ Reports 1959, 32.

CASTANEDA, J (Mexico)

(Mr Castaneda was part of the Court's composition in the Judgment of 21 March 1984 (on intervention) in the case concerning the Continental Shelf (Libyan Arab Jamahiriya/ Malta) (Application for Permission to Intervene), but appended no individual opinion to the judgment. (see ICJ Reports 1984, 3.

CASTRO, F de (Spain)

(Mr Castro was chosen by Spain as Judge ad hoc in the case concerning Barcelona Traction, Light and Power Company, Ltd (*Belgium v Spain*). The case was, however, removed from the General List before the Court had occasion to sit; see ICJ Reports 1961, 9.)

CHAGLA, M. A. C. (India)

In Judgments

Dissenting Opinion of Judge ad hoc Chagla, Right of Passage Over Indian Territory (*Portugal v India*), Judgment of 26 November 1957 on Preliminary Objections, ICJ Reports 1957, 166–180.

Dissenting Opinion of Judge ad hoc Chagla, Right of passage over Indian Territory (Portugal v India), Judgment of 12 April 1960 on Merits, ICJ Reports 1960, 116–122.

DAXNER, I. (Czechoslovakia)

In Judgments

Dissenting Opinion of Judge ad hoc Daxner, Corfu Channel (*United Kingdom v Albania*), Judgment of 25 March 1948 on Preliminary Objections, ICJ Reports 1948, 33.

DE CARA, J.-Y. (France)

Dissenting Opinion of Judge De Cara, Certain Criminal Proceedings in France, Provisional Measures Order of 17 June 2003, ICJ Reports 2003, 116.

DIMITRIJEVIC, V. (Serbia and Montenegro)

Dissenting Opinion of Judge ad hoc Dimitrijevic, Application for Revision of the Judgment of 11 July 1996 in the case Concerning Application of the Convention on the Prevention and Punishment of the Crime of Genocide (*Bosnia and Herzegovina v Yugoslavia*). Preliminary Objections (*Yugoslavia v Bosnia and Herzegovina*), Judgment of 3 February 2003, ICJ Reports 2003, 53.

DUGARD, C. J R. (South Africa)

In Orders

Separate Opinion of Judge ad hoc Dugard, Armed Activities on the Territory of Congo (New Application: 2002)(*Democratic Republic of Congo v Rwanda*), Provisional Measures Order of 10 July 2002, ICJ Reports 2002, 265–271.

ECER, B. (Czechoslovakia)

In Judgments

Dissenting Opinion of Judge ad hoc Ecer, Corfu Channel, Judgment of 9 April 1949 on Merits, ICJ Reports 1949, 115–131.

Dissenting Opinion of Judge ad hoc Ecer, Corfu Channel, Judgment of 15 December 1949 on assessment of amount of compensation, ICJ Reports 1949, 252–256.

EL-KOSHERI, A. S. (Egypt)

In Orders Relating Provisional Measures

Dissenting Opinion of Judge ad hoc El-Kosheri, Question of Interpretation and Application of the 1971 Montreal Convention arising from the Aerial Incident at Lockerbie (*Libya v UK*), Provisional Measures Order of 14 April 1992, ICJ Reports1992, 94–112.

Dissenting Opinion of Judge ad hoc El-Kosheri, Question of Interpretation and Application of the 1971 Montreal Convention arising from the Aerial Incident at Lockerbie (*Libya v United States*), Provisional Measures Order of 14 April 1992, ICJ Reports1992, 199–201

EVENSEN, J (Norway)

In Judgments

Dissenting Opinion of Judge ad hoc Evensen, Continental Shelf (Tunisia/Libyan Arab Jamahiriya), Judgment of 24 February 1982, ICJ Reports 1982 278–323.

In Orders Relating Provisional Measures

Joint Declaration of Judge Evensen, Question of Interpretation and Application of the 1971 Montreal Convention arising from the Aerial Incident at Lockerbie (*Libya v UK*), Provisional Measures Order of 14 April 1992, ICJ Reports 1992, 24

Joint Declaration of Judge Evensen, Question of Interpretation and Application of the 1971 Montreal Convention arising from the Aerial Incident at Lockerbie (*Libya v United States*), Provisional Measures Order of 14 April 1992, ICJ Reports1992, 136

FERNANDES, M. (Portugal)

In Judgments

Declaration of Judge ad hoc Farnandes, Right of Passage Over Indian Territory (*Portugal v India*), Judgment of 26 November 1957 on Preliminary Objections, ICJ Reports 1957, 153.

Dissenting Opinion of Judge ad hoc Fernandes, Right of passage over Indian Territory (*Portugal v India*), Judgment of 12 April 1960 on Merits, ICJ Reports 1960, 123–144.

FISCHER, P. H. (Denmark)

In Judgments

Dissenting Opinion of Judge ad hoc Fisher, Maritime Delimitation in the Area between Greenland and Jan Mayen (*Denmark v Norway*), Judgment of 14 June 1993, ICJ Reports 1993 304–314.

FLEISCHHAUER, C.-A. (Germany)

See under Bibliography: Judges of the International Court of Justice.

FORTIER, YL. (Canada)

Separate Opinion of Judge ad hoc Fortier, Maritime Delimitation and Territorial questions between Qatar and Bahrain (*Qatar v Bahrain*), Judgment of 16 March 2001 (merits), ICJ Reports 2001, 451.

FRANCK, T. M. (United States)

Separate Opinion of Judge ad hoc Franck, Sovereignty over Pulau Ligitan and Pulau Sipadan (Indonesia/Malaysia), Judgment of 23 October 2001 (Application by the Philippines for Permission to Intervene), ICJ Reports 2001, 652.

Dissenting Opinion of Judge ad hoc Franck, Sovereignty over Pulau Ligitan and Pulau Sipadan (Indonesia/Malaysia), Judgment of 17 December 2002, ICJ Reports 2002, 691.

GAJA, G. (Italy)

In Orders Relating Provisional Measures

Declaration of Judge ad hoc Gaja, Legality of Use of Force (*Yugoslavia v Italy*), Provisional Measures Order of 2 June 1999, ICJ Reports1999, 502

GARCIA BAUER, C. (Guatemala)

(Participated in the Judgment of 6 April 1955 in the case concerning Nottebohm (*Liechtenstein v Guatemala*), ICJ Reports 1955, 4, but appended no individual opinion to the Judgment.)

GOITEIN, D. (Israel)

In Judgments

Dissenting Opinion of Judge ad hoc Goitein, Aerial Incident of 27 July 1955 (*Israel v Bulgaria*), Judgment of 26 May 1959 on Preliminary Objections, ICJ Reports 1959, 195–204.

GONZALES CAMPOS, JD. (Spain)

Mr Gonzales Campos is chosen by Honduras as Judge ad hoc in the case concerning Maritime Delimitation between Nicaragua and Honduras in Caribbean Sea (*Nicaragua v Honduras*); the case is still pending

GUGGENHEIM, P. (Switzerland)

In Judgments

Dissenting Opinion of Judge ad hoc Guggenheim, Nottebohm, Second Phase, Judgment of 6 April 1955, ICJ Reports 1955, 50–65.

GUILLAUME, G. (France)

See under Bibliography: Judges of the International Court of Justice.

JENNINGS, Sir R. Y. (United Kingdom)

In Judgments

Dissenting Opinion of Judge ad hoc Jennings, Questions of Interpretation and Application of the 1971 Montreal Convention arising from the Aerial Incident at Lockerbie (*Libya v United Kingdom*), Judgment of 27 February 1998 on Preliminary Objections, ICJ Reports 1998 99–113.

See also under Bibliography : Judges of the International Court of Justice.

JIMENEZ DE ARECHAGA, E. (Uruguay)

In Judgments

Separate Opinion of Judge ad hoc Jemenez De Arechaga, Continental Shelf (Tunisia/Libyan Arab Jamahiriya), Judgment of 24 February 1982, ICJ Reports 1982 100–140.

Separate Opinion of Judge ad hoc Jemenez De Arechaga, Continental Shelf (Tunisia/Libyan Arab Jamahiriya), Application by Italy for permission to intervene, Judgment of 21 March 1984, ICJ Reports 1984 55–70.

KATEKA, JL. (Tanzania)

(Mr Kateka was chosen as Judge ad hoc by Uganda in the case concerning Armed Activities on the Territory of the Congo (*Democratic Republic of Congo v Uganda*). The case is at present (23 April 2005) being heard.)

KRECA, M. (Serbia and Montenegro)

In Judgments

Dissenting Opinion of Judge ad hoc Kreca, Application of the Convention on the Prevention and Punishment of the Crime of Genocide (*Bosnia and Herzegovina v Yugoslavia*), Judgment of 11 July 1996 on Preliminary Objections, ICJ Reports 1996 658–795.

Separate Opinion of Judge ad hoc Kreca, Legality of Use of Force, (*Serbia and Montenegro v Belgium*), Preliminary Objections, Judgment of 15 December 2004, ICJ Reports 2004 (still at press).

Separate Opinion of Judge ad hoc Kreca, Legality of Use of Force, (*Serbia and Montenegro v Canada*), Preliminary Objections, Judgment of 15 December 2004, ICJ Reports 2004 (still at press).

Separate Opinion of Judge ad hoc Kreca, Legality of Use of Force, (*Serbia and Montenegro v France*), Preliminary Objections, Judgment of 15 December 2004, ICJ Reports 2004 (still at press).

Separate Opinion of Judge ad hoc Kreca, Legality of Use of Force, (*Serbia and Montenegro v Germany*), Preliminary Objections, Judgment of 15 December 2004, ICJ Reports 2004 (still at press).

Separate Opinion of Judge ad hoc Kreca, Legality of Use of Force, (*Serbia and Montenegro v Italy*), Preliminary Objections, Judgment of 15 December 2004, ICJ Reports 2004 (still at press).

Separate Opinion of Judge ad hoc Kreca, Legality of Use of Force, (*Serbia and Montenegro v Netherlands*), Preliminary Objections, Judgment of 15 December 2004, ICJ Reports 2004 (still at press).

Separate Opinion of Judge ad hoc Kreca, Legality of Use of Force, (*Serbia and Montenegro v Portugal*), Preliminary Objections, Judgment of 15 December 2004, ICJ Reports 2004 (still at press).

Separate Opinion of Judge ad hoc Kreca, Legality of Use of Force, (*Serbia and Montenegro v United Kingdom*), Preliminary Objections, Judgment of 15 December 2004, ICJ Reports 2004 (still at press).

In Orders Relating Provisional Measures

Dissenting Opinion of Judge ad hoc Kreca, Application of the Convention on the Prevention and Punishment of the Crime of Genocide (*Bosnia Herzegovina v Yugoslavia*), Provisional Measures Order of 13 September 1993, ICJ Reports1993, 453–465

Dissenting opinion of Judge ad hoc Kreca, Legality of Use of Force (*Yugoslavia v Belgium*), Provisional Measures Order of 2 June 1999, ICJ Reports 1999, 216–257

Dissenting Opinion of Judge ad hoc Kreca, Legality of Use of Force (*Yugoslavia v Canada*), Provisional Measures Order of 2 June 1999, ICJ Reports1999, 327–361`

Dissenting Opinion of Judge ad hoc Kreca, Legality of Use of Force (*Yugoslavia v France*), Provisional Measures Order of 2 June 1999, ICJ Reports1999, 402–420

Dissenting Opinion of Judge ad hoc Kreca, Legality of Use of Force (*Yugoslavia v Germany*), Provisional Measures Order of 2 June 1999, ICJ Reports1999, 461–479

Dissenting Opinion of Judge ad hoc Kreca, Legality of Use of Force (*Yugoslavia v Italy*), Provisional Measures Order of 2 June 1999, ICJ Reports1999, 522–540

Dissenting Opinion of Judge ad hoc Kreca, Legality of Use of Force (*Yugoslavia v Netherlands*), Provisional Measures Order of 2 June 1999, ICJ Reports1999, 611–654

Dissenting Opinion of Judge ad hoc Kreca, Legality of Use of Force (*Yugoslavia v Portugal*), Provisional Measures Order of 2 June 1999, ICJ Reports1999, 725–759

Separate Opinion of Judge ad hoc Kreca, Legality of Use of Force (*Yugoslavia v Spain*), Provisional Measure Order of 2 June 1999, ICJ Reports 1999, 817–824

Dissenting Opinion of Judge ad hoc Kreca, Legality of Use of Force (*Yugoslavia v United Kingdom*), Provisional Measures Order of 2 June 1999, ICJ Reports1999, 886–914

Dissenting Opinion of Judge ad hoc Kreca, Legality of Use of Force (*Yugoslavia v United States of America*), Provisional Measures Order of 2 June 1999, ICJ Reports1999, 951–973.

LALONDE, M. (Canada)

(Mr Lalonde, chosen by Canada, was Judge ad hoc in the case concerning Fisheries Jurisdiction (*Spain v Canada*). To the relevant Judgment of 4 February 1998 (see ICJ Reports 1998, 432). Mr Lalonde appended no individual opinion. Mr Lalonde was chosen by Canada second time to sit as Judge ad hoc in the case concerning Legality of Use of Force (*Serbia and Montenegro v Canada*) (Preliminary Objections), Judgment of 15 December 2004, ICJ Reports 2004, p. (still in the pres). In addition to this case, there were also seven other similar, though separate, cases being heard by the Court filed by Serbia and Montenegro against Belgium, France, Germany, Italy, Netherlands, Portugal, and the United Kingdom. Hence, with regard to the phase of the procedure concerning the preliminary objections, the Court, taking into account the presence upon the Bench of judges of British, Dutch and French nationality, decided that the judges ad hoc chosen by the respondent States should not sit during the given phase. Hence, Judge Lalonede could not participate. Neither did he appen any individual opinion to the earlier Order of 2 June 1999 (see ICJ Reports 1999, 259)

LAUTERPACHT, Sir E. (United Kingdom)

In Judgments

Declaration of Judge ad hoc Lauterpacht, Application of the Convention on the Prevention and Punishment of the Crime of Genocide (*Bosnia and Herzegovina v Yugoslavia*), Judgment of 11 July 1996 on Preliminary Objections, ICJ Reports 1996 633.

In Orders

Separate Opinion of Judge ad hoc Lauterpacht, Application of the Convention on the Prevention and Punishment of the Crime of Genocide (*Bosnia Herzegovina v Yugoslavia*), Provisional Measures Order of 13 September 1993, ICJ Reports1993, 407–448

LUCHAIRE, F. (France)

In Judgments

Separate Opinion of Judge ad hoc Luchaire, Frontier Dispute (Burkina Faso/Mali) [case referred to a Chamber], Judgment of 22 December 1986, ICJ Reports 1986 652–658.

MAHIOU, A. (Algeria)

Separate Opinion of Judge ad hoc Mahiou, Application for Revision of the Judgment of 11 July 1996 in the case Concerning Application of the Convention on the Prevention and Punishment of the Crime of Genocide (*Bosnia and Herzegovina v Yugoslavia*). Preliminary Objections (*Yugoslavia v Bosnia and Herzegovina*), Judgment of 3 February 2003, ICJ Reports 2003, 70.

MAMPUYA, A. (The Republic of Congo)

(Mr Mampuya is chosen as Judge ad hoc by the Congo in the case concerning Ahmadou Sadio Diallo (*Republic of Guinea v Dmocratic Republic of the Congo*). The case is still pending)

MAVUNGU, J.-PM, (Democratic Republic of Congo)

In Orders

Separate Opinion of Judge ad hoc Mavungu, Armed Activities on the Territory of Congo (New Application: 2002)(*Democratic Republic of Congo v Rwanda*), Provisional Measures Order of 10 July 2002, ICJ Reports 2002, 272–294.

MBANEFO, Sir Louis (Nigeria)

In Judgments

Separate Opinion of Judge ad hoc Mbanefo, South West Africa (*Ethiopia v South Africa; Liberia v South Africa*), Judgment of 21 December 1962 on Preliminary Objections, ICJ Reports 1962 437–448.

Dissenting Opinion of Judge ad hoc Mbanefo, South West Africa (*Ethiopia v South Africa; Liberia v South Africa*), Second Phase, Judgment of 18 July 1966, ICJ Reports 1966 484–505.

MBAYE, K. (Senegal)

In Judgments

Declaration of Judge ad hoc Mbaye, Arbitral Award of 31 July 1989 (*Guinea- Bissau v Senegal*), Judgment of 12 November 1991, ICJ Reports 1991 80.

Separate Opinion of Judge ad hoc Mbaye, Land and Maritime Boundary between Cameroon and Nigeria (*Cameroon v Nigeria: Equatorial Guinea Intervening*), Judgment of 10 October 2002, ICJ Reports 2002, 506.

In Orders Relating Provisional Measures

Declaration of Judge ad hoc Mbaye, Land and Maritime Boundary between Cameroon and Nigeria (*Cameroon v Nigeria*), Provisional Measures Order of 15 March 1996, ICJ Reports1996, 32

See also under Bibliography: Judges of the International Court of Justice.

MORELLI, G. Italy

See under Bibliography: Judges of the International Court of Justice.

MOSLER, H. (Federal Republic of Germany)

See under Bibliography: Judges of the International Court of Justice.

OFFERHAUS, J (Netherlands)

In Judgments

Dissenting Opinion of Judge ad hoc Offerhaus, Application of the Convention of 1902 Governing the Guardianship of Infants (*Netherlands v Sweden*), Judgment of 28 November 1958, ICJ Reports 1958, 146–156.

PALMER, G. Sir (New Zealand)

In Orders Relating Provisional Measures

Dissenting Opinion of Judge ad hoc Palmer, Request for an Examination of the Situation in Accordance with Paragraph 63 of the Court's Judgment of 20 December 1974 in the Nuclear Tests (*New Zealand v France*), Provisional Measures Order of 22 September 1995, ICJ Reports1995, 381–42

PAOLILLO, FH. (Uruguay)

Dissenting Opinion of Judge ad hoc Paolillo, Application for Revision of the Judgment of 11 September 1992 in the case concerning the Land, Island and Maritime Frontier Dispute (El Salvador/Honduras): Nicaragua Intervening) (*El Salvador v Honduras*), Judgment of 18 December 2003, ICJ Reports 2003, 413.

PIRZADA, S. S. U. (Pakistan)

In Judgments

Dissenting Opinion of Judge ad hoc Pirzada, Aerial Incident of 10 August 1999 (*Pakistan v India*), Judgment of 21 June 2000 on Jurisdiction, ICJ Reports 2000 60–106.

RAO, SP. (India)
(Mr Rao is a Judge ad hoc for Singapore in the case concerning Sovereignty over Pedra Branca/Pulau Batu Puteh, Middle Rocks and South Ledge (Malaysia/Singapore). The case is still pending.)

REDDY, B. P. J (India)

In Judgments
Separate Opinion of Judge ad hoc Reddy, Aerial Incident of 10 August 1999 (*Pakistan v India*), Judgment of 21 June 2000 on Jurisdiction, ICJ Reports 2000 47.

RIGAUX, F. (Belgium)

In Judgments
Separate Opinion of Judge ad hoc Rigaux, Oil Platforms (*Islamic Republic of Iran v USA*), Judgment of 12 December 1996 on Preliminary Objections, ICJ Reports 1996 864–873.
Separate Opinion of Judge ad hoc Rigaux, Oil Platforms (*Iran v USA*), Judgment of 6 November 2003, ICJ Reports 2003, 362.

RIPHAGEN, W (Netherlands)

In Judgments
Dissenting Opinion of Judge Riphagen, Barcelona Traction, Light and Power Company, Ltd (New Application: 1962)(*Belgium v Spain*), Second Phase, Judgment of 5 February 1970, ICJ Reports 1970 334–354.

RUDA, JM. (Argentina)
See under Bibliography : Judges of the International Court of Justice.

SALMON, JJA. (Belgium)
(Mr Salmon was chosen as Judge ad hoc by Burundi in the case concerning Armed Activities on the Territory of the Congo (*Democratic Republic of the Congo v Burundi*). The case however was discontinued.)

SANDJABI, K. (Iran)
(Mr Sandjabi was chosen as Judge ad hoc by Iran in the case concerning Anglo-Iranian Oil Co. (*United Kingdom v Iran*). Mr Sandjabi was part of the Court's composition in the relevant Judgment of 22 July 1952 on Preliminary Objections, but appended no individual opinion to the decision (see ICJ Reports 1952, 93))

SETTE-CAMARA, I. (Brazil)

In Judgments
Dissenting Opinion of Judge ad hoc Sette-Camara, Territorial Dispute (Libyan Arab Jamahiriya/Chad), Judgment of 3 February 1994, ICJ Reports 1994 93–103.

SEPULVEDA, B (Mexico)

In Judgments

Separate Opinionof Judge ad hoc Sepulveda, Avena and Other Mexican Nationals (*Mexico v USA*), Judgment of 31 March 2004, ICJ Reports 2004, 99

SHAHABUDDEEN, M. (Guyana)

Se under Bibliography : Judges of the International Court of Justice.

SINGH, Nagendra (India)

In Judgments

Dissenting Opinion of Judge ad hoc Singh, Appeal Relating to the Jurisdiction of the ICAO Council (*India v Pakistan*), Judgment of 18 August 1972, ICJ Reports 1972 164–186.

See also under Bibliography : Judges of the International Court of Justice.

SKUBISZEWSKI, K. (Poland)

In Judgments

Dissenting Opinion of Judge ad hoc Skubiszewski, East Timor (*Portugal v Australia*) (POs were linked to merits), Judgment of 30 June 1995, ICJ Reports 1995 224–277.

Dissenting Opinion of Judge ad hoc Skubiszewski, The Gabcikovo- Nagymaros Project (Hungary/Slovakia), Judgment of 25 September 1997, ICJ Reports 1997 232–241.

SORENSEN, M. (Denmark)

In Judgments

Dissenting Opinion of Judge ad hoc Soresen, North Sea Continental Shelf (Federal Republic of Germany/Denmark; Federal Republic of Germany/Netherlands), Judgment of 20 February 1969, ICJ Reports 1969 241–257.

SPIROPOULOS, J (Greece)

In Judgments

Separate Opinion of Judge ad hoc Spiropoulos, Ambatielos (*Greece v United Kingdom*), Judgment of 1 July 1952 on Preliminary Objections, ICJ Reports 1952, 55–57.

STASSINOPOULOS, M. (Greece)

In Judgments

Dissenting Opinion of Judge Stassinopoulos, Aegean Sea Continental Shelf (*Greece v Turkey*), Judgment of 19 December 1978, ICJ Reports 1978 72–83.

In Orders Relating Provisional Measures

Dissenting Opinio of Judge ad hoc Stassinopoulos, Aegean Sea Continental Shelf (*Greece v Turkey*), Provisional Measures Order of 11 September 1976, ICJ Reports1976, 35–40

STEPHEN, Sir Ninian (Australia)

(Sir Stephen was Australia's Judge ad hoc in the case concerning East Timor (*Portugal v Australia*) but appended no individual opinion to the Judgment of 30 June 1995, see ICJ Reports 1995, 90)

STERZEL, FJC. (Sweden)

(Mr Sterzel was Sweden's Judge ad hoc in the case concerning Application of the Convention of 1902 Governing the Guardianship of Infants (*Netherlands v Sweden*) but appended no individual opinion to the Judgment of 28 November 1958, see ICJ Reports 1958, 55.)

THIERRY, H. (France)

In Judgments

Dissenting Opinion of Judge ad hoc Thierry, Arbitral Award of 31 July 1989 (*Guinea- Bissau v Senegal*), Judgment of 12 November 1991, ICJ Reports 1991 175–185.

In Orders Relating Provisional Measures

Dissenting Opinion of Judge ad hoc Thierry, Arbitral Award 31 Jul 1989 (*Guinea-Bissau v Senegal*), Provisional Measures Order of 2 March 1990, ICJ Reports1990, 79–84

TORRES BERNARDEZ, S. (Spain)

In Judgments

Separate Opinion of Judge ad hoc Torres Bernardez, Land, Island and Maritime Frontier Dispute (El Salvador/Honduras), Judgment of 11 September 1992, ICJ Reports 1992 629–731.

Dissenting Opinion of Judge ad hoc Torres Bernardez, Fisheries Jurisdiction (*Spain v Canada*), Judgment of 4 December 1998 on Jurisdiction, ICJ Reports 1998 582–738.

Joint Separate Opinion of Judge ad hoc Torres Bernardez, Maritime Delimitation and Territorial questions between Qatar and Bahrain (*Qatar v Bahrain*), Judgment of 16 March 2001 (merits), ICJ Reports 2001, 257.

URRUTIA HOLGUIN, F. (Colombia)

In Judgments

Dissenting Opinion of judge ad hoc Urrutia Holguin, Arbitral Award made by the King of Spain on 23 December 1906 (*Honduras v Nicaragua*), Judgment of 18 November 1960, ICJ Reports 1960, 221–239.

VALTICOS, N. (Greece)

In Judgments

Separate Opinion of Judge ad hoc Valticos, Land, Island and Maritime Frontier Dispute (El Salvador/Honduras), Judgment of 11 September 1992, ICJ Reports 1992 621–628.

Separate Opinion of Judge ad hoc Valticons, Continental Shelf (Libyan Arab Jamahiriya/Malta), Judgment of 3 June 1985, ICJ Reoprts 1985 104–113.

Separate Opinion of Judge ad hoc Valticons, Maritime Delimitation and Territorial Questions between Qatar and Bahrain (*Qatar v Bahrain*) (Jurisdiction and Admissibility), Judgment of 1 July 1994, ICJ Reports 1994 132.

Dissenting Opinion of Judge ad hoc Valticons, Maritime Delimitation and Territorial Questions between Qatar and Bahrain (*Qatar v Bahrain*) (Jurisdiction and Admissibility), Judgment of 15 February 1995, ICJ Reports 1995 74–81.

VERHOEVEN, J (Belgium)

Declaration of Judge ad hoc Verhoeven, Order of 29 November 2001 on Counter-Claims, Armed Activities on the Territory of the Congo (*Democratic Republic of Congo v Uganda*), ICJ Reports 2001, 684.

VIRALLY, M. (France)

(Mr Virally was chosen as Judge ad hoc by Honduras in the case concerning Land, Island and Maritime Frontier Dispute (El Salvador/Honduras: Nicaragua Interveining). However, he died before the case reached its final stage.)

VUKAS, B. (Croatia)

(Mr Vukas is chosen as Judge ad hoc by Croatia in the case concerning Application of the Convention on the Prevention and Punishment of the Crime of Genocide (Croatia v Serbia and Montenegro); the still is still pending)

B Vukas, 'The International Tribunal of the Law of the Sea: Some Features of the New International Judicial Institution' (1997) 37 *Indian Journal of International Law* 372.

WEERAMANTRY, C. G. (Sri Lanka)

See under Bibliography : Judges of the International Court of Justice.

WYK, J T. Van (South Africa)

In Judgments

Dissenting Opinion of Judge ad hoc Van Wyk, South West Africa (*Ethiopia v South Africa; Liberia v South Africa*), Judgment of 21 December 1962 on Preliminary Objections, ICJ Reports 1962 575–662.

Separate Opinion of Judge ad hoc Van Wyk, South West Africa (*Ethiopia v South Africa; Liberia v South Africa*), Second Phase, Judgment of 18 July 1966, ICJ Reports 1966 67–215.

WIJNGAERT, C. Van Den (Belgium)

In Judgment

Dissenting Opinion of Judge ad hoc Wijngaert, Arrest Warrant of 11 April 2000 (*Congo v Belgium*), Judgment of 14 February 2002, ICJ Reports 2002, 137–187.

In Orders Relating Provisional Measures

Declaration of Judge ad hoc Wijngaert, Arrest Warrant of 11 April 2000 (*Congo v Belgium*), Provisional Measures Order of 8–Dec–2000, ICJ Reports2000, 229–233

YAKOUB ALI KHAN, M (Pakistan)

(he was judge ad hoc in the Trial of Pakistani Prosoners of War case (1973) but did not write any individual opinion)

ZAFRULLA KHAN, M. (Pakistan)

(he was judge ad hoc in the Trial of Pakistani Prosoners of War case (1973) but did not write any individual opinion)
See also under Bibliography : Judges of the International Court of Justice.

ZOUREK, J (Czechoslovakia)
(he was judge ad hoc in the Aerial Incident of 27 July 1955(1959) but did not write any individual opinion)

INDEX